THE BEST OF

New Expanded
Edition

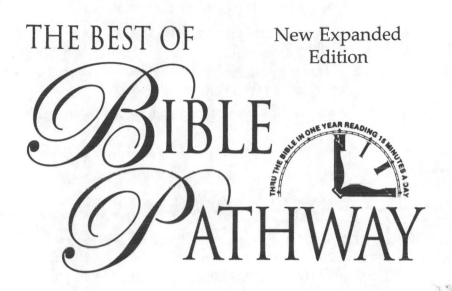

ℬIBLE ℘ATHWAY

THRU THE BIBLE IN ONE YEAR READING 15 MINUTES A DAY

366 DAILY DEVOTIONS
GENESIS THROUGH REVELATION

JOHN A. HASH

D0101184

Published By

ℬIBLE ℘ATHWAY ℳINISTRIES
I N T E R N A T I O N A L
P. O. Box 20123
Murfreesboro, Tennessee 37129

LIFE'S MOST IMPORTANT DECISION

Jesus said: *Except a man be born of water and of the Spirit, he cannot enter into the Kingdom of God* (John 3:5).

Being born again, not of corruptible seed, but of incorruptible, by the Word of God, which lives and abides for ever (I Peter 1:23).

But be doers of the Word, and not hearers only, deceiving your own selves (James 1:22).

If you know that He is righteous, you know that every one that does righteousness is born of Him (I John 2:29).

When He, the Spirit of Truth, is come,
He will guide you into all Truth (John 16:13).

We are all dependent upon the Holy Spirit to reveal His will
as we read His Word. But the Holy Spirit will not reveal
what we refuse or neglect to read.

Bible Pathway **is a Christ-centered through-the-Bible**
devotional commentary and not a theological exposition.

The devotional thought reveals how each day's Bible reading
relates to our personal relationship with God and our fellowman,
as well as our own spiritual needs.

The world's most-widely-read through-the-Bible
devotional commentary

Recommended by leaders in all major denominations.

Scripture quotations are from the *KJV Easy-Reading Edition*
Used by permission of G.E.M. Publishing

TABLE OF CONTENTS

Introductions To The Books Of The Old Testament
Maps, Charts, and Indexes

Introductions To The Books Of The New Testament
Maps, Charts, and Indexes

NOTE 1: The references given in the devotions often include more verses than the ones actually quoted to give the reader a more complete overall thought.

NOTE 2: When given consecutive Scripture references from the same book, the name of the book is only mentioned with the first reference.

Tomorrow he promised his conscience,
Tomorrow I mean to believe.
Tomorrow I'll live as I ought to;
Tomorrow my Savior receive.

Tomorrow, tomorrow, tomorrow
Thus day after day it went on.
Tomorrow, tomorrow, tomorrow
Till youth like a vision had gone.

Till age in its passion had written
The message of fate on his brow,
And forth from the shadows of death
Came that pitiful syllable, now.

—M.E.H.

FOREWORD

God gives every generation of believers a select group of saints whose unique gifts and insights help keep His people on the right track. During the past half century, the Body of Christ has been blessed by the energetic yet unassuming work of Dr. John Hash.

I was still a boy when, the year after the close of World War II, Pastor Hash began a brilliant work among the people the Lord had given into his charge. Because knowing God's Word is the key to life for any Christian, Dr. Hash made it his top ministry priority. He developed a reading plan to guide people through the entire Bible each year.

Years later, after Dr. Hash's faithful daily devotions blossomed into Bible Pathway Ministries, I had the privilege of meeting him personally. At the time, I was serving as president of the Southern Baptist Convention and so was in a position to see a remarkable variety of approaches faithful pastors and teachers could take to help people draw nearer to God. But I said to Dr. Hash, in all sincerity, that there is nothing more valuable anyone can do than to establish a daily commitment simply to read God's Word itself. For that reason, I cannot praise highly enough the vision and purpose of Bible Pathway. Its sole focus is to encourage believers to read the Bible and facilitate their understanding of Scripture.

As I reviewed the manuscript for this book, it was everything I would have expected from Dr. Hash – and a great deal more! It's ripe with some of the most helpful charts, maps, and illustrations available, and Dr. Hash offers sensitive insights into pressing issues that face today's church. Yet he always keeps foremost in mind the need of individual believers to maintain a vital, growing relationship with Jesus Christ.

If you've never read the Bible through in a year, you're in for a wonderful experience, and if you have, then you know the richness that awaits you as you do it again.

The Lord promised in Matthew 5:6 – *Blessed are they which hunger and thirst after righteousness: for they shall be filled*. There is truly no better way to be filled with the righteousness for which you thirst than to read through the Word of God each year.

May God bless your journey on your Pathway with Him!

– **James T. Draper, Jr., President**
LifeWay Christian Resources

INTRODUCTION

Know what you believe. Know why you believe it. Then live it!

That's the theme of every Greek and Hebrew language class I've ever taught. It is also the theme of one man whose ministry stands tall among those who are raised up by God to advance His Kingdom.

More than half a century ago, Dr. John Hash first grasped what should be to all of us the obvious connection between reading Scripture and knowing what you believe. All that we as Christians believe is revealed in the written Word of God. Unless you know what that Word says, you cannot know what you believe. And unless you know what you believe, you cannot know how to live it.

This book presents the wisdom Dr. Hash has gained through his years of repeated study of God's Word, and it offers direction and encouragement in a highly refined presentation of scriptural truths. The approach is essentially the same as when Dr. Hash first introduced his congregation to the idea of reading the entire Bible: *If you spend just fifteen minutes reading Scripture every day following this guide, you will read through the entire Bible in one year.*

You will find in the pages that follow, a guide to tell you which passage of Scripture to read each day. In addition, Dr. Hash explains background information about biblical history, culture, geography, and other details which bring the Bible into clearer focus. Three invaluable features deliver these insights:

(1) Each book of the Bible is introduced with an overview of the message and summary of the biblical narrative. From the outset, you will see how the message of Genesis ties to the message of the Gospel of John or the book of Hebrews or Paul's letter to the Corinthians. You will glimpse how each book of the Bible fits into the whole of God's revelation, and you will understand the impact of the events in each account on the people involved. Consequently, you will better apprehend its relevance for your own life.

(2) Every day's Scripture reading is headed by a summary statement that encapsulates what you will learn that day. For example, on March 13 when you are to read Joshua 1-3, the summary says: "God speaks to Joshua; spies sent to Jericho; pledge between the spies and Rahab; Israel crosses the Jordan River." The day's commentary shows you the significance of Joshua's faith and of Rahab's role in the ongoing revelation of God (she's part of the genealogy of Jesus). A "Thought for Today" ties the threads together and helps you grasp the Scripture's implication for your life.

(3) Maps of biblical lands and charts explaining time lines as well as other pertinent information pepper the book. Just when you need it, you'll find a

map of the Exodus from Egypt or of the boundaries of David's Kingdom; you'll review a list of the fifteen judges of Israel or study a diagram of the desert tabernacle.

Since the focus of *The Best of Bible Pathway* is Scripture itself, each devotional references several key verses relevant to the focal passage of the day. Be sure to pay close attention to scriptures cited in the book and soak in the meaning of these key verses.

Finally, let me encourage you to avoid thinking of yourself in terms of "success" or "failure." You may be tempted to think you've failed if you miss a day, or on the other extreme, become so obsessed with "succeeding" in reading the whole Bible in 365 days, that you lose sight of each day's opportunity to experience God's peace and receive His message in His timing. If you miss a day, never mind! Pick up the next day and move on. Read two days' worth, if you can, but whatever you do, don't give up!

There may be days when the clarity of a particular truth sets you on the mountaintop. Yet there may be other periods when God communicates His direction gradually over several days, or maybe even weeks. But be assured that He does have a message for you, and you will hear Him speak it in a way that you will understand. Your part is to be faithful in reading His Book.

Remember: Fifteen minutes a day is all you have to invest. Just make sure that once you read it and know it, you live it!

– **Samuel J. Gantt, III**
Former Director of Biblical Language Instruction
Fuller Theological Seminary, Pasadena, California

Art thou abiding in the Vine
In fellowship serene,
His precious Word, thy daily Bread
With naught thy Lord between?

Doth thy heart yearn new heights to gain,
Yea! new depths to explore,
To mount on eagles' sings superb
In Faith and love to soar?

My Child, if thou wouldst e'er abound
In Jesus Christ, thy Lord,
Then truly thou must e'er abide
In God's own Holy Word.

–M.E.H.

ACKNOWLEDGMENTS

I ESPECIALLY WANT TO THANK Sam Gantt for invaluable advice; our Pathway staff, Karen Hawkins, Barbara Bivens, Benjamin Wallace, Clarence Rathbone, and Ken Sharp, for their help with researching and editing this book; Rita Guerra, co-ordinator, and her assistants Barbara Jean Jackson and Charity Ryan; Gina Lesnefsky, chief typesetter; Mary Kay Wagner, proofreader; and the other invaluable team members: George Kopchak, Jim Ryan, and Pam Pendergrast for their significant contributions.

WE ARE INDEBTED TO LifeWay Christian Resources' president, James T. Draper, Jr., for his encouragement to compile *The Best of Bible Pathway*; to FaithWorks Book Distributors, Larry Carpenter and Dave Troutman

THERE IS ONE PERSON more than any other who is unequaled: my precious wife, Letha, whose spiritual insight, patience, and advice have been priceless, and whom I admire with incomparable esteem. We have experienced 60 years together sharing the abundant love of God – *above all that we ask or think* (Ephesians 3:20).

– In Memory of –

I AM DEEPLY GRATEFUL for the loving concern of my mother, Iva Ann Hash McElroy, who faithfully taught me to be loyal to Christ and His Word; an old preacher, Ted Hutchins, who was the first to tell me, as a teenager, that I ought to read through the Bible; Gerald Heskett, a preacher friend, who spent many days and weeks with me fasting and praying for God to have first place in our lives; and for M.E. Harding, a blind lady who gave me much spiritual insight 60 years ago. A few of her poems have been included in this book.

My prayer is that *The Best of Bible Pathway* will lead you to see more clearly that *All Scripture . . . is profitable . . . That the man of God may be perfect, thoroughly furnished to all good works* (II Timothy 3:16-17).

John A Hash

PREFACE

We have one supreme reason for living. The question that needs to be addressed is: Will we read how we must live to please our Creator, or suffer the consequences? Pity the person who is wasting the few short years of life chasing earthly goals to obtain financial security, popularity, or material success, but failing to achieve the purpose for which God created them. **God has allotted just one short lifetime with a threefold responsibility:**

[1]   That we may know the One True God. There is but One Living God who is a Trinity expressed in three Persons, *the Father . . . the Son* (Jesus born in Bethlehem)*, and . . . the Holy Spirit* (28:18-20), Who dwells within every Christian. All other gods are false, lifeless counterfeits that can save no one from eternal hell fire, where there is *weeping and gnashing of teeth* forever (22:13). They cannot provide for our needs, protect us from enemies, or answer our prayers. *For there is One God, and One Mediator between God and men, the Man Christ Jesus* (I Timothy 2:5; also John 14:16-17; 16:13-15; I John 5:7).

[2]   That we may know what God planned for us and how to be prepared for eternity. God has said that *the Holy Scriptures* (the Old Testament)*, which are able to make you wise to salvation through faith which is in Christ Jesus. All Scripture is given by inspiration of God, and is profitable for doctrine, for reproof, for correction, for instruction in righteousness* (in holy living, in conformity to God's will in thought, purpose, and action): *That the man of God may be perfect* (adequate), *thoroughly furnished* (efficient, well prepared) *to all good works* (II Timothy 3:16-17).

[3]   To be fully prepared to face eternity with confidence. Jesus said: *Man shall not live by bread alone, but by every Word that proceeds out of the mouth of God* (Matthew 4:4). *Bread* refers to our daily food; but, *every Word that proceeds out of the mouth of God* is vitally important to our eternal destiny. *Every Word* begins with Genesis 1:1 and ends with Revelation 22:21. If we fail to read *all Scripture* (the Bible), we will be something less than what God expects us to be to fulfill His will.

[4]   We have a responsibility to provide this message to the world. Jesus said: *Go . . . teach all nations . . . to observe ALL THINGS . . . I have commanded you* (Matthew 28:19-20).

WARNING: Without a doubt **everyone** believes they will go to heaven; but we need to take Jesus seriously, Who said: *Few there be that find it* (Matthew 7:14).

I pray as I write each day's devotion *that you might be filled with the knowledge of His will in all wisdom and spiritual understanding; That you might walk worthy of the Lord to all pleasing, being fruitful in every good work, and increasing in the knowledge of God* (Colossians 1:9-10; also II Peter 3:18).

– John A. Hash, D.D., Litt.D., Founder & Editor in Chief
Bible Pathway Ministries Inernational

JANUARY – VOLUME 1

Date	Day	Reading	Check as you read each day
1	1	Genesis 1 - 3	
2	2	Genesis 4 - 6	
3	3	Genesis 7 - 9	
4	4	Genesis 10 - 12	
5	5	Genesis 13 - 15	
6	6	Genesis 16 - 18	
7	7	Genesis 19 - 21	
8	8	Genesis 22 - 24	
9	9	Genesis 25 - 27	
10	10	Genesis 28 - 30	
11	11	Genesis 31 - 33	
12	12	Genesis 34 - 36	
13	13	Genesis 37 - 39	
14	14	Genesis 40 - 42	
15	15	Genesis 43 - 45	
16	16	Genesis 46 - 48	
17	17	Genesis 49 – Ex. 1	
18	18	Exodus 2 - 4	
19	19	Exodus 5 - 7	
20	20	Exodus 8 - 10	
21	21	Exodus 11 - 13	
22	22	Exodus 14 - 16	
23	23	Exodus 17 - 19	
24	24	Exodus 20 - 22	
25	25	Exodus 23 - 25	
26	26	Exodus 26 - 28	
27	27	Exodus 29 - 31	
28	28	Exodus 32 - 34	
29	29	Exodus 35 - 37	
30	30	Exodus 38 - 39	
31	31	Exodus 40	

MARCH – VOLUME 3

Date	Day	Reading	Check as you read each day
1	61	Deuteronomy 1 - 2	
2	62	Deuteronomy 3 - 4	
3	63	Deuteronomy 5 - 7	
4	64	Deuteronomy 8 - 10	
5	65	Deuteronomy 11 - 13	
6	66	Deuteronomy 14 - 16	
7	67	Deuteronomy 17 - 20	
8	68	Deuteronomy 21 - 23	
9	69	Deuteronomy 24 - 27	
10	70	Deuteronomy 28	
11	71	Deuteronomy 29 - 31	
12	72	Deuteronomy 32 - 34	
13	73	Joshua 1 – 3	
14	74	Joshua 4 – 6	
15	75	Joshua 7 – 8	
16	76	Joshua 9 – 10	
17	77	Joshua 11 – 13	
18	78	Joshua 14 – 16	
19	79	Joshua 17 – 19	
20	80	Joshua 20 – 21	
21	81	Joshua 22 – 24	
22	82	Judges 1 – 2	
23	83	Judges 3 - 5	
24	84	Judges 6 - 7	
25	85	Judges 8 - 9	
26	86	Judges 10 - 11	
27	87	Judges 12 - 14	
28	88	Judges 15 - 17	
29	89	Judges 18 - 19	
30	90	Judges 20 - 21	
31	91	Ruth 1 – 4	

MAY – VOLUME 5

Date	Day	Reading	Check as you read each day
1	122	II Kings 1 - 3	
2	123	II Kings 4 - 5	
3	124	II Kings 6 - 8	
4	125	II Kings 9 - 10	
5	126	II Kings 11 - 13	
6	127	II Kings 14 - 15	
7	128	II Kings 16 - 17	
8	129	II Kings 18 - 20	
9	130	II Kings 21 - 23:20	
10	131	II Kings 23:21 - 25	
11	132	I Chronicles 1 - 2	
12	133	I Chronicles 3 - 5	
13	134	I Chronicles 6 - 7	
14	135	I Chronicles 8 - 10	
15	136	I Chronicles 11 - 13	
16	137	I Chronicles 14 - 16	
17	138	I Chronicles 17 - 20	
18	139	I Chronicles 21 - 23	
19	140	I Chronicles 24 - 26	
20	141	I Chronicles 27 - 29	
21	142	II Chronicles 1 - 3	
22	143	II Chronicles 4 - 6	
23	144	II Chronicles 7 - 9	
24	145	II Chronicles 10 - 13	
25	146	II Chronicles 14 - 17	
26	147	II Chronicles 18 - 20	
27	148	II Chronicles 21 - 24	
28	149	II Chronicles 25 - 27	
29	150	II Chronicles 28 - 30	
30	151	II Chronicles 31 - 33	
31	152	II Chronicles 34 - 36	

FEBRUARY – VOLUME 2

Date	Day	Reading	Check as you read each day
1	32	Leviticus 1 - 3	
2	33	Leviticus 4 - 6	
3	34	Leviticus 7 - 8	
4	35	Leviticus 9 - 10	
5	36	Leviticus 11 - 13	
6	37	Leviticus 14 - 15	
7	38	Leviticus 16 - 18	
8	39	Leviticus 19 - 21	
9	40	Leviticus 22 - 23	
10	41	Leviticus 24 - 25	
11	42	Leviticus 26 - 27	
12	43	Numbers 1 - 2	
13	44	Numbers 3 - 4	
14	45	Numbers 5 - 6	
15	46	Numbers 7	
16	47	Numbers 8 - 9	
17	48	Numbers 10 - 11	
18	49	Numbers 12 - 13	
19	50	Numbers 14 - 15	
20	51	Numbers 16 - 18	
21	52	Numbers 19 - 20	
22	53	Numbers 21 - 22	
23	54	Numbers 23 - 25	
24	55	Numbers 26 - 27	
25	56	Numbers 28 - 29	
26	57	Numbers 30 - 31	
27	58	Numbers 32 - 33	
28	59	Numbers 34 - 35	
29	60	Numbers 36	

APRIL – VOLUME 4

Date	Day	Reading	Check as you read each day
1	92	I Samuel 1 – 3	
2	93	I Samuel 4 – 7	
3	94	I Samuel 8 – 11	
4	95	I Samuel 12 – 14:23	
5	96	I Samuel 14:24 – 16	
6	97	I Samuel 17 – 18	
7	98	I Samuel 19 – 21	
8	99	I Samuel 22 – 24	
9	100	I Samuel 25 – 27	
10	101	I Samuel 28 – 31	
11	102	II Samuel 1 – 2	
12	103	II Samuel 3 – 5	
13	104	II Samuel 6 – 9	
14	105	II Samuel 10 – 12	
15	106	II Samuel 13 – 14	
16	107	II Samuel 15 – 16	
17	108	II Samuel 17 – 18	
18	109	II Samuel 19 – 20	
19	110	II Samuel 21 – 22	
20	111	II Samuel 23 – 24	
21	112	I Kings 1 – 2:25	
22	113	I Kings 2:26 – 4	
23	114	I Kings 5 – 7	
24	115	I Kings 8	
25	116	I Kings 9 – 11	
26	117	I Kings 12 – 13	
27	118	I Kings 14 – 15	
28	119	I Kings 16 – 18	
29	120	I Kings 19 – 20	
30	121	I Kings 21 – 22	

JUNE – VOLUME 6

Date	Day	Reading	Check as you read each day
1	153	Ezra 1 – 2	
2	154	Ezra 3 – 5	
3	155	Ezra 6 – 7	
4	156	Ezra 8 – 9	
5	157	Ezra 10	
6	158	Nehemiah 1 – 3	
7	159	Nehemiah 4 – 6	
8	160	Nehemiah 7 – 8	
9	161	Nehemiah 9 – 10	
10	162	Nehemiah 11 – 12	
11	163	Nehemiah 13	
12	164	Esther 1 – 3	
13	165	Esther 4 – 7	
14	166	Esther 8 – 10	
15	167	Job 1 – 4	
16	168	Job 5 – 8	
17	169	Job 9 – 12	
18	170	Job 13 – 16	
19	171	Job 17 – 20	
20	172	Job 21 – 24	
21	173	Job 25 – 29	
22	174	Job 30 – 33	
23	175	Job 34 – 37	
24	176	Job 38 – 40	
25	177	Job 41 – 42	
26	178	Psalms 1 – 9	
27	179	Psalms 10 – 17	
28	180	Psalms 18 – 22	
29	181	Psalms 23 – 30	
30	182	Psalms 31 – 35	

JULY – VOLUME 7

Date	Day	Reading	Check as you read each day
1	183	Psalms 36 – 39	
2	184	Psalms 40 – 45	
3	185	Psalms 46 – 51	
4	186	Psalms 52 – 59	
5	187	Psalms 60 – 66	
6	188	Psalms 67 – 71	
7	189	Psalms 72 – 77	
8	190	Psalms 78 – 80	
9	191	Psalms 81 – 87	
10	192	Psalms 88 – 91	
11	193	Psalms 92 – 100	
12	194	Psalms 101 – 105	
13	195	Psalms 106 – 107	
14	196	Psalms 108 – 118	
15	197	Psalm 119	
16	198	Psalms 120 – 131	
17	199	Psalms 132 – 138	
18	200	Psalms 139 – 143	
19	201	Psalms 144 – 150	
20	202	Proverbs 1 – 3	
21	203	Proverbs 4 – 7	
22	204	Proverbs 8 – 11	
23	205	Proverbs 12 – 15	
24	206	Proverbs 16 – 19	
25	207	Proverbs 20 – 22	
26	208	Proverbs 23 – 26	
27	209	Proverbs 27 – 31	
28	210	Ecclesiastes 1 – 4	
29	211	Ecclesiastes 5 – 8	
30	212	Ecclesiastes 9 – 12	
31	213	Song of Sol. 1 – 8	

AUGUST – VOLUME 8

Date	Day	Reading	Check as you read each day
1	214	Isaiah 1 – 4	
2	215	Isaiah 5 – 9	
3	216	Isaiah 10 – 14	
4	217	Isaiah 15 – 21	
5	218	Isaiah 22 – 26	
6	219	Isaiah 27 – 31	
7	220	Isaiah 32 – 37	
8	221	Isaiah 38 – 42	
9	222	Isaiah 43 – 46	
10	223	Isaiah 47 – 51	
11	224	Isaiah 52 – 57	
12	225	Isaiah 58 – 63	
13	226	Isaiah 64 – 66	
14	227	Jeremiah 1 – 3	
15	228	Jeremiah 4 – 6	
16	229	Jeremiah 7 – 10	
17	230	Jeremiah 11 – 14	
18	231	Jeremiah 15 – 18	
19	232	Jeremiah 19 – 22	
20	233	Jeremiah 23 – 25	
21	234	Jeremiah 26 – 28	
22	235	Jeremiah 29 – 31	
23	236	Jeremiah 32 – 33	
24	237	Jeremiah 34 – 36	
25	238	Jeremiah 37 – 40	
26	239	Jeremiah 41 – 44	
27	240	Jeremiah 45 – 48	
28	241	Jeremiah 49 – 50	
29	242	Jeremiah 51 – 52	
30	243	Lamentations 1 – 2	
31	244	Lamentations 3 – 5	

SEPTEMBER – VOLUME 9

Date	Day	Reading	Check as you read each day
1	245	Ezekiel 1 – 4	
2	246	Ezekiel 5 – 9	
3	247	Ezekiel 10 – 13	
4	248	Ezekiel 14 – 16	
5	249	Ezekiel 17 – 19	
6	250	Ezekiel 20 – 21	
7	251	Ezekiel 22 – 24	
8	252	Ezekiel 25 – 28	
9	253	Ezekiel 29 – 32	
10	254	Ezekiel 33 – 36	
11	255	Ezekiel 37 – 39	
12	256	Ezekiel 40 – 42	
13	257	Ezekiel 43 – 45	
14	258	Ezekiel 46 – 48	
15	259	Daniel 1 – 3	
16	260	Daniel 4 – 6	
17	261	Daniel 7 – 9	
18	262	Daniel 10 – 12	
19	263	Hosea 1 – 6	
20	264	Hosea 7 – 14	
21	265	Joel 1 – 3	
22	266	Amos 1 – 5	
23	267	Amos 6 – 9 Obadiah 1	
24	268	Jonah 1 – 4	
25	269	Micah 1 – 7	
26	270	Nahum 1 – 3 Habakkuk 1 – 3	
27	271	Zephaniah 1 – 3 Haggai 1 – 2	
28	272	Zechariah 1 – 7	
29	273	Zechariah 8 – 14	
30	274	Malachi 1 – 4	

OCTOBER – VOLUME 10

Date	Day	Reading	Check as you read each day
1	275	Matthew 1 – 3	
2	276	Matthew 4 – 6	
3	277	Matthew 7 – 9	
4	278	Matthew 10 – 11	
5	279	Matthew 12	
6	280	Matthew 13 – 14	
7	281	Matthew 15 – 17	
8	282	Matthew 18 – 20	
9	283	Matthew 21 – 22	
10	284	Matthew 23 – 24	
11	285	Matthew 25 – 26	
12	286	Matthew 27 – 28	
13	287	Mark 1 – 3	
14	288	Mark 4 – 5	
15	289	Mark 6 – 7	
16	290	Mark 8 – 9	
17	291	Mark 10 – 11	
18	292	Mark 12 – 13	
19	293	Mark 14 – 16	
20	294	Luke 1	
21	295	Luke 2 – 3	
22	296	Luke 4 – 5	
23	297	Luke 6 – 7	
24	298	Luke 8 – 9	
25	299	Luke 10 – 11	
26	300	Luke 12 – 13	
27	301	Luke 14 – 16	
28	302	Luke 17 – 18	
29	303	Luke 19 – 20	
30	304	Luke 21 – 22	
31	305	Luke 23 – 24	

NOVEMBER – VOLUME 11

Date	Day	Reading	Check as you read each day
1	306	John 1 – 3	
2	307	John 4 – 5	
3	308	John 6 – 8	
4	309	John 9 – 10	
5	310	John 11 – 12	
6	311	John 13 – 16	
7	312	John 17 – 18	
8	313	John 19 – 21	
9	314	Acts 1 – 3	
10	315	Acts 4 – 6	
11	316	Acts 7 – 8	
12	317	Acts 9 – 10	
13	318	Acts 11 – 13	
14	319	Acts 14 – 16	
15	320	Acts 17 – 19	
16	321	Acts 20 – 22	
17	322	Acts 23 – 25	
18	323	Acts 26 – 28	
19	324	Romans 1 – 3	
20	325	Romans 4 – 7	
21	326	Romans 8 – 10	
22	327	Romans 11 – 13	
23	328	Romans 14 – 16	
24	329	I Corinthians 1 – 4	
25	330	I Corinthians 5 – 9	
26	331	I Corinthians 10 – 13	
27	332	I Corinthians 14 – 16	
28	333	II Corinthians 1 – 4	
29	334	II Corinthians 5 – 8	
30	335	II Corinthians 9 – 13	

DECEMBER – VOLUME 12

Date	Day	Reading	Check as you read each day
1	336	Galatians 1 – 3	
2	337	Galatians 4 – 6	
3	338	Ephesians 1 – 3	
4	339	Ephesians 4 – 6	
5	340	Philippians 1 – 4	
6	341	Colossians 1 – 4	
7	342	I Thessalonians 1 – 5	
8	343	II Thessalonians 1 – 3	
9	344	I Timothy 1 – 6	
10	345	II Timothy 1 – 4	
11	346	Titus 1 – 3 Philemon 1	
12	347	Hebrews 1 – 4	
13	348	Hebrews 5 – 7	
14	349	Hebrews 8 – 10	
15	350	Hebrews 11 – 13	
16	351	James 1 – 5	
17	352	I Peter 1 – 2	
18	353	I Peter 3 – 5	
19	354	II Peter 1 – 3	
20	355	I John 1 – 3	
21	356	I John 4 – 5	
22	357	II John 1 III John 1 Jude 1	
23	358	Revelation 1 – 2	
24	359	Revelation 3 – 5	
25	360	Revelation 6 – 8	
26	361	Revelation 9 – 11	
27	362	Revelation 12 – 13	
28	363	Revelation 14 – 16	
29	364	Revelation 17 – 18	
30	365	Revelation 19 – 20	
31	366	Revelation 21 – 22	

Thy Word Have I Hid in My Heart

From Psalm 119
Adapted by Ernest O. Sellers, 1869-1952

Ernest O. Sellers, 1869-1952

1. Thy Word is a lamp to my feet, A light to my path al - way,
2. For - ev - er, O Lord, is Thy Word Es - tab-lished and fixed on high;
3. At morn - ing, at noon, and at night I ev - er will give Thee praise;
4. Thro' Him whom Thy Word hath foretold, The Sav-iour and Morn-ing Star,

To guide and to save me from sin, And show me the heav'n-ly way.
Thy faith-ful-ness un - to all men A - bid - eth for - ev - er nigh.
For Thou art my por - tion, O Lord, And shall be thro' all my days!
Sal - va - tion and peace have been bro't To those who have strayed a - far.

REFRAIN

Thy Word have I hid in my heart (in my heart), That I might not sin a-gainst Thee (a - gainst Thee); That I might not sin, that I might not sin, Thy Word have I hid in my heart.

INTRODUCTION TO THE BOOK OF
GENESIS

The Book of Genesis is the first of the five books that God inspired Moses to write, except for the Ten Commandments which were written on *two tables. . . of stone, written with the finger of God* (Exodus 31:18). This points out how exceedingly important the Ten Commandments are and how ignoring them is an offense to God.

The life-giving power of His Word can be seen prior to each creative act. *And God said . . .* and at that moment it was created (Genesis 1:3,6,9,11,14,20,24,26,29). *For the Word of God is living, and powerful* (Hebrews 4:12).

Genesis is an accurate account of the origin of the universe, the creation of man, marriage, the family, sin, and the origin of the Hebrew nation. The first sentence in the Bible states: *In the beginning God created the heaven and the earth* (Genesis 1:1). This makes it clear that God is a living, personal Being Who is the Creator of all things and the Absolute Sovereign over all things (John 1:1-3; Colossians 1:16-17).

The word God used here in Genesis 1 is the Hebrew plural noun *Elohim,* even though the singular noun *Eloah* could have been used if God had so chosen (Deuteronomy 32:15,17; Habakkuk 3:3). The first chapter of Genesis also states: *Let Us make man in Our image, after Our likeness* (Genesis 1:26). By recognizing the plurality of the Hebrew noun *Elohim* and the plural Hebrew words translated as *Us* and *Our,* as well as the reference to *the Spirit of God* (1:2), we have a clear revelation that the One True God is Triune and exists as God the Father, God the Son, and God the Holy Spirit.

Jesus also made the Trinity clear when He said: *When the Comforter* (Holy Spirit) *is come, Whom I will send to you . . . the Spirit of Truth . . . He shall testify of Me. . . . He shall not speak of Himself. . . . I leave the world, and go to the Father* (John 15:26; 16:13,28).

It is of utmost importance that believers acknowledge the Lord Jesus Christ as coequal and coeternal with God the Father and God the Holy Spirit and give Him His rightful exalted place in their hearts.

The historical reliability of Genesis also becomes apparent in the Gospel of Matthew when Jesus referred to Sodom and Gomorrah as actual cities that were destroyed by fire from God and to Noah as a man who lived at the time of the flood (Matthew 10:15; 24:37-38; Genesis 6:5,13; 7:6-23; 19:24-25). Furthermore, when Jesus was questioned by His critics concerning divorce, He confirmed the validity of creation when He said: *Have you not read, that He Who made them at the beginning made them male and female, And said: For this cause shall a man leave father and mother, and shall cling to his wife: and they two shall be one flesh?* (Matthew 19:4-6; Genesis 1:27; 2:24).

Of all creation, only man has a *spirit . . . soul and body* (i.e. joined together for all eternity) (I Thessalonians 5:23). It is in His image that Adam was created like God. *God is a Spirit: and they that worship Him must worship Him in spirit and in truth* (John 4:24). No animal has a spirit, a God consciousness, or the ability to worship God.

Genesis explains how Satan deceived Eve, who then, with Adam, decided not to obey the Creator God. Because of sin, mankind inherited a sin nature, i.e. a disobedient nature, and became destined for both physical and spiritual death (Genesis 3:1-7,16-19). *For as in Adam all die, even so in Christ shall all be made alive* (I Corinthians 15:22). God prepared the way for repentant sinners to receive eternal life with the first promise of a Savior (Genesis 3:15). The woman would have a Son. The Son (Jesus Christ) would destroy Satan and provide eternal life for *as many as received Him . . . Which were born . . . of God. . . . Except a man be born again* (anew), *he cannot see the Kingdom of God* (John 1:12-13; 3:3). To illustrate how the Lord Jesus, as the Lamb of God, would die for our sin that we might be clothed with the righteousness of God in Him, God Himself killed ani-mals and *to Adam . . . and to his wife . . . made coats of skins* (causing shed blood), *and clothed them* (Genesis 3:21; also Hebrews 9:22; I Corinthians 1:30; I Peter 2:24; II Peter 1:1).

Genesis Chapters 1 – 11 record the first 2,000 years* of man's history. During that time, six major events took place: [1] the creation of all things; [2] the sin of Adam and Eve; [3] some 1600 years* later, the building of an ark by Noah; [4] the great flood; [5] 200 years* later, the building of the Tower of Babel; and [6] the diversification of tongues and scattering of people across the earth.

Chapters 12 – 50 cover the next 500 years* and focus on four men chosen by God to bless the world – Abraham, Isaac, Jacob, and Joseph. Through these men we see the love of God for His creation and His willingness to protect and to provide for those who are obedient to His revealed Word.

*Note: *Dates are approximate time periods.*

As we read through His Word our desire should be that we *walk worthy of the Lord to all pleasing, being fruitful in every good work, and increasing in the knowledge of God* (Colossians 1:10).

In Today's Reading
Creation of all things; creation of Adam and Eve; temptation by
Satan; Adam and Eve rebel against God and forfeit Garden of Eden

*G*od made mankind in His image and His likeness. He made us different from every animal. *God is a Spirit: and they that worship Him must
worship Him in spirit and in truth* (John 4:24). No animal has a God
consciousness or is capable of worshiping God.

The LORD *God took the man* (Adam), *and put him into the Garden of
Eden to dress* (cultivate) *it and to keep it* (Genesis 2:15). Man's responsi-
bility was to obey the Word of God and to take care of His garden.
However, God allowed man's love, loyalty, and obedience to be tested.

In Eden, we are introduced to Satan, the one who came in the guise
of *the serpent* (3:1). He is also called *the dragon, that old serpent . . . the
Devil. . . Satan* (Revelation 20:2; see also Isaiah 14:12; Matthew 13:39; I
Peter 5:8; Revelation 12:10). He did not reveal himself as the enemy of
God or as a wicked deceiver intent on destroying every enjoyment of
mankind (II Thessalonians 2:9-10). His intent was, and still is, to prevent
man from obeying his Creator. First, Satan tried to create doubt concerning the truth of what God had said. He implied that God was withholding the best enjoyments in life from Adam and Eve. He asked: *Has God
said, You shall not eat of every tree of the garden?* (Genesis 3:1). This was
followed by Satan's partial truth, which was a lie: *God does know that in
the day you eat thereof, then your eyes shall be opened, and you shall be as
gods, knowing good and evil* (3:5). At that moment, Eve chose to trust self
rather than God, began to "covet" what belonged only to God and
disregarded His ownership and authority. She *saw that the tree was good
for food, and . . . pleasant to the eyes, and a tree to be desired to make one wise,*
so she chose to trespass on God's property and *took of the fruit thereof,
and did eat* (3:6).

Eve yielded to lust when she coveted what God had reserved for
Himself. On that day, Adam and Eve, the father and mother of all mankind, chose to eat the forbidden fruit. They sinned, and consequently,
died spiritually. From that moment on, all of Adam's descendants
inherited his sinful, disobedient nature. *So death passed upon all men*
(Romans 5:12).

Thought for Today: The only means to heaven is through Jesus Christ (John 14:6).

Christ Revealed: As Creator (Genesis 1:1). John 1:1-4; Colossians 1:15-17; Hebrews
11:3. As the Seed of woman (Genesis 3:15; Isaiah 7:14; 9:6-7). *God sent forth His Son,
made of a woman* (Galatians. 4:4).

For definitions of unfamiliar words in today's Bible reading, see pages 468-480.

ꝆN ꝄODAY'S ꝄEADING
Sacrifices of Cain and Abel; Cain murders Abel; genealogy from Adam to Noah; Noah's ark

The physical and spiritual consequences of sin are staggering and they are eternally irreversible except for the blood of Jesus. It did not take long for Adam and Eve's sin nature to become evident. Their first-born son Cain became jealous of his brother Abel and angry with God because his sacrifice was unacceptable.

Abel ... brought ... the firstlings (firstborn) *of his flock. ... the LORD had respect to Abel and to his offering: But to Cain and to his offering He had not respect* (Genesis 4:4-5). The Lord approached Cain in love and offered him an opportunity to repent of his sin: *If you do well, shall you not be accepted? and if you do not well, sin lies at the door* (4:7). While Cain's offering of the firstfruits of the ground recognized God as Creator, it did not recognize Cain as a sinner. *Without shedding of blood is no remission* (forgiveness) *(of sin)* (Hebrews 9:22). *By faith Abel offered to God a more excellent sacrifice than Cain, by which he obtained witness that he was righteous, God testifying of his gifts* (11:4). Abel brought the best as a thanksgiving offering, but recognized himself as a sinner when he *brought. . . the firstborn of his flock* (Genesis 4:4), which means he offered a blood sacrifice of a lamb for atonement of his sins.

The genealogy of *the sons of God* (6:2,4) continued through Adam and Eve's third son Seth (5:3), through whose lineage Jesus would come (Luke 3:38). What often happens today is exactly what happened then: *The sons of God saw the daughters of men that they were fair; and they took them wives* (Genesis 6:2). It is assumed by some that marriage of believers with nonbelievers may be acceptable. The heart could swell with pride that these mixed marriages produced brilliant men. They were *mighty men . . . of old, men of renown* (6:4). But, they were not men who lived in obedience to God.

From the beginning, the biblical principle has always been: *Be not unequally yoked together with unbelievers . . . what part has he that believes with an infidel* (unbeliever)? *And what agreement has the Temple of God with idols? for you are the temple of the living God* (II Corinthians 6:14-16).

Thought for Today: Jesus is the Way that leads us from where we are to where God is.

Christ Revealed: Through Abel's blood sacrifice (Genesis 4:4-7). Christ is *the Lamb of God,* sacrificed for man's sin (John 1:29; Hebrews 9:22; 11:4). Man's best achievements can never take the place of Christ's atonement made through His own sinless blood.

For definitions of unfamiliar words in today's Bible reading, see pages 468-480.

In Today's Reading

Noah, his family, seven pairs of clean and one pair of unclean of every living creature enter the ark *as God had commanded* (Genesis 7:2,9,16); the great flood; the Rainbow Covenant

The LORD *said to Noah Come, you and all your house into the ark* (Genesis 7:1). Noah was able to save his family and preserve mankind because his faith in the spoken Word of God led him to build the ark. During the many years spent in constructing the ark, he was also known as *a preacher of righteousness* in an ungodly world (II Peter 2:5). This illustrates the New Testament truth that *faith without works is dead* (James 2:26). The ark was a secure refuge from certain death; it was also a type of Christ, Who provides spiritual refuge for believers. Christ, our spiritual ark, is calling to the lost today: *Come to Me . . . and I will give you rest* (Matthew 11:28).

For Noah and his family, there came a day, prior to the flood, when they were told to enter the ark, *and the* LORD *shut him in* (Genesis 7:16). All who wait for a more convenient time to be saved need to realize that it is an insult to God Who said *now is the accepted time . . . now is the day of salvation* (II Corinthians 6:2). *Let us therefore fear, lest, a promise being left us of entering into His rest, any of you should seem to come short of it* (Hebrews 4:1).

Just as Noah was able to rest within the ark, secure from the waters of death, so we can be assured of spiritual rest, for our lives are *hidden with Christ in God* (Colossians 3:3). As soon as he was once more on dry land, *Noah built an altar to the* LORD *. . . and offered burned offerings on the altar* (Genesis 8:20). The obedience of faith and the worship of God go hand in hand. Just as Noah was not given an exact day when the flood would come, neither do we know the day that we will face the Lord.

Of that day and hour knows no man, no, not the angels (messengers) *of heaven, but My Father only. But as the days of Noah were, so shall also the coming of the Son of Man be. For as in the days that were before the flood they were eating and drinking, marrying and giving in marriage, until the day that Noah entered into the ark, And knew* (understood) *not until the flood came, and took them all away; so shall also the coming of the Son of Man be. . . . Therefore be . . . ready* (Matthew 24:36-39,44).

Thought for Today: We don't know the day that our lives will end so be prepared.

Christ Revealed: Through the ark (Genesis 7:1,7; Acts 4:12; I Peter 3:12,20). Christ is our ark of safety. *Jesus,* Who *delivered us from the wrath to come* (I Thessalonians 1:10).

For definitions of unfamiliar words in today's Bible reading, see pages 468-480.

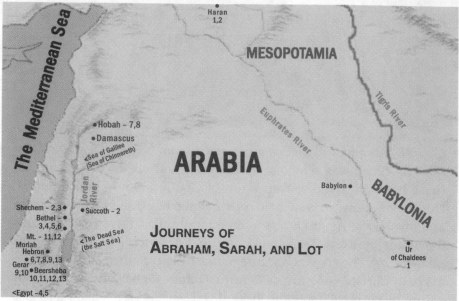

Journeys of Abraham, Sarah, and Lot

1. Ur of Chaldees [150 miles south of Babylon] **To Haran** [Genesis 11:27-31]
Distance: 600 miles
Reason for leaving Ur: Called of God
    [Acts 7:2-4; Hebrews 11:8]
Death of Abram's father [Gen. 11:32]

2. Haran to Shechem [12:1-7] [crossing Jordan at Succoth]
Distance: about 400 miles; Age: 75
First altar built; Abram worships God

3. Shechem to Bethel [12:8]
Distance: 20 miles
Second altar built; prayer offered; famine in Canaan

4. Bethel to Egypt [12:9-20]
Distance: about 225 miles south
Abram denies that Sarai is his wife;
    She was taken into Pharaoh's house

5. Egypt to Bethel [13:1-5]
Abram called on the Name of the Lord
Lot's selfish decision and separation
    from Abram [13:6-13]

6. Bethel to Mamre [Hebron] [13:14-18]
Distance: 35 miles
Third altar built
Abram promised the whole land

7. Hebron to Hobah [North of Damascus]
[14:1-17]
Distance: 160 miles
Battle of the Canaanite Kings
Lot taken captive [14:1-12]
Abram rescues Lot

8. Hobah to Mamre [Hebron] [14:18-20]
Abram gives tithes to Melchizedek and
    is blessed by Him
Promise of a son renewed [15:1-5]

Covenant renewed [15:6-18]
Ishmael born
Abram 86 years old [16:15-16]
Everlasting covenant and sign of circumcision
    at age 99 [17:1-27]
Abram and Sarai names changed to Abraham
    and Sarah [17:5-15]
Isaac, the heir promised [18:1-19]
Intercession for Sodom [18:20-32]
Sodom destroyed, Lot rescued [19:1-38]

9. Hebron to Gerar [20:1]
Distance: 40 miles
Covenant fulfilled
Isaac born when Abraham was 100
[21:1-8; Hebrews 11:11]
Hagar and Ishmael cast out [21:9-21]

10. Gerar to Beersheba [21:27-34]
Covenant with Abimelech
Abraham called on the name of the Lord

11. Beersheba to Mount Moriah [Jerusalem]
[22:1-14 Hebrews 11:17-19]
Distance: about 54 miles
Abraham built altar
Isaac prepared to be offered as a sacrifice –
    a type of God offering Jesus, His only Son,
    on same site 2,000 years later
God renews covenant [22:15-18]

12. Mount Moriah to Beersheba [22:19]
Death of Sarah [23:1-20]
Abraham sends servant to Mesopotamia
    to get wife for Isaac [24:1-67]

13. Beersheba to Hebron [25:1-4]
Distance: about 30 miles
Abraham marries Keturah
Abraham's death and burial in cave of
Machpelah at age 175 [25:7-9]

In Today's Reading

Descendants of Noah; Babel; origin of languages; God's call and
covenant with Abram; his journey to Canaan and Egypt

*N*imrod is the first king mentioned in the Bible: *The beginning of his
kingdom was Babel* (Genesis 10:10). Nimrod means "rebel." *He was a
mighty hunter before the LORD* (10:9). Later we read: *Nimrod: he began to
be mighty upon the earth* (I Chronicles 1:10).

With Nimrod as their leader, the people united to *build us a city and
a tower, whose top may reach to heaven.* They said: *Let us make us a name,
lest we be scattered abroad upon the face of the whole earth* (Genesis 11:4).
The words *make us a name* revealed their desire for power. The human
heart seeks a name for itself and has no desire to glorify God.

The *mighty* Nimrod established the first world empire and ruled it.
His ambition to build a tower *whose top may reach to heaven* did not mean
he expected to reach the throne of the Almighty God – his desire was to
make himself and his followers *mighty* enough to rule the world.
Nimrod was a *hunter* – probably meaning a *hunter* of men who would
support his ambitions. *Before the LORD* means that this rebel pursued his
own ambitious plans in defiance of God, Who had commanded Adam:
Multiply, and replenish the earth (1:28); and to Noah: *Multiply, and
replenish (fill) the earth* (9:1).

Just as in the days of Nimrod, today there is a worldwide movement
to unite and control all people and all religions into a one-world government and one church. The only assurance of not being deceived in this
age of lawlessness is knowing the Word of God as a personal relationship with Jesus. This knowlede exposes the motives behind the actions
of leaders in world affairs.

In striking contrast to Abram, who symbolizes submission to God,
Nimrod is a symbol of self-seeking independence. The call of God came to
Abram: *Get . . . out of your country . . . to a land that I will show you . . .
in you shall all families of the earth be blessed. So Abram departed* (12:1-4).

The call of God demands that we make a choice. Even the closest ties
of human loyalty or affection must be cut when they conflict with our
submission to Christ and what is written in His Word. *He that takes not
his cross, and follows after Me, is not worthy of Me* (Matthew 10:38).

Thought for Today: Nothing is more important than obeying God's Word.

Christ Revealed: As the Promised Seed of Abraham (Genesis 12:3; 18:18; Matthew 1:1;
Acts 3:25-26; Galatians 3:16). Abraham was a type of Christ Who leads the way to a far
better promised land (John 14:2-4,6; Hebrews 11:8-10). *He took on Him the seed
(offspring) of Abraham* (Hebrews 2:16).

For definitions of unfamiliar words in today's Bible reading, see pages 468-480.

ℐN ℱODAY'S ℛEADING

Abram and Lot separate; Abram moves to Hebron, builds an altar; Lot rescued; Melchizedek blesses Abram; God's covenant with Abram

The testing of Abram's faith began after he and Lot left Ur of the Chaldees on their journey of about 1000 miles to the promised land (Genesis 11:31; 12:4). Upon arrival, he discovered there was a famine and they traveled south near Sodom where the pastureland was best. Abram and Lot both had large flocks. Soon *there was a strife* (quarreling) *between the herdsmen of Abram's cattle* (livestock) *and . . . of Lot's cattle* (13:7). Abram could have taken the best for himself since he was older than his nephew, as well as being the spiritual leader. Instead, he graciously said to Lot: *Let there be no strife . . . for we are brethren* (related). *Is not the whole land before you?* (let us) *separate . . . if you will take the left . . . then I will go . . . right* (13:8-9). Lot selfishly took advantage of Abram and chose all the well-watered plain near Sodom.

It was after this experience that Abram received a promise from the Lord that He would make Abram's *seed* (descendants) as numerous as *the dust of the earth* (13:16). Abram went north to live *in the plain of Mamre . . . in Hebron, and built there an altar to the LORD* (13:18).

Lot decided to ignore his spiritual need to be in fellowship with Abram. Instead, he made friends with the people of Sodom, who were *wicked and sinners before the LORD exceedingly* (13:10-13).

Lot was typical of many Christians today who deplore our wicked society but who make decisions based on personal material advantages. Only a few listen seriously to their Savior, Who said: *No servant can serve two masters* – either Christ or Satan (Luke 16:13). Satan wants us to doubt that, when we obey the Lord, we have chosen the best in life.

The Apostle Paul wrote: *We are troubled on every side . . . perplexed* (puzzled), *but not in despair; Persecuted . . . cast down, but not destroyed. . . . we faint not. . . . our light affliction* (troubles), *which is but for a moment, works for us a far more exceeding and eternal weight of glory* (II Corinthians 4:8-17).

Thought for Today: The trials we face now will one day seem insignificant compared to what God was able to accomplish through them.

Christ Portrayed: By the high priest, Melchizedek (Genesis 14:18-20; Hebrews 4:15-16; 5:5-10; 7:1-4). Christ is our High Priest today Who is interceding in prayer for us and Who is deserving of our gifts and service to Him.

For definitions of unfamiliar words in today's Bible reading, see pages 468-480.

In Today's Reading

Ishmael; Abram's name changed; covenant of circumcision;
Sarai's name changed; Isaac promised to Abraham and Sarah;
Abraham's prayer for Sodom.

*A*bram and Sarai were childless. Although God had promised Abram a son, he still had no son when he was 85 years old. At that time, *Sarai said to Abram . . . the LORD has restrained me from bearing . . . go in to my maid; it may be that I may obtain children by* (build a family) *her* (Genesis 16:2). At the age of 86, Abram did receive a son, Ishmael, by Hagar.

Thirteen years passed after the birth of Ishmael (16:16; 17:1). Then God again spoke to Abram: *I am the Almighty God. . . . your name shall be Abraham. . . . I will establish My Covenant* (Agreement) *between Me and you and your seed* (descendants). *. . . My Covenant will I establish with Isaac, which Sarah shall bear to you at this set time . . . next year* (17:1-21).

Abraham was now 99 years old and Sarah was 90. At her age, it was humanly impossible for Sarah to have a child. But God revealed to Abraham: *I am the Almighty God*, meaning the One Who is All-Sufficient. Through Abraham, God would teach us how our faith can be strengthened when He said: *I know him . . . he will command his children and his household* (family or descendants) *after him, and they shall keep the way of the LORD, to do justice and judgment; that the LORD may bring upon Abraham that which He has spoken of him* (18:19).

One of the great tests of our faith is waiting upon the Lord. It may take two weeks, two years, or, as in Abraham's situation, 25 years for our prayers to be answered or desires fulfilled. The Holy Spirit led the Apostle Paul to write concerning Abraham's faith that he was *fully persuaded that, what He had promised, He was able also to perform. . . . Therefore it was imputed* (credited, transferred) *to him for righteousness* (Romans 4:21-22).

God had said to Abraham: *Walk before Me, and be . . . perfect* (blameless), meaning devoted to God (Genesis 17:1). We too have a responsibility in our covenant relationship with God. *Let us therefore come boldly to the throne of grace, that we may obtain mercy, and find grace to help in time of need* (Hebrews 4:16).

Thought for Today: The greatest test of our faith is waiting upon the Lord, but the outcome is always His best.

Christ Revealed: As the Seed of Isaac (Genesis 17:19). Christ was a descendant of Isaac. Jesus. . . . *Who was the son of Jacob, Who was the son of Isaac* (Luke 3:23-34; Heb. 11:18).

For definitions of unfamiliar words in today's Bible reading, see pages 468-480.

In Today's Reading

Sodom destroyed; Lot and his daughters; birth of Isaac;
Hagar and Ishmael; agreement between Abraham and Abimelech

Lot soon had a prominent position in Sodom since he *sat in the gate of Sodom* where business and legal matters were conducted (Genesis 19:1). Lot associated with the people of Sodom even though he was *vexed* (troubled) *with the filthy conversation* (conduct) *of the wicked* (II Peter 2:7). The Scriptures denounce homosexuality for which Sodom was known. Since homosexuality is so detestable in the eyes of God, we should pray for the sinner that he will repent and forsake sin (I Corinthians 9:11). The Law of God groups homosexuality with incest and bestiality (Leviticus 18:22-30; 20:13; Romans 1:24-27).

Sarah conceived, and bore Abraham a son in his old age, at the set time of which God had spoken to him (Genesis 21:2).

Isaac, the miracle child of promise, entered the family life of Abraham, Sarah, and Hagar the bondwoman. Hagar's son Ishmael soon revealed his true character through his contempt for Isaac. In the New Testament we read *that Abraham had two sons, the one by a bondmaid, the other by a free-woman. . . . these are the two covenants* (agreements); *the one from the Mount Sinai, which genders* (leads) *to bondage, which is Agar. . . . Now we, brethren, as Isaac was, are the children of promise. But as then he that was born after the flesh persecuted him that was born after the Spirit, even so it is now* (Galatians 4:22,24,28-29).

These two sons Ishmael and Isaac illustrate the dual nature of our lives. We are first *born of the flesh* (human parents) (John 3:6), symbolized by Ishmael. But the moment a sinner believes in his heart and, like the people on the Day of Pentecost, asks: "What do we do?" Peter replied: *Repent, and be baptized . . . and you shall receive the gift of the Holy Ghost* (Spirit) (Acts 2:38). The believer then becomes the possessor of the nature of God and the new life in Christ which is symbolized by Isaac, the child of faith (Romans 10:9-10; I John 3:1-2; 4:15). At the moment of conversion we do not become sinless but we are freed from the power of sin (Romans 6:7).

And they that are Christ's have crucified the flesh with the affections (passions) *and lusts. If we live in the Spirit, let us also walk in the Spirit* (Galatians 5:24).

Thought for Today: God will guide those who read His Word.

Christ Portrayed: By Isaac, the promised son of God's Covenant (Genesis 21:12) -- in contrast to Ishmael, son of a bondwoman (Galatians 4:22-31). Life in Christ sets us free from bondage of the Law because God made a new Covenant through Christ's blood (Matthew 26:28; Mark 14:24; Luke 22:20; I Corinthians 11:25; also Hebrews 12:24).

For definitions of unfamiliar words in today's Bible reading, see pages 468-480.

In Today's Reading
Abraham's willingness to offer Isaac; God's Covenant renewed;
Sarah's death; Rebekah's marriage to Isaac

After 25 years of waiting for the promised son, God said to Abraham: *Sarah your wife shall bear you a son . . . you shall call his name Isaac: and I will establish My Covenant with him* (Genesis 17:19). *It came to pass after these things, that God . . . said to . . . Abraham. . . . Take . . . your only son Isaac, whom you love, and get you into the land of Moriah; and offer him there for a burnt offering* (22:1-2).

Isaac was a young man when this final test came to Abraham's faith. A burnt offering sacrifice was always to be a male animal, was the best the offerer had, and was to be wholly consumed by fire. It was an expression of dedication to God. Abraham knew that Isaac must live since God had said: *I will establish My Covenant with him* (17:19); yet, now the command of God was to offer Isaac as a sacrifice. Obediently, *Abraham rose up . . . and took . . . Isaac his son, and split the wood for the burnt offering . . . and went to the place of which God had told him* (22:3). With unquestioned faith in God, *Abraham said to his young men, Abide . . . you here . . . I and the lad will go yonder and worship, and come again to you* (22:5).

On Mount Moriah, Abraham built an altar. When Isaac inquired how they could offer a sacrifice without a sacrificial animal, Abraham responded: *My son, God will provide Himself a lamb for a burnt offering* (22:8). Abraham's many years of trusting in the Lord gave him faith in God. This is an amazing testimony of how Abraham's faith had grown over the years until he knew that God never makes a mistake and he believed *God was able to raise him up, even from the dead* (Hebrews 11:19).

Abraham . . . took the knife to slay his son. . . . the Angel of the LORD called to him out of heaven, and said, Abraham. . . . Lay not your hand upon the lad, neither do you any thing to him: for now I know that you fear God. . . . Abraham lifted up his eyes, and looked . . . a ram (male goat) *caught in a thicket by its horns: and Abraham went and took the ram, and offered him up for a burnt offering in the stead* (instead) *of his son* (Genesis 22:10-13). Through trials and suffering, the Lord develops our faith. *God . . . will not suffer* (permit) *you to be tempted above that you are able; but will with the temptation also make a way to escape* (I Corinthians 10:13).

Thought for Today: Our faith is strengthened through stressful situations, even though they are painful.

Christ Revealed: Through Isaac's willingness to be offered (Genesis 22:7-10; compare John 10:11-18). Jesus willingly offered His life. *I lay down* (give up) *My life. . . . of Myself* (10:17-18).

For definitions of unfamiliar words in today's Bible reading, see pages 468-480.

IN TODAY'S READING

Abraham's death; birth of Jacob and Esau; Esau sells his birthright;
Isaac blesses Jacob with the Abrahamic Covenant

Esau came from the field, and he was faint: And Esau said to Jacob, Feed me . . . that same red pottage (stew); *for I am faint.* Jacob, knowing the character of his brother, replied: *Sell me this day your birthright* (Genesis 25:29-31). Esau had no interest in spiritual things so he agreed, saying: *I am at the point* (about) *to die: and what profit shall this birthright do to me?* (25:32-34). Esau could not have been *at the point to die* by missing one meal.

Though much maligned by Esau and others, the fact is, Jacob purchased the birthright for what Esau thought it was worth. More importantly, God had told Rebekah that *the elder shall serve the younger* (25:23).

Esau and Jacob were twin brothers, but Esau was born first and became legal heir to the family birthright which included, among other things, being heir to the Covenant between God and Abraham. The birthright was a link in the line of descent through which the Messiah was to come (Numbers 24:17-19). In contrast with Esau, *Jacob was a plain man, dwelling in tents* (Genesis 25:27). The Hebrew word for *plain* is the same word translated in other Scripture as *perfect, upright, undefiled;* so the word *plain* refers to Jacob's character as a man of God. God records His highest praise and blessing for Jacob: *The LORD has chosen Jacob to Himself* (Psalm 135:4). It appears that Isaac's admiration for his worldly-minded son Esau caused him to ignore the prophecy that God had revealed to Rebekah before the twins' birth (Genesis 25:23), and he chose to disregard Esau's sale of his birthright to Jacob (25:33-34).

The moment Isaac realized that Rebekah had thwarted his evil scheme, he quickly and openly conferred the Abrahamic Covenant upon Jacob, an obvious admission of how terribly wrong he had been (28:3-4). There is no hint that Isaac thought that Rebekah did wrong. The Hebrew word Jacob is translated "supplanter." One of the definitions of supplant in Webster's Dictionary is "to take the place of and serve as a substitute for, especially by reason of superior excellence."

Lest there be any fornicator, or profane (godless) *person, as Esau, who for one morsel of meat* (food) *sold his birthright* (Hebrews 12:16). The writer of Hebrews referred to Esau as a *profane* (godless) *person . . . who . . . was rejected: for he found no place of repentance* (12:16-17).

Thought for Today: How prone we are to blame others for our failures.

Christ Revealed: As the spiritual Seed (Genesis 26:4). *Now to Abraham and his Seed* (descendants) *were the promises made. . . . as of one . . . Who is Christ* (Galatians 3:16). All true believers in Christ are the children of promise. *As many as received Him, to them gave He power to become the sons of God* (John 1:12-13; I John 3:9).

For definitions of unfamiliar words in today's Bible reading, see pages 468-480.

When Isaac realized that God had overruled his scheme to confer the God-ordained birthright of Jacob upon Esau, he *trembled very exceedingly* (Genesis 27:33). He quickly conferred with Rebekah, not to accuse her of any wrongdoing, but to decide how best to plan for Jacob's future. If Jacob violated the Word of God in marrying an idol-worshiping woman, as Esau had done, Rebekah asked: *What good shall my life do me?* (27:46). *Isaac called Jacob, and blessed him, and charged him . . . You shall not take a wife of the daughters of Canaan. . . . Go to Padan-aram . . . take . . . a wife from . . . the daughters of Laban your mother's brother. And God Almighty bless you, and make you fruitful, and multiply you, that you may be a multitude of people* (28:1-3). This blessing was an obvious admission of how wrong Isaac had been in his attempt to defraud Jacob.

However, Esau was quick to blame Jacob for his trouble, saying: *He has taken away my blessing* (27:36). Esau is typical of sinners who irresponsibly blame someone else for their failures.

Isaac lived 43 years after his attempt to thwart God's plan, but there is no record of him being used again of God. For Jacob, however, his remarkable blessings began on his first night away from home.

Without map or companion, but according to the exact plan of God, Jacob left home on his journey of more than 500 miles and arrived safely in Padan-aram. God marvelously guided him to Rachel and the home of his *mother's father*, where he was received with a warm welcome (28:2).

Just as it is with everyone who lives to please the Lord, Jacob's life was set apart for a purpose. When Christians realize this truth, their attitude toward their marriage partners, workplace, physical limitations, and hardships will be seen as in the will of God.

At a much later date, Jacob's son Joseph would be sold as a slave by his brothers. But, 20 years later he would confidently say to them: *You thought evil against me; but God meant it for good* (Genesis 50:20).

Thought for Today: Eternal treasures are reserved for those who forsake earthly pleasures to do the will of God.

Christ Portrayed: By Joseph who was born (Gen. 30:23-24) in order to save and preserve his people (Genesis 50:20). Jesus was born in order to offer salvation to all mankind. *For God so loved the world, that He gave His only begotten Son, that whosoever believes in Him should not perish, but have everlasting life* (John 3:16).

For definitions of unfamiliar words in today's Bible reading, see pages 468-480.

In Today's Reading

Laban's jealousy; Jacob flees; Jacob wrestles with the Angel of God; his name changed to Israel; peace between Jacob and Esau

*T*he greed of Laban and his sons resulted in a hostile attitude toward Jacob, the servant of God. *The LORD said to Jacob, Return to the land of your fathers . . . and I will be with you. . . . I am the God of Bethel, where you . . . vowed a vow* (made a pledge) *to Me: now arise, get . . . out from this land, and return to the land of your kindred* (Genesis 31:3,13).

After 20 years, Jacob was returning home with his two wives, two concubines, 11 sons and one daughter, many servants, and flocks. Esau, who had threatened to kill Jacob (27:41-45), was approaching with 400 men and *Jacob was greatly afraid* (32:3,6-7). He hastily divided his wives, children, and flocks into two groups, reasoning that if Esau should come upon one camp and destroy it, the remaining camp would escape in the opposite direction. In the dark of night, Jacob was then left alone. He earnestly prayed and reminded the Lord that He had said: *Return to your country, and to your kindred, and I will deal well with you* (32:9). There is a lesson to learn from Jacob: first, we need to know what God has said and then, we need to remind the Lord that we are relying on His promises. But most important, Jacob was praying for the future fulfillment of the Covenant promise that God had made to His grandfather Abraham.

This godly and humble servant of the Lord spent the night alone, agonizing in prayer, until he was conferred with the highest honor given by God to any man in Old Testament history: *Your name shall be called no more Jacob, but Israel* (God Prevails): *for as a prince you have power with God and with men, and have prevailed* (overcome) (32:28). Through the centuries, the people of God would be called by his name – Israelites. Through his son Judah, Jesus the Messiah would be promised (49:10).

We too are in a covenant relationship with God through Jesus Christ our Savior and our Mediator, Who declared that the Christian life also requires struggle: *Strive to enter in at the strait* (narrow) *gate: for many, I say to you, will seek to enter in, and shall not be able* (Luke 13:24).

Thought for Today: The more we love the Word of God, the more we will love the God of the Word.

Christ Revealed: As *the Angel* (Messenger) *of God* Who guides (Genesis 31:11-13). The Angel speaks not merely in the Name of God, but as God, leaving no doubt that He is the Lord Jesus in His preincarnate state. *I and My Father are One* (John 10:30).

For definitions of unfamiliar words in today's Bible reading, see pages 468-480.

ℐN 𝒯ODAY'S ℛEADING

Dinah, daughter of Jacob and Leah, is raped; Simeon and Levi's revenge; Jacob's return to Bethel; Abrahamic Covenant renewed

*J*acob continued on toward Bethel, since the Lord had said: *I am the God of Bethel . . . return to the land of your kindred* (Genesis 31:13). But, just a short distance from Bethel, Jacob discovered the beautiful valleys and opportunities for financial gain near *Shechem* (33:18).

For ten years Jacob's stay seemed to be successful. Then we read of the tragedy of his daughter Dinah. When *Shechem . . . prince of the country, saw her, he took her, and lay with her, and defiled* (violated) *her* (34:2). In revenge for their sister Dinah's rape, Simeon and Levi slew all the men of Shechem.

Godly parents often become so involved with achieving material goals that they neglect to *train up a child in the way he should go* (Proverbs 22:6). This often results in worldly attractions gaining control of their children's hearts and leads to heartbreaking consequences.

Surely, we can learn from Jacob that material success is no assurance that we are in the will of God. But the greatest lesson we can learn from Jacob's tragedies is that he didn't give up when his situation looked hopeless. Instead, he turned to the Lord, Who said: *Arise, go up to Bethel, and dwell there: and make there an altar to God, Who appeared to you when you fled from the face of Esau your brother* (Genesis 35:1). At this time of renewal, Jacob instructed his family to *put away the strange gods that are among you, and be clean, and change your garments: And let us arise, and go up to Bethel; and I will make there an altar to God, Who . . . was with me in the way . . . I went* (35:2-3).

Three things Jacob said to his family have a parallel for Christians. He first said: *Put away the strange gods* – a reminder that old habits of sin must be forsaken; the second: *be clean, and change your garments* – a reminder to *follow . . . holiness, without which no man shall see the Lord* (Hebrews 12:14). Thirdly, we are to worship only God: *You shall worship the Lord your God, and Him only shall you serve* (Luke 4:8).

Participation in church worship is a very important way in which God can speak to us, through Bible study, hymns of praise, sermons, and presenting our tithes and offerings, and in participating in the sacred sacraments of Baptism and the Lord's Supper. *Christ also loved the Church, and gave Himself for it; That He might sanctify and cleanse it with the washing of the water by the Word* (Ephesians 5:25-26).

Thought for Today: Compromise always results in disappointments.

Christ Revealed: As *God Almighty*, El Shaddai, the All-Sufficient One (Genesis 35:11). Jesus is *the Lord . . . Who is the Almighty* (Revelation 1:18).

For definitions of unfamiliar words in today's Bible reading, see pages 468-480.

ℐN ℐODAY'S ℛEADING
Joseph's dreams; Joseph sold into slavery;
the cruel lies of Potiphar's wife; Joseph imprisoned

Joseph was the only one of Jacob's 12 sons who expressed interest in spiritual things. Joseph was deeply troubled about his older brothers' evil conduct while away from home. At 17 years of age, *Joseph . . . was feeding the flock with his brethren* and reported to his father the evil things they were doing (Genesis 37:2). The fact that Joseph *was the son of his old age* (37:3), and possibly because of Joseph's concern for his brothers' spiritual well-being, influenced Jacob to love him *more than all his brethren* (37:4).

Some people discourage exposing wrongdoing, and others say they do not want to become involved. But Joseph possessed spiritual integrity and was willing to face abuse from his brothers for exposing their evil ways. Their envy turned to hatred when Joseph shared his prophetic dreams with them (37:5-7). His brothers scoffed, saying: *Shall you indeed reign over us? . . . they hated him yet the more for his dreams* (37:8).

Joseph's brothers *went to feed their father's flock in Shechem*, which was a considerable distance from their home (37:12). Some time later, Jacob, concerned about his sons' welfare, sent Joseph to see if everything was all right with them (37:14). After a long search, Joseph found his brothers near the village of Dothan (37:17).

When his brothers saw Joseph coming, they plotted to *slay him. . . . and . . . say, Some evil beast has devoured him* (37:18-20). Shocking as it must have been, *they stripped Joseph out of his coat . . . of many colors . . . and cast him into a pit* (37:23-24). Joseph then was sold as a slave to Ishmaelites, who, in turn, sold him in the slave market to Potiphar, the captain of the royal guard (37:27-28,36; 39:1). Their last memories of their terrified younger brother were of him pleading for his life (42:21).

God used the experiences of Joseph in Egypt to prepare him to be the preserver of God's people and, thus, the lineage of the coming Messiah, Jesus Christ. *All things work together for good to them that love God, to them who are the called according to His purpose* (Romans 8:28).

Thought for Today: Faith is strengthened when trials are accepted with patience, *knowing that tribulation* (troubles) *works patience* (Romans 5:3).

Christ Portrayed: By Joseph, a type of Christ, who was rejected by his own brothers, sold for 20 pieces of silver to Gentiles and imprisoned, but eventually became their savior and a world ruler (Genesis 37:28; 41:39-40). Jesus *came to His own* (people), *and His own received Him not* (John 1:11). He was sold for 30 pieces of silver, imprisoned, crucified, and became our Savior and soon will return to rule the world (Revelation 20:6).

For definitions of unfamiliar words in today's Bible reading, see pages 468-480.

In Today's Reading

Dreams interpreted by Joseph; Joseph made a ruler of Egypt;
his brothers buy corn and bow down to him; Simeon detained

Thirteen years had passed since Joseph's brothers sold him into slavery. Following that horrible ordeal, he experienced many pitiful disappointments. Consider his many lonely nights suffering as an innocent prisoner, *Whose feet they hurt with fetters: he was laid in iron* (Psalm 105:18). Joseph spent many years as a slave but never became bitter. He remained faithful to the Lord.

At the age of 30, Joseph was called to interpret Pharaoh's dreams. *Joseph answered Pharaoh . . . God shall give Pharaoh an answer of peace* (Genesis 41:16). Because the Lord interpreted the dreams through Joseph, Pharaoh acknowledged him as the wisest man in Egypt. This former outcast then received Pharaoh's own ring as a sign of his new authority as second ruler over all the land of Egypt (41:39-44). The dreams that Joseph experienced many years before now were becoming a reality.

We may endure months, or even years, when it may appear that God either does not care about us or will not do anything about our circumstances. The faithless critic blames God for his problems and complains: "Why me?" However, God has amazing ways of developing our talents, maturing us spiritually, and honoring all who remain faithful to Him.

All of us have known someone who seemed so promising for future service for the Lord but who succumbed to Satan's temptation, such as his assistant of whom the Apostle Paul wrote: *Demas has forsaken me, having loved this present world* (II Timothy 4:10). This does not imply that Demas had rejected what Paul was preaching. By today's standards, he wanted future security, better pay, less work, and retirement benefits. Demas left the Lord's ministry for secular benefits that are often disappointing and seldom satisfying. At best, they only last for this short lifetime but then comes the awful regret. All of us need to seriously consider that Jesus said: *Take no thought for your life* (daily needs). . . . *(For after all these things does the world seek:) . . . But seek . . . first the Kingdom of God, and His righteousness* (Matthew 6:25-33).

Thought for Today: Adverse circumstances will not defeat the faithful.

Christ Revealed: By the wisdom of Joseph (Genesis 41:39). *Christ; In Whom are hidden all the treasures of wisdom and knowledge* (Colossians 2:2-3).

For definitions of unfamiliar words in today's Bible reading, see pages 468-480.

$\mathcal{I}$N $\mathcal{T}$ODAY'S $\mathcal{R}$EADING

Jacob's sons return to Egypt for food; Judah offers to take the place of Benjamin; Joseph makes himself known to his brothers

$\mathcal{B}$ecause of the great famine, Jacob was forced to send his sons to Egypt to buy food. As the second most powerful ruler of Egypt spoke to them through an interpreter, they were unaware that he was their brother Joseph, whom they had sold into slavery about 20 years earlier.

After questioning them about their family, Joseph had his brothers imprisoned for three days (Genesis 42:17). During their stay in prison, they recalled how their younger brother Joseph had pleaded with them not to be sold as a slave to the Ishmaelite traders on their way to Egypt. Now, in an Egyptian prison, they humbly confessed what a terrible act of cruelty they had committed. *And they said one to another, We are verily* (truly) *guilty concerning our brother, in that we saw the anguish of his soul, when he besought us, and we would not hear; therefore is this distress come upon us* (42:21). Simeon was then held hostage in Egypt until they brought their youngest brother to Egypt (42:24).

When Joseph's brothers returned home without Simeon, Jacob heard of the ruler's demand to bring his youngest son Benjamin to Egypt before they could buy any more food. He was deeply distressed, and said: *My son shall not go down with you* (42:38). However, as the famine continued and their food ran low, Jacob had no choice but to let Benjamin return with his brothers to Egypt.

Joseph demanded that his brothers come to his home. Imagine their shock when he said, in their Hebrew language: *I am Joseph your brother, whom you sold into Egypt* (45:4). To their amazement, he lovingly added: *Be not . . . angry with yourselves, that you sold me here: for God did send me before you to preserve life* (45:5).

For years, Joseph's brothers had deceived their father and had escaped all accountability for their cruel sin against Joseph. Now they were forced to face their brother. Joseph explained: *You sold me*; but *God did send me.* Although God used their wickedness to fulfill His will, this did not lessen their guilt. Let Joseph be our example for, regardless of how cruel someone has been, *if you forgive . . . not men their trespasses, neither will your Father forgive your trespasses* (Matthew 6:14-15).

Thought for Today: Don't wait until difficulty is past to praise God.

Christ Revealed: Through Joseph's dealings with his brothers. Christ deals with us in such a way as to bring about our confession of sin and a recognition of His forgiving love. In a similar way, He reveals His sovereignty over the affairs of life (Genesis 45:5-8,15; compare Romans 5:8; Ephesians 1:17,20-22).

For definitions of unfamiliar words in today's Bible reading, see pages 468-480.

$\mathscr{I}$N $\mathscr{T}$ODAY'S $\mathscr{R}$EADING

Jacob's vision at Beersheba; the journey to Egypt; Joseph and the famine; the best land given to Jacob; Joseph's sons blessed

$\mathscr{J}$acob knew that God had planned for his people to live in Canaan, not in Egypt, so he did not rush to Egypt for a grand reunion with his precious son Joseph. Since the will of God remained uppermost in Jacob's heart, he needed assurance from God concerning his journey to Egypt. After Jacob left Hebron, he journeyed about 25 miles *to Beersheba, and offered sacrifices to the God of his father Isaac. And God spoke to Israel in the visions of the night, and said, Jacob, Jacob. And he said, Here am I. And He said . . . fear not to go down into Egypt; for I will there make of you a great nation . . . I will also surely bring you up again* (Genesis 46:1-4).

The Lord assured Jacob that their sojourn in Egypt was not to be a permanent one, but that it would be a time of preparing his family to become *a great nation*. Earthly life is a time of preparation for eternity (Luke 12:20-21). What gets priority, and how we live, is an expression of our preparation for eternity. Our eyes should not be set on worldly securities and achievements but foremost on being the person God wants us to be in order to accomplish the purpose for which He created us.

The life of Jacob gives the believer insight into the sovereignty of God, Who assists, strengthens, and sustains all who are faithful to Him. As the years in Egypt passed, Jacob came to see how God had been directing, protecting, and providing for him all of his life.

This remarkable man of God received much abuse throughout his life, but God conferred more blessings on Jacob than any other man in Old Testament history. The name of Abraham, the father of the faithful, appears over 300 times in Scripture. The name Isaac appears only 131 times, often only in conjunction with Abraham and Jacob. Jacob, however, is mentioned over 370 times, and his new name Israel, referring to both himself and his descendants, appears over 2500 times. It is a serious thing to criticize one whom God has chosen to esteem, as He clearly said: *Jacob have I loved, but Esau have I hated* (detested, i.e. thought less of) (Romans 9:13; Malachi 1:2-3).

Thought for Today: Christians are to forgive regardless of circumstances.

Christ Portrayed: By Joseph, who was placed on the throne to sustain life and give provision (Genesis 47:15-17). Jesus said: *For the Bread of God is He Who comes down from heaven, and gives life to the world* (John 6:33).

For definitions of unfamiliar words in today's Bible reading, see pages 468-480.

Introduction To The Book Of
Exodus

The word *Exodus* means "exit, departure, the way out" (Hebrews 11:22). This book continues the history of the descendants of Jacob's 12 sons. In the first chapter of Exodus, just two short verses, 11 and 12, cover the time to which God referred when He said: *Know of a surety that your seed* (descendants) *shall be a stranger* (temporary resident) *in a land* (Egypt) *that is not theirs, and shall serve them; and they shall afflict them four hundred years* (Genesis 15:13; Acts 7:6).

Chapters 1:1 – 11:10 cover the period when the Israelites first settled in the most fertile land in Egypt until the time when they became slaves to the Egyptians and endured much suffering. To gain their release, God directed Moses to pronounce a series of ten plagues upon Egypt.

Chapters 12:1 – 14:18 At the time chosen by Him, God said: *Against all the gods of Egypt I will execute judgment: I am the LORD* (Exodus 12:12). The Israelites' miraculous deliverance from Egypt was made possible by their obedience to the Word of God as they, by faith, applied the blood of an innocent lamb to their doorposts. God had also required them to *eat the flesh in that night, roast with fire, and unleavened* (yeast-free) *bread. . . . with your loins girded, your shoes on your feet, and your staff in your hand* (12:7-11). Only after they obeyed all that God commanded were they prepared to leave Egypt. This was the beginning of a new life and their birth as a nation (12:2). It also was the beginning of a new liberty from Egyptian bondage (13:3). But, best of all, it meant a new fellowship with God through the feasts (festivals) (13:6).

Chapters 14:19 – 15:27 detail the account of Israel's victorious deliverance from Egypt and Moses' song of praise to the Lord for redeeming them. At the time they were delivered from slavery, there were about 600,000 Israelite men in addition to the women and children and a mixed multitude who were probably the result of intermarriage (12:37-38).

Chapters 16:1 – 18:27 provide an account of the Israelites' journey from Elim, along the Red Sea to Mount Sinai, which took about three months.

Chapters 19:1 – 40:38 begin in the third month of the Exodus and record the Israelites' stay at Mount Sinai, which lasted about 11 months. During this time, the Covenant relationship between God and the Israelites as a nation was established. God said to *the children of Israel . . . if you will obey My voice indeed, and keep My Covenant, then you shall be a peculiar* (select, special) *treasure to Me above all people* (Exodus 19:3-5).

The Book of Exodus reveals how God faithfully protected and provided for His people in the midst of great difficulties and fierce enemies.

THE JEWISH CALENDAR

Civil Calendar - Official calendar of kings, childbirth, and contracts   Sacred Calendar - Used to compute festivals

Month Sacred/Civil	Days in Month	Pre-Exile Name	Post Exile Name	Present-day Equivalent	Biblical References	Season	Day Feasts (Festivals)
1/7	30	Abib	Nisan	March/April	Exodus 12:2; 13:4; 23:15; 34:18; Deut. 16:1; Nehemiah 2:1	Spring, Latter rains, Barley harvest	14th Feast of Passover (Exodus 12:18; Lev. 23:5); 15-21st Feast of Unleavened Bread (Lev. 23:6); Feast of First-fruits (Lev. 23:10)
2/8	29	Zif (Ziv)	Iyyar	April/May	I Kings 6:1,37	Dry season begins	
3/9	30		Sivan	May/June	Esther 8:9	Wheat harvest, Early figs ripen	Feast of Weeks/Harvest (Pentecost) (Lev. 23:15-21)
4/10	29		Tammuz	June/July		Hot season; Grape harvest	
5/11	30		Ab (Av)	July/August		Olive harvest	9th Fast, Destruction of Temple
6/12	29		Elul	August/September	Nehemiah 6:15	Dates & Summer figs	
7/1	30	Ethanim	Tishri	September/October	I Kings 8:2	Early (former) rains, plowing time	1st Feast of Trumpets (Lev. 23:24; Num. 29:1); 10th Day of Atonement (Lev. 26:27); 15-21st Feast of Tabernacles (Lev. 23:34); 22nd Solemn Assembly (Lev. 23:36)
8/2	29	Bul	Cheshvan or Marcheshvan	October/November	I Kings 6:38	Wheat & Barley sown, Winter figs	
9/3	30		Chisleu (Chislev or Kisleu)	November/December	Nehemiah 1:1; Zechariah 7:1	Winter rains, sowing	25th 8-Day Feast of Dedication (John 10:22) added in between Old & New Testaments
10/4	29		Tebeth (Tevet)	December/January	Esther 2:16	Winter rains	
11/5	30		Sebat (Shebat, Shevat)	January/February	Zechariah 1:7	Almond trees blossom	
12/6	29		Adar	February/March	Ezra 6:15 Esther 3:7; 8:12; 9:1,15,17,19,21	Latter rains, citrus harvest	14th Feast of Purim - began with Queen Esther (Esther 9:15-19)

*The Hebrew year had 354 days based on a lunar cycle. Months were alternately 30 and 29 days long. An extra 29-day month, Vadar, was added between Adar and Nisan about every 3 years.

The Jewish day was from sunset to sunset, in 8 equal parts:

FIRST HOUR	SUNRISE TO 9 A.M.
THIRD HOUR	9 A.M. TO NOON
SIXTH HOUR	NOON TO 3 P.M.
NINTH HOUR	3 P.M. TO SUNSET

FIRST WATCH............	SUNSET TO 9 P.M.
SECOND WATCH	9 P.M. TO MIDNIGHT
THIRD WATCH	MIDNIGHT TO 3 A.M.
FOURTH WATCH	3 A.M. TO SUNRISE

IN TODAY'S READING
Jacob's prophecies; deaths of Jacob and Joseph;
the Hebrews oppressed in Egypt

*A*fter Joseph's death, the prestige the Israelites had enjoyed in Egypt gradually disappeared. *There arose up a new king over Egypt, who felt no obligation to the descendants of Joseph* (Exodus 1:8). He was fearful of the Israelites' growing numbers and said to his administrators: *Behold, the people . . . of Israel are more and mightier than we . . . let us deal wisely with them; lest . . . they join . . . our enemies, and fight against us. . . . Therefore they did set over them taskmasters to afflict them with their burdens. . . . But the more they afflicted them, the more they multiplied and grew. And they were grieved because of the children of Israel* (1:9-12).

Desperate for an answer to his dilemma, Pharaoh demanded of *the Hebrew midwives . . . if it be a son, then you shall kill him* (1:15-16). Sometime after this horrible edict was issued, *a man of the house of Levi . . . took as a wife a daughter of Levi. And the woman . . . bore a son: and . . . she hid him three months* (2:1-2). But then, fearful of being discovered, she prepared *an ark of bulrushes . . . and put the child therein; and she laid it in the flags* (reeds) *by the river's brink* (2:3).

If it had not been for Pharaoh's cruel edict, Moses would never have been rescued by Pharaoh's daughter and given all the advantages of the world's greatest empire of that time. God was preparing Moses to lead the Israelites to the promised land.

We may face suffering where we seem to be under the control of a situation where we are as powerless as the Israelites were. It could be that death has left us without a parent or spouse. We may feel defeated following a divorce or have received a terminal diagnosis from a doctor. We all will face many unforeseen sorrows.

Still, every Christian can say with the Apostle Paul: *I am persuaded* (convinced), *that neither death, nor life, nor angels, nor principalities, nor powers, nor things present, nor things to come . . . nor any other creature, shall be able to separate us from the love of God, which is in Christ Jesus our Lord* (Romans 8:38-39).

Thought for Today: The All-Sufficient God doesn't show favoritism.

Christ Revealed: As the Messiah Who would come through the tribe of Judah. *The scepter shall not depart from Judah . . . until Shiloh come* (Genesis 49:10). *Jesus . . . the son of Juda* (Luke 3:23-33).

For definitions of unfamiliar words in today's Bible reading, see pages 468-480.

In Today's Reading
Early life of Moses; his flight into Midian; the burning bush; his
commission to free the nation of Israel; his return to Egypt

*M*oses, the son of Israelite slaves, enjoyed the luxury of the Egyptian palace! *It came to pass . . . when Moses was grown, that he went out to his brethren, and looked on their burdens: and he spied an Egyptian smiting* (striking, beating) *a Hebrew, one of his brethren. And . . . when he saw that there was no man, he slew the Egyptian, and hid him in the sand* (Exodus 2:11-12).

Moses was 40 years old when he executed the cruel Egyptian. This was Moses' legal right, since he was of the royal household and possibly second only to Pharaoh in administering justice. Moses was in the prime of his life and, from a natural point of view, it would seem to be the ideal time for God to use him to set His people free from their suffering.

But Moses was forced to flee Egypt. This was followed by 40 years of loneliness as a shepherd in a desert wilderness. It must have seemed to Moses a waste of 40 years to do nothing of importance. But, with the Lord, such time is never wasted. It was in the desert that the Lord appeared to him and said: *Draw not near here: put off your shoes from off your feet, for the place whereon you stand is holy ground* (3:5). Moses could never have learned humility or been able to come closer to God in an Egyptian palace. He was too busy and too important. But both experiences were vital in preparing him to be the person God could use to lead His people out of Egypt, through the desert, and on to the borders of the promised land.

The wisdom of the world cannot qualify us to make right decisions in life. We must be taught by the Holy Spirit through reading His Word and being obedient to its truth. It is the Holy Spirit's anointing on what we do and say that makes our lives worthwhile. Like Moses, our most basic need is the removal of self-sufficiency. It was spiritually necessary for Moses to tend sheep on *the backside of the desert* to eliminate self-will and fully yield to God's will (3:1).

The highly-educated Apostle Paul wrote: *Not that we are sufficient of ourselves to think any thing as of ourselves; but our sufficiency is of God* (II Corinthians 3:5).

Thought for Today: You are a vital part of God's plan to reach others.

Christ Revealed: As the *I AM THAT I AM* Who commissioned Moses (Exodus 3:13-14; compare Hebrews 13:8). *Jesus said to them, Verily, verily* (Truly, truly), *I say to you, Before Abraham was, I am* (John 8:58).

For definitions of unfamiliar words in today's Bible reading, see pages 468-480.

𝒥ɴ 𝒯ODAY'S ℛEADING

Moses' demands to Pharaoh; Aaron to speak for Moses;
Moses' rod turned into a serpent; plague of blood

𝒢od commanded Moses to face the Pharaoh of Egypt, who referred to himself as a god, and say: *Thus says the LORD God of Israel, Let My people go, that they may hold* (celebrate) *a feast to Me in the wilderness. And Pharaoh said, Who is the LORD, that I should obey His voice to let Israel go? I know not the LORD, neither will I let Israel go* (Exodus 5:1-2).

Moses' immediate reaction was to blame God, saying: *Why have You so evil entreated* (brought harm to) *this people? why is it that You have sent me? For since I came to Pharaoh to speak in Your Name, he has done evil to this people; neither have You delivered Your people at all* (5:22-23).

How often in life our questions far outnumber our answers: "Why have I been diagnosed with cancer? Why did my husband divorce me? Why did my child become a drug addict? Why was my child born with handicaps? Why did I lose my job? Why?" God didn't answer Moses' questions, and seldom does He answer us in the way we expect.

When Moses cried out, "Why, Lord?," God merely reminded him of Who He was. What is important for us to know is that God is the unchangeable, loving, Almighty God of truth. He said: *I will bring you out from under the burdens of the Egyptians, and I will rid you out of their bondage . . . I will take you to Me for a people, and I will be to you . . . your God* (6:6-8). Before He spoke the first *I will*, God said: *I am the LORD*, meaning: "I am the only One who knows what is best and I am altogether sufficient to meet your needs" (6:2); and after His seventh *I will*, He repeated for emphasis: *I am the LORD* (6:8). God has never once failed to keep His Word; but, seldom are His promises fulfilled as soon as we expect, and almost never in the way we think.

Pharaoh persisted in keeping the Israelites under his cruel authority. However, as had been foretold, the judgment of God was poured forth on each false Egyptian deity, on every household of the Egyptians, on Pharaoh's son, and eventually on Pharaoh himself and his armies.

Today . . . hear His voice, Harden not your hearts (Hebrews 3:7-8).

Thought for Today: Some people are more concerned over present problems than being submissive to the will of God.

Christ Revealed: As the Redeemer from the bondage of sin. *I will bring you out . . . I will redeem you* (Exodus 6:6). *You are not under the Law, but under grace* (Romans 6:14). *Christ has redeemed us from the curse of the Law* (Galatians 3:13; also I Peter 1:18-25).

For definitions of unfamiliar words in today's Bible reading, see pages 468-480.

IN TODAY'S READING

Plagues of frogs, lice, flies, death of cattle, boils, hail, locusts, and darkness

*W*hile God was in the process of delivering the Israelites, the Egyptians suffered through each of the ten plagues, but the plagues did not affect the Hebrews. Even Pharaoh's magicians recognized Who was in control of the plagues. They said to Pharaoh: *This is the finger of God: and Pharaoh's heart was hardened, and he hearkened not to them* (Exodus 8:19). Following the hail that destroyed *all that was in the field, both man and beast. . . . Pharaoh sent . . . for Moses and Aaron, and said to them, I have sinned . . . the LORD is righteous, and I and my people are wicked* (9:25,27).

Pharaoh assured Moses that the Israelites could go free the moment the hail ceased. But, again Pharaoh changed his mind and hardened his heart against the will of God. Without a doubt, *Pharaoh's heart was hardened* each time he decided to reject the Word of God (7:13-14,22; 8:15,19,32; 9:7). But, the time arrived when *the LORD hardened the heart of Pharaoh* (9:12).

Eventually, Pharaoh agreed to Moses' request, saying: *Go, serve the LORD your God: but who are they that shall go? And Moses said, We will go with our young and with our old, with our sons and with our daughters, with our flocks and with our herds will we go; for we must hold a feast to the LORD* (10:8-9) – meaning that everyone from the youngest child to the most elderly person must worship the Lord. However, Pharaoh insisted that the Israelite slaves must worship on his terms. His own advisers withstood him, saying: *Let the men go, that they may serve the LORD their God: know you not yet that Egypt is destroyed?* (10:7). Disregarding his advisers, Moses and Aaron *were driven out* (dismissed) *from Pharaoh's presence* (10:8-11).

The person who is most deceived is the one who believes he can worship the Lord on his own terms. Others who are equally deceived say they will live for Jesus later in life and refuse to give up control of their lives, like Pharaoh. But there comes a day when the time for repentance is past. God alone decides how long He will be insulted.

Depart from evil, and do good; and dwell for evermore. For the LORD loves judgment (justice), *and forsakes not His saints* (Psalm 37:27-28).

Thought for Today: The real issue is: "Who is in control of your life?"

Christ Revealed: As a Light to His people. *There was a thick darkness in all the land of Egypt . . . but all the children of Israel had light in their dwellings* (Exodus 10:22-23). Jesus said: *I am the Light of the world: he that follows Me shall not walk in darkness* (John 8:12). *The LORD will lighten my darkness* (II Samuel 22:29).

For definitions of unfamiliar words in today's Bible reading, see pages 468-480.

In Today's Reading
Death of the firstborn; the Lord's Passover; the Exodus;
pillar of cloud and pillar of fire

With each miraculous plague, God proved that Egypt's gods were false deities and that He was the One True God Who controls His creation. The final plague of judgment was death. God spoke to Moses: *About midnight will I go out into the midst of Egypt: And all the firstborn . . . shall die, from the firstborn of Pharaoh . . . even to the firstborn of the maidservant* (Exodus 11:4-5). However, God lovingly provided a way for all of the Israelites who were obedient to Him to save their firstborn from death. The sentence of death would not fall on them, but upon a lamb *without blemish* (defect). They were told to *take of the blood, and strike it on the two side posts and on the upper door post* (lintel) *of the houses. . . . they shall eat the flesh in that night, roast with fire, and unleavened* (yeast-free) *bread and with bitter herbs they shall eat it. . . . with your loins girded, your shoes on your feet, and your staff in your hand; and you shall eat it in haste: it is the* LORD'S *Passover* (12:5,7-11).

The Hebrew word translated *atonement* carries the idea of covering something, thereby removing it from God's sight. However, even though an innocent lamb made a temporary atonement, sin was not fully eradicated. Even though there were numerous daily, weekly, and monthly sin offerings, the Israelites were still required to observe a full Day of Atonement annually.

The sin offering, the trespass offering, and the Day of Atonement, as the supreme act of national atonement for sins, were offered regularly. However, they were only substitute offerings until Jesus became the one True Sacrifice and died for the sins of the world.

Since God is holy, He cannot fellowship with man in his sinful state. So God has provided His sinless Son as the perfect and complete substitute to die for our sins. *How much more shall the blood of Christ, Who through the eternal Spirit offered Himself without spot* (defect) *to God, purge* (cleanse) *your conscience from dead works to serve the living God?* (Hebrews 9:14).

Thought for Today: The cross that ended the earthly life of Jesus forever ended the power of Satan to control the Christian.

Christ Revealed: Through the sacrifice of lambs without blemish. Not one of the lamb's bones was to be broken (Exodus 12:5,46). We were redeemed *with the precious blood of Christ, as of a lamb without blemish and without spot* (I Peter 1:19). It was foretold of Christ: *He keeps all His bones: not one of them is broken* (Psalm 34:20; John 19:36).

For definitions of unfamiliar words in today's Bible reading, see pages 468-480.

In Today's Reading
Crossing the Red Sea; song of Moses; the waters of Marah; murmurings; manna and quail

---

Freed from slavery in Egypt, the Israelites were on their way to the promised land. They had traveled only a short distance when they saw all the chariots of Pharaoh's army rushing toward them in a desperate effort to recover his slaves and *the Egyptians pursued after them . . . and overtook them. . . . the children of Israel . . . were sore* (very) *afraid: and . . . cried out to the LORD. And they said to Moses, Because there were no graves in Egypt, have you taken us away to die in the wilderness?* (Exodus 14:9-11). When the Israelites *cried out to the LORD*, it was not in faith, but in fear, hostility, and criticism against Moses.

The Israelites had seen the miracles in Egypt that had set them free; yet, they now chose not to trust God and His ability to provide for them. Although Moses could not see how the Lord would save them, he confidently declared: *Fear . . . not, stand still, and see the salvation* (deliverance) *of the LORD* (14:13). In a spectacular display of His power, *the LORD overthrew the Egyptians in the midst of the sea. And the waters returned, and covered the chariots . . . and all the host of Pharaoh* (14:27-28).

Although God met that need miraculously, just three days later He led the Israelites to Marah, where they could not drink the bitter water. *And the people murmured* (complained) *against Moses* (15:24). So *the LORD showed him a tree, which when he had cast into the waters, the waters were made sweet* (15:25).

The children of Israel's lack of trust in God was again evident when their food supply was exhausted. *The whole congregation of the children of Israel murmured against Moses and Aaron in the wilderness: And . . . said to them, Would to God we had died by the hand of the LORD in . . . Egypt . . . for you have brought us forth into this wilderness, to kill this whole assembly with hunger. Then said the LORD to Moses . . . I will rain bread from heaven . . . that I may prove* (test) *them, whether they will walk in My Law, or not. . . . And the house of Israel called the name thereof Manna. . . . they gathered it every morning* (16:2-4,15,31,21).

Jesus declared Himself to be *the True Bread from heaven. . . . Who . . . gives life to the world. . . . I am the Bread of Life* (John 6:32-35).

Thought for Today: A heart filled with faith in God has no room for fear.

Christ Revealed: Through the bread (manna) from heaven (Exodus 16:15). Jesus said: *I am the Living Bread Who came down from heaven* (John 6:51; also 6:32-48).

For definitions of unfamiliar words in today's Bible reading, see pages 468-480.

IN TODAY'S READING

Thirst causes murmuring against Moses; water from the rock;
Amalek defeated; Jethro's advice; God speaks at Mount Sinai

As they continued their journey toward the promised land, the Israelites faced another test of their dependence upon God. *All the congregation . . . journeyed . . . according to the commandment of the LORD, and pitched* (camped) *in Rephidim: and there was no water for the people to drink. And the people thirsted there for water; and the people murmured* (grumbled) *against Moses, and said, Wherefore* (Why) *is this that you have brought us up out of Egypt, to kill us . . . with thirst? . . . And he called the name of the place Massah* (Temptation, Testing), *and Meribah* (Strife), *because of the chiding of the children of Israel, and because they tempted the LORD, saying, Is the LORD among us, or not?* (Exodus 17:1, 3,7). The Lord knew that there was no water there and yet He directed the Israelites to that very place.

The wilderness journey exposed the Israelites' refusal to trust the Lord. God has warned us: *Harden not your hearts, as in the provocation, in the day of temptation* (testing) *in the wilderness: When your fathers tempted* (tested) *Me, proved Me, and saw My works forty years. . . . I was grieved with that generation, and said, They do alway err* (go astray) *in their heart* (Hebrews 3:8-10).

Israel's release from bondage and the wilderness journey is symbolic of the Christian's release from sin pilgrimage through life. From their experiences, we should learn to trust God even when anticipated resources are not available. Just as the Israelites blamed Moses, we are tempted to blame others. Frustration on the job, emotional stress, discontent, finding fault with uncomfortable situations, hate, jealousy, fits of anger – these are all evidence of the selfish life demanding its own way. Even more serious, it is an expression of distrust in the wisdom, competence, and goodness of God.

The Christian's faith cannot based on favorable circumstances, but on our all-wise Creator. The key to peace of mind and overcoming all life's problems is confidence in His Word. The Christian is admonished to express faith when *you are in heaviness through manifold temptations* (various testings): *That the trial of your faith, being much more precious than of gold that perishes, though it be tried with fire, might be found to praise and honor and glory at the appearing of Jesus Christ* (I Peter 1:6-7).

Thought for Today: To complain exposes a lack of faith in God.

Christ Revealed: As the Rock and the Water that came forth (Exodus 17:6). *They drank of that spiritual Rock (Petra in Greek) that followed them: and that Rock was Christ* (I Corinthians10:4).

For definitions of unfamiliar words in today's Bible reading, see pages 468-480.

> ## *In Today's Reading*
> Ten Commandments and other laws and regulations given

The Ten Commandments are very sacred because they were *written with the finger of God* (Exodus 31:18). It is no surprise that pagans hate to see them displayed. They are an expression of the spiritual and moral conduct of the people of God. Eight are expressed negatively: *You shall not*. Six present requirements for our relationship with others. Four reveal the perfection of the Holy, One True God, Who alone is to be worshiped.

God spoke all these words, saying, I am the LORD your God.... You shall have no other gods before Me. You shall not make to you any graven image, or any likeness of any thing . . . in heaven above, or . . . the earth . . . for I the LORD your God am a jealous God . . . showing mercy to . . . them that love Me, and keep My Commandments. You shall not take the Name of the LORD your God in vain; for the LORD will not hold him guiltless that takes His Name in vain. Remember the Sabbath (rest) *day, to keep it holy. . . . Honor your father and your mother . . . . You shall not kill. . . . commit adultery. . . . steal. . . . bear false witness against your neighbor. . . . covet* (20:1-17).

We are warned that it is wrong to steal – wrong whether it is done by shoplifting, cheating on income tax, or failing to give an employer a full day's work. It is wrong to bear false witness against a neighbor, and it is wrong to commit adultery. *The . . . unbelieving, and the abominable, and murderers, and whoremongers, and sorcerers, and idolaters, and all liars, shall have their part in the lake which burns with fire and brimstone* (Revelation 21:8). We are also warned against the practices of witchcraft, sorcery, bestiality, and sacrificing *to any god, save to the LORD only* (Exodus 22:18-20). All who were guilty of these sins were to be put to death immediately. We need to remember that obedience should come from the heart. If I have love toward my neighbor, I will not steal his property, commit adultery with his wife, or commit fornication with his daughter. I will protect and respect his loved ones because they are the property of God.

The Law is a mirror that reveals what we should be with absolute accuracy. The Apostle Paul said: *Nay, I had not known sin, but by the Law: for I had not known lust* (evil desire), *except the Law had said, You shall not covet* (Romans 7:7).

Thought for Today: We enjoy the peace of God when our desire is: "Whatever pleases You, Lord, pleases me."

Christ Revealed: The perfection of Christ is revealed through the Ten Commandments (Exodus 20:1-17). He was perfect and *without sin* (Hebrews 4:15). He also gave us a new Commandment – *That you love one another, as I have loved you, that you also love one another* (John 13:34).

For definitions of unfamiliar words in today's Bible reading, see pages 468-480.

In Today's Reading

Laws instituted; three feasts which must be kept; the Angel
promised for a guide; instructions for Tabernacle furnishings

The Israelites were commanded: *Serve the LORD your God* (Exodus
23:25). This was followed by 14 blessings which God promised the Israelites for their obedience, including the assurance: *I will deliver the inhabitants of the land into your hand; and you shall drive them out* (23:31).
Then a warning concerning the Canaanites followed: *You shall make no
covenant* (agreement) *with them, nor with their gods* (23:32). The people
responded, saying: *All the words which the LORD has said will we do* (24:3).

God alone determines what is acceptable conduct as well as worship
to Him. Thus, He gave Moses detailed instructions for building the Tabernacle where He would accept the worship of His people.

The Tabernacle provided a way for man to maintain a right relationship with God and a place for man to worship the Lord. But, most importantly, it was a place for God to dwell among His people. In outward
appearance, covered with *rams' skins* (26:14), it was unattractive, like
Jesus, of whom Isaiah prophesied: *He has no form nor comeliness; and
when we shall see Him, there is no beauty that we should desire Him* (Isaiah
53:2). But, like Jesus, nothing could be more inspiring from within, for
it was the only place on earth where God met with His people.

The court of the Tabernacle was a rectangular enclosure with only
one entrance through which sinful man could approach God (Exodus
26:36; 27:16-18). Our Lord Jesus declared: *I am the Door: by Me if any man
enter in, he shall be saved* (John 10:9). Its white linen wall of separation was
symbolic of the holiness of God and excluded all Gentiles. Consequently, they could not so much as look over the curtain fence to observe
what was going on inside the courtyard or come near it, or they would
be put to death (Numbers 1:51). This linen curtain illustrates that sin has
separated sinful man from the Holy Presence of God.

The Bible says: *The Law was given by Moses, but grace and truth came
by Jesus Christ. . . . Behold the Lamb of God, Who takes away the sin of the
world* (John 1:17,29).

Thought for Today: Unless you have something good to say about someone, it's best
not to say anything.

Christ Revealed: As the Ark of the Covenant (Testimony). The wood demonstrates His
humanity; the gold overlay His deity; only through His blood sprinkled on it could one
receive forgiveness; God dwelt above the Mercy Seat (Exodus 25:10-22). *Neither by the
blood of goats and calves, but by His own blood He entered in once into the Holy
Place, having obtained eternal redemption for us* (Hebrews 9:12).

For definitions of unfamiliar words in today's Bible reading, see pages 468-480.

The Tabernacle

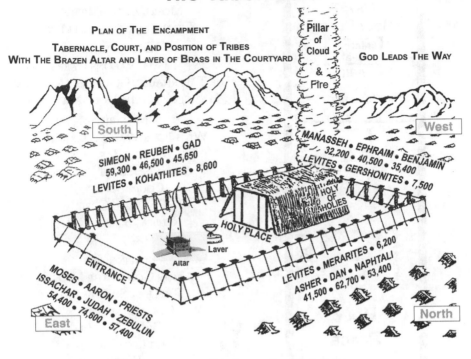

PLAN OF THE ENCAMPMENT

TABERNACLE, COURT, AND POSITION OF TRIBES
WITH THE BRAZEN ALTAR AND LAVER OF BRASS IN THE COURTYARD

Pillar of Cloud & Fire

GOD LEADS THE WAY

South

West

MANASSEH • EPHRAIM • BENJAMIN
32,200 • 40,500 • 35,400
LEVITES • GERSHONITES • 7,500

SIMEON • REUBEN • GAD
59,300 • 46,500 • 45,650
LEVITES • KOHATHITES • 8,600

HOLY OF HOLIES

HOLY PLACE

Laver

Altar

ENTRANCE

LEVITES • MERARITES • 6,200
ASHER • DAN • NAPHTALI
41,500 • 62,700 • 53,400

MOSES • AARON • PRIESTS
ISSACHAR • JUDAH • ZEBULUN
54,400 • 74,600 • 57,400

East

North

Look that you make them after their pattern,
which was showed you in the mount (Exodus 25:40).

Court of the Tabernacle – Brazen Altar – Laver of Brass – The Tabernacle
The Holy Place – Gold Candlestick – Table of Showbread – Altar of Incense
Most Holy Place – The Ark of the Covenant with its Mercy Seat

All things according to the pattern (Hebrews 8:5).

THE TABERNACLE

The Tabernacle was a rectangular structure, about 45 feet long and 15 feet wide, and was set up in the center of the encampment of the 12 tribes. It was protected by an outer court that was about 150 feet long and 75 feet wide based on a pattern the Lord had shown Moses. Nothing was left to human opinion.

Sixty posts, 7½ feet high, were equally spaced around the Tabernacle. This wall separated the unbeliever from the worshiper and was symbolic of the righteousness of God that bars the sinner from His presence.

There was only one door through which sinful man could approach God (Exodus 26:36). It was symbolic of Christ, Who said: *I am the Door: by Me if any man enter in, he shall be saved, and shall go in and out, and find pasture* (John 10:9).

TABERNACLE ENCLOSURE

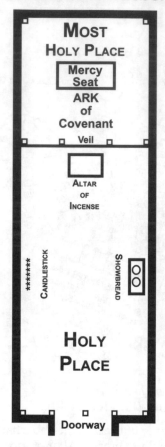

MOST
HOLY PLACE

Mercy
Seat

ARK
of
Covenant

Veil

ALTAR
OF
INCENSE

CANDLESTICK

SHOWBREAD

HOLY
PLACE

Doorway

PILLAR OF CLOUD & FIRE
GOD LEADS THE WAY

MOSES, AARON, PRIESTS
JUDAH, ISSACHAR, ZEBULUN

GERSHONITES
WITH TWO WAGONS CARRYING
THE TABERNACLE, CURTAINS, COVERINGS,
HANGINGS, GATE, DOOR AND CORDS

MERARITES
WITH FOUR WAGONS CARRYING
THE BOARDS, BARS, PILLARS,
SOCKETS, COURT PILLARS,
COURT SOCKETS,
PINS, AND CORDS
REUBEN, SIMEON, GAD

KOHATHITES
BEARING THE
ARK – GOD IN THE MIDST
TABLE OF SHOWBREAD
GOLD CANDLESTICK
BRAZEN ALTAR
ALTAR OF INCENSE
VESSELS
LAVER OF BRASS

EPHRAIM, MANASSEH, BENJAMIN,
DAN, ASHER, NAPHTALI

THE BRAZEN ALTAR
(Exodus 38:1-7)

After passing through the gate into the fenced courtyard, the worshiper approached the Brazen Altar, also called the Altar of Burned Offering. It was about 7½ square

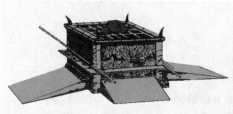

feet and 4½ feet high, with a grate in the center. At this altar the worshiper received covering for his sin through offering the sin and trespass sacrifices.

All sacrifices were offered on the Brazen Altar with the exception of the sin offering which was burned outside the camp, except for its fat which was burned on the Brazen Altar. The blood of the sin offering was sprinkled upon the Altar of Incense and the remainder poured out at the Brazen Altar (Leviticus 4:4-12). Our Lord was both *the Lamb of God, Who takes away the sin of the world* (John 1:29), and our High Priest. *We have such a High Priest . . . on the right hand of the throne of the Majesty in the heavens*(Hebrews 8:1; 9:11-14; Ephesians 2:13; I Peter 2:24).

THE LAVER OF BRASS
(Exodus 29:4; 30:18-21; 38:8)

After the priest offered the sacrifice, he approached the Laver of

Brass that contained water for the priests to cleanse their hands and feet before ministering in the Holy Place. It was symbolic of the Word of God that reveals our sins and is the cleansing power in our lives (John 15:3; Titus 3:5; James 1:23,25).

THE TABLE OF SHOWBREAD
(Exodus 25:23-30; 37:10-16)

After the priest washed his hands and feet at the Laver of Brass, he proceeded toward the Tabernacle, passing through the linen veil, the only door to the Holy Place. Inside the Holy Place

on the right was the Table of Showbread, made of shittim (acacia) wood and overlaid with pure gold. Twelve loaves of unleavened bread sprinkled with incense were placed in two rows of six upon the Table. They were eaten only by the priests in the Holy Place. Its name "Bread of the Presence" meant more than physical nourishment; it indicated gaining spiritual insight that was not obtainable in any other way.

The Holy Spirit is able to do something beyond our ability to explain. He enlightens, empowers, and then transforms the lives of those who prayerfully continue to read the Word of God with a desire to do His will. Jesus said: *I am the Living Bread which came down from heaven: if any man eat of this bread he shall live for ever* (John 6:51; also 6:29-38; 12:24-33).

THE GOLD CANDLESTICK
(Exodus 37:17-24)

Inside the holy place on the left was the seven-branched pure Gold Candlestick that provided the only source of light. Without this light, the room would have been in total darkness. The Candlestick represents Christ, the *Light of the World*, Who makes Himself known through His Word (compare John 8:12 and Revelation 1:12-20).

THE GOLD ALTAR
(Exodus 30:1-10; 27:25-28; 40:5; Leviticus 16:12-13)

Just in front of the veil leading to the Holy of Holies was a gold altar called the Altar of Incense (I Kings 6:22; Hebrews 9:4). This Altar was about 3 feet high, 1½ feet wide, and 1½ feet deep, made of acacia (shittim) wood overlaid with pure gold.

The Altar of Incense was used exclusively to burn incense morning and evening. A coal of fire from the Brazen Altar was placed on this Altar each morning and incense put on it. Only the high priest was permitted to offer incense, a type of intercessory prayer that ascended toward heaven day and night.

The Altar of Incense was the smallest piece of furniture in the Tabernacle and, as such, may seem insignificant. But it was symbolic of Christ as our Intercessor (John 17:1-26; Hebrews 7:25). It is through Him that the praise as well as the prayers of undeserving people become precious to God (Hebrews 13:15).

THE ARK OF THE COVENANT with THE MERCY SEAT
(Exodus 37:1-9; Numbers 10:33)

The Ark of the Covenant was made of acacia (shittim) wood, covered within and without with pure gold. The Ark contained Aaron's rod that budded, a golden pot of manna, and the two tables of stone on which were written the Ten Commandments (Exodus 16:33; 31:18; 34:29; Numbers 17:10; Deuteronomy 10:5; Hebrews 9:4).

The Mercy Seat, or lid of the ark, was made of pure gold. On this lid were two gold cherubim with outstretched wings, facing each other, but looking down on the Mercy Seat. Between the cherubim dwelt the manifestation of the Presence of God, which lighted the Holy of Holies.

Only one man, the high priest, symbolic of Christ, could enter the

Holy of Holies. Once each year, on the Day of Atonement, he sprinkled the blood of the sacrificed animal on the Mercy Seat and then before it seven times, symbolic of the perfect and complete salvation and forgiveness of sins made possible by Jesus Christ.

Christ, our High Priest, presented His blood as His sacrifice so that we might be acceptable to God (Hebrews 9:11-15; 10:19).

In Today's Reading

Directions given for constructing the Tabernacle, court, furniture, and enclosure; plans for Altar; Aaron's priestly garments; ephod

*J*ust inside the courtyard which surrounded the Tabernacle stood the Brazen Altar (Exodus 27:1-8; 38:30), also called *the Altar of Burnt Offering* (30:28). God had said to Moses: *You shall make an Altar of shittim wood. . . . overlay it with brass* (27:1-2). Throughout the Bible, brass is a symbol of the judgment of God on sin (compare Numbers 21:6-9; John 3:14-16). All sacrifices were offered on the Brazen Altar, with its fire which was kindled by an act of God and which was never to go out (Leviticus 6:13).

In sacrificing an unblemished animal, the Israelite understood that the animal's life was being forfeited in his place because of sins he had committed. He knew that it was only through the sinless animal being slain on his behalf that he was restored to a right relationship with God. The worshiper entered the one door into the outer court and approached the Brazen Altar. Then he placed his hands upon his sacrifice to signify his guilt being transferred to the innocent animal.

Between the Altar and the Tabernacle was the large Brass Laver made out of many brass mirrors which the women of the camp had provided (Exodus 38:8). Each day after the priest had offered a sacrifice, he approached the *Laver of Brass* (30:17-19) and washed his hands and feet before ministering in the Holy Place. The mirrors and water were symbolic of the Word of God which both reveals our sins and is the cleansing power to remove sin from our lives (Titus 3:5; James 1:23,25).

God used the Romans to destroy Herod's Temple: its Brazen Altar, Brass Laver, Gold Candlestick, Table of Showbread, and Altar of Incense. The Ark of the Lord's Covenant, with its Mercy Seat, had been missing since the Babylonian captivity. All of these had symbolized Christ, Who fulfilled them (Hebrews 9:1 – 10:22; 13:10-12). Since the crucifixion, bodily resurrection, and ascension of Christ, both Jews and Gentiles have but one God-appointed means of cleansing from sin.

Christ gave Himself for the Church *that He might sanctify* (make holy) *and cleanse it with the washing of water by the Word* (Ephesians 5:26). Jesus also said: *Now you are clean through the Word which I have spoken to you* (John 15:3).

Thought for Today: What will I do today to honor the Lord?

Christ Revealed: Through the Brazen Altar, upon which the sin sacrifice was burned (Exodus 27:1-8; Leviticus 4:1-12). Jesus' sacrifice was the fulfillment of all Old Testament altars as well as all sacrifices. *In Whom we have redemption through His blood* (Ephesians 1:7; John 1:36).

For definitions of unfamiliar words in today's Bible reading, see pages 468-480.

IN TODAY'S READING

The rules and sacrifices for the priests; continual burnt offering;
Altar of Incense; the ransom of souls; the holy anointing oil;
Sabbath regulations; Moses receives two tablets of stone

The priests, who ministered in the Tabernacle, had to be cleansed before entering. *The LORD spoke to Moses . . . make a Laver* (tub) *of Brass, and its foot also of brass . . . put it between the Tabernacle . . . and the Altar, and . . . put water therein. For Aaron and his sons shall wash their hands and their feet thereat* (Exodus 30:17-19). After a priest had washed his hands and feet at the Laver, which provided cleansing from the activities of life, he then was qualified to enter the Tabernacle through a heavy linen veil which was the only entrance into the Holy Place.

On the right was the Table of Showbread with its 12 loaves of unleavened bread sprinkled with incense. The name Showbread suggests more than just bodily nourishment. It implies spiritual insight that is not obtainable anywhere else. The Showbread is symbolic of Christ, Who said: *I am that Bread of Life. . . . the Living Bread which came down from heaven: if any man eat of this Bread, he shall live for ever* (John 6:48,51; 6:29-38; 12:24). Just as physical food is assimilated to sustain our physical lives, so too, as we continue to "read" the Word of God which is the Bread of Life, the Holy Spirit enlightens and then transforms our lives. *Laying aside all malice and all guile* (deceit), *and hypocrisies, and envies, and all evil speakings, As newborn babes, desire the sincere* (unadulterated, pure) *milk of the Word, that you may grow thereby* (I Peter 2:1-2).

On the left was the seven-branched Candlestick made of solid, beaten gold. Its seven lamps burned with pure olive oil. It provided the only source of light in the Holy Place (Leviticus 24:2-4).

God has provided just one book – the Holy Bible – as the source of *light* for understanding His will. It is written: *Your Word is a lamp to my feet, and a light to my path. . . . The entrance of Your words gives light; it gives understanding to the simple* (Psalm 119:105,130; also Proverbs 6:23).

Christ said: *I am the Light of the World: he that follows Me shall not walk in darkness, but shall have the Light of Life* (John 8:12).

Thought for Today: Ignoring God's Word always leads to deception.

Christ Revealed: Through the Laver, Christ is revealed as both the container and the dispenser of *Living Water* (Exodus 30:18; John 4:10). *Jesus . . . cried, saying, If any man thirst, let him come to Me, and drink. . . . you are clean through the Word which I have spoken to you* (John 7:37, 15:3; compare I Corinthians 10:4).

For definitions of unfamiliar words in today's Bible reading, see pages 468-480.

*J*N *T*ODAY'S *R*EADING
Moses delayed on Mount Sinai; Aaron's golden calf; its destruction;
death of 3,000 Israelites; Law renewed; God's Covenant; three feasts

*M*oses was on Mount Sinai when God gave him *two tables of testimony, tables of stone, written with the finger of God* (Exodus 31:18). At the same time, something tragic was taking place at the base of the mountain. *When the people saw that Moses delayed to come down out of the mount, the people gathered themselves together to Aaron, and said to him, Up, make us gods* (an image to remind us of God), *which shall go before us; for as for this Moses, the man that brought us up out of the land of Egypt, we know not what is become of him* (32:1). It didn't take Aaron long to make a golden calf and *he built an altar before it. . . . And they rose up early on the morrow, and offered burnt offerings, and brought peace offerings* (32:2-6).

A true burnt offering was a delight to the Lord since it symbolized full surrender to Him; but these idolatrous sacrifices were hypocrisy.

Returning to the camp, Moses saw how quickly the Israelites had *corrupted themselves* (done wrong) (32:7). Did they think that a golden calf, which they could see, was a better reminder of Whom they were to worship than the invisible, yet ever present God? Had they turned to Apis, an Egyptian god in the form of a bull? Only six weeks before, the whole congregation had sworn: *All that the LORD has spoken we will do* (19:8).

False worship leads to irresponsible immoral conduct. Let us compare the Israelites' sins with our own behavior. Most of us would reject man-made idols; but think how easily money, possessions, talents, hobbies, and success become idols for many. The Apostle Paul spoke of others who, although *they knew God, they glorified Him not as God, neither were thankful; but became vain* (empty, worthless) *in their imaginations, and their foolish heart was darkened* (Romans 1:21).

The golden calf stands as a symbol of human intellect which devises its own system of worship apart from, or added to, the Word of God. The world admires the independent person who is determined to be in control. They *rejoiced in the works of their own hands* (Acts 7:41).

Thought for Today: Following the opinions of people, instead of listening to God, results in disaster.

Christ Revealed: As the One Who is ever-present. *My Presence shall go with you, and I will give you rest* (peace) (Exodus 33:14). *He has said, I will never leave you, nor forsake you* (Hebrews 13:5; compare Matthew 11:28).

For definitions of unfamiliar words in today's Bible reading, see pages 468-480.

In Today's Reading

Freewill offerings for the Tabernacle; construction of the Tabernacle;
the Ark of the Covenant (Testimony);
Mercy Seat; Table of Showbread; Candlestick; Altar of Incense

The Altar of Incense was *made . . . of shittim wood. . . . and. . . . a crown*
(moulding) *of gold round about. . . . And he made the holy anointing oil, and
the pure incense* (Exodus 35:15; 37:25-26,29). Moses was also directed to
put it before the veil that is by the Ark of the Covenant (Testimony), *before
the Mercy Seat that is over the Covenant, where I will meet with you. . . .
Aaron shall burn thereon sweet incense every morning. . . . a perpetual
incense before the* LORD *throughout your generations* (Exodus 30:6-8).

The priests were permitted in the Holy Place, but only the High
Priest could enter the Holy of Holies, once a year on the Day of Atonement. In front of the veil was a Gold Altar that was much smaller than
the Brazen Altar. But the Brazen Altar sacrifices dealt with the judgment
of sin. It was near the entrance to the courtyard.

The Altar of Incense was symbolic of Christ as our Intercessor (John
17:1-26; Hebrews 7:25). Each morning, Aaron the high priest would
refill the lamps with pure olive oil and burn incense upon the altar. He
would take a coal of fire from the Brazen Altar and place it on the Altar
of Incense and then place the incense, symbolic of our prayers, on it for
a sweet fragrance that ascended toward heaven day and night. God
alone was the source of fire on both of the altars.

Only Jesus Christ can make it possible for us to approach the
Heavenly Father in prayer. *My little children . . . if any man sin, we have
an advocate with the Father, Jesus Christ the righteous* (I John 2:1). *It is* (the
sinless) *Christ Who died* (for our sins), *yea rather, that is risen again, Who
is even at the right hand of God, Who also makes intercession for us* (Romans
8:34). In Hebrews, we read: *He is able also to save them . . . that come to
God by Him, seeing He ever* (forever) *lives to make intercession for them*
(Hebrews 7:25). Christ our High Priest is interceding for us each time we
pray. We are encouraged: *in every thing by prayer and supplication with
thanksgiving let your requests be made known to God. And the peace of God
. . . shall keep your hearts* (Philippians 4:6-7).

Thought for Today: It is through Christ that the prayers of sinful, undeserving people
become precious to God.

Christ Revealed: Through the Candlestick (Exodus 35:14). Christ is *the Light of the
World* (John 1:6-9; 8:12; 9:5; compare Luke 1:78-79).

For definitions of unfamiliar words in today's Bible reading, see pages 468-480.

IN TODAY'S READING
Brazen Altar of burned offering; Tabernacle courtyard;
priest's garments

At Mount Sinai, the Tabernacle was completed according to the instructions the Lord commanded Moses: *Thus was all the work of the Tabernacle . . . finished. . . . and all its furniture . . . The Ark of the Testimony . . . and the Mercy Seat* (Exodus 39:32-35). *The Ark of the Testimony* (25:22) – also known as the *Ark of the Covenant* (Numbers 10:33) – contained the Covenant between God and His people Israel. It was a wooden chest overlaid with gold, both inside and out. The Ark was a type of Jesus the Messiah, the Son of God, Who alone can atone for sin. The wood represented His human nature, as foretold by Isaiah: *He shall grow up before Him as a tender plant, and as a root out of a dry ground* (Isaiah 53:2). The gold represented His divine nature, for **He is both fully God and fully man**. The Ark was made from the wood of the acacia tree which grew in the deserts, symbols of the world system of things.

The "lid" of the Ark was made of pure gold and was called the *Mercy Seat*. It covered the Law that had been placed in the Ark. Everyone is a sinner, but Christ, the perfect, sinless Son of God became our High Priest. By His perfect atonement for our sins, He provided us with mercy and salvation represented by the *Mercy Seat*.

The Ark was behind the veil, inside the Holy of Holies. Without the Presence of the Lord above the Ark, all the services of the Tabernacle would have been meaningless. You can be sure that, as you prayerfully read the Word of God daily and worship the Lord, His indwelling presence will bring meaning to your life.

On the Day of Atonement, the high priest sprinkled the blood of an innocent goat on the Mercy Seat, then in front of it seven times (Leviticus 16:14). The number seven is symbolic of the perfect and complete salvation and forgiveness of sins which would be made possible by Jesus Christ.

The Law provides the "knowledge" of sin, but not the "forgiveness" of sin (Galatians 2:16; 3:11). *The Law was given by Moses, but grace and truth came by Jesus Christ* (John 1:17). Jesus is the One *in Whom we have redemption through His blood, even the forgiveness of sins* (Colossians 1:14).

Thought for Today: The more we recognize our unworthiness, the more we will appreciate the Lord's mercy in saving us.

Christ Revealed: Through *the golden Altar of Incense* and the incense – representing prayers going up to heaven (Exodus 39:38). Christ prayed for us. *Neither pray I for these alone, but for them also which shall believe on Me through their word* (John 17:20).

For definitions of unfamiliar words in today's Bible reading, see pages 468-480.

In Today's Reading

Tabernacle completed and erected; furnishings arranged;
consecration of Aaron and sons; glory of the Lord fills theTabernacle

*I*n Mount Sinai, God instructed Moses: *Make Me a Sanctuary; that I may dwell among them. According to all that I show you* (Exodus 25:8-9). After nine months, the building of the Tabernacle was completed (39:32; compare 19:1; 40:2). Moses did *according to all that the LORD commanded him* (40:16). This phrase emphasizes the supreme importance of obedience to the will of God (40:16-32). Moses' obedience was complete in every detail for making about 40 different items, including the tent, altars, vessels, Brass Laver, garments, pins, sockets, loops, posts, and furniture (25:40; 26:30; 39:42-43).

The first thing to be placed within the Tabernacle was the Ark of the Testimony which contained the Ten Commandments of God: *On the first day of the first month you shall set up the Tabernacle of the tent of the congregation. And you shall put therein the Ark of the Testimony* (witness). . . . *He took and put the testimony* (tablets of the Law) *into the Ark . . . And he brought the Ark into the Tabernacle . . . as the LORD commanded* (40:2-3,20-21).

After the Tabernacle was constructed, the cloud of the Lord's presence (Exodus 13:21) and the Tabernacle were inseparable throughout the Israelites' journeys. If the cloud lifted and moved forward, the Tabernacle and the people then followed; if the cloud stopped, the people remained until it moved again (40:36-37).

God's Word and His Holy Spirit provide all of the wisdom, spiritual guidance, and strength necessary to live for Him. It is vital that we, like Moses, do all that *the LORD commanded*. In order to understand all of what He has commanded, we must read all of His Word.

Soon, the glorious presence of God will again be seen on earth, as the Apostle John revealed while imprisoned on Patmos, when he wrote: *I John saw the holy city, new Jerusalem, coming down from God out of heaven, prepared as a bride adorned for her husband. And I heard a great voice out of heaven saying, Behold, the Tabernacle of God is with men, and He will dwell with them, and they shall be His people, and God Himself shall be with them, and be their God* (Revelation 21:2-3).

Thought for Today: Allow Christ to take charge of the affairs of your life. You will be so glad you did.

Christ Portrayed: By Aaron as the high priest (Exodus 40:13). *Christ being come a High Priest . . . to appear in the Presence of God for us* (Heb. 9:7-24).

For definitions of unfamiliar words in today's Bible reading, see pages 468-480.

Introduction To The Book Of
*L*eviticus

The purpose of this book was to explain how the Israelites could have a personal relationship with God. The first seven chapters are occupied with the five sacrifices. Chapters 8 – 10 cover the priesthood; chapters 11 – 16 express the qualifications for sanctification and explain the Day of Atonement; and chapter 17 emphasizes the Brazen Altar as the place where sacrifices were to be offered. All five of the Levitical sacrifices were necessary to give a complete understanding of the death of *our Lord Jesus Christ, Who gave Himself for our sins, that He might deliver us from this present evil world* (Galatians 1:3-4).

Chapters 18 – 27 reveal how fellowship with God is maintained. The basic principle is the same today, *because it is written, Be . . . holy: for I am holy* (I Peter 1:16; Leviticus 11:44-45; 19:2; 20:7). Chapters 18 – 22 express God's standard of holiness for all the people and the regulations of sanctification for the priests. Chapters 23 – 27 are concerning *feasts of the LORD* and describe how they were to maintain fellowship with the holy God (Leviticus 23:44).

The seven feasts were timed so that after they had settled in the promised land the men could go to Jerusalem without neglecting their crops. *Three times in the year all your males shall appear before the Lord GOD* (Exodus 23:17).

The first journey to Jerusalem was to be in the first month of the religious year. Three feasts were celebrated in this month. The Passover Feast was on the 14th; the Feast of Unleavened Bread began on the 15th and lasted 7 days; and the Feast of First-fruits began *on the morrow after the Sabbath* of the Passover week, which was always on a Sunday (Leviticus 23:1-14). Jesus Christ is the perfect Passover Lamb, as well as the Unleavened Bread, Who arose on Sunday, the day of First-fruits: *But now is Christ risen from the dead, and become the First-fruits of them that slept* (died) (I Corinthians 15:20).

The second journey was seven weeks later. It commemorated the early harvest and was called the Feast of Weeks. It also occurred on a Sunday, the first day of the week (Leviticus 23:16).

The third group of feasts was during the seventh month of the religious year. Included were the Feast of Trumpets (beginning of their civil year) on the first day, the Day of Atonement on the 10th day, and the Feast of Tabernacles from the 15th through the 21st.

The Sabbaths were occasions free from work. They were times to teach the Word of God and worship Him (23:2-4, 7-8, 21, 24-25, 27-28, 35-37).

*I*N *T*ODAY'S *R*EADING
Burned offering; meat (meal, grain) offering; peace offering

The first three offerings mentioned in the first three chapters of Leviticus are called *sweet savor offerings*, which means they were voluntary and pleasing to God. *Speak to the children of Israel, and say to them, If any man of you bring an offering to the LORD, you shall bring your offering of the cattle, even of the herd, and of the flock. If his offering be a burned sacrifice of the herd, let him offer a male without blemish: he shall offer it of his own voluntary will at the door of the Tabernacle of the congregation before the LORD. And he shall put his hand upon the head of the burned offering; and it shall be accepted for him to make atonement for him* (Leviticus 1:2-4,9).

The first offering mentioned is called *the burned sacrifice*. It symbolized the offerer giving his own life in full submission to God and without a selfish motive. The offering was to be a bull, lamb, goat, turtledoves, or pigeons, according to the financial ability of the offerer (1:3,10,14). If the offerer owned a herd, then he offered a bull. If, however, the offerer possessed only flocks, then his offering would be a lamb or a goat; for either of these men to offer pigeons would have been offensive to God. But, if the offerer were so poor that he did not own a herd or a flock, then an acceptable offering could be the less-expensive turtledoves or young pigeons. This was the offering made by Joseph and Mary, the mother of Jesus, which points out how very poor they were before the wise men arrived with their expensive gifts (Luke 2:22-24; Matthew 2:11; see Leviticus 12:2-8).

The procedure for the offering was for the offerer to lay his hands heavily upon the head of the animal, symbolizing the transfer of sin from the guilty to the sinless to atone for his sin. Next, the offerer had to *kill the bullock before the LORD: and the priests, Aaron's sons, shall bring the blood, and sprinkle the blood round about upon the altar* (1:5). The blood offered to God indicated that a life had been given as a substitute for the one who had sinned. This was a foreshadowing of the crucifixion of Jesus Christ, *Who gave Himself for us, that He might redeem us from all iniquity* (lawlessness), *and purify to Himself a peculiar* (special) *people, zealous of good works* (Titus 2:13-14).

Thought for Today: It's the spirit of giving that counts most.

Christ Revealed: Through the meat (meal, grain) offering which was made without leaven (symbolic of sin) (Leviticus 2:11). Christ was *without sin* (Hebrews 4:15).

For definitions of unfamiliar words in today's Bible reading, see pages 468-480.

IN TODAY'S READING
Sin offering; trespass offering; further directions concerning
burned, meat (meal, grain), and sin offerings

The *meat offering* is also translated meal or grain offering. It could be brought with either the burned offering or the peace offering; but it was never to be brought with the sin or trespass offerings. *And this is the law* (rule) *of the meat* (grain) *offering: the sons of Aaron shall offer it before the LORD. . . . the remainder thereof shall Aaron and his sons eat: with unleavened* (yeast-free) *bread shall it be eaten. . . . in the court of the Tabernacle of the congregation they shall eat it. It shall not be baked with leaven. . . . it is most holy, as is the sin offering, and as the trespass offering* (Leviticus 6:14-17).

The Hebrew word translated *meat* (meal) *offering* is *minchah*, "a gift" given by an inferior to a superior, in the sense of a required tribute paid to a king by a peasant. The Lord's portion was burned on the altar, signifying that the offerer was now in a right relationship with the Most High God.

The fine flour reminded the people that God provided their food and that they, in turn, owed Him their lives. The grain was usually crushed and ground into fine flour which was sometimes mixed with oil and/or frankincense, but always with salt, and then baked. Frankincense, as it burned with the offering, gave forth a satisfying odor symbolizing that the prayers and intercessions of all who are in covenant relationship with God are satisfying to Him.

While the *burned offering* expressed a consecration of self, the *meat offering* was a consecration of service. It also illustrates the life of Christ, the sinless Savior, Who laid aside His glory as the God of creation to be crushed as a grain of wheat by the mill of humiliation. *He was wounded for our transgressions, He was bruised for our iniquities* (Isaiah 53:5). He endured beatings and intense suffering, was crowned with thorns in mockery, and was finally put to death on the cross for the sins of the world, but it is only effective for all repentant sinners who receive Him as their Savior and Lord. The atonement of Christ secured for the sinner the benefits of forgiveness from God and peace and fellowship with Him. *The Son of Man came . . . to give His life a ransom for many* (Matthew 20:28).

Thought for Today: Loyalty and dependability are of far more value than outstanding abilities.

Christ Revealed: Through the body of the young bull which was burned outside the camp (Leviticus 4:12). This pictures Jesus as He suffered *outside the gate* (Hebrews 13:11-12).

For definitions of unfamiliar words in today's Bible reading, see pages 468-480.

THE FIVE OFFERINGS

THE OFFERING	PURPOSE	MEANING FOR TODAY
SIN OFFERING [REQUIRED FIRST] LEV. 4:1-35; 6:24-30 Bulls, goats, or lambs were acceptable – the whole animal was burned outside the camp. The poor could bring two young pigeons or two turtledoves.	This offering provided atonement for the convicted sinner who was separated from God by sin. It was the first offering, because *all have sinned, and fall short of the glory of God* [Romans 3:23]; no one was exempt. It was offered for all the people on feast days. It was a type of Christ crucified outside Jerusalem.	Christ, the perfect, sinless Son of God, gave Himself as the final sacrifice for our sins. *For He has made Him to be sin for us, Who knew no sin* [II Cor. 5:20-21; Gal. 1:4; Heb. 10:3-4; 13:12], thereby providing a cleansing from sin and reconciliation with God for all who accept Christ as their Savior and Lord [John 1:12].
TRESPASS OFFERING [REQUIRED] SIMILAR TO SIN OFFERING LEV. 5:1-19; 6:1-7; 14:12-18	The sinner was required to *make restitution for the harm that he has done* [Leviticus 5:16], whether the sin was against another or against God.	The injured person was compensated. Restitution included an additional 20% of the value restored. Fellowship with the wronged person and with God also was restored.
MEAT OFFERING [VOLUNTARY] GRAIN, MEAL, CEREAL LEV. 2:1-16; 6:14-23; 7:9-10 "Fine" flour, unleavened bread, cakes, wafers, and grain were offered – always with salt and oil, and with frankincense. This always followed the morning and evening burned offerings.	This freewill offering was an expression of thanksgiving: *A sweet savor* (pleasing aroma) *to the LORD* [Leviticus 2:2]. Grain ground into fine flour signifies Christ's brokenness by His crucifixion on our behalf. Jesus was wholly devoted to His Father's will. *Christ also has loved us, and has given Himself for us an offering and a sacrifice to God for a sweet-smelling savor* (pleasing aroma) [Ephesians 5:2].	The individual grains being ground into fine flour and mixed with oil symbolize our need to lose our identity to become part of the Body of Christ. Our unreserved submission to God's will, under the guidance of the Holy Spirit, today arises as *a sweet savor* (pleasing aroma) *to the Lord* [Leviticus 2:2]. *For we are to God a sweet savor* (the fragrance) *of Christ, in them that are saved, and in them that perish* [II Corinthians 2:15].
BURNED OFFERING [VOLUNTARY] LEV. 1:1-17; 5:7; 6:8-13 Based on financial ability: bull for the rich; two turtledoves or young pigeons for the poor.	After sin, trespass, and meat (meal) offerings, the offerer was now reconciled to God and came to worship Him. A bull, ram, goat, turtledoves, or young pigeons were completely burned to ashes on the altar. This was a freewill offering.	This offering illustrates the complete act of self-surrender [Matthew 22:37]. We too are to present our bodies to God as *a living sacrifice* [Romans 12:1-2] – this means we are to give the best of our time, talents, and possessions.
PEACE OFFERING [VOLUNTARY, LAST] LEV. 3:1-17; 7:11-36 *From the herd. . . . flock. . . . a goat. . . . the priest shall burn them upon the altar* [3:1,6,12,16].	This is the only offering shared in fellowship with God, the priests, and families expressing praise to God. It was a symbol of enjoyment and unity and was always a joyful occasion [Ephesians 2:14-15; 5:2; also 1:2; Colossians 1:20; 3:12-16].	Christ is "our peace offering." He alone makes possible true peace and fellowship between God and believers. His prayer was: *That they may be one* [John 17:22]. Jesus promised: *Peace I leave with you, My peace I give unto you* [14:27].

IN TODAY'S READING

Regulations concerning offerings; consecration of Aaron and his
sons for the priesthood, and the priests' offerings

The *peace offering* was the only offering shared by three parties. First:
*The priest shall burn the fat upon the altar: but the breast shall be Aaron's and
his sons'. And the right shoulder you shall give to the priest for a heave* (lifted
up and waved before the Lord as a gift) *offering of the sacrifices of your peace
offerings* (Leviticus 7:31-32) and all that was left was eaten by the offerer
and his family. The sacrifice for the *peace offering* was to be a bull and a ram
(9:3-4). But birds were not acceptable for a *peace offering*. The animal had to
be unblemished, characteristic of the perfect, sinless Christ.

The *peace offering* could be brought for answered prayer, in connection with a vow, or as an act of thanksgiving. It was not required, but
strict regulations had to be followed. To offer a *peace offering*, the offerer
*shall lay his hand upon the head of his offering, and kill it at the door of the
Tabernacle of the congregation: and Aaron's sons the priests shall sprinkle
the blood upon the altar round about* (3:2). The priest burned the fat on the
altar. The fat was always God's portion and was never to be eaten.
*Whosoever eats the fat of the beast, of which men offer an offering made by
fire to the LORD, even the soul* (person) *that eats it shall be cut off from his
people* (7:25).

In all the offerings, the Lord's portion was presented first from all
income. We are never to give the Lord whatever is left over after every
other desire is met. Furthermore, a right relationship with God results
in love and peace in fellowship with other believers. *Therefore, being
justified by faith, we have peace with God through our Lord Jesus Christ*
(Romans 5:1). "Justification" means "being put into a right relationship
with God."

The *peace offering* expressed a peaceful relationship with God, as
well as with others. It was a time of sharing, and friendship, a perfect
illustration which foreshadowed the church, a reminder that we are not
to forsake *the assembling of ourselves together, as the manner of some is:
but exhorting* (encouraging) *one another: and so much the more, as you
see the day approaching* (Hebrews 10:25).

Thought for Today: Pride and jealousy are deadly to health, happiness, fellowship
with others, and peace with God.

Christ Portrayed: By Moses as he consecrated the priests who were called for the work
(Leviticus 8:23-24). Christ is the One Who sets the believer apart for service. *You have
not chosen Me, but I have chosen you, and ordained* (appointed) *you* (John 15:16).

For definitions of unfamiliar words in today's Bible reading, see pages 468-480.

In Today's Reading
First offerings of Aaron; offerings for the people; sin and deaths
of Nadab and Abihu; restrictions for the priesthood

The sin offering and the *trespass offering* (Leviticus 5:6-7) were man-
datory and were the first two *offerings* to be presented. They were
required to restore the broken relationship between God and sinful
man. *Moses said to Aaron . . . offer your sin offering, and your burned
offering, and make an atonement for yourself, and for the people* (9:7).

*And the LORD spoke to Moses . . . Speak to the children of Israel, say-
ing, If a soul* (person) *shall sin through ignorance against any of the Commandments of the LORD concerning things which ought not to be done,
and shall do against any of them: If the priest that is anointed* (placed in
office) *do sin according to the sin of the people; then let him bring for his
sin, which he has sinned, a young bullock without blemish to the LORD for
a sin offering* (4:1-4). This also served as a reminder that the innocent
animal died in the sinner's place. The animal's body was then taken outside the camp for burning.

Scripture points out that ignorance is not an excuse for failing to
obey the Law of God (Romans 2:12-16). Disobedience to the will of God
is sin and must be repented of and atoned for.

No animal could be an absolute substitute for a sinner, but could
only provide a temporary covering for sin. Christ is our sin offering.
God sent forth His Son, made (born) *of a woman, made under the Law*
(Galatians 4:4). Jesus died in the sinner's place for the sins of all mankind. *He* (God) *has made Him* (Christ) *to be sin for us, Who knew no
sin; that we might be made the righteousness of God in Him* (II
Corinthians 5:21).

Christ is also our *trespass offering. You, being dead in your sins and
the uncircumcision of your flesh, has He quickened* (made alive) *together
with Him, having forgiven you all trespasses; Blotting out the handwriting
of ordinances (commands) that was against us . . . and took it out of the way,
nailing it to His cross* (Colossians 2:13-14), so that we have *escaped the
pollutions* (corruptions) *of the world through the knowledge of the Lord and
Savior Jesus Christ* (II Peter 2:20).

Thought for Today: We cheat ourselves when we give less than our best to the Lord.

Christ Revealed: Through the sacrifice of a lamb without defect (Leviticus 9:3). *Behold
the Lamb of God, Which* (Who) *takes away the sin of the world* (John 1:29).

For definitions of unfamiliar words in today's Bible reading, see pages 468-480.

In Today's Reading

Health and dietary laws; the cleansing (purification) of women
after childbirth; signs and laws concerning leprosy

Over 40 times in Leviticus we read: *I am the LORD* or *I am the LORD your God*; and more than six times the Lord demands: *You shall be holy; for I am holy.* Both inward and outward, morally and spiritually, we must separate ourselves from all that defiles: *For I am the LORD your God: you shall therefore sanctify* (consecrate) *yourselves, and you shall be holy; for I am holy* (Leviticus 11:44). The Israelites were to eat clean food (chapter 11); have clean bodies (chapters 12-13), clean clothes (13:47-59), clean houses (14:33-57), clean personal hygiene (chapter 15); and be a clean nation (chapter 16).

The word *unclean* is used about 100 times in chapters 11 through 16, implying that God required every unclean thing to be removed from their lives. God also required that the Israelites separate themselves from heathens, idolatry, immorality, and even unsanitary habits. The people of God were not to intermarry with Gentile unbelievers. The many sacrifices, rules, and regulations concerning what is *clean* and *unclean* (what defiles a person), lead us to understand how sin separates us from God.

This is also a daily reminder to every Christian today that *whether therefore you eat, or drink, or whatsoever you do, do all to the glory of God* (I Corinthians 10:31).

The Holy Spirit led the Apostle Paul to write: *I beseech* (beg) *you therefore, brethren, by the mercies of God, that you present your bodies a living sacrifice, holy, acceptable to God, which is your reasonable service* (Romans 12:1). And, to the church at Corinth, he wrote: *Know you not that you are the temple of God, and that the Spirit of God dwells in you? If any man defile the temple of God, him shall God destroy; for the temple of God is holy, which temple you are* (I Corinthians 3:16-17). To the Ephesians, he wrote: *Be holy and without blame before Him in love* (Ephesians 1:4). *For God has not called us to uncleanness, but to holiness* (I Thessalonians 4:7). And it is also written: *Follow peace with all men, and holiness, without which no man shall see the Lord* (Hebrews 12:14).

Thought for Today: The worldly-minded person never perceives what God reveals to those who are *pure in heart* (Matthew 5:8).

Christ Revealed: Through the clean food of the believer (Leviticus 11:47). Our Lord is the *Bread of Life* (John 6:35), supplies living water (4:10,14), and His Father's will was His *meat* (food, nourishment) (4:34).

For definitions of unfamiliar words in today's Bible reading, see pages 468-480.

In Today's Reading
Purification after having skin diseases; signs of leprosy; uncleanness
of men and women; sacrifice for cleansing from defilements

*W*hen the priest declared that an Israelite was a leper, God said: *The priest shall pronounce him utterly unclean . . . . his clothes shall be rent* (torn), *and his head bare, and he shall put a covering upon his upper lip, and shall cry, Unclean, unclean. . . . he shall dwell* (live) *alone; outside the camp shall his habitation be* (Leviticus 13:44-46). To express his extreme grief and deep humiliation, this poor, wretched person had to pass through the camp for one last time, crying: *Unclean! Unclean!*

When leprosy first appears, it seems harmless – just a small white or pink spot on the skin and, in its earliest stages, it is totally painless. The spot might remain for months or even years before it begins to develop further. Eventually, leprosy produces an extremely repulsive disfigurement of the entire body, including spongy tumor-like swellings on the face and head. The movement of joints causes deep, painful, bleeding fissures. The fingers and toes become misshapen, rough, and ragged. The fingernails swell, curl up, and fall off. And, as leprosy progresses, the flesh develops offensive, running sores, and the gums begin to bleed. Eventually, as the years pass, the leper becomes thin and weak, plagued with diarrhea, an incessant thirst, and burning fever.

During the ministry of Jesus many lepers were healed, which attested to His deity.

On one occasion, *ten. . . lepers, which stood afar off . . . lifted up their voices, and said, Jesus, Master, have mercy on us. . . . One of them, when he saw he was healed . . . glorified God. . . . And He* (Jesus) *said, Arise, go your way: your faith has made you whole* (Luke 17:12-13,15,19).

Leprosy illustrates how insignificant a sin may first appear, but how dreadful, loathsome, and fatal it can become. **Sin immediately separates us from God**, for we are "unclean." People controlled by sin exist in a state of living death, unless they turn to Christ, truly repent, and forsake their sins.

Before Jesus came, there were only two recorded cases of leprosy that were healed – Miriam (Numbers 12:10-16) and Naaman the Syrian (II Kings 5:1-14), both of whom were sovereignly healed by God. *The blood of Jesus Christ His Son cleanses us from all sin* (I John 1:7).

Thought for Today: The lust of the flesh and the eye are never satisfied.

Christ Portrayed: By the priest who made atonement for the leper (Leviticus 14:20). *Our Lord Jesus Christ, by Whom we have now received the atonement* (reconciliation) (Romans 5:11).

For definitions of unfamiliar words in today's Bible reading, see pages 468-480.

In Today's Reading
Day of Atonement; the scapegoat; the eating of blood forbidden;
civil and religious laws; immorality forbidden

On the annual Day of Atonement, Aaron the high priest was first required to present a young bull as a sacrifice for his own sins before he could proceed with the sin offering for the people. God had said that *Thus shall Aaron . . . . take the two goats, and present them before the LORD at the door of the Tabernacle of the congregation. . . . Then shall he kill the goat of the sin offering . . . and bring his blood within the veil . . . and sprinkle it upon the Mercy Seat, and before the Mercy Seat. . . . And Aaron shall lay both his hands upon the head of the live goat, and confess over him all the iniquities of the children of Israel, and all their transgressions in all their sins, putting them upon the head of the goat, and shall send him away by the hand of a fit man into the wilderness: And the goat shall bear* (carry) *upon him all their iniquities. . . . For on that day shall the priest make an atonement* (to cover, a reconciliation) *for you* (Leviticus 16:3-30).

Two goats were necessary to express our Lord's twofold atonement. One goat was sacrificed upon the altar for a *sin offering.* Then Aaron laid his hands upon the head of the remaining goat, the scapegoat, and confessed the sins of the congregation, thereby transferring their sins to the scapegoat which was led away by another *to a land not inhabited: and he shall let go the goat in the wilderness* (16:22) where it disappeared from sight, a symbol that *as far as the east is from the west, so far has He removed our transgressions from us* (Psalm 103:12). There was no justification but merely a "covering" of another year's sins for the Israelites. But Christ, our great High Priest, did not need to present a sacrifice for Himself, for He *is holy . . . Who needs not daily, as those high priests, to offer up sacrifice, first for His own sins, and then for the people's: for this He did once, when He offered up Himself* (Hebrews 7:26-27).

We too should both forgive and choose not to remember offenses against ourselves or others. Therefore, *let all bitterness, and wrath, and anger, and clamor, and evil speaking, be put away from you, with all malice: And be . . . kind one to another, tenderhearted, forgiving one another, even as God for Christ's sake has forgiven you* (Ephesians 4:31-32).

Thought for Today: We should never condemn ourselves or others over sins confessed and forsaken – because God has forgiven them.

Christ Revealed: Through two goats used on the Day of Atonement (Leviticus 16:8). The slaying of the first goat typifies that our peace with God was restored by the blood of Christ. The second goat represents the precious mercy of God in forever removing from His sight the sins of His people -- *as far as the east is from the west* (Psa. 103:12). *Their sins and iniquities will I remember no more* (Heb. 10:17).

For definitions of unfamiliar words in today's Bible reading, see pages 468-480.

𝓘ɴ 𝒯ᴏᴅᴀʏ's 𝓡ᴇᴀᴅɪɴɢ

Laws of holiness and justice for the people and priests; penalties for idolatry and immorality; laws regarding defilement of priests

𝒯he priests were to represent the Lord God at all times. They were also to represent Him in their own personal lives and family relationships, lest the sanctuary of God be profaned. *And the LORD said to Moses, Speak to the priests the sons of Aaron, and say to them: There shall none be defiled for the dead among his people . . . . he shall not defile himself, being a chief man among his people, to profane himself. . . . They shall not take a wife that is a whore, or profane; neither shall they take a woman put away from her husband: for he is holy to his God. . . . Neither shall they take for their wives a widow, nor her that is put away: but they shall take maidens of the seed of the house of Israel, or a widow that had a priest before* (Leviticus 21:1,4,7; Ezekiel 44:22). The marriage status of a priest was so important that God repeated: *A widow, or a divorced woman, or profane, or a harlot, these shall he not take: but he shall take a virgin of his own people as a wife* (Leviticus 21:14). Since the priest represented the Most High God, surely a higher standard of conduct should be required of an elder, minister, pastor, or priest today (Titus 1:6-7; I Timothy 3:12).

The priest's right ear, right thumb, and big toe of his right foot were to be anointed with blood. The blood-anointed ear was a reminder to listen to the voice of God above all others; the blood-anointed hand was a reminder of the priests' privilege to serve in the Tabernacle; and the blood-anointed foot was a reminder to walk in obedience to the Word of God.

Since he was the spiritual leader among his people, the sacrifice for the sins of a priest required a young bull, the most highly valued animal. In comparison, this was the same sacrifice required for all the sins of the congregation. The priest was a spiritual role model who could influence the entire congregation to sin (Leviticus 4:3,22-23). As representatives of God, a priest who disregarded the qualifications for service *shall be cut off from My presence: I am the LORD* (22:3-7).

As Christians we must set the example and abstain from any conduct that may influence others to be less than their best for Christ. He *has made us kings and priests to God and His Father; to Him be glory and dominion for ever and ever* (Revelation 1:6).

Thought for Today: A Christian represents the Lord God at all times.

Christ Revealed: As the source of true guidance, in contrast to evil guidance through spiritualist mediums (Leviticus 20:6-8). Jesus, Who is *the Truth* (John 14:6) also sent us *the Spirit of Truth* Who guides us *into all truth* (16:13).

For definitions of unfamiliar words in today's Bible reading, see pages 468-480.

THE ANNUAL FEASTS ALL MEN WERE REQUIRED TO ATTEND

FEASTS	SIGNIFICANCE TO ISRAEL	MEANING TODAY
PASSOVER 1 DAY NISAN 14 [MARCH/APRIL] AND	Beginning of the religious year [Lev. 23:5-8].The Passover commemorated Israel's deliverance from death by placing a lamb's blood on the door post, eating the lamb, and preparing for the exodus.	Our deliverance from the death penalty of sin by Christ, the Lamb of God, Who died in our place [John 1:29; I Cor. 5:7; I Pet. 1:18-19].
UNLEAVENED BREAD NISAN 15-21 [MARCH/APRIL]	Leaven is symbolic of sin and was prohibited during this week. This feast involved careful house cleaning, including ceilings, walls, floors, and every piece of furniture. All cooking utensils were boiled in water. It was a reminder that they were a holy people, a people separated unto the Lord.	Unleavened bread illustrates the sinlessness of Christ, the *Bread of Life* (John 6:35). *Wherefore come out from among them, and be you separate, says the Lord, and touch not the unclean* (unfit) *thing; and I will receive you* [II Cor. 6:17].
FIRST-FRUITS [DAY AFTER SABBATH OF PASSOVER WEEK] [MARCH/APRIL]	A sheaf of the firstfruits of the barley harvest was presented as a wave offering, indicating the beginning of harvest.	Jesus arose on First-fruits. *Now is Christ risen from the dead, and become the first-fruits of them that slept* (died) (I Cor. 15:20).
PENTECOST [OR FEAST OF WEEKS/HARVEST] 1 DAY SIVAN [MAY/JUNE]	Celebrated 7 weeks [50 days] after First-Fruits. Thanksgiving for the harvest [Lev. 23:15-22; Deut. 16:9-12]. It included presenting two loaves of leavened bread from the first-fruits of the wheat harvest commemorating the end of the summer harvest.	The outpouring of the Holy Spirit took place at Pentecost, 50 days after the resurrection of Christ [Acts 2]. Pentecost means 50th in Greek. Two loaves of leavened bread illustrate the sinful nature of both Jew and Gentile.
TRUMPETS 1 DAY TISHRI 1 [SEPTEMBER/OCTOBER]	Beginning of the civil year. Symbolic of the voice of God. Special sacrifices were brought [Lev. 23: 23-25; Num. 29:1-6].	The Word of God preached is His trumpet [II Tim. 4:1-2; Rev. 4:1].
DAY OF ATONEMENT 1 DAY TISHRI 10 [SEPTEMBER/OCTOBER]	The high priest made atonement for the nation's sins of the past year. He first offered a sacrifice, then sprinkled the blood on the Mercy Seat and at the base of the Brazen Altar. Two goats were also selected for a Sin Offering – one by death and the other by confessing over it the sins of the people and taking it into the wilderness where it was loosed [Lev. 23:26-32].	Christ, our High Priest, gave Himself as the perfect sacrifice. He did this not only by dying on the cross for our sins, but also by removing the guilt and consequences of sin. Our sins are never to be remembered [Heb. 7:27; 8:12; 10:17; I John 1:7-9].
TABERNACLES [OR BOOTHS OR FEAST OF INGATHERING] 7 DAYS TISHRI 15-21 [SEPTEMBER/OCTOBER]	During this feast they lived in temporary shelters in commemoration of God's gracious provisions during the 40 years in the wilderness [Ex. 23:16; Lev. 23:36; Num. 29:12-34; Deut. 16:13-15].	Jesus revealed Himself as the source of Living Water at this feast [John 7:37-39]. *The Word* (sayings of God) *was made* (became) *flesh, and dwelt* (tabernacled) among us [John 1:14].

In Today's Reading
Death penalty for defiled priests who eat holy things; acceptable
offerings; Sabbath, Passover, feasts, and other requirements

The Passover was the first feast of the Israelite's religious year. *In the fourteenth day of the first month at evening is the LORD's Passover. And on the fifteenth day of the same month is the Feast of Unleavened Bread to the LORD: seven days you must eat unleavened bread* (Leviticus 23:5-6). The *Feast of Unleavened Bread* lasted seven days during which unleavened bread was the only bread eaten (Exodus 34:18). Unleavened bread represented the sinless nature of Christ. *Then Jesus said to them, Verily, verily, I say to you, Moses gave you not that bread from heaven; but My Father gives you the True Bread from heaven. For the Bread of God is He Which (Who) comes down from heaven, and gives life to the world* (John 6:32-33). Israel's abstinence from leaven for seven days was a reminder that they were a holy people separated to their Lord God.

It took seven weeks to harvest all the crops, beginning with the barley crop that ripened in the spring. After that came the harvest of olives and the vineyards, followed by wheat, the final summer harvest. There was a day of First-fruits in the spring to indicate faith in the coming harvests, Feast of Weeks, also known as Feast of Harvest. It expressed thankfulness for the completion of the summer harvest (Exodus 23:16). Later it was also called *Pentecost*, from the Greek "pente" meaning "five" and "pent→kovra" meaning "50." This feast took place on the 50th day after the one sheaf offering of the Feast of First-fruits (Leviticus 23:15-16).

In contrast to the unleavened bread required for Passover were the *two wave loaves* that were to be baked with leaven for the *Feast of Weeks* (Pentecost) (23:17). Leaven is symbolic of our sin nature and was required in the *two wave loaves* because they were symbolic of both Jewish and Gentile believers who would later make up the Church.

Purge out therefore the old leaven, that you may be a new lump, as you are unleavened. For even Christ our Passover is sacrificed for us: Therefore let us keep the feast, not with old leaven, neither with the leaven of malice and wickedness; but with the unleavened bread of sincerity and truth (I Corinthians 5:7-8).

Thought for Today: Christians desire to please the Lord, be clean in mind and body.

Christ Revealed: Leviticus 23 -- in the seven great feasts of the Lord: Passover, Feast of Unleavened Bread, Feast of First-fruits, Feast of Pentecost, Feast of Trumpets, Day of Atonement, Feast of Tabernacles (Booths) -- all of which typified Jesus Christ. *Christ our Passover* (I Corinthians 5:7); *Bread of Life* (John 6:35); *Christ . . . the first-fruits of them that slept* (I Corinthians 15:20).

For definitions of unfamiliar words in today's Bible reading, see pages 468-480.

ℐɴ 𝒯ODAY'S ℛEADING

The Tabernacle, Candlestick, Showbread; blasphemy; year of jubilee;
laws concerning redemption of property and the poor

ℱollowing the command for *the children of Israel, that they bring to you pure oil olive beaten for the light, to cause the lamps to burn continually* (Leviticus 24:2), they were given detailed instructions for making the Showbread. *And you shall take fine flour, and bake twelve cakes thereof. . . . And you shall set them in two rows, six on a row, upon the pure table before the LORD. . . . Every Sabbath he* (Aaron) *shall set it in order before the LORD continually, being taken from the children of Israel by an everlasting covenant* (24:5-9).

The term Showbread literally means "bread of the face" and "presence of God," signifying that He and His Word alone sustained their very lives. When the priests ate the bread, it ratified Israel's dependence upon Him. The loaves were made of *fine flour* – coarse flour could not be used, for these loaves represented Christ, the perfect One, *holy, harmless, undefiled, separate from sinners, and made higher than the heavens* (Hebrews 7:26).

The aromatic frankincense that was required to be placed on the loaves is symbolic of praise to God as well as a reminder that Christ, as *the Bread of Life*, provides true satisfaction. *How sweet are Your words to my taste! yea, sweeter than honey to my mouth!* (Psalm 119:103).

The loaves also picture Christ, Who faced the fierce oven of affliction and crucifixion to come forth as *the Bread of Life*. Jesus declared: *He that comes to Me shall never hunger; and he that believes on Me shall never thirst* (John 6:35). The 12 identical loaves were a reminder that the Lord was the satisfier and sustainer of all 12 tribes.

Light is a revealer of truth, and the Golden Candlestick's light shone upon the sacred Showbread that also typified Christ. *For the Bread of God is He Which* (who) *comes down from heaven, and gives life to the world* (6:33). As we read His Word, the Holy Spirit, Who indwells believers, provides light on the moral and spiritual values of life. This light enables Christians to fulfill one of their essential missions to the world: *Let your light so shine before men, that they may see your good works, and glorify your Father Which* (Who) *is in heaven* (Matthew 5:16).

Thought for Today: Everything we possess is a gift from God.

Christ Portrayed: By the kinsman-redeemer (Leviticus 25:47-55). Christ is our Savior and Redeemer (Isaiah 60:16) Who made us His kinsmen: *The Spirit Itself bears witness with our spirit, that we are the children of God* **(Romans 8:16).**

For definitions of unfamiliar words in today's Bible reading, see pages 468-480.

*I*N *T*ODAY'S *R*EADING
Blessings for obedience; judgment for disobedience; redeeming
persons and property; tithes shall be holy to the Lord

*T*he Lord warns His people: *You shall make no idols nor graven image
. . . to bow down to it: for I am the* LORD *your God. You shall keep My
Sabbaths, and reverence My sanctuary: I am the* LORD. *. . . . keep My
Commandments. . . . and you shall be My people. . . . But if you will not
hearken* (listen) *to Me, and will not do all these Commandments. . . . I will
set My face against you, and you shall be slain before your enemies. . . . And
I will scatter you among the heathen* (Leviticus 26:1-33). The Israelites
were reminded that the first and fourth of the Ten Commandments are
the foundation of a right relationship with our Creator and for all true
worship of Him.

Numerous blessings were recorded as benefits of obedience to the
Word of God (26:3-13). Also recorded were clear warnings regarding sin
and disobedience to His Word which later were fulfilled (26:14-39).

Although the Book of Leviticus was written to Israelites, its basic
truths are just as relevant for us today. The God of holiness is *Jesus Christ
the same yesterday, and to day, and for ever* (Hebrews 13:8).

The majority of Jews continue to reject Jesus as their Messiah, but
they will eventually recognize their spiritual blindness, repent, and
worship their Messiah Jesus, the true source of eternal peace. Just as God
foretold: *I will bring them again to this land. . . . for they shall return to Me
with their whole heart* (Jeremiah 24:6-7). The times of the Gentiles that
began with King Nebuchadnezzar will soon end and Jesus Christ, the
King of kings, will rightfully rule the world from Jerusalem.

The marvelous compassion and love of God is seen in His desire to
forgive and restore the sinner to Himself. *If we confess our sins, He is
faithful and just to forgive us our sins, and to cleanse us from all
unrighteousness* (I John 1:9). Recognizing the eternal consequences of
sin, confession is of utmost importance. *Confess your faults one to
another, and pray one for another, that you may be healed. The efectual
fervent prayer of a rightous man avails much* (James 5:16).

Thought for Today: The tragic losses of a wasted lifetime cannot be relived or restored,
but the sins can be forgiven.

Christ Revealed: As the Tabernacle to be sent to dwell among us (Leviticus 26:11). *The
Word was made* (became) *flesh, and dwelt* (tabernacled) *among us* (John 1:14).

For definitions of unfamiliar words in today's Bible reading, see pages 468-480.

Introduction To The Book Of
*N*umbers

The Book of Numbers continues the history of the Israelites where the Book of Exodus left off. Just one month had passed between the completion of the Tabernacle (Exodus 40:17) and the command of God to number the people (Numbers 1:1-2). During that time, the instructions in the Book of Leviticus were given. The first census of all men 20 years old and older records that 603,550 men were qualified to serve in the army of Israel (1:1-46).

And it came to pass on the twentieth day of the second month, in the second year, that the cloud was taken up from off the Tabernacle of the testimony (10:11), and the Israelites followed the cloud as it moved toward Kadesh Barnea, about 160 miles to the north (10:11 – 14:45). It was not long, however, before the people complained and then rebelled.

After the Israelites arrived at Kadesh Barnea, 12 spies were sent out to investigate the land (Numbers 13 – 14; Deuteronomy 1:22-40). When they returned 40 days later, *Caleb stilled the people before Moses, and said, Let us go up at once, and possess it; for we are well able to overcome it* (Numbers 13:30). Ten of the spies strongly protested, saying: *We be not able to go up against the people; for they are stronger than we* (13:31). However, Joshua and Caleb pleaded: *The LORD is with us: fear them not.* But the people agreed with the ten disbelieving spies (14:1-45). Because of their unbelief God pronounced His judgment of death upon that generation (14:26-35). Thus, they wasted 38 years wandering in the wilderness until all the people from the first generation who were 20 years of age or older at the first census had died (15:1 – 21:35).

Later, the Lord commanded Moses and Eleazar, Aaron's son and successor, to take a second census of the new generation of men 20 years of age and older, whose parents had left Egypt (26:1-65). This second numbering took place almost 40 years after the first census, in the 10th month of the 40th year (1:19; 26:4; compare Exodus 1:1-5; Deuteronomy 1:3).

Only Joshua and Caleb, the two men of faith from the first generation of Israelites, lived to enter the promised land. The new generation was estimated to be more than two million people. They gathered on the Plains of Moab, north of the Dead Sea and east of the Jordan River, across from Jericho, ready to take the land their parents had refused.

One of the greatest illustrations of New Testament doctrine is found in this book. *These things were our examples, to the intent we should not lust after evil things, as they also lusted. . . . Wherefore let him that thinks he stands take heed lest he fall* (I Corinthians 10:6-12).

*I*N *T*ODAY'S *R*EADING

First numbering (census) of the Israelites for military purposes
and encampment location of each tribe in relation to the Tabernacle

*A*bout 70 times in the Book of Numbers, we read: *The LORD said* or
the LORD spoke to Moses. These were the words of our Heavenly Father
speaking to His children. The desire of God was to have a people that
would love, obey, and follow Him without reservation. He, in turn,
would be their God, and lead them into the promised land. While the
Israelites remained at Mount Sinai, it was twice said of them: *And the
children of Israel did according to all that the LORD commanded Moses*
(Numbers 1:54; 2:34). As long as the Israelites were neither accomplishing anything for the Lord nor going anywhere, but were just talking
about it, they were satisfied. But, just days after *they departed from the
mount of the LORD . . . to search out a resting place for them. . . . the people
complained. . . . Who shall give us flesh to eat? . . . our soul* (body) *is dried
away* (up): *there is nothing at all, beside this manna* (10:33; 11:1,4,6). Rather
than see their difficulties as an opportunity to believe that God would
continue to meet their needs and lead them to the promised land, they
chose to be dissatisfied with their circumstances.

In much the same way, our lives are also a wilderness journey, a
march each day through unfamiliar territory. Let us not forget that,
from the time the Israelites were led to move forward in obedience to
God's Word, Satan was there to create discontent, faultfinding and
unbelief in the promises of God.

When Christians complain about their hardships, as the Israelites
did, they too disqualify themselves from the Lord's best. Only a faithful
few, like Caleb, Joshua, and Moses, recognize that God is in control and
has arranged His plan for our lives. We all can avoid wasted years. As
we faithfully read the Bible with an unreserved desire to know His will,
His Word enables us to be all that He would have us be, and to do all that
He would have us do. His indwelling Holy Spirit enlightens our minds
and stirs our hearts to pray and *the effectual* (effective) *fervent prayer of
a righteous man avails* (accomplishes) *much* (James 5:16).

Thought for Today: Don't disqualify yourself from the Lord's best blessings because
of faultfinding and dissatisfaction with your circumstances.

Christ Portrayed: By Moses as he led the people (Numbers 1:54). Jesus said: *I am the
Good Shepherd, and know My sheep. . . . My sheep . . . follow Me* (John 10:14,27).

For definitions of unfamiliar words in today's Bible reading, see pages 468-480.

IN TODAY'S READING

Census and duties of the Levites: the Kohathites, the Gershonites,
and the Merarites; the redemption of the firstborn

Nadab and Abihu, Aaron's two oldest sons, had been greatly honored by being included with Moses and Aaron and 70 elders on Mount Sinai to hear the voice of God (Exodus 24:1,9). They had been given national recognition and God-ordained spiritual leadership. But, all this did not protect them from the consequences of their disobedience. The newly-ordained priests *Nadab and Abihu died before the LORD, when they offered strange fire before the LORD, in the wilderness of Sinai* (Numbers 3:4). They presumed to burn incense, symbolic of the prayers of the people, with unauthorized fire, that is, fire not kindled by God on the Brazen Altar (Leviticus 9:23-24; 10:1-2).

Their unauthorized fire underlined the seriousness of departing from the Commandments of God. It points out that no one becomes so important or popular as a "spiritual" leader that God will overlook disobedience to His Word. To be a minister, or even to become a member of a church, with no intent to submit one's life to please Christ, is hypocrisy.

The decision to ignore any command of God is sin. We are not to use circumstances to justify an exception to His Word. Neither is there a choice of what part of His Word we can neglect or reject, for all is God-breathed (inspired). The Word of God is the source of meeting the needs of the human heart; it is the final and only source of absolute truth.

All Scripture is given by inspiration of God, and is profitable (II Timothy 3:16). All New Testament doctrine is based on Old Testament principles. *For if we sin willfully after that we have received the knowledge of truth, there remains no more sacrifice for sins, But a certain fearful* (terrifying) *looking for of judgment. . . . He that despised* (rejected) *Moses' law died without mercy under two or three witnesses: Of how much sorer* (more severe) *punishment, suppose you, shall he be thought worthy, who has trodden under foot the Son of God, and has counted the blood of the covenant* (agreement), *wherewith he was sanctified, an unholy thing, and has done despite* (insult) *to the Spirit of Grace?* (Hebrews 10:26-29).

Thought for Today: No Christian is worthy, but we have been accepted by our Savior because of God's forgiving love and grace.

Christ Portrayed: By Aaron, the high priest, who was served by the Levites (Numbers 3:6). As a *holy* and *royal priesthood,* we serve Christ, our great High Priest (John 12:26; I Peter 2:5,9; Hebrews 4:14).

For definitions of unfamiliar words in today's Bible reading, see pages 468-480.

In Today's Reading

Laws concerning cleansing, confession and restitution, jealousy;
the Nazarite vow

The Nazarite vow committed an individual to a life set apart to God for a specific period of time or even for life. The Nazarite vow prohibited drinking *any liquor* (juice) *of grapes, nor eat moist grapes, or dried.... he shall come at* (touch) *no dead body. . . . All the days of his separation he is holy* (consecrated) *to the LORD* (Numbers 6:2-8).

The Nazarite's separation to God was expressed in several ways including abstinence from grape juice and eating fresh grapes or raisins, representative of the best of physical satisfaction; and by refusing to be defiled by the dead, representative of spiritual deadness (vss 6-12). However, the Nazarite was still responsible for offering all the usual sacrifices, such as the sin offering. This points out that even in doing our very best to separate ourselves from the world we still fall far short of being free from all spiritual defilement.

Only two people in the Old Testament are recorded as lifelong Nazarites. One was Samson (Judges 13:7), who failed in his separation from the world and consequently did not fulfill his opportunities to lead the Israelites to victory over the Philistines. In contrast Samuel's dedication (I Samuel 1:28) to the Lord led him to free the nation from Philistine domination and unite the tribes in preparation for a united kingdom. Although the Nazarite vow no longer applies, our personal consecration and dedication is vital to fulfilling the will of God.

There was nothing sinful about eating grapes, for God created the fruit of the vine; but, often, even the "good" things of life can take the place of Christ. Those who have a desire to dedicate their lives to Christ will abstain from pleasures that interfere with serving Him and also *abstain from all appearance of evil* (I Thessalonians 5:22).

The Apostle Paul was led to write: *I beseech* (beg) *you therefore, brethren, by the mercies of God, that you present* (offer) *your bodies a living sacrifice, holy, acceptable to God, which is your reasonable service. And be not conformed to this world: but be . . . transformed by the renewing of your mind, that you may prove* (approve) *what is that good, and acceptable, and perfect, will of God* (Romans 12:1-2).

Thought for Today: Accomplishing the will of God often requires self-denial, even of things which in themselves may not be sinful.

Christ Revealed: Nazarite is the transliteration of a Hebrew term meaning "dedication by separation" (Numbers 6:1-8). Jesus dedicated Himself to do the will of His Father separating Himself from sin even to death: *Your will be done* (Matthew 26:39,42).

For definitions of unfamiliar words in today's Bible reading, see pages 468-480.

In Today's Reading
The princes' offerings for the dedication of the Tabernacle

And it came to pass on the day that Moses had fully set up the Tabernacle, and had anointed it, and sanctified it, and all the instruments thereof, both the altar and all the vessels thereof, and had anointed them, and sanctified them; That the princes of Israel, heads of the house of their fathers, who were the princes of the tribes, and (who) were over them that were numbered, offered: And they brought their offering before the LORD, six covered wagons, and twelve oxen; a wagon for two of the princes, and for each one an ox: and they brought them before the Tabernacle. And the LORD spoke to Moses, saying, Take it of them, that they may be to do the service (used in the work) of the Tabernacle of the congregation; and you shall give them to the Levites, to every man according to his service (Numbers 7:1-5).

These gifts were not equally divided among the Levites. The family of the Gershonites received two wagons and four oxen for their duties (compare Numbers 4:25-26; 7:7). The Merarites, who had much heavier burdens to bear (4:31-32; 7:8), received four wagons and eight oxen. But the Kohathites received none. They were required to carry the Tabernacle furniture: *To the sons of Kohath he gave none: because the service of the sanctuary belonging to them was that they should bear upon their shoulders,* the Golden Candlestick, Table of Showbread, Altar of Incense, Brass Laver, Brazen Altar, and Mercy Seat on the Ark of the Lord's Covenant (7:9; see also 3:29-31; 4:1-15). These were all symbolic of Jesus Christ.

Although all the gifts were identical, each prince was recognized for his gift. From this we learn that every gift and act of service to our Lord is faithfully remembered. Mount Sinai is often associated with the severity of the Law. But the Tabernacle that was built there illustrates the loving concern of God to communicate and fellowship with His people and to direct them through life. All the princes revealed their gratitude through their generous freewill gifts. All responded equally to the need.

Giving always benefits the giver. Your gift to missions can lift burdens, provide happiness, answer prayers, and save a soul from eternal hell. God has said: *Give, and it shall be given to you; good measure . . . running over, shall men give into your bosom. For with the same measure that you mete* (use to benefit on others) *withal it shall be measured to you again* (Luke 6:38).

Thought for Today: When our thoughts are to please God, not self, we enjoy peace of mind.

Christ Revealed: Through the voluntary offerings of the leaders which were sufficient to meet the needs (Numbers 7). Jesus gave his life to meet our very need. *My God shall supply all your need according to His riches in glory by Christ Jesus* (Phil. 4:19).

For definitions of unfamiliar words in today's Bible reading, see pages 468-480.

𝓘N 𝓣ODAY'S 𝓡EADING

Cleansing of the Levites; observance of the second Passover; the
Lord's guiding presence in the cloud and the fire over the Tabernacle

---

*T*he Israelites gained their freedom from Egypt after they observed
the first Passover. The blood was placed on the doorpost but, equally
important, they were commanded to eat the lamb.

Freedom from the cruel slavery of Pharaoh in Egypt meant that
now they were free to follow the leadership of the One True God.

*And the LORD spoke to Moses in the wilderness of Sinai, in the first
month of the second year . . . Let the children of Israel also keep the Passover at its appointed season. In the fourteenth day of this month, at evening,
you shall keep it in its appointed season: according to all the rites of It, and
according to all the ceremonies thereof, shall you keep it* (Numbers 9:1-3).

The Passover was a reminder of how the Israelites gained their freedom. Not only were they to partake of the Passover Feast, but they
were also required to bring the Lord's offering: *But the man that is
clean, and is not in a journey, and forbears to keep the Passover, even the
same soul* (person) *shall be cut off* (destroyed) *from among his people;
because he brought not the offering of the LORD in its appointed season*
(time), *that man shall bear his sin* (9:13).

Our observance of the Lord's Supper is a participation in our freedom from sin, that we have become children of God, and are prepared
for our wilderness journey through life. *For even Christ our Passover is
sacrificed for us* (I Corinthians 5:7). Paul bears witness to Jesus' words
by saying: *For as often as you eat this bread, and drink this cup, you do
show* (proclaim) *the Lord's death till He come* (11:26).

Just as the Lord determined the journey of the Israelite tribes, He
has a plan for you as you journey through life. Our supreme aim
should be to accomplish His purpose for creating us. When God is our
Guide, what is there to fear? He has provided a reliable threefold
Guide for direction – His perfect Word, the indwelling Holy Spirit,
and the power of prayer: *For it is God which works in you both to will and
to do of His good pleasure* (Philippians 2:13).

Thought for Today: Our objective in life should be to accomplish God's purpose for
creating us to let God's life live through us.

Christ Revealed: The Passover serves as a beautiful illustration of the redemption
Christ accomplished at Calvary as *the Lamb of God* (Numbers 9:2; compare John 1:29;
I Corinthians 5:7).

For definitions of unfamiliar words in today's Bible reading, see pages 468-480.

IN TODAY'S READING

Two silver trumpets; the Israelites leave Sinai; complaint of the
people; the 70 elders chosen; the Lord sends a plague

It was the responsibility of the priest to *make . . . two trumpets of
silver; of a whole piece shall you make them: that you may use them for the
calling of the assembly, and for the journeying of the camps* (Numbers
10:2). The trumpets were long, straight tubes of silver with bell-shaped
mouths. They could not be made from inferior metal, nor from silver
fragments; instead they were to be fashioned from one whole piece of
silver. Regardless of how far away one was from the Tabernacle, the
clear tones of the silver trumpets would communicate various messages: *They shall blow an alarm for their journeys. But when the congregation is to be gathered together, you shall blow, but you shall not sound an
alarm. . . . And if you go to war in your land against the enemy that oppresses
you, then you shall blow an alarm with the trumpets; and you shall be
remembered before the LORD your God, and you shall be saved from your
enemies. Also in the day of your gladness, and in your solemn* (appointed)
*days, and in the beginnings of your months, you shall blow with the
trumpets over your burned offerings, and over the sacrifices of your peace
offerings* (10:6-10; also Leviticus 23:24; II Chronicles 5:12-14; 7:6; 29:26-
29; Ezra 3:10; Nehemiah 12:35,41).

Whether they worshiped, went to war, or journeyed, every move of
the people was to be in obedience to the various sounds of the
trumpets. The two silver trumpets represent the truth of God's Word
and remind us that both the Old and the New Testaments are each a
part of the whole Word of God.

God's people are to be fully dependent upon and subject to the will
of God as revealed in His Word. If our hearts are accustomed to hearing
the true silver trumpet, His voice through His Word, we will then be in
harmony with the Holy Spirit's prompting as to what we should or should
not do. His Word will keep us from missing the will of God.

Our Lord assures us that, *when He, the Spirit of Truth, is come, He will
guide you into all truth: for He shall not speak of Himself; but whatsoever He
shall hear, that shall He speak: and He will show you things to come* (John 16:13).

Thought for Today: The most insignificant person in man's eyes is important to Christ.

Christ Revealed: The two trumpets were made of silver (Numbers 10:2). Silver in the
Bible stands for truth. Christ is *the Way, the Truth, and the Life* (John 14:6).

For definitions of unfamiliar words in today's Bible reading, see pages 468-480.

IN TODAY'S READING
Miriam and Aaron speak against Moses; Miriam stricken with
leprosy; Moses prays; 12 spies sent to Canaan; their report

Miriam was the sister of Moses and of Aaron the high priest. She was honored above all the women of Israel, had a prophetic anointing, and was gifted in music and singing (Exodus 15:20; Micah 6:4).

Miriam and Aaron spoke against Moses because of the Ethiopian (Cushite) woman whom he had married: for he had married an Ethiopian woman. And they said, Has the LORD indeed spoken only by Moses? has He not spoken also by us? And the LORD heard it (Numbers 12:1-2).

Suddenly, the Lord demanded to meet with Miriam, Aaron, and Moses. Miriam may have been delighted, thinking that God was just as displeased with Moses as she was and would agree with her criticism. Undoubtedly, she experienced an overwhelming shock when God said to her: *With him will I speak mouth to mouth . . . wherefore (why) then were you not afraid to speak against My servant Moses? And the anger of the LORD was kindled against them. . . . and, behold, Miriam became leprous, white as snow: and Aaron looked upon Miriam, and, behold, she was leprous. And Aaron said to Moses, Alas, my lord, I beseech you, lay not the sin upon us, wherein we have done foolishly, and wherein we have sinned* (12:8-11).

Covetousness and pride are never satisfied. Even the possession of spiritual gifts can lead to pride which, in turn, can lead to jealousy if others with similar spiritual gifts appear to be competitors. When someone we have known as less qualified is promoted above us in our office or given recognition, we may be tempted to fall into Miriam's sin of criticizing. Pride takes many forms. It can be based on physical beauty, wealth, education, or talents; but pride is a self-destructive and self-deceptive sin.

Miriam succeeded, as many others have, in making it appear that her concern came from a "spiritual" motive. But God saw through her jealousy, envy, pride, and hurt feelings. It was the God-ordained leadership of Moses, not his choice of a wife or what he was teaching, that was being questioned. God has clearly declared: *Touch not My anointed, and do My prophets no harm* (I Chronicles 16:22; Psalm 105:15).

Thought for Today: Covetous people never get enough money, proud people never get enough praise, and self-centered people never get enough attention.

Christ Portrayed: By Moses, who *was very meek* (humble), *above all the men which were upon the face of the earth* (Numbers 12:3). Jesus said: *I am meek* (gentle, mild) *and lowly in heart* (Matthew 11:29).

For definitions of unfamiliar words in today's Bible reading, see pages 468-480.

In Today's Reading
Moses interceded in prayer for the Israelites; Israel's wasted life;
laws concerning offerings, sins, and the Sabbath

Leaving the wilderness of Sinai, the Israelites were led northward until they reached Kadesh-barnea where, for the first time, the people could actually see the promised land lying before them. The march from Egypt, including the 12-month stay at Mount Sinai (Horeb), had taken about 16 months. Now they stood on the threshold of that glorious promised land. A leader from each tribe had taken 40 days to spy out the land. When they returned carrying a single cluster of grapes so large it took two men to carry it, the Israelites were assured by all of them that Canaan *flows with milk and honey; and this is the fruit of it* (Numbers 13:27). This was a confirmation of its extraordinary fruitfulness. Caleb, one of the 12, was quick to say: *Let us go up at once, and possess* (take, occupy) *it; for we are well able to overcome it* (13:30). However, ten of the spies discouraged the people, saying: *The people be strong that dwell in the land, and the cities are walled, and very great* (13:28,31). *And all the congregation lifted up their voice* (made loud lament), *and cried; and the people wept that night. And all the children of Israel murmured* (grumbled) . . . *Would God* (we wish) *that we had died in the land of Egypt! or would God* (we wish) *we had died in this wilderness!* (14:1-2). This marked the end of their journey to the land of promise and the beginning of 38 years of wilderness wanderings.

The Israelites who *wept that night* remind us of Esau who had grown up disregarding his holy calling and had sold his birthright. *For you know how that afterward, when he would have inherited the blessing, he was rejected: for he found no place of repentance, though he sought it carefully with tears* (Hebrews 12:17); but his prayers were not heard. His only interest had been in what he had to gain, not in how he could be used by the Lord.

Satan's objective is that your decisions be like Esau or the unbelieving Israelites and not like Caleb's. Satan seeks to divert a Christian's thoughts from trust in the Lord. Such diversion is in opposition to the single eye that takes God at His Word and that puts the Lord first and foremost above all other considerations. *Let us draw near with a true heart in full assurance of faith* (Hebrews 10:22).

Thought for Today: *Faithful is He that call you, who also will do it* (I Thess. 5:24).

Christ Revealed: As God's glory (Numbers 14:22). Jesus Christ is *the brightness of His* (God's) *glory, and the express image of His person* (Heb. 1:3).

For definitions of unfamiliar words in today's Bible reading, see pages 468-480.

ISRAEL'S UNBELIEF

The Lord said. . . . all those men which have seen My glory, and My miracles, which I did in Egypt and in the wilderness, and have tempted Me now these ten times, and have not hearkened to My voice; Surely they shall not see the land which I swore to their fathers (Numbers 14:20-23).

PLACE	REBELLION	GOD'S MERCY REVEALED	KEY THOUGHT
RED SEA Ex. 14:10-12	Israelites murmuring against Moses at the sight of Egyptian chariots	In destroying their enemies and providing a way of deliverance (Ex. 14:21-31)	There is a great temptation for a person to desire the things of his sinful past (I John 2:15-17).
MARAH Ex. 15:23-24	Grumbling because God took them to bitter water	By sweetening the water (15:25-26)	Disappointments provide opportunities to exercise faith (II Cor. 4:16-17).
DESERT Ex. 16:2-3	Grumbling – they feared starvation	By providing manna (16:14-15)	God supplies all our needs *according to His riches in glory* (Phil. 4:19).
DESERT Ex. 16:20	Disbelieving God by keeping manna overnight	Provision continued for 40 years (16:35)	God's Word is essential and must be obeyed (II Tim. 3:16-17).
DESERT Ex. 16:26-27	Ignoring God and searching for manna on the Sabbath	In still providing a day of rest (16:28-30)	We must show proper respect for the Lord's day (Heb. 10:25).
REPHIDIM Ex. 17:1-3	Quarreling with Moses over the lack of water	In providing water from the rock (17:6)	Christians must depend on God (Matt. 6:33).
HOREB Ex. 32:1-10	Worshiping the golden calf	In sparing those who did not sin (32:32-33)	Satan will provide opportunities for us to return to sin (II Tim. 4:10).
TABERAH Num. 11:1	Complaining against God about adversity	Answering Moses' prayer (11:2-3)	Remedy for sin is loving obedience (John 14:21).
KIBROTH-HATTAAVAH Num. 11:10-15,34	Weeping for a variety of food with the people of the world	By providing quail in abundance (11:31-32)	Discontentment is a lack of trust in the love of God (I Tim. 6:8; Phil. 4:11; Heb 13:5).
KADESH-BARNEA Num. 14:2-10	Refusing to believe God and enter the promised land	In sparing Joshua, Caleb, and the children (14:20-31)	God always rewards the faithful (Heb. 11:6).

In Today's Reading

Korah leads a rebellion against Moses and Aaron; plague sent by God; Aaron's rod; duties for priests; the tithe offering

*K*orah, Dathan, and Abiram *rose up before Moses, with certain of the children of Israel, two hundred and fifty princes of the assembly, famous in the congregation, men of renown. . . . And Korah gathered all the congregation* (Numbers 16:2,19).

Once again, Moses was confronted with opposition, this time from his own cousins and the key leaders of the 12 tribes. Two hundred fifty of the leading men of Israel were influenced by Korah, Dathan, and Abiram and they rebelled against Moses and Aaron. They accused Moses and Aaron of assuming too much authority, and their argument seemed very convincing: *They gathered themselves together against Moses and against Aaron, and said to them, You take* (assume) *too much upon you, seeing all the congregation are holy, every one of them, and the LORD is among them: wherefore then lift you up yourselves above the congregation of the LORD?* (16:3). They refused to recognize that Moses and Aaron were appointed by God to lead the people and that they were actually *gathered together against the LORD* (16:11).

Korah did not just make a mistake, but committed a serious sin, as recorded by Jude, who wrote: *I will therefore put you in remembrance . . . how that the Lord, having saved the people out of the land of Egypt, afterward destroyed them that believed not. . . . Woe to them! for they have gone in the way of Cain, and ran greedily after the error of Balaam for reward, and perished in the gainsaying* (rebellion) *of Core* (Korah) (Jude 1:5,11).

Korah was a believer in God from the chosen tribe of Levi. The Kohathites were responsible for bearing the sanctuary and later would be *set over the service of song in the House of the LORD* (I Chronicles 6:31) and *over the Showbread, to prepare it every Sabbath* (9:32). However, it appears that Korah would serve the Lord only if it resulted in bringing recognition to himself. Self-willed people need to recognize that God has said: *Obey them that have rule over you, and submit yourselves: for they watch for your souls* (Hebrews 13:17).

Thought for Today: It is God's life living in us rather than our decision to live as we choose.

Christ Portrayed: By Aaron and his sons who were responsible for making proper atonement for all of the iniquity of Israel (Numbers 18:1). Jesus *was wounded for our transgressions, He was bruised for our iniquities* (Isaiah 53:5); He *gave Himself for us, that He might redeem us from all iniquity* (lawlessness) (Titus 2:14).

For definitions of unfamiliar words in today's Bible reading, see pages 468-480.

In Today's Reading

Red heifer sacrifice; Miriam's death; Moses strikes the rock twice;
Edom refuses Israel passage; Aaron's death

The red heifer sacrifice was instituted in the wilderness of Paran at a time when all Israel was under the sentence of death. The Law required that *whosoever touches the dead body of any man that is dead, and purifies not himself, defiles the Tabernacle of the LORD* (Numbers 19:13).

The blood of the red heifer was burned with the carcass, and its ashes were mixed with "running water" (19:17) and sprinkled upon the defiled ones in order to restore them to the holy God. The Hebrew word for "running" also means "living" – implying not only cleansing from sin, but renewal of life. The water of purification was made from the ashes of just one heifer, which was sufficient for all the people.

Through the red heifer ordinance, God gave a new revelation of the importance of cleansing from defilement – whether it be through our thoughts, our conversations, the books we read, our associations with unbelievers, or whatever we may do that defiles our minds or bodies. God has said: *Be . . . holy: for I am holy* (I Peter 1:16).

The red heifer sacrifice is symbolic of Christ. Through His death on the cross, He has *given to us exceeding great and precious promises: that by these you might be partakers of the divine nature, having escaped the corruption that is in the world through lust* (II Peter 1:4). It is the plan of God that Christ's own life be reproduced in Christians.

Since humility is a means of overcoming pride, jealousy, greed, and envy, some assume we should pray for humility; but the real need is to pray that Christ be magnified in our lives. God does not give humility or patience or love as separate gifts of His grace. The indwelling Christ is the answer to every need. As we pray for Him to live out His life in us, we will express humility, patience, love, and everything else that reveals His character. Paul said: *I am crucified with Christ; nevertheless I live; yet not I, but Christ lives in me: and the life which I now live in the flesh I live by the faith of the Son of God, Who loved me, and gave Himself for me* (Galatians 2:20).

Thought for Today: When we try to impress others with our importance, the Lord will not be glorified.

Christ Revealed: Through the rock that Moses struck (Exodus 17:6; Numbers 20:8-11). Christ, our Rock, Who was struck once through His death on the cross, does not need to be struck again. *That spiritual Rock* (Petra) *that followed* (accompanied) *them . . . was Christ* (I Corinthians 10:4). *For in that He died, He died to sin once* (Romans 6:10). **For definitions of unfamiliar words in today's Bible reading, see pages 468-480.**

In Today's Reading

Fiery serpents; brass serpent; Israel defeats King Arad, Amorites, Moabites; Balaam hired to curse the Israelites

---

The Israelites were near their last encampment and would soon cross the Jordan River to enter into the promised land. Some of these people were children when, with their parents, they had left Egypt; others had been born in the wilderness. *The soul of the people was much discouraged because of the way. And the people spoke against God, and against Moses, Wherefore* (why) *have you brought us up out of Egypt to die in the wilderness? for there is no bread, neither is there any water; and our soul loathes* (detests) *this light bread* (Numbers 21:4-5). At this point, *the LORD sent fiery serpents . . . and many people of Israel died* (21:6). When the people repented, *Moses prayed for the people* (21:7).

The response to Moses' *prayer* was immediate. *The LORD said to Moses, Make . . . a fiery serpent, and set it upon a pole: and it shall come to pass, that every one that is bitten, when he looks upon it, shall live* (21:8). The brass serpent was a symbol both of God's judgment against their sin and of His mercy and love for all who repented and truly believed in Him.

Many centuries later, in His conversation with *Nicodemus, a ruler of the Jews* (John 3:1-21), Jesus said that the *serpent* which had been lifted up by Moses in the wilderness illustrated Himself as the One to *be lifted up* on the cross as the only way for sinners to be saved from eternal death (3:14; 12:32). Jesus did not tell Nicodemus how he should live to have eternal life, rather He told him how to be made alive. Jesus replied to Nicodemus: *Verily, verily, I say to you, Except a man be born of water and of the Spirit, he cannot enter into the Kingdom of God* (3:5). This is far more than changing one's way of life, giving up bad habits, or turning over a new leaf. All mankind, with One exception (Jesus), was *dead in trespasses and sins* (Ephesians 2:1). Each of us was born with our parents' human nature and, when we receive Christ as our Savior, we are "born again" and receive His spiritual nature: *But as many as received Him, to them gave He power to become the sons of God, even to them that believe on His Name* (John 1:12).

As children of our Heavenly Father, we are reminded: *Let not sin therefore reign* (rule) *in your mortal body, that you should obey it in the lusts* (evil desires) *thereof. . . . but yield yourselves to God* (Romans 6:12-13).

Thought for Today: It is impossible to have a right attitude toward God while maintaining a wrong attitude toward delegated authority.

Christ Portrayed: By Moses who was faithful to pray to God for the people (Numbers 21:7). *Christ Jesus; Who was faithful to Him that appointed Him, as also Moses was faithful in all his house* (Hebrews 3:1-2).

For definitions of unfamiliar words in today's Bible reading, see pages 468-480.

In Today's Reading
Prophecies of Balaam; Israel sins; the plague stopped because of the intercession of Phinehas

The last encampment of the Israelites on the eastern side of the Jordan River was on the Plains of Moab just northeast of the Dead Sea near Mount Nebo, a few miles south of today's Amman, Jordan (Numbers 33:49; Joshua 2:1; 3:1). Everything seemed peaceful, with no apparent dangers. However, upon seeing this vast multitude of Israelites who had defied Pharaoh, left Egypt, and conquered everyone who opposed them on their way to Canaan, the Moabites who lived nearby, were fearful that they too would soon be destroyed. This fear led King Balak to form an alliance with his Midianite neighbors against Israel (Numbers 22:4-7). Even then, believing they could never defeat Israel in battle, Balak sent for the prophet Balaam to put a curse on Israel. He lived in Pethor, a city of northern Mesopotamia (modern Iraq). This was in the vicinity where Abraham had lived. *God said to Balaam, You shall not go with them; you shall not curse the people: for they are blessed* (22:12).

Knowing the judgment of God would come upon Israel if he could cause the Israelites to sin, and coveting the king's rewards, Balaam wickedly suggested that the Moabite women make friends with the men of Israel. The friendliness of the Moabite women quickly led the Israelite men to become involved in sexual immorality and idol worship, thus breaking their covenant vow of allegiance to the One True God.

Disobedience resulted in a plague of death that swept through the tribes of Israel and *those that died in the plague* (pestilence) *were twenty and four thousand* (25:9).

Some will say that we should not be judgmental, that we should be tolerant of the immoral (alternative) lifestyles that are growing in popularity. But sexual sins are still an outrage against God: *Know you not that your bodies are the members of Christ? shall I then take the members of Christ, and make them the members of a harlot? God forbid. . . . he that commits fornication sins against his own body. What? know you not that your body is the temple of the Holy Ghost* (Spirit) *which is in you, which you have of God, and you are not your own? For you are bought with a price: therefore glorify God in your body* (I Corinthians 6:15-20).

Thought for Today: Covetousness is always self-defeating.

Christ Revealed: As the prophesied Star and Scepter (Numbers 24:17). Christ is coming to reign in great glory, not only over Israel, but over all men (Rev. 19:15-16). *To the Son He says, Your throne, O God, is for ever and ever: a scepter of righteousness is the scepter of Your Kingdom* (Heb. 1:8). *I Jesus . . . am the Root and the Offspring of David, and the Bright and Morning Star* (Rev. 22:16).

For definitions of unfamiliar words in today's Bible reading, see pages 468-480.

69

> ## In Today's Reading
> Second numbering (census) of the Israelites;
> law of inheritance; Joshua to succeed Moses

Almost 40 years had passed since the exodus of the Israelites from Egypt. All the 603,550 men included in that first census, except Joshua, Caleb and Moses had died. This second generation was now near the promised land. *The LORD spoke to Moses and to Eleazar the son of Aaron the priest, saying, Take the sum* (a census) *of all the congregation of the children of Israel, from twenty years old and upward* (Numbers 26:1-2). This took place *in the plains of Moab by Jordan near Jericho* (26:3).

Another major event was to take place before the Israelites could enter the promised land. *The LORD said to Moses, Get . . . up into this mount Abarim, and see the land which I have given to the children of Israel. And when you have seen it, you also shall be gathered to your people* (will die), *as Aaron your brother was gathered* (died). *For you rebelled against My commandment in the Desert of Zin, in the strife of the congregation, to sanctify Me* (make My holiness apparent) *at the water before their eyes: that is the water of Meribah. . . . And the LORD said to Moses, Take you Joshua the son of Nun, a man in whom is the Spirit, and lay your hand* (transfer authority) *upon him* (27:12-18).

Despite his rebuke and his great disappointment in not being allowed to enter the promised land, *Moses did as the LORD commanded him: and he took Joshua, and set him before Eleazar the priest, and before all the congregation: And he laid his hands upon him, and gave him a charge* (commission) (27:22-23). And, without hesitation, he stepped down from leadership and announced that his helper, Joshua, would become his successor to lead the Lord's people. Moses blessed Joshua and *laid his hands upon him,* symbolically transferring his leadership which God had given to him.

God has said that Moses was the meekest man on earth (12:3). One test of meekness is our willingness to yield our prominent position to another. As a follower of Christ, we are taught: *Let nothing be done through strife or vainglory* (conceit)*; but in lowliness of mind let each esteem other better than themselves* (Philippians 2:3).

Thought for Today: Remain faithful to serving the Lord – even when you must step down and release your position.

Christ Portrayed: By the man (Joshua) who would lead the people like a shepherd (Numbers 27:17). Jesus said: *I am the Good Shepherd* (John 10:11).

For definitions of unfamiliar words in today's Bible reading, see pages 468-480.

IN TODAY'S READING
The daily and weekly offerings (sacrifices), Sabbath and
monthly offerings (sacrifices), and the offerings (sacrifices)
at the appointed feasts

The Israelites' civil year began in the fall with the Feast of Trumpets: *In the seventh month, on the first day of the month, you shall have a holy convocation* (sacred assembly); *you shall do no servile* (to serve another) *work: it is a day of blowing the trumpets to you* (Numbers 29:1). This joyous *day of blowing the trumpets* was followed 10 days later by the solemn Day of Atonement. This was followed by the Feast of Tabernacles (Booths), which was also called the Feast of Ingathering because the work in the fields was finished and the time had come for the people to rest from their labors. It was a time of great rejoicing and lasted for seven days, from the 15th through the 21st of Tishri (Sept/Oct) (Exodus 23:16; 34:22; Leviticus 23:33-44). It was followed by an eighth day of holy convocation on the 22nd which, though closely connected with the Feast of Tabernacles, was not a part of that feast for the people no longer lived in "booths."

The Feast of Tabernacles was the last feast of the religious year. For seven days, all the residents of Israel dwelt in temporary booths (shelters) as an annual reminder of the time when they dwelt in tents during the 40 years in the wilderness. The trees used for these temporary dwellings also had symbolic meanings. The trees provided shade, as well as reminded the people of the Lord's protection and provision. The palm tree was the emblem of victory and the olive tree was a symbol of peace and God's presence (Nehemiah 8:15). The willow tree of the brook signified a thriving and blessed people, a reminder that a blessed man *shall be like a tree planted by the rivers of water, that brings forth its fruit in its season; its leaf also shall not wither; and whatsoever* (whatever) *he does shall prosper* (Psalm 1:3).

The life of a Christian is a journey. It should be a great adventure of going on with the Lord into deeper experiences and greater faith. With the Apostle Paul, let us each say: *I press toward the mark* (goal) *for the prize of the high calling of God in Christ Jesus* (Philippians 3:14).

Thought for Today: It is impossible to gain God's best when our hearts are obsessed with gaining more and more things of the world.

Christ Revealed: By the Tabernacles (Booths) (Numbers 29:12-39; Leviticus 23:34). *The Word* (logos, i.e. the sayings of God) *was made* (became) *flesh, and dwelt among us* (John 1:14). The Greek word translated *dwelt* means to "tabernacle or live in a tent temporarily."

For definitions of unfamiliar words in today's Bible reading, see pages 468-480.

The Exodus Out of Egypt
& Route to the Promised Land

Scholars do not agree on
the route, but the traditionally
accepted route is located near
the vicinities shown
[Also Exodus 12:37 – 19:1
for Exodus from Egypt to Sinai].

1. **Rameses** – (Numbers 33:3)
2. **Succoth** – (Numbers 33:5)
3. **Etham** – (Numbers 33:6)
4. **Migdol / Pi-Hahiroth**
   – (Numbers 33:7-8)

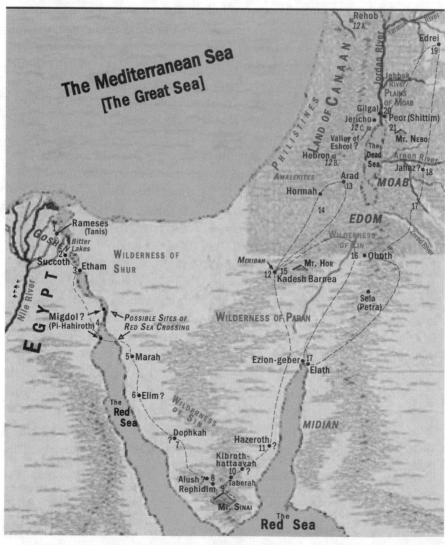

5. **Marah** – (Numbers 33:8)

6. **Elim** – (Numbers 33:9)

7. **Wilderness of Sin** – (Numbers 33:11-12)

8. **Rephidim** – (Numbers 33:14) – People complain of thirst, Moses smites the rock in Horeb and brings forth water (Exodus 17:1-7); Victory over Amalekites (17:8-16)

9. **Wilderness at the base of Mount Sinai** – (Numbers 33:15; Exodus 19:1 – 40:38) – Moses receives 10 Commandments (Exodus 20:1-17); Golden calf worshiped; Moses intercedes; People repent; Moses prays; Covenant is renewed (32:1 – 34:35); Moses receives instructions for building the Tabernacle (25:1 – 31:18); Tabernacle is built (35:1 – 40:38); Passover observed at Sinai (Numbers 9:1-14)

10. **Taberah/Kibroth-hattaavah** – 3 days' journey from Mount Sinai (Numbers 10:33; 33:16-17); People murmur and then die from eating too much quail (11:31-35)

11. **Hazeroth** – (Numbers 33:17) – Miriam and Aaron rebel against Moses; Miriam becomes a leper; Moses intercedes for Miriam and she is restored (12:1-16)

12. **Wilderness of Paran** (Numbers 12:16)/**Kadesh Barnea** – Numbers 33:18) – Spies sent out from Kadesh Barnea and they explore: A. Rehob (North end of Jordan Valley); B. Hebron; C. Valley of Eschol; The people refuse to believe Joshua and Caleb's good report (14:6-10); Rebellion against God; God's judgment was that they would die in the wilderness (14:11-38)

13. **Arad** *top of the mountain* – People attempt to enter the promised land without the Lord (Numbers 14:40-45)

14. **Hormah** – Amalekites and Canaanites defeat Israel *even to Hormah* (Numbers 14:44-45); Israelites return to Kadesh-barnea

WILDERNESS WANDERINGS FOR 38 YEARS – Miriam dies at Kadesh Barnea (12)

15. **Meribah** – No water; People complain; Moses sins by striking rock (Numbers 20:2-13); Refused passage through Edom(20:14-21); Aaron dies on Mount Hor in 40th year (20:22-29; 33:38-39); Victory over king of Arad at Hormah(21:1-3)

16. **Oboth** – Between Kadesh Barnea and Oboth, sin results in *fiery serpents*; God has Moses make a brass serpent to save those who would look upon it (Numbers 21:4-10)

VARIOUS OTHER UNIDENTIFIED LOCATIONS – (Numbers 33:12-47; 21:10-20)

17. **Plains of Moab** – From Kadesh Barnea to the plains of Moab via Elath and Ezion-geber (Numbers 33:37-49; Deuteronomy 2:8)

18. **Jahaz** – The Amorite king, Sihon, refuses Israel passage through his territory; Israel defeats him at Jahaz (Numbers 21:21-32)

19. **Edrei** – After defeating the Amorites, they defeat Og, the king of Bashan (Numbers 21:33-35); King Balak, a Moabite, hires Balaam to curse Israel (22:1 – 24:25)

20. **Peor (near Shittim)** – (Numbers 25:1-18) – Israelites' apostasy with the Midianites;
Second Census (26:1-65)

21. **Mount Nebo** (Pisgah in Abarim mountain range) – (Numbers 27:12-23; Deuteronomy 34:1-4) - Moses appoints Joshua his successor (Numbers 27:12-23); Israelites defeat Midianites and kill 5 kings and the prophet Balaam (31:1-8); Moses ascends to the top of Mount Pisgah (Mount Nebo) and views the promised land; Moses dies there and God Himself buries Moses (Deuteronomy 34:5-6)

JOSHUA ASSUMES LEADERSHIP OF THE ISRAELITES – (Deuteronomy 34:8-9; Joshua 1:1-2)

In Today's Reading

Law concerning vows; Midianites conquered; division of booty;
officers and captains bring an offering to the Lord

The Midianites were descendants of Abraham through his second
wife Keturah, whom he married after Sarah died (Genesis 25:1-2). The
Midianites had devastated Israel, not as enemies who had won a war
but as friendly idol worshipers who seduced the Israelites into committing spiritual adultery. Israel became involved in the worship of their
pagan deity Baal-peor followed by physical adultery with their women.
This had resulted in the death of 24,000 Israelites (Numbers 25:9). Some
time later, God spoke to Moses, saying: *Avenge the children of Israel of the
Midianites* (31:2).

In this war, *Moses sent . . . a thousand of every tribe . . . and Phinehas
the son of Eleazar the priest, to the war, with the holy instruments, and the
trumpets to blow in his hand* (31:6) to execute the judgment of God upon
the Midianites. The *trumpets* were symbols of truth and God's direction.
Not one Israelite died in this battle which resulted in the deaths of all five
kings of the confederation and every Midianite male (31:7-9,15-17). *And
they slew the kings of Midian . . . Balaam also the son of Beor they slew
with the sword* (31:8). It was not incidental that Balaam had chosen to
live in luxury among the Midianites while enjoying the esteem of the
king and the people.

Balaam was from Mesopotamia which included Ur of the Chaldees,
where Abraham had lived before his call from God (Deuteronomy 23:4;
see also Genesis 15:7; Acts 7:2). Balak had said to Balaam: *Come, curse me
Jacob, and come, defy Israel* (Numbers 23:7). Like Balaam, how easy it is
to say: *I cannot go beyond the Word of the LORD my God, to do less or more*
(compare 22:18, see also 22:38; 23:26; 24:13). *Let me die the death of the
righteous, and let my last end be like his* (Jacob)! (23:10). But, like Balaam,
greed and compromise have deceived many who did not *die the death
of the righteous*. Their destiny is eternal hell. *But you, beloved, building up
yourselves on your most holy faith, praying in the Holy Ghost* (Spirit), *Keep
yourselves in the love of God, looking for the mercy of our Lord Jesus Christ
to eternal life* (Jude 1:20-21).

Thought for Today: All earthly treasures cannot compare to an eternal inheritance.

Christ Revealed: As the Ruling One who will righteously judge the wicked (Numbers
31:1-17). *In righteousness He does judge* (Revelation 19:11; II Thessalonians 1:7-9;
Jude 1:14-15).

For definitions of unfamiliar words in today's Bible reading, see pages 468-480.

*M*ore than 40 years had passed since Moses, while still in Egypt, foretold that God would lead the Israelites to the land He had promised to
Abraham, Isaac, and Jacob. While moving with great anticipation toward
the fulfillment of that promise, and almost in view of the promised land,
two of the twelve tribes, those of Reuben and Gad, who *had a very great
multitude of cattle,* decided they would be financially better off if they
remained on the eastern side of the Jordan, so they said to Moses: *The
country which the LORD smote* (conquered) *before the congregation of
Israel, is a land for cattle, and your servants have cattle: Wherefore, said
they . . . let this land be given to your servants for a possession, and bring
us not over Jordan* (Numbers 32:4-5). Moses replied: *Wherefore* (Why)
discourage (frustrate, restrain) *. . . the heart of the children of Israel from
going over into the land which the LORD has given them?* (32:7). They
were joined by half the tribe of Manasseh. Humanly speaking, it was a
wise financial decision; but spiritually, it was an act of compromise. The
unity of the nation and being near the Tabernacle with the presence of
God should have been uppermost in their desires.

History records that they gradually became involved in idol worship
and ignored the Lord's instructions : *These words, which I command you
this day, shall be in your heart: And you shall teach them diligently* (impress
them on) *to your children, and shall talk of them when you sit in your house,
and when you walk by the way, and when you lie down, and when you rise up.
And you shall bind them for a sign upon your hand, and they shall be as
frontlets between your eyes. And you shall write them upon the posts of your
house, and on your gates* (Deuteronomy 6:6-9).

These tribes typify self-indulgent "Christians" who foolishly allow
physical advantages to be their first consideration. They stand as a warning
to those whose business interests, social advancements, or attainment of
prominence are chosen over how they can best serve the Lord. Some who
claim to be Christians are consumed with worldly pursuits that keep them
from giving their time and/or tithes to the Lord. *Wherefore take to you the
whole armor of God, that you may be able to withstand in the evil day. . . . take
. . . the sword of the Spirit, which is the Word of God* (Ephesians 6:13,17).

Thought for Today: Men of faith find ways to obey God – others settle for excuses.

Christ Revealed: Through the promised land -- filled with abundance, as well as
protection, for those who live in harmony with His Word (Num. 33:50-54). *I am come
that they might have life, and that they might have it more abundantly* (John 10:10).

For definitions of unfamiliar words in today's Bible reading, see pages 468-480.

In Today's Reading
Dividing the land of Canaan; inheritance of the Levites

*U*nlike the other tribes, the tribe of Levi, which included the priests, did not have a separate inheritance in the land. They were to depend on the people's tithes, as God had commanded. Forty-eight cities and pasturelands scattered throughout the other tribes were assigned to them as permanent residences (Joshua 21:1-42). Of their 48 cities, six were assigned as cities of refuge which were easily accessible throughout the 12 tribes. For those suspected of manslaughter, these cities were vitally important as places of safety until a trial could determine their guilt or innocence (Numbers 35:6-7,11,13).

Our Creator demands that, *whoso kills any person, the murderer shall be put to death by the mouth of witnesses: but one witness* (accuser) *shall not testify against any person to cause him to die. Moreover you shall take no satisfaction* (ransom) *for the life of a murderer, which is guilty of death: but he shall be surely put to death. . . . So you shall not pollute the land wherein you are: for blood it defiles the land: and the land cannot be cleansed of the blood that is shed therein, but by the blood of him that shed it* (35:30-31,33).

When it was proven to the satisfaction of the congregation that the accused person was guilty of murder, he had to be put to death, regardless of age or whether it was a man or a woman. There was to be no consideration of being sentenced to time in prison, the possibility of parole, rehabilitation, or any kind of financial settlement.

Without a doubt, the prosecution and execution of criminals is an exceedingly painful situation that everyone would prefer to avoid; yet it is necessary to maintain justice and order, the welfare of our society, and, most importantly, the approval of God. *Blessed are they that do His commandments, that they may have right to the tree of life, and may enter in through the gates into the city. For outside are dogs, and sorcerers, and whoremongers, and murderers, and idolaters, and whosoever loves and makes a lie* (Revelation 22:14-15).

Thought for Today: God demands the highest respect for human life, for He created man in His image.

Christ Revealed: By the city of refuge (Numbers 35). Christ is our Refuge from the judgment of God and the curse of the Law. *We . . . have fled for refuge to lay hold upon the hope set before us: Which hope we have as an anchor of the soul . . . even Jesus* (Hebrews 6:18-20). As *the inheritance of the children of Israel* (Numbers 36:7). *Christ . . . In Whom also we have obtained an inheritance* (Ephesians 1:10-11).

For definitions of unfamiliar words in today's Bible reading, see pages 468-480.

Five of *the daughters of Zelophehad . . . of the families of Manasseh the son of Joseph. . . . stood before Moses, and before Eleazar the priest, and before the princes and all the congregation, by the door of the Tabernacle* (Numbers 27:1-2), awaiting a decision concerning their tribal territory after they married. *Moses brought their cause before the LORD* (27:5). The Lord declared through Moses: *saying, Let them marry to whom they think best; only to the family of the tribe of their father shall they marry. . . . for every one of the children of Israel shall keep himself to the inheritance of the tribe of his fathers* (36:6-7).

Although they had the legal right to marry anyone they like, they were to consider the responsibility that rested on their actions. To marry someone from another tribe would forfeit their father's inheritance. The decision involved an important principle of denying one's own personal satisfaction and remaining faithful to fulfilling the will of God. *Even as the LORD commanded Moses, so did the daughters of Zelophehad* (36:10).

No one should overlook how perfectly the request of the five *daughters of Zelophehad* corresponds to our relationship with Christ. We too are often faced with personal satisfaction that is not sinful, but which can cause us to relinquish other spiritual opportunities.

In contrast, no one who remains true to Christ forfeits the best in life. A commitment to God's Word preserves and enhances, rather than hinders, the enjoyment of one's life. Our enemy Satan often appears as an angel of light, seeking our consent to yield, just once, so that he can gain a foothold, and then he gradually takes control of one's life.

The Book of Hebrews continues the warning of God: *Harden not your hearts, as in the provocation, in the day of temptation* (testing) *in the wilderness. Take heed, brethren, lest there be in any of you an evil heart of unbelief, in departing* (turning away) *from the living God* (Hebrews 3:8,12-13; see also Psalm 95:8).

Thought for Today: We always miss God's best when we neglect His Word.

Christ Revealed: As *the inheritance of the children of Israel* (Numbers 36:7). While they were given an inheritance of the land that will pass away, we have been given a greater inheritance, one that will not pass away. *Blessed be the God and Father of our Lord Jesus Christ, Which* (Who) *according to His abundant mercy has begotten* (i.e. through spiritual birth) *us again to a lively* (living) *hope by the resurrection of Jesus Christ from the dead, To an inheritance incorruptible* (imperishable), *and undefiled, and that fades not away, reserved in heaven for you* (I Peter 1:3-4).

For definitions of unfamiliar words in today's Bible reading, see pages 468-480.

Introduction To The Book Of
DEUTERONOMY

The events of the Book of Deuteronomy took place in the 40th year after the Israelites left Egypt and during the final weeks of Moses' life. At that time, Moses reviewed the 40 years in the wilderness and the reason their parents had failed to enter the promised land (Numbers 14:22-24; Deuteronomy 1:22-38). The first generation of adults, except for Joshua, Caleb, and Moses, had all died because of their unbelief that led to disobedience. Now the new generation of Israelites was camped on the Plains of Moab, about to enter the promised land (29:1-5).

From Genesis through Numbers, the love of God was never mentioned; but now, four times Moses revealed: *He loved your fathers, therefore He chose their seed* (descendants) *after them. . . . and redeemed you out of the house of bondmen* (slavery) (4:37; 7:7-8; 10:15; 23:5). *And He brought us out . . . that He might bring us in, to give us the land which He swore to our fathers* (6:23).

Moses stated that the Lord had made a Covenant with their parents at Horeb (Mount Sinai), but they had continually failed to keep it. After giving the Mosaic Law to the new generation, Moses stressed the importance of obedience to God's Word and of teaching it to their children (4:1-9,44; 5:31-33; 11:19). *And it shall be, if you . . . walk after other gods, and serve them, and worship them . . . you shall surely perish* (8:19).

Moses reminded them of the importance of their loyalty to God, saying: *And now, Israel, what does the LORD your God require of you, but to fear the LORD your God to walk in all His ways, and to love Him, and to serve the LORD your God . . . for your good?* (10:12-13; 27:1 – 29:1; 30:20). The two key words *for your good* are **obey** and **do** which occur more than 170 times in this book. This key to success is the central message of Deuteronomy as well as the entire Bible.

Instructions were also given concerning the importance of tithes and offerings. Of particular significance is the revelation that *the LORD your God will raise up to you a Prophet from the midst of you, of your brethren, like to me; to Him you shall hearken* (18:15,18-19). Fifteen hundred years later, Peter applied this prophecy to Jesus (Acts 3:20-23), as did both Stephen and Philip (7:37; John 1:45).

The Book of Deuteronomy ends with the death of Moses after his commission of Joshua, a man *full of the spirit of wisdom* to lead the Israelites into the promised land (Deuteronomy 34:1-9). The seven different Hebrew names used for God in Deuteronomy reveal Him as *the Strong One, the Mighty One, the Almighty, the Self-Existing One, Jehovah (Yahweh) is Lord, the Lord God,* and *the Most High God.*

IN TODAY'S READING
Moses' review of Israel's past 40 years;
command to leave Mount Sinai;
refusal to enter the promised land; 38 years of wanderings

In his first message to the new generation (Deuteronomy 1:1 – 4:43), Moses reminded them that *there are eleven days' journey from Horeb by the way of Mount Seir to Kadesh-barnea* (about 165 miles) (1:2). This message was given *in the fortieth year* after leaving Egypt (1:3). Despite their miraculous deliverance from Egypt, the older generation sinned against the Lord by not believing that He would give them victory over the Canaanites. By faith, the promised land could have been theirs.

The adult Israelites who had left Egypt did not recognize that their hardships were designed to test their faith and prepare them to defeat the Canaanites. As a consequence of their sin of unbelief, that first generation failed to accomplish the will of God and wasted their lives wandering in the wilderness until they all died. The new generation would also be tested. Would they take God at His Word?

We too have a choice. We can choose to be like the many Israelites who found fault with everything, or choose to be like Caleb and Joshua whose faith in God's Word overcame all fears and frustrations.

Like the Israelites, some today, although they have accepted Christ as their Savior, have made little or no spiritual progress since they first believed. They do as little as possible to help others spiritually for they have not made Him Lord of their lives. It is our responsibility to be *doers of the Word, and not hearers only* (James 1:22).

Loving submission to the Lord develops our faith in His ability to guide, protect, and provide for our every need. Just as God had a plan for Israel, so He has a plan for each of us.

In the midst of giant problems, the Holy Spirit is available to all who, like Caleb and Joshua, trust in the Lord to overcome their giants. God's Word is our only infallible Guide. *For we are His workmanship, created in Christ Jesus to good works, which God has before ordained* (planned) *that we should walk in them* (Ephesians 2:10).

Thought for Today: In the midst of "giant" problems, strength to be an overcomer through the Holy Spirit is available to all who trust in Him.

Christ Portrayed: By Moses, who *spoke to the children of Israel, according to all that the LORD ... commanded* (Deuteronomy 1:3). Jesus faithfully told others everything God told Him to say. *I do nothing of Myself; but as My Father has taught Me, I speak these things* (John 8:28).

For definitions of unfamiliar words in today's Bible reading, see pages 468-480.

In Today's Reading
Division of land east of the Jordan; Moses' prayer; cities of refuge
established east of the Jordan

*M*oses reminded the new generation of Israelites that living according to God's Word would bring lasting fulfillment. He began to explain the Law that God had given their parents 40 years earlier at Mount Sinai (Deuteronomy 1:3-5). *To declare this Law* meant more than merely "repeating" the Law; it meant to explain its meaning. Moses' first message highlighted the importance of keeping all the Word of God, *that you may live, and go in and possess* (live in) *the land. . . . keep* (obey) *the Commandments of the LORD your God. . . . and do them; for this is your wisdom and your understanding. . . . For what nation is there so great, who has God so near to them?* (4:1-7).

That you may live (4:1) meant that the Israelites would enjoy the best in life. The one essential requirement for remaining in the land of promise was **obedience** to God's Word. He warned them that when you *shall do evil in the sight of the LORD your God . . . you shall soon utterly perish* (4:25-26). God desires that we *seek Him with all our heart and with all our soul* (4:29) *for our good* (10:13).

Obedience to the One True God would have enabled Israel to be successful and morally and spiritually unique among all other nations.

We too need a daily reminder to *take heed to* (be careful for) *yourself, and keep your soul* (watch yourselves) *diligently, lest you forget the things which your eyes have seen, and lest they depart from your heart . . . teach them to your sons, and to your sons' sons* (4:9).

Children begin developing respect for God by first being taught to behave in a respectful way toward their parents. Unfortunately, unless children learn respect for their parents, they seldom learn to respect and obey God, Who said: *Train up a child in the way he should go: and when he is old, he will not depart from it* (Proverbs 22:6).

The Bible provides our only source of knowing the will and character of our Creator. *Keep therefore His Statutes, and His Commandments, which I command you this day, that it may go well with you, and with your children after you* (Deuteronomy 4:40).

Thought for Today: It is our faith in God – not our strength or wisdom – that leads to victory.

Christ Portrayed: By Joshua, who led the Israelites into their inheritance (Deuteronomy 3:28). Through Jesus we receive His promised *inheritance among them which are sanctified* (set apart) *by faith that is in Me* (Acts 26:18).

For definitions of unfamiliar words in today's Bible reading, see pages 468-480.

> ## In Today's Reading
> Review of the Covenant made on Horeb (Mount Sinai);
> chosen to be a holy people; command to destroy idol worship

Moses reminded the Israelites that *the LORD our God is one LORD* (Deuteronomy 6:4). The Hebrew word translated *our God* is *Elohenu*, meaning "our Gods." This, then, is what Moses said: *Hear, O Israel: The LORD our Gods is one LORD* (6:4). The word *one* ('echad) expresses "one" in the collective sense. It signifies a compound unity. The *one LORD* is a glorious revelation of the One True God as being one, yet three distinct persons: Father, Son, and Holy Spirit. *Let Us make man in Our image* (Genesis 1:26); *as one of Us* (3:22); *let Us go* (11:7); and *who will go for Us?* (Isaiah 6:8).

The same Hebrew word *'echad* is used in Genesis 2:24 where man and woman became *one flesh* and, even with numerous children, they are still called "one" family, as soldiers become *one troop* (II Samuel 2:25).

The Hebrew word for "one" in the sense of absolute oneness is the word *yacheed*, meaning an "absolute one." Moses had the word *yacheed* available to him; but obviously God led Moses to accurately refer to Himself by the word *echad*, meaning a compound unity. Those who reject Jesus as fully God, as well as fully Man, are rejecting the true revelation of God the Father, God the Son, and God the Holy Spirit. *For there are three that bear record in heaven, the Father, the Word, and the Holy Spirit: and these three are One. And there are three that bear witness in earth, the Spirit, and the water, and the blood: and these three agree in one. If we receive the witness of men, the witness of God is greater: for this is the witness of God which He has testified of His Son* (I John 5:7-9).

It is of utmost importance that we understand that worshipers of any other "gods" are deceived. *For there is one God, and one Mediator between God and men, the Man Christ Jesus* (I Timothy 2:5).

In the beginning was the Word (logos, sayings of God) , *and the Word was with God, and the Word was God. The Same was in the beginning with God. All things were made by Him; and without Him was not any thing made that was made. . . . And the Word was made* (became) *flesh, and dwelt among us* (John 1:1-3,14).

Thought for Today: Rejoice! Jesus will soon return to rule the world as King of kings.

Christ Revealed: Through the land flowing with milk and honey (Deuteronomy 6:3). This pictures Christ Who provides for our needs. *Seek first the Kingdom of God, and His righteousness; and all these things shall be added to you* (Matthew 6:33).

For definitions of unfamiliar words in today's Bible reading, see pages 468-480.

IN TODAY'S READING
Keep the commandments; reminder of parents' rebellion,
golden calf; the second tablets of stone

---

*J*esus began His earthly ministry by quoting from Deuteronomy: *Man shall not live by bread alone, but by every word that proceeds out of the mouth of God* (Matthew 4:4; compare Deuteronomy 8:3). This was His response to Satan, who tempted Him to make bread for Himself from stones after His 40-day fast. Satan had said: *If You be the Son of God, command that these stones be made bread* (Matthew 4:3), meaning: "Why should You, of all people, go hungry?"

Satan the tempter quoted Scripture, but he misapplied its meaning. Jesus again quoted Deuteronomy at the second temptation, saying: *You shall not tempt the Lord your God* (4:7; Deuteronomy 6:16). Jesus did not compromise even once – a lesson some Christians need to learn. At the third temptation, Jesus once again quoted Deuteronomy: *It is written: You shall worship the Lord your God, and Him only shall you serve* (Matthew 4:10; Deuteronomy 6:13). A vital key to overcoming Satan is knowing God's Word through which we are empowered to be overcomers. *For the Word of God is quick* (living), *and powerful* (Hebrews 4:12) and it is the only weapon needed to defeat Satan. As we continue reading all of God's Word, the Holy Spirit brings it to our minds when it is needed.

We need to remember Moses' warning to Israel: *Beware that you forget not the* LORD *your God, in not keeping His Commandments. . . . And you say in your heart* (to yourself) *my power and the might of my hand has gotten me this wealth. But you shall remember the* LORD *your God for it is He that gives you power to get wealth* (Deuteronomy 8:11,17-18).

After reviewing the Commandments, Moses added: *What does the* LORD *your God require of you, but to fear the* LORD *your God to walk in all His ways, and to love Him, and to serve the* LORD *your God with all your heart and with all your soul, To keep the Commandments of the* LORD, *and His Statutes, which I command you this day for your good* (benefit) (10:12-13).

Jesus not only quoted these verses as applying to His followers, but said that *he that has My Commandments, and keeps them, he it is that loves Me. . . . If a man love Me, he will keep My words* (John 14:21-23).

Thought for Today: Does Jesus get all the credit for your achievements?

Christ Revealed: Through the shittim (acacia) wood used to make the Ark of the Covenant (Deuteronomy 10:3). Acacia wood, a desert growth, is symbolic of Christ in His human form as a *root out of a dry ground* (Isaiah 53:2). Jesus took on human form to redeem us. *God sent forth His Son, made of a woman* (born), *made* (born) *under the Law, To redeem them that were under the Law* (Galatians 4:4-5).

For definitions of unfamiliar words in today's Bible reading, see pages 468-480.

In Today's Reading

Israel is to love and obey God; warning against false gods and
adding to or taking away anything from His Word

To perpetuate loyalty and love to God in future generations, every Israelite was to live in subjection to the Word of God. To accomplish this God said: *Teach them* (to) *your children* (Deuteronomy 11:19). Our foremost concern every day should be to teach our children to love the Lord and be obedient to Him. They should have no doubt that we also truly love the Lord and are obedient to Him. If our hearts are filled with the Word of God, it will overflow from our lives: *When you sit in your house, and when you walk by the way, when you lay down, and when you rise up* (11:19).

Moses repeated to the new generation what the Lord had said to their parents, reminding them of how important it is to *diligently keep all these Commandments which I command you, to do them, to love the LORD your God, to walk in all His ways, and to cleave* (hold fast) *to Him* (11:22).

God has said: *You shall rejoice in all that you put your hand to, you and your households, wherein the LORD your God has blessed you* (12:7).

What our children will become is usually dependent upon what they learn about our values in life. What we are in great measure is what our children become. That is why it is so important that parents devote time to molding the rapidly developing minds of their young children. It is of utmost importance that parents guide even the youngest children to reverence God, to worship Him, to pray, and to recognize the Bible as the voice of God speaking to them.

Influences outside the home often send strong messages to our children that are opposite in character to the values we desire them to live by. It becomes increasingly important in this time of moral chaos to provide our children with a strong spiritual environment.

Children need to fear (have a reverential attitude of deep concern to be obedient to) God and to know that He said: *Honor your father and mother; (which is the first commandment with promise;) That it may be well with you, and you may live long on the earth* (Ephesians 6:2-3).

Thought for Today: Christian parents are responsible to teach their children the way they should live (Proverbs 22:6).

Christ Revealed: Through the burned offerings which were totally consumed. These typified Christ's total offering of Himself to death (Deuteronomy 12:6; see Hebrews 10:5-7). *For the bodies of those beasts, whose blood is brought into the sanctuary (Holy Place) by the high priest for sin, are burned outside the camp. Wherefore Jesus also, that He might sanctify (make holy) the people with His own blood, suffered without the gate* (Hebrews 13:11-12).

For definitions of unfamiliar words in today's Bible reading, see pages 468-480.

*I*N *T*ODAY'S *R*EADING
Clean and unclean food; the Law of the tithe; dedication of the
firstborn; three festivals to be observed; judges and justice

*T*he prosperity of Israel in the promised land did not depend on advanced agricultural techniques but on obedience to the Word of God (Deuteronomy 11:10-15). The Israelites were taught: *You shall truly tithe all the increase of your seed* (produce from what you sow) . . . *year by year. . . . that you may learn to fear* (revere) *the LORD your God always* (14:22-23).

Tithing reminded the people that they, as well as the land, belonged to the Lord, and Who and What should occupy first place in their lives. Since all they possessed was the result of His loving provision, before all other considerations, their tithes to the Lord were to be given first. Furthermore, no Israelite could come before the Lord without an offering commensurate with his income. To merely bring leftovers or a small pittance of one's income would be an expression of disobedience and ingratitude.

The command was clear: *They shall not appear before the LORD empty* (empty-handed): *Every man shall give as he is able, according to the blessing of the LORD your God which He has given you* (16:16-17).

The Israelites were not only taught to bring their tithes to the Lord as a spiritual and moral obligation, but they were to "rejoice" with a heartfelt appreciation for the privilege of honoring God with their tithes and offerings; *that the LORD your God may bless you* (14:29).

Five hundred years before the Law was given to Moses, Abraham, father of the faithful (Romans 4:11), paid a tenth (tithe) as an acceptable offering to the Lord. That principle continued throughout the Bible, and includes all believers today who are called *the children of Abraham* (Galatians 3:7). Today, the Lord's ministries, missionaries, churches, Bible schools, Bible publishers, translators, and other agencies are being sustained through the tithes and offerings of His people. Unexpected expenses test the sincerity of our faith. All of us were born selfish and self-centered, desiring to keep everything for self. However, all of what we call our possessions, even ourselves, belongs to God. Jesus said: *Render* (give) *therefore to Caesar the things which are Caesar's; and to God the things that are God's* (Matthew 22:21).

Thought for Today: Tithing is acknowledgment of God's ownership of everything!

Christ Revealed: Through the year of release, which typifies Christ's forgiveness of our sins (Deuteronomy 15:1). This should teach us to forgive others, even as He has forgiven us (Matthew 6:14-15). *Be you kind one to another, tenderhearted, forgiving one another, even as God for Christ's sake has forgiven you* (Ephesians 4:32).

For definitions of unfamiliar words in today's Bible reading, see pages 468-480.

IN TODAY'S READING
Idolaters and obedience to authority; offerings due priests and Levites; heathen practices; prophecy concerning the coming of Christ; cities of refuge

*M*oses foretold: *The LORD your God will raise up to you a Prophet* (Jesus) *from the midst of you, of your brethren, like to me; to Him you shall hearken. . . . the LORD said to me. . . . I* (God) *. . . will put My words in His mouth; and He shall speak to them all that I shall command Him. . . . whosoever will not hearken to My words which He shall speak in My Name, I will require it of him* (Deuteronomy 18:15,17-19). The prophet Jeremiah foretold that, in the end times, God will make a new Covenant with His people (Jeremiah 31:31-34).

In conversation with His critics, Jesus said that Moses and the Scriptures bore witness of Him: *For had you believed Moses, you would have believed Me: for he wrote of Me. But if you believe not his writings* (Genesis – Deuteronomy), *how shall you believe My words?* (John 5:46-47).

Jesus declared to Pilate: *My kingdom is not of this world,* meaning it has no earthly origin, but is a spiritual kingdom without end (18:36). On the Day of Pentecost, Peter boldly proclaimed that Jesus fulfilled the prophecy of Moses, who said: *A Prophet shall the Lord your God raise up to you of your brethren, like to me; Him shall you hear in all things whatsoever He shall say to you. And it shall come to pass, that every soul, which will not hear that Prophet, shall be destroyed from among the people. Yea, and all the prophets from Samuel and those that follow after, as many as have spoken, have likewise foretold of these days* (Acts 3:22-24; Deuteronomy 18:18-19). The Prophet whom Moses foretold is Jesus, Who said: *He that follows Me shall not walk in darkness* (John 8:12).

The writer of the Book of Hebrews wrote: *He that despised* (rejected) *Moses' Law died without mercy . . . how much sorer* (more severe) *punishment, suppose you, shall he be thought worthy, who has trodden under foot the Son of God, and has counted the blood of the Covenant* (Agreement), *wherewith he was sanctified, an unholy thing, and has done despite* (insulted) *to the Spirit of grace?* (Hebrews 10:28-29).

Thought for Today: Christ makes intercession for all who come to the Father through Him.

Christ Revealed: Through the Old Testament sacrifices which were made without blemish or defect (Deuteronomy 17:1). Christ was perfectly pure from all sin and all appearance of evil. *Christ . . . without blemish and without spot* (I Peter 1:19).

For definitions of unfamiliar words in today's Bible reading, see pages 468-480.

IN TODAY'S READING
Laws concerning murder; female war captives, their marriage and
divorce; another's property; sanitation and human relations

The Israelites had been taught that everything belonged to God and
they were only caretakers of His possessions. Because of their Covenant relationship with the Lord, they even were responsible for the
welfare of their neighbor's property: *You shall not see your brother's ox
or his sheep go astray, and hide yourself from them: you shall in any case
bring them again to your brother* (Deuteronomy 22:1-4).

Under the laws of our country, we may not be held legally responsible for failing to prevent someone else's financial loss. But our stew-
ardship responsibility to God requires that we respond to another's
needs in a spirit of Christlike love.

In our Lord's Sermon on the Mount, He taught His followers to
go far beyond merely helping preserve the property of a neighbor.
Jesus commanded His followers: *Love your enemies, bless them that
curse you . . . That you may be the children of your Father which is in
heaven* (Matthew 5:44-45). As His disciples we must do the same.

The person we help may or may not appreciate or deserve the
kindness shown. Our responsibility, however, is not to the person
who needs our help but to the Lord, Who is the true Owner of all
creation, and Who provides the opportunities for us to express His love.

Jesus illustrated this by saying: *A certain man went down from
Jerusalem to Jericho, and fell among thieves . . . leaving him half dead.
. . . a certain priest. . . . And . . . a Levite . . . looked on him, and passed by.*
Perhaps they had completed their religious responsibilities in Jerusalem and were on their way home to Jericho, the city of palm trees,
where many of the Temple priests lived. To stop and help this man
could have defiled them and made them ceremonially unclean. *But a
certain Samaritan* wasn't looking for excuses as to whether the hurt-
ing man was deserving of being helped. *He had compassion* (pity) *on
him* (Luke 10:30-34).

The Apostle John was led to remind us we must *not love in word,
neither in tongue* (talk); *but in deed* (action) *and in truth* (I John 3:18).

Thought for Today: We should take advantage of every opportunity to express Christ's love
to those around us.

Christ Revealed: Christ died on a tree (cross) in our place, submitting to the penalty of death
imposed by the Law for our sins (Deuteronomy 21:23). In the evening He was taken down
from the cross, signifying the Law had been satisfied (John 19:31). *Christ has redeemed
us from the curse of the Law, being made a curse for us: for it is written, Cursed is
every one that hangs on a tree* (Galatians 3:13).

For definitions of unfamiliar words in today's Bible reading, see pages 468-480.

In Today's Reading

Divorce; domestic relations; first-fruits and tithes;
the Law on Mount Ebal; an altar on Mount Gerizim

*M*oses, the lawgiver and prophet, placed great emphasis on the necessity of honesty and truthfulness in all areas of life. He warned against two sets of weights and measures – one for buying and the other for selling: *You shall not have in your house divers* (different) *measures, a great and a small. But you shall have a perfect and just weight, a perfect and just measure . . . that your days may be lengthened in the land which the LORD your God gives you. For all that do . . . unrighteously, are an abomination* (detestable) *to the LORD your God* (Deuteronomy 25:14-16).

God hates lying and bribery. Each of us has the opportunity to exercise the principles of justice and equity or to take advantage of others, which take some form of dishonesty such as wasting time on the job, taking what doesn't belong to us, unethical business transactions, lies, fraud, or any other dishonest act.

Our relationship with others goes much deeper than either word or deed; it goes to the hidden motives of our hearts and reveals what we truly are. This means that the thoughts of a Christian should always be the expression of what Jesus would do.

The attitude of fairness and consideration for others' well-being applies to a Christian's daily conduct. The self-centered "I" must give way to Christ and His control.

It is possible to have bitter thoughts while doing kind deeds and to say loving words while having wrong attitudes and motives. But, our Adamic nature and its self-serving conduct can be overcome by the Christ-centered nature that He has bestowed within us.

Abraham, the father of the faithful (Romans 4:11), exemplified this as he gave up his right to the possession of the best land to his nephew Lot in order to settle a dispute (Genesis 13:8-9).

For the weapons of our warfare are not carnal (fleshly), *but mighty through God to the pulling down of strong holds . . . bringing into captivity every thought to the obedience of Christ* (II Corinthians 10:4-5).

Thought for Today: A Christian should resist all temptation to lie, cheat, or steal. These evils will result in the judgment of God.

Christ Revealed: Through the deliverance of the Israelites from Egypt and Pharaoh (Deuteronomy 26:8). *Our Lord Jesus Christ, Who gave Himself for our sins, that He might deliver us from this present evil world* (Galatians 1:3-4).

For definitions of unfamiliar words in today's Bible reading, see pages 468-480.

In Today's Reading
Blessings for obedience; consequences for disobedience

*M*oses related to the Israelites the blessings the people would receive: *If you shall hearken diligently to the voice of the LORD your God, to observe and . . . do all His Commandments which I command you this day. . . . The LORD shall open . . . the heaven to give the rain to your land in its season, and to bless all the work of your hand* (Deuteronomy 28:1,12). The Israelites could choose either to live as His Word directed and enjoy the Lord's blessings or to reject His Word, as their parents had done, and suffer the consequences. Moses further warned: *The LORD shall make the pestilence* (disease) *cling to you, until He has consumed* (destroyed) *you from off the land, where you go to possess it. The LORD shall smite you . . . with the sword. . . . you shall not prosper in your ways; and you shall be only oppressed and spoiled* (robbed) *evermore, and no man shall save you* (28:21-22,29).

Almost four times as many verses warn of the curses resulting from disobedience than of the blessings for obedience. The obvious conclusion of God's Word is that each sin has a consequence – and it definitely does. However, this fact can also be misapplied, as in the case when Jesus' *disciples asked Him, saying, Master, who did sin, this man, or his parents, that he was born blind? Jesus answered, Neither has this man sinned, nor his parents: but that the works of God should be made manifest* (revealed) *in him* (John 9:2-3). What seemed to be a curse became a blessing, for it brought this man to his Savior.

This points out that not all misfortunes are the result of sin, and that not all wealth and good health are necessarily a blessing from God. Consider the rich young ruler who chose to keep his wealth but it kept him from denying self and becoming a follower of Jesus (Matthew 19:16-22).

Victory over our present-day "Canaanite" giants – *the lust of the flesh, and the lust of the eyes, and the pride of life* (I John 2:16) – is achieved, not because of our abilities but because of our commitment to do the will of God. Overcoming power is found in cooperating with the Spirit of Christ, Who dwells within us. We too can say with the Apostle Paul: *I can do **all things*** (that He calls me to do) *through Christ Who strengthens me* (Philippians 4:13).

Thought for Today: God takes note of every thought of the heart.

Christ Revealed: As the One from Whom our blessings come (Deuteronomy 28:1-2). *Blessed he the God . . . Who has blessed us with all spiritual blessings . . . in Christ* (Eph. 1:3).

For definitions of unfamiliar words in today's Bible reading, see pages 468-480.

In Today's Reading

New generation's covenant; warnings against disobedience;
Joshua, Moses' successor; Moses' last counsel

The Creator chose the small Israelite nation as the people through whom He would reveal Himself as the One True Self-Existent God. *Keep therefore the words of this Covenant, and do them, that you may prosper in all that you do. . . . That He may establish you to day for a people to Himself, and that He may be to you a God . . . as He has sworn to your fathers, to Abraham, to Isaac, and to Jacob* (Deuteronomy 29:9,13). Moses continued to warn the people of the consequences of disregarding their Covenant responsibilities: *Lest there should be among you man, or woman, or family, or tribe, whose heart turns away this day from the LORD your God to go and serve the gods of these nations; lest there should be among you a root that bears gall and wormwood* (29:18-19).

God's chosen people confirmed their Covenant with God with promises to keep the agreement. It implied much more than a contract agreement. The Covenant was a permanent arrangement and covers a person's total being.

When the Israelites entered the promised land, they were surrounded by influences that would test their loyalty to the One True God. They were faced with people who seemed to have "advantages" such as chariots for war and an "attractive" religious system with images they could see and touch. The Israelites were tempted to depart from loyalty to their God. In Joshua's last message, he proclaimed: *When you . . . have gone and served other gods . . . then shall the anger of the LORD be kindled against you, and you shall perish quickly from off the good land* (Joshua 23:16). Israel's God, the One True God, is our God. There is no other. Israel's Messiah is our Savior. There is no other. Christians are the people of God by a far more precious covenant (Hebrews 8:6) than that in Abraham and we too are tempted by false gods.

As the nations of the world have become our near neighbors, some are deceived and assume that their false gods are also the One True God Who is just called by another name and that their faith is but one of many ways to worship the Almighty God. But all worshipers of these false gods reject *that blessed hope, and the glorious appearing of the great God and our Savior Jesus Christ* (Titus 2:13).

Thought for Today: Our love for the Lord is the same as our love for God's Word.

Christ Revealed: As Life (Deuteronomy 30:15). Jesus is *the Resurrection, and the Life* (John 11:25).

For definitions of unfamiliar words in today's Bible reading, see pages 468-480.

The Israelites were to proclaim *greatness to our God . . . for all His ways are judgment; a God of Truth*. The Almighty Rock will never forsake the faithful. *The Rock, His work is perfect: for all His ways are . . . without iniquity, just and right is He* (Deuteronomy 32:3-4). Moses foretold of the blessings and happiness that would be theirs if they lived in obedience to the Word of God (33:6-29).

After conferring spiritual blessings upon each of the tribes, Moses concluded with praise to God: *The eternal God is your refuge, and underneath are the everlasting arms: and He shall thrust out the enemy from before you* (33:27). Although it is written: *There arose not a prophet since in Israel like to Moses, whom the LORD knew face to face* (34:10), Moses forfeited the privilege of leading Israel into Canaan because of his sin (32:48-52; compare Numbers 20:1-13). Thus Moses became an example for all Israel that God is holy and cannot allow His Law to be broken without consequences.

Moses' life had been almost perfect. However, even though he had been the Lord's lawgiver, he had also broken the Law once, and the Law did not permit exceptions. Moses is last seen alone, climbing one of the most prominent mountain peaks in Moab from which he was allowed to view the promised land, though he could not enter it. Moses' penalty illustrates that even forgiveness of sin does not remove its earthly consequences (James 2:10).

Centuries later, Moses, symbolizing God's Law, stood on Mount Hermon in the promised land with Elijah, who symbolized the prophets of God. Together they talked with Jesus as He *was transfigured before them: and His face did shine as the sun, and His raiment was white as the light. And, behold, there appeared to them Moses and Elias* (Elijah) *talking with Him. Then answered Peter, and said . . . let us make three tabernacles; one for You, and one for Moses, and one for Elias* (Elijah). *While He yet spoke, behold, a bright cloud overshadowed them: and behold a voice out of the cloud . . . said, This is My beloved Son, in Whom I am well pleased; hear . . . Him* (Matthew 17:2-5).

Thought for Today: Express the same patience to others that you expect to receive from the Lord.

Christ Portrayed: As *our Rock* (Deuteronomy 32:31). Christ was *that spiritual Rock* (Petra) *that followed* (accompanied) *them* (I Corinthians 10:4).

For definitions of unfamiliar words in today's Bible reading, see pages 468-480.

Introduction To The Book Of
Joshua

The Book of Joshua covers a period of about 25 years and is a continuation of the history of Israel recorded in Numbers.

Through Moses God spoke to Joshua, saying: *This Book of the Law shall not depart out of your mouth but you shall meditate therein day and night, that you may observe to do according to all that is written therein: for then you shall make your way prosperous, and then you shall have good success* (Joshua 1:8).

Major events in the Book of Joshua:

1. Two men spy out the land and make a covenant with Rahab (2:1-24).

2. The Israelites move from Shittim to the eastern bank of the Jordan River and remain three days to *sanctify* themselves (3:1-5).

3. The flood waters of the Jordan are miraculously parted (3:9-17).

4. The Israelites cross the Jordan. *Joshua set up twelve stones in the midst of Jordan* (4:9-24).

5. In the promised land, the Israelites first camped at Gilgal, near the banks of the Jordan, where *the LORD said to Joshua, Make you sharp knives, and circumcise* (all men of the new generation) *the children of Israel* (5:2,5). A second memorial was built at Gilgal (4:20).

6. The first Passover is observed in the promised land (5:10).

7. Jericho and Ai are conquered (6:1 – 8:29).

8. Joshua offered a burned sacrifice and peace offering on Mount Ebal, near Jacob's Well. *He wrote there upon the stones a copy of the Law of Moses, which he wrote in the presence of the children of Israel* (8:32).

9. Deception by the Gibeonites is followed by a peace treaty (9:1-27).

10. War is declared by kings in the south. Joshua conquered them through the miraculous intervention of the Lord (10:1-43).

11. The remaining kings in the land were defeated along with their armies (11:1-23). The key to conquering the Canaanites is clear: *As the LORD commanded Moses his servant, so did Moses command Joshua, and so did Joshua; he left nothing undone of all that the LORD commanded Moses* (11:15).

12. Territory is assigned to the tribes (13:1 – 22:34), except to the tribe of Levi (21:41) which was given 48 cities throughout all the tribes. *There failed nothing of any good thing which the LORD had spoken to the house of Israel; all came to pass* (21:43-45; see also 1:1-6).

13. Joshua's farewell message was clear: *Be . . . very courageous to keep and to do all that is written in the Book of the Law of Moses, that you turn not aside . . . to the right hand or to the left* (23:6).

In Today's Reading
God speaks to Joshua; spies sent to Jericho;
pledge between the spies and Rahab; Israel crosses the Jordan River

Joshua was born into Egyptian slavery. While the majority were complaining and finding fault with Moses during their desert trials, Joshua remained a faithful coworker with Moses.

Israel's first encounter with the Canaanites in the promised land was at the powerful walled city of Jericho. The people of Jericho had *heard how the LORD dried up the water of the Red Sea for you, when you came out of Egypt; and what you did to the two kings of the Amorites . . . whom you utterly destroyed* (Joshua 2:10). Rahab *said to the men, I know that the LORD has given you the land. . . . for the LORD your God He is God in heaven above, and in earth beneath* (2:9-11). She then turned from her false gods, left her life as a prostitute, and trusted in the mercy of the One True God. It was no accident that the spies came to her home to bring God's protection upon her and her family.

Because of her faith in the Lord, Rahab became an ancestor of King David and was included in the genealogy of Jesus Christ (Matthew 1:5; Luke 3:32). She is listed in the "Faith Hall of Fame" (Hebrews 11:31).

Moses gave up life in the palace and possibly his right to be a Pharaoh of Egypt, *choosing rather to suffer affliction with the people of God, than to enjoy the pleasures of sin for a season* (short time); *Esteeming the reproach of Christ greater riches than the treasures in Egypt* (11:25-26). Joshua remained faithful to God when the majority threatened to kill him (Numbers 14:6-10). Moses, Joshua and Rahab forsook their sins, lived to please the Lord, and made themselves available for God to accomplish His will through them.

All of us have faced, or will face, choices similar to those of Moses, Joshua and Rahab. Let us not be like the majority, but *looking diligently* (carefully) *lest any man fail of the grace of God; lest any root of bitterness springing up trouble you, and thereby many be defiled; Lest there be any fornicator, or profane* (godless) *person, as Esau, who for one morsel of meat* (food) *sold his birthright* (Hebrews 12:15-16).

Thought for Today: Most of us will pass into eternity with unfinished goals; but if our life's work is of God, it will continue to bless others.

Christ Revealed: Through the *scarlet line in the window* that saved Rahab and her household—symbolic of the blood of Christ (Joshua 2:21; Hebrews 11:31; James 2:25. *The blood of Jesus Christ His Son cleanses us from all sin* (I John 1:7).

For definitions of unfamiliar words in today's Bible reading, see pages 468-480.

JOSHUA'S CONQUEST OF CANAAN

For hundreds of years Israel had hoped to occupy the land promised to Abraham; now that time had come. The Israelites were encamped at Shittim (Acacia) where Moses had delivered his farewell address, and Joshua had taken command. The qualifications of his success were very clear for the Lord commanded and promised: *This Book of the Law shall not depart out of your mouth but you shall meditate therein day and night, that you may observe to do according to all that is written therein: for then you shall make your way prosperous, and then you shall have good success* [Joshua 1:8]. Outline for this map:

1.   **Crossing the Jordan** [chapter 3:1 – 5:1]

The priests bearing the Ark of the Covenant led the way as the nation followed at a distance. As their feet touched the water at flood stage, it ceased to flow and they walked across *on dry land* [4:22]. This was a repetition of the Exodus miracle.

2.   **Preparation that preceded any battle – circumcision and Passover** [chapter 5:2-15]

The nation of Israel then encamped at Gilgal, a site which remained their base of operation for about seven years during the conquest. *The Captain of the Lord's host* reminded Joshua that this new land was holy ground and that He (Christ Pre-incarnate) was *leading Israel* [5:15].

3.   **The Central Campaign** [chapters 6:1 – 8:35]   ➡ ➡ ➡

In obedience to God's Word, the walls of Jericho fell [6:20]. Because of Achan's sin, the Israelites were at first defeated at Ai, but after obeying God's command in dealing with the sin, the city of Ai was reduced to a ruin and the king hanged [8:18-29]. Then Israel assembled together at the ancient site of Shechem, between Mount Ebal and Mount Gerizim. An altar was built as the Lord had commanded through Moses and the Law was recorded on stones in Mount Ebal [Deuteronomy 27:1-8; Joshua 8:30-35].

4.   **The Southern Campaign** [chapters 9:1 – 10:43]   ☛ ☛ ☛

The Gibeonites decided the only wise course was to join their enemy Israel [9:3-27]. The Amorite kings of Jerusalem, Hebron, Jarmuth, Lachish, and Eglon were next to fall [10:1-5]. The Lord sent giant hailstones from heaven and the sun and moon stood still to help the Israelites in battle [10:10-14]. These five kings fled to Makkedah, where they were found hidden in a cave. Later Joshua slew them, hanged their bodies on trees, and then buried them in the same cave [10:17-27]. Joshua next struck deep into the south and west and conquered all the towns of any importance [10:40-42].

5.   **The Northern Campaign** [chapter 11:1-15]   ✦ ✦ ✦

With the central and southern parts of the land under Israel's control, a northern coalition made up of the Canaanite, Amorite, Hittite, Perizzite, Jebusite, and Hivite kings united in a vast federation led by Jabin, king of Hazor. Jabin enlisted the kings and their soldiers from as far north as Lake Huleh and as far east as Damascus in Syria; all the kingdoms east of Jordan as far south as the Dead Sea and from the Jezreel Valley on the west bank of the Jordan. He united his armies at the waters of Merom, with all their chariots awaiting the Israelite invasion. In this last and final battle of the conquest, Hazor was burned to the ground; 31 kings had been defeated without one horse or one chariot to aid the Israelites. All of the Promised Land was now under the control of the Israelites, although pockets of resistance would continue for centuries.

6.   **Summary of Israel's wars** [chapters 11:16 – 12:24]

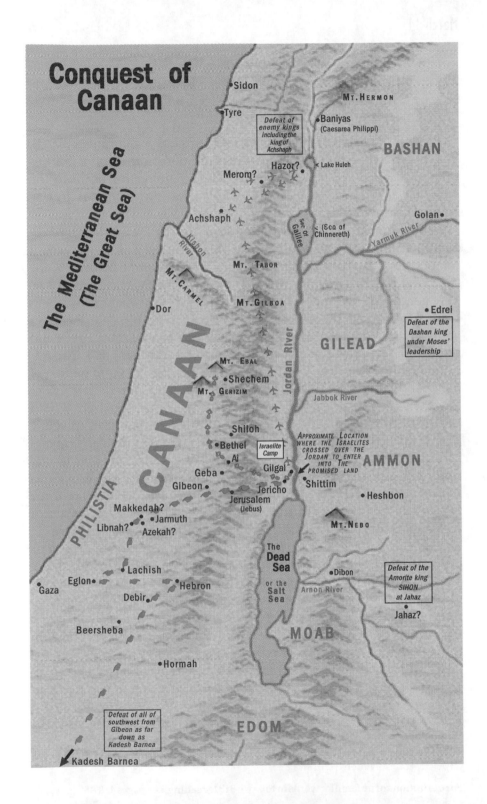

Conquest of Canaan

The Mediterranean Sea
(The Great Sea)

Sidon

Tyre

MT. HERMON

Baniyas
(Caesarea Philippi)

Defeat of
enemy kings
including the
king of
Achshaph

BASHAN

Hazor?

Lake Huleh

Merom?

Achshaph

Sea of
Galilee

(Sea of
Chinnereth)

Golan

Yarmuk River

Kishon
River

MT. CARMEL

MT. TABOR

Dor

MT. GILBOA

Edrei

Defeat of the
Bashan king
under Moses'
leadership

Jordan River

GILEAD

CANAAN

MT. EBAL

Shechem

MT. GERIZIM

Jabbok River

Shiloh

Bethel

Ai

Israelite
Camp

Geba

Gibeon

Gilgal

Jericho

Jerusalem
(Jebus)

APPROXIMATE LOCATION
WHERE THE ISRAELITES
CROSSED OVER THE
JORDAN TO ENTER
INTO THE
PROMISED LAND

Shittim

AMMON

Heshbon

PHILISTIA

Makkedah?

Libnah?

Jarmuth

Azekah?

MT. NEBO

The
Dead
Sea

or the
Salt
Sea

Gaza

Eglon

Lachish

Hebron

Debir

Dibon

Arnon River

Defeat of the
Amorite king
SIHON
at Jahaz

Beersheba

Jahaz?

Hormah

MOAB

Defeat of all of
southwest from
Gibeon as far
down as
Kadesh Barnea

EDOM

Kadesh Barnea

95

In Today's Reading
Memorial at Gilgal; circumcision; Passover at Gilgal;
manna ceases; Jericho besieged and destroyed

*G*od said: *I have given you the land to possess it* (Numbers 33:53); but, the promises of God always include personal responsibilities for the receivers of those promises. Before going further into the land, *the LORD said to Joshua . . . circumcise again the children of Israel* (Joshua 5:2-5).

The rite of circumcision had been instituted by the Lord with Abraham, the father of the faithful, as a visible sign of the people's Covenant relationship with Him (Genesis 17:9-14). It was required before anyone could eat the Passover (Exodus 12:48). After being circumcised, the new generation became identified as the Lord's Covenant people and were qualified to keep the Passover (Joshua 5:8,10). The Passover commemorated the Lord's deliverance of His people from Egypt and pointed the way to the messianic Deliverer (I Corinthians 5:7). Circumcision and the Passover foreshadowed the ordinances (commands) of believer's baptism and the Lord's Supper for the Church.

At His last Passover, our Lord Jesus revealed that His death would fulfill and replace the Passover. The Apostle Paul spoke of this new Covenant, saying: *That the Lord Jesus the same night in which He was betrayed took bread: And when He had given thanks, He broke it, and said, Take, eat: this is My body, which is broken for you: this do in remembrance of Me. After the same manner also He took the cup, when He had supped* (finished eating), *saying: This cup is the New Testament* (covenant) *in My blood: this do you, as often as you drink it, in remembrance of Me. For as often as you eat this bread, and drink this cup, you do show the Lord's death till He come* (I Corinthians 11:23-26).

The Christian's circumcision is also explained by Paul: *In Whom also you are circumcised with the circumcision made without hands, by putting off the body of the sins of the flesh by the circumcision of Christ: Buried with Him in baptism, wherein also you are risen with Him through the faith of the operation of God, who hath raised Him from the dead . . . being dead in your sins and the uncircumcision of your flesh, He has quickened* (made alive) *together with Him, having forgiven you all trespasses* (Colossians 2:11-13).

Thought for Today: The Holy Spirit through the Word of God enables us to rise above temptations.

Christ Revealed: As the *Captain of the host of the LORD* (Joshua 5:14). Christ is the Captain of our salvation (Hebrews 2:10).

For definitions of unfamiliar words in today's Bible reading, see pages 468-480.

In Today's Reading
Sin of Achan; Israel defeated by Ai; judgment of Achan;
Ai defeated; altar on Mount Ebal; Covenant renewed; Law read

The Lord held back the waters of the Jordan River at the time of year when the Jordan River overflowed its banks *and all the Israelites passed over on dry ground* into Canaan (Joshua 3:6-17). After the victory over Jericho, the Israelites were rejoicing. However, without seeking direction from God the Israelites attacked the city of Ai. *The men of Ai smote of them about thirty and six men: for they chased them from before the gate even to Shebarim, and smote them in the going down* (on the descent or slope) (7:5).

Nine times in the first six chapters of this book it is said that the Lord had directed Joshua (1:1; 3:7; 4:1,8,10,15; 5:2,15; 6:2). By not consulting the Lord, Israel's defeat was inevitable (7:2-5). Joshua had momentarily failed to consider that the Lord Himself was their Commander-in-Chief, that He alone could issue orders that would result in success (1:5). First, the evil sin by Achan had to be judged. Then, Joshua called on the Lord Who directed him in the complete victory over Ai.

The Israelites' reasoning that led to their defeat at Ai has been repeated by most of us. When no serious problems seem to exist, we become overconfident, seemingly self-sufficient, and assume the Lord expects us to use "our own good judgment." However, apart from our submission to the indwelling presence of the Holy Spirit, the smallest temptation will prove to be too powerful for us. He alone imparts discernment as we read and desire to obey the Word of God.

Many begin their Christian lives in prayer and daily Bible reading but eventually become self-confident and forget that *pride goes before destruction, and a haughty spirit before a fall* (Proverbs 16:18). The truth here is we don't win our victories because we are Christians any more than Joshua won the battle at Ai because he was an Israelite.

The Word of God is quick (living), *and powerful, and sharper than any twoedged sword, piercing even to the dividing asunder* (in two) *of soul and spirit, and of the joints and marrow, and is a discerner* (judge, critic) *of the thoughts and intents of the heart* (Hebrews 4:12).

Thought for Today: Any of our accomplishments that are worthwhile are the result of God working through us.

Christ Revealed: Through the uncut stones of the altar (Joshua 8:31). Daniel saw Christ as a Stone which was not cut by human hands (Daniel 2:34,45). Jesus is our *Chief Corner Stone* (I Peter 2:6-8).

For definitions of unfamiliar words in today's Bible reading, see pages 468-480.

In Today's Reading
Israel's treaty with Gibeon; Gibeon attacked; God intervenes,
causing the sun and moon to stand still; Amorite kings defeated

*A*fter Joshua's victories over Jericho and Ai, five kings united to fight the Israelites. However, the Gibeonites, located between the land of the Canaanite kings and the encampment of Israel (Joshua 9:17), decided their chances of survival would be greater by making a league with the Israelites than by joining with the Canaanite kings in their war with Israel. They told Joshua: *From a very far country your servants are come because of the Name* (reputation) *of the LORD your God: for we have heard the fame of Him, and all that He did in Egypt. . . . Wherefore our elders and all the inhabitants of our country spoke to us, saying, Take victuals* (provisions, food) *with you for the journey, and go to meet them, and say to them, We are your servants: therefore now make you a league* (treaty) *with us. . . . And the men took of their victuals, and asked not counsel at the mouth of the LORD. And Joshua made peace with them, and made a league with them, to let them live* (9:9-11,14-15) – a violation of the Law (see Exodus 23:32-33; 34:12). This points out that ignorance of God's Word does not nullify its results.

This league with the Gibeonites should impress upon us the enemy's skill in deception. We should also learn how fallible our human reasoning is. If Joshua had prayed for the Lord's guidance, the league never would have been agreed to.

The Israelites did not break their oath, even though the Gibeonites deceived them. However, over 400 years later, King Saul broke this covenant and it resulted in a 3-year famine in Israel (II Samuel 21:1). Through this, the Lord teaches us that the wrong done by another does not give us the right to do a similar wrong. One sin never justifies another. The characteristic of the children of God that distinguishes us from all other people is that we *overcome evil with good* (Romans 12:21). God wants us to learn from the Gibeonites' covenant how important it is to have personal integrity and keep our commitments.

The moldy bread and worn clothing seemed to be visible proof of the strangers' words (Joshua 9:12-13). Too often we are foolish in making decisions based on what we see or think. *Trust in the LORD with all your heart; and lean not to your own understanding. In all your ways acknowledge Him, and He shall direct your paths* (Proverbs 3:5-6).

Thought for Today: Faith dispels fear of the future (I John 4:18-19).

Christ Revealed: As the One through Whom we have victory (Joshua 10:25). *Thanks be to God, Who gives us the victory through our Lord Jesus Christ* (I Corinthians 15:57).

For definitions of unfamiliar words in today's Bible reading, see pages 468-480.

In Today's Reading

Conquest of the northern kings; Joshua's obedience; conquered
kings; 2-1/2 tribes settle on the east side of the Jordan River

Everyone in Jericho knew the reputation of Israel's God as did
Rahab who confessed: *As soon as we had heard these things, our hearts
did melt, neither did there remain any more courage in any man,
because of you; for the LORD your God, He is God in heaven above, and
in earth beneath* (Joshua 2:11). Rahab alone put her faith in the God of
the Hebrews and was not only saved but was included in the
genealogy of Jesus (Matthew 1:5; Hebrews 11:31; James 2:25). The
Canaanite kings had known what the Gibeonites knew but they
decided to defend their heathen gods against the true God.

News of Joshua's invasion quickly spread throughout Canaan.
Jabin, King of Hazor in the north, enlisted the kings and their soldiers
from far into the northern mountains (Joshua 11:1-2,8).

Joshua's comparatively small army received a report that they were
facing *many people, even as the sand that is upon the sea shore in
multitude, with horses and chariots very many. And when all these kings
were met together. . . . the LORD said to Joshua, Be not afraid because of
them: for tomorrow about this time will I deliver them up all slain before
Israel. . . . So Joshua came, and all the people of war with him, against
them by the waters of Merom suddenly. . . . they smote them, until they
left them none remaining* (11:4-8).

*So Joshua took the whole land, according to all that the LORD said
to Moses. . . . And the land rested from war* (11:23). Thirty-one kings
(12:24) had been defeated. Joshua established military control over all of
the promised land. However, the individual tribes were to complete the
destruction of the Canaanites (Exodus 23:29-30; Deuteronomy 7:22).

The judgment of the Canaanites foreshadows the final judgment of
all who continue in their sins. *And to you who are troubled rest with
us, when the Lord Jesus shall be revealed from heaven with His mighty
angels, In flaming fire taking vengeance on them that know not God,
and that obey not the Gospel of our Lord Jesus Christ: Who shall be
punished with everlasting destruction from the presence of the Lord, and
from the glory of His power* (II Thessalonians 1:7-9).

Thought for Today: Obedience to God's Word is the key to victory.

Christ Portrayed: By *Moses the servant of the LORD* (Joshua 12:6). Jesus was the Servant
of God. *Behold My Servant, Whom I have chosen* (Matthew 12:18).

For definitions of unfamiliar words in today's Bible reading, see pages 468-480.

IN TODAY'S READING
Canaan divided among the tribes; territories given to
Judah, Caleb, Ephraim, and Manasseh

The Anakim (giants) had been driven out of Hebron by Joshua, perhaps five years before this time (Joshua 10:2-11; 11:21-22). Now they were back and in control of the territory – undoubtedly, with a much greater determination to retain the land promised to Caleb.

At Caleb's "retirement" age of 85, he recounted to Joshua how God had brought him that far: *Forty years old was I when Moses the servant of the LORD sent me from Kadesh-barnea to espy* (spy) *out the land; and I brought him word again as it was in my heart. Nevertheless my brethren that went up with me made the heart of the people melt: but I wholly* (wholeheartedly) *followed the LORD my God* (14:7-8). Caleb's unshakable faith can be seen in his report as a spy: *I brought him word again as it was in my heart.* He spoke his convictions as he faced the opposition of the other spies and the people. He stood alone with Joshua. We are sometimes afraid to speak about our faith when our convictions are unpopular; but the person blessed of God speaks what is in his heart on spiritual issues.

Caleb boldly said: *I wholly followed the LORD my God.* His decision was unaffected by what others said or did. The loyal few who have their hearts fixed on the Lord and trust in His Word are not afraid to speak out or move forward to accomplish the Lord's will regardless of what others say or do.

Caleb's courageous spirit reminds us that *they that wait upon the LORD shall renew their strength; they shall mount up with wings as eagles; they shall run, and not be weary; and they shall walk, and not faint* (Isaiah 40:31). The truly blessed are faithful to God.

Yes, most of us will face giant "Canaanite" difficulties in life as well as friends who attempt to discourage us. Surely our faith ought to exceed Caleb's, inasmuch as *It is Christ . . . at the right hand of God, Who also makes intercession for us. Who shall separate us from the love of Christ? shall tribulation, or distress, or persecution, or famine, or nakedness, or peril, or sword* (war)? *. . . in all these things we are more than conquerors through Him that loved us* (Romans 8:34-35,37).

Thought for Today: God honors faith that is established in His Word.

Christ Portrayed: By Caleb, who *followed the LORD* (Joshua 14:8,14). Our Savior said: *Lo, I come . . . to do Your will, O God* (Hebrews 10:7).

For definitions of unfamiliar words in today's Bible reading, see pages 468-480.

In Today's Reading

Distribution of land to all the tribes; Manasseh fails to drive out
Canaanites; Tabernacle set up at Shiloh; Joshua's inheritance

The conquest of Canaan was completed and the land was divided,
not by majority vote, but by the Lord. When *the whole congregation
of the children of Israel assembled together at Shiloh, and set up the
Tabernacle of the congregation. . . . the land was subdued before them.
. . . Joshua cast lots for them in Shiloh before the LORD: and there Joshua
divided the land to the children of Israel* (Joshua 18:1,10).

Although they had received some of the best territory in the promised land, the tribes of Manasseh and Ephraim complained that they
should have more territory given to them because of their great numbers and what they perceived as their prominent position among the
tribes (17:14-18). The Ephraimites were proud of their history as descendants of Joseph and that Joshua, the victorious commander who
had led in the conquest of Canaan, was also from their tribe.

Sadly, these two tribes chose the easy way of compromise with the
Canaanites. The blessings of God often depend upon faith and *faith
without works is dead* (James 2:20). It is sometimes wise to refuse to help
those who will not help themselves.

When we have our priorities centered upon the Lord, we need not
fear losing our share of anything. In fact, we gladly accept less to maintain peace with others. True children of God do not expect others to
serve or praise them.

In a striking contrast to the tribes of Manasseh and Ephraim,
Joshua chose to be the last to lay claim to any territory (Joshua 19:49).
As captain, we could expect him to be first and to take the best for
himself. Instead, he chose last. His choice was a very small area near
Shiloh where the Tabernacle was erected and where he could best
worship and serve the Lord. It was there, in the nearness of the Lord's
presence, that Joshua built his small city. Joshua illustrates the
importance of being *fervent in spirit; serving the Lord. . . . Submit
yourselves therefore to God. Resist the devil, and he will flee from you.
. . . Humble yourselves in the sight of the Lord, and He shall lift you up*
(Romans 12:11; James 4:7,10).

Thought for Today: Meekness is not weakness.

Christ Revealed: Through Shiloh. *The children of Israel assembled together at
Shiloh, and set up the Tabernacle* (Joshua 18:1). Shiloh was the dwelling place of God's
presence which was prophetic of Jesus. *The Word* (Jesus) *. . . dwelt* (tabernacled) *among
us* (John 1:14).

For definitions of unfamiliar words in today's Bible reading, see pages 468-480.

In Today's Reading

Six cities of refuge appointed; 48 cities given to the Levites;
the Israelites possess the land

*U*nlike all the other tribes of Israel, Levi was not given separate
territory (Joshua 14:3). *To the tribe of Levi Moses gave not any inheritance:
the LORD God of Israel was their inheritance, as He said to them* (13:33).
*But the Levites have no part among you; for the priesthood of the LORD
is their inheritance* (18:7).

The Levites were divided into three groups according to the
descendants of Levi's three sons, Gershon, Kohath, and Merari. But
only those Israelites who were descendants of Levi through Kohath's
grandson Aaron could be priests and serve in the Tabernacle. However, even some of these descendants were physically disqualified to be
ministers at the altar because of disabilities and defects; and some were
spiritually disqualified because they violated one or more of the
Commandments (Leviticus 21:1-23). The priests were responsible for
preserving, transcribing, teaching, and interpreting the Law. They
were also the civil officers responsible for the administration of the
Law (Deuteronomy 17:9-12; 31:9,11-12,26). All the Levites, not merely
the ones who were responsible for the worship at the Tabernacle, were
to receive an equal share of the tithes from the other tribes. Each tribe
was to provide for the physical welfare of the priests within its own
territory. This was not left up to the goodwill of the people, but was
a command from God.

God devoted 42 of the 45 verses in Joshua 21 to emphasizing the Israelites' obligation to support the ministers of His Word. No one is too
poor or exempt from giving his tithe which is a tenth of his income and,
thus, proportionately equal for all. When Israel was faithful in this, God
mightily blessed them. When they failed, they suffered.

The Apostle Paul illustrated this saying: *For it is written . . . You
shall not muzzle the mouth of the ox that treads out the corn. Does God
take care for oxen? Or says He it altogether for our sakes? For our sakes,
no doubt, this is written. . . . If we have sown to you spiritual things, is
it a great thing if we shall reap your carnal* (material) *things?. . . the
Lord ordained that they which preach the Gospel should live of the
Gospel* (I Corinthians 9:9-11,14).

Thought for Today: Nothing is too hard for God! (Philippians 4:13).

Christ Portrayed: By Eleazar, the chief priest (Joshua 21:1; 3:32). Christ is our High Priest.
The . . . High Priest of our profession (confession), *Christ Jesus* (Hebrews 3:1).

For definitions of unfamiliar words in today's Bible reading, see pages 468-480.

When God told Joshua: *Every place that the sole of your foot shall
tread upon, that have I given to you, as I said to Moses* (Joshua 1:3),
Joshua did not merely "trust the Lord" that He would force the
Canaanites to voluntarily give up their land. The fact is, the Israelites
received their inheritance by faith; but they were to fight for every foot
of land that God had promised them.

After about seven years, the Israelites under the leadership of
Joshua had conquered Canaan. *And the LORD gave them rest round
about, according to all that He swore to their fathers: and there stood
not a man of all their enemies before them; the LORD delivered all their
enemies into their hand* (21:44).

The Israelites' greatest danger was yet to be faced. *Joshua said to the
people. . . . If you forsake the LORD, and serve strange* (foreign) *gods, then
He will . . . do you hurt* (bring disaster) *and consume* (destroy) *you,
after that He has done you good. . . . Now therefore put away . . . the
strange gods which are among you, and incline* (yield) *your heart to the
LORD God of Israel* (24:19-20,23). "Jesus" (the same as "Joshua" in
Hebrew) freed us from sin by His substitutionary death on the cross
and His triumphant physical resurrection.

We too need to be reminded daily to *incline our heart to the LORD*.
What a tragedy that so many people assume once a person has accepted
Jesus Christ as Savior, he has nothing to do but "just leave everything
up to the Lord." The truth is, the Lord has left it up to us. *Wherefore
take to **you** the whole armor of God, that **you** may be able to withstand
in the evil day, and having done all, to stand. Stand therefore, having
your loins girt* (belted) *about with truth, and having on the breastplate
of righteousness; And **your** feet shod with the preparation of the Gospel
of peace; Above all, taking the shield of faith, wherewith **you** shall be
able to quench* (put out, extinguish) *all the fiery darts* (arrows, shots)
*of the wicked. And take the helmet of salvation, and the sword of the
Spirit, which is the Word of God* (Ephesians 6:13-17).

Thought for Today: Every day serve only the Lord.

Christ Revealed: Through the peace offering (Joshua 22:27). Our Lord offered Himself to
God as our means of peace with the Father. *Being justified by faith, we have peace with
God through our Lord Jesus Christ* (Romans 5:1).

For definitions of unfamiliar words in today's Bible reading, see pages 468-480.

INTRODUCTION TO THE BOOK OF
*J*UDGES

The Book of Judges covers about 450 years of Israel's history in the promised land. It relates fragments of what took place from the death of Joshua to the beginning of Samuel's ministry.

The key to the conquest of Canaan is clear: *And the people served the LORD all of the days of Joshua, and all the days of the elders that outlived Joshua, who had seen all the great works of the LORD, that He did for Israel* (Judges 2:7). After Joshua's death there was no God-appointed national leader so each tribe acted independently (1:1 – 2:23).

Most of the Israelite tribes disregarded the Lord's command to drive out all the Canaanites who remained in their territories. Instead, they compromised by gradually enslaving them. This compromise eventually led to intermarriage with the Canaanites and, ultimately, to Israel's worship of their false gods.

The reason for this failure is obvious: *Also all that generation were gathered to their fathers* (died): *and there arose another generation after them, which knew not the LORD, nor yet the works which He had done for Israel. . . . And they forsook the LORD, and served Baal* (the chief god of the Canaanites) *and Ashtaroth* (2:10,13). Without a central leader or government, a time of spiritual failure and confusion prevailed.

Because of their sins, surrounding nations and tribes, including the Philistines, Moabites, and Midianites were used of God to defeat them and cause them to realize why they had lost their freedom.

Seven major apostasies are recorded when *the children of Israel did evil in the sight of the LORD, and served Baalim* (false gods) (2:11; 3:7,12; 4:1; 6:1; 10:6; 13:1). In each case, the Israelites were overcome by their enemies, lost their freedom, and were greatly impoverished; but, when the people prayed, God once again delivered them from their oppressors. These judges acted under the authority of God, Who was Israel's invisible King. As each successive judge was in submission to the Lord, a period of peace and prosperity would follow.

Chapters 17 – 21 contain insight into the Israelites' moral and spiritual degradation that prevailed preceding the time when Samuel became a prophet of God and their judge. The Book of Judges illustrates that we can never enjoy freedom, peace of mind, and the blessings of God for long if we are only partially **obedient** to His Word. When we become involved in questionable acts or relationships which may seem harmless, just like the Israelites we will soon find ourselves overcome by the desires of fleshly interests.

In Today's Reading
Judah chosen to lead wars; Israel fails to drive Canaanites out;
Angel of the Lord's rebuke; Joshua's death

The Israelites were chosen by the One True God to reveal Him to the heathen nations and to glorify Him by being obedient to His Word. The first few verses of Judges give us a sense of high hope for the total conquest of the land as begun by Joshua: *Judah went with Simeon his brother, and they slew the Canaanites that inhabited Zephath, and utterly destroyed it* (Judges 1:17). One by one, Canaanite cities fell to the Israelites – then the Philistine cities (1:10-11,13,17-18). *And the people served the LORD all the days of Joshua, and all the days of the elders that outlived Joshua, who had seen all the great works of the LORD, that He did for Israel* (2:7).

The Israelites who were living at the time of Joshua's death recognized that God was their Captain and King and that He had given them victory over the Canaanites. But a new era in the history of the 12 tribes began soon after the death of Joshua.

The Lord's command to complete the conquest of Canaan was not fulfilled because of the people's compromise with the pagan inhabitants of the land. It is disappointing to read: *There arose another generation after them, which knew not the LORD, nor yet the works which He had done for Israel. And the children of Israel did evil in the sight of the LORD, and served Baalim. And they forsook the LORD. . . . And the anger of the LORD was hot against Israel; and He said, Because . . . this people has transgressed My Covenant . . . I also will not hereafter drive out any from before them of the nations which Joshua left when he died: That through them I may prove* (test) *Israel, whether they will keep the way of the LORD* (2:10-22).

The Israelites chose to do what they thought was more "humanitarian" and created peaceful coexistence with the enemies of God. Perhaps they argued: "How could a God of love destroy 'innocent' people?" This, of course, is human reasoning. The concept of innocence disappears when we see sin for what it really is and that false gods are robbing God of love and worship, and are deceiving people so that they will be eternally lost. *And whosoever was not found written in the Book of Life was cast into the lake of fire* (Revelation 20:15).

Thought for Today: Considering our guilt God's mercy is amazing.

Christ Revealed: By *the Angel of the LORD* (Judges 2:1,4). The *Angel of the LORD* is understood to be the Lord Jesus Himself preincarnate, for He speaks as God Himself (*I made you . . . I swore . . . I said . . . I will*). Jesus said to them, Verily, verily, I say to you, Before Abraham was, I am (John 8:58).

For definitions of unfamiliar words in today's Bible reading, see pages 468-480.

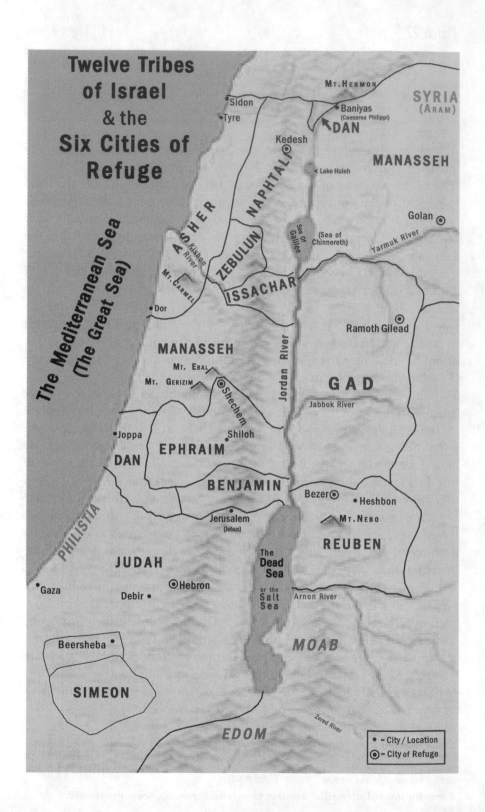

Twelve Tribes
of Israel
& the
Six Cities of
Refuge

MT. HERMON

SYRIA
(ARAM)

Sidon

Tyre

Baniyas
(Caesarea Philippi)

DAN

Kedesh

MANASSEH

Lake Huleh

Golan

ASHER

Kishon River

ZEBULUN

NAPHTALI

Sea Of Galilee

(Sea of Chinnereth)

Yarmuk River

MT. CARMEL

ISSACHAR

Dor

The Mediterranean Sea
(The Great Sea)

MANASSEH

MT. EBAL

MT. GERIZIM

Shechem

Ramoth Gilead

GAD

Jordan River

Jabbok River

Joppa

EPHRAIM

Shiloh

DAN

BENJAMIN

Bezer

Heshbon

Jerusalem
(Jebus)

MT. NEBO

REUBEN

PHILISTIA

JUDAH

The
Dead
Sea

or the
Salt
Sea

Gaza

Hebron

Debir

Arnon River

Beersheba

MOAB

SIMEON

Zered River

EDOM

• = City / Location

◉ = City of Refuge

106

Judges of the Israelites (Judges – I Samuel 7)

Judge	From the Tribe of	Text	Oppressor	Oppressed Years	Peace Years
Othniel	Judah	Judges 3:7-11	Mesopotamians	8	40
Ehud	Benjamin	Judges 3:12-30	Moabites, Ammonites, Amalekites	18	80
Shamgar	Naphtali	Judges 3:31; 5:6	Philistines		
Deborah/Barak	Ephraim	Judges 4:1 – 5:31	Canaanites	20	40
Gideon	Manasseh	Judges 6:1 – 8:32	Midianites, Amalekites	7	40
Abimelech (A Usurper)	Ephraim	Judges 8:30 – 9:57	No Peace, Only chaos		
Tola	Issachar	Judges 10:1-2			23
Jair	Manasseh	Judges 10:3-5			22
Jephthah	Manasseh (East of Jordan River)	Judges 10:6 – 12:7	Ammonites, Philistines	18	6
Ibzan	Judah	Judges 12:8-10			7
Elon	Zebulun	Judges 12:11-12			10
Abdon	Ephraim	Judges 12:13-15			8
Samson	Dan	Judges 13:24-16:31	Philistines	40	20
Eli	Ephraim	I Samuel 4:18	Philistines	40	
Samuel	Ephraim	I Samuel 1:20-7:17	Philistines		About 40

The Six Cities of Refuge (See Map on opposite page)

KEDESH – located about 15 miles north of the Sea of Galilee in the mountains bordering the west side of the Huleh Valley in the territory of Naphtali

SHECHEM - located in the valley between Mount Ebal and Mount Gerizim in the mountains of Ephraim

HEBRON (KIRIATH-ARBA) – located in Judah about 20 miles south of Jerusalem

BEZER – located east of the Jordan River in the tribe of Reuben

RAMOTH GILEAD – located about 50 miles north of Bezer in the highlands of Gilead in the tribe of Gad

GOLAN – located in the highlands of the tribe of Manasseh, east of the Jordan River

Since the Law required a near relative of the one killed to become an avenger of blood (Deuteronomy 19:6,12), the cities of refuge provided a sanctuary for those who had killed by accident. Under the law, the slayers had to remain in the city until after the death of the high priest (Numbers 35:25).

The law did not provide for any sacrifice for the manslayer. The guilt of the man who killed accidentally was removed only by the death of the high priest. He could not pay a fine or be set free any sooner.

There is a sharp distinction between an accidental death and a willful murder. God demands that a murderer be put to death. The Levites and the elders in each city were designated to investigate to determine if a death was accidental or a willful murder.

*J*N *T*ODAY'S *R*EADING
Israel intermarries with Canaanites, worships false gods, is defeated;
the Lord raises up judges to deliver Israel; Deborah and Barak

*A*lthough Joshua had executed all the Canaanite kings, the Canaanite people occupied the promised land. *They were to prove (test) Israel by them, to know whether they would hearken to the Commandments of the LORD, which he commanded their fathers* (Judges 3:4).

The first major step in the downfall of the Israelites was their disregard for *the Commandments of the LORD.* The next step was that they became friendly neighbors and *dwelled among the Canaanites* (3:5). The third step in their decline soon followed: *They took their daughters to be their wives, and gave their daughters to their sons, and served their gods* (3:6). The fourth step was inevitable because the Israelites' heathen wives who worshiped idols could not teach their children to worship the One True God. Sadly, the final step: *The children of Israel did evil in the sight of the LORD . . . and served Baalim and the groves* (idol worship) (3:7). The outcome was certain; sin separates the sinner from the protective love of God and they were soon under the control of an enemy nation after years of suffering. *The children of Israel cried to the LORD, the LORD raised up a deliverer to the children of Israel, who delivered them* (3:9,15).

We learn from Israel's history that, regardless of how far we have backslidden and sinned, our merciful God in heaven always hears the prayers of those who confess their sins and commit their lives to Him. Often we are so taken up with condemning ourselves and others when we fall short of being what our heart tells us is right that we forget that God does love us *as a Father pities his children* (Psalm 103:13). So don't give up. We need to recognize that God loves to forgive even *seventy times seven* (Matthew 18:22). But, the sad fact is that wasted years of opportunity cannot be relived.

Who is he that condemns? It is Christ that died, yea rather, that is risen again, Who is even at the right hand of God, Who also makes intercession for us (Romans 8:34).

Thought for Today: Wealth and pleasures can be deceptive snares to keep the believer from accomplishing God's eternal purposes.

Christ Portrayed: By Othniel, a deliverer upon whom the Spirit of the Lord rested (Judges 3:9-11). The Spirit of God was also upon Christ, our Deliverer (Matthew 3:16). *There shall come out of Sion the Deliverer, and shall turn away ungodliness from Jacob* (Romans 11:26). Jesus declared: *The Spirit of the Lord is upon Me, because He has anointed Me . . . to preach deliverance to the captives* (Luke 4:18).

For definitions of unfamiliar words in today's Bible reading, see pages 468-480.

In Today's Reading

Israel forsakes God; Midianites oppress Israel for seven years;
Israel prays; God sends a prophet; Gideon destroys altar of Baal

*O*nce more the Israelites were enslaved, this time by the Midianites. *And the children of Israel did evil* (sinned) *in the sight of the LORD: And the LORD delivered them into the hand* (under the control) *of Midian seven years. . . . Israel was greatly impoverished . . . and the children of Israel cried to the LORD* (Judges 6:1,6). The answer to their prayers began with reproof: *The LORD sent a prophet . . . which said to them, Thus says the LORD God of Israel: I brought you up from Egypt . . . out of the hand of all that oppressed you . . . and gave you their land . . . but you have not obeyed My voice* (6:8-10). There was no word of comfort, only reproof. The people were left with the consciousness of their sins and with no hope of relief. They needed to recognize that their miserable suffering was the direct result of their disregarding the Word of God.

It would appear that this unnamed prophet may have had only one convert – Gideon: *And the Angel of the LORD appeared to him, and said . . . The LORD is with you, you mighty man of valor. . . . Go in this your might, and you shall save Israel from the hand of the Midianites* (6:12,14).

Gideon was deeply conscious of his poverty and in his own ability, and confessed: *Oh my Lord, wherewith shall I save Israel? behold, my family is poor in Manasseh, and I am the least in my father's house* (6:15). We tend to think that the only people God can use are those who have influence in their communities. But, often these people are too busy, want to do it their way, or would rather compromise than lose their popularity. Gideon was truly a man of inexperience and uncertainty, but he unconditionally obeyed the Lord without fear of the opposition. Gideon was ready to worship the God of Israel and *built an altar there to the LORD, and called it Jehovah (Yahweh)-Shalom* (the LORD is peace) (6:24). We too must get our eyes off circumstances and fix our faith on the Word of God. *Hearken* (listen), *my beloved brethren, Has not God chosen the poor of this world rich in faith, and heirs of the kingdom which He has promised to them that love Him?* (James 2:5).

Thought for Today: Faith in God, not our wisdom, brings success.

Christ Portrayed: As *the Sword of the LORD* (Judges 7:20). In the Apostle John's revelation of Jesus, *out of His mouth went a sharp two-edged sword* (Revelation 1:16). We know that the sword is *the Word of God* (Ephesians 6:17) and that Jesus is the Word of God *made* (became) *flesh* (John 1:14).

For definitions of unfamiliar words in today's Bible reading, see pages 468-480.

In *Today's* *Reading*
Gideon makes an ephod; his death; Gideon's son Abimelech
murders 70 of his brothers; Abimelech's accident and death

Gideon was called of God to deliver the Israelites from the Midianites. Thirty-two thousand men responded to Gideon's call to war; but God chose to use just 300 men to defeat the Midianites. The other Israelites were sent home; and, with only 300 men, God defeated 135,000 Midianite soldiers in battle. *And the country was in quietness forty years in the days of Gideon* (Judges 8:28). This illustrates a wonderful principle. God would not act without man's cooperation, and man could not overcome without the wisdom and power of God.

The Israelites urged Gideon to be their king. It was an appeal to his pride. But Gideon knew that it was not he who had saved his people, but God who was the true King. *And Gideon said to them, I will not rule over you . . . the LORD shall rule over you* (8:23). Gideon knew that, as a judge of Israel, he would need God to guide him.

The Israelites soon forgot that God was the One who had miraculously delivered them from the Midianites.

After Gideon's death, with an appetite for power, his cruel and crafty son Abimelech negotiated a large sum of money from the Baal temple treasury to pay men to murder his 70 brothers. *Jotham the youngest son of Jerubbaal was left; for he hid himself* (9:5). Following the execution of his competition, *all the men of Shechem . . . made Abimelech king* (9:6). However, at the moment of Abimelech's proudest achievements, Jotham, the son of Gideon who had escaped execution, warned that they would soon discover that this self-made king would bring suffering and death upon them as well as himself (9:7-21). As Jotham had foretold, they soon brought about their own destruction (9:22-57).

Abimelech is an example of a person controlled by the deceptive and destructive forces of pride and ambition. He was determined to gain selfish ends regardless of whom he hurt. He is a reminder: *Be not deceived; God is not mocked: for whatsoever a man sows, that shall he also reap. For he that sows to his flesh shall of the flesh reap corruption* (destruction); *but he that sows to the Spirit shall of the Spirit reap life everlasting* (Galatians 6:7-8).

Thought for Today: Surrender to God ensures victory.

Christ Portrayed: By Gideon, who delivered the Israelites from Midian (Judges 8:22-23). The Lord Jesus has delivered us out of the hands of our spiritual enemies, and it is fitting that He should rule over us. *Our Lord Jesus Christ, Who gave Himself for our sins, that He might deliver us from this present evil world* (Galatians 1:3-4; II Peter 2:9; Romans 11:26).

For definitions of unfamiliar words in today's Bible reading, see pages 468-480.

In Today's Reading

Israel forsakes the Lord and worships idols; Israel oppressed by
Ammonites for 18 years; Jephthah's daughter dedicated to God

*A*fter much suffering because they worshiped false gods (Judges
10:8), *the children of Israel said to the LORD, We have sinned. . . . And
they put away the strange* (foreign) *gods from among them, and served
the LORD* (10:15-16). *And it was so, that when the children of Ammon
made war against Israel, the elders of Gilead. . . . said to Jephthah,
Come, and be our captain, that we may fight with the children of
Ammon* (11:5-6).

Jephthah prayed: *If You shall without fail deliver the children of
Ammon into my hands, Then it shall be, that whatsoever comes forth
of the doors of my house to meet me . . . shall surely be the LORD's,
and I will offer it up for a burned offering* (11:30-31). God arranged
that Jephthah's daughter should be the first to meet him. Jephthah
knew the Scriptures well and human sacrifices were condemned by
God (Leviticus 20:2-5; Deuteronomy 12:29-31; 18:10-12). How could
one imagine that this man of God would cut the throat of his
daughter to offer her as a burned offering? To do that would have
made God, as well as this man of faith, responsible for a vile murder,
since it was *the Spirit of the LORD* Who gave Jephthah his victory
(Judges 11:29,32).

How he fulfilled his vow becomes clear as we consider all the facts.
She was his only child; beside her he had neither son nor daughter
(11:34). The Lord had declared that the firstborn were to be "sanctified"
– not sacrificed: *It is Mine* (Exodus 13:2; Numbers 3:13). And his
daughter's response to Jephthah's vow made the outcome unmistak-
ably clear. She asked for *two months* to go up and down *the mountains*
to *bewail* (lament) *my virginity* (Judges 11:37) – meaning to "bewail
that I will never marry." Undoubtedly, in lifelong chastity, she became
one of the servants of God in the Tabernacle.

Jephthah was highly honored as one of the heroes of faith: *Who
through faith subdued kingdoms, wrought righteousness, obtained
promises* (Hebrews 11:32-33).

Thought for Today: Trust and obey ... for there's no other way.

Christ Portrayed: By Jephthah's only child as she wholly submitted to her father's will even
as Jesus wholly submitted to His Father's will (Judges 11:34-40). On the night He was
betrayed, Jesus prayed: *Not as I will, but as You will* (Matthew 26:39).

For definitions of unfamiliar words in today's Bible reading, see pages 468-480.

*I*N *T*ODAY'S *R*EADING
Jephthah's victory over the Ephraimites; Israel under Philistine
control; Samson's Philistine wife in Timnath

*I*n the area of Dan and Ephraim, the Israelites were oppressed by the
Philistines for 40 years. During that time, Samson was born. Unlike
Jephthah, Samson had a godly mother and father who desired to train
him to do what the Angel of the Lord had instructed. Samson's mother
was deeply concerned that her son be fully dedicated to the Lord
(Judges 13:3-21).

From time to time, the Spirit of God came upon Samson and *began
to move* (stir) *him* (Judges 13:25). Eventually, Samson ruled as a judge.
However, early in his life, we see his disregard for his holy calling. His
first recorded act of unfaithfulness was friendship with the enemies of
God. It seemed that Samson was easily distracted with his own
physical desires and satisfactions, as in Timnath, when he fell in love
with a Philistine woman. He ignored Israel's Covenant relationship
with the Lord *and told his father and his mother . . . get her for me as
a wife. . . . at that time the Philistines had dominion over Israel* (14:1-4).

Samson's life typified the spiritual condition of Israel during that
period of the Judges and revealed how a self-willed life results in sorrow
and suffering for self as well as others.

All of us are tempted to please ourselves. Self-pleasing comes in
many forms: pride, jealousy, theft, refusing to tithe, sexual sins, hate,
avoidance of responsibility, using drugs or alcohol, and a host of other
things. Every day that we continue in willful sin, Satan's hold becomes
stronger, and our chances of deliverance become less likely. Perhaps
the greatest deceptive sin is that of presuming the mercy and long-
suffering of God will continue indefinitely.

As a Nazarite, Samson was meant to be an example before all Israel
of loyal commitment to God. We too are called upon to be separated
from the world with a desire to fulfill the Lord's will. *The night is far
spent* (almost gone), *the day is at hand: let us therefore cast off the works
of darkness, and let us put on the armor of light* (Romans 13:12).

Thought for Today: A person's conscience can only be a safe guide when it is guided by God's
Word.

Christ Portrayed: By Samson, who, as a Nazarite, was to be separated or consecrated *to
God from the womb* (birth) *to the day of his death* (Judges 13:7). Jesus was also set
apart and consecrated to God from the womb to the day of His death on the cross. Unlike
Samson, who failed God, Jesus totally fulfilled God's plan as He said He would do when He
left heaven saying: *Lo, I come . . . to do Your will, O God* (Hebrews 10:7).

For definitions of unfamiliar words in today's Bible reading, see pages 468-480.

In Today's Reading

Samson loses his wife; 1,000 Philistines slain; Delilah;
Samson defeated, blinded, dies with the Philistines; Micah's idols

---

The early life of Samson is recorded in chapters 13, 14, and 15 of the Book of Judges. Then it appears that many years passed for which we have no record until we read the tragic events in chapter 16.

There is no record that Samson ever expressed a desire to be used by the Lord to deliver the Israelites from the Philistine's oppression. So it is not a surprise that he neither prayed for guidance nor protection. He also chose the enemies of God for his friends.

Early in life, Samson disregarded the spiritual significance of his Nazarite dedication by marrying a Philistine woman. He became deeply involved in sin as he made friends with Delilah, another Philistine woman. When Samson saw Delilah, he should have thought of his sacred Nazarite vow and his high calling as a judge. But sin had blinded him to his high calling and to the reason he was gifted with great strength. And, as always, with each person who presumptuously believes that God's mercy and long-suffering will continue indefinitely, we see Samson yield to Delilah's treachery. *And she said, the Philistines be upon you, Samson. And he awoke out of his sleep, and said, I will go out as at other times before, and shake myself. And he knew not that the LORD was departed from him* (Judges 16:20).

Consequently, *the Philistines took him, and put out his eyes, and brought him down to Gaza, and bound him with fetters* (chains) *of brass; and he did grind in the prison house* (16:21). Not only did he suffer the gruesome torture of having his eyes gouged out, but he was forced to take the place of an animal and spend his time turning the mill to grind corn into meal.

The story of Samson should send a strong message to every Christian who has fallen into the treacherous web of sinful pleasures. Samson is not the only servant of God who ever lost his power through worldliness and self-indulgence (16:19).

In contrast, *By faith Moses* delivered his people from bondage *rather to suffer affliction with the people of God, than to enjoy the pleasures of sin for a season* (Hebrews 11:24-25).

Thought for Today: Oh, the high cost of lust and its treachery.

Christ Revealed: Through the strength God gave to Samson for his last victory over the Philistines (Judges 16:28-30). *I can do all things through Christ Who strengthens me* (Philippians 4:13).

For definitions of unfamiliar words in today's Bible reading, see pages 468-480.

ℐN ℐODAY'S ℛEADING
Danites force Micah's Levite to be their priest, attack Laish, then occupy it; a concubine is victimized

ℐsrael continued to ignore God's Word. Consequently, we read: *In those days there was no king in Israel, but every man did that which was right in his own eyes* (Judges 17:6; 21:25; compare 18:1; 19:1). This means doing whatever seemed most gratifying.

To illustrate the deplorable moral condition that existed at that time, a Levite, representing spiritual leadership, and his concubine are introduced. We are disappointed to read of the violation of the Law by his relationship with his concubine (Leviticus 21:7) who *played the whore against him, and went away from him to her father's house to Bethlehem-judah* (Judges 19:2). But, after *four months*, the Levite decided that he wanted her back, so he went to her father's house. *When the father of the damsel* (young woman) *saw him, he rejoiced to meet him* (19:2-3).

When the Levite decided to return home several days later, it was too late to complete their journey before nightfall, so they stopped in Gibeah (19:14). An old man offered them hospitality in his house, which they accepted. *The men of the city, sons of Belial, beset the house round about, and beat at the door, and spoke to the master of the house . . . saying, Bring forth the man that came into your house, that we may know him.* The old man said: *Do not this folly. Behold, here is my daughter a maiden, and his concubine* to rape (19:22-24). Every decision was in violation of the Word of God, confirming the fact that *in those days there was no king in Israel: but every man did that which was right in his own eyes* (Judges 17:6; 21:25; compare 18:1; 19:1).

The vileness of the homosexuals is confirmed in the New Testament where we read: *For this cause God gave them up to vile affections* (degrading passions): *for even their women did change the natural use into that which is against nature: And likewise also the men, leaving the natural use of the woman, burned in their lust one toward another; men with men working that which is unseemly, and receiving in themselves that recompence* (penalty) *of their error which was meet* (fitting) (Romans 1:26-27).

Thought for Today: The morally perverted need our prayers.

Christ Revealed: *In those days there was no king in Israel* (Judges 18:1). Christ was the rejected King of Israel. *Pilate says to them, Shall I crucify your King? The chief priests answered, We have no king but Caesar* (John 19:15).

For definitions of unfamiliar words in today's Bible reading, see pages 468-480.

In Today's Reading
Civil war between Benjamites and other tribes; Benjamites defeated;
wives provided for few remaining Benjamites

The tribe of Benjamin refused to allow justice to be done to the homosexual mob that gang-raped a defenseless Israelite woman causing
her death (Judges 20:13). All the other tribes of Israel united to execute
judgment against them and *came to the House of God, and wept, and
sat there before the LORD, and they fasted that day until evening, and
offered burned offerings and peace offerings before the LORD* (20:26). In
deep humility, they committed themselves to the Lord.

It was only after they had built an altar and offered the sacrifices for
their own needs that *the LORD said, Go up; for tomorrow I will deliver
them into your hand* (20:28). The tribe of Benjamin was almost destroyed
before the consequences of this wicked sin had been meted out.

There is growing indifference to immorality in our society that is
similar to what existed in the tribe of Benjamin. We have redefined sin.
Adultery is now called "having an affair." *Homosexuality* is replaced
with "gay and lesbian" or "alternative lifestyles." *Fornication* is referred
to as "live-in lovers." The purpose is to remove the sense of guilt for
violating God's moral Law and to make the sinner feel comfortable, as
they did when *in those days . . . every man did that which was right in
his own eyes* (21:25). However, while hating and exposing sin, we must
also show mercy and kindness as we pray for and lovingly entreat
sinners to come to Christ and allow Him to change their lives.

All sin is abominable to our holy God; however, all sin that is truly
repented of and forsaken is forgiven through the atoning blood of
Jesus Christ. The Apostle Paul reminded the Corinthians that some of
them had been delivered from sexual sins when he wrote: *Be not
deceived: neither fornicators, nor idolaters, nor adulterers, nor effeminate, nor abusers of themselves with mankind . . . shall inherit the
Kingdom of God. And such were some of you: but you are washed, but
you are sanctified* (set apart), *but you are justified in the Name of the
Lord Jesus, and by the Spirit of our God* (I Corinthians 6:9-11).

Thought for Today: We cheat ourselves when withholding what we should give to God.

Christ Revealed: As our Deliver (Judges 20:26,28). As we pray and seek the Lord's will,
He delivers us from all evil forces. *Our Lord Jesus Christ, Who gave Himself for our sins,
that He might deliver us from this present evil world* (Galatians 1:3-4).

For definitions of unfamiliar words in today's Bible reading, see pages 468-480.

Introduction To The Book Of
*R*UTH

The events of the Book of Ruth occurred when the judges ruled (Ruth 1:1). *In those days there was no king in Israel: every man did that which was right in his own eyes* (Judges 21:25). The Book of Ruth provides insight on faithfulness to God during the lawless period of the judges. The purpose of the book is to reveal how the mercy and providential care of God extends to both Jew and Gentile.

The Book of Ruth highlights our Lord's loving-kindness in selecting a Moabite woman to be included in His Covenant with Israel and to be one of only two women after whom books of the Bible are named. Ruth was one of only four women, other than Mary, mentioned in the genealogy of Jesus (Matthew 1:3,5-6,16) demonstrating the love of God for all people.

The Law provided for Boaz, as a kinsman-redeemer, to reclaim the deceased Elimelech's inheritance, to marry Ruth, and to raise a child to continue the lineage of Elimelech. An unnamed near kinsman (symbolic of the Law) had the first legal right to redeem Elimelech's lost inheritance. He refused by saying that to marry Ruth, a Moabite, would *mar* (endanger) *my own inheritance . . . I cannot redeem it* (Ruth 4:6). The Law stated: *An Ammonite or Moabite shall not enter into the congregation* (assembly) *of the LORD; even to their tenth generation* (Deuteronomy 23:3). The Law cannot forgive or make exceptions; it can only expose our sins and condemn us. But, Ruth had forsaken her false gods by confessing her faith in the God of Israel Who also said: *And now, Israel, what does the LORD your God require of you, but to fear the LORD your God to walk in all His ways, and to love Him* (Deuteronomy 10:12-16; compare Jeremiah 4:4; Romans 2:29; Galatians 3:29; Philippians 3:3; Colossians 3:11).

Boaz, a type of Christ who assumed the right of "kinsman-redeemer," purchased the property inheritance of Naomi and took Ruth as his wife. After making the necessary arrangements, *Boaz said to the elders . . . You are witnesses this day, that I have bought all that was Elimelech's . . . of the hand of Naomi. Moreover Ruth the Moabitess, the wife of Mahlon, have I purchased to be my wife, to raise up the name of the dead upon his inheritance, that the name of the dead be not cut off* (Ruth 4:9-10; Leviticus 25:25-34,47-48; Deuteronomy 25:5-10).

Through the marriage of Boaz and Ruth, for the third time God united both Jew and Gentile in the ancestry of David and of our Lord Jesus, the Messiah (Matthew 1:3,5; Luke 3:32-33). *There is neither Jew nor Greek, there is neither bond nor free, there is neither male nor female: for you are all one in Christ Jesus. And if you be Christ's, then are you Abraham's seed* (offspring), *and heirs according to the promise* (Galatians 3:28-29).

ℐN ℐODAY'S ℛEADING

Famine; Elimelech and Naomi move from Bethlehem to Moab;
Naomi and Ruth return to Bethlehem; marriage of Boaz and Ruth

𝓑ethlehem, the land of promise, was experiencing a severe famine. All Israel knew the Lord's warning: *If . . . you will not do all My Commandments. . . . your land shall not yield her increase, neither shall the trees of the land yield their fruits* (Leviticus 26:15-16,19-20).

Perhaps, while standing in their unproductive fields in the Judean hills, Elimelech, his wife Naomi, and their sons Mahlon and Chilion looked down on Moab, where it was reported that all was prosperous. They decided to abandon their God-given inheritance in Bethlehem, and *sojourn* (temporarily live) *in the country of Moab* (Ruth 1:1-2).

However, unforeseen tragedy struck in the idol-worshiping country of Moab. Elimelech died, then his sons ignored their Covenant relationship with God and married Ruth and Orpah, who were Moabite women. Sometime later, Mahlon and Chilion also died (1:3-5). The three childless widows were left without a means of support. *Then* (Naomi) *arose with her daughters in law. . . . and they went on the way to return to the land of Judah* (1:6-7).

Soon Orpah returned to her earthly securities, *back to her people, and to her gods* (1:15). But Ruth was no longer a Moabite in her heart, for she had forsaken the gods of Moab and confessed her loyalty to the God of Israel by saying to Naomi: *Your people shall be my people, and your God my God* (1:16).

Ruth and Naomi arrived in Bethlehem where Ruth married Boaz. Ruth became the mother of *Obed: he is the father of Jesse, the father of David* (4:17). The Book of Ruth highlights our Lord's loving-kindness to Gentiles in selecting a Moabite woman to become the great-grandmother of King David. Ruth is one of three Gentile women mentioned in the genealogy of Jesus (Matthew 1:3,5-6). These historical facts illustrate the love of God for all mankind.

For he is not a Jew, which is one outwardly . . . But he is a Jew, which is one inwardly; and circumcision is that of the heart, in the Spirit, and not in the letter (Romans 2:28-29).

Thought for Today: We cheat ourselves if we fail to give God our best.

Christ Revealed: Through Bethlehem (Ruth 1:1), which means *House of Bread.* Jesus, the *Bread of Life,* satisfies the spiritual hunger of all who come to Him. *Then Jesus said to them. . . . I am the Bread of Life: he that comes to Me shall never hunger* (John 6:32-35).

For definitions of unfamiliar words in today's Bible reading, see pages 468-480.

ISRAEL'S KINGS AND PROPHETS

UNITED KINGDOM ABOUT 1051 BC

KING	REIGN	PROPHET
Saul	40 Years	Samuel I Samuel 3:20; 9:15-27; 10:16-27;11:7-12
David	40 Years Note: Kingdom divided first 71/2 years; David reigned over Judah at Hebron I Kings 2:10-11 II Samuel 5:5	Samuel I Samuel 16:11-13; 19:8 Nathan II Samuel 7:2-17; 12:1-25 Gad I Sam 22:5; II Sam 24:11-19
Solomon	40 Years	Ahijah the Shilonite I Kings 11:29-39 Iddo II Chronicles 9:29

THE DIVIDED KINGDOM ABOUT 933 BC
SOUTHERN KINGDOM (Judah)   NORTHERN KINGDOM (Israel)

KING	REIGN	PROPHET	KING	REIGN	PROPHET
Rehoboam	17 Years	Shemaiah I Kings 12:22-24 II Chronicles 11:1-4; 12:5-8 Iddo II Chronicles 12:15	Jeroboam I	22 Years	Ahijah I Kings 11:29-39; 12:15; 14:1-18 15:29; II Chron 9:29; 10:15 A man of God from Judah I Kings 13:1-32
Abijam (Abijah)	3 Years	Iddo II Chron 13:22			
Asa	41 Years	Azariah II Chron 15:1-7 Hanani II Chron 16:7-10	Nadab	2 Years	
			Baasha	24 Years	Jehu I Kings 16:1-4,7,12
			Elah	2 Years	
			Zimri	7 Days	
			Omri [& Tibni] I Kings 16:21-28	12 Years	
Jehoshaphat	25 Years	Jehu II Chron 19:1-3; 20:34 Jahaziel II Chron 20:14-17 Eliezer II Chron 20:35-37	Ahab	22 Years	Elijah I Kings 17 – II Kings 2 Micaiah I King 22:8-28 II Chron 18:7-27
			Ahaziah	2 Years	Elijah II Kings 1:1-18
			Jehoram (Joram)	12 Years	Elisha
Joram (Jehoram)	8 Years	Elijah II Chron 21:12-15			
Ahaziah	1 Year		Jehu	28 Years	Elisha II Kings 9 – 10
Queen Athaliah [Usurper]	6 Years				
Joash (Jehoash)	40 Years	Joel ? **Zechariah (1) II Chron 24:20-22	Jehoahaz	17 Years	Elisha

119

ISRAEL'S KINGS AND PROPHETS

SOUTHERN KINGDOM (Judah)			NORTHERN KINGDOM (Israel)		
KING	REIGN	PROPHET	KING	REIGN	PROPHET
Joash (cont'd)			Jehoash (Joash)	16 Years	Elisha II Kings 13:10-20
Amaziah	29 Years		Jeroboam II	41 Years	Jonah II Kings 14:25 Hosea 1:1 *Amos 1:1; 2:6 – 9:10
Uzziah (Azariah)	52 Years	**Zechariah (2) II Chron 26:5 Isaiah 1:1 Micah 1:1			
Jotham	16 Years	Isaiah 1:1 Micah 1:1	Zechariah	6 Months	
			Shallum	1 Month	
			Menahem	10 Years	
			Pekahiah	2 Years	
Ahaz	16 Years	Isaiah 1:1 Micah 1:1	Pekah	20 Years	Oded II Chron 28:9-11
Hezekiah	29 Years	Isaiah 1:3 II Kings 19:1 – 20:19; II Chron 32:20-32; Isaiah 37:5-35; 38:1-8; 39:3-8 Micah 1:1	Hoshea	9 Years	
Manasseh	55 Years	The Lord's Servants II Kings 21:10-15	The Northern Kingdom ended when its people were taken captive by Assyria under Shalmaneser in 723/722 BC.		
Amon	2 Years				
Josiah	31 Years	Jeremiah 1:1-2 Zephaniah 1:1 Nahum/Habakkuk? Prophetess Huldah II Kings 22:14-20			

RISE OF BABYLONIA-CHALDEAN DYNASTY ABOUT 625 BC

KING OF JUDAH	REIGN	PROPHET
Jehoahaz (Shallum)	3 Months	Jeremiah 22:10-12
Jehoiakim	11 Years "Puppet-king" under Egypt & then Babylon	Jeremiah 1:3; 22:13-19; 25:1; 27:1; 35:1; 36:11,32; 45:1 Urijah (Uriah) Jeremiah 26:20-23 Habakkuk ?

FALL OF ASSYRIA ABOUT 612-607 BC
by Nabopolassar, king of Babylon & father of Nebuchadnezzar

KING OF JUDAH	REIGN	PROPHET
Jehoiachin (Jeconiah/Coniah)	3 Months	Jeremiah 1:3; 22:24-30 Habakkuk ?
Zedekiah	11 Years	Jeremiah 1:3; 21:1 – 22:9 Obadiah ?

Note: Dates shown are approximate; scholars vary. There are difficulties in the chronology which may, in part, be accounted for by "overlapping reigns," "associated sovereignty," and "part of year as years."
* Amos was from Judah but prophesied in Israel.
** Zechariah (1) & Zechariah (2) are not the same as Zechariah the prophet after the Exile.

Introduction To The Books Of
I & II Samuel

The First Book of Samuel covers about 125 years from the birth of Samuel, the last judge of Israel, through the forty-year reign of Saul, the first king. It continues the Book of Judges during the transition from a loose federation of the 12 tribes under the rule of judges to a united kingdom.

Samuel grew up in the home of Eli who was judge of Israel and in charge of the Tabernacle at Shiloh, the center of Israel's worship.

And all Israel from Dan even to Beersheba knew that Samuel was established (confirmed) *to be a prophet of the LORD* (I Samuel 3:20; compare Acts 3:24). When Samuel assumed both civil and spiritual leadership, the Israelites were entrenched in apostasy and were politically fragmented. Through his loyalty to the Word of God, Samuel restored the nation's moral and spiritual condition to the highest level since the days of Joshua.

Samuel founded the first school of the prophets, faithfully teaching God's Word (I Samuel 10:5; 19:20). Because Samuel was a man of prayer and obedient to the Word of God (7:5-9; 8:6; 12:17-18,23; 15:11), he was able to unite the tribes of Israel into one great nation. But as he grew old, the people insisted on a king such as the other nations. God directed Samuel to anoint as king, *Saul, a choice young man* (9:2) and Saul reigned for 40 years.

II Samuel opens with a brief report of the events surrounding the death of Saul. The tribe of Judah immediately anointed David as their king. However, Abner, captain of Saul's army as well as Saul's cousin (I Samuel 14:50), influenced the other tribes to accept Ish-bosheth, Saul's son, as their king over the eleven tribes (II Samuel 2:8-9).

After seven years, Joab, David's nephew and military commander, killed Abner. Ish-bosheth was assassinated by two of his own captains (4:5-6). *So all . . . Israel . . . anointed David king over Israel* (5:3).

David . . . reigned forty years. In Hebron . . . over Judah seven years and six months: and in Jerusalem . . . thirty and three years over all Israel and Judah (5:4-5) to build the most powerful nation on earth.

David's first conquest as king of the united kingdom was the fortress of Jebus. *David took the strong hold of Zion: the same is the city of David* (5:7). The Messianic Covenant was then foretold to David by the prophet Nathan: *I will establish the throne of his kingdom for ever* (7:13). Much later the prophet Isaiah foretold: *Of the increase of His government and peace there shall be no end, upon the throne of David, and upon His kingdom, to order it, and to establish it with judgment and with justice from hereafter even for ever* (Isaiah 9:7; 11:1; Jeremiah 23:5-6; Ezekiel 37:25).

IN TODAY'S READING

Samuel, the last judge; his mother and her sorrow; her song;
Samuel hears the voice of God; all Israel knows Samuel as a prophet

Near the end of the period of the Judges, we are introduced to Hannah, a godly woman who had lived many years in deep sorrow and humiliation because she could not have children. Since the Hebrew culture considered this a disgrace, *year by year . . . she went up to the house of the LORD, so she* (Hannah's adversary) *provoked her; therefore she* (Hannah) *wept, and did not eat. . . . And she vowed a vow, and said, O LORD of hosts, if You will indeed look on the affliction of Your handmaid, and remember me, and not forget Your handmaid, but will give to Your handmaid a man* (male) *child, then I will give him to the LORD all the days of his life* (I Samuel 1:7,11). *And it came to pass, as she continued praying before the LORD, that Eli marked* (noticed) *her mouth. Now Hannah . . . spoke in her heart; only her lips moved . . . therefore Eli thought she had been drunken. And Eli said to her, How long will you be drunken?* (1:12-14). Although she was wrongfully accused, Hannah did not become angry, but graciously answered Eli: *No, my lord, I am a woman of a sorrowful spirit: I have drunk neither wine nor strong drink, but have poured out my soul before the LORD* (1:15-16).

It was Eli's responsibility to rebuke those who did evil. In this case, Eli's misjudgment was truly a test of the genuineness of Hannah's humility. Had she reacted in indignation and anger toward Eli for being so judgmental, she would have returned home with a bitter attitude. However, instead of being angry, she entreated Eli, telling him of her sorrow. *Then Eli answered and said, Go in peace: and the God of Israel grant you your petition that you have asked of Him* (1:17). Hannah's son Samuel united the tribes of Israel into one nation.

Hannah lived centuries before the New Testament experience of being filled with the Holy Spirit; and yet we see her maintaining a godly attitude while being rebuked. The acceptance of such an undeserved rebuke in a right spirit often brings an answer to our prayers.

Put on therefore, as the elect (chosen) *of God, holy and beloved, bowels of mercies* (compassion), *kindness, humbleness of mind, meekness, long-suffering* (Colossians 3:12).

Thought for Today: When parents are living to please God their children are likely to do the same.

Christ Portrayed: By Samuel who grew in favor with God and men (I Samuel 2:26). *And Jesus increased in wisdom and stature, and in favor with God and man* (Luke 2:52).

For definitions of unfamiliar words in today's Bible reading, see pages 468-480.

ℐN ℱODAY'S ℛEADING
Consequences of sin; death of Eli; Ark of the Covenant taken;
Israel defeated; Ark is returned

The hostile Philistines lived on the coastal plains of the Mediterranean Sea, on the southwestern border of Israel, often declared war on God's people. *And when they joined battle, Israel was smitten* (defeated) *before the Philistines* (I Samuel 4:2). In desperation, *the elders of Israel said, Wherefore* (Why) *has the LORD smitten us to day before the Philistines? Let us bring the Ark of the Covenant of the LORD out of Shiloh . . . that, when it comes among us, it may save us out of the hand of our enemies* (4:3-5).

Because of a lack of spiritual insight, the Israelites' hopes were on the Ark, not on God who dwelt *above the Mercy Seat* and who alone has power to save (Exodus 25:10-22). The Israelites marched into battle against the Philistines, confident of victory. But the two sons of Eli who carried the Ark were evil men at that time (I Samuel 2:12).

Eli, who was old and blind, sat near the Tabernacle anxious to hear the outcome of the battle. A messenger returned and reported: *Israel is fled before the Philistines, and there has been . . . a great slaughter . . . your two sons . . . Hophni and Phinehas, are dead, and the Ark of God is taken. . . . When he* (the messenger) *made mention of the Ark of God . . . he* (Eli) *fell . . . backward . . . and he died* (4:17-18).

After the death of Eli, *Samuel spoke to all . . . Israel . . . prepare your hearts to the LORD, and serve Him only: and He will deliver you out of the hand of the Philistines. . . . And Samuel said, Gather all Israel to Mizpeh, and I will pray for you to the LORD. . . . they . . . said there, We have sinned against the LORD* (7:3,5-6). When the Philistines learned that the Israelites were worshiping God, they assumed it was an opportune time to attack. *And as Samuel was offering up the burned offering, the Philistines drew near to battle against Israel: but the LORD thundered with a great thunder on that day upon the Philistines, and discomfited* (overwhelmed) *them; and they were smitten before Israel* (7:10-13).

The satisfying truth is that God works through men and women of faith, like Samuel, who display their trust in Him by their **obedience** to His Word. *Let us hold fast* (firmly) *the profession of our faith without wavering; (for He is faithful that promised)* (Hebrews 10:23).

Thought for Today: The most profitable part of our day is the time we spend in God's presence, praying, reading, and obeying His Word.

Christ Revealed: Through the rock called *Ebenezer*, which means the *Stone of Help* (I Samuel 7:12). Jesus is our Rock of salvation; our help comes from Him (Psalms 18:2; 121:2). *I can do all things through Christ which strengthens me* (Philippians 4:13).

For definitions of unfamiliar words in today's Bible reading, see pages 468-480.

IN TODAY'S READING

Samuel's evil sons; Israel demands a king; Saul chosen;
Saul begins as a humble ruler, defeats the Ammonites,
and delivers Jabesh-gilead

During the history of the judges, Samuel accomplished more as a spiritual leader than any other judge. *And it came to pass, when Samuel was old . . . he made his sons judges over Israel. . . . And his sons . . . took bribes, and perverted judgment* (I Samuel 8:1-3). Eventually, *all the elders of Israel . . . came to Samuel . . . And said . . . you are old, and your sons walk not in your ways: now make us a king to judge us like all the nations. But the thing displeased Samuel* (8:4-6). *And the LORD said to Samuel . . . they have not rejected you, but they have rejected Me, that I should not reign over them* (8:7). Then Samuel anointed Saul king in Ramah as the Lord had directed him. After a brief time, *Samuel called the people together to the LORD to Mizpeh; And said . . . you have . . . rejected your God, Who Himself saved you out of all your adversities and your tribulations* (10:17-19). He then presented Saul to them as the man *whom the LORD has chosen. . . . And all the people shouted . . . God save* (long live) *the king* (10:24).

The first test of the new king came when Saul was told that Nahash the Ammonite king had put his army in position to attack. The Ammonites had not attacked the Israelites since Jephthah, a hero of faith (Hebrews 11:32), had defeated them many years before (Deuteronomy 2:19; 23:3-4; Judges 3:13; 10:7; 11:5). Responding to this current threat, Saul called together men from all the tribes of Israel to be his soldiers.

Saul led the Israelites in a spectacular victory. As he finished his first battle, he shouted: *To day the LORD has wrought salvation in Israel* (I Samuel 11:13).

Saul had a good beginning, but pride and self-will soon became his way of life that resulted in a succession of failures. This illustrates the temptation that often follows success, the deception of pride that inevitably leads to a self-centered life where Christ is no longer Lord (Matthew 16:24-27). The assumption that we have the ability to make decisions as to what is best for our lives and no longer need to pray for guidance is a reminder that Jesus said: *Without* (Apart from) *Me you can do nothing* (that has eternal value) (John 15:5).

Thought for Today: There are many ways in which God works in our lives, but most often through ordinary circumstances, allowing God's life to live through us.

Christ Portrayed: Through Samuel who faithfully served Israel as judge, prophet and priest. Jesus was the Prophet promised through Moses (Deuteronomy 18:15); He is our High Priest (Hebrews 4:14); and one day He will judge all mankind: *For the Father judges no man, but has committed all judgment to the Son* (John 5:22).

For definitions of unfamiliar words in today's Bible reading, see pages 468-480.

In Today's Reading
The people have their king; other battles with the Philistines;
office of The Priesthood usurped by Saul

*S*aul, the first king of Israel, was a man of great ability, but he had a fatal flaw. Perhaps three years after Saul became king, his first great failure occurred when he trusted his own judgment and not the Lord. *The Philistines gathered . . . to fight with Israel, thirty thousand chariots, and six thousand horsemen, and people as the sand which is on the sea shore in multitude* (I Samuel 13:5). The Israelites appeared to be doomed to defeat.

Realizing the military might of the Philistines, the majority of Saul's army hid *themselves in caves* (13:6). Saul realized that their only hope was in God. *He tarried seven days . . . but Samuel came not. . . . And Saul. . . . offered the burned offering. . . . as soon as he had made an end of offering the burned offering . . . Samuel came* (13:8-10). Saul's decision to assume the role of a priest violated the Word of God. Saul first made an excuse: *Because I saw that the people were scattered from me . . . Therefore, said I, The Philistines will come down now upon me to Gilgal, and I have not made supplication to* (prayed to, asked the favor of) *the LORD: I forced myself therefore, and offered a burned offering* (13:11-12).

The burnt offering symbolized surrender to God; but, when Saul assumed the God-ordained position of a priest, the sacrifice became an abomination to the Lord (15:22-23; see Numbers 16:1-40; Proverbs 21:27).What seemed to Saul a tardiness in Samuel's arrival was, in reality, a test by God of Saul's obedience to Him. Samuel spoke bluntly to *Saul, You have done foolishly: you have not kept the Commandment of the LORD your God, which He commanded you* (I Samuel 13:13-14).

Though some may consider Saul's disobedience of little consequence, the Lord said that what Saul did was a sin. How easily we can deceive ourselves into believing that God will be pleased with our accomplishments "for Him" even though we obey only what pleases us.

We may be tempted at times to disregard what the Bible states is sin, assuming that circumstances justify our actions. Saul's presumption demonstrates the importance of always obeying God's Word. *For the LORD gives wisdom: out of His mouth comes knowledge and understanding* (Proverbs 2:6).

Thought for Today: A true servant of the Lord willingly follows his Master's instructions without exception.

Christ Portrayed: By Samuel the intercessor (I Samuel 12:23). Right now Jesus is interceding for believers. *It is Christ that died, yea rather, that is risen again, Who is even at the right hand of God, Who also makes intercession for us* (Romans 8:34; Hebrews 7:25).

For definitions of unfamiliar words in today's Bible reading, see pages 468-480.

In Today's Reading

Saul's foolish oath; Saul commanded to destroy all Amalekites; he sins by sparing the enemy king; David anointed Israel's next king; Saul rejected by God as king

*F*ew kings in biblical history were blessed with as many advantages as Saul. But he soon forgot the source of his success. He became more concerned with impressing the people than with pleasing the Lord. It was not long before Saul exposed his true character when Samuel came to him and said: *Thus says the LORD of hosts, I remember that which Amalek did to Israel, how he laid wait for him in the way, when he came up from Egypt. Now go and smite Amalek, and utterly destroy all that they have* (I Samuel 15:2-3).

Saul defeated the Amalekites and then erected a memorial to himself at Carmel to commemorate his victory (15:12). He then returned. When Samuel met him, *Saul said to Samuel, Yea, I have obeyed the voice of the LORD . . . and have brought Agag the king of Amalek, and have utterly destroyed the Amalekites* (15:20). Although there had been a great victory, Saul had disobeyed the command of God by "sparing" the Amalekite king. He tried to shift the blame by saying: *But the people took of the spoil* (plunder), *sheep and oxen . . . to sacrifice to the LORD your God in Gilgal* (15:21). Saul seemed blind to his own disobedience. To *utterly destroy* would have been a true burned offering to God. But, when people kept the best, it was for themselves to eat at their next festival.

Saul was more concerned about his public image before the elders of Israel than with his right relationship with God. *Has the LORD as great delight in burned offerings and sacrifices, as in obeying the voice of the LORD? Behold, to obey is better than sacrifice, and to hearken than the fat of rams. . . . Because you have rejected the Word of the LORD, He has also rejected you from being king* (15:22-23). Saul finally confessed his partial disobedience, saying: *I have transgressed the Commandment of the LORD, and your words: because I feared the people, and obeyed their voice. . . . I have sinned: yet honor me now, I pray you, before . . . Israel* (15:24,30).

There is nothing so self-deceiving than professing Christ as Savior and Lord when the real motive is to gain personal recognition and praise.

Then said Jesus . . . If you continue in My Word, then are you My disciples indeed (John 8:31).

Thought for Today: We form opinions about people, but only God knows their hearts.

Christ Revealed: Through David's name (I Samuel 16:13) which means "beloved." David is a type of Jesus, Whom the Heavenly Father called: *My beloved Son* (Matthew 3:17; 17:5; Mark 1:11; 9:7; Luke 3:22; 9:35).

For definitions of unfamiliar words in today's Bible reading, see pages 468-480.

In Today's Reading

David kills Goliath; Saul appoints David captain of his guard;
he marries Saul's daughter Michal; Jonathan's loyalty to David

Early in Saul's reign, the giant warrior Goliath challenged the Israelite army to send a man to fight him and let the outcome of their fight decide who won the war. Apparently Saul was unwilling to accept his challenge.

But, when young David came into the camp and heard Goliath's taunts, he agreed to fight him and said *to the Philistine, You come to me with a sword, and with a spear, and with a shield: but I come to you in the Name of the LORD of hosts, the God of the armies of Israel, Whom you have defied. This day will the LORD deliver you into my hand; and I will smite* (strike you down) *you. . . . that all the earth may know that there is a God in Israel* (I Samuel 17:45-46).

Following his spectacular victory over Goliath, David was welcomed into the palace of King Saul, was made his trusted captain of the guard, and soon became his son-in-law by marrying the king's daughter Michal (18:27). We are not told how much time passed after David was welcomed into the king's court until Saul was determined to destroy him. But, when Saul heard women singing David's praises, he became exceedingly jealous and attempted to kill David by throwing a javelin at him as he was playing his harp (18:10-11).

David fled and escaped with the help of his wife Michal. He *came to Samuel at Ramah, and told him all that Saul had done to him* (19:12,18). He once had enjoyed acceptance in the king's palace but now he was reduced to hiding in caves. Difficulties, handicaps, and suffering in life are permitted by the Lord to develop godly character and to enable us to accomplish His purposes. Like David, we are put to the test to see if we will remain faithful and prove worthy of our high calling. We each are accountable for the effect which trials, suffering, or handicaps will have on us. They can be used to develop our faith in the Lord, or we can become bitter and resentful, blaming God and others for our troubles. *We must through much tribulation enter into the Kingdom of God* (Acts 14:22).

Thought for Today: Faith is developed as we trust the Lord when we face difficult disappointments. *Knowing that tribulation works patience* (Romans 5:3-5).

Christ Portrayed: By Jonathan, who knew the will of God was to make David king and stripped himself of his royal robes and made a covenant promising all that he had to David (I Samuel 18:3-4). Jesus, knowing the will of God, cast off His heavenly robes and *took upon Him the form of a servant, and became obedient to death, even the death of the cross* (Philippians 2:5-8).

For definitions of unfamiliar words in today's Bible reading, see pages 468-480.

ℐN 𝒯ODAY'S ℛEADING

Saul attempts to kill David; Jonathan's covenant with David;
David's flight to Nob; David flees for his life to Gath
in Philistine territory

David became a national hero and, as time passed, King Saul became increasingly jealous of his popularity. *And Saul spoke to Jonathan his son, and to all his servants, that they should kill David. But Jonathan Saul's son delighted much in David: and Jonathan told David . . . Saul my father seeks to kill you . . . abide in a secret place, and hide yourself* (I Samuel 19:1-2).

Prior to this, Saul had manipulated circumstances to expose David to the Philistines, hoping they would kill him (18:25). *And Jonathan spoke good of David to Saul his father, and said to him, Let not the king sin against his servant . . . For he did put his life in his hand, and slew the Philistine, and the LORD wrought a great salvation for all Israel: you saw it, and did rejoice: why then will you sin against innocent blood, to slay David without a cause?* (19:4-5).

Saul had become violent, with an uncontrolled temper. He considered any opposition as treason. Jonathan revealed remarkable spiritual insight and courage when he confronted his father the king in defense of David. The risk was very real for in a fit of rage, Saul denounced his son and, on one occasion, he even attempted to kill Jonathan (20:33).

Jonathan could have avoided any risk to himself if he had decided not to get involved in defending David. To defend an innocent person from slander or harm's way, whatever the cost to self, is to remain faithful to biblical principles by doing what is morally right.

We too may find ourselves in situations where people whom we know are being threatened, accused, maligned, intimidated, or taken advantage of. We are then faced with the decision of whether or not to get involved. We should not be an accomplice to evil by remaining silent, but respond as Jonathan did. There is a direct connection between what we truly believe and how we behave. The Apostle James urged believers: *Be . . . doers of the Word, and not hearers only, deceiving your . . . selves* (James 1:22).

Jesus declared: *But I say to you, Love your enemies . . . and pray for them which . . . persecute you; That you may be the children of your Father Who is in heaven* (Matthew 5:44-45).

Thought for Today: The Bible was not given to merely inform us, but to transform us.

Christ Portrayed: By David, who, as a servant of Saul, suffered at the hands of the one whom he chose to serve (I Sam. 19:1,10-11). Jesus suffered at the hands of the ones He came to serve and to save. *From that time forth began Jesus to show to His disciples, how that He must go to Jerusalem, and suffer many things of the elders and chief priests and scribes, and be killed, and be raised again the third day* (Matthew 16:21).

For definitions of unfamiliar words in today's Bible reading, see pages 468-480.

In Today's Reading
David's escape; Saul murders the priests of Nob;
David protects the Israelites in Keilah; David will not kill Saul

---

*N*ob was located just northeast of Jerusalem, where the sacred vessels had been kept by the priests since the destruction of Shiloh. Ahimelech the priest had given David food and allowed him to take the sword that had belonged to Goliath.This was reported to Saul in Gibeah by Doeg, an Edomite servant. In a rage of anger, *the king sent to call Ahimelech the priest . . . and all his father's house, the priests that were in Nob: and they came all of them to the king* (I Samuel 22:11). Saul then accused Ahimelech of conspiracy. *Then Ahimelech answered the king, and said, And who is so faithful among all your servants as David, which is the king's son in law, and goes at your bidding, and is honorable* (respected) *in your house?* (22:14).

Blinded by jealousy and hatred, Saul ordered the execution of all the priests and their families. *And the king said to the footmen* (guards) *that stood about him, Turn, and slay the priests of the LORD; because their hand also is with David, and because they knew when he fled, and did not show it to me. But the servants of the king would not put forth their hand to fall upon the priests of the LORD* (22:17). Without hesitation, *Doeg the Edomite . . . slew on that day fourscore and five* (85) *persons that did wear a linen ephod* (priestly garments). *And Nob, the city of the priests, he smote with the edge of the sword, both men and women, children and sucklings, and oxen, and asses, and sheep, with the edge of the sword. And one of the sons of Ahimelech . . . named Abiathar, escaped, and fled after David* (22:18-20). This was one of numerous attempts by Saul to murder David (I Samuel 18:11,21-25; 19:1,10,11,15,20-22; 20:24-31; 23:11-25; 24:2; 26:2).

There are times in the lives of most Christians when everything seems hopeless, as it must have for David who was forced into hiding for many years. In fact, we all experience times when we need to be encouraged about ourselves, our gifts and talents, our work, our children, or even our relationship with the Lord.

This was also true of David, who received spiritual direction and comfort from Abiathar and prophets such as Gad (22:5).

We can take comfort in knowing: *The Angel of the LORD encamps round about them that fear Him, and delivers them* (Psalm 34:7).

Thought for Today: Loving our enemies means sharing God's love with those who need it most.

Christ Revealed: By David's refusal to take the kingdom by force or before the appointed time set by God (I Samuel 24:10-13). Christ refused to become King of Israel. *When Jesus . . . perceived* (knew) *that they would come and take Him by force, to make Him a king, He departed . . . into a mountain Himself alone* (John 6:15).

For definitions of unfamiliar words in today's Bible reading, see pages 468-480.

IN TODAY'S READING
Death of Samuel; Nabal, a wicked landowner, dies;
David marries his widow Abigail; Saul's pursuit of David

Samuel was one of the greatest spiritual giants in Israel's history and is listed as one of the heroes of the faith (Hebrews 11:32), but just one sentence records the death of this grand, old prophet at this treacherous time in Israel's history. *And Samuel died; and all the Israelites . . . buried him in his house at Ramah.* Because of Saul, David could not attend the funeral; instead he *went down to the wilderness of Paran* (I Samuel 25:1). The Israelites were now without spiritual leadership. But the all-wise God, Who controls the universe, knew what was best.

We are tempted at times to think that death has come to the wrong person or has come at the wrong time, especially when a child is left without a mother, or when children die at a young age. Familiar as we are with death, the ways of God regarding it often seem strange to us. But, without a doubt, God never abandons His children. He leads us to look beyond our grief and trust in His wisdom and His tender love to comfort our broken spirit. Jesus said: *Let not your heart be troubled: you believe in God, believe also in Me* (John 14:1).

Death for the Christian is a promotion from this world's suffering to a welcome home by our wonderful Lord. Soon, *God shall wipe away all tears from their eyes; and there shall be no more death, neither sorrow, nor crying, neither shall there be any more pain: for the former things are passed away* (Revelation 21:4).

At times we all need comfort. This is especially true during experiences of distress and grief when a loved one dies. Those of us who have lost loved ones know what a word of compassion can mean. As we see others suffering, let us also remember that our Heavenly Father has commanded: *Comfort . . . My people* (Isaiah 40:1).

Last, but not least, the death of loved ones makes heaven all the more desirable for we who remain. *Precious in the sight of the LORD is the death of His saints* (Psalm 116:15). The words of our Savior are most comforting: *Let not your heart be troubled. . . . I will come again, and receive you to Myself; that where I am, there you may be also* (John 14:1,3).

Thought for Today: Comfort and pray for someone you know who seems discouraged.

Christ Revealed: By Abigail's efforts to make peace between David and Nabal (I Samuel 25:21-28). *God was in Christ, reconciling the world to Himself* (II Corinthians 5:19).

For definitions of unfamiliar words in today's Bible reading, see pages 468-480.

IN TODAY'S READING

David stays in Philistine territory; Saul is troubled over the Philistine army and consults a witch who claims to contact the dead

After Samuel became judge, the Philistines were so badly defeated because of his prayer meeting at Mizpeh that *they came no more into the coast* (territory) *of Israel: and the hand of the LORD was against the Philistines all the days of Samuel* (I Samuel 7:13). But, *there was sore* (severe) *war against the Philistines all the days of Saul* (14:52).

In the final year of Saul's reign, *the Philistines gathered to gether all their armies to Aphek* (29:1). Saul panicked when he realized the size and power of the Philistine armies that were ready to attack. Could Saul forget that Samuel had said: *Because you have rejected the Word of the LORD, He has also rejected you from being king?* (15:23). Out of jealousy, Saul also had attempted to kill David and forced him into exile. Finally, in desperation, Saul *inquired of the LORD* (28:6). Since he had murdered the priests of God, how could he expect an answer? How pathetic it is to see Saul riding through the night, frantically seeking counsel from a fortune-teller in Endor. He knew that mediums, spiritualists, witches, and fortune-tellers *are an abomination to the LORD* (Deuteronomy 18:10-12). In fact, earlier Saul had banished them from the land (I Samuel 28:3). This fortune-teller was no help. Instead his fears increased even more after the appearance of Samuel, who said: *Why then do you ask of me, seeing the LORD is departed from you, and is become your enemy?* (28:16). The next day Saul, along with his sons, including Jonathan, was killed in battle. At last Saul reaped what he had sown.

Saul's worst enemy was himself. He had lived a self-serving life. Power, wealth, popularity, and talents are often great hindrances to a spiritual life. Some seek guidance from psychics, fortune-tellers, palm readers, and other demon-controlled people, rather than crying out to the Lord in times of great distress and relying upon Him alone.

True success is the result of seeking the Lord's will through reading His Word, while at the same time praying to the Lord for guidance. *No good thing will He withhold from them that walk uprightly* (Psalm 84:11).

Thought for Today: Ignoring God's Word leads to deception.

Christ Revealed: Through the Urim (I Samuel 28:6), which was used to determine God's will. Today Christ speaks to us through His Spirit when we read His Word. *God . . . Has in these last days spoken to us by His Son* (Hebrews 1:1-2). *However when He, the Spirit of Truth, is come, He will guide you into all Truth: for He shall not speak of Himself; but whatsoever He shall hear, that shall He speak: and He will show you things to come* (John 16:13).

For definitions of unfamiliar words in today's Bible reading, see pages 468-480.

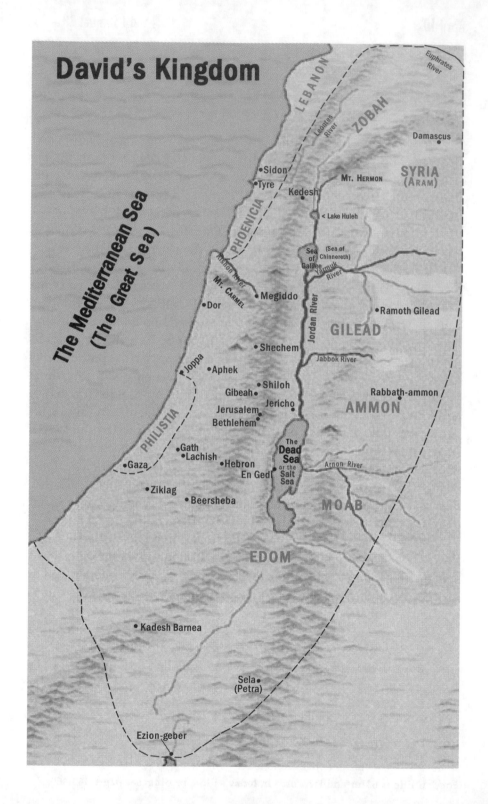

David's Kingdom

Euphrates River

LEBANON

ZOBAH

Leontes River

Damascus

•Sidon

•Tyre

Kedesh

Mt. Hermon

SYRIA
(Aram)

< Lake Huleh

PHOENICIA

Sea of Galilee

(Sea of Chinnereth)

The Mediterranean Sea
(The Great Sea)

Yarmuk River

Kishon River

Mt. Carmel

•Megiddo

Jordan River

•Ramoth Gilead

•Dor

GILEAD

•Shechem

Jabbok River

•Joppa

•Aphek

•Shiloh

Gibeah•

Jericho•

Rabbath-ammon

Jerusalem•

AMMON

Bethlehem•

PHILISTIA

The
Dead
Sea
or the
Salt
Sea

•Gath
•Lachish

•Hebron

Arnon River

•Gaza

En Gedi

•Ziklag

•Beersheba

MOAB

EDOM

• Kadesh Barnea

Sela•
(Petra)

Ezion-geber

ℐN ℐODAY'S ℛEADING

Saul killed in battle; David mourns the deaths of Saul and Jonathan;
David crowned king of Judah; Ish-bosheth made king of Israel

*S*aul had driven David from his family, his wife, his friends, and then into exile as a fugitive far from the palace. An Amalekite nomad, who carried in his hand the crown of Saul, mistakenly thought David would be pleased that he had executed him. The Amalekite could not conceive of David not rejoicing over the death of such an enemy. But, David *mourned, and wept, and fasted until evening . . . because they were fallen by the sword. . . . David lamented. . . . The beauty of Israel is slain upon your high places: how are the mighty fallen! Tell it not in Gath, publish it not in the streets of Askelon; lest the daughters of the Philistines rejoice* (II Samuel 1:12,17,19-20).

The world delights in the failures of Christians. Surely no Christian should ever be involved in gossip about the failures of fellow Christians. *If any man among you seem to be religious* (God-fearing), *and bridles* (controls) *not his tongue, but deceives his own heart, this man's religion is vain* (worthless) (James 1:26).

Now that Saul was dead, who would reign in his place? Israel was without a king. David had been anointed long ago by Samuel the prophet to be the next king of Israel (I Samuel 16:13). However, Abner, Saul's cousin and the powerful commander of Saul's army, was determined to retain his position. He persuaded the elders of Israel to put Saul's son Ish-bosheth on the throne over the 10 tribes. David could have felt justified to face Abner in battle for his right as God's chosen successor. Instead, *David inquired of the LORD, saying, Shall I go up into any of the cities of Judah? And the LORD said to him, Go up. And David said, Where shall I go up? And He said, To Hebron. . . . And the men of Judah came, and there they anointed David king over the house of Judah* (II Samuel 2:1,4).

How prone we are to jump at opportunities for personal advancement rather than seek God and His plan for our lives. But we need not fight for our rights. David prayed for God's will to be done in His way and at His time. It is comforting for Christians to know that: *Great peace have they which love Your Law: and nothing shall offend them* (Psalm 119:165).

Thought for Today: Spiritual victory is not dependent on human strength or reasoning, but on submission to the Holy Spirit.

Christ Revealed: In David's noble poem of sorrow (II Samuel 1:17-27). David forgot all his years of suffering at the hand of Saul and considered only the pleasant things. Here David typifies Christ, Who loved us even when we *were dead in trespasses and sins* (Ephesians 2:1).

For definitions of unfamiliar words in today's Bible reading, see pages 468-480.

In Today's Reading

Abner deserts Ish-bosheth to join David; Abner murdered by Joab;
Ish-bosheth murdered; David declared king of all Israel;
the city of Jebus (Jerusalem) is captured

Following the death of Saul, Abner, the powerful commander of Saul's armies, proclaimed Saul's son Ish-bosheth king of Israel. He then controlled both the puppet-king and his kingdom.

About seven years later, there was a fierce quarrel between Abner and Ish-bosheth (II Samuel 3:6-11). Because of this, *Abner sent messengers to David on his behalf, saying . . . Make your league with me, and , behold, my hand shall be with you, to bring about all Israel to you* (3:12-16). Abner contacted the elders of Israel, reminding them: *The LORD has spoken of David, saying, By the hand of My servant David I will save My people Israel out of the hand of the Philistines, and out of the hand of all their enemies* (3:18). A short time after Abner met with David, he was murdered by Joab, the commander of David's army, and then Ish-bosheth was assassinated by two of his own guards.

So all the elders of Israel came to the king to Hebron . . . and they anointed David king over Israel (5:3). The time had come for David to move his capital from Hebron to a more central location where the Jebusites held a stronghold in the heart of the promised land. *The king and his men went to Jerusalem. . . . David took the strong hold of Zion: the same is the city of David* (5:6-7).

There could never have been a Temple for the dwelling place of God in the place that He had chosen until the Jebusites, who held the central position in the promised land, were cast out. This *strong hold of Zion* is symbolic of strongholds which lie deep within our minds and which may not be known to anyone, either by our conduct or by our conversation. They depict secret thoughts that keep Christ from becoming Lord of our lives. These secret strongholds may not conflict with giving the Lord our time, talents, or tithes. But the *fleshly mind* (Colossians 2:18), with its physical impulses subtly demands to remain within our hearts. It is overcome as we daily read and **obey** God's Word, and are *filled with the knowledge of His will in all wisdom and spiritual understanding* (Colossians 1:9).

Thought for Today: Genuine devotion to God brings eternal rewards.

Christ Portrayed: By David, the anointed *king over Israel* (II Samuel 5:3). Christ is the Lord's Anointed. "Christ" is Greek for the Hebrew word *Messiah*, "Anointed One" (Psa. 2:2; John 1:41). Jesus is the King of the world. *And Pilate wrote a title, and put it on the cross. And the writing was, JESUS OF NAZARETH THE KING OF THE JEWS. . . . and it was written in Hebrew, and Greek, and Latin* (John 19:19-20).

For definitions of unfamiliar words in today's Bible reading, see pages 468-480.

IN TODAY'S READING
David brings the Ark of God into Jerusalem;
God makes a covenant with David; David's prayer of thanksgiving;
his victories; David's kindness to Mephibosheth

David was now king of the united kingdom. He desired to honor God by bringing the Ark of the Covenant, the dwelling place of God, to Jerusalem which would be the religious and political capital of David's kingdom. For about 75 years, during most of Samuel's leadership and during Saul's 40-year reign, the Ark had remained with Abinadab at Kirjath-jearim.

David often *inquired of the LORD* about what to do (I Samuel 23:2,4; II Samuel 2:1; 5:19,23), but he saw no need to pray about moving the Ark to Jerusalem.

David gathered together all the chosen men of Israel, thirty thousand. *. . . to bring up from there* (to Jerusalem) *the Ark of God. . . . they set the Ark of God upon a new cart* as the Philistines had done many years before when they captured it, and proceeded toward Jerusalem with great rejoicing. *Uzzah and Ahio, sons of Abinadab, drove the new cart* (II Samuel 6:1-4). David made the procession a national day of rejoicing to impress all Israel with the importance of putting God in the center of their nation.

Attempting to keep the Ark from toppling off the cart, *Uzzah put forth his hand to the Ark of God, and took hold of it; for the oxen shook it.* *. . . and God smote him there for his error; and there he died by the Ark of God* (6:6-7). David was humiliated and *displeased* (6:8). David was sincerely seeking to honor God but had overlooked two very important instructions in the Word of God: The Ark had to be carried by poles on the shoulders of the priests, and the penalty for touching the Ark of God's Presence was death (Exodus 25:10-15; Numbers 3:30-31; 4:15; 7:9).

This incident should teach us that it is a serious error to believe that, as long as a person is sincere, it makes no difference what he believes or does. It should also teach us the importance of knowing God's Word: *Study to show yourself approved to God, a workman that needs not to be ashamed, rightly dividing the Word of Truth* (II Timothy 2:15).

Thought for Today: Is your chief concern that God be honored? Then tell your friends to read His directions.

Christ Revealed: By the Ark of the Covenant which *they . . . set . . . in the midst of the Tabernacle* (II Samuel 6:17). The Ark contained God's Word given to Moses (Deuteronomy 10:1-5). Christ is the Living Word and dwells within us. *Christ in you, the hope of glory* (Colossians 1:27).

For definitions of unfamiliar words in today's Bible reading, see pages 468-480.

IN TODAY'S READING
The Ammonites and Syrians defeated; Bathsheba and David;
Nathan's parable and David's repentance; birth of Solomon

David, king of Israel, had never lost a war and had grown accustomed to getting what he wanted. *And it came to pass, after the year was expired* (in the spring), *at the time when kings go forth to battle, that David sent Joab, and his servants with him, and all Israel. . . . But David tarried still at Jerusalem* (II Samuel 11:1). Satan always has something or someone to attract us when we are in a position to gratify our fleshly desires. He always presents sin as both attractive and satisfying.

For David, his spiritual defeat began with a look of lust at the beautiful Bathsheba. David knew that adultery was a wicked sin against God and was punishable by death (Leviticus 20:10). *And David sent messengers, and took her; and she came in to him, and he lay with her. . . . and she returned to her house* (II Samuel 11:4). One sin usually leads to another, to unforeseen complications as well as other evils.

From the moment David first lusted after Bathsheba until their marriage, no one interfered with their pleasure. However, about one year later, Nathan the prophet boldly confronted David: *Wherefore have you despised the Commandment of the LORD, to do evil in His sight?* (12:9). Because of David's adultery, Nathan foretold: *Now therefore the sword shall never depart from your house; because you have despised Me, and have taken the wife of Uriah the Hittite to be your wife. Thus says the LORD, Behold, I will raise up evil against you out of your own house, and I will take your wives before your eyes, and give them to your neighbor, and he shall lie with your wives in the sight of this sun* (publicly) (12:10-11). Deeply grieved and repentant, David confessed: *I have sinned against the LORD. And Nathan said to David, The LORD also has put away your sin; you shall not die* (12:13). Although forgiven, the next twenty years – the entire last half of his reign – until his death – David's sorrows and sufferings never ceased from that one night of yielding to his lust. Because of David's sincere repentance, as recorded in Psalm 51, God forgave him. **But forgiveness does not remove the results.**

In addition to facing God on Judgment Day, no one can avoid the bitter consequences of yielding to the temptation of lust. *Be not deceived; God is not mocked: for whatsoever a man sows, that shall he also reap* (Galatians 6:7).

Thought for Today: We must live in the world, but we don't have to live by its standards.

Christ Revealed: In the prophet Nathan giving Solomon the name Jedidiah, which means beloved of the Lord (II Samuel 12:24-25). Christ was greatly loved by the Father. Jesus prayed: *You loved Me before the foundation of the world* (John 17:24).

For definitions of unfamiliar words in today's Bible reading, see pages 468-480.

In Today's Reading

Rape, incest, and murder occur among David's children;
Absalom flees to Geshur in Syria (Aram); Absalom's return

*A*bsalom's sister Tamar was the beautiful daughter of King David by *Maacah . . . of Geshur* (in Syria). David's oldest son, Amnon, by *Ahinoam the Jezreelitess*, was about 20 years of age when he pretended to be sick and asked his father David to send his half-sister Tamar to prepare him a meal (II Samuel 3:2-3; I Chronicles 3:1-2).

And when she had brought them to him to eat, he took hold of her, and said to her, Come lie with me, my sister. And she answered him, Nay, my brother, do not force (degrade) *me; for no such thing ought to be done in Israel: do not . . . this folly* (disgusting thing). . . . *However he would not hearken to her voice: but, being stronger than she, forced her, and lay with her. Then Amnon hated her exceedingly* (intensely). . . . *And Amnon said to her, Arise, be gone* (II Samuel 13:11-15). After his brief moment of lustful gratification, he forced her out of his home and locked the door. *So Tamar remained desolate in her brother Absalom's house* (13:20).

When David learned of Amnon's deception and wicked sin against his daughter, *he was very angry. And Absalom spoke to his brother Amnon neither good nor bad: for Absalom hated Amnon, because he had forced* (raped) *his sister Tamar* (13:21-22). Amnon was David's firstborn son and heir to the throne. David took no legal action, even though the Law of God demanded the death sentence for rape (Leviticus 20:17).

After two full years . . . Absalom invited all the king's sons (to a great feast). *. . . Now Absalom had commanded his servants . . . when I say to you, Smite* (strike) *Amnon; then kill him. . . . And the servants of Absalom did to Amnon as Absalom had commanded* (II Samuel 13:23-29). Absalom fled for safety to Geshur where he lived with his grandfather for *three years* (13:37-38).

A parent can experience no greater suffering than to see his own sin repeated in his children's lives. We cannot undo past sins, failures, and wasted time, but Christians are assured that, *if any man sin, we have an Advocate* (a Defender, a Defense Attorney) *with the Father, Jesus Christ the Righteous: And He is the propitiation* (the atoning sacrifice) *for our sins* (I John 2:1-2).

Thought for Today: *Sin is a reproach to any people* (Proverbs 14:34).

Christ Revealed: Through David's restoration of Absalom (II Samuel 14:33). If an earthly father's compassion reconciles him to his estranged son, how much more will our loving Heavenly Father reconcile us to Himself when we confess our sins. *God was in Christ, reconciling the world to Himself, not imputing* (counting, crediting) *their trespasses to them; and has committed to us the word of reconciliation* (II Corinthians 5:19).

For definitions of unfamiliar words in today's Bible reading, see pages 468-480.

IN TODAY'S READING

Absalom wins over national leaders; he leads a revolt and overthrow of David; David flees in fear of his son; Absalom's death

After Absalom had been in exile three years (II Samuel 13:34-38),
Joab, commander-in-chief of David's army, initiated a clever plot which
persuaded David to bring Absalom home.

About two years after Absalom had returned from exile (14:28),
with an arrogant, shameless, and defiant attitude, he demanded that
Joab arrange to have the king see him. David promptly forgave Absalom,
who then began an ambitious and deceptive scheme of conspiracy to
overthrow his father and declare himself king of Israel. *Absalom prepared him chariots and horses, and fifty men to run before him. And
Absalom rose up early, and stood beside the way of the gate: and it was so,
that when any man that had a controversy came to the king for judgment* he
pretended a deep concern. *And Absalom said to him, See, your matters are
good and right; but there is no man deputed of* (representing) *the king to
hear you. . . . Oh that I were made judge in the land, that every man which
has any suit or cause might come to me, and I would do him justice!* (15:1-
4). Soon the shocking news reached David that *the hearts of the men of
Israel are after* (with) *Absalom* (15:13).

It is sad to read that David, the brokenhearted old king, left
Jerusalem, running barefoot down the rocky, rugged hills to the Brook
Kidron and up the Mount of Olives, weeping, fleeing Jerusalem in fear
of his own beloved son (15:30). During this time, he had no thought of
self-pity, bitterness, or revenge. David's great concern was to avoid
bloodshed in Jerusalem, the city of God.

After learning he had been betrayed by his trusted counselor, David
committed himself to God and prayed: *O LORD, I pray* that *You, turn the
counsel of Ahithophel into foolishness* (15:31). Then, he sent Hushai his
longtime friend (15:37; I Chronicles 27:33) back to Jerusalem with
instructions as to how he could become Absalom's adviser and, thus,
refute Ahithophel's counsel (II Samuel 15:33-35).

Wicked men are often used by our holy God to correct those whom
He loves. David later confessed: *Before I was afflicted I went astray: but
now have I kept Your Word* (Psalm 119:67).

Thought for Today: In contrast to the accepted immoral principles of the world, the
Word of God reveals the vileness of sin.

Christ Portrayed: By David as he rebuked his followers when they wanted to execute his
enemies (II Samuel 16:10-11; compare I Samuel 26:8-9). When Jesus' disciples wanted to
do the same, He rebuked them saying: *You know not what manner of spirit you are of. For
the Son of Man is not come to destroy men's lives, but to save them* (Luke 9:54-56).

For definitions of unfamiliar words in today's Bible reading, see pages 468-480.

*I*N *T*ODAY'S *R*EADING

Absalom follows advice of Hushai; David's troops battle Absalom
and his followers; Absalom killed by Joab; David grieves bitterly

*I*t often takes a crisis to reveal who our true friends are. Ahithophel (David's adviser) was invited by Absalom to join his conspiracy. *And the conspiracy was strong; for the people increased* (in numbers) *continually with Absalom* (II Samuel 15:12). David was old and feeble and it appeared that Absalom had successfully won the confidence of most of the key leaders of the nation. When Ahithophel decided to desert David and join with Absalom, he revealed his true character with the words "me" and "I." *Let **me** now choose out twelve thousand men, and I will arise and pursue after David this night: And I will come upon him . . . I will smite* (murder) *the king only: And I will bring back all the people to you* (17:1-3). At first, *the saying pleased Absalom* (17:4). Apparently, Absalom realized that he would be in a secondary position to Ahithophel. God did not forget David's prayer: *O LORD . . . turn the counsel of Ahithophel into foolishness* (15:31).

David had sent his friend Hushai to join Absalom. Undoubtedly, his coming appealed to Absalom's ego, for he now had gained his father's two top advisers. Ahithophel assumed Absalom would accept his plan. But it had offended Absalom as well as Amasa. This led them to consider the counsel of Hushai, who reminded Absalom that *all Israel knows . . . your father is a mighty man, and they which be with him are valiant* (brave) *men* (17:10).

As Absalom considered the possibility of losing his first battle, he realized this could produce panic and the loss of his followers. Hushai advised *that all Israel be generally gathered to you, from Dan even to Beersheba . . . and that you go to battle in your own person* (17:11). This appealed to Absalom's ego, and gave David and his men time to prepare for the battle that would lead to Absalom's defeat. The Bible clearly warns that *pride goes before destruction, and a haughty spirit before a fall* (Proverbs 16:18). Undoubtedly, Hushai's advice was an answer to David's prayer.

Pity the ignorant who are unaware of the "Unseen Presence" of God, Who defends those who trust in Him (Hebrews 4:13; Psalm 40:17).

For promotion comes neither from the east, nor from the west, nor from the south. But God is the judge: He puts down one, and sets up another (Psalm 75:6-7).

Thought for Today: No one can defeat God's purposes for you.

Christ Revealed: Through Mahanaim, a city of refuge where David went when he was fleeing from Absalom (II Samuel 17:27). Christ is our Refuge. *We . . . have fled for refuge to lay hold upon the hope set before us . . . even Jesus* (Hebrews 6:18-20).

For definitions of unfamiliar words in today's Bible reading, see pages 468-480.

IN TODAY'S READING
Joab rebukes David; he returns; Sheba revolts and is killed

---

*A*bsalom was a traitor who was determined to destroy his father, so that he could be king. The battle ended when Joab killed Absalom.

David's soldiers returned expecting a celebration; instead they heard the king weeping: *O Absalom, my son, my son!* (II Samuel 19:4). In deep sorrow, David ignored his loyal followers who had defended him. *The victory that day was turned into mourning* and the soldiers slipped away *as people being ashamed steal away when they flee in battle* (19:2-3).

David had faced many sorrows throughout his life. When Bathsheba's first child became sick, David had prayed and fasted. Then, when he received word the child had died, David confidently said: *I shall go to him, but he shall not return to me* (12:23). David knew heaven would be all the more precious because his child was with the Lord. But David expressed no hope that he would see Absalom in heaven. David may have felt that if Joab had only given Absalom one more chance perhaps he would have turned from his wicked ways. But, had he lived, Absalom would have been in fierce competition with Solomon, God's choice to take David's place as king.

All of us, at times, are responsible for the adversities and sorrows which we experience. It is also natural to condemn ourselves for our faults and failures, or even to blame others for the things that disappoint us. Like David, we can grieve too long over what might have been. If we are out of the will of God, we need to repent of our sins, ask God to forgive us, and be like the Apostle Paul, who proclaimed: *Forgetting those things which are behind, and reaching forth to those things which are before, I press toward the mark* (goal) *for the prize of the high calling of God in Christ Jesus* (Philippians 3:13-14).

In our darkest moments, we all need friends to remind us to trust the Lord. In turn, we need to be a friend who can share comforting words with a despondent sufferer. By God's grace, we should encourage them to become involved in a local church where others can help deepen and nurture their faith in the love of God *for we are members of His body. . . . This is a great mystery* (hidden truth)*: but I speak concerning Christ and the Church* (Ephesians 5:30,32).

Thought for Today: Christ heals the brokenhearted who trust Him.

Christ Portrayed: By David, who wished to be invited back as king (II Samuel 19:11). Our Lord Jesus wants to be invited into the hearts of all mankind. He only comes in by our invitation. *Behold, I stand at the door, and knock: if any man hear My voice, and open the door, I will come in to him* (Revelation 3:20).

For definitions of unfamiliar words in today's Bible reading, see pages 468-480.

In Today's Reading
God punishes Israel with a 3-year famine; seven members of Saul's
family put to death; victories over Philistine giants

*T*he days of harvest had once again come, but there was nothing to eat because *there was a famine . . . three years, year after year* (II Samuel 21:1). The famine was the judgment of God: *If you will not hearken* (listen) *to the voice of the LORD your God, to observe to do all His Commandments . . . . your heaven that is over your head shall be brass* (not emitting rain), *and the earth that is under you shall be iron* (unproductive) (Deuteronomy 28:15,23).

It is assumed that this three-year famine occurred during the early years of David's reign, even though it is recorded here more than 25 years later. Recognizing the famine as the judgment of God, *David inquired of the LORD. And the LORD answered, It is for Saul, and for his bloody house, because he slew the Gibeonites* (II Samuel 21:1). Saul had violated the covenant that Israel had made with the Gibeonites 400 years earlier. That treaty was still sacred because the covenant had been sworn to in the Name of God (Joshua 9:3,15-19).

The surviving Gibeonites did not ask David for silver or gold to compensate for the murder of loved ones or for the loss of their property (II Samuel 21:4). From their many years of association with the Israelites, the Gibeonites had to have known the Commandment of God. *Moreover you shall take no satisfaction for the life of a murderer, which is guilty of death: but he shall be surely put to death* (Numbers 35:31). Disobedience to this command meant Israel would be defiled.

The Gibeonites asked permission to hang seven men who were descendants of Saul. Therefore, David was responsible before God to deliver the seven men to the Gibeonites. Because of his covenant with Jonathan, an exception was made for his crippled son, Mephibosheth (II Samuel 21:7; I Samuel 20:14-17; 23:16-18).

Throughout the Old Testament, we learn the value God has placed on keeping our promises. Let us recognize the danger of disregarding our moral and spiritual responsibilities. In God's eyes, not even the king of a nation is above its laws. *For the LORD knows the way of the righteous: but the way of the ungodly shall perish* (Psalm 1:1-6).

Thought for Today: God expects us to keep our promises. Can you be trusted to fulfill what you said you would do?

Christ Portrayed: As the One we call upon for salvation (II Samuel 22:4). *Neither is there salvation in any other: for there is no other Name under heaven given among men, whereby we must be saved* (Acts 4:12).

For definitions of unfamiliar words in today's Bible reading, see pages 468-480.

In Today's Reading
The last words of David; David's last recorded sin;
David builds an altar; his sacrifice; the three-day plague

David never lost a battle in his 40-year reign. Although he had often prayed for the Lord's direction during his early years of conquest, his desire at this time to take a census of his army was obviously not based on any threat by invaders. When we begin feeling proud or desiring a feeling of security, Satan is quick to suggest wrong thoughts, as he did with David. *And Satan stood up against Israel, and provoked* (incited) *David to number* (take a census in) *Israel* (I Chronicles 21:1). The Chronicles passage further explains the incident in II Samuel. From the standpoint of the absolute sovereignty of God over everything, including Satan, we read: *And again the anger of the LORD was kindled against Israel, and He moved David against them to say, Go, number Israel and Judah. . . . And David's heart smote him after that he had numbered the people. And David said to the LORD, I have sinned greatly in what I have done: and now, I beseech You, O LORD, take away the iniquity of your servant; for I have done very foolishly. . . . So the LORD was entreated for the land, and the plague was stayed* (ceased) *from Israel* (II Samuel 24:1,10,25).

It would be inconceivable for God to actually force David to commit this sin and then, before the census was completed, to destroy 70,000 people because of it (24:15; I Chronicles 27:24). The Holy Spirit directed the writing of II Samuel to let us see that everyone is under the sovereign will of God, but that He allows us to stubbornly go our own way, for He will not violate our free will.

There is no record that taking a census was prohibited. But the Law did state: *When you take the sum of the children of Israel after their number, then shall they give every man a ransom for his soul* (himself) *to the LORD . . . that there be no plague among them. . . . This they shall give, every one that passes among them that are numbered, half a shekel . . . shall be the offering of the LORD* (Exodus 30:12-13).

Because of this violation, a plague spread over the land. David's tragic experience is a reminder of how important it is that we pray one for another that: *The God of peace . . . Make you perfect in every good work to do His will, working in you that which is well-pleasing in His sight, through Jesus Christ* (Hebrews 13:20-21; Titus 3:8).

Thought for Today: The weapons of our spiritual warfare are mighty.

Christ Revealed: Through the silver which David used to purchase *the threshingfloor* upon which he built *an altar to the LORD* (II Samuel 24:24-25). Silver symbolizes Christ's redemption offered for all. *And (Judas) said to them, What will you give me . . . And they covenanted* (agreed) *with him for thirty pieces of silver* (Matthew 26:15).

For definitions of unfamiliar words in today's Bible reading, see pages 468-480.

Introduction To The Books Of
I & II $\mathcal{K}$INGS

All the kings of Judah and Israel are recorded in I & II Kings except for Saul. The purpose of I & II Kings is to illustrate the blessings that result from faithfulness and obedience to the Lord and His judgment upon unfaithfulness and disobedience. The first 11 chapters of I Kings focus attention primarily on the reign of Solomon. Chapters 12 – 22 cover about the first 80-100 years of the divided kingdom. During that time, four kings reigned over the southern kingdom and eight over the northern kingdom.

David's final words to Solomon were: *Keep the charge* (require-ments) *of the LORD your God, to walk in His ways, to keep . . . His Commandments . . . that you may prosper in all that you do* (I Kings 2:3; Joshua 1:7). But Solomon ignored David's advice. Consequently, His reign resulted in a divided kingdom soon after his death.

The first 17 chapters of II Kings focus on the prophets Elijah and Elisha as well as record the decline of both the southern and northern kingdoms. Nineteen kings ruled the northern kingdom of Israel during its approximately 210-year history as a divided kingdom. Chapter 17 ends with the conquest and removal of the people of the northern kingdom of Israel by the Assyrians. Most of the Israelites were scattered throughout the Assyrian Empire, while captives from other nations were brought into Samaria. These pagans intermarried with the few remaining Israelites. Their descendants became known as Samaritans, a people despised by the Jews.

The smaller southern kingdom of Judah remained independent for another 135 years, existing for a total of about 465 years. Including the 120 years of the united kingdom, Judah had 19 kings and one usurper, Queen Athaliah (I Kings 11:42 – II Kings 25:30). The closing eight chapters of II Kings are devoted to the southern kingdom of Judah.

By the end of the last chapter, we read that Jerusalem was destroyed and Solomon's Temple burned by the Babylonians. Most of Judah's population then was taken captive and dispersed throughout Babylonia.

The prophets Elijah and Elisha prophesied in Israel, as did Amos, Hosea, and Jonah. Obadiah, Joel, Isaiah, Micah, Nahum, Habakkuk, Zephaniah, and Jeremiah prophesied during this time in Judah. These men of God exposed the nation's sins and appealed to the people to reject their idols and repent or experience defeat and judgment.

IN TODAY'S READING
David's son, Adonijah, revolts; Joab defects; Abiathar defects;
King David charges Solomon to be obedient to God's Word

*A*s we grow old, all of us want to remain useful; but increasing age continues to diminish our strength and narrow our options. *Now King David was old and stricken in years* (I Kings 1:1). Just like everyone else, the beloved king became physically feeble. But his spiritual insight had grown even stronger. Spiritual alertness is maintained as we continue to take in and share God's Word with others.

David said nothing to Solomon about amassing wealth or enlarging his kingdom. Instead, he stressed the true values of living in **obedience** to the Supreme King of Israel. His last words to Solomon express his heartfelt desire for his son: *I go the way of all the earth: be . . . strong therefore, and show yourself a man* (stand firm against all pressure to compromise); *And keep the charge* (requirements) *of the LORD your God* (2:2-4). Compromise for us could include active involvement in secular organizations that rob us of time that could be invested in Christ-centered goals with the Church and other ministries.

God had commanded that Israel's king must not *cause the people to return to Egypt, to the end that he should multiply horses: forasmuch as the LORD has said to you, You shall hereafter return no more that way* (Deuteronomy 17:16). But Solomon's first years as king were occupied in accumulating 40,000 horses for himself (I Kings 4:26).

God had also commanded all the kings to intimately know His Word: *He shall write him a copy of this Law in a book out of that which is before the priests the Levites: And it shall be with him, and he shall read therein all the days of his life: that he may . . . do* (follow) *them* (Deuteronomy 17:18-20). The division and eventual destruction of the kingdom of Israel can be attributed to the sins of Solomon. He failed *to keep all the words of this Law and these statutes* (decrees), *to do them* (17:19). Let us *look not at the things which are seen, but at the things which are not seen: for the things which are seen are temporal; but the things which are not seen are eternal* (II Corinthians 4:18).

Thought for Today: You are precious to the Lord.

Christ Revealed: By the oil used to anoint Solomon (I Kings 1:39). Christos (Greek) and Messiah (Hebrew) mean "The Anointed One." Oil, symbolic of the Holy Spirit, was poured out upon those chosen by God for special service. Jesus is God's Anointed One: *The Spirit of the Lord is upon Me, because He has anointed Me* (Luke 4:18).

For definitions of unfamiliar words in today's Bible reading, see pages 468-480.

In Today's Reading
Abiathar banished from priesthood; Joab put to death; Shimei
executed; Solomon's control of the kingdom becomes secure

Soon after Solomon became king, we read: *Solomon loved the LORD,
walking in the statutes of David his father: only he sacrificed and burned
incense in high places* (I Kings 3:3). The Tabernacle and the Altar of
Burned Offering were still located at Gibeon, about six miles northwest
of Jerusalem (I Chronicles 16:37-40; 21:29). The last major event to take
place at Gibeon was Solomon's great dedication service as king (II
Chronicles 1:1-13). On the night of that great sacrifice, Solomon had a
remarkable dream in which he asked God for *an understanding heart to
judge Your people, that I may discern between good and bad* (I Kings 3:9).
God was trying to get Solomon's attention through a dream to remind
him that he needed to meditate upon the Scripture, *discern between good
and bad*. Then, *Solomon awoke; and, behold, it was a dream* (3:15). But this
remarkable dream had no lasting affect on his life.

Solomon ignored God's Word concerning the kings of Israel: *He
shall not multiply horses to himself. . . . Neither shall he multiply* (take
many) *wives to himself . . . neither shall he greatly multiply to himself silver
and gold* (Deuteronomy 17:16-17). He not only turned to Egypt for
horses, but also *took Pharaoh's daughter* as a wife (I Kings 3:1).

Solomon offered enormous sacrifices to God, built the world famous Temple, and offered the longest recorded prayer in the Bible; but
his disregard for God's Word, his many marriages to pagan wives, and
his worship at their Canaanite *high places* (3:3) were all acts of rebellion
against God. These actions eventually led to his apostasy.

Solomon refused to follow his godly father's advice to *keep the charge*
(requirements) *of the LORD your God . . . keep . . . His Commandments* (2:3).
He is typical of the brilliant, multitalented people who compromise biblical
principles and assume that God is pleased since they are successful and
popular. But compromise is the first foothold of sin that sooner or later
destroys one's spiritual usefulness and influence for Christ.

Solomon eventually confessed: *I have seen all the works that are done
under the sun; and, behold, all is vanity and vexation of spirit* (chasing after
the wind) (Ecclesiastes 1:14). But, later he wrote: *Fear God, and keep His
Commandments* (12:13).

Thought for Today: Surely the highest of all wisdom is to obey the Lord.

Christ Revealed: Through the wisdom which God gave Solomon (I Kings 3:12). We
are *in Christ Jesus, Who of God is made to us wisdom, and righteousness, and
sanctification, and redemption* (I Cor. 1:30). Wonderful Counselor and justice will
be distinguishing characteristics of the Messianic King and His reign (Isaiah 9:6-7).

For definitions of unfamiliar words in today's Bible reading, see pages 468-480.

In Today's Reading
Solomon builds the Temple;
furnishings of the Temple and his own palace

Solomon's Temple was twice the size of the Tabernacle, but it was still comparatively small, only 90 feet long, 30 feet wide, and 45 feet tall. The interior was divided into two rooms. The first room was called the Holy Place and was 60 by 30 feet; the second room was called the Holy of Holies and was a 30 x 30 x 30 foot cube.

In the four hundred and eightieth year after the children of Israel were come out of the land of Egypt, in the fourth year of Solomon's reign over Israel . . . that he began to build the House of the LORD (I Kings 6:1). No other building in the world compared with Solomon's Temple. The most costly materials and treasures were lavished upon it. But the world observed only the external beauty of the Temple; its true glory was in the presence of God Who chose to dwell within the Holy of Holies.

The Temple was built without the noise of craftsmen since the stones were shaped in the quarry and made ready to fit together on Mount Moriah (6:7). This should remind us not to mistake noise for spiritual progress. We are transformed into His glorious likeness, not by noisy human efforts, but silently by the power of the Holy Spirit, as day by day God perfects His temple within every believer (Zechariah 4:6).

Every child of God is more precious to our Heavenly Father than Solomon's Temple. *You are the temple of God* (I Corinthians 3:16). *We are His workmanship, created in Christ Jesus* (born anew) *to good works, which God has before ordained* (planned) *that we should walk in them* (Ephesians 2:10).

Every day is a sacred trust that becomes more meaningful with the awareness that the God of heaven lives within every believer. The miracle of the new birth and the indwelling Holy Spirit are the differences between the true Christian and the "religious world." Jesus said: *I am the Way, the Truth, and the Life: no man comes to the Father, but by Me* (John 14:6). The Apostle Peter attested: *Neither is there salvation in any other: for there is no other Name . . . whereby we must be saved* (Acts 4:12).

For you are bought with a price (belong to God); *therefore glorify God in your body* (I Corinthians 6:20).

Thought for Today: The true beauty of a Christian is the presence of God Who dwells within and radiates without for our bodies truly belong to Him.

Christ Revealed: Through the Temple (I Kings 6). Christ is the true Temple (John 2:21). Through Christ all may have access to God (Romans 5:12-21). *For through Him we . . . have access by one Spirit to the Father* (Ephesians 2:18).

For definitions of unfamiliar words in today's Bible reading, see pages 468-480.

In *Today's* *Reading*
Ark brought into the Temple; glory of the Lord fills the Temple;
Solomon's sermon, prayer, and dedication

*T*he day had arrived for the dedication of the glorious Temple in Jerusalem. *Then Solomon assembled the elders of Israel . . . in Jerusalem, that they might bring up the Ark of the Covenant of the LORD out of the city of David, which is Zion. . . .the priests brought in the Ark of the Covenant of the LORD . . . into . . . the Most Holy Place* (I Kings 8:1,6). The Ark is where the presence of God dwelt above the Mercy Seat. *There was nothing in the Ark save the two tables of stone, which Moses put there at Horeb. . . . when the priests were come out of the Holy Place . . . the glory of the LORD . . . filled the House of the LORD* (8:9-11). The people stood in the courtyard and worshiped the Lord at the dedication of the Temple.

Solomon offered a sacrifice . . . to the LORD, two and twenty thousand oxen, and a hundred and twenty thousand sheep. So the king and all the children of Israel dedicated the House of the LORD (8:63). The word "sacrifice" does not mean "a great loss." A sacrifice to the Lord is never a deprivation, but is a gift of something dedicated to the Lord. However, sacrifices are an abomination if they don't represent an expression of our true inner devotion to the Lord.

Solomon prayed the longest recorded prayer in the Bible and stressed to the Israelites the faithfulness of God, Who, *keeps covenant and mercy with Your servants that walk before You with all their heart* (8:22-23).

The Israelites were chosen to let the world know there is only One True God. Solomon prayed: *That all people of the earth may know Your Name, to fear You, as do Your people Israel.* Then *he . . . blessed . . . Israel . . . saying. . . . That He may incline our hearts to Him, to walk in all His ways, and to keep His Commandments. . . . That all the people of the earth may know that the LORD is God, and that there is none else* (8:43,55,58,60). Buddha, Allah, and all other "gods" are false gods.

The One True God includes all three persons of the Trinity: God the Father, Jesus, Who is God the Son, and God the Holy Spirit. A Christian's daily conversation and conduct should express love and loyalty to the One True God. *For there is one God, and one Mediator between God and men, the Man Christ Jesus* (I Timothy 2:5-6).

Thought for Today: The holiness of God reveals the vileness of sin.

Christ Revealed: As the perfect Temple of God before whom all kings of the earth one day must bow (I Kings 8:54; John 2:19-21). *Wherefore God also has highly exalted Him, and given Him a Name which is above every name* (Philippians 2:9-10).

For definitions of unfamiliar words in today's Bible reading, see pages 468-480.

In Today's Reading
Warning to Solomon; alliance with King Hiram of Tyre;
Solomon's riches and wisdom

The Lord gave Solomon special privileges far exceeding those of other kings. But the Lord's continued blessings are conditional, as He said to Solomon: *If you will walk before Me, as David your father walked, in integrity of heart, and in uprightness, to do . . . all that I have commanded you . . . Then I will establish . . . your kingdom . . . for ever* (I Kings 9:4-7).

Did Solomon assume that building the most sacred Temple in history, praying the longest prayer, and offering the most sacrifices meant that God would overlook his sins? In disregard for the Word of God, Solomon amassed thousands of horses and chariots, and lived in an atmosphere of unparalleled luxury. He also violated the command of God by accumulating 700 wives and 300 concubines (Deuteronomy 17:16-17). Did Solomon deceive himself into thinking that, as king, he could ignore the Word of God in his personal life?

Solomon not only chose daughters of foreign kings for his wives, but he encouraged them to worship their idols. This had been expressly forbidden in the Law (18:9-12). There is no indication that Solomon made an effort to encourage any of his wives to worship the One True God. To do this would have interfered with his political agenda, since his foreign wives were daughters of kings who would insure peace with their countries. His power, prestige, and wealth eventually became his undoing. We are shocked to read that Solomon eventually *went* (followed) *after Ashtoreth the goddess of the Zidonians, and after Milcom the abomination* (detestable idol) *of the Ammonites. . . . And the LORD was angry with Solomon, because his heart was turned from the LORD God of Israel, which had appeared to him twice* (I Kings 11:5-9).

What happened to Solomon can happen to all who allow an abundance of "things" to crowd out one's loyalty to the Lord. We are to *be content with such things as you have* (Hebrews 13:5).

How solemn is the warning: *For the love of money is the root of all evil: which while some coveted after, they have erred* (wandered) *from the faith, and pierced themselves through with many sorrows* (I Timothy 6:10).

Thought for Today: God's Word has solutions to all of life's problems.

Christ Portrayed: By David who walked before the Lord *in integrity of heart* (I Kings 9:4). *Jesus increased in wisdom and stature, and in favor with God and man* (Luke 2:52).

For definitions of unfamiliar words in today's Bible reading, see pages 468-480.

*I*n *T*oday's *R*eading
Solomon's death; ten tribes revolt; Jeroboam rebuked
by an unnamed prophet; death of the disobedient prophet

*K*ing Solomon *was buried in the city of David his father* (I Kings 11:43). His son Rehoboam inherited power and a treasury full of wealth. However, Solomon left the kingdom morally and spiritually bankrupt.

Jeroboam and all the congregation of Israel came, and spoke to Rehoboam, saying, Your father made our yoke grievous (harsh, hard): *now therefore make . . . his heavy yoke which he put upon us, lighter, and we will serve you* (12:3-4).

King Rehoboam consulted with the old men . . . and said, How do you advise that I may answer this people? And they spoke to him, saying, If you . . . this day . . . speak good words to them, then they will be your servants for ever. But he forsook the counsel of the old men, which they had given him, and consulted with the young men that were grown up with him, and which stood before (served) *him* (12:6-8).

Note that Rehoboam said to the wise old men: *How do **you** advise?* But, he said to his newly-appointed cabinet of young friends: *What counsel* (advice) *give you **that we may answer this people?*** (12:9). Taking the young men's counsel, Rehoboam foolishly threatened the nation with additional taxes and even more cruel treatment. This blunder caused the people to rebel and declare a new king: *And it came to pass. . . . all Israel . . . made him* (Jeroboam) *king* (12:19-20).

Jeroboam provided his new northern kingdom with two "more convenient" places of worship located at Bethel in the south and Dan in the north. This violated the Word of God that clearly commanded that all worship sacrifices must be conducted at the Temple in Jerusalem. *And He shall give Israel up because of the sins of Jeroboam, who did sin, and who made Israel to sin* (14:16).

A similar departure from the fundamental doctrines of the Word of God is prevalent today. Pitiful as this is, some people neglect to read His Word and simply do not know the difference between God's truth and religious traditions or "political incorrectness." *Beware of false prophets, which come to you in sheep's clothing, but inwardly they are ravening* (greedy) *wolves. . . . Not every one that says to Me, Lord, Lord, shall enter into the Kingdom of Heaven; but he that does the will of My Father Who is in heaven* (Matthew 7:15,21).

Thought for Today: Pity the one who compromises the Word of God.

Christ Portrayed: Through *Shemaiah* who spoke for the Lord (I Kings 12:22). Jesus spoke only what the Father told Him. *All things that I have heard of My Father I have made known to you* (John 15:15).

For definitions of unfamiliar words in today's Bible reading, see pages 468-480.

In Today's Reading
Ahijah's prophecy; reign and death of Rehoboam;
Abijam's wicked reign and Asa's good reign in Judah

*J*eroboam set up worship centers at Bethel in the south and at Dan in the north for his kingdom. The southern kingdom of Judah was greatly influenced to worship the Lord because *the Levites* (in the northern kingdom) *left . . . their possession, and came to Judah and Jerusalem. . . . So they strengthened the kingdom of Judah . . . for three years they walked in the way of David* (II Chronicles 11:14,17).

In the fifth year of Rehoboam's reign in Jerusalem, *Rehoboam . . . forsook the Law of the LORD* (12:1-2). Rehoboam followed the policy of his father Solomon in being "broad-minded" and "tolerant" of other religions. This could be expected of Rehoboam since *his mother . . . was . . . an Ammonitess* (I Kings 14:21).

Although the kingdom of Judah did not forsake the prescribed order of the Temple services, *Judah did evil in the sight of the LORD, and they provoked Him to jealousy. . . . And there were also sodomites* (male cult prostitutes) *in the land: and they did according to all the abominations* (detestable practices) *of the nations which the LORD cast out before the children of Israel* (14:22-24). When Israel first entered the land, God declared: *There shall be no whore of the daughters of Israel, nor a sodomite of the sons of Israel* (Deuteronomy 23:17).

Because of their sin, God withdrew His blessings and protection from Judah. *And it came to pass in the fifth year of king Rehoboam, that Shishak king of Egypt came up against Jerusalem: And he took away the treasures of the House of the LORD, and the treasures of the king's house; he even took away all* (I Kings 14:25-26). The kingdom was not only emptied of all its wealth but now it was under the control of Egypt.

In his later years, Solomon encouraged the worship of false gods and it continued to gain popularity during the reign of his son Rehoboam. Biblical history confirms that once cults and false worship become acceptable in a nation, they are followed by the acceptance of homosexuality and lesbianism.

For the wrath of God is revealed from heaven against all ungodliness and unrighteousness of men, who hold (suppress) *the truth in unrighteousness* (Romans 1:18).

Thought for Today: *Blessed* (Divinely favored) *are the pure in heart* (Matthew 5:8).

Christ Revealed: In Asa's ridding the land of idols and sodomites (I Kings 15:11-14). Christ cleansed the Temple (Matthew 21:12-13; John 2:13-16). As Christians, we are the temples of God, bought with His own blood (I Corinthians 6:19-20; II Corinthians 6:16-17), and are cleansed of all unrighteousness when *we confess our sins* (I John 1:9).

For definitions of unfamiliar words in today's Bible reading, see pages 468-480.

In Today's Reading
Evil kings of Israel; Elijah's pronouncement of drought;
Elijah fed by ravens and the widow; he raises the widow's son;
his contest with prophets of Baal

Ahab promoted Baal worship as a result of his marriage to Jezebel. During his reign, Israelite worshipers of God hid in caves in fear for their lives. Then the prophet Elijah declared to Ahab: *As the LORD God of Israel lives, before Whom I stand, there shall not be dew nor rain these years, but according to my word* (I Kings 17:1). Elijah's faith was in God, Who had said: *Take heed to yourselves, that your heart be not deceived, and you turn aside, and serve other gods, and worship them; And . . . He shut up the heaven, that there be no rain* (Deuteronomy 11:16-17).

After 3½ years of no rain, Elijah again informed the king that Israel's drought was the result of rejecting *the Commandments of the LORD. Now therefore send, and gather to me all Israel to Mount Carmel, and the prophets of Baal four hundred and fifty, and the prophets of the groves four hundred* (I Kings 18:18-19).

Elijah challenged the 850 false prophets to *call on the name of your gods* to consume their sacrifice (18:25). After a full day of Jezebel's prophets frantically praying to no avail, Elijah called the people to *come near to me. . . . And he repaired the altar of the LORD that was broken down* (18:30). Then he prayed: *LORD God . . . let it be known this day that You are God in Israel, and that I am Your servant, and that I have done all these things at Your Word. . . . Then the fire of the LORD fell, and consumed the burned sacrifice, and the wood, and the stones, and the dust. . . . And when all the people saw it, they fell on their faces: and they said, The LORD, He is the God; the LORD, He is the God* (18:36-39).

Elijah then demanded that all false prophets be executed (Deuteronomy 13:1-5). After their execution, *Elijah said to Ahab . . . there is a sound of abundance of rain* (I Kings 18:41; see James 5:17-18).

Elijah illustrates how the power of God is released when we pray and are obedient to His Word. We are to pray *always with . . . all perseverance and supplication for all saints* (Ephesians 6:18).

Thought for Today: Through difficulties, exercise faith in the Lord.

Christ Portrayed: By Elijah, whom God used to provide flour and oil for the needy widow at Zarephath (I Kings 17:13-16). Christ is our Provider, Who supplies all our needs *according to His riches in glory* (Philippians 4:19).

For definitions of unfamiliar words in today's Bible reading, see pages 468-480.

IN TODAY'S READING
Jezebel's threat against Elijah; Elijah's flight; the call of Elisha;
Ahab's death foretold

*A*pparently, Elijah believed that the miraculous fire from heaven and the end of the drought would prove Baal to be a false god, and it would result in Ahab and Jezebel's conversion to the One True God.

Ahab headed toward his palace to tell Jezebel what had happened. Responding immediately, *Jezebel sent a messenger to Elijah, saying, So let the gods do to me, and more also, if I make not your life as the life of one of them by tomorrow about this time. And when he saw that, he arose, and went* (ran) *for his life* (I Kings 19:2-3). Avoiding the ruthless Jezebel was not weakness, but wisdom. However, feeling defeated and discouraged, he prayed: *O LORD, take away my life; for I am not better than my fathers* (19:4).

There is no indication that Elijah contemplated suicide; he believed that God was the Creator and Lord of life and only He had the right to take life. What he meant was: "I'm a failure. I have not achieved my mission, and there seems to be no hope of restoring the nation to worship You as the One True God." However, God lovingly provided for Elijah's physical needs by sending an angel to supply nourishment after his long journey (19:5-6). Often our mountaintop spiritual victories will be quickly followed by opposition or a time of desert testing.

When we stand before the Lord, each person's work shall be judged, not by how spectacular it was but by its true eternal worth. All of us have moments of disappointment when it seems we have failed. Often our estimation of what we should achieve and God's estimation are far apart. We are not called to be successful but to be available and to remain faithful to God (I Corinthians 1:9).

Although he did not know it, Elijah did accomplish what God wanted him to do. One of his great successes was that the leaders in Ahab's kingdom went home with a renewed conviction that *The LORD, He is the God* (I Kings 18:39). Elijah has given encouragement to millions of believers that: *The LORD is near to all them that call upon Him, to all that call upon Him in truth. . . . The LORD preserves all them that love Him: but all the wicked will He destroy* (Psalm 145:18,20).

Thought for Today: God has a purpose for disappointments we face.

Christ Portrayed: By the unnamed prophet who prophesied victory to King Ahab so that he would know his victory was controlled by God: *I am the LORD* **(I Kings 20:13,28).** *Thanks be to God, Who gives us the victory through our Lord Jesus Christ* **(I Corinthians 15:57).**

For definitions of unfamiliar words in today's Bible reading, see pages 468-480.

In Today's Reading

The covetousness of Ahab leads Jezebel to murder Naboth;
death of Ahab and Jezebel foretold

Ahab ruled the northern kingdom of Israel. His capital was the city of Samaria. His life is summed up in just a few words: *But there was none like . . . Ahab, which did sell himself to work wickedness in the sight of the LORD, whom Jezebel his wife stirred up* (incited). *And he did very abominably* (behaved in a very vile, detestable manner) *in following idols* (I Kings 21:25-26).

Ahab invited Jehoshaphat, his daughter's father-in-law who was the king of Judah, to join him in a war to regain Ramoth-gilead, a strategic fortress on the Syrian border. Four hundred of Ahab's paid prophets unanimously assured the two kings of a great victory. But godly Jehoshaphat must have felt uneasy and asked Ahab: *Is there not here a prophet of the LORD besides, that we might inquire of him?* (22:7). Reluctantly, Ahab replied: *There is yet one man, Micaiah . . . by whom we may inquire of the LORD: but I hate him; for he does not prophesy good concerning me, but evil* (22:8).

The messenger who was sent to bring Micaiah from prison *spoke to him, saying, . . . let your word, I pray you, be like the word of one of them, and speak that which is good. And Micaiah said, As the LORD lives, what the LORD says to me, that will I speak* (22:13-14). If Micaiah had cooperated, no doubt he would have immediately gained his freedom. But Micaiah knew that obedience to God was far more important than his freedom, and he courageously proclaimed: *I saw all Israel scattered upon the hills, as sheep that have not a shepherd* (22:17).

Micaiah had bluntly foretold Ahab's death. *And the king of Israel said to Jehoshaphat, Did I not tell you that he would prophesy no good concerning me, but evil?* (22:18). He then ordered Micaiah to be taken back to prison. Proving the obedient prophet correct, Ahab was killed on the first day of battle (22:34,37).

The tragic consequences of Ahab's disregard for the Word of God should be a warning to all who are making the same fatal mistake. In contrast, a follower of Christ can express unlimited peace of mind with the psalmist: *I have set the LORD always before me: because He is at my right hand, I shall not be moved* (Psalm 16:8).

Thought for Today: All who do God's will will receive eternal rewards.

Christ Portrayed: By Micaiah, who would say only what God instructed him to say (I Kings 22:14). Jesus faithfully told others everything God told Him to say. *Then said Jesus to them . . . I do nothing of Myself; but as My Father has taught Me, I speak these things* (John 8:28; 12:49-50).

For definitions of unfamiliar words in today's Bible reading, see pages 468-480.

In Today's Reading

Death of Ahaziah King of Israel; Elijah taken up by a whirlwind;
Elisha purifies Jericho's water; Elisha mocked by the children

Ten years before Elijah's departure in a "chariot of fire," the LORD said to him: *You shall . . . anoint Jehu to be king over Israel: and Elisha . . . you shall anoint to be prophet in your room* (place). *. . . So he departed from there, and found Elisha . . . who was plowing with twelve yoke of oxen before him, and he with the twelfth . . . Elijah passed by him, and cast his mantle upon him* (I Kings 19:16,19), designating Elisha to replace him. At the time Elijah called Elisha to join him, it appears that Elisha was a prosperous young farmer. To accept Elijah's calling to be his servant would mean that Elisha would have to forsake his family and friends as well as financial securities. His friends probably thought that to be the servant of a prophet would be a lonely, menial occupation. But, Elisha knew the true values of life and immediately converted his plows into firewood and *took a yoke of oxen, and slew them, and boiled their flesh with the instruments* (implements) *of the oxen, and gave to the people, and they did eat. Then he arose, and went after Elijah, and ministered to him* (19:21). Elisha's actions demonstrate that the key to one's usefulness in the Kingdom of God is to immediately respond to our opportunities to serve the Lord, regardless of how great or how insignificant the task may appear.

Just prior to Elijah's translation into heaven, Elisha again revealed his spiritual discernment and loyalty to God, which qualified him to be Elijah's successor. *Elijah said to Elisha, Tarry here . . . for the LORD has sent me to Bethel. And Elisha said to him, As the LORD lives . . . I will not leave you. So they went down to Bethel* (II Kings 2:2). Elisha was determined to continue with Elijah on his journey from Gilgal to Bethel, on to Jericho, and then across the Jordan River (2:3-8).

Like Elisha, circumstances have placed each of us where we are today to determine the sincerity of our commitment to the Lord. *Therefore, my beloved brethren, be . . . steadfast, unmovable, always abounding in the work of the Lord, forasmuch as you know that your labor is not in vain in the Lord* (I Corinthians 15:58).

Thought for Today: The Lord is present in every circumstance. *My grace is sufficient. . . . Therefore I take pleasure* (comfort) *in infirmities* (II Corinthians 12:9-10).

Christ Revealed: In the taking up of Elijah in the whirlwind and the dropping of the mantle – a symbol of the presence of God and power that remains with His faithful servants (II Kings 2:8-15). This is a type of the ascension of the Lord Jesus Christ and the sending of the Holy Spirit to indwell the believers, giving us power to evangelize the world. *He was parted from them, and carried up into heaven* (Luke 24:51-53; also Acts 1 – 2).

For definitions of unfamiliar words in today's Bible reading, see pages 468-480.

*I*N *T*ODAY'S *R*EADING

Widow's oil; Elisha and the Shunammite woman; Elisha's miracles;
Elisha feeds 100 men; Naaman cured of leprosy; Gehazi's leprosy

*D*esperate to be healed of his leprosy, Naaman appeared before King Jehoram in Israel with *ten talents of silver, and six thousand pieces of gold, and ten changes of raiment. And . . . the letter* (from King Ben-hadad of Syria that read) . . . *I have therewith sent Naaman my servant to you, that you may recover him of his leprosy* (II Kings 5:2-6). Jehoram had no faith in God and thought that King Ben-hadad was seeking an excuse to declare war. *And it was so, when Elisha the man of God had heard . . . that he sent to the king, saying. . . . let him now come to me, and he shall know that there is a prophet in Israel* (5:8). When Naaman obeyed the words of the prophet, he was miraculously healed. Elisha refused the huge reward that Naaman offered him. But his greedy servant Gehazi persuaded himself that God had blessed him with the opportunity to be wealthy. He probably did not think it was much of a sin to gain wealth that he didn't deserve from someone who was ungodly and didn't need it.

When Naaman saw him running after him, he . . . said, Is all well? (5:21). Gehazi then told him this lie: *My master has sent me, saying . . . there be come to me . . . two young men of the sons of the prophets: give them, I pray you, a talent of silver, and two changes of garments* (5:22). The schemer thought he could rush back before Elisha discovered he was missing. After Gehazi's return, Elisha said: Where were you, Gehazi? *Your servant went no where. And he said to him . . . Is it a time to receive money, and to receive garments, and oliveyards, and vineyards, and sheep, and oxen, and menservants, and maidservants? The leprosy therefore of Naaman shall cling to you, and to your seed for ever. And he went out from his presence a leper as white as snow* (5:25-26).

Gehazi forfeited his opportunity to be the next honored prophet of God. Instead, he became a leper! When Gehazi was tested, he exposed his true character as a covetous hypocrite.

Ask yourself the question Elisha asked Gehazi: *Is it a time to receive money?* – meaning: "What is your goal in life?" How will you respond to Christ, Who said: *Seek you first the Kingdom of God?* (Matthew 6:33).

Thought for Today: Remain faithful in your trials, God has His purposes.

Christ Revealed: By the meal that took the poison out of the pot (II Kings 4:40-41). Meal, made of crushed corn, speaks of Christ, Who *was wounded for our transgressions, He was bruised* (crushed) *for our iniquities* (Isaiah 53:5) thereby removing the poison of our sin.

For definitions of unfamiliar words in today's Bible reading, see pages 468-480.

In Today's Reading

The ax head made to float; Syrians (Arameans) attack Israel;
famine in Samaria; Elisha's prophecy fulfilled

Ben-hadad, the king of Syria, could not have "forgotten" that, when the Syrian (Aramean) soldiers had attempted to capture the prophet Elisha, they had been miraculously blinded and were then led by Elisha inside the walls of the capital city of Samaria. The soldiers then were trapped and at the mercy of the king of Israel. However, at Elisha's command, the king *prepared great provision* (a great feast) *for them: and when they had eaten and drunk, he sent them away, and they went to their master. So the bands of Syria came no more into the land of Israel. And it came to pass after this, that Ben-hadad king of Syria gathered all his host, and went up, and besieged Samaria* (II Kings 6:23-25).

The once-powerful, luxurious, fortress-city of Samaria was faced with all the horrors of an extended famine. To surrender to Syria meant death for King Jehoram (Joram) and slavery for his people. But, remaining within the walls eventually reduced the people to starvation, some even resorted to cannibalism. These appalling conditions were the result of Israel's disobedience as God had forewarned (Leviticus 26:14-29).

When it appeared there was no hope, the Lord again brought Jehoram face to face with Elisha, who proclaimed: *Hear . . . the Word of the LORD . . . Tomorrow about this time shall a measure of fine flour be sold for a shekel, and two measures of barley for a shekel, in the gate of Samaria* (II Kings 7:1). One of the king's officials ridiculed him, saying: *Behold, if the LORD would make windows in heaven, might this thing be?* Elisha replied: *Behold, you shall see it with your eyes, but shall not eat thereof* (7:2).

The prophecy was miraculously fulfilled when God, in His great mercy, sent fear into the hearts of the Syrian army and they hurriedly abandoned their camp leaving their food in abundance for the Israelites. The king's official was trampled to death in the rush for food (7:17).

Obedient Christians need not fear for tomorrow! Instead, we can rejoice in the promises of God, Who *shall supply all your need according to His riches in glory by Christ Jesus* (Philippians 4:19).

Thought for Today: The answers to our prayers are sometimes postponed because God has a better plan.

Christ Portrayed: By Elisha, who wept when he realized what Hazael would do to Israel and its people (II Kings 8:11-12). We are reminded of Jesus as He wept over Jerusalem. *O Jerusalem, Jerusalem . . . how often would I have gathered your children together . . . and you would not!* (Matthew 23:37-38).

For definitions of unfamiliar words in today's Bible reading, see pages 468-480.

In Today's Reading
Jehu anointed king of Israel; Jehu kills Joram and Ahaziah;
Jezebel killed; Ahab's family killed; Baal worshipers executed

*A*fter Ahab's death, his son Ahaziah reigned over Israel for two years, followed by the 12-year reign of another son, Jehoram (also known as Joram). These two kings zealously promoted Baal worship, which had been initiated by their wicked mother Jezebel. Baal worship had also become popular in the southern kingdom of Judah due to its king, who was also named Jehoram. The southern king had married Jezebel's daughter Athaliah, and their son, also named Ahaziah, was equally wicked.

During this time of spiritual decline, the Lord was preparing Jehu, the military commander of the armies of the northern kingdom, as His instrument of judgment. God had earlier revealed to Elijah that Jehu would become king of Israel (I Kings 19:16). Perhaps 20 years passed before the Lord directed Elisha to send a young prophet east of the Jordan River to Ramoth-gilead, where Jehu was stationed with his army. The prophet anointed Jehu as king of Israel and the God-appointed executioner of Israel's evil King Jehoram and all the descendants of Ahab.

Jehu drove his chariots furiously to Jezreel where he executed Joram (Jehoram), king of Israel, and then Ahaziah, king of Judah. Then Jehu had Jezebel thrown out of a window and he trampled her with his horse. And, as foretold by Elijah, the dogs ate her body (II Kings 9:33-37).

Jehu zealously executed all the family of Ahab in Samaria (I Kings 21:17-24). However, Athaliah, the daughter of Jezebel, continued to promote Baal worship as queen in Judah. Jehu had bragged to Jehonadab: *Come with me, and see my zeal for the LORD* (II Kings 10:16). But Jehu's *zeal for the LORD* was just enough to achieve his own selfish ends. *Jehu took no heed to walk in the Law of the LORD God of Israel with all his heart: for he departed not from the sins of Jeroboam, which made Israel to sin* (10:31-32). This illustrates that it is possible for one to be used by God and yet never be in submission to Christ as Lord of one's life. Hypocrites serve the Lord for their own self-interests. *This is the will of God . . . That every one of you should know how to possess his vessel* (control his body) *in sanctification and honor. . . . For God has not called us to uncleanness, but to holiness* (I Thessalonians 4:3-4,7).

Thought for Today: God may cut short a life that is disobedient to Him.

Christ Portrayed: By Elisha who sent one of the sons of the prophets with oil to anoint Jehu (II Kings 9:1-6). Oil symbolizes the Holy Spirit, and the Lord sent the Holy Spirit to anoint believers (John 14:16-17; 16:13; Acts 1:8; compare I Samuel 16:13). *The anointing which you have received of Him abides* (lives) *in you* (I John 2:27).

For definitions of unfamiliar words in today's Bible reading, see pages 468-480.

IN TODAY'S READING
Athaliah reigns; David's descendants murdered;
Joash crowned king; he repairs the Temple;
worship restored; evil reign of Jehoahaz

When Athaliah, daughter of Ahab and Jezebel, received word that her son, King Ahaziah, was dead, she seized the throne of Judah and proclaimed herself queen. To make sure she had no competition, she ruthlessly murdered her own grandsons. She thought she had killed all of David's descendants (II Kings 11:1; II Chronicles 22:10).

However, God intervened and saved the one-year-old Joash (Jehoash), the sole link that preserved the dynasty of David and the lineage of Jesus Christ (II Kings 11:2-3; II Chronicles 22:11-12). *And He was with her hidden in the House of the LORD six years. And Athaliah did reign over the land* (II Kings 11:3).

Joash remained in the protective care of Jehoiada the high priest. When Joash was about seven years old, Jehoiada *brought forth the king's son, and put the crown upon him, and gave him the testimony; and they made him king, and anointed him; and they clapped their hands, and said, God save* (long live) *the king* (11:12). The excited shouts caught the attention of Athaliah, who ran into the Temple court just in time to hear Jehoiada the high priest command the captains of the guard to execute her. *And Jehoiada made a covenant between the LORD and the king and the people, that they should be the LORD's people* (11:17-18).

And Jehoash did that which was right in the sight of the LORD all his days wherein Jehoiada the priest instructed him (12:2; II Chronicles 24:2). *Now after the death of Jehoiada came the princes of Judah, and made obeisance* (bowed down) *to the king. Then the king hearkened* (listened) *to them. And they left the House of the LORD God of their fathers, and served . . . idols: and wrath came upon Judah and Jerusalem for this their trespass. Yet He sent prophets to them . . . but they would not give ear. . . . And . . . his own servants conspired against him . . . and slew him* (24:17-18,20,25; also II Kings 12:20). The account of Joash illustrates that to forsake the Word of God results in untold miseries, *and with all deceivableness* (deception) *of unrighteousness in them that perish; because they received not the love of the truth, that they might be saved* (II Thessalonians 2:10).

Thought for Today: What a privilege to trust God for guidance!

Christ Portrayed: By Jehoiada, who protected Joash and, in holy judgment, had Athaliah slain (II Kings 11:4-16). Christ keeps us safe to fulfill His will and will return to judge all who *obey not the Gospel of our Lord Jesus Christ* (II Thessalonians 1:8).

For definitions of unfamiliar words in today's Bible reading, see pages 468-480.

Following the death of his father Jehoash, Jeroboam II ruled the northern kingdom of Israel in Samaria for 41 years (II Kings 14:16-29). However, *he did that which was evil in the sight of the LORD: he departed not from all the sins of Jeroboam the son of Nebat, who made Israel to sin* (14:24). Immorality and idolatry flourished during the reign of Jeroboam II. Finally, God commanded the prophet Amos, from the southern kingdom of Judah, to go to Bethel and prophesy the destruction of Jeroboam's kingdom (Amos 7:9). Both Hosea and Amos spoke out against sweeping religious and moral decay during Jeroboam's reign (Hosea 6:4-10; 10:1-15; Amos 2:6-8; 3:13 – 5:27). For about 30 years the nation enjoyed peace, prosperity, and political prestige unparalleled since the days of David and Solomon. Jeroboam *restored the coast* (boundaries) *of Israel from the entering of Hamath to the sea of the plain, according to the Word of the LORD God of Israel, which He spoke by the hand of His servant Jonah, the son of Amittai, the prophet* (II Kings 14:25).

Sadly, Israel's prosperity did not cause the people to worship the Lord. It appears that they attributed their prosperity to idols. Thus, immorality and violence continued to permeate the nation (17:13-17).

After Jeroboam's death, anarchy prevailed and Israel rapidly degenerated. Jeroboam was succeeded by his son Zechariah (14:29) who reigned only six months (15:8).This was the fourth and last generation of the house of Jehu (15:12).

About 30 years after Jeroboam's death, the words of the prophets were fulfilled. The northern kingdom was destroyed and its people taken captive by the Assyrians (17:1-18). Material success is often deceptive, as it was for King Jeroboam II. We cannot measure men's character by the length of their lives, nor by their material prosperity for only God *knows the secrets of the heart* (Psalm 44:21).

Surely the goodness of God should lead us, in gratitude, to do the will of Jesus Christ our Lord. He (the Father) *has delivered us from the power of darkness, and has translated us into the kingdom of His dear Son* (Colossians 1:13).

Thought for Today: We forfeit His best when we fail to keep and obey His Word.

Christ Revealed: When the Lord struck King Azariah with leprosy and thrust him out from being king (II Kings 15:5-7). This foreshadows the time when all who ignore the merciful gift of salvation shall be *cast into the lake of fire* (Revelation 20:15).

For definitions of unfamiliar words in today's Bible reading, see pages 468-480.

IN TODAY'S READING

Ahaz reigns in Judah, defiles the Temple; Hoshea reigns in Israel;
fall of Samaria; captivity and deportations of Israel

Fearing the growing power of Assyria, Pekah, king of Israel, made an alliance with Rezin, king of Syria (Aram) (II Kings 15:37). Together, they attempted to force Ahaz, king of Judah, to join them. When Ahaz refused, Aram's King Rezin and Israel's King Pekah came up to wage war against Jerusalem. *They besieged Ahaz, but could not overcome him* (16:5). In retaliation, Ahaz made an alliance with Tiglath-pileser, king of Assyria, to attack Syria and Israel. This cost Ahaz all *the silver and gold that was found in the House of the LORD, and in the treasures of the king's house . . .* (which he) *sent . . .* as *a present* (required payment) *to the king of Assyria* (16:8). The king of the Assyrian Empire conquered the small kingdom of Syria and killed Rezin, its king (16:9). Tiglath-pileser also defeated the tribes of Reuben and Gad and the half-tribe of Manasseh on the eastern side of the Jordan. He then took control of the northern part of the Jordan Valley, making Galilee and Gilead into Assyrian provinces (15:29; compare Isaiah 9:1). All that was left of the ten-tribe northern kingdom of Israel was the capital city of Samaria and the surrounding hill country of Ephraim.

The captivity and dispersion of the northern kingdom throughout Assyria took place because the Israelites *served idols, whereof the LORD had said to them, You shall not do this thing. Yet the LORD testified against Israel, and against Judah, by all the prophets, and by all the seers, saying, Turn . . . from your evil ways, and keep My Commandments and My statutes, according to all the Law which I commanded your fathers, and which I sent to you by My servants the prophets. Notwithstanding they would not hear* (II Kings 17:12-14; 15-23).

They lived as if God did not exist. We must remember, whoever or whatever receives our loyalty becomes our idol, be it a person, purpose, or possession.

Jesus said: *Strait is the gate, and narrow is the way, which leads to life, and few there be that find it* (Matthew 7:14).

Thought for Today: Compromise is a characteristic of the doubleminded person.

Christ Revealed: Through the Brazen (bronze) Altar made by Solomon (II Kings 16:14; II Chronicles 4:1). The Brazen Altar is a type of the cross on which Christ, our whole burnt offering, offered Himself to God (Hebrews 9:14). Unlike the necessary daily sacrifices on the Brazen Altar, on the cross, *this He did once* (once for all), *when He offered up Himself* (Hebrews 7:27).

For definitions of unfamiliar words in today's Bible reading, see pages 468-480.

In Today's Reading
Hezekiah's reign; Assyria invades Judah; Hezekiah and
Isaiah pray; Hezekiah's miraculous healing

Hezekiah the son of Ahaz king of Judah began to reign. Twenty and five years old was he when he began to reign; and he reigned twenty and nine years in Jerusalem. . . . And he did what was right in the sight of the LORD, according to all that David his father did (II Kings 18:1-3). When Hezekiah became king, he did not follow the ways of his evil father Ahaz; instead, he believed the prophets of God, including the unpopular Micah. Hezekiah not only benefited from the ministry of Micah, but he also gained spiritual encouragement from the prophet Isaiah. *He removed the high places, and broke the images* (sacred pillars), *and cut down the groves* (Asherah idols). . . . *He trusted in the LORD God of Israel; so that after him was none like him among all the kings of Judah, nor any that were before him. For he clung to the LORD, and departed not from following Him, but kept His Commandments, which the LORD commanded Moses* (18:4-6).

Hezekiah led the nation to keep the Passover and renew its covenant with the Lord. *So there was great joy in Jerusalem* (II Chronicles 30:26-27). Hezekiah's spiritual reformation was followed by a radical reorganization of the entire administration of both the secular and religious affairs of the kingdom. We learn from Hezekiah that people will be blessed, and prayers will be answered, when the Word of God is obeyed.

The greatest opposition to Isaiah, Micah, and Hezekiah's reformation did not come from the pagan nations around Judah, but from the false prophets within their own country, as well as those who worshiped the idols which had been introduced earlier by King Solomon.

Some popular religious leaders today seem to do nothing to encourage people to forsake their sins, live godly lives, and read the Bible. Instead, they preach what appeals to man's physical desires. Others cry out: "Cooperate with the majority, compromise, be tolerant, avoid the extreme right, keep up with the times, don't offend anyone but let everyone believe what he wishes." Still, there are always the faithful few who desire to *be blameless and harmless, the sons of God, without rebuke, in the midst of a crooked and perverse nation* (Philippians 2:15-16).

Thought for Today: It is not enough merely walking through life; we must be on the narrow road that leads to heaven.

Christ Portrayed: By Hezekiah, who was faithful in leading the kingdom of Judah back to the Word of God (II Kings 19) – a reminder of Jesus' words to the Pharisees in His attempt to awaken their need to see themselves as sinners and recognize Him as their Savior (Mark 2:17).

For definitions of unfamiliar words in today's Bible reading, see pages 468-480.

IN TODAY'S READING
Evil reigns of Manasseh and Amon; Josiah's good reign; book of
the Law discovered; true worship restored; idolatry destroyed

*H*ezekiah was one of the best kings in the history of Judah; but his
son Manasseh was even more wicked than Hezekiah's grandfather
Ahaz, who had closed the Temple (II Chronicles 28:24). Manasseh *did
that which was evil in the sight of the LORD, after the abominations* (detestable practices) *of the heathen. . . . And he built altars for all the host of
heaven in the two courts of the House of the LORD. And he made his son pass
through the fire* (thrown into a raging fire to the Canaanite god Molech).
. . . he wrought (did) *much wickedness in the sight of the LORD, to provoke
Him to anger* (II Kings 21:2-6).

Manasseh's wickedness resulted in his being defeated by the fierce
Assyrians. *The captains of the host . . . took Manasseh among the thorns*
(with hooks), *and bound him with fetters, and carried him to Babylon. And
when he was in affliction* (misery, suffering), *he besought the LORD his
God, and humbled himself greatly before . . . God . . . And prayed to Him:
and He was entreated of him* (moved by his plea) *. . . and brought him again
to Jerusalem into his kingdom. Then Manasseh knew that the LORD He was
God* (II Chronicles 33:10-13). The Lord permitted him to return to
Jerusalem and be reinstated as king. This was an answer to Manasseh's
prayers for mercy and forgiveness, as well as to the prayers of his godly
father Hezekiah many years before. God forgives even the most evil of
sinners when they truly repent and pray for forgiveness. Upon being
restored as king, Manasseh immediately destroyed the false gods and
altars he had previously built and rebuilt the altar and returned to true
worship of the Lord.

But Manasseh could not relive the wasted years of his wicked rule
or even convince his own son to reject idols and worship the Lord. After
Manasseh's death, his son Amon reinstated all the wicked, idolatrous
practices of his father's earlier reign (II Chronicles 33:22). *And he . . .
served the idols . . . and worshiped them* (II Kings 21:21). This points out
the irreversible law of nature: *Be not deceived . . . whatsover a man sows,
that shall he also reap. For he that sows to his flesh shall of the flesh reap
corruption* (destruction); *but he that sows to the Spirit shall of the Spirit
reap life everlasting* (Galatians 6:7-8).

Thought for Today: The measure of a person's surrender determines his usefulness to God.

Christ Portrayed: By the prophets (II Kings 21:10). *God, Who . . . spoke in time past
to the fathers by the prophets, Has in these last days spoken to us by His Son*
(Hebrews 1:1-2).

For definitions of unfamiliar words in today's Bible reading, see pages 468-480.

> ## *In Today's Reading*
> Passover restored; destruction of Jerusalem and Temple foretold;
> death of Josiah; fall of Jerusalem; captivity of Judah

*J*osiah was the last godly king of Judah before the destruction of Jerusalem, *and he did what was right in the sight of the LORD* (II Kings 22:2; II Chronicles 34:2). He destroyed all the idolatrous practices in Jerusalem and Judah. *And the king went up into the House of the LORD . . . and he read . . . all the words of the Book of the Covenant which was found in the House of the LORD. And the king . . . made a covenant . . . to walk after the LORD, and to keep His Commandments. . . . And he broke down the houses of the sodomites* (male cult prostitutes) (II Kings 23:2-3,7).

Josiah went beyond Judah, into the Assyrian-controlled former northern kingdom to Bethel, where Jeroboam had built one of the golden calves. *And he broke in pieces the images, and cut down the groves* (Asherah idols). *. . . Josiah . . . sent, and took the bones out of the sepulchres* (tombs), *and burned them upon the altar . . . according to the Word of the LORD* prophesied almost 300 years before (23:14-16; I Kings 13:1-3).

And the king commanded . . . Keep the Passover to the LORD your God, as it is written in the Book of this Covenant. . . . Moreover the workers with familiar spirits (mediums), *and the wizards* (spiritists), *and the images, and the idols, and all the abominations* (detestable things) *that were spied in the land of Judah and in Jerusalem, did Josiah put away, that he might perform the words of the Law . . . found in the House of the LORD* (II Kings 23:21,24).

The last four kings who followed Josiah were all evil, puppet rulers, appointed by and subject first to Egypt and then to Babylon.

Finally, Nebuchadnezzar marched his army into Judah and destroyed Jerusalem.

The destruction of the once-glorious kingdom of Judah and Solomon's Temple reminds us that even the greatest present-day nation on earth, with all its wealth, military might, and nuclear defense, cannot survive – regardless of how much the people may pray – if they continue to ignore the Word of God (23:25-27). *He that turns away his ear from hearing the Law, even his prayer shall be abomination* (Proverbs 28:9).

Thought for Today: A nation is successful when it is faithful to the Word of God.

Christ Revealed: Through the Passover (II Kings 23:21-23), which was a type foreshadowing how Jesus Christ, our Redeemer will keep us from spiritual death. *I am He that lives, and was dead; and, behold, I am alive for evermore, Amen; and have the keys of hell* (the grave) *and of death* (Revelation 1:18).

For definitions of unfamiliar words in today's Bible reading, see pages 468-480.

Introduction To The Books Of
I & II Chronicles

The Books of II Samuel and I & II Kings cover about the same period in history as I & II Chronicles. The Books of Kings primarily focus on the political history of Israel and Judah, while the Chronicles primarily present the religious history of Judah, Jerusalem, and the Temple as it relates to the Davidic Covenant. The northern tribes are of little significance in Chronicles. At this time in their history few were alive when Nebuchadnezzar destroyed their kingdoms. With no central place of worship and their long captivity, only a few could have been familiar with the Word of God and how to worship Him.

I Chronicles opens with the longest genealogical history in the Bible and covers about 4000 years (chapters 1 – 9). Its second chapter is devoted to the descendants of Judah because the promised Messiah would descend from this tribe (Genesis 49:8-12). The record begins with Adam (I Chronicles 1:1); then to Abraham, Isaac, and Jacob; then Judah; and on to David, through whom the Messiah would come. These families are the vital links connecting the legal genealogy of Christ through Joseph, who was His legal, but not His biological, father (Matthew 1:1-17; II Samuel 7:12-13; Psalms 89:3-4; 132:11; Isaiah 11:1; Jeremiah 23:5). The rightful Heir to the throne of David is the Messiah Jesus, Who was born through the virgin Mary, as recorded in Luke 2:7,11; 3:23-38. The Messianic lineage passed from David to Nathan, Solomon's brother (II Samuel 5:14; I Chronicles 3:5; 14:4; Luke 3:31). The line of Solomon was eliminated (Jeremiah 22:22-30). While Abraham and David were ancestors of both Joseph and Mary, the royal Davidic lineage of Jesus as the Messiah is traced to Joseph in Matthew and the actual human bloodline is traced through Mary in Luke.

Saul's last battle and death are mentioned in chapter ten of I Chronicles. Chapters 11 – 29 cover the 40-year reign of David.

II Chronicles continues with the reign of Solomon. It records the division of the kingdom and covers the history of Judah until the exile of the people to Babylon. The last verses contain the proclamation of the Persian King Cyrus for their return to Jerusalem, according to the prophecy of Jeremiah (II Chronicles 36:22-23; Jeremiah 29:10-14).

The first seven chapters of II Chronicles record the building of the Temple on Mount Moriah in Jerusalem after the pattern of the Tabernacle. The Temple was completed and dedicated to God in the 11th year of Solomon's reign (chapter 5; compare I Kings 6:38). II Chronicles ends with the fall of Jerusalem and the destruction of Solomon's Temple in 586 B.C. (chapters 10 – 36).

In Today's Reading
Jesus' lineage through Adam, Noah, Abraham,
Israel (Jacob), and Judah

The first nine chapters of I Chronicles may first appear to be an unimportant list of names. But, this ancient genealogy reveals the exact plan and choices of our Creator in selecting the people whom He qualified to serve Him, beginning with *Adam, Sheth . . . Noah. . . . Abraham; Isaac. . . . Henoch. . . . and Israel* (I Chronicles 1:1,4,28,33-34; compare Genesis 5:1-32). Here Jacob is called by his God-given name *Israel* (compare 35:9-12).

This genealogy was exceedingly important after the Israelites' captivity. It showed how God continued to protect the family line of the coming Messiah, Whose descent was traced from Adam through Abraham and David. In Luke 3:23-38, we see the genealogy of the last Adam, Jesus Christ (I Corinthians 15:22,45), traced through the very names recorded in Chronicles. Unless a man's name had been included in the genealogy of Levi, he could not minister in the Temple.

Our Lord is now drawing to Himself *a holy nation, a peculiar* (God's own) *people* (I Peter 2:9), united not by a human genealogical bloodline that dates back to Adam, but united by a spiritual rebirth into the family of God through the blood of the last Adam, Jesus Christ.

Christ is Lord of our lives and oversees every detail. You can be sure that things that happen to believers are never "accidents"; they are allowed by our Lord, the Master Engineer, to prepare us to be the person He can use to accomplish the purpose for which He created us. As we prayerfully read all His Word, He continually reveals His will to us. Although we do not understand many of the things that God allows a Christian to suffer, His Word makes it clear that He has an eternal purpose for them and our new life in Christ is the beginning of life eternal.

This recorded genealogy is a reminder that soon the final books in heaven will be opened. Jesus promised: *He that overcomes, the same shall be clothed in white raiment* (clothing); *and I will not blot out his name out of the Book of Life, but I will confess his name before My Father, and before His angels* (Revelation 3:5).

Thought for Today: There are no "accidents" with God's children. He is in charge.

Christ Revealed: By the first Adam (I Chronicles 1:1). Christ is the last Adam. We have eternal life because *the last Adam was made a living* (life-giving) *Spirit* (I Corinthians 15:45,47).

For definitions of unfamiliar words in today's Bible reading, see pages 468-480.

In Today's Reading
Descendants of David, Solomon, Judah, Simeon, Reuben,
Gad and Manasseh

God compares the small tribe of Simeon that chose to live in the promised land to the much larger tribe of Reuben that chose not to settle in the promised land. *Of the sons of Simeon, five hundred men, went to Mount Seir. . . . And they smote* (destroyed) *the rest of the Amalekites that were escaped, and dwelled there to this day* (I Chronicles 4:42-43). What a contrast this is to the more powerful *sons of Reuben. . . . They transgressed against the God of their fathers, and went a whoring* (played the harlot) *after the gods of the people of the land, whom God destroyed before them. And the God of Israel stirred up the . . . king of Assyria , and he carried them away, even the Reubenites . . . and brought them to Halah . . . and to the river Gozan, to this day* (5:1,25-26).

The Reubenites chose to live in the fertile lands outside the promised land on the eastern side of the Jordan River, even though it was far from the Tabernacle, which was the only place where God had chosen for people to worship Him (Numbers 32). They chose what they believed would bring them greater material success rather than spiritual blessings, direction and protection.

Jacob's prophecy regarding Reuben truly came to pass. By birthright, the descendants of the firstborn son should have had preeminence over all the other tribes. But Jacob had prophesied: *Reuben, you are . . . the excellency of power: Unstable as water, you shall not excel, because you went up to your father's bed; then you defiled it* (Genesis 49:3-4). Water is a good illustration, because it naturally flows to the lowest possible level. Water is also unstable in that it can be driven by the winds as well as evaporate with the heat. The Reubenites are an example of some today who become so involved in the things of the world that little time is left for serving the Lord and for reading His Word. They too consider the plan of God for their lives less important than satisfying personal ambitions and pleasures. We need not fear that we are not talented enough, strong enough, or good enough. Everything God wants us to be or to do He makes possible. *O LORD, I know that the way of man is not in himself: it is not in man that walks to direct his steps* (Jeremiah 10:23).

Thought for Today: Those who commit their all to God receive His best.

Christ Revealed: Through the genealogy of David (I Chronicles 3:1-24). Christ the Son of God was also called the Son of David. *The book of the generation of Jesus Christ, the Son of David* (Matthew 1:1; Luke 3:23-38; Romans 1:3).

For definitions of unfamiliar words in today's Bible reading, see pages 468-480.

In Today's Reading

Descendants of Levi; Temple singers and keepers appointed;
descendants of Aaron; cities of the Levites; numerous genealogies

The long and seemingly uninteresting genealogy in these chapters reveals that God does not look on mankind as just a multitude of human beings who populate the earth. The name of every individual priest and Levite, along with the family and tribe he belonged to, was carefully registered. In gratitude for their spiritual leadership, the other tribes were given the responsibility of sustaining the Levites who lived within their communities through their tithes and offerings. We see a striking contrast in the character of the men mentioned in these chapters.

Of first consideration in this listing was the high priest, who was chosen only from the family of Aaron (I Chronicles 6:3). Aaron, Eleazar, and Ithamar were devoted to their calling as priests, but Aaron's two oldest sons Nadab and Abihu were struck dead when they ignored the Commandments of God. Samuel was a godly judge, but *the sons of Samuel; the firstborn Vashni, and Abiah* (6:28) were evil.

The Israelites knew that they had returned to holy ground. God had said *the land is Mine* (Leviticus 25:23). But it was equally important for the Israelites to recognize that they were a *peculiar people* (Deuteronomy 14:2; 26:18; Titus 2:14; I Peter 2:9) – this means a special, privileged people who belonged to God. And these facts remind us that we too belong to the Lord, as well as all that we possess. *You are not your own. For you are bought with a price: therefore glorify God in your body, and in your spirit, which are God's* (I Corinthians 6:19-20).

Consequently, there must be a practical expression in every aspect of our life, of the allocation of our time, talent and tithes– for maintaining His work in spreading His Word. Where these aspects of one's daily life are ignored, then it is meaningless to say that we belong to God and are looking forward to hear Him say: *Well done, good and faithful servant; you have been faithful over a few things, I will make you ruler over many things: enter . . . into the joy of your lord* (Matthew 25:23).

Thought for Today: Your name is recorded in the Book of Life when you receive Christ as your Savior.

Christ Revealed: By the cities of refuge (I Chronicles 6:57,67,69). For a person to have protection from the avenger of blood, he had to flee to a city of refuge. God provided His only begotten Son Jesus Christ to be our Refuge from His judgment against sin. (Compare John 3:14-18; 10:24-30; Galatians 2:16; 3:1-14; Hebrews 10:1-18; I John 2:2; Revelation 1:5.) When, by faith, in obedience to His Word, we come to Christ, He becomes our Refuge (Hebrews 6:18).

For definitions of unfamiliar words in today's Bible reading, see pages 468-480.

In Today's Reading

Descendants of Benjamin; priests and Levites in Jerusalem
and their responsibilities; genealogy of Saul;
tragic deaths of Saul and his sons

*O*nly a small minority of Israelites were willing to leave the comforts of the new Persian kingdom and return to Jerusalem to rebuild the Temple.

Now the first inhabitants that dwelled in their possessions in their cities were, the Israelites, the priests, Levites, and the Nethinims (the Temple servants) (I Chronicles 9:2-3; Nehemiah 11:3). The work of *the Nethinims* may seem rather insignificant, but it was essential work that needed to be done for the Lord. Loyalty to their heavenly King made them willing to work and to serve wherever needed. Of the Levites, *certain of them had the charge of the ministering vessels, that they should bring them in and out by tale* (count) (I Chronicles 9:28). This responsibility appears to be of little importance. Some overseers *were appointed to oversee the vessels, and all the instruments* (utensils) *of the sanctuary, and the fine flour, and the wine, and the oil, and the frankincense, and the spices* (9:29-30), which perhaps required a little more skill; still others were responsible for *things that were made in the pans* (9:31). All were ordinary laborers and, to us, may seem hardly worth mentioning. But God esteemed each responsibility as indispensable and worthy of recording and, collectively, all tasks were necessary to fulfill the service to the Lord in the Tabernacle.

Now there are diversities of gifts, but the same Spirit. . . . But all these works that one and selfsame Spirit, dividing (distributing) *to every man severally* (individually) *as He will*, and not necessarily as we prefer (I Corinthians 12:4,11). Regardless of the seeming importance or insignificance of our abilities, they are a sacred trust from God. The Lord does not expect the person who is given one talent to fulfill the responsibility of the person who has five talents (Matthew 25:24-28). But, though his talents may be minimal, everyone can do something. Paul reminded Titus that *many profess that they know God; but in works they deny Him, being . . . disobedient* (Titus 1:16).

We are required to be faithful stewards (managers) of our lives and the abilities and opportunities that God has entrusted to us. *Whatsoever you do, do it heartily, as to the Lord, and not to men* (Colossians 3:23).

Thought for Today: Faith becomes stronger as we read and obey God's Word.

Christ Revealed: By Jerusalem, which means "foundation of peace" (I Chronicles 9:3). Christ is the only foundation of peace upon which man can stand before God. Jesus said: *My peace I give to you* (John 14:27; II Corinthians 5:18; Ephesians 2:14).

For definitions of unfamiliar words in today's Bible reading, see pages 468-480.

𝒥N 𝒯ODAY'S 𝑅EADING
David made king over Judah; Israel anoints David king;
He reigns in Jebus (Jerusalem)

𝒟avid did not see any possibility that he could ever be king of Israel when Saul, the first anointed king of Israel, with all his authority and other resources, was determined to kill him. Saul was also far from being an old man, and he had sons who were the expected heirs to the throne. Moreover, how could David expect that the large and jealous tribe of Ephraim would agree that David, from the tribe of Judah, should rule over them? How would Saul's tribe, the Benjamites, permit the monarchy to be taken from them? David suffered under very difficult circumstances until it seemed he again had to flee to the land of the Philistines. But then, Saul died a violent death, and eventually the leaders of *all Israel gathered themselves to David to Hebron, saying, Behold, we are your bone and your flesh. And moreover in time past . . . the LORD your God said to you, You shall feed My people Israel, and you shall be ruler over My people Israel. . . . and they anointed* (consecrated) *David king over Israel, according to the Word of the LORD by Samuel* (I Chronicles 11:1-3).

In many respects, David's problems parallel situations that some of us face today. Just as surely as the Lord gives us a desire to accomplish something for His honor, obstacles will appear. It may be a financial situation that seems hopeless, or simply a feeling of inability to cope with problems. For some of us, not much opposition is needed before we feel there is no use in trying. Whatever the case, overcoming these difficulties may seem as impossible for us as it was to David becoming king. The Lord never promised an easy road for any of His followers. In fact, Jesus said: *If any man will come after Me, let him deny himself, and take up his cross daily, and follow Me* (Luke 9:23). The way of the cross is often long and lonely and it is never popular. Once we submit to the authority of Christ over our lives, we will patiently look to Him for direction and strength. *Whoso looks into the perfect Law of liberty, and continues* (remains) *therein, he being not a forgetful hearer, but a doer of the work, this man shall be blessed in his deed* (James 1:25).

Thought for Today: We never build ourselves up by putting others down.

Christ Portrayed: By David, the anointed king (I Chronicles 11:3). Christ is the Anointed One who will soon reign as *KING OF KINGS, AND LORD OF LORDS* (Revelation 19:16).

For definitions of unfamiliar words in today's Bible reading, see pages 468-480.

IN TODAY'S READING

King Hiram's kindness to David; Philistines defeated;
Ark brought to Jerusalem; David's psalm of thanksgiving

*S*oon after establishing his capital in Jerusalem, David united the nation for a glorious time of praising the Lord while bringing the Ark of God from the house of Obed-edom to Jerusalem. To demonstrate his reverence for God, and in recognition that God was the Supreme Ruler, David humbly laid aside his kingly garments and dressed in a plain linen ephod, a garment the priests wore when ministering before the Lord. In doing this, David was publicly acknowledging his submission to the authority of the supreme King and expressing adoration and praise to his Lord as Almighty God and the true King of Israel.

On that day, David provided an inspiring psalm for his choir to sing. It still lifts our spirits as we worship our wonderful Lord. David proclaimed to the world: *Give thanks to the LORD, call upon His Name; make known His deeds among the people. . . . Sing psalms to Him, talk you of all His wondrous works. . . . rejoice. . . . Be you mindful always of His Covenant* (Agreement); *the Word which He commanded to a thousand generations. . . . Declare His glory among the heathen. . . . For great is the LORD, and greatly to be praised. . . . bring an offering, and come before Him: worship the LORD in the beauty of holiness. . . . The LORD reigns* (16:8-31). Is it any surprise that David was a man after God's own heart (I Samuel 13:14; Acts 13:22)? Yes, the Lord reigns. He is still Sovereign and the world needs to hear us praise the Lord and to talk of all His wondrous works.

David also stands out as a man of prayer; thus, we see the often-repeated phrase: *David inquired of God* (I Chronicles 14:10,14; note: I Samuel 23:2,4; 30:8; II Samuel 2:1; 5:19,23; 21:1). As a result of these basic, God-honoring characteristics, *the fame of David went out into all lands; and the LORD brought the fear* (respect) *of him upon all nations* (I Chronicles 14:17).

When we complain and are despondent, it is truly a victory for Satan and an insult to God for we are demonstrating lack of faith in God's Word (Romans 8:28), as well as dissatisfaction with God. *It is a good thing to give thanks to the LORD, and to sing praises to Your Name, O Most High: to show forth* (declare) *Your lovingkindness in the morning, and Your faithfulness every night* (Psalm 92:1-2).

Thought for Today: People who complain can't sing praises to the Lord.

Christ Revealed: Through David's fame and exaltation (I Chronicles 14:17). God highly exalted Christ, our Redeemer, and gave Him a *Name which is above every name* (Philippians 2:9-11).

For definitions of unfamiliar words in today's Bible reading, see pages 468-480.

ℐN 𝒯ODAY'S ℛEADING

David forbidden to build the Temple; God makes a Covenant
with David; his prayer; God extends David's kingdom

𝒫rayer and praise to God were distinguishing characteristics in the
life of David. It is often recorded: *David inquired of the LORD* (I Samuel
23:2,4; 30:8; II Samuel 2:1; 5:19,23; 21:1; I Chronicles 14:10,14).

David's prayer life was often words of praise. David prayed: *O
LORD, there is none like You, neither is there any God beside You, according
to all that we have heard with our ears* (17:20). Although almost everyone
is aware of the importance of prayer, few make it a vital part of their
lives. But prayer has led many Christians to make right decisions.

As we pray, we are speaking to our Father, and as we read His Word,
He is speaking to us. That is "open communication" in the family of
God. Prayer and knowing God's Word are vital links in releasing
heaven's power to answer our prayers. With utmost confidence, *I will
say of the LORD, He is my refuge and my fortress* (Whose power the enemy
forces cannot penetrate): *my God; in Him I will trust* (Psalm 91:2).

There is no other how-to-pray manual, nor any better reading plan,
than beginning in Genesis and ending with Revelation. It is an attitude
of foolish pride to believe we are qualified to choose what not to read
when the Lord has clearly said: *All Scripture is . . . profitable* (II Timothy
3:16). If it is *all . . . profitable* and we don't read all of it, then we fail to gain
the best preparation for prayer that God has provided. When we recognize
the Bible as His unique prayer manual written for us, we will give it
priority far above all other "important matters" in our daily schedules.

Open your Bibles reverently, daily, praying *that the God of our Lord
Jesus Christ, the Father of glory, may give to you the spirit of wisdom and
revelation in the knowledge of Him: The eyes of your understanding* (mind)
*being enlightened; that you may know what is the hope of His calling, and
what the riches of the glory of His inheritance in the saints, And what is the
exceeding greatness of His power to us-ward* (toward us) *who believe, according to the working of His mighty power* (Ephesians 1:17-19).

Let the dominating motive in all your reading of God's Word be *that
you might walk worthy of the Lord to all pleasing, being fruitful in every
good work, and increasing in the knowledge of God* (Colossians 1:10).

Thought for Today: A problem? Pray, then trust God for the outcome!

Christ Portrayed: By David, the shepherd-king (I Chronicles 17:7; compare Matthew
1:1-2; Romans 1:3), symbolic of Christ as the *Good Shepherd* (John 10:11) and *King of
kings* (Revelation 19:16).

For definitions of unfamiliar words in today's Bible reading, see pages 468-480.

*I*N *T*ODAY'S *R*EADING
David's sin in taking a military census; his preparation for building
the Temple and instructions to Solomon; duties of the Levites

*S*olomon was about 20 years of age when he was anointed king. Since young people do not have the years of experience that their elders do, they often underestimate the things that are of greatest importance. Consequently, David was not satisfied with just providing Solomon with the materials needed to build the Temple. *Only the LORD give you wisdom and understanding, and give you charge concerning Israel, that you may keep the Law of the LORD your God. Then shall you prosper, if you take heed to fulfill the statutes and judgments which the LORD charged Moses with concerning Israel. . . . Now set your heart and your soul to seek the LORD your God; arise therefore, and build you the sanctuary of the LORD God, to bring the Ark of the Covenant of the LORD, and the holy vessels of God, into the house that is to be built to the Name of the LORD* (I Chronicles 22:12-13,19).

David's accumulation of materials for the Temple were now in the possession of his son. But Solomon ignored the spiritual advice of his father David to *set your heart . . . to seek the LORD. . . . arise therefore, and build you the sanctuary.* Building the Temple should have been his first priority, but Solomon put personal interests first and did not begin building the Temple until the fourth year of his reign. Instead, he began to amass chariots and horses as well as wives (II Chronicles 1:14; 3:1-2; I Kings 10:26 - 11:4). This was in violation of the Law for the kings of Israel (Deuteronomy 17:16-18).

David's appeal to Solomon is still the need of every Christian. True faith is demonstrated by our commitment and obedience to the Word of God and our dependency upon Him to answer prayer while we do all we can to bring it to pass. We should not assume that we can just "leave it up to the Lord and do nothing." The Lord expects our participation in all that we can do. Christ calls every believer to *seek you first the Kingdom of God, and His righteousness; and all these things shall be added to you* (Matthew 6:33). Then consider this fact: *Was not Abraham our father justified by works, when he had offered Isaac his son upon the altar? See you how faith wrought* (working) *with his works, and by works was faith made perfect?* (James 2:21-22).

Thought for Today: Satan will tempt you to sin, but by God's grace you can resist him.

Christ Revealed: Through the altar David built to sacrifice unto the Lord that Israel might be restored to a right relationship with God (I Chronicles 21:18,26). Only through Christ can we be restored to a relationship right with God. *Being justified freely by His grace through the redemption that is in Christ Jesus* (Romans 3:24).

For definitions of unfamiliar words in today's Bible reading, see pages 468-480.

$\mathscr{I}$N $\mathscr{T}$ODAY'S $\mathscr{R}$EADING

Duties assigned to priests; musicians and singers; divisions of the
porters (gatekeepers); treasurers and other officials

$\mathscr{D}$avid . . . *separated* (set apart) *to the service*, Levites, singers, porters
(gatekeepers), treasurers, and other workers (I Chronicles 25:1; 9:22-29)
of the Temple who were entrusted with responsibilities for worship in
the Temple. The gatekeepers were called *able men for strength for the
service* (26:8). They were the Korahites and Merarites, descendants of
Levi (Genesis 46:11). Twenty-four gatekeepers guarded the entrances
day and night lest an unqualified person attempted to enter (I Chronicles
26:17-18).

Every position was equally important to maintain worship in the
Temple as required by the Lord. Today, thee are no unimportant tasks
in the Church (the Body of Christ). The ministries dedicated to fulfilling
the great commission are also a sacred responsibility from God.

Earlier, David had planned to make Jerusalem the religious center
of Israel by bringing the Ark of the Covenant there. After Uzzah was
struck dead for touching the Ark, it was taken to the home of Obed-
edom. When he received the Ark containing the Word of God; he also
received the very presence of God (Exodus 25:22; I Samuel 4:4; II Samuel
6:2). The presence of the Lord brought blessing on the home of Obed-edom.
In like manner, the presence of the Lord will also bless our families and
homes when the Word of God is prominent in our lives.

Some people ignore the Master's ownership rights to their lives and
do not recognize their position as His managers of their talents, time,
and even the Lord's tithe. All these are meant to be used for His purposes
rather than for our own pleasures and personal interests. Each day is
given to us as a trust that we may become like Christ and glorify Him.
What God has entrusted to us can become multiplied blessings to
others; but, when kept for selfish purposes, it can become a curse.

In our family devotions, let us thank our Heavenly Father for each
of our children and help them to know their importance to Him. *He that
is faithful in that which is least is faithful also in much. . . . If therefore you
have not been faithful in the unrighteous mammon* (wealth), *who will
commit to your trust the true riches?* (Luke 16:10-11).

Thought for Today: Uppermost in our thoughts should be Christ and His Word.

Christ Revealed: Through the Temple treasures (I Chronicles 26:20-28). *Christ; In
Whom are hidden all the treasures of wisdom and knowledge* (Colossians 2:2-3). In
Christ are treasures of wisdom, knowledge, and riches to supply all a believer needs
(Philippians 4:19).

For definitions of unfamiliar words in today's Bible reading, see pages 468-480.

$\mathcal{I}$N $\mathcal{T}$ODAY'S $\mathcal{R}$EADING

Solomon encouraged to build the Temple; David's gifts for the
Temple; his thanks and prayer; Solomon made king; David's death

---

$\mathcal{D}$avid had reigned over Israel *forty years; seven years . . . in Hebron,
and thirty and three years . . . in Jerusalem* (I Chronicles 29:27). In his last
year, David assembled all the tribal princes and military captains. He
told them how God had chosen Solomon to build His Temple and that
their greatest concern should be to be obedient to *all the Commandments
of the LORD your God* (28:8). Then David charged Solomon: *Know . . . the
God of your father, and serve Him with a perfect heart and with a willing
mind: for the LORD searches all hearts, and understands all the imaginations of the thoughts: if you seek Him, He will be found of you; but if you
forsake Him, He will cast you off for ever* (28:9).

David then offered one of the most inspiring prayers recorded in the
Scriptures. *David prayed, Blessed be You, LORD God of Israel our Father,
for ever and ever. Yours, O LORD, is the greatness, and the power, and the
glory, and the victory, and the majesty: for all that is in the heaven and in
the earth is Yours; Yours is the kingdom, O LORD , and You are exalted as
Head above all. . . . and in Your hand is power and might . . . to make great,
and to give strength to all. Now therefore, our God, we thank You, and praise
Your glorious Name* (29:10-13).

David's heartfelt prayer is a reminder to all of us that prayer should
be a time of praising, and worshiping God with thanksgiving for Who
He is, as well as for what He has given us. As we recognize our total
dependence upon God for everything, we will praise Him for His
provision.When we neglect to praise the Lord daily, our worship often
becomes a mere ritual. Every day, under every circumstance, *in every
thing give thanks* (I Thessalonians 5:18). To grumble about our circumstances is to express dissatisfaction with God and to question His
wisdom and His love for us.

Kneeling, bowing the head, and stretching forth hands are all
expressions of worship. David was inspired by the Holy Spirit to write:
Lift up your hands in the sanctuary, and bless the LORD (Psalm 134:2). *I will
therefore that men pray every where, lifting up holy hands, without wrath
and doubting* (I Timothy 2:8).

Thought for Today: Let us freely offer praise to God *today.*

Christ Revealed: Through the gold offered for the Temple by David from his personal wealth (I Chronicles 29:3-5). Gold is the purest metal (Revelation 21:21) and
represents the preciousness and great worth of Christ. *He is pure* (I John 3:2-3).

For definitions of unfamiliar words in today's Bible reading, see pages 468-480.

IN TODAY'S READING
Solomon's sacrifices; his dream; his accumulation of chariots
and horsemen; Solomon builds the Temple

King Solomon began his reign in submission to *the LORD his God* (II Chronicles 1:1). *So Solomon, and all the congregation with him, went to . . . the Tabernacle of the congregation of God, which Moses . . . had made in the wilderness. . . . And Solomon . . . offered a thousand burned offerings. . . . In that night did God appear to Solomon, and said to him, Ask what I shall give you* (1:3-7). In I Kings, we have more complete details of this event. *In Gibeon the LORD appeared to Solomon in **a dream** by night: and God said, Ask what I shall give you. . . . And Solomon awoke; and, behold, **it was a dream*** (I Kings 3:5,15). **In this dream,** *Solomon said to God. . . . Give me now wisdom and knowledge . . . for who can judge* (rule) *this Your people, that is so great?* (II Chronicles 1:8-12). Through this dream, the Lord was revealing to Solomon that his greatest need was to be obedient to the Word of God.

Following the sacrifices at Gibeon, Solomon began accumulating massive numbers of *chariots and horsemen* (II Chronicles 1:14; 9:25; I Kings 4:26). However, God had commanded that the king *shall not . . . cause the people to return to Egypt, to the end that he should multiply horses; forasmuch as the LORD has said to you, You shall hereafter return no more that way* (Deuteronomy 17:16). But he even married the daughter of Pharaoh (I Kings 11:1). He again defied God, Who had said: *Neither shall he multiply* (take many) *wives to himself, that his heart turn not away: neither shall he greatly multiply to himself silver and gold* (Deuteronomy 17:17). Solomon ignored all three of these commandments. But his most serious neglect was his indifference toward the fourth commandment to Israel's kings: *When he sits upon the throne . . . he shall write him a copy of this Law in a book out of that which is before the priests the Levites. . . . he shall read therein all the days of his life . . . to keep all the words of this Law* (17:18-19).

It makes little difference whether or not we become famous, powerful, or wealthy. But, it is most important for us to recognize that, as He is our Creator, God has first claim on our wisdom and abilities, and on our use of them, *according as His divine power has given to us all things that pertain to life and godliness, through the knowledge of Him that has called us to glory and virtue* (II Peter 1:3).

Thought for Today: God is the True and only Source of wisdom.

Christ Revealed: By the thousand burned offerings of Solomon (II Chronicles 1:6). We can be thankful that the one perfect offering of Christ on the cross did away with the need for many and continual individual offerings. *He died to sin once* (for all) (Romans 6:10; Hebrews 10:10-12,14).

For definitions of unfamiliar words in today's Bible reading, see pages 468-480.

In Today's Reading

The Temple's furnishings; the Ark brought into the Temple; the cloud of the Lord fills the Temple; Solomon's prayer of dedication

*T*he Israelites gathered around Solomon as *he stood before the altar of the LORD . . . and spread forth his hands: For Solomon had made a brazen scaffold . . . and kneeled down upon his knees before all the congregation of Israel, and spread forth his hands toward heaven* (II Chronicles 6:12-13). It was not uncommon for the people of God to lift their hands in prayer and praise (Psalm 63:3-4). Hands lifted toward heaven are a sign of wholehearted submission and worship. Surely it should be natural to lift up our hands or to kneel in humility before the living God.

Solomon began his prayer, saying: *O LORD God of Israel, there is no God like You in the heaven, nor in the earth; which keeps covenant* (agreement), *and shows mercy to Your servants, that walk before You with all their hearts. . . . Then hear You from the heavens . . . and do according to all that the stranger calls to You for; that all the people of the earth may know Your Name, and fear You, as do Your people Israel, and may know that this House* (Temple) *which I have built is called by Your Name* (II Chronicles 6:14,33). Sadly, Solomon's talk didn't match his conduct.

Solomon also had prayed: *If Your people . . . have sinned . . . and confess Your Name, and pray and make supplication* (appeal) *before You . . . Then . . . forgive the sin of Your people Israel. . . . that all the people of the earth may know Your Name, and fear You* (6:24-25,33). It is pathetic to realize there is no record that Solomon ever repented of any of his sins.

Somewhere, at this moment, on a hospital bed or in a prison cell, facing unemployment or the cruel experiences of family problems, there are people repenting of their sins, reading God's Word for direction, being restored to Him, and coming forth stronger in their faith. It is wonderful to know how much the Lord loves us. *But when we are judged, we are chastened of the Lord, that we should not be condemned with the world* (I Corinthians 11:32). The best years of our lives can be the outcome of failure, heartbreak, or loneliness that lead to a true commitment to Christ as Lord of our lives. We can become the people God meant us to be. Suffering could be caused by God, Satan, or our own foolish decisions; but it can, and will, be used of God, if we have faith to turn to Him. *For I reckon that the sufferings of this present time are not worthy to be compared with the glory which shall be revealed in us* (Romans 8:18).

Thought for Today: Are we so occupied expecting recognition, we fail to praise God?

Christ Revealed: Through Solomon's prayer (II Chronicles 6:14). Jesus is that God: *For there is One God, and One Mediator* (Arbitrator, Negotiator) *between God and men, the Man Christ Jesus* (I Timothy 2:5).

For definitions of unfamiliar words in today's Bible reading, see pages 468-480.

*I*N *T*ODAY'S *R*EADING

Solomon's sacrifices; glory of the Lord; God appears to Solomon;
Queen of Sheba visits Solomon; his riches and fame; his death

*W*hen *Solomon had made an end of praying, the fire came down from
heaven, and consumed the burned offering and the sacrifices; and the glory
of the LORD filled the House* (II Chronicles 7:1).

After that great dedication, the Lord again appeared to Solomon by
night, saying: *If I shut up heaven that there be no rain, or if I command the
locusts to devour the land, or if I send pestilence among My people; If My
people, which are called by My Name, shall humble themselves, and pray,
and seek My face, and turn from their wicked ways; then I will hear from
heaven, and will forgive their sin, and will heal their land* (7:13-14).

Carefully consider the qualifications for God to *heal their land*. First,
He is speaking of *My people*. This implies our need to receive Christ according to His Word. Then, to *humble* ourselves means, first and foremost, a confession of our sin of neglecting His Word, as if we could live
by our own good judgment and do not need His advice. To humble one's
self also includes acknowledgment of all sin, a sorrow for sin, and
genuine repentance of sin. God alone can, and does, forgive and cleanse
us from all confessed sin (I John 1:9).

When God says: *Seek My face*, He means for us daily to seek Him in
His Word that we may know what life is all about. As we read His Word,
the Holy Spirit not only enlightens our understanding of how to know
His will, but He empowers us to live it. God has warned: *He that turns
away his ear from hearing the Law, even his prayer shall be abomination*
(Proverbs 28:9).

We need to consider and ask ourselves: "Will what I'm seeking in
prayer bring honor to the Father or merely benefit me?"

Our great need is to prayerfully read all of His Word. Jesus said: *If
a man abide not in Me, he is cast forth as a branch, and is withered; and men
gather them, and cast them into the fire, and they are burned. If you abide
in Me, and My words abide in you, you shall ask what you will, and it shall
be done to you* (John 15:6-7).

Thought for Today: *The LORD is near all . . . that call upon Him* (Psalm 145:18).

Christ Revealed: Through the glory of Solomon's kingdom (II Chronicles 9:1-28).
Even though Solomon had a rich and glorious kingdom, it cannot begin to compare
to Christ's coming kingdom. *The throne of God and of the Lamb shall be in it* (Revelation 22:1-5).

For definitions of unfamiliar words in today's Bible reading, see pages 468-480.

The Divided Kingdom (During the ministries of Elijah & Elisha)

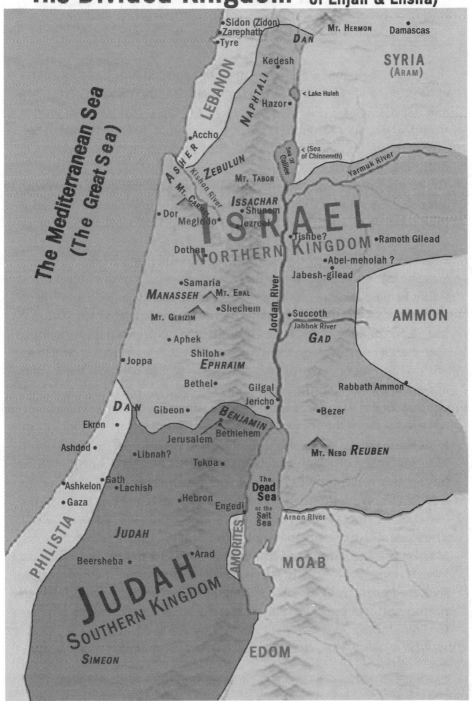

IN TODAY'S READING

Rehoboam succeeds Solomon; Jeroboam leads revolt of the 10 tribes;
Rehoboam forsakes *the Law* of God; Shishak invades Judah

When Solomon was made king, David urged him: *Keep the charge of the LORD your God, to walk in His ways . . . and . . . keep . . . His Commandments . . . as it is written in the Law of Moses, that you may prosper in all that you do* (I Kings 2:3). Sadly, however, there is no record of Solomon urging his own son, Rehoboam, to read God's Word and remain faithful to the Lord.

Neither is there any mention that Rehoboam began his reign with altar sacrifices and prayer as his father had done. What we do read is that, three years after Rehoboam became king, *he forsook the Law of the LORD, and all Israel with him. . . . And he did evil, because he prepared not his heart to seek the LORD* (II Chronicles 12:1-14; also 11:17).

The leaders of Israel met with Rehoboam with a reasonable request – that he ease the excessive taxes his father had imposed upon them. They also asked that he discontinue the forced labor which had persisted since Solomon first began building the luxurious palaces, stables, and chariot houses, magnificent parks, and other spectacular structures within his famous kingdom. If Rehoboam would consent, the leaders agreed to pledge their loyalty to him.

Rehoboam's first decision as king was a major blunder. His intolerance led most of the tribes to secede and form the northern kingdom. Rehoboam was left with only a small part of the original promised land. Only the tribes of Judah and Benjamin remained. But, how could he have made wise choices, since *he prepared not his heart to seek the LORD?* (12:14). Notice that it does not say to "serve the Lord." It was not better service that the Lord expected, but for Rehoboam to *seek the LORD*. The same spiritual principles hold true today. The difference between Martha "serving" Jesus and Mary who "sat at Jesus' feet and heard the Word" (Luke 10:38-42). Though we may be unaware of it, if we humbly seek the Lord, our lives will be guided by His Spirit to accomplish His perfect will and purpose. *But He gives more grace. Wherefore He says, God resists the proud, but gives grace to the humble* (James 4:6).

Thought for Today: Without God, the most clever strategy of the wisest counselors is worthless.

Christ Revealed: Through the gold candlestick (lampstand) (II Chronicles 13:11). Jesus is *the Light of the world* (John 9:5).

For definitions of unfamiliar words in today's Bible reading, see pages 468-480.

In Today's Reading

King Asa's reforms; his covenant with God;
his treaty with Syria (Aram); Asa rebuked by Hanani;
Asa's death; Jehoshaphat succeeds Asa

King Asa was the grandson of Rehoboam and the great-grandson of Solomon. But Asa rejected their pagan idols (II Chronicles 14:1-7). Asa was greatly encouraged by the prophet *Azariah the son of Oded* (15:1). When Azariah spoke, *Asa . . . took courage, and put away the abominable* (detestable) *idols out of all the land of Judah and Benjamin, and out of the cities which he had taken from Mount Ephraim, and renewed* (restored) *the altar of the LORD, that was before the porch of the LORD. And he gathered all Judah and Benjamin, and the strangers with them out of Ephraim and Manasseh, and out of Simeon: for they fell* (defected) *to him out of Israel in abundance, when they saw that the LORD his God was with him. . . . And they entered into a covenant* (agreement) *to seek the LORD God of their fathers with all their heart and with all their soul. . . . and the LORD gave them rest* (peace) *round about* (from war for 10 years) (15:8-9,12,15).

Asa left no room for compromise. *He took away the sodomites* (male cult prostitutes) *out of the land, and removed all the idols that his fathers had made* (I Kings 15:12). He even removed his own grandmother Maachah *from being queen, because she had made an idol in a grove* (shrine for the goddess Asherah); *and Asa destroyed her idol, and burned it by the brook Kidron* (15:13; II Chronicles 15:16).

You can be sure that, when anyone takes a firm stand for moral and spiritual values, Satan will instigate opposition and then seek to bring about a compromise in that person's positive declaration of faith.

As his wealth and power increased, Asa's dependence upon God decreased. *Hanani the seer came to Asa king of Judah, and said to him, Because you have relied on the king of Syria, and not relied on the LORD your God, therefore is the host of the king of Syria escaped out of your hand* (16:7).

Hanani was put in prison for his faithful witness. But his words have imparted immeasurable faith and boldness for all of us to remain faithful in the midst of a hostile world: *For the eyes of the LORD run to and fro throughout the whole earth, to show Himself strong in the behalf of them whose heart is perfect toward Him* (II Chronicles 16:9).

Thought for Today: Only the unsaved are powerless against Satan.

Christ Revealed: Through the rest that God gave Judah (II Chronicles 14:7). Jesus declared: *Take My yoke* (yoke of burden) *upon you . . . and you shall find rest to your souls* (Matthew 11:29).

For definitions of unfamiliar words in today's Bible reading, see pages 468-480.

IN TODAY'S READING
Jehoshaphat allied himself with Ahab; death of Ahab;
Jehoshaphat's national reformation; death of Jehoshaphat

Jehoshaphat was one of the most godly kings in the history of Judah. He appointed Levites throughout the country to read and instruct people in the Law of God. He forced the Baal and Ashtoreth cult followers, as well as the male prostitutes (homosexuals), out of his country (I Kings 22:46; II Chronicles 17:3-9).

Jehoshaphat made a serious mistake when he associated with Ahab, the Baal-worshiping king of the northern kingdom. Their friendship led to the marriage of Jehoshaphat's son Jehoram to Ahab's daughter Athaliah (18:1; 21:1,6). Ahab then asked Jehoshaphat to join him in a battle with Syria to regain his border city of Ramoth-gilead (18:3). Godly Jehoshaphat also made a serious mistake when he accepted an invitation to a feast with Ahab and Jezebel.

Following Jehoshaphat's request for a word from God, a fearless prophet named Micaiah boldly foretold that Ahab would not return alive from that war (18:4,13,16). In disregard of the prophet's warning, Jehoshaphat joined Ahab and almost lost his life. When surrounded by Syrians, *Jehoshaphat cried out, and the LORD helped him; and God moved them to depart from him* (18:31). *Jehoshaphat the king of Judah returned to his house in peace to Jerusalem* (19:1). God sent the prophet Jehu to rebuke him: *Should you help the ungodly, and love them that hate* (despise) *the LORD? therefore is wrath upon you from . . . the LORD* (19:2).

The marriage of Jehoshaphat's son Jehoram to the daughter of Jezebel opened the door to Baal worship in Judah and the massacre of all of Jehoshaphat's sons and grandsons, except for one-year-old Jehoash (Joash) who was hidden by the high priest Jehoiada (22:10-12).

All of our relationships should be guided by the Scriptures: *Be not unequally yoked together with unbelievers: for what fellowship has righteousness with unrighteousness? and what communion has light with darkness? . . . Come out from among them, and be separate, says the Lord* (II Corinthians 6:14,17). *And have no fellowship with the unfruitful works of darkness* (Ephesians 5:11).

Thought for Today: A marvelous transformation takes place when anyone – even the most wretched sinner – prays for mercy. The prayer for mercy covers everything needed in our lives.

Christ Portrayed: By Micaiah, who told the truth even though it was unpopular with his listeners (II Chronicles 18:12-27). We are reminded of Christ when He spoke the unpopular truth to the Pharisees (Matthew 12:1-14). Jesus responded: *Now you seek to kill Me, a Man that has told you the truth, which I have heard of God* (John 8:40).

For definitions of unfamiliar words in today's Bible reading, see pages 468-480.

IN TODAY'S READING

Jehoram's, Ahaziah's and Athaliah's reigns;
prophecy of Elijah; Joash becomes king and repairs the Temple;
the nation turns to idolatry

*D*uring most of Jehoshaphat's reign, he maintained friendly relations with Ahab, the idol-worshiping king of the northern kingdom. His
son's marriage to Ahab's daughter resulted in a heritage of wicked
leadership for Judah. Jehoshaphat's life should serve as a warning to
those today who say: "I know God said we should not have close
relationships with unsaved people, but I don't let them affect me."
However, just as it was with Jehoshaphat, though it did not influence
him personally, he could not control the way it affected his sons and his
grandchildren.

After the death of Jehoshaphat, his son Jehoram took control of the
kingdom. He proceeded to destroy all the godly influence of his father's
reign. He also *slew all his brethren with the sword. . . . And he walked in
the way of the kings of Israel . . . for he had the daughter of Ahab to wife: and
he wrought* (did) *that which was evil in the eyes of the LORD. . . . Moreover
he . . . caused the inhabitants of Jerusalem to commit fornication, and com-
pelled* (led) *Judah thereto* (II Chronicles 21:4,6,11).

Although the prophet Elijah lived in the northern kingdom, he sent
a letter to the ungodly Jehoram, king of the southern kingdom, and
rebuked his evils, saying: *Because you have not walked in the ways of
Jehoshaphat your father . . . But have walked in the way of the kings of Israel
. . . Behold, with a great plague will the LORD smite your people, and your
children, and your wives . . . And you shall have great sickness by disease
of your bowels. . . . After the end of two years . . . he died* (21:12-19).

Godly Jehoshaphat could not have realized the tragic consequences
that resulted from his friendship with Ahab and his son's marriage to an
unbeliever. Some Christian parents' hearts have been broken as a result
of permitting a son or daughter to date an unsaved person who seems
so desirable in many other ways. Every Christian young man and
woman should recognize why there are strong warnings against dating
the unsaved. *Wherefore come out from among them, and be you separate,
says the Lord; and touch not the unclean* (unfit) *thing; and I will receive you*
(II Corinthians 6:17).

Thought for Today: Neglecting the Bible and ceasing to obey it has caused many to
lose their sense of spiritual direction.

Christ Portrayed: By Jehoiada, the high priest, who faithfully hid and protected Joash
(II Chronicles 23:1-11). Jesus is our High Priest (Hebrews 5:5-10); we are *hidden with
Christ in God* (Colossians 3:3).

For definitions of unfamiliar words in today's Bible reading, see pages 468-480.

IN TODAY'S READING

Amaziah reigns in Judah; war against Edom; Israel defeats Judah;
Uzziah reigns in Jerusalem; Uzziah stricken with leprosy

After Joash was murdered by his servants, his son Amaziah became king of Judah (II Chronicles 24:25-27; also II Kings 12:20-21). As he began his reign, *he did what was right in the sight of the LORD, but not with a perfect heart* (II Chronicles 25:2; also II Kings 14:3-6). On one occasion, he hired soldiers from the northern kingdom to help him fight against Edom (descendants of Esau) in an effort to regain lost territory (II Chronicles 25:6). After *a man of God* rebuked him for not fully trusting in the Lord, Who alone *has power to help, and to cast down* (25:7-8), Amaziah dismissed the Israelite army and was successful in defeating the Edomites. But, instead of praising the Lord for victory, he *brought the gods of the children of Seir, and set them up to be his gods, and bowed down himself before them, and burned incense to them. Wherefore the anger of the LORD was kindled against Amaziah* (25:14-16).

One of the most successful kings in Judah's history was his 16-year-old son Uzziah (26:1). The key to his success was unmistakable: *He sought God in the days of Zechariah, who had understanding in the visions of God. . . . And his name spread far abroad; for he was marvelously helped, till he was strong. But when he was strong, his heart was lifted up to his destruction: for he transgressed against the LORD his God, and went into the Temple of the LORD to burn incense* (26:5,15-16). Only priests were qualified to offer incense to God; but Uzziah refused to stop, even when rebuked by Azariah and 80 other priests (26:17). Consequently, God struck Uzziah with leprosy. Even though he was a great king, God still judged him, for no man is above the Law of God. Because of his leprosy, Uzziah was an outcast from both his own palace as well as the Temple.

Few sins are as deceptive and destructive as overestimating one's importance. *For I say, through the grace given to me, to every man that is among you, not to think of himself more highly than he ought to think; but to think soberly, according as God has dealt to every man the measure of faith* (Romans 12:3).

Thought for Today: You glorify Jesus when saying: "Praise the Lord." (Hebrew word "Hallelujah")

Christ Portrayed: By Azariah the high priest who stood between Uzziah and the altar, because there was only one proper way to approach the Lord God of Israel and that was through the service of the priests (II Chronicles 26:17-18). Jesus, our great High Priest (Hebrews 4:14), is the only way for anyone to come to God. *Jesus said to him, I am the Way, the Truth, and the Life: no man comes to the Father, but by Me* (John 14:6).

For definitions of unfamiliar words in today's Bible reading, see pages 468-480.

In Today's Reading

Ahaz reigns in Judah; Syria (Aram) and Israel defeat Judah;
death of Ahaz; Hezekiah's reign; worship restored in the Temple

---

Ahaz had the wonderful heritage of a godly father Jotham (II Chronicles 27:6). But Ahaz was one of the most wicked kings in Judah's history, *for he . . . made . . . molten images* (cast idols) *for Baalim. Moreover, he burned incense in the valley of the son of Hinnom, and burned his children in the fire, after the abominations of the heathen whom the LORD had cast out before the children of Israel. . . . Wherefore the LORD his God delivered him into the hand of the king of Syria; and they smote* (defeated) *him, and carried away a great multitude of them captives, and brought them to Damascus. And he was also delivered into the hand of the king of Israel, who smote him with a great slaughter* (28:2-3,5).

Because of the great wickedness of King Ahaz, the kingdom of Judah continued to suffer serious losses of territory. The Edomites gained their independence from Judah on the southeast. The Philistines raided the cities in the southwest and occupied them (28:17-18). Thousands of his people were taken as slaves into other countries (28:5-17).

Regrettably, the many defeats of Ahaz never caused him to humble himself and repent. He fiercely rejected the Lord and *sacrificed to the gods of Damascus* (28:23). *And Ahaz gathered together the vessels of the House of God, and cut in pieces the vessels . . . and shut up the doors of the House of the LORD, and he made him altars in every corner of Jerusalem. And in every . . . city of Judah he made high places to burn incense to other gods, and provoked to anger the LORD God of his fathers* (28:24-25).

In this tragic account of Ahaz, king of Judah, the Lord is warning us of the awful fate of those who turn from Him. Just as Ahaz attempted to suppress the worship of the One True God, the unsaved world, with all of its deceptive attractions, attempts to suppress our loyalty and obedience to the Lord. To overcome these hindrances and remain faithful we need to pray each day: *Give me understanding, and I shall keep Your Law; yea, I shall observe it with my whole heart. Make me to go in the path of Your Commandments; for therein do I delight. Incline my heart to Your testimonies, and not to covetousness. Turn away my eyes from beholding vanity; and quicken* (renew) *. . . me in Your way* (Psalm 119:34-37).

Thought for Today: Someone today needs to hear how the Lord answers prayers.

Christ Portrayed: By King Hezekiah who offered an intercessory prayer for *every one. That prepares his heart to seek God* (II Chronicles 30:18-19). Jesus Christ our King, now seated *at the right hand of God*, intercedes in prayer for all who continue to seek Him (John 17:9; Romans 8:34). *Seek those things which are above, where Christ sits on the right hand of God* (Colossians 3:1).

For definitions of unfamiliar words in today's Bible reading, see pages 468-480.

*A*fter the death of wicked King Ahaz, his godly son Hezekiah became king and assumed leadership of a nation where idol worship was both popular and prevalent. Furthermore, his father had placed the kingdom of Judah in subjection to Assyria, which was fast becoming the world's most powerful kingdom. Its seemingly invincible armies had seized control of both Syria and the northern kingdom of Israel. In addition, Sennacherib, king of Assyria, had jurisdiction over 46 walled cities inside the kingdom of Judah.

Hezekiah could have mourned over the mess he inherited, either hating his father or blaming God for the wretched moral and economic conditions that prevailed throughout the nation. Instead, he *appointed the courses of the priests. . . . He appointed also the king's portion* (share) *of his substance for the burned offerings. . . . he commanded the people . . . to give the portion of the priests and the Levites. . . . And . . . the LORD . . . blessed His people* (II Chronicles 31:2-10).

Hezekiah observed the Passover (30:1-27). He reopened the Temple which his wicked, idol-worshiping father had desecrated, and restored worship of the true God.

As with Hezekiah, who inherited serious problems because his father was evil, we too may be the victim of other people's sins. But Christians never need to fear the future or "unfortunate circumstances" of the past. We should not be concerned about our parents' mistakes, which we may have inherited, or other situations over which we have no control. Dwelling on one's past mistakes, or those of others, never provides helpful solutions, and can create depression, suspicion, self-hatred, and hatred of others. How encouraging it is to know that, when Hezekiah and Isaiah prayed with no hint of ill will, the Lord protected them.

With the Apostle Paul, let us say: *This one thing I do, forgetting those things which are behind, and reaching forth to those things which are before, I press toward the mark* (goal) *for the prize of the high calling of God in Christ Jesus* (Philippians 3:13-14).

Thought for Today: Don't give up. Even the vilest sinner can be saved.

Christ Revealed: By Hezekiah's offering of *the king's portion* (share) *of his substance for the burned offerings* (II Chronicles 31:3). The burned offerings were wholly consumed, symbolic of total surrender, and offered as a sweet savor to the Lord (Leviticus 8:28; Numbers 15:3). God offered His King's portion in Christ Jesus Who, in total surrender on the cross, was wholly consumed, even unto death. *Christ . . . has given Himself for us an offering and a sacrifice to God for a sweet-smelling savor* (Ephesians 5:2).

For definitions of unfamiliar words in today's Bible reading, see pages 468-480.

IN TODAY'S READING
Josiah's reign; book of the Law found; fall of Jerusalem;
captivity of Judah; decree of Cyrus to rebuild the Temple

*O*ne of the highest honors ever attributed to a king was given to
Josiah, when it was recorded: *He did that which was right in the sight of
the LORD, and walked in the ways of David his father, and declined* (turned
aside) *neither to the right hand, nor to the left. . . . And he read in their ears
all the words of the Book of the Covenant that was found in the House of the
LORD* (II Chronicles 34:2,30).

But the last four kings of Judah – Jehoahaz, Jehoiakim, Jehoiachin, and
Zedekiah – were all evil, and led the nation in a descending course to its
disastrous end morally, politically, and spiritually. During his reign of
11 years (36:11), Zedekiah (Mattaniah), the youngest son of Josiah, *did
that which was evil in the sight of the LORD* (36:12), and rebelled against
Babylon's domination because he thought he had the support of Egypt.
This time, the Lord left the Israelites to their ruin. Nebuchadnezzar
showed no mercy and surrounded Jerusalem until *there was no bread for
the people of the land* (II Kings 25:3). The horrors of the starving defenders
of Jerusalem are recorded in Lamentations 2:19; 4:3-10 and Ezekiel 5:10.

Nebuchadnezzar's soldiers eventually broke through the north
wall and mercilessly butchered both young and old. Then *they burned
the House of God, and broke down the wall of Jerusalem, and burned all the
palaces thereof with fire, and destroyed all the goodly* (valuable) *vessels
thereof* (II Chronicles 36:17-19; II Kings 25:4-11; Jeremiah 52:5-23).

Most of those who had escaped the massacre were driven off as
slaves to become exiles in a foreign land (II Chronicles 36:20-21).

Because of His great love for Israel and His covenants with Abraham,
Isaac, Jacob, and David, the Lord made a precious promise to the Jewish
people that is fast approaching fulfillment. They will soon recognize
Jesus of Nazareth as their Messiah. *Blindness in part is happened to Israel,
until the fullness of the Gentiles be come in. And so all Israel shall be saved:
as it is written, There shall come out of Zion the Deliverer, and shall turn
away ungodliness from Jacob: For this is My Covenant* (Agreement) *to
them, when I shall take away their sins* (Romans 11:25-27).

Thought for Today: Can others always depend on what you say?

**Christ Revealed: Through the messengers of God who were rejected by His people (II
Chronicles 36:15-16; compare Isaiah 53:3; Mark 9:12). Jesus *came to His own* (own
people), *and His own received Him not* (John 1:11; also Matthew 21:42; Mark 8:31;
12:10; Luke 9:22; 17:25; 20:17).**

For definitions of unfamiliar words in today's Bible reading, see pages 468-480.

Introduction To The Book Of
Ezra

The Book of Ezra begins with the history of the Jews from the time Cyrus, king of Persia released them from Babylonian exile. He permitted them to return to Jerusalem to rebuild the Temple under the leadership of Zerubbabel, a descendant of King David and the great-grandson of Jehoiakim. He was considered a prince of Judah by Cyrus (Ezra 1:8). Cyrus was not a believer in the One True God; he was just promoting goodwill for his own newly-won empire.

Most of the older generation of Israelites, who had been taken into captivity by Nebuchadnezzar, had died; and the majority of the new generation did not desire to return to a homeland they had never seen.

Ezra records that the first expedition was made up of 42,360 Jews and 7,337 of their servants (Ezra 2:64-65) led by Zerubbabel, who was appointed governor by King Cyrus (5:14; Haggai 1:1,14; 2:2,21).

The original Temple, built by King Solomon, had been destroyed by King Nebuchadnezzar of Babylon in 586 B.C. After arriving in Jerusalem with Zerubbabel, the returned exiles built an altar and observed the Feast (Festival) of Tabernacles (Booths) which commemorates the Israelites' 40 years in the wilderness. Ezra records that *in the second year of their coming to the House of God at Jerusalem, in the second month, began Zerubbabel . . . to set forward* (oversee) *the work of the House of the LORD* (Ezra 3:8; 5:16). It took about two years to complete the foundation, after which the work ceased because of opposition from surrounding adversaries (chapters 3 – 4).

About 15 years later, stirred by the preaching of the Word of God by the prophets Haggai and Zechariah, the Israelites *began to build the House of God* (5:2). They completed it in about five years despite intense opposition (chapters 5 – 6). Between chapters 6 and 7 there is an interval of about 60 years. During this time, Zerubbabel, Haggai, and Zechariah died and the events in the Book of Esther probably took place.

Perhaps 80 years after Zerubbabel's expedition, Ezra, a descendant of Aaron the first high priest, received authority from the king to lead another expedition to Jerusalem *according to the Law of your God . . . . Whatsoever is commanded by the God of heaven, let it be diligently* (zealously) *done* (7:11-14,23). At that time, Ezra led about 5,000 people, from the Persian capital of Babylon to Jerusalem (7:28 – 8:32). The Book of Ezra reveals how God controls the destiny of all mankind and, thus, the Book of Ezra is a message of God's continuing Covenant grace.

$\mathcal{I}$N $\mathcal{T}$ODAY'S $\mathcal{R}$EADING
Cyrus' proclamation to rebuild the Temple;
list of the Jews who returned from captivity

$\mathcal{A}$bout 200 years before the time of Ezra, Isaiah had prophesied that Babylon would be overthrown by a man named Cyrus. The Lord said of this heathen king of Persia: *He . . . shall perform all My pleasure: even saying to Jerusalem, You shall be built; and to the Temple, Your foundation shall be laid. . . . and he shall let go My captives* (Isaiah 44:28; 45:13). These prophecies reassured the Israelites that, following the judgment foretold by Jeremiah of 70 years of captivity due to their sins, God would restore them once again to the promised land (Jeremiah 25:11-12).

To fulfill that prophecy, *the LORD stirred up the spirit* (moved the heart) *of Cyrus king of Persia, that he made a proclamation. . . . Who is there among you of all His people? his God be with him, and let him go up to Jerusalem, which is in Judah, and build the House of the LORD God of Israel, (He is the God,) which is in Jerusalem. . . . Then rose up the chief of the fathers of Judah and Benjamin, and the priests, and the Levites, with all them whose spirit God had raised, to go up to build the House of the LORD which is in Jerusalem* (Ezra 1:1,3,5).

Neither a pillar of fire by night nor a cloud by day to guide the way, and no manna fell from heaven as experienced many years before by their ancestors (Numbers 9:15-16,22-23), but there is not one complaint recorded. This is in sharp contrast to the continual complaints of their ancestors, who had been miraculously released from Egypt (20:24; 27:14; Deuteronomy 1:26,43; 9:23).

When we recognize that our Sovereign Creator controls everything that affects our lives, we can truly enjoy the peace of God, regardless of what happens, since *all things work together for good to them that love God* (Romans 8:28). Believing this will remove all fear, depression, and discouragement, as well as faultfinding, anger, and strife. Our loving Lord is sovereign over all that takes place in our lives, including suffering and pain, and will use whatever happens in our lives to our ultimate advantage. Because of this, we can *live in peace; and the God of love and peace shall be with you* (us) (II Corinthians 13:11).

Thought for Today: *Rejoice in the LORD, you righteous; and give thanks at the remembrance of His holiness* (Psalm 97:12).

Christ Portrayed: By Sheshbazzar, another name for Zerubbabel, the prince (governor) of Judah (Ezra 1:8). Christ is both The Prince of Peace (Isaiah 9:6) and the Lion of the tribe of Judah (Revelation 5:5).

For definitions of unfamiliar words in today's Bible reading, see pages 468-480.

The Exiles & Return

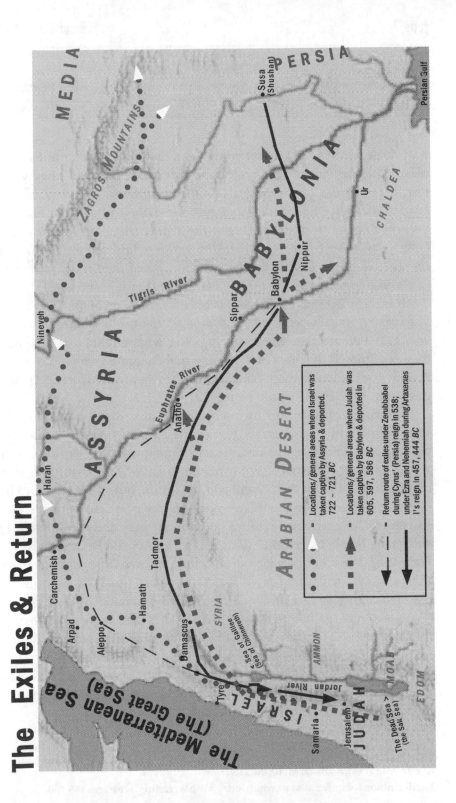

Legend:

- •••• Locations/general areas where Israel was taken captive by Assyria & deported. 722 – 721 BC
- ▪▪▪▪ Locations/general areas where Judah was taken captive by Babylon & deported in 605, 597, 586 BC
- – – Return route of exiles under Zerubbabel during Cyrus' (Persia) reign in 538; under Ezra and Nehemiah during Artaxerxes I's reign in 457, 444 BC

MEDIA

PERSIA

Susa (Shushan)

ZAGROS MOUNTAINS

BABYLONIA

Ur

CHALDEA

Tigris River

Nineveh

Nippur

ASSYRIA

Sippar

Babylon

Euphrates River

Anatho

Haran

ARABIAN DESERT

Carchemish

Arpad

Aleppo

Hamath

Tadmor

Damascus

SYRIA

Sea of Galilee
(Sea of Chinnereth)

AMMON

Tyre

Jordan River

MOAB

ISRAEL

Samaria

Jerusalem

JUDAH

The Dead Sea
(the Salt Sea)

EDOM

The Mediterranean Sea
(The Great Sea)

Persian Gulf

In Today's Reading
Restoration of the altar and worship; rebuilding Temple begun;
adversaries stop work, it resumes; Tatnai writes to Darius

After returning to Jerusalem, the Jews first built *the altar of the God of Israel, to offer burned offerings. . . . for fear was upon them* (they were terrified) *because of the people of those countries: and they offered burned offerings . . . morning and evening. They kept also the Feast of Tabernacles, as it is written. . . . But the foundation of the Temple of the LORD was not yet laid. . . . When the builders laid the foundation of the Temple of the LORD . . . the priests . . . and the Levites. . . . sang . . . praising and giving thanks to the LORD* (Ezra 3:2-4,6,10-11).

It is recorded that many men, *when the foundation of this House was laid before their eyes, wept with a loud voice; and many shouted aloud for joy* (3:12). Perhaps they were weeping over what might have been had they not ignored the prophet's warning that continued sin would result in their destruction. Perhaps others rejoiced as they looked forward to the day when the Temple would be rebuilt.

It is right for us to sorrow over our past sins which have brought the judgment of God upon us, just as the Israelites did. But, after repenting and forsaking our sins, *He is faithful and just to forgive us our sins* (I John 1:9). We should not continue to grieve over past losses that blur opportunities for the present and the future, but thank Him for His mercy and grace. Nor should we glory in our past achievements and successes. Daily we need to move on with our lives and join in *praising and giving thanks to the LORD* (Ezra 3:11). The Apostle Paul reminds us: *Forgetting those things which are behind, and reaching forth to those things which are before, I press toward the mark* (goal) *for the prize of the high calling of God in Christ Jesus* (Philippians 3:13-14).

A lesson we gain from these devout Jews is that, as we seek to serve the Lord, we will face opposition. During the rebuilding of the Temple's foundation *the people of the land . . . troubled them in building. . . . Then ceased the work of the House of God which is at Jerusalem* (Ezra 4:4,24).

Let us look ahead with confidence, not in ourselves, but in God *and in the power of His might* (Ephesians 6:10).

Thought for Today: Winners never quit and quitters never win.

Christ Revealed: Through the great (huge) stones used in building the Temple of God (Ezra 5:8). Christ is the Stone which the builders rejected and He has become the Cornerstone of our faith (Psalm 118:22; Matthew 21:42).

For definitions of unfamiliar words in today's Bible reading, see pages 468-480.

*T*he prophets Haggai and Zechariah reminded the Israelites in Jerusalem that the real reason the Lord's work went unfinished was because their first interest was in building their own homes. These anointed men boldly preached the Word of God and inspired the people to rebuild the Temple: *And the elders of the Jews built, and they prospered through the prophesying of Haggai the prophet and Zechariah . . . according to the Commandment of the God of Israel* (Ezra 6:14).

Nothing is recorded about the Jews in Jerusalem between the time of Haggai and Zechariah's ministry and the coming of Ezra from Persia about 60 years later. Zerubbabel, Haggai, and Zechariah had all died leaving the next generation to grow up without spiritual leadership.

Ezra was born during the Babylonian captivity. He was a descendant of Aaron, Israel's first high priest (7:1-5; I Chronicles 6:3-15). The key to Ezra's great effectiveness in accomplishing the will of God is clear: *For Ezra had prepared his heart to seek* (study) *the Law of the LORD, and to do it, and to teach in Israel statutes* (laws) *and judgments* (what God declares is right and wrong) (Ezra 7:10). Note carefully the threefold key to Ezra's great success: Ezra *had prepared his heart to seek the Law of the LORD.* The word *prepared* implies a steadfast effort to know all of God's Word. The second qualification for the Lord's blessings upon his life was that Ezra committed himself *to do it* (obey the Law). And third, he planned to teach its *statutes and judgments.*

Ezra was committed to seeking, doing, and teaching God's Word. This should be a reminder that, if we want God to bless our lives, we too must set our hearts upon the whole counsel of God. *Above all, taking the shield of faith, wherewith you shall be able to quench* (put out, extinguish) *all the fiery darts* (arrows, shots) *of the wicked. Take . . . the sword of the Spirit, which is the Word of God* (Ephesians 6:16-17).

Ezra is an example of how God will use anyone who will take His Word seriously, *rightly dividing the Word of Truth* (II Timothy 2:15).

Thought for Today: Living to please the Lord will encourage others to be obedient to Him.

Christ Revealed: Through *the Feast of Unleavened* (Yeast-free) *Bread* (Ezra 6:22). Jesus is the *Bread of Life* (John 6:35), and He was *without sin;* leaven is symbolic of sin (Hebrews 4:15).

For definitions of unfamiliar words in today's Bible reading, see pages 468-480.

IN TODAY'S READING

Genealogy of Ezra's companions; Ezra proclaims a fast;
treasures delivered to the priests; Ezra's prayer and confession

*E*zra knew the Scriptures and decided to be responsible for leading perhaps five thousand men, women, and children on the treacherous, possibly 800-mile journey from Babylon to Jerusalem. Added to this was the responsibility for priceless treasures of *silver . . . gold, and the vessels . . . of the House of our God, which the king . . . had offered* (Ezra 8:25). Ezra was also aware of the danger of bandits who could murder and plunder. The people would face physical and emotional hardships as well.

It would have been easier to remain in Babylon and just pray for the people in Jerusalem. But Ezra decided to do what he could. Furthermore, Ezra did not ask the king for a protective military guard; rather it is recorded that Ezra *proclaimed a fast there . . . that we might afflict* (humble) *ourselves before our God, to seek of Him a right way. . . . I was ashamed to require of the king a band of soldiers . . . to help us against the enemy . . . because we had spoken to the king, saying, The hand of our God is upon all them for good that seek Him* (8:21-22).

Ezra and all his followers arrived safely in Jerusalem about four months after leaving Babylon (7:8-9; 8:31). However, Ezra was grief stricken upon hearing about the low moral and spiritual state of affairs in Jerusalem since the Temple had been rebuilt. Ezra was told: *The people of Israel, and the priests, and the Levites, have not separated themselves from the people of the lands, doing according to their abominations* (detestable practices) (9:1). Again, he did not say: "It's not my problem, so I'll leave it up to someone else." Instead, he became involved and *every one that trembled at the words of the God of Israel . . . were assembled to me* (9:4). At the evening sacrifice, he fell on his knees and spread out his hands to the Lord, and prayed: *O my God, I am ashamed . . . for our iniquities . . . . for we have forsaken Your Commandments* (9:6,10).

When the Word of God is neglected, we too need to be as concerned as Ezra. *Was not Abraham our father justified by works, when he had offered Isaac his son upon the altar? See . . . how . . . by works faith was made perfect* (James 2:21-22).

Thought for Today: *Faith without works is dead* (James 2:20).

Christ Portrayed: By Ezra, who mourned over the sins of the people of Jerusalem (Ezra 9:5). Twice it is recorded that, when Jesus looked upon Jerusalem, He also mourned for the people (Luke 19:41; 13:34).

For definitions of unfamiliar words in today's Bible reading, see pages 468-480.

IN TODAY'S READING
Foreign wives and children

The Israelites had married Canaanites. Consequently, many were worshiping their idols. The Law of God, had warned: *Neither shall you make marriages with them. . . . For they will turn away your son from following Me . . . so will the anger of LORD . . . destroy you* (Deuteronomy 7:3-4).

As the Israelites listened to Ezra proclaim the Word of God, they were convicted of their sins. Shechaniah, spokesman for the offenders, said to Ezra: *We have trespassed against* (been unfaithful to) *our God, and have taken strange wives. . . . let us make a covenant* (agreement) *with our God to put away all the* (idol worshiping) *wives* (Ezra 10:2-3).

One by one, each man who had married a Canaanite had to present himself with his wife and children before a court of *the elders of every city, and the judges thereof* (10:14) to determine if they were involved in idol worship or were worshipers of the true God of Israel. If the only consideration had been the excommunication of all Canaanite wives, it would have been a simple, immediate decision. But, something more than simple separation was being considered in their courts. There was an examination of each family to determine if the Canaanite wives had forsaken their idols and converted to the One True God of Israel. If these men had led their wives to reject their idols and worship the One True God, their wives would have become Israelites and would not have been called *strange wives.* This precedent had been set by Joshua when he welcomed and protected Rahab, the harlot of Jericho, who had rejected her idols and sinful life to place her trust in the One True God of Israel. Much later, Ruth, a Moabitess, joined with Naomi, confessing: *Your God . . . will be . . . my God* (Ruth 1:16). Ruth rejected her people's idols and became an Israelite. In the providence of God, both she and Rahab became a part of the genealogy of Jesus.

We are prone to underestimate the heartbreak and suffering that results from disobedience to the Word of God. The price of sin is much greater than anyone suspects! *He that sows to his flesh shall of the flesh reap corruption* (doomed to destruction) *. . . but he that sows to the Spirit shall of the Spirit reap life everlasting* (Galatians 6:8).

Thought for Today: Self-denial that honors Christ may result in suffering, but the outcome is peace and satisfaction.

Christ Revealed: Through the ram (male sheep) offered for the offenses of the sons of the priests (Ezra 10:19). Christ offered Himself up for the sins and offenses of all mankind (Hebrews 7:27; Acts 8:32).

For definitions of unfamiliar words in today's Bible reading, see pages 468-480.

Introduction To The Book Of
Nehemiah

The Book of Nehemiah is a continuation of the history recorded in the Book of Ezra. Nehemiah grew up in Persia among the Jews who had been exiles in Babylon before Cyrus restored their freedom. Nehemiah had the honored position of cupbearer to King Artaxerxes, the son of Xerxes, known as Ahasuerus in the Book of Esther. His position was one of great trust and responsibility (I Kings 10:5; II Chronicles 9:4).

Nehemiah was heartbroken when he received a report of the spiritual and physical poverty that existed in Jerusalem. Upon learning of Nehemiah's great concern, the Persian king appointed him governor of Judah and gave him the authority to return to his homeland and rebuild the walls (Nehemiah 2:5-7; 5:14). This was about 100 years after Zerubbabel arrived in Jerusalem to rebuild the Temple (Ezra 1:5) and about 14 years after Ezra had gone to Jerusalem to restore the Temple worship (7:6). After much opposition the work ceased. Darius issued the second decree to rebuild the Temple in 519 B.C. In 458, Ezra dedicated the Temple (6:6).

The walls had remained in ruins since Nebuchadnezzar had completely destroyed Jerusalem about 140 years before (II Kings 25:8-11). The Jewish remnant had no protection against surrounding nations which could easily come in and rob them of their harvests and possessions. In 444 B.C. Artaxerxes issued the third decree permitting Nehemiah to rebuild the wall. Restoring the broken-down walls which had once protected Jerusalem from its enemies was Nehemiah's first major project. Yet some of the leading citizens of Jerusalem who would benefit from those walls refused to cooperate with him (Nehemiah 2:19; 3:5; 4:1-12).

Although faced with many problems (4:12-23; 6:2-4,10-13), by continual prayer, fasting, and faith in the Word of God, Nehemiah led the people to complete the walls in the short time of 52 days (6:15). There was great emphasis placed upon hearing the Word, as well as understanding and applying it, which led to a revival among the people (8:2-3,7-8,12).

After the walls of Jerusalem were dedicated by Ezra and Nehemiah (12:27-43), Nehemiah continued in Jerusalem as governor of Judah for about 12 years (5:14). He then returned to the Persian court for an indefinite period of time. During Nehemiah's absence from Jerusalem, the Word of God was once again disregarded and corruption and immorality gained acceptance (13:6). Nehemiah again obtained leave from the Persian king and returned to Jerusalem. With great fervor, he turned the nation from its sins, reestablished its Covenant relationship with God, and restored the people to true worship (13:7-31).

In Today's Reading
Nehemiah's prayer for Jerusalem and his leave of absence;
Nehemiah inspects Jerusalem's walls; the builder of the walls

When Nehemiah's relative Hanani arrived in Persia from Jerusalem, he told Nehemiah of the pitiful conditions that existed there. Nehemiah said: *When I heard these words . . . I sat down and wept, and mourned certain days, and fasted, and prayed before the God of heaven. . . . both I and my father's house have sinned. . . . and have not kept the Commandments* (Nehemiah 1:4,6-7). Over a period of about four months, he continued to pray.

When King Artaxerxes asked why he was so sad, Nehemiah told him that it was because *the city, the place of my fathers' sepulchers* (tombs), *lies waste* (2:1-3). The king graciously responded by appointing him governor over Judah and commissioned him to rebuild the walls of Jerusalem. The king even provided some of the materials (2:6-8).

Three basic characteristics made Nehemiah's efforts a success. First, his desire to do the will of God (1:1,11). This led him to leave the luxury and security of living in the king's palace in Persia and to endure the hardships in Jerusalem in order to restore the city of God.

Second, he not only *fasted and prayed*, but he confessed: *We. . . . have not kept the Commandments* (1:4-11). He recognized that obedience to the Word of God is essential to answered prayer.

Third, he was determined to persuade his people to join him in rebuilding the walls, regardless of opposition. Sanballat and his crowd expressed their hostility to Nehemiah: *They laughed us to scorn, and despised us* (2:19). Their ridicule then turned to slander: *Will you rebel against the king?* (2:19). In addition, Judah's *nobles put not their necks to the work of their lord* (supervisor) (3:5).

Nehemiah refused to become discouraged and give up. Accomplishing the will of God is dependent upon remembering that He is Sovereign over the affairs of our lives. *Be content with such things as you have: for He has said, I will never leave you, nor forsake you. So that we may boldly say, The Lord is my helper, and I will not fear what man shall do to me* (Hebrews 13:5-6).

Thought for Today: Much can be accomplished when Christians work together.

Christ Revealed: Through Nehemiah's prayer for his people (Nehemiah 1:4-11). Christ also prayed for His own throughout the ages which includes us today (John 17:20).

For definitions of unfamiliar words in today's Bible reading, see pages 468-480.

IN TODAY'S READING

Builders opposed and ridiculed; Nehemiah's prayer; weapons for
the workers; evils corrected; plots of adversaries; walls completed

*N*ehemiah determined to rebuild the walls around Jerusalem, even
though there was fierce opposition. He armed workers *with their
swords, their spears, and their bows* (Nehemiah 4:13). He also said: *Be
not . . . afraid of them: remember the Lord, Who is great and terrible* (to
be reverenced). *. . . our God shall fight for us. So we labored in the
work: and half of them held the spears from the rising of the morning
till the stars appeared* (4:14,20-21; compare Numbers 14:9; Exodus
14:13-14). Working about 12 hours a day left little time for anything
else. The Israelites' faith had been strengthened through the reading of
God's Word.

Sanballat again attempted to stop their work, saying: *Come, let us
meet together in some one of the villages in the plain of Ono* (Nehemiah
6:2), about 28 miles northwest of Jerusalem. Nehemiah replied: *I am
doing a great work, so that I cannot come down: why should the work
cease, while I leave it, and come down to you?* (6:3).

After Sanballat made five attempts to meet with Nehemiah, he then
accused him of rebelling against the king of Persia (6:5-7). When this
failed, Sanballat hired a prophet to foretell Nehemiah's death.

Eleven times it is recorded that Nehemiah prayed (1:4-11; 2:4; 4:4-5,9;
5:19; 6:9,14; 13:14,22,29,31). He encouraged his workers, saying: *The
God of heaven . . . will prosper us. . . . for the people had a mind to work.
. . . So the wall was finished . . . in fifty and two days* (2:20; 4:6; 6:15).

Once we recognize that *the battle is the LORD's* (I Samuel 17:47),
and God is the One Who allows the opposition, we will not panic.
Instead, we will seek to learn what the Lord expects of us in order to
qualify to have our prayers answered. People of faith, though a
minority, will always find a way to accomplish God's will. In serving
the Lord, one great temptation is that many will find excuses to wait
for a more convenient time rather than to put the Lord first and doing
their best with what they have. Jesus said: *I must work the works of Him
that sent Me, while it is day: the night comes, when no man can work*
(John 9:4).

Thought for Today: Prayerless Christians weaken their effectiveness.

Christ Portrayed: By Nehemiah and other Jews who had bought back (redeemed) some Jews
who had been sold to the heathen as slaves while in Persia (Nehemiah 5:8). When we were
enslaved by sin, we were redeemed with the precious lifeblood of Jesus when we accepted
Him as our Lord and Savior (Romans 7:14; I Peter 1:18-19; Leviticus 25:42).

For definitions of unfamiliar words in today's Bible reading, see pages 468-480.

---

*I*N *T*ODAY'S *R*EADING

Nehemiah's appointment of leaders; genealogy of returned exiles;
Scriptures read and explained;
the Feast (Festival) of Tabernacles (Booths) observed

---

*T*he ultimate purpose of God for His people was more than the restoration of His Temple and the walls of Jerusalem. These man-made
structures were powerless to protect the Israelites from their enemies
unless the people knew and obeyed the Word of God. The Hebrew language in which *the Book of the Law* (Nehemiah 8:3) was written was
no longer the common language of the people. During their captivity,
they spoke Aramaic, which was the international trade language used by
the Aramaeans (Syrians), Persians, and Babylonians at that time.

After the wall was completed under Nehemiah's supervision, thousands of Jews assembled in Jerusalem day after day from sunrise until
noon to hear Ezra and the Levites read and explain the Book of the Law.
This resulted in a renewal of the Covenant relationship of the Israelites
with God and the restoration of scriptural worship.

A revival took place, *for all the people wept, when they heard the words
of the Law* (8:9).

The most pressing need today is for Christians to become seriously
concerned about reading all of God's Word because it is *a discerner*
(judge, critic) *of the thoughts and intents of the heart* (Hebrews 4:12).
God speaks to us through His Word and, as we read it, our various acts
of disobedience, whether by ignorance, omission or commission, are
brought to mind. This will lead to our conviction, confession, and
cleansing. We will then become *doers of the Word, and not hearers only*
(James 1:22).

Furthermore, the guilt which results from sins we have committed
should no longer remain after we have confessed and repented. We dare
not dig up past confessed and forgiven sins of our own or of others;
instead, we should rejoice in the merciful, forgiving love of God through
Christ our Savior. In our Lord's parable, the unforgiving servant was
delivered to the tormentor. *So likewise shall My Heavenly Father do
also to you, if you from your hearts forgive not every one his brother their
trespasses* (Matthew 18:35).

Thought for Today: Obeying God's Word prepares our hearts for the Holy Spirit to work
in and through us.

Christ Revealed: Through the names required to be registered for priestly service
(Nehemiah 7:64). Christ, our Great *High Priest* (Hebrews 3:1), will soon return wearing
His Name, *KING OF KINGS, AND LORD OF LORDS* (Revelation 19:16).

For definitions of unfamiliar words in today's Bible reading, see pages 468-480.

IN TODAY'S READING

Fasting and confession of sins; reading of the Law; confession of
God's goodness; new covenant to keep the Law

The completion of the wall provided protection from the surrounding
enemies but provided peace of mind to hear what God had to say. It was
symbolic of our necessity to *have no fellowship with the unfruitful works
of darkness, but rather reprove them. . . . See then that you walk
circumspectly* (watchful of various dangers, hidden or visible). *. . .
understanding . . . the will of the Lord* (Ephesians 5:11,15,17).

Ezra stands out as a godly man who led the people to "understand the
will of the Lord." Ezra and other Levites *read in the Book of the Law of God
distinctly, and gave the sense* (meaning), *and caused them to understand the
reading* read from the Law (Nehemiah 8:8). The importance of teaching
the Word of God was of such grave consequences that it is mentioned seven
times in one chapter (8:2,3,7,8,9,12,13). This points out how essential it is to
read all the Bible from Genesis to Revelation.

On the 24th day of Tishri (September/October), *the children of Israel
were assembled with fasting* (Nehemiah 9:1). There was a movement of
the Holy Spirit following the reading of the Scriptures. *They stood up
in their place, and read in the Book of the Law of the LORD their God one
fourth part of the day; and another fourth part they confessed, and
worshiped the LORD their God* (9:2-3). The Levites were led to say to the
people: *Stand up and bless the LORD your God for ever and ever: and
blessed be Your glorious Name, which is exalted above all blessing and
praise* (9:5).

The priests revealed how God, in *manifold* (great) *mercies*, had
provided His *good Spirit to instruct them . . . they lacked nothing* (9:19-
21). It is the same Holy Spirit Who still guides believers, as Jesus
promised: *When He is come, He will reprove* (convict) *the world of sin.
. . . when He, the Spirit of Truth, is come, He will guide you into all Truth*
(John 16:8,13). The Holy Spirit also seeks to guide all Christians into the
occupation or position God has chosen for us to most effectively serve
Him and to prepare us for our eternal inheritance. The Holy Spirit alone
can enlighten our minds, impart conviction of sin, and empower us to
live a sanctified (holy) life (I Corinthians 2:16; 6:11).

*For this cause I bow my knees to the Father . . . That He would grant
you, according to the riches of His glory, to be strengthened with might
by His Spirit in the inner man* (Ephesians 3:14,16).

Thought for Today: If we live by faith, we never need to fear regardless of circumstances.

Christ Revealed: As the Creator (Nehemiah 9:6). God created all things by Jesus Christ
(Colossians 1:16).

For definitions of unfamiliar words in today's Bible reading, see pages 468-480.

✐N ꞆODAY'S ℛEADING

Residents of Jerusalem; priests and Levites with Zerubbabel;
dedication of the walls; Temple offices restored

*O*rdinary people, although not skilled in building walls, had willingly gone to work under Nehemiah's leadership and did the best they could to rebuild the walls around Jerusalem.

Only a minority of the people who left Persia to rebuild Jerusalem actually lived inside the city's walls. Most of the Jews lived in suburbs where they could grow crops, pasture their animals, and make a living more easily. Because of this, there were not enough people living in Jerusalem to maintain and protect it. *And the rulers of the people dwelled at Jerusalem: the rest of the people also cast lots, to bring one of ten to dwell in Jerusalem the holy city* (Nehemiah 11:1).

The Israelites could now assemble within the rebuilt walls of Jerusalem and worship without fear of their enemies. *At the dedication of the wall of Jerusalem they sought the Levites out of all their places, to bring them to Jerusalem, to keep* (observe) *the dedication with gladness, both with thanksgivings, and with singing. . . . Also that day they offered great sacrifices, and rejoiced: for God had made them rejoice with great joy. . . . the joy of Jerusalem was heard even afar off* (12:27,43).

The Israelites' worship demonstrated a heartfelt commitment to the Lord in their renewed relationship to Him. Though all true Christians love the Lord, not all are willing to give up personal interests and financial security to do what is needed to accomplish His purposes.

It is no less important for followers of Christ to consider "the walls" that may need to be rebuilt in their own lives where worldly interests have broken through and devastated their zeal for the Lord.

In our Christian walk, we need to be on guard against anything, including good, wholesome activities, which may cause us to divert either our time or our money from their usefulness to God and from becoming *treasures in heaven . . . For where your treasure is, there will your heart be also* (Matthew 6:20-21).

We all will want to hear our Lord say what the earthly master said in the parable of the talents: *Well done, you good and faithful servant: you have been faithful over a few things, I will make you ruler over many things: enter . . . into the joy of your lord* (Matthew 25:21).

Thought for Today: God can use the least servant to fulfill His needs.

Christ Portrayed: By the priests and Levites who purified (sanctified) themselves and the people (Nehemiah 12:30). Christ our High Priest, through His perfect sacrifice, purified His believers by His Word. The Word of God has the power to cleanse our lives as we read it and then seek to live it (John 15:3; 17:17).

For definitions of unfamiliar words in today's Bible reading, see pages 468-480.

In Today's Reading
Reading of the Law; separation from the heathen; tithes given;
Sabbath-breaking forbidden; mixed marriages condemned

*D*uring Nehemiah's absence, the Israelites' worship of God and the Sabbath observance were neglected. Intermarriage with Canaanite idol worshipers was common. Nehemiah again *came . . . to the king, and after certain days obtained . . . leave* (permission) *of the king: And . . . came to Jerusalem* (Nehemiah 13:6-7). He was grieved over the people's disregard of the Law and took firm action to return the nation to God. *On that day they read in the Book of Moses . . . therein was found written, that the Ammonite and the Moabite should not come into the congregation of God for ever* (13:1).

The greatest evils were committed by those who held the highest positions of spiritual leadership. *Eliashib the priest . . . was allied to Tobiah* (through marriage). *. . . And one of the sons of Joiada, the son of Eliashib the high priest, was son in law to Sanballat the Horonite* (13:4,28). Other priests had also married Canaanite women.

Added to these sins, Nehemiah *understood . . . the evil that Eliashib did for Tobiah, in preparing him a chamber* (room) *in the courts of the House* (Temple) *of God* (13:7). This was not only forbidden by . . . God (Deuteronomy 23:3-4), but Tobiah formerly had opposed Nehemiah's work in rebuilding the walls around Jerusalem (Nehemiah 2:10,19; 4:3-8; 6:17-19). Nehemiah *cast forth all the household stuff of Tobiah out of the chamber* (room). *. . . and . . . contended . . . with the rulers, and said, Why is the House* (Temple) *of God forsaken?* (13:8-9,11). The reason was obvious. The nobles of Judah had violated the Law by marrying heathen women, and consequently *defiled the priesthood* (13:29).

Nehemiah continued his reformation while facing much opposition. He warned the people concerning marriage with the Canaanites: *You shall not give your daughters to their sons, nor take their daughters to your sons. . . . Did not Solomon king of Israel sin by these things? . . . him did outlandish* (unbelieving) *women cause to sin* (13:25-26). Like Nehemiah we too can make a difference in our world. He was mightily used of God because he knew the Scriptures and refused to compromise.

Draw near to God. . . . you sinners; and purify your hearts, you double minded (doubters) (James 4:8).

Thought for Today: Give all praise to the Lord for all achievements.

Christ Portrayed: By Nehemiah who cleansed the priests and Levites and defined their duties (Nehemiah 13:30). Christ cleanses us from all our sins when we confess them (I John 1:9). Through Him we have been made *a royal priesthood* to serve the Lord (I Peter 2:9).

For definitions of unfamiliar words in today's Bible reading, see pages 468-480.

INTRODUCTION TO THE BOOK OF
ESTHER

The Book of Esther centers around the descendants of the Israelites who remained in Persia after the 70-year captivity and the Hebrew maiden Hadassah, who was given the Persian name Esther. The events in this book probably took place in the time period between chapters six and seven of the Book of Ezra, occurring about 40 years after the Temple had been rebuilt (Ezra 3:10; 5:14-15), but about 30 years before the walls of Jerusalem were rebuilt (Nehemiah 6:15). It is quite possible that Esther, who was by then the queen mother, was used of God to prepare the way for her fellow Israelite Nehemiah to become the cupbearer to her Persian stepson King Artaxerxes I. This trusted position and relationship with the king was probably the basis for Nehemiah to receive the king's support for rebuilding the walls in Jerusalem.

Ahasuerus is the Hebrew name and *Xerxes* (Esther 1:1) the Greek name, of Khshayarsha, king of Persia. He ruled *from India even to Ethiopia, over a hundred and seven and twenty provinces*. It is assumed that, at the banquet which opens the Book of Esther, he was planning a battle against Greece which eventually led to his defeat. Ahasuerus reigned in Shushan (Susa) which was located in modern Iran near the eastern border of Iraq. The rule of his son Artaxerxes I is recorded in Ezra 7-10 and Nehemiah 1-13.

The Book of Esther, as well as the Books of Ezra and Nehemiah, confirm that our Creator can accomplish His perfect will through a helpless minority of faithful servants, even when they are ruled by evil men (Jeremiah 32:27).

COMFORT

But the Comforter, Who is the Holy Spirit . . . shall teach you (John 14:26).

These things I have spoken to you, that My joy might remain in you, and that your joy might be full (John 15:11).

Wherefore comfort (encourage) *one another with these words* (I Thessalonians 4:18).

This is my comfort in my affliction: for Your Word has quickened me (given me life) (Psalm 119:50).

My soul melts (weeps) *for heaviness* (sorrow): *strengthen You me according to Your Word* (Psalm 119:28).

In Today's Reading

Vashti removed as queen; Esther made queen; Mordecai saves
the king's life; Haman's plan to destroy all the Jews

Hadassah was the Hebrew name for the Jewish orphan whose Persian name was Esther (Star). She was taken to the king's palace along with other maidens, either to be made queen or to become a part of the king's harem. Esther found herself in a situation over which she had no control. She and her faithful, older cousin Mordecai, who had adopted her (Esther 2:7,15), could only trust God for direction and protection. To complicate their situation, the man given the power to enforce the king's commands was the evil and self-serving Haman (3:10,15; 6:6-10; 7:9). Haman was an Amalekite, a descendant of Esau (3:1; also Genesis 36:12; I Samuel 15:2-3, 32-33), who hated all Jews (Deuteronomy 25:17-19). When Mordecai refused to bow down in "reverence" (Esther 3:2), Haman was determined to use his authority to destroy Mordecai and all Jews in the kingdom. Haman's plan was declared law with the king's approval and the lot (*Pur*) was cast to determine the best day to execute all Jews (3:7-13). However, Mordecai and Esther used every legal means to defend the interests of the people of God, even risking their own well-being.

God expects us to do all we can to resolve our own health, job, and financial problems. However, we should never doubt that God is in ultimate control to protect us and provide what we can't do. God never makes a mistake, is never partial, and never overlooks one of His children. We should not give in to self-pity and defeat but remain faithful and look to the Lord and His Word for guidance and strength. Like Mordecai, we must not bow down to the Hamans of this world who would seek to destroy our loyalty to Christ.

Like Esther, you may feel hopelessly trapped where you are and may long for the time when you would be free to do what you desire. But, Jesus explained the importance of doing your best now with the parable of a man with *two talents . . .* (who) *said* (to his master), *Lord, you delivered to me two talents: behold, I have gained two other talents beside them. His lord said to him, Well done, good and faithful servant; you have been faithful over a few things, I will make you ruler over many things* (Matthew 25:22-23).

Thought for Today: God does hear and answer your prayers.

Christ Portrayed: By Mordecai, who adopted Esther (Esther 2:15). We are adopted into the family of God by Jesus Christ (Ephesians 1:5), and we are now called children of God (I John 3:1).

For definitions of unfamiliar words in today's Bible reading, see pages 468-480.

In Today's Reading
Fasting among the Jews; Esther's banquet for Haman and the
king; Haman forced to honor Mordecai; Haman executed

About five years after Esther became queen, Haman was promoted *above all the princes that were with him* (Esther 3:1-7). When his decree was proclaimed that all Jews would be destroyed, Mordecai urged Esther *that she should go in to the king, to make supplication to him, and to make request before him for her people* (4:8). No one knew that Esther was a Jew because Mordecai had forbidden her to reveal her nationality. Esther was fearful and reminded him that Persian law stated that anyone who approached the king uninvited could be put to death. The risk was real, for she had *not been called to come in to the king these thirty days* (4:11). Esther could easily have reasoned: "If the king has lost interest in me or even discovered that I am a Jew, how could I favorably influence him?" But Esther believed that the risk of losing her prestigious position as queen Vashti had done, or even losing her own life, was not as important as doing what she could to save her people.

After three days of fasting, queen Esther *stood in the inner court of the king's house* (5:1) and waited to see if she would face life or death. The king welcomed her and offered to grant her request. *If it seem good to the king, let the king and Haman come this day to the banquet that I have prepared for him* (5:4). The king accepted and then, at a second banquet, he again asked Esther what her request might be. He was shocked to hear her pleading for her own life: *O king . . . let my life be given me . . . For we are sold, I and my people, to be destroyed. . . . The adversary* (foe) *and enemy is this wicked Haman* (7:3-6). Angrily, *the king said, Hang him. . . . So they hanged Haman on the gallows that he had prepared for Mordecai* (7:9-10).

Esther is an encouragement to all of us to use whatever talents, position, popularity, or wealth we have been blessed with to tell a lost world that our King gave His life to save them from the eternal torment of hell. *For whosoever will save his life shall lose it; but whosoever shall lose his life for My* (the Lord Jesus Christ's) *sake and the Gospel's, the same shall save it* (Mark 8:35).

Thought for Today: Throughout the ages, Satan has tried to destroy God's witnesses, but the Lord guides and guards His children.

Christ Portrayed: By Esther, whose death was demanded by others although she was innocent. She went before the king's court willing to die for her people (Esther 3:6-14; 4:16). Jesus also was innocent and His death was demanded by others (Mark 15:13-14). He was taken before rulers and was willing to die for His people—and He did die for them and for all mankind (Luke 23:8; John 10:17-18; I John 2:2).

For definitions of unfamiliar words in today's Bible reading, see pages 468-480.

IN TODAY'S READING

Esther's plea to reverse Haman's decree; enemies of the Jews
destroyed; Festival of Purim instituted; Mordecai
promoted to great honor

Haman's "wise counselors" *had cast Pur* (lot) to determine the most favorable time for the execution of all Jews. Haman's "lucky day" fell on the 13th day of the twelfth month (Esther 3:7-13; 9:1,24). Undoubtedly Haman felt fortunate that the lot had fallen on the last month of the year so that he would have plenty of time to make his evil plans to murder every Jew in the kingdom.

The fixed day of execution, which came to be known as Purim (Lots), was turned from death to deliverance by the intervening providence of God. Haman did not realize that Mordecai's God is always in control of the affairs of earth. Even though *the lot is cast into the lap . . . the whole disposing thereof is of the LORD* (Proverbs 16:33).

Following Haman's execution, the king allowed Mordecai to write a new decree giving the Jews the right to defend themselves.

In the day that the enemies of the Jews hoped to have power over them . . . (it was turned to the contrary, that the Jews had rule over them that hated them) (Esther 9:1). The Book of Esther demonstrates how God uses faithful servants to change world affairs in order to fulfill His Word.

In days of peace and prosperity, we are prone to be less concerned about the presence of God. But, when our situation seems critical, we seek His presence, and when He wonderfully intervenes, we praise Him for His merciful protection and provision.

Esther is a testimony to the fact that, even in a secular society dominated by a heathen power, our God can protect His people. But, He expects us, like Esther, to respond courageously in faith to the threats of the Hamans of this world.

The peace and satisfaction enjoyed by Mordecai and Esther can only be experienced by those who share our Lord's compassion for a lost world. Everyone has a right to know how to be saved. Jesus said: *No man comes to the Father, but by Me* (John 14:6).

Thought for Today: No sin works more deceitfully than pride.

Christ Revealed: By Mordecai's exaltation from servanthood to a position of honor and glory next to the king (Esther 8:2,15; 10:3). Christ came to earth as a servant and was exalted to *the right hand of God* (Philippians 2:7-9; Mark 16:19).

For definitions of unfamiliar words in today's Bible reading, see pages 468-480.

INTRODUCTION TO THE BOOK OF
*J*OB

The Book of Job opens with a brief history of a godly, praying man named Job, *the greatest of all the men of the east* (Job 1:3). In the first two chapters, we read of Satan's accusations against Job and the ordeal God permitted him to experience to test his faith. Job proved God could trust him to be faithful even through life's most painful experiences.

God said: *There was a man in the land of Uz, whose name was Job* (1:1). Uz was a descendant of Noah's third son Shem, through whom the Messiah would come (Genesis 10:22-23). The *land of Uz* (Job 1:1) is not specifically located, but it was situated in the area of the tribes of the Temanites, the Shuhites, and the Naamathites, as well as the Buzites (2:11; 32:2; compare Genesis 22:20-22). It also would have been within raiding distance of the Sabeans and Chaldeans (Job 1:15,17). Jeremiah wrote of *all the kings of the land of Uz, and all the kings of the land of the Philistines* (Jeremiah 25:20). Most of these are well-documented places. In Lamentations 4:21 it appears that Uz was located in Edom, just below the Dead Sea: *O daughter of Edom, that dwell in the land of Uz.* The exact locations are unimportant, but the spiritual insight concerning how we should understand and accept our circumstances and suffering is of utmost importance, relevant, and applicable to every age.

In the Book of Job we see the reasonings of God, Job, his wife, his three friends, Elihu the Buzite, and Satan who is exposed as the instigator of all suffering. As you read through each chapter, carefully distinguish between the wisdom of godly Job and the well-meaning, but inaccurate, half-truths and misleading humanistic arguments of his friends. God highly complimented Job as being *perfect* (blameless) *and upright* (Job 1:1,8,22; 2:10) for having spoken the truth.

Job's friends and Elihu reveal how deceptive and unreliable human reasoning can be. The only satisfying answers to the needs of all of us are found in the only infallible, Holy Word of God.

In each day's reading, note the intensifying of Job's suffering but also the development of his spiritual insight. In the final chapter, God once again removes all doubt concerning Job's righteousness and truthfulness when the Lord said to Eliphaz: *My wrath is kindled against you, and against your two friends: for you have not spoken of Me the thing that is right, as My servant Job has* (42:7).

𝒥N 𝒯ODAY'S 𝒭EADING

Job's wealth and godliness; Satan permitted to afflict Job; critical
counsel by Job's wife and his three friends

𝒲ithout the Holy Scriptures, we would never understand the reason for suffering. Job, the faithful servant of the Lord, was stripped of his family, possessions, reputation, and health. But his suffering was not misfortune or bad luck, nor was it punishment from God for his sins as his friends mistakenly assumed. Our Creator, Who knows our innermost thoughts, declared that Job *was perfect and upright, and one that feared* (revered) *God, and eschewed* (shunned) *evil* (Job 1:1).

Behind all the world's evil is Satan, *going to and fro in the earth . . . walking up and down in it* (1:7) in his continuous effort to destroy all that is good. But Satan is under the constant surveillance of God and can do nothing without His permission.

Satan assumed that, like every self-serving person, Job was faithful only because God would reward him. During his intense suffering and testing, Job's wife even suggested that he *curse* (renounce) *God, and die* (2:9). She too had suffered loss, but it seems that her greatest loss was her faith in God. Job realized he was not the owner of all he possessed, not even of his children, but he was merely the Lord's manager of things entrusted to his care. From there, it was just one more step of faith for Job to accept that God, in His infinite wisdom, had the right to reclaim His possessions anytime He chose. Instead of cursing God, Job worshiped Him, saying: *The LORD gave, and the LORD has taken away; blessed be the Name of the LORD* (1:21).

Just as Satan used Job's "friends" to criticize, belittle, and condemn him, Satan still delights in using family, friends, coworkers, and even fellow church members to do the same today. *Be sober, be vigilant; because your adversary the devil, as a roaring lion, walks about, seeking whom he may devour* (I Peter 5:8). But Satan is not a *lion*; he only appears like a lion, and his *roaring* is all bluff.

Our God, the Master Planner, is still in full control. *Jesus Christ the same yesterday, and to day, and for ever* (Hebrews 13:8).

Thought for Today: It is good to praise the Lord, to sing praise to His Name (Psalm 92:1).

Christ Revealed: In the conversation between Satan and God Almighty (Job 1:6-12). We can see the meaning of Christ's statement to Peter that Satan wanted to sift him *as wheat* (Luke 22:31). It is comforting to know that Satan cannot test us beyond the will of God.

For definitions of unfamiliar words in today's Bible reading, see pages 468-480.

In Today's Reading

Eliphaz' rebuke of Job continues; Job's response; Job reproaches his friends; Bildad's theory about Job's affliction

---

*A*fter one full week of silent contemplation about Job's suffering, Eliphaz, his eldest friend spoke first (Job 2:13). He tried to convince Job to confess his secret sin, saying: *Happy is the man whom God corrects: therefore despise not . . . the chastening of the Almighty* (5:17). Eliphaz then went on to elaborate on the blessings Job could expect if he would only confess his sin, and he confidently concluded: *Lo . . . we have searched it, so it is; hear it, and know . . . it for your good* (5:27).

In addition to Job's physical sufferings, his financial loss, the death of his children, and his wife's bitterness toward God, all three of his friends misjudged his integrity and continued to unmercifully attack him day after day. Job felt the bitter sting of Eliphaz's condemnation and his insinuation that Job was a hypocrite. Job did not understand why God had not come to his defense. Even worse, it seemed to him that he had even been struck down by *the arrows of Almighty* (6:4).

However, through Job's sufferings we see how the Lord was bringing to light deeper spiritual insight, when Job said: *What is man, that You should magnify him? and that You should set Your heart upon him? And that You should visit* (examine) *him every morning, and try* (test) *him every moment?* (7:17-18).

We too recognize our insignificance in comparison to the eternal, holy, and Almighty God. Although He created us, by nature we are defiled by sin and deserve eternal punishment. But, through the miraculous new birth, we have the joy of being eternally with our loving Creator. However, all who reject Christ as personal Savior and Lord will be *cast into the lake of fire. This is the second death* (Revelation 20:14-15).

It is not our Heavenly Father's will *that any should perish, but that all should come to repentance* (II Peter 3:9). However, God *tries* (proves) *us* – either with afflictions or with blessings. Through it all, He is seeking to develop in us a genuine love for and commitment to Him.

All that God does and allows is for our ultimate good. *For to you it is given in the behalf of Christ, not only to believe on Him, but also to suffer for His sake* (Philippians 1:29).

Thought for Today: Every trial gives us an opportunity to draw closer to God and can make us more the person He wants us to become.

Christ Revealed: Through Job's sorrowful condition (Job 7:1-6). Christ was known as *a Man of sorrows . . . acquainted with grief.* On the cross separated from God in His humanity, Jesus felt that pain in addition to all our sins which He bore (Isaiah 53:3; Mark 15:34).

For definitions of unfamiliar words in today's Bible reading, see pages 468-480.

In Today's Reading
Job acknowledges God's justice; his weariness of life;
Zophar's accusation; Job's affirmation of faith in God's wisdom

*A*ll of us will benefit by listening carefully to the spiritual discernment of Job, whom God said *was perfect and upright, and one that feared God, and eschewed evil* (Job 1:1).

This man of spiritual insight proclaimed with confidence: *Are not his* (man's) *days also like the days of a hireling* (hired worker)? . . . *So I am made to possess months of vanity, and wearisome nights are appointed to me* (7:1,3). His friend Bildad incorrectly believed that God had appointed *wearisome nights* of suffering only for sinners, and his response to Job was critical and cynical: *How long will you speak these things? . . . If you were pure and upright; surely now He would awake* (rouse Himself) *for you, and make the habitation of your righteousness prosperous* (8:2,6).

Bildad concluded that those who enjoy good things in this life are righteous, and all suffering is the result of sin. But, in a parable given by Jesus, the rich man who built bigger barns for "greater blessings" was not one who pleased the Lord (Luke 12:18,20). Another time, Jesus revealed that the man was not born blind because of sin (John 9:2-3).

Job's suffering led him to experience deep, spiritual maturity as he recognized God as far superior to himself and he spoke with confidence, saying: *Remember . . . that You have made me as the clay. . . . You have granted me life and favor, and Your visitation has preserved my spirit* (Job 10:9,12). However, Job knew that he and God could not meet on the same level; *For He is not a man, as I am, that I should answer Him, and we should come together in judgment* (court). *Neither is there any daysman* (arbitrator) *between us* (9:32-33). Job expressed the desperate need for a mediator, someone who would stand in the gap between the Holy God and sinful man.

Our Lord Jesus Christ is the only Mediator who can restore man's broken fellowship with God (Romans 5:8-10). *For there is One God, and One Mediator between God and men, the Man Christ Jesus* (I Timothy 2:5). We now have access to the Father through our Mediator Jesus Christ, Who has entered *into heaven itself, now to appear in the presence of God for us* (Hebrews 9:24).

Thought for Today: You will be blessed when you love the person who is unlovely.

Christ Portrayed: Through the daysman (mediator) Job longs for (Job 9:33). Christ is the only *Mediator between God and* sinful *men* (I Timothy 2:5).

For definitions of unfamiliar words in today's Bible reading, see pages 468-480.

$\mathcal{I}$N $\mathcal{T}$ODAY'S $\mathcal{R}$EADING
Job's defense of his integrity; his desire to die; Eliphaz' intensified
condemnation; Job's complaint of God's dealing with him

$\mathcal{S}$atan prompted the attacks on Job by his wife and by his "devoted" friends in an attempt to substantiate his own accusation that Job would curse God if his many blessings were removed.

Job's suffering intensified with days and weeks of sleeplessness and painful, ulcerating boils that would only become more intense since he had no painkillers. It may appear that he wavered at times, but Job always ended his comments on a high note of praise. Job could say with utmost confidence: *Though He slay me, yet will I trust in Him. . . . I know that I shall be justified* (Job 13:15,18).

Although Job gave up hope of recovering his health, wealth, children, or high esteem among the people, he did not become bitter or resentful toward his accusers or toward God. Instead, he looked forward to being with the Lord after his death, saying: *If a man die, shall he live again? all the days of my appointed time will I wait, till my change come* (14:14), meaning: "After death, I shall live again and I will be changed."

How different Job's attitude was from many today who blame fate, circumstances, God, or others for what goes wrong in their lives. Some easily become dissatisfied, bitter, pessimistic, or engulfed in self-pity. Their self-image depends on others' reactions. When others praise them, their self-esteem rises; when they are criticized or their plans fail, they feel defeated. Job didn't need praise from people to maintain his faith since he retained his confidence in the wisdom and justice of his Creator.

Christians can thank God for the perfect Savior and great High Priest, Who *ever lives to make intercession for them* (us) (Hebrews 7:25). Having accepted Jesus as Savior and Lord of our lives, we should have a sincere desire to know His will by reading all His Word.

Job's unshakable faith in God resulted from his obedience to the revealed Word of God. He said: *Neither have I gone back from the commandment of His lips; I have esteemed the words of His mouth more than my necessary food* (Job 23:12).

Thought for Today: Treasures laid up in heaven pay high dividends.

Christ Revealed: Through the smiting of Job (Job 16:10). Christ also was struck by those who ridiculed Him (Matthew 27:29-44; John 18:22-23; Psalms 22:7-8; 109:25; Isaiah 53).

For definitions of unfamiliar words in today's Bible reading, see pages 468-480.

IN TODAY'S READING
Job's appeal to God; Bildad's cruel accusation; Job's reaffirmation of faith; Zophar refers to Job as a wicked man

Job assumed all hope of recovery was gone when he said: *My breath* (spirit) *is corrupt, my days are extinct, the graves are ready for me. . . . all my members are as a shadow. . . . My days are past, my purposes are broken off* (Job 17:1,7,11).

Bildad interrupted this suffering saint with scathing words that were even more cruel and critical than his first speech. He assumed that Job's sufferings exposed him as a sinful hypocrite who was hopelessly condemned: *For he is cast into a net by his own feet. . . . He shall be driven from light into darkness, and chased out of the world* (18:8,18). Bildad went on to say: *Surely such are the dwellings of the wicked, and this is the place of him that knows not God* (18:21). This mistaken accusation from Job's "friend" must have been a bitter blow. Not only was Job facing death, but to die misjudged as a hypocrite when he knew his heart was right with God must have been heartbreaking.

Our hearts are deeply stirred with compassion as this pitiful, lonely, suffering saint looked beyond his "friends." With great spiritual discernment and assurance, Job said: *I know that my Redeemer lives, and that He shall stand at the latter day upon the earth . . . I shall see God* (19:25-26). This revelation of life after death is one of the greatest in the Old Testament. God leads us to see, through Job, that we have no valid excuse for complaining about our suffering, material loss, or being misunderstood by others.

According to the Law, a redeemer was the next of kin who was responsible for redeeming (buying back) an enslaved kinsman or his lost inheritance (Leviticus 25:25). The kinsman-redeemer foreshadowed the coming of Jesus Christ, our Savior-Redeemer. We were hopeless, lost sinners condemned to die and to be cast into eternal hell. *By the deeds of the Law there shall be no flesh* (body) *be justified in His sight: for by the Law is the knowledge of sin. But now the righteousness of God without the Law. . . . which is by faith of Jesus Christ to all and upon all them that believe . . . Being justified freely by His grace through the redemption that is in Christ Jesus* (Romans 3:20-22,24).

Thought for Today: The Christian has a personal, living Savior to guide him.

Christ Revealed: As the *Redeemer* (Job 19:25). Jesus Christ is our Redeemer. By His death, He provided the required sacrifice for our sins (Acts 20:28; Ephesians 1:14; Revelation 5:9).

For definitions of unfamiliar words in today's Bible reading, see pages 468-480.

*I*N *T*ODAY'S *R*EADING
Job declares that wicked men sometimes prosper; Eliphaz
accuses Job of sin; Job's desire to plead his case before God

*F*ew men in Bible history are so highly esteemed by God as Job. God
said of him: *There is none like him in the earth, a perfect* (blameless) *and
an upright man, one that fears* (reveres) *God, and eschews* (shuns) *evil*
(Job 1:8). His friends mistakenly supposed that all his problems were
the result of his secret sins. They assumed that wicked men are miserable and, since Job was exceedingly miserable, he must be very wicked!

It is shocking to read how wrong Eliphaz could be with his blunt,
critical, and cruel condemnation of Job, saying: *Acquaint now yourself
with Him, and be at peace. . . . Receive, I pray you, the Law from His
mouth, and. . . . put away iniquity far from your tabernacles* (22:21-23).
In striking contrast, God said to Job's friend Eliphaz: *You have not
spoken of Me the thing that is right, as My servant Job has* (42:7).

There are still self-righteous, overbearing, opinionated people like
Eliphaz, who are quick to pass judgment on anyone who doesn't believe as they do or who experience difficulties or sickness. Job's faith
was unshakable because he could truthfully say: *His way I have kept,
and not declined. Neither have I gone back from the commandment of
His lips; I have esteemed the words of His mouth more than my necessary
food* (23:11-12). He believed that, since God was faithful to His Word,
He also would be faithful to His obedient servant.

We often do not understand why we face disappointments, sufferings, or being misunderstood. But, we can believe and trust in God, since
He always gives His best to all who desire to do His will.

The devotion of Job should be an inspiration to all of us who are
not as concerned about knowing the "reason" for our suffering as with
knowing God and His Word, the only true source of guidance.

It seemed to Job that God was nowhere to be found. But, regardless
of this, Job said: *He knows the way that I take: when He has tried me,
I shall come forth as gold* (Job 23:10).

Thought for Today: Strength from God's Word on a day-to-day basis upholds our faith in
Him in times of testing.

Christ Revealed: Through Job's faithfulness to God throughout his suffering (Job 23:10-12).
Christ's faithfulness to the Father is seen as He prayed for the Father's will to be done (Luke
22:42).

For definitions of unfamiliar words in today's Bible reading, see pages 468-480.

In Today's Reading

Bildad's answer; Job's reproof of Bildad; Job's praise to God;
Job's truthfulness; source of wisdom; recalling past wealth

The Book of Job is the inspired Word of God. Job was not searching for answers when he said: *But where shall wisdom be found? and where is the place of understanding? Man knows not the price thereof; neither is it found in the land of the living. . . . neither shall silver be weighed for the price thereof. . . . Where then comes wisdom? . . . Seeing it is hidden from the eyes of all living* (Job 28:12-13,15,20-21).

Job was expressing his utmost confidence that God is the Author and Revealer of true wisdom. There is no substitute for reading all of His Word to understand His perfect plan for our lives. This means that it is important to read through every book of the Bible, from Genesis to Revelation, with a sincere desire to apply its instruction to our own lives. We can be sure that Satan will attempt to distract us from the true source of wisdom and cause us to make decisions based on circumstances or contemporary standards.

The worldly-minded find fault with God, just as the Israelites did as they journeyed through the wilderness. They complained about their circumstances instead of acknowledging that God was in control. We too can make unwise decisions when we allow ourselves to become frustrated. To illustrate, we may say to someone: "You make me angry." But the fact is, we choose to be angry. Or we may say: "I am depressed today." However, the sad truth is that we have refused to see God in the circumstances He has allowed to take place in our lives. We can be sure that our Lord is far more concerned with our best interests than we are. *Wherefore let them that suffer according to the will of God commit the keeping of their souls to Him in well doing, as to a faithful Creator* (I Peter 4:19). We always have the choice to move above and beyond anger and disappointments by permitting the indwelling Christ to rule our lives. This is the key to experiencing *the peace of God* (Philippians 4:7). *The entrance of Your words gives light; it gives understanding to the simple* (Psalm 119:130).

Thought for Today: Our faith in God is revealed by the way we react to both our sorrows and our sufferings.

Christ Revealed: Through Job's compassion for others (Job 29:15-17,21-25). Jesus was moved to compassion when He saw great crowds in need of healing and feeding (Matthew 14:14; 15:30-39).

For definitions of unfamiliar words in today's Bible reading, see pages 468-480.

*N*o one in biblical history, other than Christ, suffered so much public humiliation and intense physical and emotional pain as Job did. He had held the chief administrative position in his country and had *dwelled as a king* (Job 29:25). *I delivered the poor that cried, and the fatherless, and him that had none to help him. . . . I was eyes to the blind, and feet was I to the lame. I was a father to the poor: and the cause which I knew not I searched out* (29:12,15-16). In chapter 31 he listed 12 common sins that no one could accuse him of committing. Yet, in his time of need, no one expressed compassion or a kind word to him.

For Job, there seemed to be no end to the cruelty of the people who made his suffering even more painful and miserable: *They push away my feet. . . . Terrors are turned upon me: they pursue my soul as the wind: and my welfare passes away as a cloud. And now my soul is poured out upon me; the days of affliction have taken hold upon me* (30:12-17). But, by far, the most troubling to Job was that it seemed that God did not care and was not hearing his prayers: *I cry to You, and You do not hear me* (30:20).

At such times our faith is put to the test, *For we walk by faith* (II Corinthians 5:7) and are not dependent upon "the things that are seen." We are to trust the Lord and the promises of His Word. Faith does not originate with us but it is a gift from God (Ephesians 2:8).

Job's three friends mistakenly judged his relationship to God, but he did not allow them to destroy his faith. As we consider Job, whom God declared the most perfect man on earth (Job 1:8), should we be surprised when we are falsely criticized? The most devoted Christian often suffers the worst indignities and humiliation from thoughtless, inconsiderate people – even from some who profess to be Christians.

So that we ourselves glory in (speak proudly of) *you in the churches of God for your patience and faith in all your persecutions and tribulations* (afflictions) *that you endure: Which is a manifest* (visible, evident) *token of the righteous judgment of God, that you may be counted worthy of the Kingdom of God, for which you also suffer* (II Thessalonians 1:4-5).

Thought for Today: If you are confronted with gossip, immediately turn the conversation to something commendable (Philippians 4:8).

Christ Revealed: Through the ridicule and affliction which Job suffered (Job 30:10-11). Christ was afflicted and spat upon. After Pilate delivered Jesus to the Roman soldiers, they flogged Him, hit Him with a stick and spat on Him (a sign of great contempt) – and then they crucified Him (Mark 15:15-20; also Isaiah 50:6; 53:2-5; Matthew 27:26-30; John 19:1-3).

For definitions of unfamiliar words in today's Bible reading, see pages 468-480.

In Today's Reading
Elihu continues his accusations against Job

*E*lihu did not speak until Job's three friends had ended their accusations. He condemned Job's three friends but expressed even greater hostility toward Job. Four times in five verses we read variations of the phrase that Elihu's *wrath was kindled* (Job 32:1-5).

This young egotist referred to himself by the words "me," "my," and "I" at least 55 times to inform Job that he alone was chosen to intercede on Job's behalf and that he was *according to your* (Job's) *wish in God's stead* (32:6 – 33:33). Elihu's accusations against Job's testimony are, at best, half-truths and misinterpretations (33:8-13).

One of Elihu's accusations was that Job had claimed to be sinlessly perfect (34:5). The fact is Job acknowledged his imperfection as sin in 7:21 and 13:26. However, the Lord proclaimed Job as *My servant . . . that there is none like him in the earth, a perfect and an upright man* (1:8). Elihu falsely stated that Job *has said, It profits a man nothing that he should delight himself with God* (34:9). But Job never said that. Elihu continued his vicious attack on this dear, godly man, saying: *Job has spoken without knowledge, and his words were without wisdom. My desire is that Job may be tried to the end because of his answers for* (like) *wicked men. For he adds rebellion to his sin . . . and multiplies his words against God* (34:35-37).

Elihu's conclusions were in direct opposition to the testimony of God, Who said that Job had *spoken of Me the thing which is right* (42:7-8).

During times of personal afflictions, heartbreaking bereavement, persecution, or financial struggles, we are often tempted to become depressed and even fail to pray. That is when we need someone's loving comfort and assurance that our Lord ultimately controls every situation that comes into our lives. Regardless of how bad it may seem, He wants to use it for our good and for His glory (Romans 8:28; also Genesis 50:20).

Have faith in the wisdom of God, *casting all your care* (anxiety) *upon Him; for He cares for you* (I Peter 5:7).

Thought for Today: Enjoying fellowship with God, among other things, is dependent upon one's attitude toward others.

Christ Revealed: As the One Who watches how we live and all we do (Job 34:21). The Lord keeps His eyes on the righteous (I Peter 3:12).

For definitions of unfamiliar words in today's Bible reading, see pages 468-480.

In Today's Reading
Elihu's speech interrupted by God; God's challenge to Job;
man's weakness and ignorance; Job humbled

*I*s it any surprise that God interrupted Elihu's speech and *answered Job out of the whirlwind, and said, Who is this that darkens counsel by words without knowledge?* (Job 38:1-2).

For the first time since his suffering started, Job began hearing words of comfort rather than condemnation. When the God of love said: *Gird up now your loins like a man* (38:3), He seemed to be saying: "Step out of the ashes; you have suffered long enough; you have proven Satan a liar; get ready to move a little closer to Me. I'm not as far away from you as it seemed when you said: *I cannot perceive Him . . . I cannot see Him* (23:8-9). I want you to see that I, and I alone, control the vast universe and yet am greatly concerned with even the smallest detail of your life."

The second statement of God to Job was equally comforting: *I will demand of you, and answer you Me* (38:3). The Lord was saying to Job: "You no longer have to listen to the insults of cruel men, for I am in control and will reveal to you the most amazing wisdom concerning the universe ever given to mankind." First, God wanted Job to consider the limitations of his own wisdom compared to the wisdom of the One Who created the universe: *Can you bind the sweet influences* (chains) *of Pleiades, or loose the bands of Orion?* (38:31). God asked Job about 60 questions in this first cycle of conversation (38:1 – 40:2), and over 80 questions altogether (38 – 41). The wisest astronomer can't explain or change one star in the marvelous array of Pleiades, one of the most beautiful clusters of stars.

The Mighty God, Who created the universe, also created us, cares for us, patiently listens to our prayers, and provides us with what is best for us in the light of our eternal destination. We need to see how un-qualified we are to question His wisdom. Nothing is unforeseen and no one is overlooked, slighted, or left out by our Heavenly Father. He imparts inner strength and sustains us by His indwelling Holy Spirit.

God's words to the Apostle Paul were also for us: *My grace is suf-ficient for you: for My strength is made perfect in* (perfects your) *weakness* (II Corinthians 12:9).

Thought for Today: The vastness of the universe reveals God's unlimited resources and matchless wisdom.

Christ Revealed: As the One Who *laid the foundations of the earth* (Job 38:4). By Christ, God created our universe (Hebrews 1:1-2; also John 1:1-3).

For definitions of unfamiliar words in today's Bible reading, see pages 468-480.

IN TODAY'S READING
God's great power reviewed; Job's submission to God;
his prayer for his friends; God blesses Job

Through a series of over 80 questions, God revealed to Job many of the wonders of the universe, some of which have only recently been "discovered" by science. Because of his faith in God and his patience through suffering, Job acknowledged the supreme authority of God compared to how little is known by mankind. It is no surprise to read that Job confessed to God: *I know that You can do every thing, and that no thought can be withheld from You. . . . I uttered that I understood not; things too wonderful for me, which I knew not* (Job 42:2-3). By this he meant: "Although I did not understand, I will never again question what God does or what He allows to happen, since His love and wisdom are perfect." All of us need to be reminded that our limited knowledge and ability to cope with life's problems should cause us to realize how foolish, as well as sinful, it is to question the wisdom and love of God for His children. We need to accept, with submissive hearts, the circumstances He allows in our lives, which He will use to fulfill His loving, eternal purpose.

During his suffering, Job experienced glorious revelations of the incomparable greatness of God and His ways. Job's spiritual understanding continued to grow as he said: *I have heard of You by the hearing of the ear: but now my eye sees You. Wherefore I abhor* (despise) *myself, and repent in dust and ashes* (42:5-6). Those who trust in the Lord, as Job did, are not searching for the answers to all of life's problems, nor asking the questions: "Why?" or "Why me?" They are simply trusting our loving, all-wise Father, Who always knows what we need and will give the best to those who trust Him.

Job's friends must have been astounded to hear the Voice from heaven say to Eliphaz: *My wrath is kindled against you, and against your two friends: for you have not spoken of Me the thing that is right, as My servant Job has* (42:7). Job could have become proud after God came to his defense. Instead, he humbly prayed for God to forgive his three friends who had so cruelly misjudged him. Jesus also set an example when He said: *Bless them that curse you, and pray for them which despitefully use you* (Luke 6:28).

Thought for Today: Can the Lord say to you: *Well done, you good and faithful servant* (Matthew 25:21,23)?

Christ Revealed: Through Job's praying for his "friends" (Job 42:10). We are reminded of Christ's command to pray for those who curse or falsely accuse us (Luke 6:28).

For definitions of unfamiliar words in today's Bible reading, see pages 468-480.

Introduction To The Book Of
Psalms

The Book of Psalms includes songs of praise and thanksgiving. Each of the last five psalms begins and ends with the phrase: *Praise . . . the LORD,* which is the English translation of the Hebrew word *Hallelujah.* It has become a universal word, for it is the same in every language. It is impossible to be praising the Lord while being dissatisfied with our circumstances. The psalms teach us to forgive others, as well as to express gratitude to God for His forgiveness of our many sins and our restoration to fellowship with Him.

The psalms also include prayers seeking mercy and help, as well as expressing confidence. Prominent in the Book of Psalms is the high esteem God has given to the Scripture itself. He inspired the psalmist to write: *Blessed are they that keep His testimony, and that seek Him with the whole heart. . . . Then shall I not be ashamed, when I have respect to all your Commandments. . . . Your Word have I hidden in my heart, that I might not sin against you* (Psalm 119:2,6,11). The vital importance of the Scriptures is brought to our attention at least 170 times in Psalm 119. The psalmist was led to write: *I will . . . praise Your Name for Your lovingkindness and for Your truth: for You have magnified Your Word above all Your Name* (138:2). Because God has exalted His Word above all else, we are made to see that the Scriptures are exceedingly important for our personal well-being.

Although written about a thousand years before the birth of Jesus, many psalms refer to the coming of the Messiah – His birth, life, betrayal, crucifixion, resurrection, and ascension into heaven, as well as His return to reign on earth. In the New Testament, the following psalms are applied to Jesus Christ: 2; 8; 16; 22; 40; 41; 45; 68; 69; 72; 89; 102; 109; 110; 118; and 132. In Psalm 2, the Messiah is God's Son Who is to be worshiped; 16:10-11 proclaims His resurrection; chapter 22 His suffering; and chapter 40 His sacrifice. In Psalm 45:6 the Messiah is God; in chapter 89 He is the One promised to fulfill God's covenant with David. In Psalm 110 He is *the LORD* (vs 1), *a rod of Your strength* (Ruler) (vs 2), *in the beauties of holiness* (vs 3), *a Priest for ever* (vs 4), *shall strike through* (shatter, be Conqueror of) *kings* (vs 5), *judge among the heathen* (nations) (vs 6).

After His resurrection, Jesus opened the eyes of two of His disciples: *And beginning at Moses and all the Prophets, He expounded* (explained) *to them in all the Scriptures the things concerning Himself. . . . And He said to them . . . all things must be fulfilled, which were written in the Law of Moses, and in the Prophets and in the Psalms, concerning Me* (Luke 24:27,44).

> ## In Today's Reading
> The blessed and the ungodly; David's confidence in God;
> prayer for protection, mercy, and deliverance

The key to receiving a blessing from God begins with three negative statements. The first is: *Blessed* (Divinely favored, Fortunate) *is the man Who walks not in the counsel of the ungodly* (Psalm 1:1). The *ungodly* may live acceptable lifestyles that conform to the basic moral standards of society, but live and act as though the Creator God does not exist. Therefore, they assume that any religion, or none at all, is equally acceptable. In doing this, they feel no accountability to God and see no need of a Savior.

The second negative statement is: *Nor stands in the way of sinners.* Sinners speak, act, think, and live to please themselves. They may be honest, upright, and generous in the eyes of the majority of people. They may even believe there is a God and may live a good, moral life. Consequently, they are deceived and see no need to repent of sin because they do not think they are sinners. The Christian life is centered in God, but the sinner's life is centered on himself.

The third negative statement is: *Nor sits in the seat of the scornful.* The *scornful* makes known his belittling, antagonistic attitude against God the Father as Creator of all things and against worshiping Jesus Christ as God the Son – *the great God and our Savior Jesus Christ* (Titus 2:13). The *scornful*, for the most part, stand firmly and openly against the Bible and Jesus Christ as the only way to be saved and reach heaven.

The *blessed* person has an attitude of *delight . . . in the Law of the LORD; and in His Law he does meditate day and night* (Psalm 1:2). If we delight in pleasing Jesus Christ, we will "meditate" upon His Word. As we meditate prayerfully *in His Law,* the Holy Spirit speaks to our hearts, revealing the meaning of His Word for our lives. Such people have a desire to be led by *the Spirit of Truth* (John 16:13).

One of the great blessings that is imparted to those who meditate upon God's Word comes silently and unnoticed, *like a tree planted by the rivers of water, that brings forth its fruit in its season; its leaf also shall not wither; and whatsoever* (whatever) *he does shall prosper* (Psalm 1:3).

Thought for Today: Only to the extent that we love God will we enjoy obeying His Word.

Christ Revealed: As the Son of God (Psalm 2:7). God loved the world and gave us His only Son, that whoever *believes in Him* will not perish, but will have life everlasting (John 3:16; also Acts 13:33; Hebrew 1:5).

For definitions of unfamiliar words in today's Bible reading, see pages 468-480.

In Today's Reading
Judgment upon the wicked; David's desire for justice;
those who shall dwell with God; prayer for protection

David asked a question that has eternal consequences: *LORD, who shall abide* (dwell) *in Your Tabernacle* (Tent)? *who shall dwell in Your holy hill?* (Psalm 15:1). David focused on two of the all-important issues of life when he asked: *Who shall dwell?* and *Who shall abide?* The Holy Spirit provided the answer: *He that walks uprightly, and works righteousness, and speaks the truth in his heart* (15:2). To *work righteousness* can only take place after one becomes a child of God through faith in Christ. Jesus told Nicodemus: *Except a man be born of water and of the Spirit, he cannot enter into the Kingdom of God* (John 3:5). To *speak the truth in his heart* comes from knowing God's Word.

Although the Book of Psalms foretells the resurrection of Christ, it also offers assurance that all who believe in Him will rise to share in His resurrection and life eternal. *For the Lord Himself shall descend from heaven . . . and the dead in Christ shall rise first* (I Thessalonians 4:16). How wonderful to *dwell* in Him and to look forward to *living* in the presence of our Lord forever. Like David, let us rejoice: *I have set the LORD always before me: because He is at my right hand, I shall not be moved. Therefore my heart is glad, and my glory rejoices: my flesh also shall rest in hope* (Psalm 16:8-9). The Almighty God fulfilled the prophecy of David: *For You will not leave my soul in hell* (16:10). Forty days after His resurrection, Jesus Christ ascended heavenward to take His place at the right hand of the Father as had been prophesied. *You will show me the path of life: in Your presence is fullness of joy; at Your right hand there are pleasures for evermore* (16:11).

On the *Day of Pentecost*, Peter quoted from this psalm to assure about three thousand people that Jesus was the Christ of Whom David had prophesied (Acts 2:1,25-28,31).

The risen Christ is the Good News of the Gospel upon which our faith is based. *As in Adam all die, even so in Christ shall all be made alive* (I Corinthians 15:22).

Thought for Today: Christ died to reconcile you to Himself.

Christ Revealed: In the prophecy that God would not allow His Holy One to see decay (Psalm 16:10). This foretells of the resurrection of our Lord Jesus Christ (Acts 2:25-27; 13:35-39). When Jesus spoke the Revelation to John, He declared He had been dead but now is alive and that He has the keys of death and hell in His possession (Revelation 1:18).

For definitions of unfamiliar words in today's Bible reading, see pages 468-480.

$\mathscr{I}$N $\mathscr{T}$ODAY'S $\mathscr{R}$EADING
Thanksgiving for deliverance; creation and Covenants of God;
a prayer for God's people; cry of anguish and song of praise

The effects of the Word of God are beyond compare, for it was by His Word that the worlds were created and by which they are still upheld (Hebrews 1:3). *The heavens declare* (are telling of) *the glory of God; and the firmament* (expanse) *shows His handiwork* (Psalm 19:1). Most exciting is the transforming power of Jesus, the Word of God made flesh, upon all who receive Him as Lord.

The first six verses of Psalm 19 refer to the works of God in the world, and the remaining eight refer to the marvelous influence of His Word on the lives of all who love and obey Him.

In this short psalm, six names are used to express the Word of God:
1.   It is the *Law of the* LORD and, as such, *is perfect* (complete), *converting the soul* (restoring the whole person) *making wise the simple* (19:7). It is as far superior to the words of man as the heavens are above the earth. Then why should anyone settle for less than to *receive with meekness the engrafted* (implanted) *Word, which is able to save* (deliver, preserve) *your souls* (James 1:21)?
2.   The *testimony of the* LORD *is sure* (never fails), *making wise the simple* (Psalm 19:7). The Apostle Paul confirmed this to Timothy, saying: *You have known the Holy Scriptures, which are able to make you wise to salvation* (II Timothy 3:15).
3.   It is the *statutes* (precepts) *of the* LORD and, therefore, *right* (Psalm 19:8), because they are founded solely on the righteousness of God. His Word reveals what we are, as well as what God has planned for us to be.
4.   It is the *Commandment of the* LORD (19:8) – not merely suggested alternatives of popular opinion; it is the expression of the holiness of God. His Commandments provide a new life free from sin's bondage.
5.   It reveals the *fear of the* LORD (19:9), a reverential admiration for His holiness and a fear of offending His majesty.
6.   It is the *judgments of the* LORD (which) *are true and righteous altogether* (19:9).

The psalmist expresses well what our feelings should be concerning the incomparable Word of God. *More to be desired are they than gold, yea, than much fine gold: sweeter also than honey* (Psalm 19:10).

Thought for Today: Thank the Lord for His Presence in your life today!

Christ Revealed: As the One to Whom the psalms refer when they speak of the nails that pierced His hands and feet on the cross and the parting of His clothing (Psalm 22:16,18; John 19:18). See also Matthew 27:35; Mark 15:24; Luke 23:34.

For definitions of unfamiliar words in today's Bible reading, see pages 468-480.

ℐN ℐODAY'S ℛEADING
The Great Shepherd; King of Glory; prayer for guidance;
love for God's House; prayer for God's help;
adoration of God's mighty power

𝒟avid, the old shepherd-king who saw himself as nothing more than a sheep that needed to be led, was inspired by the Holy Spirit to say: *The LORD is my shepherd; I shall not want* (lack nothing) . . . . *He leads me in the paths of righteousness for His Name's sake* (Psalm 23:1-3). No other livestock requires more attention than sheep. Left alone, they can easily become separated from the flock and lose their way. Of all domesticated animals, sheep are the most defenseless and helpless.

By nature, we are all like sheep. We may blindly follow the same paths that have ruined the lives of others. Or we can become so caught up in our own affairs that we lose sight of the *Good Shepherd* and find ourselves separated from Him (John 10:11,14).

The trouble with most of us is that many times we try to be our own shepherd. There is something almost terrifying about the consequences of the destructive, self-willed stubbornness of those who refuse to be led in *the paths of righteousness*. They are determined to go their own way, even though the path they take will inevitably lead to trouble. It is a fact that without the *Good Shepherd* we are helpless, defenseless sheep. When we recognize this we will fully trust the *Good Shepherd*. We are comforted and encouraged by knowing that *though I walk through the valley of the shadow of death, I will fear no evil: for You are with me* (Psalm 23:4).

Even *Your rod and Your staff they comfort me* (23:4). We know that *whom the Lord loves He chastens* (disciplines) (Hebrews 12:6).

The utmost desire of every one of God's sheep should daily be *bringing into captivity every thought to the obedience of Christ* (II Corinthians 10:5). God will guide and provide for every need that will better prepare us for eternity with Him.

We should pray each day: Lord lead *me in the paths of righteousness for His* (Your) *Name's sake* (Psalm 23:3).

Thought for Today: Often God's ways differ from our expectations!

Christ Revealed: As our *Shepherd* (Psalm 23). Christ called Himself *the Good Shepherd* and vowed to lay down *His life for the sheep* (John 10:11).

For definitions of unfamiliar words in today's Bible reading, see pages 468-480.

IN TODAY'S READING

David's trust in God; the blessedness of forgiveness;
the Lord hears the righteous; David's prayer for safety

What a privilege we have to join with David and the multitudes since his time, saying: *I will bless the LORD at all times; His praise shall continually be in my mouth. . . . O magnify the LORD with me, and let us exalt His Name together. . . . This poor man cried, and the LORD heard him, and saved him out of all his troubles. The Angel of the LORD encamps round about them that fear Him, and delivers them* (Psalm 34:1,3,6-7). Praise in our worship services, at mealtime, and during daily devotions is good and right and fills our hearts with joy. But, the psalmist went beyond the expected times of worship and praise because he was continually expressing love and devotion to the Lord. He wrote: *My tongue shall speak of Your righteousness and of Your praise all the day long* (35:28).

We are expected to praise the Lord even when everything seems to go wrong, since we know that *many are the afflictions of the righteous: but the LORD delivers him out of them all* (34:19). *We know that all things work together for good to them that love God* (Romans 8:28). David suffered numerous injustices at the hands of enemies of God. He refers to himself *like a broken vessel. . . . they devised to take away my life* (Psalm 31:12-13). He could have become bitter or could have blamed others. Instead, he declared: *I trusted in You, O LORD,* and confidently said: *My times are in Your hand* (31:14-15). Only in yielding our lives to God will we find the assurance, peace, and security we long for. This is not "holding on" to Him, but abiding in Him – trusting that He is holding on to us, for He has promised we are in the Heavenly Father's hand (John 10:28-29).

Though, at times, we may not feel like praising God because of some pressing concern or problem, we should remember that God is still on the throne. With David we can *be glad in the LORD, and . . . shout for joy* (Psalm 32:11). Yes! Without hesitation, and regardless of circumstances, David said: *I will bless the LORD at all times: His praise shall continually be in my mouth* (Psalm 34:1).

Thought for Today: Unwavering confidence in God brings a spontaneous spirit of gratitude and praise.

Christ Revealed: In the prophecy that not one of His bones would be broken as recorded concerning His crucifixion (Psalm 34:20). This was fulfilled as recorded in John 19:36.

For definitions of unfamiliar words in today's Bible reading, see pages 468-480.

> ## ℐN ℐODAY'S ℛEADING
> David's confidence in God; destruction of the wicked;
> the prayer of a penitent heart; brevity of life

𝒟avid sat watching a fire burning and recorded: *While I was musing the fire burned* (Psalm 39:3), its bright flames slowly turned to ashes. He was reminded of how the most satisfying life soon fades and ends in death. This is a reminder to all of us that life will soon end. David then prayed: *LORD, make me to know . . . the measure* (length) *of my days* (life) (39:4). David realized how easy it is to get so caught up with material achievements that we would forget our most important purpose in life. Life is short and opportunities for fulfilling the will of God will soon *be no more* (39:13). David's prayer points out that the brevity of life is an issue everyone should consider, not just senior citizens.

Compared to eternity, earthly life is very, very short. Yet, strangely enough, it is easy to be so involved with daily activities that we forget that we are just one breath away from death.

In our brief journey on earth, we may sometimes retrace our steps or repeat a task; but wasted time can never be recovered. This points out how seriously we need to consider what God would have us do today and take advantage of every opportunity to wholeheartedly serve Him. Only as we read through the Bible will we fully know what God expects of us and how best to be prepared to serve Him.

Much of our time and energy are devoted to preparations for earthly securities or pleasures. Many make the fatal mistake of waiting too long for a "convenient time" to serve the Lord. But the clock of time will soon stop without notice. Just as the sun is seen rising in the east, it will soon set in the west, and another day brings us that much closer to eternity. For the majority of us, death will come unexpectedly, and much sooner than we think. Let us reconsider our secular goals. Do they rob us of opportunities to help reach a lost world with the words of eternal life?

It is of utmost importance that, just as our Lord did, we need to fulfill our purpose for existence. Jesus said: *I must work* (do) *the works of Him that sent Me, while it is day: the night comes, when no man can work* (John 9:4).

Thought for Today: Side by side with special privileges are temptations to test our willingness to sacrifice in order to gain God's best.

Christ Revealed: As *the Fountain of Life* (and the) *Light* (Psalm 36:9). *In Him was Life; and the Life was the Light of men. . . . That was the True Light, which lights every man that comes into the world* (John 1:4-9; compare 4:10,14; Revelation 22:1).

For definitions of unfamiliar words in today's Bible reading, see pages 468-480.

In Today's Reading

Praise for answered prayer; David's enemies; his longing for God's presence; prayer for deliverance from present troubles

*I*t was foretold by the psalmist that the Messiah, our wonderful Lord Jesus Christ and King of kings, would always defend *truth . . . meekness and righteousness* (Psalm 45:4) in His reign. In contrast, most kings are known for their ruthless, oppressive cruelty. Because the Lord Jesus is the only begotten sinless Son of God, David was inspired to write: *Your throne, O God, is for ever and ever: the scepter of Your kingdom is a right* (true) *scepter* (divine right to rule) (45:6). The Father has anointed Jesus and poured out abundantly on Him *the oil of gladness* (45:7) far above all others. After His resurrection, Jesus told His disciples: *All things must be fulfilled, which were written in the Law of Moses, and in the Prophets, and in the Psalms, concerning Me* (Luke 24:44).

The Apostle Paul quoted from Psalm 45 concerning Jesus as the Son of God, saying: *Your throne, O God, is for ever and ever: a scepter* (kingdom) *of righteousness. . . . God, has anointed You with . . . oil* (Hebrews 1:8-9). Loving only what is right and hating all wrong is one of numerous attributes of Christ.

Although we often fall short, those who have received Jesus Christ as their Lord and Savior desire to express the attributes of loving righteousness and hating lawlessness. Since Christians are also the Bride of Christ, we desire to express the characteristics of the One we represent. The King sees only beauty in His Bride and we, in turn, recognize Him as our Lord and worship Him (Psalm 45:11). This means that He must have our undivided allegiance.

In the midst of trying and uncertain circumstances, the Lord has assured us of His loving care over our lives. No Christian needs to fear what the future may be. We are to trust the Lord for today's necessities and seek not . . . *what you shall eat, or what you shall drink. . . . For all these things do the nations of the world seek after: and your Father knows that you have need of these things. But rather seek* (desire) *the Kingdom of God; and all these things shall be added to you* (Luke 12:29-31). Jesus taught us to pray: *Our Father. . . . Give us day by day our daily bread* (whatever is needed for today) (Luke 11:2-3).

Thought for Today: Why worry? God knows what is best, so trust Him.

Christ Revealed: As One Who will do the will of God (Psalm 40:6-8). Jesus said that His purpose on earth was *to do the will of Him that sent Me, and to finish His work* (John 4:34; Hebrews 10:7-9).

For definitions of unfamiliar words in today's Bible reading, see pages 468-480.

In Today's Reading
The psalmist's confidence and praise of God; deception of
worldly wealth; a prayer for mercy and forgiveness

David disregarded the Word of God when he lusted after the beautiful wife of his neighbor, Uriah the Hittite, one of his most loyal soldiers. While Uriah was at war, David committed adultery with Uriah's wife. Through a planned military maneuver initiated by David, Uriah was killed, allowing David to legally marry Bathsheba.

It appeared to be a happy ending for David and Bathsheba until Nathan, the fearless prophet of God, appeared and denounced the king's selfish and wicked sins. Nathan asked: "Why did you despise the Word of God by killing Uriah the Hittite with the sword and then taking his wife to be your wife?" (II Samuel 12:9). Both acts were forbidden under the Law. He deserved to die and he knew it (Leviticus 20:10). He cast himself on the mercy of God as a brokenhearted sinner and he humbly prayed: *Have mercy upon me, O God, according to Your lovingkindness. . . . cleanse me from my sin. . . . Create in me a clean heart, O God; and renew a right spirit within me* (Psalm 51:1-2,10).

The Holy Spirit inspired David to record his own cry of sorrow and repentance. God is merciful to all repentant sinners. In answer to David's sincere prayers, God forgave him. But the result of his sin was personal shame and suffering for the rest of his life, as well as many tragic personal and national consequences.

We wish that this blight upon David's life had not happened. But it was recorded, not only to reveal the deception and never-ending devastation of lust, but to let us know that God forgives our sins when we repent and pray as David did. This holds out hope to the sinner who truly repents that he can experience the mercy and forgiving love of God. It also teaches the inescapable consequences of sin. David's prayer for mercy is a prayer for release from the presence and power of sin. He prayed: *Blot out my transgressions. Wash me thoroughly from my iniquity, and cleanse me from my sin* (51:1-2). To *blot out* illustrates the way a debt would be erased or forgiven. *Wash me . . . cleanse me* illustrates the same way that dirty clothes would be washed.

If we walk in the light, as He is in the light . . . the blood of Jesus Christ His Son cleanses us from all sin (I John 1:7).

Thought for Today: God does not overlook the sin of anyone. No one is above God's Law.

Christ Revealed: As the One Who will *judge His people* (Psalm 50:4). *The Lord Jesus Christ . . . shall judge the quick* (living) *and the dead at His appearing* (II Timothy 4:1). For definitions of unfamiliar words in today's Bible reading, see pages 468-480.

228

IN TODAY'S READING
Tendency of corrupt tongue; foolishness of atheism; a prayer for
protection; a cry against deceitful friends; the psalmist's trust in God

God must judge all unconfessed sin. It is fitting that David, the man
after God's own heart (I Samuel 13:14), expressed the exceeding hatred
God has for the evil which corrupts His creation. Included in Psalm 59
is David's prayer: *O my God: defend me from them that rise up against
me* (Psalm 59:1). He also prays that God would not be merciful to his
enemies, since God cannot be merciful to any sinner who does not
repent of his sins (59:5,13). True repentance prepares our hearts to
receive Christ as our Savior and allows Him to become Lord of our lives
in obedience to His Word (Acts 2:38; 4:12).

David recognized that sinful acts are rebellion against God as well
as against others. David identified himself with God, Who hates sin,
and declared that he too hated those who rebel against God and
counted them his enemies as well. For David it was the expression of
a king who loved the Lord and His ways and recognized that he was
the anointed representative of God on earth and, therefore, was
responsible to administer justice on the Lord's behalf.

There is coming a day of reckoning when God *will render to every
man according to his deeds: To them who by patient continuance in
well doing seek for glory and honor and immortality, eternal life:
But to them that are contentious, and do not obey the truth, but obey
unrighteousness, indignation and wrath, Tribulation* (Distress) *and
anguish,* (will be) *upon every soul of man that does evil* (Romans 2:6-
9). You can be among those who look forward to Christ's return if you
repent and forsake your sins. Let Christ be Lord of your life and read
His Word in order to do His will. Life is fleeting and judgment is sure.
Behold, now is the accepted time; behold, now is the day of salvation (II
Corinthians 6:2).

Though Jesus first came as the "Suffering Servant," when He returns, it will be as the Conquering King, Who will make war against the
forces of Satan and will judge all mankind by His righteousness. The
sharp sword that will go forth out of His mouth is the Word of God.
Jesus said: *He that rejects Me, and receives not My words, has One that
judges him: the Word that I have spoken, the same shall judge him in the
last day* (John 12:48).

Thought for Today: Obedience to Jesus insures where you spend eternity.

Christ Revealed: As the One Who saves those who will call on Him (Psalm 55:16-17; compare
Romans 10:13).

For definitions of unfamiliar words in today's Bible reading, see pages 468-480.

IN TODAY'S READING

David's prayer for deliverance from his enemies;
his confidence in God's promises;
David's exhortation to praise God for His goodness

*B*ecause of Saul's relentless search and his efforts to kill David, he was forced to flee to a desolate area outside the promised land. Exiled from his loved ones and the physical comforts of the palace, he prayed: *Hear my cry, O God: attend* (listen) *to my prayer. From the end of the earth I will cry to You, when my heart is overwhelmed: lead me to the Rock that is higher than I. For You have been a shelter for me, and a strong tower from the enemy* (Psalm 61:1-3).

David was overwhelmed with sorrow and loneliness, even as we would be. He prayed intensely, asking God to hear his prayer. He confessed his distress but also his confidence in God as *the Rock that is higher than I. . . . a shelter . . . and a strong tower from the enemy.* Although his desolate situation seemed like the end of the earth, David was confident that his True Source of security from his enemies was the living God Himself, Who was like a great *tower* of protection.

Making God our *strong tower* means recognizing that His followers are in the protective care of the invincible God. Depression and frustration need not exist in the life of one who believes that God is the *strong tower* in the face of evil forces. We have His assurance that *no good thing will He withhold from them that walk uprightly* (84:11). Like David, we can depend upon the Lord for protection and provision, regardless of how hopeless our circumstances may seem, since the Lord has assured us: *Behold, I am the LORD, the God of all flesh: is there any thing too hard for Me?* (Jeremiah 32:27).

Although David's difficult circumstances remained the same for many years, he continued to declare: *Truly my soul waits upon God. . . . He only is my Rock and my Salvation* (Psalm 62:1-2). David then turned his thoughts to others who faced trials and suffering, and continued to encourage all of us to *trust in Him at all times . . . pour out your heart before Him: God is a Refuge for us* (62:8). It is a comfort to know that everything we face in life is to prepare us for eternity.

We are reminded that nothing *shall separate us from the love of Christ* (Romans 8:35).

Thought for Today: Our confidence in the Lord's power and protection will be increased as we daily read God's Word.

Christ Revealed: As *the Rock* – the unmovable, eternal, unchanging Savior (Psalms 61:2; 62:2,6-7). Jesus is the Rock of our salvation and *that spiritual Rock* (Petras) *that followed* (accompanied) *them* (I Corinthians 10:4).

For definitions of unfamiliar words in today's Bible reading, see pages 468-480.

In Today's Reading
The blessings of God upon His people; His judgment
upon His enemies; David's prayer in time of trouble;
prayer of praise and thanksgiving

The psalmist encourages everyone to rejoice *and sing for joy* (Psalm 67:4). Furthermore, singing and giving praise to the Lord always brings satisfaction and peace of mind. While we await Jesus' return from heaven, the psalmist reminds us to rejoice: *Let the righteous be glad; let them rejoice before God: yes, let them exceedingly rejoice. Sing to God, sing praises to His Name: extol* (praise) *Him that rides upon the heavens by His Name JAH, and rejoice before Him* (68:3-4). *JAH* is short for the Name of Jehovah (Yahweh), Who is ever in the present.

Let us join with the psalmist in a proclamation of praise and adoration for Jesus Christ, our wonderful Savior and Lord, Who generously pours out His blessings upon us.

The psalmist also foretold the resurrection of Christ. A numerous host of people will proclaim the glorious news of His victory. Jesus *ascended on high, You have led captivity captive. . . . and to GOD the Lord belong the issues from death* (68:18,20). All the kingdoms of the earth *sing praises to the Lord* (68:32) as they express their heartfelt worship. Paul explained the meaning of this psalm as a prophecy concerning Christ, Who *ascended up on high, He led captivity captive*. This means that He conquered death and Satan, who had held mankind in bondage (Hebrews 2:15) *and gave gifts to men* (Ephesians 4:8). These gifts were given to apostles, prophets, evangelists, pastors, and teachers for equipping God's people to do His work, to help them mature and grow in the likeness of Christ (4:11-12).

Verily, verily, I say to you, He that hears My Word, and believes on Him that sent Me, has everlasting life, and shall not come into condemnation; but is passed from death to life. . . . Marvel not at this . . . all that are in the graves shall hear His voice, And shall come forth; they that have done good, to the resurrection of life; and they that have done evil, to the resurrection of damnation (John 5:24,28-29).

Thought for Today: Life is like the uncontrollable sea until we turn to the Lord who imparts His perfect peace.

Christ Revealed: As the One Who *led captivity captive* (Psalm 68:18). With His resurrection power, Jesus broke the captive power of Satan. When He led the Old Testament saints from paradise into heaven, *He led captivity captive* (compare Ephesians 4:8; also Galatians 5:1; Revelation 1:18).

For definitions of unfamiliar words in today's Bible reading, see pages 468-480.

> ## In Today's Reading
> David's prayer for Solomon; mystery of the prosperity of the
> wicked; the wicked and the proud rebuked; Majesty of God praised

The psalmist praised the Lord for the assurance that no effort against the faithful people of God, regardless of how powerful, can hinder His ability to protect and bless those who are obedient to His Word. *For promotion comes neither from the east, nor from the west, nor from the south. But God is the judge; He puts down one, and sets up another* (Psalm 75:6-7). God controls both the present and the future of His people. His judgment is impartial and always righteous.

When confronted by problems, we need to praise our Almighty God, Who *has said, I will never leave you, nor forsake you* (Hebrews 13:5). However, the psalmist was also led to proclaim that the proud and self-willed who love to boast will be judged (Psalm 75:4-5).

To illustrate this fact, in this Psalm God is referred to as *the God of Jacob* (75:9); God wonderfully blessed Jacob. Esau had threatened to murder his brother, Jacob, over the birthright God had foretold would rightfully be Jacob's although Esau was the firstborn. God knew that Esau would despise the birthright and that Jacob would cherish the covenant blessing to Abraham and Isaac (Genesis 25:21-23).

When Esau threatened to kill Jacob, he left home to live with his uncle Laban more than 500 miles north. Twenty years later, when Esau received word that Jacob was returning home, Esau went out to meet him with 400 of his servants (32:6). It appeared that Esau would now fulfill his vow to kill Jacob in order to regain his birthright. This threat led Jacob to pray all night, after which God marvelously blessed him and gave him a new name, Israel. He is referred to far more times than all other men in Old Testament history (32:24-29).

Now that we have seen how God blessed Jacob because he wrestled all night in prayer, we should take this lesson to heart. We too need to be persistent and spend more time in prayer. God assures us that: *The wicked . . . I will cut off; but the horns* (strength) *of the righteous shall be exalted* (Psalm 75:10).

Thought for Today: Choose to set your heart on the *strait* (confining) . . . *gate . . . which leads to life . . . few . . . find it* (Matthew 7:14).

Christ Revealed: As the Righteous Judge Who will crush the oppressors (Psalm 72:4). Psalm 75:8 describes the judgment of God upon those who refuse to accept the salvation so freely offered by Jesus, *the Lamb of God* (John 1:29,34-36; compare II Thessalonians 1:8-9).

For definitions of unfamiliar words in today's Bible reading, see pages 468-480.

In Today's Reading
The Lord's judgment against disobedience;
prayer against enemies; prayer for mercy and restoration

God had chosen Israel to be His witness to the world. As His people, they were to be an example of how He would bless all who honor Him and His Word; but, they failed miserably and the glorious city of God was destroyed. We are reminded of the pitiful heartbreak and awesome horror felt by the Israelites following the destruction of the Temple and Jerusalem. They had assumed that, since they were the chosen Covenant people of God, they were secure. But they had chosen to disobey God's Covenant and His Commandments. The awful consequences of sin are inevitable. The psalmist cried out: *O God, the heathen* (nations) *are come into Your inheritance; Your holy Temple they have defiled; they have laid Jerusalem on heaps* (in ruins) (Psalm 79:1).

The few remaining faithful Israelites pleaded: *Help us, O God of our salvation, for the glory of Your Name: and deliver us, and purge away our sins, for Your Name's sake* (79:9).

Since the destruction of Jerusalem in A.D. 70, there has been no Temple, no Brazen Altar, no Laver, no Golden Candlestick, no Table of Showbread, no Ark of the Covenant, no Altar of Incense, and no biblical Day of Atonement as commanded by God through Moses. All that was essential to cover their sins was destroyed. Israel's sacrifices and feasts were symbols created by God to foreshadow all that was to be accomplished by Jesus the Messiah.

With Jesus' death, all of the Old Testament sacrifices for sins were made obsolete and the old sacrificial system under the Law was destroyed. For the Israelites, the blood sacrifices of animals could only temporarily atone for (cover) sins. *How much more shall the blood of Christ . . . purge* (cleanse) *your conscience from dead works to serve the living God?* (Hebrews 9:14).

The sacrifice of Christ on the cross made it possible for both Jews and Gentiles, who recognize themselves as lost sinners, truly repent, and receive Jesus as their Savior, to be forgiven of their sins. *For as many of you as have been baptized into Christ have put on Christ. There is neither Jew nor Greek, there is neither bond nor free, there is neither male nor female: for you are all one in Christ Jesus* (Galatians 3:27-28).

Thought for Today: True success in life depends on living in accordance with God's Word – not on our own well-laid plans.

Christ Revealed: As the true *Shepherd* (Psalm 80:1). Christ is the Good Shepherd and the Door through Which one must enter to be saved. He alone is the Way to heaven (John 10:9,11).

For definitions of unfamiliar words in today's Bible reading, see pages 468-480.

The Holy Spirit guided David to unite the only two weapons of
our spiritual warfare – prayer and the inspired Word of God. Psalm
86 expresses the power we have when these become our way of life.

When David prayed: *Bow down Your ear, O LORD, hear me: for I
am poor and needy* (Psalm 86:1), he was acknowledging his dependence on God (86:2). He continued to pray: *Be merciful to me, O Lord:
for I cry to You daily* (86:3). Although David was the king of Israel he
recognized the lordship of God over his life (86:4). He often spoke of
himself as the *servant* of the Lord in the Psalms.

David continued in worship to confess God's mercy and readiness
to forgive. He expressed the utmost confidence that God listens to His
people's prayers and delivers them from all harm regardless of our
circumstances (86:5,7,13,15).

David then asked God to teach him to obey Him. The godly person does not depend upon previous learning to continue a day-by-
day walk in the way of truth, but upon the continual daily guidance
of God through His Word. Instruction is much more than just information; it is also the means to understand His will and to be obedient, for it carries the thought of correction (86:11). The child of God
never graduates from God's school of instruction; that is why all of
us need to read His Word each day.

A sincere commitment to the Lord is essential. The Apostle Peter
recognized this when he admonished us to diligently build upon our
faith virtue (moral excellence), then *knowledge*, then *temperance* (self-
control), then *patience*, then *godliness*, then *brotherly kindness*, which
will produce in us genuine *charity* (love) to do the will of God (II Peter
1:5-8). The God Who created us has made everything which pertains to
life and godliness available to us. His power is made possible as we read
His Word, *for the Word of God is quick* (living and active), *and powerful* (Hebrews 4:12). We have the potential to live in obedience to His
Word. But, we must take the initiative to build our faith. *Faith comes
by hearing, and hearing by the Word of God* (Romans 10:17).

Thought for Today: God's grace is sufficient for you.

Christ Revealed: By Jerusalem, from where the psalmist declared all of the springs (source)
of joy and happiness emanate (Psalm 87:7). Jesus is the source of our joy as the angel
announced at His birth (Luke 2:10). Jesus also declared: *These things have I spoken to
you, that My joy might remain in you, and that your joy might be full* (John 15:11).

For definitions of unfamiliar words in today's Bible reading, see pages 468-480.

In Today's Reading

A cry for deliverance from death; praise for God's Covenant and
promises; frailty and brevity of life; the faithful protected

*He that dwells in the secret place of the Most High shall abide under
the shadow of the Almighty* (Psalm 91:1). This is one whose heart is set
on being obedient to the Lord. To *abide under the shadow of the
Almighty* there is a need to *draw near to God, and He will draw near
to you. Cleanse your hands, you sinners; and purify your hearts, you
double minded* (James 4:8). When in doubt, *abstain from all appearance of evil* (I Thessalonians 5:22).

The psalmist expressed the utmost confidence in the loving care of
God when he said: *You shall not be afraid for the terror by night; nor
for the arrow that flies by day* (Psalm 91:5). The psalmist then assured
the faithful, saying: *Because you have made the LORD . . . your habitation* (dwelling place); *There shall no evil befall you. . . . For He shall
give His angels charge over you, to keep you in all your ways* (91:9-12).

Satan, a fallen angel, quoted these verses to Jesus after His 40-day
fast in an attempt to persuade Jesus to leap off the pinnacle of the
Temple. Satan said: *If You be the Son of God* (meaning: Since You are
the Son of God), *cast Yourself down: for it is written, He shall give His
angels charge concerning You: and in their hands they shall bear You
up, lest at any time You dash Your foot against a stone* (Matthew 4:6;
Luke 4:9-11; Psalm 91:11-12). In tempting our Lord, Satan was like some
today who love the promises of God, but who disregard the conditions
of those promises. Our Lord set the example when He responded to
Satan by quoting Scripture which warns not to tempt the Lord God:
It is written again, you shall not tempt (test) *the Lord your God*
(Matthew 4:7; also Deuteronomy 6:16). We have no assurance that the
Lord's angels will keep us if we choose "ways" that ignore His Word.

Satan has deceived many by saying: "Your situation is an exception" or "Just this one time" or "Be broad-minded, everyone is doing it."
He also uses examples of hypocrites to deceive some by pointing out:
"Religious people do these things, so why shouldn't you?" We must
continually be *casting down imaginations, and every high thing that
exalts itself against the knowledge of God, and bringing into captivity
every thought to the obedience of Christ* (II Corinthians 10:5).

Thought for Today: *Wherefore be not unwise, but understanding what the will of the
Lord is* (Ephesians 5:17).

Christ Revealed: By the seed (descendants) **of David** (Psalm 89:3-4). *Concerning His Son
Jesus Christ our Lord, Who was made of the seed* (descendants) *of David according
to the flesh* (Romans 1:3; also Matthew 1:1; Luke 3:31-32).

For definitions of unfamiliar words in today's Bible reading, see pages 468-480.

IN TODAY'S READING

Praise for the loving-kindness of the Lord; appeal for justice;
a call to sing, worship, and praise the Lord

By the inspiration of the Holy Spirit, the psalmist invites the faithful to *come, let us sing to the LORD: let us make a joyful noise to the Rock of our salvation. . . . O come, let us worship and bow down: let us kneel before the LORD our Maker. For He is our God; and we are the people of His pasture, and the sheep of His hand* (Psalm 95:1,6-7). Singing with a heartfelt attitude of gratitude and *thanksgiving* (95:2) is a vital part of worship. Singing joyfully carries with it the thought of expressing devotion to our Lord.

Praise to the Lord will lift worship beyond the level of personal needs to the higher plane of love and adoration as we glorify the Heavenly Father, our precious Savior Jesus Christ, and the indwelling Holy Spirit. A "self-centered" person assumes the "worship" service was meant for his personal satisfaction. Consequently, we hear such people say: "I didn't get much out of the service." The reason is clear – they didn't put much into it.

Worship is not a "time" set aside for receiving personal satisfaction or for the enjoyment of a "sermon." Worship should be an active, heartfelt expression of prayer, praise, and adoration, demonstrating our esteem for our Heavenly Father and our Savior Jesus Christ. Following this, all else, including the sermon, becomes more meaningful.

Some lack spiritual fulfillment because they have decided to reflect the mood and attitude of unbelievers when confronted with adverse circumstances, such as the loss of a job, the death of a loved one, a divorce, the betrayal of a friend, or some other painful experience. By deciding to be unhappy and dissatisfied, we deprive ourselves of the joy of an abundant, peaceful life.

When you think of all our Lord has done for you, in you, and with you, and all He has promised to you for all eternity, you cannot help but decide to praise, worship, and *serve the LORD with gladness* and *come before His presence with singing* (100:2). Our *gladness* will be in direct proportion to our faith in His unfailing presence and promises. *For the LORD is good; His mercy is everlasting; His truth endures to all generations* (Psalm 100:5).

Thought for Today: How much of Christ will others see in you today?

Christ Revealed: As the Creator: *It is He that has made us* (Psalm 100:3; John 1:3; Ephesians 3:9; Colossians 1:16; Revelation 4:11).

For definitions of unfamiliar words in today's Bible reading, see pages 468-480.

In Today's Reading

Personal commitment to the Lord's ways; a cry in distress;
gratitude to God for His mercy; His mighty power;
God's providence over Israel

David was inspired by the Holy Spirit to prophesy of Jesus' coming kingdom reign when He will administer equal justice for all the world. Because of this, David declared: *I will walk within my house with a perfect heart. I will set no wicked thing before my eyes* (Psalm 101:2-3). To maintain this attitude, David chose his friends wisely, saying: *A froward* (deceitful, perverted) *heart shall depart from me: I will not know* (have anything to do with) *a wicked person* (101:4).

A few of the many reasons for praising the Lord are given in Psalm 103, but it is our loving Lord Himself Who is our highest reason for praise. First, we praise Him for Who He is, the all-powerful, all-wise, righteous Creator, and then for His mercy and forgiving love in cleansing us from all our sins. We also thank and praise Him because *He has not dealt with us after our sins; nor rewarded us according to our iniquities. For as the heaven is high above the earth, so great is His mercy toward them that fear Him* (103:10-11). Just think, His forgiving love toward those who fear Him is as great as the height of the heavens above the earth. Therefore, it is an act of unbelief on our part, a deception of Satan, and contrary to the nature of our loving Lord, for us to bring up former sins – either ours or those of others. Forgiven means no longer remembered, not only by God, but by us as well (I John 1:9; II Peter 1:9). As you begin praying, always remember to forgive anyone you feel has wronged you. When you do that, your Father will forgive your evil deeds; but, if you do not forgive others, your Father will not forgive you or answer your prayers (Psalm 66:18).

We are reminded that unlimited forgiveness should characterize every true disciple of Christ, for He said: *When you stand praying, forgive, if you have anything against any: that your Father also which is in heaven may forgive you your trespasses. But if you do not forgive, neither will your Father . . . forgive your trespasses* (Mark 11:25-26).

Thought for Today: God often overrules our wishes and plans in order to accomplish His highest purpose in our lives.

Christ Revealed: As the One *Who forgives all your iniquities; Who heals all your diseases* (Psalm 103:3). Forgiveness of sin and the healing power of God describe the ministry of our Lord Jesus, Who was sent *to preach deliverance to the captives, and recovering of sight to the blind, to set at liberty them that are bruised, To preach the acceptable year of the Lord* (Luke 4:18-19; Matthew 9:6).

For definitions of unfamiliar words in today's Bible reading, see pages 468-480.

*I*N *T*ODAY'S *R*EADING

Israel's rebellion in the wilderness; God's mercies to Israel;
exhortation to praise God for His goodness

*A*lthough God had faithfully blessed Israel, miraculously delivered them from Egyptian slavery, provided the promised land, and
given them victory over the Canaanites and great prosperity, *they soon
forgot His works; they waited not for His counsel . . . and tempted God
in the desert* (Psalm 106:13-14). Israel's unfaithfulness and numerous
sins are brought to our attention. Among them: *They made a calf in
Horeb, and worshiped the molten image* (vs 19); *forgot God their
Savior* (vs 21); *despised the pleasant land, they believed not His Word*
(vs 24); *murmured in their tents* (vs 25); *did not destroy the nations,
concerning whom the LORD commanded them* (vs 34); *But . . . mingled
among the heathen, and. . . . served their idols* (vss 35-36).

The psalmist then points out the inevitable consequences of sin:
*Therefore was the wrath of the LORD kindled against His people,
insomuch that He abhorred His own inheritance. And He gave them into
the hand of the heathen* (nations); *and they that hated them ruled over
them* (vss 40-42). But, the Lord's judgment on Israel was mingled with
His mercy. When *they cried unto the LORD in their trouble . . . He
delivered them out of their distresses. . . . Oh that men would praise
the LORD for His goodness. . . . He sent His Word, and healed them*
(107:6-9,20).

Note carefully that Israel's method of deliverance is the same for
everyone today: *He sent His Word, and healed them.* The psalmist could
have simply said: *He delivered them out of their distresses.* Instead, he
chose to say: *He sent His Word, and healed them.* His Word is Jesus
come in the flesh as well as His Written Word: *In the beginning was the
Word, and the Word was with God, and the Word was God* (John 1:1).
His Written Word, when believed and acted upon, is the means God
has chosen to supply and satisfy man's every need.

*Oh that men would praise the LORD for His goodness, and for His
wonderful works to the children of men! . . . The righteous shall see it, and
rejoice. . . . Whoso is wise, and will observe these things, even they shall
understand the lovingkindness of the LORD* (Psalm 107:8,15,21,31,42-43).

Thought for Today: How much of the Word do you make available for God to use in your
life?

Christ Revealed: As the One Who makes *the storm a calm* (Psalm 107:29). When Jesus
calmed the storm, His awestruck disciples exclaimed: *What manner of Man is this, that
even the winds and the sea obey Him!* (Matthew 8:27). Jesus offers to calm the storms
of our lives and give us His peace (John 14:27).

For definitions of unfamiliar words in today's Bible reading, see pages 468-480.

In Today's Reading

David's praise to God for His sovereignty over nations; prayer for judgment upon the wicked; exhortation to trust in God, not idols

*W*hen Jesus Christ ascended into heaven, He fulfilled the prophecy which the Holy Spirit had earlier inspired David to write: *The LORD said to my Lord* (God the Son), *Sit . . . at My right hand, until I make Your enemies Your footstool* (Psalm 110:1). Jesus quoted this psalm as referring to Himself (Mark 12:36).

Israel, as a nation, rejected their Messiah King. But, *the Stone* (Christ) *which the builders refused is become the Head Stone* (Christ) *of the corner. This is the LORD'S doing; it is marvellous in our eyes. . . . Blessed be he that comes in the Name of the LORD. . . . God is the LORD, Which has showed us light.* David then gives praise to God and we too can say: *You are my God, and I will praise You: You are my God, I will exalt You. O give thanks to the LORD . . . for His mercy endures for ever* (Psalm 118:22-23,26-29).

Jesus quoted this psalm, saying: *What is this then that is written, The Stone which the builders rejected, the same is become the Head of the corner? Whosoever shall fall upon that Stone shall be broken; but on whomsoever It shall fall, It will grind him to powder* (Luke 20:17-18; Mark 12:10-11).

Paul quoted this psalm when he wrote to the Ephesians: *Now therefore you are no more strangers and foreigners, but fellowcitizens with the saints* (believers), *and of the household of God; And are built upon the foundation of the apostles and the prophets, Jesus Christ Himself being the chief Corner Stone; In Whom all the building fitly framed together grows to a holy temple in the Lord* (Ephesians 2:19-21).

After a miracle of healing, *Peter, filled with the Holy Ghost, said to them, You rulers of the people, and elders of Israel . . . Be it known to you all, and to all the people of Israel, that by the Name of Jesus Christ of Nazareth, Whom you crucified, Whom God raised from the dead, even by Him does this man stand here before you whole* (well). Peter then quoted Psalm 118 when he said: *This is the Stone which was set at nothing of you builders, which is become the Head of the corner. Neither is there salvation in any other: for there is no other Name under heaven given among men, whereby we must be saved* (Acts 4:8,10-12).

Thought for Today: Fears vanish as we daily trust God.

Christ Revealed: Christ quoted Psalm 118:22: *The Stone which the builders rejected* – to the chief priests and the Pharisees when they rejected Him (Matthew 21:42-45).

For definitions of unfamiliar words in today's Bible reading, see pages 468-480.

> ## 𝒥n 𝒯oday's 𝒭eading
> The greatness, power, and perfection of God's Word

𝒯he purpose of the longest chapter in the Bible is to focus our attention on the only infallible Guide to Life given by our Creator. In it, God has provided everything we need to be the person He planned for us to be and to accomplish the purpose for which He created us. It is equally emphasized how indispensable it is to know our Creator, Savior, and soon-coming Messiah King. The chapter opens with: *Blessed are the undefiled* (Divinely favored, blameless, whose conduct is beyond reproach) *in the way, who walk in the Law of the LORD. . . . and that seek Him with the whole heart* (Psalm 119:1-2). *The undefiled* means much more than just avoiding sin or living a good life. We are specially blessed as we seek to please God Himself *with the whole heart*.

Like David, all who seek God, will pray: *With my whole heart have I sought You: O let me not wander from Your Commandments. Your Word have I hid in my heart, that I might not sin against You* (vss 10-11). It is by taking daily delight in God's Word, *as much as in all riches* (vs 14), that our fellowship with the Lord is assured. The psalmist continues: *I will not forget Your Word* (vs 16). This kind of forgetting is more than a momentary memory lapse. It is drifting away from God as a result of becoming so involved in other interests that His Word is neglected.

Daily we need to pray: *Make me to go in the path of Your Commandments; for therein do I delight. Incline my heart to Your testimonies, and not to covetousness* (119:33-36). As we do this, we have something to sing about regardless of circumstances (vs 54). The child of God can also say with the psalmist: *Before I was afflicted I went astray: but now I have kept Your Word. . . . It is good for me that I have been afflicted; that I might learn Your statutes* (vss 67,71).

Though he had been afflicted, the psalmist did not find fault with God, nor did he doubt the Lord's wisdom or His justice. For many, it is in times like these that we painfully recognize that we have made wrong choices in the past which have led to unwholesome consequences. In such circumstances we realize that the Bible is priceless, for it alone reveals life's true values and prepares us for eternity. All who love the Lord can say: *I rejoice at Your Word, as one that finds great spoil* (Psalm 119:162).

Thought for Today: Spiritual growth is dependent on the time we spend with the Lord letting Him speak to us from His Word.

Christ Revealed: By the psalmist who delighted in the Commandments of God (Psalm 119:47). Christ said: *I came down from heaven, not to do My own will, but the will of Him that sent Me* (John 6:38; 15:10).

For definitions of unfamiliar words in today's Bible reading, see pages 468-480.

In Today's Reading
Prayer for deliverance from lying lips; sustaining power;
prayer for the peace of Jerusalem; blessing of trusting God

*T*he Law required all male Jews physically able and ceremonially clean to go to Jerusalem three times a year to participate in the seven feasts (Exodus 23:14-17; Deuteronomy 16:16).

With confidence in the Lord's protection on the journeys, the Israelite worshiper could sing: *My help comes from the LORD. . . . The LORD shall preserve our going out and our coming in . . . for evermore* (Psalm 121:2,8).

The psalms were sung as they traveled toward Jerusalem to participate in the festivals (feasts), sacrifices, and worship. Even though some may have traveled from one to three weeks to arrive in Jerusalem, these were to be journeys of great joy. They sang with assurance that the Lord would protect their homes and possessions during their absence: *Behold, He that keeps Israel shall neither slumber nor sleep* (121:4). The psalmist said: *In His Word do I hope. . . . with Him is plenteous redemption* (130:5,7). The Israelites were taught to trust in the Lord for provisions and protection, as well as for forgiveness of their sins.

David was inspired to foresee that glorious time when the Messiah will reign in Jerusalem, when *the kingdoms of this world are become the kingdoms of our Lord* (Revelation 11:15).

This prophecy foretells the reign of Christ: *Many people shall go and say, Come . . . and let us go . . . to the House of the God . . . and He will teach us of His ways, and we will walk in His paths: for out of Zion shall go forth the Law, and the Word of the LORD from Jerusalem* (Isaiah 2:3).

Centuries have passed since this prophecy was first given, but the day will soon arrive when Israel's throne will be occupied by a descendant of David – the promised Messiah, Jesus Christ.

Let all believers praise our loving Heavenly Father and echo the words of the Apostle Paul: *Blessed be the God and Father of our Lord Jesus Christ, Who has blessed us with all spiritual blessings . . . that we should be holy and without blame before Him in love. . . by Jesus Christ. . . . In Whom we have redemption through His blood, the forgiveness of sins* (Ephesians 1:3-5,7).

Thought for Today: Being satisfied is the key to praising the Lord.

Christ Revealed: As our Protector – the One Who *shall preserve your going out and your coming in* (Psalm 121:8). *By Me if any man enter in, he shall be saved, and shall go in and out, and find pasture* (John 10:9).

For definitions of unfamiliar words in today's Bible reading, see pages 468-480.

IN TODAY'S READING

A prayer for God's blessing; joy of unity; exhortation to praise
the Lord; God's enduring mercy; God's Word magnified

The psalmist reminds us of *how good and how pleasant it is for
brethren to dwell together in unity! It is like the precious ointment upon
the head, that ran down upon the beard, even Aaron's beard: that went
down to the skirts of his garments* (Psalm 133:1-2; Exodus 30:25,30;
Leviticus 8:12). The holy anointing oil that was poured upon the head
of Aaron, the first high priest, is a foreshadowing of the anointing,
indwelling, and outflowing of the Holy Spirit upon believers today.
The oil poured out symbolized the Holy Spirit Who, in love, covers as well
as permeates the lives of those who have submitted themselves to Him.

The same indwelling Holy Spirit lives within all true Christians (I
John 2:27). Therefore, in a spirit of love, we should express our oneness
without partiality, regardless of race, nationality, education, or wealth,
for we are the Body of Christ (I Corinthians 12:27).

The key to true unity is to *let nothing be done through strife or
vainglory* (empty conceit, self-seeking or petty ambition); *but in
lowliness of mind let each esteem other better than themselves* (Philippians
2:3). Our fallen nature is ever prone to distort unwelcome encounters
with others and our emotions can create a crisis out of unimportant
incidents. Added to this, we all too often selfishly demand our own
rights and blame our frustrations on others. Pride, self-will, and an
independent spirit are all enemies of the Spirit-filled life. It is Christlike
to accept personal offense with patience rather than to react to
someone's rudeness. We need to recognize that people's bad attitudes
are often momentary frustrations caused by conflicts, sorrows, sufferings, or bad news. God permits difficult people to come into our lives
to give us an opportunity to express His love and patience toward them
– just as our Lord has made known His love and mercy toward us.

The unity of believers can be compared to a great orchestra with
many instruments creating beautiful harmony. To maintain that
harmony, we each must stay in tune by following the Master Conduc-
tor. *With all lowliness and meekness, with long-suffering, forbearing
one another in love; Endeavoring* (making every effort) *to keep the unity
of the Spirit in the bond of peace* (Ephesians 4:2-3).

Thought for Today: All Christians are members of the Body of Christ.

Christ Revealed: As the descendant of David, Who would sit upon David's throne (Psalm
132:11). *He shall be great, and shall be called the Son of the Highest: and the Lord
God shall give to Him the throne of His father David* (Luke 1:32; Acts 2:29-30).

For definitions of unfamiliar words in today's Bible reading, see pages 468-480.

In Today's Reading
The all-seeing providence of God; David's prayer for deliverance
from Saul; comfort in prayer; prayer for mercy in judgment

*O*ur Creator inspired David to write: *O LORD, You. . . . are acquainted with all my ways* (from the time I was conceived to this very day). . . . *Such knowledge is too wonderful for me* (beyond my understanding). . . . *For You have possessed my reins* (formed my inward spirit and heart): *You have covered me in my mother's womb. . . . when I was made in secret. . . . Your eyes did see my substance . . . when as yet there was none* (Psalm 139:1-16). God reveals that, at conception, David became a person, a living soul. Although, as an unborn infant, he was hidden from human view, as if buried in the earth, his body was no mystery to his Creator, Who was skillfully preparing him for his God-ordained destiny on earth.

The Holy Spirit inspired the beloved physician Luke to record what the Angel Gabriel announced to the virgin Mary: *Behold, you shall conceive in your womb, and bring forth a son, and shall call His Name JESUS* (Luke 1:31). Note that the Lord Jesus Christ was announced as a Person at conception.

God also led Isaiah to prophesy concerning Christ: *The LORD has called Me from the womb; from the bowels* (body, internal parts) *of My mother has He made mention of My Name. . . . in the shadow of His hand has He hidden Me. . . . And now, says the LORD Who formed Me from the womb to be His Servant. . . . I will also give You for a* **Light to the Gentiles** (Isaiah 49:1-6).

God revealed to Jeremiah: *Before I formed you in the belly I knew you; and before you came forth out of the womb I sanctified you, and I ordained you a prophet to the nations* (Jeremiah 1:5). If the mothers of David, Isaiah, or Jeremiah had aborted them, they would have murdered great men of God. But the world's records today would have just shown more unnamed fetuses. Life is sacred and is given by the Creator for His own purposes. Even if there are unplanned or regrettable circumstances surrounding a conception, God permitted it.

Jesus said, Suffer (Permit) *little children, and forbid them not, to come to Me: for of such is the Kingdom of Heaven* (Matthew 19:14).

Thought for Today: *The one who finds Me finds life* (Proverbs 8:35).

Christ Revealed: As the One Who delivers souls from prison (Psalm 142:7). Jesus said: *He has sent Me . . . to preach deliverance to the captives* (Luke 4:18).

For definitions of unfamiliar words in today's Bible reading, see pages 468-480.

In Today's Reading

David's praise for God's mercy and goodness; benefits of trusting in God; all creation to praise the Lord; triumph in the God of Israel

The psalmist begins and ends each of the last five psalms saying: *Praise the LORD. While I live will I praise the LORD; I will sing praises to my God while I have any being. . . . We praise the LORD* that we can look to Him for our needs. *Happy is he that has the God of Jacob for his help, whose hope is in the LORD his God; Which made heaven, and earth, the sea, and all that therein is. . . . Praise the LORD* (Psalm 146:1-2,5-6,10).

The psalmist continues by saying: *Praise . . . the LORD. . . . He heals the broken in heart, and binds up their wounds. . . . He sends forth His Commandment upon earth: His Word runs very swiftly* (147:1,3,15). *Kings of the earth, and all people; princes, and all judges of the earth . . . Let them praise the Name of the LORD: for His Name alone is excellent* (148:11,13).

The more we are determined to truly put Christ first in our lives, the more we will experience interruptions which demand our time and attention. Many times, we allow even "good things" keep us from "the best" that God would give us. The loss of "good things" may also be a test of our faithfulness, to see if, like Job, we can say: *He knows the way that I take: when He has tried me, I shall come forth as gold* (Job 23:10).

The Psalms make us aware that nothing comes into our lives by accident. Everything God permits is to develop His highest good in us.

These closing psalms assure us we have a loving, Heavenly Father Who wants the best for His children. To make this possible, He has provided His Word as the One True Guide that reveals how we should live to please Him. Our Lord has provided His Church where we can sing praises to Him, share our testimonies with others who love Him, and receive instruction and inspiration from spiritual leaders. As Christians, we were never meant to be self-sufficient, independent loners but responsible members of His Church. Christ is *the Head . . . From Whom the whole body fitly joined together and compacted* (held together) *by that which every joint supplies* (Ephesians 4:15-16).

The Book of Psalms concludes by proclaiming: *Let every thing that has breath praise the LORD. Praise you the LORD* (Psalm 150:6).

Thought for Today: Trusting in the Lord's unsearchable ways is better than hoping in man's predictable, fallible ways.

Christ Revealed: As the One Who gives sight to the blind (Psalm 146:8). Jesus Christ opened blind eyes. *Then touched He their eyes. . . . And their eyes were opened* (Matthew 9:27-30; Mark 10:46-52; John 9:1-41).

For definitions of unfamiliar words in today's Bible reading, see pages 468-480.

Introduction To The Book Of
Proverbs

Solomon spoke *three thousand proverbs: and his songs were a thousand and five* (I Kings 4:32), but the wisdom revealed to and through him was inspired of God. Solomon also collected many of the proverbs written by others (Proverbs 30:1; 31:1).

The Book of Proverbs begins by stating its purpose: *To know wisdom and instruction; to perceive the words of understanding* (1:2), and then it is clearly stated that *the fear of the LORD is the beginning of knowledge; but fools despise wisdom and instruction* (1:7). Wisdom is an attribute of our Creator revealed in the Word of God. We need His wisdom to gain the most in life.

Our Lord quoted frequently from Proverbs. He often said positively what Proverbs say negatively. Compare Proverbs 4:19 with John 12:35; Proverbs 5:23 with John 8:24; Proverbs 8:35 with John 6:47; Proverbs 14:31 with Matthew 25:31-46; Proverbs 18:21 with Matthew 12:37; and Proverbs 23:7 with Matthew 12:34.

The Proverbs focus primarily on the daily conduct of the "wise" in contrast to the fool. Worldly achievements are worthless vanity compared to the eternal values that are gained by knowing His will: *For the LORD gives wisdom: out of His mouth comes knowledge and understanding* (Proverbs 2:1-2,6). God gives His people wisdom for daily direction. Wisdom is more than knowledge; it is a distinct representation and application of Christ in all areas of our lives (8:12-36).

Every word of God is pure; He is a shield to them that put their trust in Him (30:5), and *he that turns away his ear from hearing the Law, even his prayer shall be abomination* (28:9).

Cast thy bread upon the waters
With a steadfast faith sublime,
All of which in His Name one scatters
Will return to Him in time.

E'en if some give no reception
God's own Truth is not denied
But, in spite of their rejection
God is truly glorified.

Nothing lost in any service
Rendered to our gracious Lord
Whether it seem glad or grievous
There will be a full reward.

— M.E.H.

IN TODAY'S READING
Fear of God is the beginning of wisdom; necessity of searching for wisdom; importance of trusting in the Lord

Solomon, as well as all the writers of the Bible, was inspired of God to record exactly what God wanted us to know in order to be the person He created us to become. Consequently, we read: *Receive My (God's) words and hide* (treasure) *My Commandments with you; So that you incline your ear to wisdom, and apply your heart to understanding; Yea, if you seek after knowledge, and lift up your voice for understanding; If you seek her as silver, and search for her as for hid treasures; Then you shall understand the fear of the LORD, and find the knowledge of God* (Proverbs 2:1-5).

Speaking through Solomon, God is saying: "Take My Word seriously." It alone can provide you with true wisdom that will guide you to *understand righteousness, and judgment, and equity;* and, *every good path. When wisdom enters into your heart, and knowledge is pleasant to your soul; Discretion shall preserve you, understanding shall keep you* (2:9-11).

Despite the Lord's urging, some people spend little, or no, time reading the Bible, even though the Apostle Paul said: *Study* (Be diligent) *to show yourself approved to God, a workman that needs not to be ashamed, rightly dividing the Word of Truth* (II Timothy 2:15). Only a few ever pray for spiritual achievements so they may accomplish the purpose for which God created them. Discerning Christians will put their personal goals in harmony with God's purposes and *seek . . . first the Kingdom of God, and His righteousness* (Matthew 6:33) while making all secular goals secondary. *For our conversation* (citizenship) *is in heaven; from where also we look for the Savior, the Lord Jesus Christ* (Philippians 3:20).

The choice of whom we will serve is of utmost importance, for it affects everything else in life. With the same intense energy by which worldly success is pursued by many, Christians should seek achievements of eternal value for the good of others and the glory of God.

One of life's most sobering thoughts is that *the Son of Man shall come in the glory of His Father with His angels; and then He shall reward every man according to his works* (deeds) (Matthew 16:27).

Thought for Today: Read God's Word with an intense desire to accept His wisdom and reproof in order to mature spiritually.

Christ Revealed: As the Creator Who *founded the earth . . . He established the heavens* (Proverbs 3:19). *All things were created by Him, and for Him* (Colossians 1:16; Ephesians 3:9; Hebrews 1:2-3).

For definitions of unfamiliar words in today's Bible reading, see pages 468-480.

In Today's Reading

The power of wisdom to protect from evil; the seven sins most hated by God; the necessity of keeping God's Commandments

*S*exual sins are so deceptive and so destructive that more space is given in Proverbs to warnings of their wickedness than to any other sin. Sexual sin defiles the body which, for believers, is the temple of the Holy Spirit (I Corinthians 6:19). The warnings against such sins are found in Proverbs in all of chapter 5; 6:23-35; all of chapter 7; 9:13-18; and 22:14. God reveals that the only sure way of safety is found *when wisdom enters into your heart, and knowledge is pleasant to your soul . . . understanding shall . . . deliver you from the strange woman, even from the stranger which flatters with her words* (Proverbs 2:10-11,16, also 19). Indulging in a sinful relationship may provide momentary physical gratification; but *whoso commits adultery with a woman lacks understanding: he that does it destroys his own soul* (6:32).

God warns that disastrous results are inevitable: *He goes after her immediately, as an ox goes to the slaughter, or as a fool to the correction of the stocks* (7:22). Some people assume that adultery and fornication are acceptable when they occur between consenting adults; but God says: *Be not deceived: neither fornicators, nor idolaters, nor adulterers, nor effeminate, nor abusers of themselves with mankind . . . shall inherit the Kingdom of God* (I Corinthians 6:9-10) .

Satan can only tempt us, but sin begins as we dwell upon the temptation. Therefore, we must obey God's Word by *bringing into captivity every thought to the obedience of Christ* (II Corinthians 10:5).

Anyone who has been drawn into sexual sins should genuinely repent of this evil and ask God for forgiveness, for *he that covers his sins shall not prosper: but whoso confesses and forsakes them shall have mercy* (Proverbs 28:13). *But this Man* (the Lord Jesus Christ), *after* (when) *He had offered one sacrifice for sins for ever, sat down on the right hand of God. . . . For by one offering He has perfected for ever them that are sanctified* (cleansed from sin, made holy). . . . *And their sins and iniquities will I remember no more. Now where remission* (forgiveness) *of these is, there is no more offering* (sacrifice) *for sin* (Hebrews 10:12,14,17-18).

Thought for Today: We are cautioned that as a man *thinks within himself, so he is* (Proverbs 23:7).

Christ Revealed: By the teacher of *wisdom* (Proverbs 4:7,11). Christ is the Teacher *in Whom are hidden all the treasures of wisdom and knowledge* (Colossians 2:3).

For definitions of unfamiliar words in today's Bible reading, see pages 468-480.

In Today's Reading
Benefits of wisdom; wise and foolish contrasted

Nothing in life is more to be treasured, more priceless, than knowing the Word of God. As Solomon spoke these proverbs to his "son," God is also speaking to us as His "sons." *All the words of my mouth are in righteousness; there is nothing froward* (crooked, deceitful) *or perverse* (wrong) *in them. They are all plain to him that understands, and right to them that find knowledge. Receive my instruction, and not silver; and knowledge rather than choice gold. For wisdom is better than rubies; and all the things that may be desired are not to be compared to it* (Proverbs 8:8-11).

Is it any surprise that Satan seeks so relentlessly to keep Christians from reading what God has written, the only sure way of knowing right from wrong? When we commit ourselves to obedience of God's Word, our first considerations are love, loyalty, and service to our Lord.

The fear of the LORD is the beginning of wisdom: and the knowledge of the Holy is understanding (9:10). This wisdom and understanding covers every aspect of life: physical, moral, spiritual, financial, and our social well-being. *The fear of the LORD is to hate evil: pride, and arrogancy, and the evil way, and the froward* (perverted) *mouth, do I hate. Counsel is Mine, and sound wisdom: I am understanding; I have strength. . . . I love them that love Me; and those that seek Me early shall find Me. . . . Now therefore hearken to Me, O . . . children: for blessed are they that keep My ways. . . . For whoso finds Me finds life, and shall obtain favor of the LORD. But he that sins against Me wrongs his own soul: all they that hate Me* (God's Word) *love death* (8:13-14,17,32,35-36).

The basic difference between the wise man and the fool is in the use each makes of his time, talents, and material possessions. When we rely on God and His Word it will result in loving obedience to Him (3:5-6).

We all are on one of two roads in our journey through life. The road followed by the wise is narrower and more difficult, but it brings happiness, satisfaction, peace, and eternal life; however, the broad road of the fool inevitably leads to vanity (a life of self-interest) and, ultimately, into the eternal lake of fire. *Death and hell were cast into the lake of fire. This is the second death. And whosoever was not found written in the Book of Life was cast into the lake of fire* (Revelation 20:14-15).

Thought for Today: Failure to give help to others is motivated by selfishness.

Christ Revealed: As the Creator Who *prepared the heavens* **(Proverbs 8:27-31).** *The heavens are the works of Your hands* **(Hebrews 1:10, John 1:3).**

For definitions of unfamiliar words in today's Bible reading, see pages 468-480.

God, in His infinite wisdom, has declared: *He that spares his rod hates* (disregard for) *his son: but he that loves him chastens him betimes* (diligently) (Proverbs 13:24).

The greatest acts of love we can make to our children's future is to teach them obedience and respect – first to Christ as their personal Savior and Lord of their lives, then to their parents and all who are in authority, including schoolteachers and law enforcement officers. This obedience should also extend to the laws of our government. As a prerequisite to teaching a child submission to authority, it is vital that parents consistently show submission to authority by their own example.

The rod is the symbol of authority that God has committed to parents for training their children. To apply the rod means to exercise authority. The rod must be administered firmly yet lovingly. Using the rod of authority does not mean that parents should release their bottled-up frustrations by shouting demands, slapping faces, or severely spanking. These are examples of mental and physical abuse. We must not expect adult maturity from our children. They need the same loving-kindness and patience from us that we desire from our Heavenly Father. Even mature Christians are prone to forget how many times the Lord, with long-suffering love, has forgiven our sins and failures through the years.

Biblical discipline follows the example of our loving Father in heaven, Who corrects and disciplines everyone Whom He loves (Hebrews 12:6). The psalmist expressed it this way: *Before I was afflicted* (punished) *I went astray: but now have I kept Your Word* (Psalm 119:67).

We can develop our children's respect for God-ordained authority and, at the same time, provide them with an assurance of both our love and God's love for them. It is important to spend time with our children, especially reading the Bible and praying with them, to develop a concern for the things of God (Deuteronomy 6:2-9; Proverbs 22:6).

Children, obey your parents in the Lord: for this is right. Honor your father and mother; (which is the first Commandment with promise) (Ephesians 6:1-2; also Exodus 20:12).

Thought for Today: Prayerfully think before you act or speak.

Christ Revealed: As One Who hates *lying* (Proverbs 12:22). *He that sat upon the throne said. . . . all liars, shall have their part in the lake which burns with fire and brimstone* (Revelation 21:5,8).

For definitions of unfamiliar words in today's Bible reading, see pages 468-480.

> ## In Today's Reading
> The values of pleasing the Lord and choosing wisdom

*N*o one is naturally humble. Our human nature is permeated with pride passed down from Adam; only the indwelling Christ can develop true humility in our lives. This will manifest itself in kindness toward the unkind, long-suffering toward those who annoy us, and love toward our enemies. How inconsistent it is to think we have "humbly given ourselves to Christ" when we snub or react harshly to anyone.

The Lord leads us to see the end result of pride and false humility: *Pride goes before destruction, and a haughty spirit before a fall. Better it is to be of a humble spirit with the lowly, than to divide the spoil with the proud* (Proverbs 16:18-19).

It is natural to think of ourselves as humble, at least more humble than others. But humility, or a lack of it, is apparent by our attitude when we are with someone who irritates us. If our replies are expressed in an unkind way, either outwardly in our words or actions or inwardly in our thoughts, then our "humility" is not real; it is a mere pious mask. Knowing the destructive power of pride, let us look upon people who seem difficult to love as those chosen by God to provide us with the opportunity to cleanse ourselves of self-righteousness and to express Christlike humility and the love of God.

Humble people will feel no jealousy or envy when they are ignored while others are praised. God reminds us: *Let nothing be done through strife or vainglory* (pride, empty conceit); *but in lowliness of mind let each esteem other better than themselves* (Philippians 2:3).

The Christlike nature of a Christian moves him to not respond with a sharp, unfriendly attitude when differences of opinion exist. Personal views often create ill will. We are admonished: *Be of the same mind one toward another. Mind not high things, but condescend to men of low estate. Be not wise in your own conceits* (opinions) (Romans 12:16).

To be Christlike is to see others through the eyes of Jesus and to give equal consideration to all people, regardless of their race, position, abilities, or wealth, for *God is no respecter of persons* (Acts 10:34).

Thought for Today: Avoid worldly-minded associates.

Christ Revealed: As the One Who punishes the proud (Proverbs 16:5). Jesus said: *Whosoever exalts himself shall be abased* (humbled); *and he that humbles himself shall be exalted* (Luke 14:11). As the *Friend that sticks closer than a brother* (Proverbs 18:24). Jesus is our Friend (John 15:14-15) and *will never leave* (us), *nor forsake* (us) (Hebrews 13:5).

For definitions of unfamiliar words in today's Bible reading, see pages 468-480.

In Today's Reading
Deception of wine; sovereignty of God over kings of the earth;
moral virtues rewarded

*A*lcohol is amazingly deceptive. The insidious "occasional" drink, in moderation, seems harmless. It even gives the appearance of making life more enjoyable. But many a "social" drinker eventually discovers that he is an alcoholic and has exchanged a meaningful life for a degrading existence. Brilliant people who were once successful and influential have been reduced to uselessness because of alcohol. And, strange as it may seem, in their own minds they are convinced that they can take it or leave it and stop drinking at any time. God has warned that *wine is a mocker, strong drink is raging: and whosoever is deceived thereby is not wise* (Proverbs 20:1).

Pity the person who tries to escape the pressures of life and relax with a "little" drink, unaware of where it might lead. No words can express the pitiful results of continued use of alcohol. The warning from God of alcohol's poisoning effects is clear: *At the last it bites like a serpent, and stings like an adder* (23:32).

Alcohol takes control both chemically and emotionally, with both physical and psychological effects. Once a person is "hooked," dependence upon it robs him of good judgment and, eventually, may destroy his life as well as those of others. Alcohol can produce unavoidable, irreversible, and far-reaching physical and emotional wounds.

The longer the victim of intoxication continues indulging in alcohol, the more insensible he becomes to the consequences of his behavior. Gradually, millions have allowed themselves to be in direct violation of the Word of God. The only release from these tragic consequences is the mercy of God. When a person truly repents, turns to Christ, and allows Him to be Savior and Lord of his life, the Holy Spirit becomes his source of strength to overcome sin. *Wherefore be you not unwise, but understanding what the will of the Lord is. And be not drunk with wine, wherein is excess; but be filled with* (controlled by) *the Spirit* (Ephesians 5:17-18).

Let us walk honestly (properly) *. . . not in rioting* (wild parties) *and drunkenness, not in chambering* (sexual indulgence) *and wantonness* (unbridled lust). *. . . . But put . . . on the Lord Jesus Christ, and make not provision for the flesh* (Romans 13:13-14).

Thought for Today: Play it safe — *Abstain from all appearance of evil* (I Thessalonians 5:22).

Christ Revealed: As the King Who sits on *the throne of judgment* (Proverbs 20:8). *For the Father judges no man, but has committed all judgment to the Son* (John 5:22).

For definitions of unfamiliar words in today's Bible reading, see pages 468-480.

ℐN 𝒯ODAY'S ℛEADING
Moral, ethical, and spiritual teachings; the excellence of wisdom

*ℐ*t seems normal to stand up for our rights – to fight back against those who treat us unjustly or to get even by inflicting suffering upon those who offend us. But, it is a serious sin to be delighted when an enemy suffers and seems to reap what we think he deserves. It is even more serious to harbor a secret hatred and a desire to bring about his downfall: *Rejoice not when your enemy falls, and let not your heart be glad when he stumbles: Lest the* LORD *see it, and it displease Him, and He turn away His wrath from him* (Proverbs 24:17-18).

Attitudes of bitterness, revenge, hatred, or ill will toward anyone are self-destructive and they are indications that we are not living nearly as close to Christ as we should. *Let us not love in word, neither in tongue* (talk); *but in deed* (action) *and in truth* (I John 3:18). We are not to regard anyone as an enemy, since we were all created in the image of God and Christ died to save all of us without an exception. Let us pray that those whom we might consider "enemies" may become disciples of Christ and our brothers and sisters in Him.

No one is justified in taking revenge; we are definitely not qualified to be judge, jury, or executioner. We dare not assume the position of God, Who said: *Dearly beloved, avenge not yourselves, but rather give place to wrath* (opportunity for God's wrath): *for it is written, Vengeance is Mine; I will repay, says the Lord* (Romans 12:19; Deuteronomy 32:35; Hebrews 10:30). If we are unjustly treated, we should pray for our offender. All thoughts of hatred and revenge are temptations of Satan; but the indwelling Holy Spirit will enable the Christian to reject them and be merciful and forgiving rather than hateful toward a wrongdoer.

Our reaction to the unkind behavior of our offenders reveals whether we are controlled by the Holy Spirit or by our old sinful nature (Romans 8:1-9). *Blessed are the meek* (submission to the will of God): *for they shall inherit the earth. . . . Blessed are they which are persecuted for righteousness' sake: for theirs is the Kingdom of Heaven* (Matthew 5:5,10).

Thought for Today: To love the unlovely is an expression of Christ's love.

Christ Revealed: As the One Who rewards those who repay evil with good (Proverbs 25: 21-22). *If your enemy hunger, feed him; if he thirst, give him drink* (Romans 12:20). Jesus said: *Love your enemies* (Matthew 5:44; Luke 6:27,35).

For definitions of unfamiliar words in today's Bible reading, see pages 468-480.

ℐN ℐODAY'S ℛEADING
Advice to the wise; Agur's confession of his faith;
the words of King Lemuel; praise of a good wife

ℐf we love someone, we want to be with them and to know what pleases them so that we can develop a lasting relationship. We also want to know what they dislike so that we can avoid decisions that would displease them. Surely, this should also be an important consideration in our relationship with our Lord.

God said: *Whoso keeps the Law is a wise son. . . . He that turns away his ear from hearing the Law, even his prayer shall be abomination* (Proverbs 28:7,9). Why should God be attentive to what we have to say if we are not interested in reading His qualifications for acceptable prayer?

The Apostle John reminded believers: *If our heart condemn us not, then have we confidence toward God. And whatsoever we ask, we receive of Him, because we keep* (obey) *His Commandments, and do those things that are pleasing in His sight* (I John 3:21-22). But, we can't keep all His Commandments if we don't read all of His Word to know what they are.

Strange as it may seem, some people pray for solutions to their problems, but ignore the one place where God provides the answers. Why is there such widespread failure among Christians to read all of what God has said? Do they assume that, like the unregenerate world, their own "good judgment" can take the place of the wisdom of our Creator?

The prophet Jeremiah exposed the reason for Israel's problems, saying: *The Word of the LORD is to them a reproach; they have no delight in it* (Jeremiah 6:10). The Lord further declared through His prophet: *I will bring evil . . . because they have not hearkened to My words, nor to My Law, but rejected it* (6:19). Throughout history, God has rejected His people when they continued to refuse His guidance. Without a doubt, God was heartbroken when He said to the prophet Hosea: *My people are destroyed for lack of knowledge* (Hosea 4:6) – knowledge of His Word they had chosen to ignore.

Jesus emphasized the need to read His Word when He said: *If you keep My Commandments, you shall abide in My love* (John 15:10).

Thought for Today: Christ is the only Savior and the world needs to know.

Christ Revealed: As the One Who descended from and ascended to heaven (Proverbs 30:4). *Jesus came down from heaven, even the Son of Man Who is* (now) *in heaven* **(John 3:13).**

For definitions of unfamiliar words in today's Bible reading, see pages 468-480.

Solomon listed 27 achievements in his life and ended by saying: *Whatsoever my eyes desired I kept not from them, I withheld not my heart from any joy* (Ecclesiastes 2:10). But Solomon repeatedly used the expression: *All is vanity* (1:2). The word *vanity* means it has no lasting satisfaction. However, during that time, he violated all four commands given to kings in the Word of God by amassing horses, wealth, and wives (Deuteronomy 17:16-17).

By the end of his 40-year reign, the people had been oppressed with excessive taxes to support his massive personal building projects.

After living his life in vain, Solomon conceded that a man is a fool who thinks he can achieve fulfillment in life by amassing material possessions – because he is never satisfied (5:10-20; 6:1-9). Solomon described himself when he wrote: *Better is a poor and a wise child than an old and foolish king, who will no more be admonished* (4:13).

The Book of Ecclesiastes is a confession of the worthlessness of all earthly treasures. It is impossible to find lasting satisfaction apart from reading the Word of God and living according to His will. Everything is indeed futile if Christ is not Lord of our lives.

After a lifetime of searching for satisfaction through wealth, women, and possessions, Solomon eventually recognized that man's true contentment lies only in full obedience to God. He concluded by cautioning others: *Remember now your Creator in the days of your youth, while the evil days come not, nor the years draw near, when you shall say, I have no pleasure in them* (12:1).

JUDGE

And if any man hear My words, and believe (obeys) not, I judge him not: for I came not to judge the world, but to save the world. He that rejects Me, and receives not My words, has one that judges him: the Word that I have spoken, the same shall judge him in the last day (John 12:47-48).

For I testify (forth-telling or fore-telling) to every man that hears the words of the prophecy (teaching) of this Book, If any man shall add to these things, God shall add to him the plagues that are written in this Book: And if any man shall take away from the words of the Book of this prophecy, God shall take away his part out of the Book of Life, and out of the holy city, and from the things which are written in this Book (Revelation 22:18:19).

In Today's Reading

The vanity (emptiness) of living for pleasure and material gain;
a reason for everything; varied proverbs of wisdom

*I*t would be easy to be impressed by the achievements of Solomon. He wrote: *I built me houses; I planted me vineyards: I made me gardens and orchards, and I planted trees in them . . . all kind of fruits: I made me pools of water, to water* (irrigate) *therewith the wood that brings forth trees: I got me servants and maidens, and had servants born in my house; also I had great possessions of great and small cattle above all that were in Jerusalem before me: I gathered me also silver and gold . . . I got me . . . delights of the sons of men. . . . So I was great, and increased more than all that were before me in Jerusalem. . . . And whatsoever my eyes desired, I kept not from them* (Ecclesiastes 2:4-10).

The key word here is "me." Solomon did all of these things for himself. With each increasing excess, he found less and less pleasure. Jesus declared success in life with one simple statement: *Seek . . . first the Kingdom of God, and His righteousness; and all these things* (material necessities) *shall be added to you* (Matthew 6:33).

Solomon eventually concluded: *I looked on all the works that my hands had wrought, and on the labor that I had labored to do: and, behold, all was vanity and vexation of spirit* (chasing after the wind), *and there was no profit under the sun.* Solomon was rightly troubled when he said: *I hated* (abhorred) *life; because the work that is wrought under the sun is grievous to me: for all is vanity and vexation of spirit* (Ecclesiastes 2:11,17). Sadly, many today are still trying to gain fulfillment with earthly pursuits while ignoring the will of God.

It is recorded that, when *Solomon* began his reign, he *loved the LORD, walking in the statutes of David his father . . .* (But Solomon's heart was divided); *he sacrificed and burned incense in high places* (I Kings 3:3). Consequently, his priorities became distorted and he gradually set his heart on material projects, wealth, and women.

Each of us needs to consider: "What is God's purpose for my brief life?" Can we expect to hear Jesus say: *Well done, good and faithful servant; you have been faithful over a few things, I will make you ruler over many things: enter into the joy of your Lord* (Matthew 25:23).

Thought for Today: Possessions and pleasures are no substitute for the Person to whom we owe our supreme devotion – the Lord Jesus.

Christ Revealed: As God, the true source of *wisdom, and knowledge, and joy* – the One Who truly satisfies (Ecclesiastes 2:26). *We have the mind of Christ* which is wisdom, knowledge, and joy (I Corinthians 2:16; see also Luke 21:15; John 15:11; Romans 15:14).

For definitions of unfamiliar words in today's Bible reading, see pages 468-480.

In Today's Reading
Caution against hasty vows; the emptiness of riches;
wisdom and goodness upheld; respect for rulers

At Gibeon, the Lord appeared to Solomon in a dream in which Solomon asked for wisdom. Yet, we have no record that Solomon ever copied the Law in his own hand, as God had instructed Israel's kings to do, and he broke all of the laws specifically given to kings (Deuteronomy 17:14-20). As the years passed, he searched for satisfaction everywhere except from the Lord and His Word (Psalm 119:97-98). Following years of an extravagant lifestyle, in his old age Solomon observed that rich and poor were equally obsessed with such fruitless endeavors.

Solomon's thoughts then turned from the secular to the religious life, and he noted that many attended the House of God offering insincere prayers and making vows that were never kept. The Holy Spirit, speaking through him, warned: *Keep your foot when you go to the House of God, and be more ready to hear, than to give the sacrifice of fools* (Ecclesiastes 5:1). Hypocrisy is an insult to God, as well as spiritually self-destructive. He further warned: *Be not rash with your mouth* (5:2).

True worship requires a heart-inspired obedience to the Word of God. When we assemble to worship, we are to open our hearts to adore, praise, and exalt the Lord. Jesus defined worship when He said: *God is a Spirit: and they that worship Him must worship Him in spirit and in truth* (John 4:24). After creating Adam, God *breathed into his nostrils the breath of life; and man became a living soul* (Genesis 2:7). That eternal spirit and soul life is what must worship God; mere physical speech and to go through religious ritual are not sufficient. The inner man, the eternal man, is what Jesus was saying must recognize and worship his Creator.

The place where we worship the Lord is not important. It may be a magnificent cathedral, a thatched hut, a disciple's home, or a cave since *you are the temple of God, and . . . the Spirit of God dwells in you* (I Corinthians 3:16). There is no time or place where God is not with His children (John 14:16; Hebrews 13:5). Because of this, we should always praise the Lord – be it in a palace or a prison. *At midnight Paul and Silas prayed, and sang praises to God* (Acts 16:25).

Thought for Today: Do not envy the wealth of evildoers – it is only temporary.

Christ Revealed: As One Who expects us to keep our vows made to Him (Ecclesiastes 5:4). *So then every one of us shall give account of himself to God* (Romans 14:12).

For definitions of unfamiliar words in today's Bible reading, see pages 468-480.

In Today's Reading
Struggles of the righteous and the wicked; wisdom better than
strength; the wise versus the foolish; the Creator to be remembered

Solomon was famous for his wisdom, but he could be misunderstood when he said: *Rejoice, O young man, in your youth; and let your
heart cheer you in the days of your youth, and walk in the ways of your
heart, and in the sight of your eyes* (Ecclesiastes 11:9). Not continuing
his message would imply he was encouraging youth to let passion and
pleasure go unchecked; but he continued: *Know you, that for all these
things God will bring you into judgment.*

Solomon spent his lifetime searching for pleasure from every
worldly source, but he used the word *vanity* (emptiness) over 30 times
in the Book of Ecclesiastes and concluded that ignoring the Word of
God was *vanity of vanities* (12:8). Before finishing his message,
Solomon restated the basis for true wisdom: *Remember now your
Creator in the days of your youth, while the evil days come not, nor the
years draw near, when you shall say, I have no pleasure in them. . . . Let
us hear the conclusion of the whole matter: Fear God, and keep His
Commandments: for this is the whole duty of man* (12:1,13). Since all of
us are part of the purposes of God, all else in life should be seen as
opportunities to advance the Kingdom of God.

Satisfaction in life results from giving one's time, talents, and
resources to fulfill the will of God. This is the only true source of
happiness, peace of mind, and genuine enjoyment in life, for we were
created to fulfill His purpose. *We are His workmanship, created in
Christ Jesus to good works, which God has before ordained* (planned)
that we should walk in them (Ephesians 2:10).

Therefore, it is foolish to seek riches, security, power, popularity, or
fleeting goals in life merely for earthly self-satisfaction. It is also vanity
to give way to *the lust of the flesh* (gratification of the physical nature),
and the lust of the eyes, and the pride of life (I John 2:16).

*Let no man deceive himself. If any man among you seems to be wise
in this world, let him become a fool, that he may be wise. For the wisdom
of this world is foolishness with God* (I Corinthians 3:18-19).

Thought for Today: Genuine enjoyment in life is to be like Jesus.

Christ Revealed: In the statement: *For God shall bring every work into judgment*
(Ecclesiastes 12:14). Jesus will judge all, *for the Father* (God) *judges no man, but has
committed all judgment to the Son* (Jesus) (John 5:22).

For definitions of unfamiliar words in today's Bible reading, see pages 468-480.

Introduction To The Book Of
The Song of Solomon

Jewish rabbis regard this book as an illustration of the marriage relationship between God and Israel as His wife (Isaiah 54:4; Jeremiah 2:2; Ezekiel 16:8-14; Hosea 2:16-20). Many Christian leaders believe that it expresses the love that exists between Christ and His Church. It expresses the longing of the Christian for the presence of the Heavenly Bridegroom and the precious union of the bride with Jesus Christ, our Bridegroom, and the King of kings (Revelation 19:7-9,16; 21:9). This beautiful love story also expresses the love of a marriage relationship planned by the Creator.

There are many difficulties in the spiritual interpretation of some of these passages, just as there are some difficulties in the interpretation of the Church as the Bride of Christ and He as our Bridegroom.

The importance of this Song is recognized in two ways. First, the Creator Who controls the king's heart led the compilers of Scripture to include *the song of songs, which is Solomon's* (The Song of Solomon 1:1). Second, through Paul, the Lord Himself said: *All Scripture is given by inspiration of God, and is profitable for doctrine* (teaching), *for reproof, for correction, for instruction in righteousness* (II Timothy 3:16). Because God inspired this book to be written, we should seek to know Him better through it.

The Song of Solomon is about a king's love for a maiden and her desire for everyone to admire him. It illustrates the relationship between Christ and those who will not be satisfied with anyone's love but His.

I love Thee, Lord; I love Thy will.
Do Thou Thy plan through me fulfill
That glory may return to Thee
For time and for eternity.

In natural strength no honor lies;
Thy grace alone sin's power defies,
but Satan's power is nullified
Through all in whom Christ does abide.

The victory of Christ - complete -
Through all the ages stands replete
As any humble, trusting soul
Yields fully to Thy blest control.

- M.E.H.

This poem describes the wholesome enjoyment of married love between a man and a woman. It expresses the delight of the bridegroom
in the bride and of the bride in her husband. The bride describes her
wonderful memories as her bridegroom tarries. The whole narrative
has a dreamlike quality. The circumstances are vague and not such as
occur in ordinary life. The longing, the wondering, and the searching
represent the images of dreams. The bride was asleep on her bed, but
her thoughts were continually about her absent bridegroom. *By night
on my bed I sought him whom my soul loves: I sought him, but I
found him not* (The Song of Solomon 3:1).

Every believer is assured that *my beloved is mine, and I am his*
(2:16), for Jesus Christ has entered into our very lives. Our love
relationship continues to grow and deepen as we listen to Him speak
to us as we read His Word. We become different persons by virtue of
our relationship with the coming Bridegroom. With Paul, we too can
say: *I live; yet not I, but Christ lives in me: and the life which I now
live in the flesh I live by the faith of the Son of God, Who loved me,
and gave Himself for me* (Galatians 2:20).

Sometimes we enjoy a very close sense of the presence of Christ.
But, all too often, His presence seems far away. Yet our love for Him
continues to grow as we wait expectantly for that first glimpse of Him
when He welcomes us home.

As the bride, we also wait with great anticipation for the return of
our Bridegroom Jesus when we too will be able to say: *He brought me
to the banqueting house, and His banner over me was love* (The Song of
Solomon 2:4).

*Let not your heart be troubled: you believe in God, believe also in Me.
In My Father's house are many mansions: if it were not so, I would have
told you. I go to prepare a place for you. And if I go and prepare a place
for you, I will come again, and receive you to Myself; that where I am,
there you may be also* (John 14:1-3).

Thought for Today: Be prepared for the Lord's return.

Christ Revealed: As *the chiefest* (outstanding) *among ten thousand* (The Song of
Solomon 5:10). Jesus is the *KING OF KINGS, AND LORD OF LORDS* (Revelation
19:16).

For definitions of unfamiliar words in today's Bible reading, see pages 468-480.

Introduction To The Book Of
Isaiah

Isaiah's ministry extended about 60 years during the reigns of Judah's kings Uzziah (Azariah), Jotham, Ahaz, and Hezekiah (II Kings 14:21; Isaiah 1:1; II Chronicles 26:22; 32:20-23). This was during the same period of time that Micah was prophesying in Judah, while Jonah, Amos, and Hosea were prophets to the northern kingdom of Israel.

The Book of Isaiah is addressed to the entire world: *Hear, O heavens, and give ear . . . for the LORD has spoken* (Isaiah 1:2). In its pages, we learn how God uses the nations of the world as His instruments for working out His perfect will for mankind. The message throughout the book is: *Hear the Word of the LORD* (1:10). This means not only to seriously read His Word, but also to carry out and obey His will.

The Lord made a wonderful promise, through Isaiah, for sinners. His invitation was: *Come now, and let us reason together, says the LORD: though your sins be as scarlet, they shall be as white as snow* (1:18). It was an appeal for the Israelites to return to the Lord and once again live in obedience to His Word when He said: *O house of Jacob, come and let us walk in the light of LORD* (2:5). It is also a warning of judgment upon those who reject His Word (2:6 – 3:26). A severe warning of six woes is pronounced upon the faithless (2:12; 5:8,11,18,20-22).

A new vision of the glorious Messiah King is described: *In the year that King Uzziah died I saw also the Lord sitting upon a throne, high and lifted up, and His train* (trailing edge of His robe) *filled the Temple. . . . my eyes have seen the King, the LORD of hosts* (6:1,5). Isaiah was blessed with the rare privilege of actually seeing the Lord sitting in His heavenly Temple. The Book of Isaiah closes with God's promises of comfort and peace for His children, as well as a warning that eternal punishment awaits those who reject Him (66:22-24).

Jesus Christ is the Supreme theme of this book. Isaiah prophesied the birth of Christ and His deity (7:14; 9:6-7), His ministry (42:1-7; 61:1-2), His sufferings and death (52:1-3; 53:1-12), His coming reign which will follow the great tribulation, and His triumph over the Antichrist (2:11; 9:7; 25:1-27:13; 42:4-7; 49:5-6; 52:13; 63:1-6). Isaiah frequently refers to God as *the Holy One of Israel* (1:4; 5:19,24; 10:20; 12:6; 17:7; 29:19,23; 30:11-12,15; 31:1; 37:23; 41:14,16,20; 43:3,14; 45:11; 47:4; 48:17; 49:7; 54:5; 55:5; 60:9,14).

Visions of *the* (coming) *Day of the LORD of hosts*, sometimes simply called *that day*, are prominent (2:11-12,17,20; 3:7,18; 4:1-2; 5:30; 28:5; 29:18; 30:23; 31:7) with special attention given to it (10:20; 11:10-11; 12:1,4; 13:6,9,13; 14:3; 17:4,7,9; 19:16,18-19,21,23-24; 22:5,12,20,25).

PARTIAL LIST OF NAMES AND TITLES OF CHRIST IN ISAIAH

Angel of His Presence 63:9

Arm of the Lord 51:9-10

Banner for the Peoples 11:10

Boy 7:16

Branch of Jesse 11:1

Branch of the LORD 4:2

Channels of Water 32:2

Child 9:6

Chosen One of the Lord 42:1

Commander & Leader 55:4

Counselor 9:6

Covenant of the People 42:6

Creator of Israel 43:15

Crown/Diadem 28:5

Eliakim 22:20

Eternal Father 9:6

Everlasting Rock 26.4

Everlasting Light 60:20

Glorious One 33:21

Glory of the Lord 40:5

God of Israel, Savior 45:15

God of All the Earth 54:5

Great Light 9:2

Heritage of Jacob 58:14

Highway/Roadway/Pathway 35:8

Holy, Holy, Holy 6:3

Holy One of Israel 41:14; 49:7

Husband 54:5

Immanuel 7:14

Israel 49:3

Lord 40:3

King in His Beauty 33:17

King Lord of Hosts 6:5

Lawgiver 33:22

Light to the Nations 42:6

Lord God [Jehovah] 40:10

Lord [Jehovah] of Hosts 6:3; 54:5

Lord, your Holy One 43:15

Lord, your Redeemer 43:14

Man of Pains 53:3

Mighty God 9:6

Mighty One of Jacob 49:26

Mighty to Save 63:1

My Chosen,
  in Whom I Myself Delight 42:1

My Messenger 42:19

My Servant 49:3

Place to Hide; to Find Cover 32:2

Polished Arrow 49:2

Precious CornerStone 28:16

Prince of Peace 9:6

Redeemer 59:20; 60:16

Refuge from the Rain 25:4

Righteous Servant 53:11

Rock of Israel 30:29

Rock to Trip Over 8:14

Root of Jesse 11:10

Salvation of
  the Daughter of Zion 62:11

Sanctuary 8:14

Savior 19:20

Servant 42:1,19

Servant of Rulers 49:7

Shade from the Heat 25:4

Shadow of a Massive Rock 32:2

Sharp Sword 49:2

Shoot and Branch 11:1

Son given 9:6

Stone 28:16

Stone Laid in Zion 28:16

Stone to Stumble Over 8:14

Stronghold for the Poor 25:4

Sure Foundation 28:16

Tested Stone 28:16

Witness to the Peoples 55:4

Wonderful 9:6

In *Today's* *Reading*

Israel's sin; Isaiah's exhortation for repentance;
coming of Christ's kingdom; Jerusalem's glorious future

*T*he God of Creation chose the Israelites to reveal Himself as the One True God, as revealed in His incarnate and written Word to all nations. It must have been with deep sorrow that God led Isaiah to say: *Hear . . . and give ear . . . for the LORD has spoken, I have nourished and brought up children, and they have rebelled against Me. The ox knows its owner, and the ass its master's crib* (manger): *but Israel does not know. . . . they have provoked the Holy One of Israel to anger, they are gone away backward* (turned away from Him) (Isaiah 1:2-4). Isaiah recorded how the Lord had chosen and provided for the Israelites, only to have them turn against Him by worshiping idols. The Lord lamented that even the animals He had created knew Who their Master was, but the sinful Israelites refused to recognize their responsibility to their Creator.

Like our Heavenly Father, it must have been heartbreaking for King David, the great prophet Samuel, and godly King Josiah of Judah, all of whom had children who were rebellious and did not obey the Word of God. The Lord has provided His written Word which, through the guidance of the indwelling Holy Spirit, will teach us how to experience the joy of forgiveness and deliverance from guilt and condemnation of sin.

Many godly parents are heartbroken when they see their children turning from the Lord. Like our Heavenly Father, they too feel sorrow over children who are uncommitted to the Lord, to reading the Bible, or to regular worship in a local church. Whether or not our children succeed or fail in their earthly goals, by comparison, it is of little eternal consequence, for only their spiritual achievements will bring true success and eternal rewards.

Isaiah was called to comfort those who were faithful to the Holy One (40:1). Isaiah prophesied of a coming King Who would reign in righteousness and peace over children who had returned to Him. When the Messiah comes, *many people shall go and say, Come you, let us go up to the mountain of the LORD, to the House of the God of Jacob; and He will teach us of His ways, and we will walk in His paths: for out of Zion shall go forth the Law, and the Word of the LORD from Jerusalem* (Isaiah 2:3).

Thought for Today: Continued disobedience blinds one's eyes and hardens one's heart to the will of God.

Christ Revealed: As the One Who will judge the nations (Isaiah 2:2-4). *The Lord Jesus Christ . . . shall judge the quick and the dead at His appearing* (II Timothy 4:1).

For definitions of unfamiliar words in today's Bible reading, see pages 468-480.

IN TODAY'S READING

God's judgment upon sinners; Isaiah's vision of God's holiness;
his message for King Ahaz; Christ's birth and Kingdom foretold

The prophet Isaiah foretold the judgment of God against the kingdom of Judah for the people's sins.

Ahaz, king of Judah, was facing war. The prophet appealed to him, saying: *Ask a sign of the LORD* (7:11). Although Ahaz refused, Isaiah spoke a glorious prophecy of the true King of kings Who was yet to come. The sign Isaiah offered was the declaration of a special Child: *The virgin shall conceive, and bear a Son, and shall call His Name Immanuel* (God With Us) (7:14). Seven hundred years later, the Angel Gabriel confirmed to the Virgin Mary: *The Holy Ghost* (Spirit) *shall come upon you, and the power of the Highest shall overshadow you: therefore also that Holy Thing* (One) *which shall be born of you shall be called the Son of God* (Luke 1:35). In fulfillment of Isaiah's prophecy, Jesus, the Son of God, was born. To reject the virgin birth and question either the deity or the humanity of Jesus of Nazareth is to miss the significance that Jesus was both Holy God and sinless Man. Only He could atone for the sins of mankind and redeem what Adam had forfeited.

The prophet Isaiah received another glorious revelation of the eternal King of kings of Whom he foretold: *To us a Child* (Jesus Christ) *is born, to us a Son is given: and the government shall be upon His shoulder: and His Name shall be called Wonderful, Counselor, The Mighty God, The Everlasting Father, The Prince of Peace* (9:6). We recognize the fulfillment of that prophecy in Jesus, Who was born and later crucified, providing eternal life to all believers by dying on the cross for our sins, and by His triumph over death. Not only was His first advent declared, but also His second. We can rejoice as we look forward to the time when He will reign in righteousness on earth as the most *Wonderful Counselor*.

Jesus is the Second Person of the Godhead. *The Same was in the beginning with God. All things were made by Him; and without Him was not any thing made that was made* (John 1:2-3; also Hebrews 1:3).

Thought for Today: All of our own righteousness is as filthy rags before a Holy God. Self-righteous people assume they are "good enough" without the Savior.

Christ Revealed: Isaiah reveals that a Child shall be born; a Son shall be given; *and that the government shall be upon His shoulder* (Isaiah 9:6). *The kingdoms of this world are become the kingdoms of our Lord, and of His Christ; and He shall reign for ever and ever* (Revelation 11:15).

For definitions of unfamiliar words in today's Bible reading, see pages 468-480.

ℐN 𝒯ODAY'S ℛEADING

Assyria to be broken; promise of Israel's restoration;
Christ, the Branch; thanksgiving for God's mercies;
Babylon's doom predicted; Israel to be preserved

𝒞oncerning the return of Jesus to earth and His glorious millennial reign, Isaiah foretold: *The Spirit of the LORD shall rest upon Him, the Spirit of wisdom and understanding, the Spirit of counsel and might, the Spirit of knowledge and of the fear of the LORD . . . . The earth shall be full of the knowledge of the LORD, as the waters cover the sea. And in that day there shall be a Root of Jesse, which shall stand for an ensign* (rallying flag) *of the people; to it shall the Gentiles seek: and His rest shall be glorious* (Isaiah 11:2,9-10). The promise made through Isaiah, of the Ruler Who would come from King David, the Root of Jesse, is far-reaching and anticipates the new heavens and the new earth that are yet to be. *In that day you shall say, Praise the LORD, call upon His Name, declare His doings among the people, make mention that His Name is exalted. Sing to the LORD; for He has done excellent things: this is known in all the earth. Cry out and shout, you inhabitant of Zion: for great is the Holy One of Israel in the midst of you* (12:4-6).

Isaiah the prophet also looked beyond the defeat of the northern kingdom by Assyria to the future when Babylon would carry the people of Judah into captivity. Surprisingly, about 180 years before it took place, he also foretold Babylon's defeat and destruction saying: *Babylon, the glory of kingdoms, the beauty of the Chaldees' excellency, shall be as when God overthrew Sodom and Gomorrah* (13:19-20). In striking contrast, Isaiah prophesied Israel's future restoration: *The LORD will have mercy on Jacob, and will yet choose Israel, and set them in their own land: and the strangers shall be joined with them, and they shall cling to the house of Jacob. And the people shall take them, and bring them to their place . . . and they shall rule over their oppressors* (14:1-2).

Until that day, let us proclaim to the world with Isaiah: *Behold, God is my salvation. . . . the LORD JEHOVAH (YAHWEH) is my strength and my song; He also is become my salvation. Therefore with joy shall you draw water out of the wells of salvation* (Isaiah 12:2-3).

Thought for Today: Our Lord's love is inexhaustible.

Christ Revealed: As the Descendant of Jesse, King David's father (Isaiah 11:1; compare Luke 3:31-32). Isaiah 11 reveals Christ's coming earthly rule of righteousness. One day soon Jesus will return to earth in all the fullness of His glory and accompanied by His angels. Then He will set up the millennial kingdom of His creation; this will be the beginning of His eternal rule (Matthew 25:31-46; also Revelation 20-22).

For definitions of unfamiliar words in today's Bible reading, see pages 468-480.

In Today's Reading

Moab's ruin foretold; Syria (Aram) and Israel threatened;
God's judgments; Egypt to worship the Lord;
captivity of Egypt foretold

The prophet Isaiah was led to turn his thoughts from the glorious future reign of the King of Peace to proclaim the judgment of God upon the unbelieving. First it was pronounced upon the idolatrous northern kingdom, saying: *The fortress also shall cease from Ephraim* (Isaiah 17:3). He then included Judah, saying: *In that day it shall come to pass, that the glory of Jacob shall be made thin. . . . there shall be desolation. Because you have forgotten the God of your salvation* (17:4,9-10).

The fortress of Ephraim refers to the ten-tribe northern kingdom, a symbol of wealth, power, and self-glory, which would be ruthlessly destroyed by Assyria. Surprisingly, he also prophesied that Judah, the *glory of Jacob*, would fade, a reminder that the kingdom of Judah and the holy city of God would eventually be destroyed because they too had become involved in worldly pursuits, numerous sins, and idolatry.

Nothing hides the will of God from view as deceptively as success and pride, both of which foster self-sufficiency. Perhaps this is why our Savior cautioned: *Lay not up for yourselves treasures upon earth, where moth and rust does corrupt* (destroy), *and where thieves break through and steal* (Matthew 6:19). Wealth accumulated for self-interest may lead to greed and can weaken faith, as James pointed out, saying: *My beloved brethren, Has not God chosen the poor of this world rich in faith, and heirs of the kingdom which He has promised to them that love Him?* (James 2:5). Covetousness leads to an endless pursuit of earthly possessions.

Our Lord Jesus warns: *Beware of covetousness: for a man's life consists not in the abundance of the things which he possesses* (Luke 12:15).

The Lord is able to speak to each of us personally as to how He would have us invest in transforming lives and fulfilling His Great Commission. Paul wrote to Timothy: *Charge* (Instruct, Command) *them that are rich in this world, that they be not high-minded* (conceited), *nor trust in uncertain riches, but in the living God, Who gives us richly all things to enjoy* (I Timothy 6:17; also Deuteronomy 8:18).

Thought for Today: Be vigilant and prepared for Jesus' return.

Christ Revealed: As the One Who will sit on the throne of David (Isaiah 16:5). Gabriel told the Virgin Mary that the *Lord God shall give to Him the throne of His father David* (Luke 1:32-33). Christ also was revealed as the Savior (Isaiah 19:20; compare Matthew 1:21; Luke 2:11).

For definitions of unfamiliar words in today's Bible reading, see pages 468-480.

In Today's Reading
Prophecy about Jerusalem; Babylon and Tyre to be destroyed;
Isaiah glorifies God; God's dominion over Judah

*I*saiah's prophecy was first directed to Judah, then to Israel, then to the surrounding Gentile nations, and finally to all the world: *He will swallow up death in victory; and the Lord GOD will wipe away tears from off all faces. . . . And it shall be said in that day, Lo, this is our God; we have waited for Him, and He will save us . . . we will be glad and rejoice in His salvation. . . . You will keep Him in perfect peace, whose mind is stayed on You* (Isaiah 25:8-9; 26:3).

Just as surely as many of the prophecies were fulfilled in ancient history, we can also expect that the Messiah Jesus will return as Christ the King. *As the Mighty God* (Jesus Christ), *The Everlasting Father, The Prince of Peace* (9:6), He will give eternal life to both Jews and Gentiles who have received Him as Lord of their lives.

Jesus has imparted His indwelling Holy Spirit into every believer and assured us: *You are of God, little children, and have overcome them* (spirits of Antichrist): *because greater is He that is in you, than he* (Satan) *that is in the world* (I John 4:4). We need not live in slavery to Satan and our fleshly passions; we can *be strong in the Lord, and in the power of His might. Put on the whole armor of God, that you may be able to stand against the wiles* (schemes, trickery) *of the devil* (Ephesians 6:10-11).

We are slaves to what we allow to control us, including our thoughts and conduct. In the beginning, all are slaves to sin because we descended from Adam (Romans 5:12). However, our Creator, through Christ, has given us freewill to choose. Once we choose to obey Him, we no longer remain slaves to sin. God's Word provides a simple revealing test: *Know you not, that to whom you yield yourselves servants to obey, his servants you are to whom you obey; whether of sin to death, or of obedience to righteousness? But God be thanked, that you were the servants of sin, but you have obeyed from the heart. . . . Being then made free from sin, you became the servants of righteousness* (Romans 6:16-18).

Thought for Today: Suffering, hardships, and handicaps have helped many come to know God's will for their lives.

Christ Portrayed: By Eliakim, master of Hezekiah's household (Isaiah 22:20-22); what was said of him is true of Christ Who is also Master over the household of faith. *Christ . . . a Son over His own house; Whose house are we* (Hebrews 3:6; Galatians 6:10).

For definitions of unfamiliar words in today's Bible reading, see pages 468-480.

In Today's Reading
Judgment of Ephraim; Jerusalem warned;
Israel rebuked for its alliance with Egypt; future destiny assured

The magnificent northern kingdom of Israel was enjoying great prosperity when the Lord led Isaiah to prophesy its coming captivity by Assyria. He proclaimed: *Woe to the crown of pride, to the drunkards of Ephraim, whose glorious beauty is a fading flower. . . . The crown of pride, the drunkards of Ephraim, shall be trodden under feet* (Isaiah 28:1-3,).

The people of Samaria, the capital of the large and powerful northern kingdom, were enjoying the luxury of both summer and winter homes, ivory palaces, and a wealth of gardens. They were content in their affluence and unwilling to hear the Lord's prophet. With a heavy heart, Isaiah warned them that all would soon be destroyed because they had rejected the Word of God and turned to idols.

Samaria's *beauty* was likened to *a fading flower* that would soon disappear. The prophet foretold a horrible future: *Ephraim, shall be trodden under feet* – and, without God, the nation would be helpless to withstand the fierce Assyrian army. Like most worldly-minded people today, they did not believe judgment would or could happen to them.

Isaiah also warned Judah that, since they had refused to live in obedience to the Covenant of God, they had made a covenant with death and would be destroyed by the Assyrians. They would pay the same price for their sins as the northern kingdom.

Times and circumstances change; but one fact remains the same – all who have not received Christ as their Savior have made an eternal *covenant with death* [i.e. eternal separation from God] (28:15,18), whether knowingly or unknowingly. For all who have not heard the Gospel and don't possess a Bible, it is our responsibility to let them know.

We can praise the Lord that while there is life, there is still hope. *The Lord is not slack* (slow) *concerning His promise, as some men count slackness* (slowness); *but is long-suffering to us-ward, not willing that any should perish, but that all should come to repentance* (II Peter 3:9). *Let every one that names the Name of Christ depart from iniquity* (unrighteousness, sin) (II Timothy 2:19).

Thought for Today: If it seems there is no hope, we are relying on human resources instead of the promises of God's strength.

Christ Revealed: As the *precious* (Chief) *Corner Stone, a sure foundation* (Isaiah 28:16; Ephesians 2:20-21; Matthew 21:42; Acts 4:10-12; Romans 9:33; I Peter 2:6-8).

For definitions of unfamiliar words in today's Bible reading, see pages 468-480.

In Today's Reading

Righteous King foretold; judgment upon nations pronounced;
Jerusalem threatened; Hezekiah's prayer;
destruction of the Assyrians

In the fourteenth year of King Hezekiah . . . Sennacherib king of Assyria came up against all the defensed cities of Judah, and took them (Isaiah 36:1). Even the walled cities were no match for the might of Sennacherib's army. In one military campaign he quickly defeated 46 of the towns and villages of the small southern kingdom. He carried away into captivity about 200,000 of its inhabitants, but he was not able to conquer Jerusalem. At that time, all of western Asia was under Assyria's control, including the once powerful Babylonia, Media, Armenia, Syria, Phoenicia, Philistia, Edom, and most of the promised land.

Eventually, the king of Assyria demanded unconditional surrender. Feeling secure in the might of his army, Sennacherib sent word to the people of Jerusalem: *Let not Hezekiah deceive you: for he shall not be able to deliver you. Neither let Hezekiah make you trust in the LORD, saying, The LORD will surely deliver us* (36:14-16).

Upon hearing this demand, King Hezekiah immediately did what we all should do when we receive bad news. *Hezekiah went up to the House of the LORD. . . . And Hezekiah prayed . . . O LORD of hosts, God of Israel . . . You are the God, even You alone, of all the kingdoms of the earth. . . . hear all the words of Sennacherib, which* (he) *has sent to reproach the living God. . . . save us . . . that all the kingdoms of the earth may know that You are the LORD, even You only* (37:14-17,20).

Isaiah sent a word to Hezekiah, saying: *Thus says the LORD God of Israel, Whereas* (Because) *you have prayed to Me against Sennacherib king of Assyria. . . . I will defend this city to save it for My own sake, and for My servant David's sake* (37:21,35). That night *the Angel of the LORD went forth, and smote . . . the Assyrians* (37:36), destroying 185,000 soldiers.

It is important that, like Hezekiah, we pray and trust the Lord for all of our needs. It is foolish to think we can *stand against the wiles* (schemes, trickery) *of the devil* in our own might (Ephesians 6:11). God is waiting for us to place our trust in Him. The Lord is still urging us: *Call to Me, and I will answer you, and show you great and mighty* (unsearchable) *things, which you know not* (Jeremiah 33:3; also Ephesians 3:20).

Thought for Today: You can depend on God's promises; they cannot fail.

Christ Revealed: As the One, Who in judgment, wields *the sword of the LORD* (Isaiah 34:6). *Out of His mouth goes a sharp sword, that with it He should smite the nations* (Revelation 19:15).

For definitions of unfamiliar words in today's Bible reading, see pages 468-480.

> ## $\mathscr{I}$N $\mathscr{T}$ODAY'S $\mathscr{R}$EADING
> Hezekiah's life lengthened; Babylonian captivity foretold;
> comfort for God's people; song of praise to the Lord

$\mathscr{A}$bout 13 years had passed since Isaiah brought Hezekiah, king of Judah, the exciting news that the southern kingdom would be miraculously saved from the "invincible" armies of the Assyrian Empire.

But this time Isaiah said to Hezekiah, who was gravely ill: *Thus says the LORD, Set your house in order: for you shall die, and not live* (Isaiah 38:1; II Kings 20:1; II Chronicles 32:24-26).

Hezekiah knew of the precedent of Moses praying for the people when God's anger would have destroyed them, but God had relented in response to Moses' intercession (Exodus 32:7-14). With intense weeping, *Hezekiah turned his face toward the wall, and prayed to the LORD, And said, Remember now, O LORD, I beseech* (beg) *You, how I have walked before You in truth and with a perfect* (sincere) *heart, and have done that which is good in Your sight. And Hezekiah wept sore* (bitterly) (Isaiah 38:2-3; compare 38:17). He reminded the Lord how he had served Him faithfully and had not departed from the Lord's Commandments. He had sincerely lived to please the Lord. Isaiah again heard the voice of God say: *Go, and say to Hezekiah, Thus says the LORD . . . I have heard your prayer, I have seen your tears: behold, I will add to your days 15 years* (38:5). Surely the additional years were not only due to Hezekiah's tears and prayer but to his faithfulness during the previous 40 years of his life.

We should never hesitate to pray, regardless of how hopeless our circumstances may appear. However, this does not mean that God always answers every prayer in the way we want or according to our timing.

Since we often fall short in our desire to be like Jesus, many people find it easy to accept the condemnation of Satan that we are too unworthy for God to answer our prayers. Although it is right to assess our faults and confess our sins, it also magnifies the grace of God to recognize the good in our lives just as Hezekiah did. We can also remind the Lord of our sincere endeavors to live God-honoring lives, which are only produced as we surrender to the inner working of the Holy Spirit.

Not by works of righteousness which we have done, but according to His mercy He saved us, by the washing of regeneration, and renewing of the Holy Ghost (Spirit) (Titus 3:5; also James 5:16).

Thought for Today: Trusting in anything or anyone but the Lord for your eternal salvation is deception and will result in eternal death.

Christ Revealed: As the *Creator* (Isaiah 40:28; compare John 1:1-3); as the *Shepherd* (Isaiah 40:11; compare John 10:11); as the *Redeemer* (Isaiah 41:14; compare Galatians 3:13; I Peter 1:18-19; Revelation 5:9).

For definitions of unfamiliar words in today's Bible reading, see pages 468-480.

ℐN 𝒯ODAY'S ℛEADING
God's care for Israel; folly of idolatry;
Jerusalem and the Temple to be rebuilt; God's purpose for Cyrus;
power of the Lord and weakness of idols

---

*W*hen Isaiah was a prophet, the people felt very secure. Jerusalem was the City of God and the sacred Temple stood there. Therefore, Isaiah's prophecy concerning the "ruins" of Jerusalem was rejected by the people. Through Isaiah, God foretold both the destruction and the rebuilding of the Temple while the nation was still enjoying freedom and prosperity. He also foretold: *The cities of Judah . . . shall be built, and I will raise up the decayed places* (ruins) (Isaiah 44:26).

At that time, Babylon, the capital city of the Chaldean dynasty, was surrounded by massive walls about 300 feet high. The Babylonians were certain that no one could invade their great city. However, Isaiah foretold that a man named Cyrus would conquer Babylon 150 years before it took place. *Thus says the LORD . . . of Cyrus, he . . . shall perform all My pleasure: even saying to Jerusalem, You shall be built; and to the Temple, Your foundation shall be laid* (44:24,28).

Babylon thought itself invincible because of its walls, as well as the great brass gates spanning the Euphrates which ran through its center. However, God declared exactly how the city would be taken by the armies of Cyrus. The river would dry up and the Lord would see that the gates across it would be left unlocked. And that is exactly what happened when Darius, the Mede, under the rule of Cyrus entered the city the same fateful night that King Belshazzar of Babylon saw the handwriting of God on the wall (Daniel 5:1-31). Only God could have given Isaiah such remarkable details concerning the defeat of Babylon by saying that *Babylon . . . shall be as . . . Sodom* (Isaiah 13:19). At the end of the kingdom of Judah's 70 years of captivity, this was fulfilled exactly as foretold by the prophet. This fact should dispel all doubt regarding the Lord's loving concern and care for His followers. It is a fact that even the *king's heart is in the hand of the LORD, as the rivers of water: He turns it wherever He will* (Proverbs 21:1).

Thought for Today: God is not limited; He will keep His Word.

Christ Revealed: As the Redeemer (Isaiah 43:1; 44:22-24). Through His death on the cross, Christ has redeemed (bought back) all who trust Him as their Savior (I Corinthians 6:20; Galatians 4:4-5; Titus 2:13-14; I Peter 1:18-19).

For definitions of unfamiliar words in today's Bible reading, see pages 468-480.

In Today's Reading

Judgment on Babylon; Israel rebuked; Christ, a Light to the
Gentiles; restoration of Israel; suffering of the Lord's servant

*W*e expect judgment upon the ungodly, or upon the backslider, but
many Christians do not understand why sincere believers experience so
many critical situations. The prophet Isaiah encourages us to remain
faithful, regardless of the circumstances, even though we cannot see
why we face so many difficulties. *Who is among you that fears* (reveres)
*the LORD . . . that walks in darkness, and has no light? let him trust in the
Name of the LORD, and stay* (rely) *upon his God* (Isaiah 50:10). God will
bring blessings out of suffering and triumph out of tragedy for every
child of God, just as He did for Job. Heartbreaking experiences are a test
of our faith, as well as a means of our developing greater faith. God twice
said Job was the most perfect man on earth, yet he suffered more than
anyone in biblical history except Jesus, Who bore the sins of the world
on the cross. Job's faith remained strong because he knew that God was
in control of his life. He testified confidently, even while suffering
intensely, saying: *He knows the way that I take: when He has tried me, I
shall come forth as gold* (Job 23:10).

Each of us can expect testing from the Lord, as well as temptation
from the forces of evil; so do not be dismayed if one day your whole
world crumbles and it seems that the Lord has abandoned you.

The Apostle James, who later suffered martyrdom for his faith in
Jesus as the Christ, encouraged believers to *take . . . the prophets, who have
spoken in the Name of the Lord, for an example of suffering affliction, and
of patience* (James 5:10). Jesus explained to His disciples that, because the
world hated Him, it would also hate them. Another time, He promised
a hundredfold return to those who forsook home and family for Him,
but He cautioned that they too would suffer persecution (John 15:18,20-
21; Mark 10:29-30).

Rejoice, inasmuch as you are partakers (sharers) *of Christ's sufferings;
that, when His glory shall be revealed, you may be glad . . . with exceeding
joy* (I Peter 4:13). But Paul warned: *If we deny Him, He will also deny us*
(II Timothy 2:12). Let us express gratitude to *the God of all grace Who has
called us to His eternal glory by Christ Jesus, after that you have suffered
a while, make you perfect, stablish* (stabilize), *strengthen, settle you* (I
Peter 5:10).

Thought for Today: Regardless of circumstances, God is in control.

**Christ Revealed: As the *Light* to the nations (Gentiles) (Isaiah 49:6). Jesus said: *I am
the Light of the world* (John 8:12,9:5; Luke 2:32; Acts 13:47).**

For definitions of unfamiliar words in today's Bible reading, see pages 468-480.

IN TODAY'S READING

Christ to bear our grief, suffering, and sin; the Lord's everlasting
love for Israel; everyone a sinner; a call to faith and repentance

God revealed to Isaiah that the Messiah, the King of kings, would
first be *My Servant . . .* (then) *He shall be exalted* (Isaiah 52:13). Jesus first
came as the *Servant* (of God), as the Suffering Savior; but He will soon
return highly *exalted* as the King of kings.

The Jews of the first century were looking for a warrior-king, like
David, to deliver them from the oppression of Rome. However, Isaiah
had foretold of the Messiah: *He shall grow up before Him* (the Lord) *as a
tender plant, and as a root out of a dry ground: He has no form nor
comeliness; and when we shall see Him, there is no beauty that we should
desire Him* (53:2). During the time of Jesus the religious leaders' only
concern was for a Messiah who would overthrow the Roman government. But their greater need was to be in subjection to the Word of God
and this they refused to do.

Dry ground illustrates the spiritual condition of the religious world
without Jesus. He alone provides eternal life for all who confess their
guilt, repent of their sins, and seek to obey His Word. That's why it's
important to read all of it. Even though we fall short of what God desires
us to be, Jesus continues to make intercession for us with the Father.

Surely He has borne our griefs, and carried our sorrows (53:4). This
means He has met our emotional and spiritual, as well as physical,
needs of every kind. Although Isaiah was prophesying about the future,
he wrote as if it was already an established fact – the Messiah *was
wounded for our transgressions, He was bruised for our iniquities: the
chastisement of our peace was upon Him; and with His stripes* (whip-
lashes) *we are healed* (made whole) (53:5). Jesus' death on the cross
provided the means to end the enmity between sinful man and the
Righteous Holy Creator God. This means that all repentant believers,
Jew and Gentile alike, receive eternal life and become acceptable to Him
through the death of the sinless Son of God when they pray to God to
receive Jesus as their Savior and Lord. All other gods are false and
cannot save anyone. *There is none other name under heaven given
among men, whereby we must be saved* (Acts 4:12).

Thought for Today: Praise God today for His amazing grace.

Christ Revealed: As the One Who was rejected by His own people (Isaiah 53:3;
compare Luke 23:18; John 1:11); remained silent when He was falsely accused (Isaiah
53:7; Mark 15:3-5); was buried with the rich (Isaiah 53:9; Matthew 27:57-60); and was
crucified with sinners (Isaiah 53:12; Mark 15:27-28).

For definitions of unfamiliar words in today's Bible reading, see pages 468-480.

In Today's Reading

True fasting; sin, confession, and redemption; future glory of
Jerusalem; the day of vengeance; God's loving-kindness to Israel

*D*uring Isaiah's time, the Israelite leaders complained to God: *Why
have we fasted . . . and You see not? why have we afflicted our soul, and You
take no knowledge?* (Isaiah 58:3). They accused Him of not paying attention to what they were doing and they felt they had wasted their
time. The Lord answered: *In the day of your fast you find pleasure*
(continue to seek selfish interests), *and exact* (exploit) *all your labors*
(laborers). . . . *you fast for* (continue your) *strife and debate, and to smite
with the fist of wickedness* (occupied with personal conflicts) (58:3-4).

Even more serious was their hypocrisy. The Lord said: *Is it such a
fast that I have chosen? . . . is it to bow down his head as a bulrush, and to
spread sackcloth and ashes under him* (to impress others with pretended
humility)? (58:5; also Luke 18:10-14). Through Isaiah, God reminded the
Israelites that acceptable fasting was not to impress the world of how
religious they were, but it was to seek the will of God through intercession. The Lord said the fast He would accept would be preceded by acts
of kindness such as: *To loose the bands* (bonds) *of wickedness . . . undo the
heavy burdens . . . to let the oppressed go free? . . . to deal* (divide) *your bread
to the hungry, and that you bring the poor that are cast out* (wandering) *to
your house? . . . when you see the naked, that you cover him; and that you
hide not yourself from your own flesh* (never neglect your responsibility
to your own family) (Isaiah 58:6-7).

If what we do for someone (or for the Lord) is meant to impose (or
implies) expecting special favors in return, prayers and fasting will be
futile. Our prayers are effective only when our attitude and our relationship with others expresses the mercy and love of God unconditionally.

Often, being a Christian is thought of as the sum total of things we
don't do. But a Christian is first and foremost both who we are and what
we do. *Let your light so shine before men, that they may see your good
works, and glorify your Father Who is in heaven* (Matthew 5:16).

Thought for Today: Graciously submit to God's arrangements in your life, and under
no circumstances grieve the Holy Spirit.

Christ Revealed: As the One anointed *to preach Good Tidings* (Isaiah 61:1). Jesus
preached this passage to the rulers of the synagogue (Luke 4:16-22) but stopped before
the completion of the second verse, thus showing that He fulfilled the first part but,
the second part, the day of judgment, was yet to be fulfilled.

For definitions of unfamiliar words in today's Bible reading, see pages 468-480.

Most of the northern kingdom of Israel was carried away captive by the Assyrians during the reign of wicked King Pekah (Isaiah 7:1; II Kings 15:27-29). Having witnessed the destruction of the northern kingdom before he came to the throne, undoubtedly godly King Hezekiah of the southern kingdom was greatly encouraged by the prophet Isaiah. Sadly, after Hezekiah's death, his son Manasseh became one of the most wicked kings in Judah's history.

During this time, the Word of God, as proclaimed by Isaiah, had been ignored and now God spoke through him these pitiful words: *I have spread out My hands all the day to a rebellious people, which walks in a way that was not good, after their own thoughts* (Isaiah 65:2). Although God had reached out to them, they had not responded to Him. They had gone their own ways. The Lord continued: *I also will choose their delusions, and will bring their fears* (dread, terrors) *upon them; because when I called, none did answer; when I spoke, they did not hear: but they did evil before My eyes, and chose that in which I delighted not* (66:4).

The Apostle Paul quoted from Isaiah 64:4 to encourage the Corinthian church, and wrote: *But as it is written, Eye has not seen, nor ear heard, neither have entered into the heart of man, the things which God has prepared for them that love Him* (I Corinthians 2:9). The magnificence of His wisdom and glory are now revealed to us as we read His Word. Paul goes on to state that believers in Jesus also receive the very thoughts of Christ through the written Word of God. Through Isaiah, God declared things which were beyond the comprehension of His creation, but these very things were later bestowed through the Messiah upon those *that love Him.* At any time, in any place, we may pray to our loving God. While we have an opportunity to serve Him, we should determine to make His will the priority in our lives.

To the small minority who remained faithful then, as well as to the faithful today, Isaiah is saying: *Hear the Word of the LORD, you that tremble at His Word; Your brethren that hated* (despised) *you, that cast you out for My Name's sake . . . shall be ashamed. . . . For thus says the LORD, Behold, I will extend peace to her like a river* (Isaiah 66:5,12).

Thought for Today: Sin breaks our fellowship with the Lord and keeps us from receiving His true peace and wisdom.

Christ Revealed: As the Creator of *new heavens and a new earth* (Isaiah 65:17; 66:22; compare John 1:1-3; II Peter 3:13). As the One Whose glory will be declared among the nations (Isaiah 66:18-19; Revelation 5:12-13).

For definitions of unfamiliar words in today's Bible reading, see pages 468-480.

Introduction To The Book Of
*J*EREMIAH

Jeremiah prophesied during the last 40 years of the small southern kingdom of Judah. This was more than 100 years after the Assyrians destroyed the northern kingdom of Israel. As the years passed, the Assyrian empire weakened and was overthrown by the Babylonians.

Jeremiah's public ministry began in the 13th year of the reign of godly King Josiah (Jeremiah 1:2), who ruled for 31 years (II Chronicles 34:1). He continued his ministry through the reigns of the last four kings of Judah, all of whom were wicked: Jehoahaz (Shallum); followed by his brother Jehoiakim (Eliakim), *in his days Nebuchadnezzar* (was) *king of Babylon* (II Kings 24:1); Jehoiachin (Coniah, Jeconiah); and Mattaniah (Zedekiah).

After Nebuchadnezzar defeated Egypt in the battle at Carchemish, the key city of northern Syria, the kingdom of Judah was then brought under his control. Seven years later, in the eleventh year of Zedekiah's reign, Jerusalem and the Temple were destroyed by Nebuchadnezzar and his Babylonian armies who then controlled all of the area now known as the Middle East (25:2-21).

It was at a time in Judah's history that Jeremiah exposed their hypocrisy and declared: *From the least of them even to the greatest of them every one is given to covetousness; and from prophet even to priest every one deals falsely* (Jeremiah 6:13). *The prophets prophesy falsely, and the priests bear rule by their means; and My people love to have it so* (5:31).

After most of the people were carried off into captivity by Nebuchadnezzar, the remaining people fled to Egypt and forced Jeremiah to accompany them. He faithfully continued to declare God's Word to the unrepentant, defiant people (II Kings 24:20 – 25:21; Jeremiah 39:1-10).

Although the kingdom of Judah was defeated and Jerusalem and the Temple were destroyed, the people as a nation were not finished. God had made a Covenant with Abraham, Isaac, and Jacob, and then with David, of a glorious future for His people. The God of mercy had also promised, through Jeremiah: *Again I will build you, and you shall be built. . . . this shall be the Covenant that I will make with the house of Israel; After those days, says the LORD, I will put My Law in their inward parts, and write it in their hearts; and will be their God, and they shall be My people* (31:4,33; also Romans 11:25-27).

The events in this book are not arranged in chronological order, but by similar subjects to let us see more clearly the tragic results of sin.

ℐN 𝒯ODAY'S ℛEADING

Jeremiah's call; his message to sinful Judah;
its apostasy results in idolatry; Judah entreated to repent

𝒢od revealed to Jeremiah that He has a plan and purpose for each
of us **even before our birth**: *The Word of the* LORD *came to me, saying,
Before I formed you in the belly I knew you . . . I sanctified* (set apart for
God) *you, and I ordained you a prophet to the nations* (Jeremiah 1:4-5).

Through Jeremiah's revelation concerning the origin of human life,
it is revealed that our birth is not our real beginning, nor will our death
be our end. Since God is the Giver of life, let us recognize the sanctity
of all human life. Just think! **God knew you and had a plan for your
life even before the day you were born.**

The Holy Spirit led King David to write: *I will praise You; for I am
fearfully and wonderfully made: marvellous are Your works; and that my
soul knows right well. My substance was not hidden from You, when I was
made in secret, and curiously wrought in the lowest parts of the earth*
(Psalm 139:14-15). Both mother and father have the biblical responsibility to recognize that every unborn child, from the moment of conception, belongs to its Creator God. Both parents are responsible as
faithful stewards of God to teach their children to know, love, and be
obedient to God.

God revealed that *He* (God) *has chosen us in Him* (Christ) *before the
foundation* (beginning) *of the world, that we should be holy and without
blame before Him in love. . . . In Whom* (Christ) *also we have obtained an
inheritance. . . . That . . . the Father of glory, may give to you . . . The eyes
of your understanding* (mind) *being enlightened; that you may know what
is the hope of His calling, and what the riches of the glory of His inheritance in the saints* (Ephesians 1:4-5,11,17-18).

We are special! Even before God laid the foundation of the world,
He chose us to be His children through Jesus Christ, and it is because
of Christ that we have received this inheritance from God.

God has chosen each of us for His sacred purpose. However, He
has also given us the **freedom to choose** whom we will serve. Jesus
stated an often overlooked fact when He said that *no man can serve two
masters: for either he will hate the one, and love the other; or else he will
hold to the one, and despise the other* (Matthew 6:24).

Thought for Today: Without reading the Word of God we have no way of knowing the
truth of God and the standards He has set for His creation.

Christ Revealed: As the *Fountain of Living Waters* (Jeremiah 2:13). *Jesus stood and
cried, saying, If any man thirst, let him come to Me, and drink* (John 7:37; also 4:1-26).

For definitions of unfamiliar words in today's Bible reading, see pages 468-480.

IN TODAY'S READING
God's call to Israel; Jeremiah's lamentations for Judah; spiritual and civil corruption; destruction of Judah

The prophet Jeremiah began his public ministry during the reign of King Josiah of Judah (Jeremiah 1:2). He exposed the worldly, compromising lifestyle of the Israelites when he called them a *foolish people, and without understanding; which have eyes, and see not; which have ears, and hear not. . . . this people has . . . a rebellious heart. . . . your sins have withheld good things from you* (5:21,23,25). The reason for their lack of understanding was clear – they were rebellious against God in their hearts. Jeremiah lamented: *The Word of the LORD is to them a reproach; they have no delight in it. . . . every one is given to covetousness; and from the prophet even to the priest every one deals falsely* (6:10-13;). Josiah's grandfather Manasseh and his father Amon were wicked kings who had led the people to forsake God and had encouraged worship of false gods.

However, young Josiah *did what was right in the sight of the LORD, and walked in all the way of David his father* (ancestor), *and turned not aside to the right hand or to the left* (II Kings 22:2). No doubt, Jeremiah was a great encouragement and influence on Josiah. After *he had purged the land*, Josiah began repairing the Temple and restoring worship of the One True God (II Chronicles 34:8-33). He then initiated a Passover feast unequaled in Israel's history *from the days of the judges . . .* (and) *in all the days of the kings* (II Kings 23:22).

Following Josiah's death (23:30-32), his son, Jehoahaz reverted to the evil ways of his grandfather Manasseh and great-grandfather Amon. With deep concern, we see a parallel between the false gods and immorality of Judah that led to its fall and in the growth of false religions, moral decline, and sexual deviation in America today.

A true Christian desires to worship only the Lord and especially enjoys doing so with other believers where there is reading, studying, and obeying the Word of God. The Apostle Paul was lead by the Holy Spirit to warn us: *The time will come when they will not endure sound doctrine; but after their own lusts . . . they shall turn away their ears from the truth, and shall be turned to fables* (II Timothy 4:3-5).

Thought for Today: The more we read the Bible, the more the Lord's ways become our ways, and His thoughts our thoughts, and His actions our actions.

Christ Portrayed: By Jeremiah, whom God commissioned to reveal His truth (Jeremiah 4:2). Jesus shall one day judge all mankind. *In the day when God shall judge the secrets of men by Jesus Christ. . . . Every man's work shall be made manifest* (known): *for the day shall declare it, because it shall be revealed by fire; and the fire shall try* (test) *every man's work of what sort it is* (Romans 2:16; I Corinthians 3:13).

For definitions of unfamiliar words in today's Bible reading, see pages 468-480.

ℐN 𝒯ODAY'S ℛEADING

Plea for repentance; punishment for Judah's rebellion;
mourning over the people's sins; idols will perish

*A*ll adult men who were physically able were required by the Law to attend three major feasts annually in Jerusalem. These occasions were to be joyful celebrations of praise to God for His provision and protection. But, on this occasion Jeremiah did not give the crowd a warm welcome; instead, he pronounced a harsh condemnation: *Hear the Word of the LORD, all you of Judah, that enter in at these gates to worship the LORD. . . . Will you steal, murder, and commit adultery, and swear falsely . . . and walk after other gods whom you know not; And come and stand before Me in this house, which is called by My Name, and say, We are delivered to do all these abominations?* (Jeremiah 7:2,9-10).

The people considered Jeremiah's preaching far too narrow-minded, so they would not tolerate this prophet of God. They had declared: *We are wise, and the Law of the LORD is with us* (8:8). The physical presence of the Scriptures and the Temple gave them a false sense of security. The prophet warned them: (You) *have rejected the Word of the LORD. . . . every one from the least even to the greatest is given to covetousness, from the prophet even to the priest every one deals falsely* (8:9-11). They were confident that God would never allow them to be destroyed since they were His chosen people. But the Lord's Covenants do not give His people license to sin or to ignore His Word.

Then, as now, people foolishly assume that each person should have the freedom to worship whomever, or whatever, he chooses according to his own conscience. But Jesus declared: *I am the Way, the Truth, and the Life: no man comes to the Father, but by Me* (John 14:6). Some today call themselves Christians, but they harbor secret sins and have unsubmitted hearts. Jesus asks those who say they are Christians while still living sinful lives: *Why call you Me, Lord, Lord, and do not the things which I say?* (Luke 6:46). He reminds us: *If you continue in My Word, then you are My disciples indeed; And you shall know the Truth, and the Truth shall make you free. . . . Whosoever commits sin is the servant of sin* (John 8:31-32,34). He also declared: *Not every one that says to Me, Lord, Lord, shall enter into the Kingdom of Heaven; but he that does the will of My Father Who is in heaven* (Matthew 7:21).

Thought for Today: The best of religious accomplishments are never a substitute for godly living.

Christ Revealed: As the One Who demanded a cleansed Temple (Jeremiah 7:1-11). Jesus said: *My House shall be called of all nations the house of prayer* (Mark 11:17).

For definitions of unfamiliar words in today's Bible reading, see pages 468-480.

ℐN ᴛODAY'S ℛEADING

Jeremiah's proclamation of God's Covenant; plot against Jeremiah;
Jeremiah's complaint; ruined girdle (belt); filled bottles; famine

All Israelites were called to be holy and to serve the Lord, as He said
to Moses: *I am the LORD your God: you shall therefore sanctify* (set apart
to serve the Lord) *yourselves, and you shall be holy* (Leviticus 11:44). And,
in return, God promised to provide all their needs. Instead, the majority
of the people had forsaken the Lord to worship idols. To illustrate their
failure, the Lord directed Jeremiah to *get a linen girdle* (sash-like belt)
and put it upon your loins, and put it not in water (to wash it) (Jeremiah
13:1). Hebrew men wore tunics – long, loose, gown-like garments. To
hold the tunic close to the body while working, they wore a sash-like belt
around the waist called a "girdle." The girdle represented the close
relationship of the Israelites to Jehovah (Yahweh).

Jeremiah reports that, eventually, *the Word of the LORD came to me
the second time, saying, Take the girdle . . . and . . . go to Euphrates, and hide
it there in a hole of the rock. So I went, and hid it by Euphrates, as the LORD
commanded me. And it came to pass after many days, that the LORD said
to me, Arise, go to Euphrates, and take the girdle from there, which I
commanded you to hide there. Then I went to Euphrates, and dug, and took
the girdle from the place where I had hidden it: and, behold, the girdle was
marred* (rotted, ruined), *it was profitable for nothing* (13:3-7). The girdle
represented the spiritual condition of the Israelites. Then Jeremiah
spoke: *Thus says the LORD. . . . This evil people . . . refuse to hear My words
. . . and walk after other gods, to serve them, and to worship them, shall even
be as this girdle, which is good for nothing* (13:9-10).

Like the Israelites, some today are intent on satisfying self-interests
with their talents, time, and tithes, and reject their opportunities to use
them in serving the Lord. Unfortunately, many will **discover too late
that they have forfeited their God-given opportunities**.

Lest there be any fornicator, or profane (godless) *person, as Esau, who
for one morsel of meat* (food) *sold his birthright. . . . See that you refuse not
Him that speaks. For if they escaped not who refused Him that spoke on
earth, much more shall not we escape, if we turn away from Him that speaks
from heaven* (Hebrews 12:15-17,25).

Thought for Today: Wholeheartedly living for the Lord provides the assurance that *all
things work together for good* **(Romans 8:28).**

Christ Revealed: As *the Hope of Israel, the Savior* **(Jeremiah 14:8). Christ is the only**
Hope **of all mankind.** *Looking for that blessed Hope, and the glorious appearing of the
great God and our Savior Jesus Christ* **(Titus 2:13).**

For definitions of unfamiliar words in today's Bible reading, see pages 468-480.

$\mathcal{I}$N $\mathcal{T}$ODAY'S $\mathcal{R}$EADING

Jeremiah's prayer; signs of Judah's captivity; Sabbath regulations;
lesson from the potter; God's absolute power over the nations

---

$\mathcal{T}$he LORD said, Verily (truly) . . . I will cause the enemy to entreat (treat) you well in the time of evil and in the time of affliction (Jeremiah 15:11). But, when the Israelites rejected God and His Word as their way of life, they forfeited the privilege of His protection and suffered tragic spiritual and physical loss.

To understand the Israelites' problems and their final outcome, Jeremiah was sent to the potter's house to see a live illustration of what God was about to do. God said to Jeremiah: Arise, and go down to the potter's house, and there I will cause you to hear My words. Then I went down to the potter's house, and, behold, he wrought (was making) a work on the wheels. And the vessel that he made of clay was marred (ruined) in the hand of the potter: so he made it again another vessel, as seemed good to the potter to make it (18:2-4). Then the Lord said: O house of Israel. . . . as the clay is in the potter's hand, so are you in My hand. . . . If it do evil in My sight, that it obey not My voice, then I will repent of the good, wherewith I said I would benefit them (18:6,10).

When the vessel (God's chosen people) was marred in the hand of the potter, it was the hardness within the clay itself and not the failure of the potter that made the vessel worthless. Israel had rejected the will of God and was marred (hardened) by its sin. Consequently, the vessel, Israel, was broken and taken into captivity by Babylon, a nation used as the instrument of God. After 70 years of captivity (25:11), God made the clay into another vessel which was the small group of Jews who willingly returned to Jerusalem to rebuild the Temple and worship Him.

We are like earthen vessels and God has a special plan for each of us to be a vessel for His use, even though we too are distorted by sin. When we yield ourself to the Master Potter, with loving hands He will mold us again into another vessel, one better prepared to contain and express the Presence of Christ Himself. Therefore if any man be in Christ, he is a new creature: old things are passed away; behold, all things are become new (II Corinthians 5:17).

Thought for Today: We were created for God's glory.

Christ Revealed: By Jeremiah's words to God: Your Word was to me the joy and rejoicing of my heart (Jeremiah 15:16). Jesus said: The words that I speak to you, they are Spirit, and they are Life (John 6:63).

For definitions of unfamiliar words in today's Bible reading, see pages 468-480.

In Today's Reading

Jeremiah beaten and imprisoned by Pashur; Jeremiah's grief;
destruction of Jerusalem foretold; the way of life or death

During the last days of the kingdom of Judah, Jeremiah courageously faced the son of the chief governor of the high priest and said: *Thus
says the LORD, Behold, I will make you a terror to yourself, and to all your
friends: and they shall fall by the sword of their enemies . . . and I will give
all Judah into the hand of the king of Babylon, and he shall carry them captive
into Babylon, and shall slay them with the sword. . . . And you, Pashur, and
all that dwell in your house shall go into captivity: and you shall come to
Babylon, and there you shall die, and shall be buried there, you, and all your
friends, to whom you have prophesied lies* (Jeremiah 20:4,6).

Soon the people of Judah learned of the defeat of Assyria and then
of Egypt. With Nebuchadnezzar's victory in the battle at Carchemish,
Babylon emerged as the new dominant world power. This confirmed
what Isaiah had foretold about 100 years earlier (Isaiah 39:6-7).

Even after being fully informed of the results of rejecting the Word
of God, the religious leaders not only refused to repent, but they began
a campaign to discredit Jeremiah before the king and the nation.
Jeremiah sat alone in prison and was momentarily discouraged when he
said: *I will not make mention of Him, nor speak any more in His Name. But
His Word was in my heart as a burning fire shut up in my bones, and I was
weary with forbearing, and I could not stay* (hold it in) (Jeremiah 20:9).

Jeremiah may have thought that he had failed to communicate to the
people the importance of obeying the Word of God. Most spiritual
leaders have, at some time, felt that they failed in fulfilling their God-
given responsibility. But, far beyond all his own expectations, Jeremiah
has been an inspiration to millions of believers for many centuries. Our
Creator has assured us: *My Word . . . shall not return to Me void* (without
result) *. . . but it shall prosper . . . in the thing whereto I sent it* (Isaiah 55:11).

No one who is devoted to teaching the Word of God personally, or
by providing the money to make it possible for others to teach His Word,
and who lives by it is a failure. Jesus promised: *Verily* (truly) *. . . I say to
you, He that hears My Word, and believes on Him that sent Me, has
everlasting life, and shall not come into condemnation; but is passed from
death to life* (John 5:24).

Thought for Today: Pray like Jesus: *Not My will, but Yours, be done* (Luke 22:42).

Christ Revealed: As the One Who pronounces judgment upon those who refuse to
obey His Word (Jeremiah 19:15). *For the Father . . . committed all judgment to the Son*
(John 5:22).

For definitions of unfamiliar words in today's Bible reading, see pages 468-480.

In Today's Reading
Future restoration; Christ's rule promised; lying prophets;
good and bad figs; judgment on Babylon foretold

---

*O*nly a few months remained before the Babylonians' destruction of the kingdom of Judah. It was now too late to pray for Jerusalem or for the Temple to be saved from destruction. Judah's last king, Zedekiah, would have his eyes gouged out and be taken to Babylon in chains (II Kings 25:7). These prophecies are all horrifying reminders that sin and suffering are inseparable and that judgment is inevitable whenever the Word of God is disregarded.

Jeremiah's message turned from one of the coming judgment to one of comfort to them. To illustrate, the Lord showed him *one basket* (that) *had very good figs, even like the figs that are first ripe; and the other basket had very naughty* (bad, rotten) *figs, which could not be eaten* (Jeremiah 24:2).Then the Lord said: *Like these good figs, so will I acknowledge* (regard) *them that are carried away captive of Judah, whom I have sent out of this place into the land of the Chaldeans for their good. For I will set My eyes upon them for good, and I will bring them again to this land* (24:5-6). There were three fig harvests – June, August, and November. The first figs, in June, were considered a great delicacy (Isaiah 28:4; Hosea 9:10; Micah 7:1). Thus the Lord was lovingly sending the chosen "good figs" into captivity to correct them "for their own good."

Even while the armies of Babylon were besieging Jerusalem, Jeremiah assured those who were faithful to God's Word: *Behold, the days come, says the LORD, that I will raise to David a righteous Branch, and a King shall reign and prosper, and shall execute judgment and justice in the earth. In His days Judah shall be saved, and Israel shall dwell safely: and this is His Name whereby He shall be called: THE LORD OUR RIGHTEOUSNESS* (Jeremiah 23:5-6; 33:15-16). At the proper time the Lord Jesus Christ will fulfill this prophecy concerning Himself.

When we receive Christ as our Savior He becomes for us *THE LORD OUR RIGHTEOUSNESS.* We too are comforted as we continue to look forward to the coming return of the Messiah Jesus, Who is that Righteous Branch. *He* (God) *has made Him* (Jesus) *to be sin for us, Who knew no sin; that we might be made the righteousness of God in Him* (II Corinthians 5:21).

Thought for Today: Give a friend *Bible Pathway* – a gift they'll use all year.

Christ Revealed: As *THE LORD OUR RIGHTEOUSNESS* (Jeremiah 23:5-6). *Of Him are you in Christ Jesus, Who of God is made to us wisdom, and righteousness, and sanctification, and redemption* (I Corinthians 1:30).

For definitions of unfamiliar words in today's Bible reading, see pages 468-480.

During the early part of Zedekiah's reign, God commanded Jeremiah to make a yoke and put it on his own neck, symbolizing the coming captivity of the kingdom of Judah. *Now have I given all these lands into the hand of Nebuchadnezzar the king of Babylon, My servant; and the beasts of the field have I given him also to serve him* (Jeremiah 27:6).

Jeremiah proclaimed that, because of their sin, along with that of Moab, Ammon, Tyre and Sidon, God had appointed Nebuchadnezzar as ruler over all these nations (27:2-11; compare Daniel 2:37-38). Sometime earlier, when he had prophesied something similar, the priesthood was determined to kill Jeremiah. *Then spoke the priests and the prophets to the princes and to all the people, saying, This man is worthy to die; for he has prophesied against this city, as you have heard with your ears* (Jeremiah 26:11).

When Jeremiah's prophecy was fulfilled and the Israelites were defeated by Nebuchadnezzar, it began *the times of the Gentiles* (Luke 21:24). We are near the close of that final generation when *the times of the Gentiles* (will) *be fulfilled*. God, in His sovereign power, has caused the Jews to return to Jerusalem and once again become a nation before the coming of the Messiah, King Jesus – just as He declared centuries ago. God has not indicated when it will take place. Therefore, we do not look for signs, but prepare for that day.

Let us faithfully and diligently tell others how they can be prepared for His return. Failure to do so will result in eternal damnation for all who do not receive Christ as their Savior and Lord.

The grace of God that brings salvation has appeared to all men, Teaching us that, denying ungodliness and worldly lusts, we should live soberly (sensibly), *righteously, and godly, in this present world; Looking for that blessed hope, and the glorious appearing of the great God and our Savior Jesus Christ; Who gave Himself for us, that He might redeem us from all iniquity* (lawlessness), *and purify to Himself a peculiar* (special) *people, zealous of good works* (Titus 2:11-14).

Thought for Today: Speak boldly for the Lord; it will influence others.

Christ Portrayed: By Jeremiah, who was falsely accused by the priests and the false prophets (Jeremiah 26:8-9). Our Lord was threatened and falsely accused by the religious rulers of His day. *The elders . . . and the chief priests and the scribes. . . . began to accuse Him, saying, We found this fellow perverting* (misleading) *the nation, and forbidding to give tribute* (tax) *to Caesar, saying that He Himself is Christ a King* (Luke 22:66 – 23:2; also John 8:48,59).

For definitions of unfamiliar words in today's Bible reading, see pages 468-480.

IN TODAY'S READING

Letter to captives in Babylon; Jews' deliverance foretold;
full restoration of all things foretold

A full end of the powerful kingdoms of Assyria and Babylon did take place. These two powerful world empires were destroyed just as the Lord foretold through Jeremiah. Jeremiah also prophesied the destruction of Jerusalem and the captivity of the small kingdom of Judah. *Thus says the LORD; Behold, I will bring again the captivity of Jacob's tents, and have mercy on his dwellingplaces; and the city shall be built upon her own heap* (ruin) (Jeremiah 30:18).

The Lord also revealed to Jeremiah that, at a future time, He would make a New Covenant: *I will put My Law in their inward parts, and write it in their hearts; and will be their God, and they shall be My people* (31:33). During their Babylonian captivity, through His prophet Jeremiah, the Lord taught the people to *seek the peace of the city where I have caused you to be carried away captives, and pray to the LORD for it: for in the peace thereof shall you have peace* (29:7). This means they were to pray for, and be a blessing to, their captors; and the Israelites, in turn, would be blessed by God. The Lord reminds us also of the self-destructive results of hatred, of holding grudges, or of seeking revenge when we are mistreated or faced with opposition.

Pity the person who, even though physically free, remains shackled with dissatisfaction about his circumstances and is longing for a time when he can be free and enjoy living. Perhaps he is waiting until he has a promotion or a better home, or for retirement. But he is always waiting for release from his present situation. An even more serious example is the person who has been offended and has quit attending church. Often such people are engulfed in bitter resentment and have made themselves prisoners of their own miserable attitudes (Hebrews 13:5-6).

The Apostle Peter was led to write: *Gird up the loins of your mind . . . As obedient children, not fashioning* (conforming) *yourselves according to the former lusts in your ignorance: But as He Who has called you is holy, so be you holy in all manner of conversation* (behavior); *Because it is written, Be you holy: for I am holy* (I Peter 1:13-16).

Thought for Today: Every reader of the Bible will be richly rewarded.

Christ Revealed: As the One Who forgives sin (Jeremiah 31:34). *That you may know that the Son of Man has power* **(authority)** *on earth to forgive sins, (then says He to the sick of the palsy,) Arise, take up your bed, and go* **(Matthew 9:6; compare John 8:10-11).**

For definitions of unfamiliar words in today's Bible reading, see pages 468-480.

In Today's Reading

Jeremiah imprisoned, then buys a field at Anathoth; return to
Jerusalem promised; Christ, the Branch of Righteousness, promised

*The king of Babylon's army besieged Jerusalem: and Jeremiah the prophet
was shut up in the court of the prison, which was in the king of Judah's house*
(Jeremiah 32:2). Yet, under such adverse circumstances when the destruction of the nation was imminent, the Lord told Jeremiah: *Buy the
field for money, and take witnesses; for the city is given into the hand of the
Chaldeans* (32:25). Without hesitation Jeremiah paid for the land, took
receipts, registered the purchase, then handed over the documents in
the presence of many witnesses (32:9-12).

This business transaction would have seemed ridiculous to those
who had heard Jeremiah's repeated warnings of approaching destruction and captivity. But, Jeremiah had also proclaimed that the people
would be restored to the land, and this purchase of land was evidence
of his faith that the Sovereign God would fulfill His Word.

Although Jeremiah could not see how God would accomplish this
prophecy, his faith was in the unfailing Word of God, Who also said: *I
am the LORD, the God of all flesh: is there any thing too hard for Me?* (32:27).

God gave Jeremiah a fresh assurance concerning the future of Israel
by saying: *I will gather them out of all countries, where I have driven them
. . . and I will bring them again to this place . . . to dwell safely* (32:37). How
wonderful to know that, in the midst of the most difficult circumstances,
we can rest assured that God is merciful and will protect and provide
for the needs of His faithful servants. The Lord's invitation still is: *Call
to Me, and I will answer you, and show you great and mighty things* (33:3).

Our faith in the Word of God can be measured by the influence we
allow it to have upon our conduct. *The day of the Lord will come as a thief
in the night; in the which the heavens shall pass away with a great noise, and
the elements shall melt with fervent heat, the earth also and the works that
are therein shall be burned up. Seeing then that all these things shall be
dissolved* (destroyed), *what manner of persons ought you to be in all holy
conversation* (conduct) *and godliness. . . . that you may be found of Him in
peace, without spot, and blameless* (II Peter 3:10-14).

Thought for Today: What occupies your thoughts most is a revelation of who or what
is your god.

Christ Portrayed: By Jeremiah who acted as a kinsman-redeemer by purchasing the
land of his cousin Hanameel even though he was in prison (Jeremiah 32:6-14; also
Leviticus 25:25,49; Ruth 2:20; 3:12-13). Jesus is our Kinsman-Redeemer Who purchased
our freedom from sin, hell, and the grave with His own blood on Calvary (I Corinthians
6:20; Galatians 4:4-5; Titus 2:13-14; Hebrews 13:12).

For definitions of unfamiliar words in today's Bible reading, see pages 468-480.

IN TODAY'S READING
Jeremiah's warning to Zedekiah; obedience of the Rechabites;
scroll read by Jehudi and destroyed by King Jehoiakim

Four years after the Egyptians conquered Judah and appointed Jehoiakim as its king, Nebuchadnezzar defeated the Egyptians, invaded Jerusalem, and appointed Jehoiakim as his servant-king. Unlike his godly father Josiah, Jehoiakim was a ruthless, cruel ruler.

At that time, Jeremiah instructed his secretary Baruch to record the judgment of God on *a roll* (scroll) *of a book, and write therein all the words that I have spoken to you against Israel, and against Judah . . . and against all the nations* (Jeremiah 36:2).

Then *Jeremiah commanded Baruch . . . go . . . and read . . . the words of the LORD . . . in the LORD'S House. . . . to all Judah. . . . It may be they will . . . return every one from his evil way* (36:5-7). The princes (leaders) were disturbed by the prophet's words and immediately informed the king, who *sent Jehudi to bring the roll* (scroll) (36:21).

After *Jehudi had read three or four leaves* (of the scroll, Jehoiakim flew into a rage, snatched it from Jehudi, and), *he cut it with the penknife, and cast it into the fire that was on the hearth, until all the roll* (scroll) *was consumed in the fire* (36:23). But, that was all he could do. It was beyond his power to destroy the truth that the scroll contained.

In the third year of the reign of Jehoiakim king of Judah came Nebuchadnezzar king of Babylon to Jerusalem, and besieged it. And the Lord gave Jehoiakim . . . into his hand (Daniel 1:1-2).

Like Jehoiakim, some today seal their fate by refusing to read the truth that God considers necessary to fulfill His will. History records many Bible burnings; but what is the difference between burning it or not reading it?

Without a doubt, the godly, such as Daniel and his friends, suffer because of the sins of others. But, God is able to bless the faithful as he did Daniel. Without exception: *All things work together for good to them that love God, to them who are the called according to His purpose* (Romans 8:28).

Thought for Today: Those who seek counsel from the Lord through His Word will never be deceived.

Christ Revealed: As the One Who desires liberty for all in bondage (Isaiah 61:1). Jesus said: *The Spirit of the Lord is upon Me . . . to preach deliverance to the captives* (Luke 4:18-19).

For definitions of unfamiliar words in today's Bible reading, see pages 468-480.

ℐN ℐODAY'S ℛEADING

Jeremiah imprisoned in a dungeon; his counsel rejected; Jerusalem destroyed; Jeremiah set free; Ishmael's plan to assassinate Gedaliah

*D*uring the 11th year of Zedekiah's evil reign, the armies of Nebuchadnezzar surrounded Jerusalem and Zedekiah frantically said to Jeremiah: *Inquire . . . of the LORD for us; for Nebuchadnezzar . . . makes war against us* (Jeremiah 21:2). But the answer from the Lord was firm: *I have set My face against this city . . . the king of Babylon . . . shall burn it with fire* (21:10). Neither Zedekiah, *nor the people of the land, did hearken* (listen) *to the words of the LORD, which He spoke by the prophet Jeremiah* (37:2).

Believing that Egypt would protect his kingdom, Zedekiah sent his officials to Egypt to make an alliance. Because it also seemed wise to show "good will" to the prophet, *Zedekiah the king sent . . . the priest to the prophet Jeremiah, saying, Pray now to the LORD our God for us* (37:3). Instead of praying, Jeremiah replied: *Thus says the LORD; Deceive not yourselves . . . The Chaldeans shall. . . . burn this city with fire* (37:9-10).

When the Chaldean army retreated from Jerusalem, the Israelites believed their alliance with Egypt had been successful without the prayers of the prophet. Yet Zedekiah was uneasy. He removed Jeremiah from prison *and . . . asked him secretly in his house . . . Is there any word from the LORD? And Jeremiah said, There is . . . you shall be delivered into the hand of the king of Babylon* (37:17).

The fortified city of Jerusalem held out for nearly a year and a half. During this time the people suffered the horrors of famine, pestilence, and cannibalism. When Zedekiah finally attempted to escape the city at night, he was captured near Jericho, where Joshua had victoriously begun the conquest of the promised land (39:5).

Zedekiah was blinded, taken to Babylon, and imprisoned (39:7). He is an example of the consequences of those who refuse to seek the Lord's forgiveness for their sins. Regarding those, the Apostle Paul wrote: *The god of this world has blinded the minds of them which believe not* (II Corinthians 4:4).

Thought for Today: A person who rejects the Lord and His Word is blindly moving toward his own destruction.

Christ Portrayed: By Jeremiah, who stood as a faithful witness to the revealed will of God (Jeremiah 38:2-9). *Now the chief priests, and elders, and all the council, sought false witness* (testimony) *against Jesus, to put Him to death* (Matthew 26:59).

For definitions of unfamiliar words in today's Bible reading, see pages 468-480.

*J*N *T*ODAY'S *R*EADING
Gedaliah's assassination; Jeremiah taken to Egypt;
desolation of Judah because of idolatry

*G*od allowed Nebuchadnezzar to defeat His rebellious people and fulfill His prophecy of the destruction of Jerusalem. *The king of Babylon . . . made Gedaliah . . . governor in the land, and . . . committed to him . . . them that were not carried away captive to Babylon* (Jeremiah 40:7).

Gedaliah set up his government at Mizpah, about five miles northwest of the ruins of Jerusalem. He then held a banquet in honor of Ishmael at Mizpah. Ishmael was a leader of an anti-Babylonian nationalist party. At this event, Ishmael and his ten companions murdered Gedaliah (II Kings 25:25; Jeremiah 40:7 – 41:18). The Israelites who remained in the land evidently expected Nebuchadnezzar to retaliate and escaped into Egypt, forcing Jeremiah to go with them.

In Egypt, Jeremiah watched the Israelites sink further into sin as they worshiped the Egyptian goddess Ashtoreth. When confronted with their sins by the prophet, they *answered Jeremiah, saying, As for the word that you have spoken to us in the Name of the LORD, we will not hearken to you. . . . We will . . . burn incense to* (sacrifice, worship) *the queen of heaven* (female deity idol), *and . . . pour out drink offerings to her* (44:15-17). Because of their sins and rejection of the Word of God, faith in the living God did not exist. Like so many today, they distorted the facts to fit their decision and said to Jeremiah: In Egypt we *had plenty of victuals, and were well, and saw no evil. But since we left off to burn incense to the queen of heaven . . . we have wanted* (lacked) *all things* (44:17-19).

Some would say the godly prophet Jeremiah surely deserved better treatment than this for his loyalty to the Lord. However, though distressed over the unbelief of his people, Jeremiah had nothing to fear. He knew his life was in the hands of the living God. Jeremiah never compromised, but remained loyal to God regardless of the consequences.

Centuries have passed and you can be sure that in heaven Jeremiah has no regrets. May it also be our desire to say with God's servant, the Apostle Paul: *I count all things but loss for the excellency of the knowledge of Christ Jesus my Lord: for Whom I have suffered the loss of all things, and do count them but dung* (rubbish), *that I may win Christ* (Philippians 3:8).

Thought for Today: Shed God's Light on someone's path today.

Christ Revealed: By *My servants the prophets* (Jeremiah 44:4). God the Father called Jesus *My Servant, Whom I have chosen* (Matthew 12:17-18; also Acts 3:20-21).

For definitions of unfamiliar words in today's Bible reading, see pages 468-480.

In Today's Reading
Jeremiah's message to Baruch;
judgment against Egypt, Philistia, and Moab

*A*mong all the prophecies of Jeremiah, the Lord included a personal message to just one man, Baruch, Jeremiah's discontented assistant. *Thus said the LORD . . . to you, O Baruch; You did say, Woe is me now! for the LORD has added grief to my sorrow; I fainted in my sighing, and I find no rest* (Jeremiah 45:2-3). Perhaps he had hoped that his service as a scribe would be a means of achieving personal ambitions and recognition, or other self-serving goals.

Baruch's grandfather Maaseiah had been governor of Jerusalem during Josiah's reign (32:12; II Chronicles 34:8). Did Baruch secretly think he was "overqualified" to be a mere scribe to an unpopular prophet?

Instead of rewards, or even words of sympathy for his frustrations, Baruch received a strong rebuke from the Lord: *Seek you great things for yourself? seek them not* (Jeremiah 45:5).

Baruch expressed no heartfelt grief regarding the impending destruction of Jerusalem and the Temple of God or the pitiful slavery of the people, as Jeremiah had foretold. Instead, he only expressed sorrow over his own lack of personal fulfillment.

Although Baruch was recording the Word of God spoken through Jeremiah, he did not have the spiritual concern or insight of the prophet, who was deeply concerned for the people to repent of their sins and avoid destruction. Baruch should have considered it a great privilege to be a coworker in Jeremiah's ministry.

Our time and talents are precious treasures invested in us by the God of all creation to accomplish His will through us. True fulfillment comes only when we recognize that God has arranged the circumstances in our lives.

Baruch is typical of those who are dissatisfied with their circumstances or position of less esteem than they think they deserve. In contrast are those who realize that *godliness with contentment is great gain* (I Timothy 6:6; also Hebrews 13:5-6).

Thought for Today: Look at the birds of the sky: they don't sow or reap or gather into barns, yet your Heavenly Father feeds them.

Christ Revealed: As the One Who corrects His people (Jeremiah 46:28). *Whom the Lord loves He chastens* **(disciplines),** *and scourges* **(whips)** *every son whom He receives* **(Hebrews 12:6).**

For definitions of unfamiliar words in today's Bible reading, see pages 468-480.

*I*N *T*ODAY'S *R*EADING

Judgments against Ammon, Edom, Damascus, Kedar, Hazor,
Elam, and Babylon foretold; redemption of Israel promised

*J*eremiah prophesied that the Ammonites, descendants of Lot who were historically hostile to the Israelites, would be destroyed (Jeremiah 27:3-6; also II Chronicles 20:1-3; II Kings 24:1-2). *Rabbah of the Ammonites* (now known as Amman, Jordan) . . . *shall be a desolate heap, and her daughters* (villages) *shall be burned with fire* (49:2). The Lord then turned to Moab, saying: *Behold, I will bring a fear* (terror) *upon you, says the Lord GOD of hosts . . . and you shall be driven out* (49:5).

Our attention is turned to Edom, a nation that descended from Jacob's twin brother Esau. Edom had always been a jealous enemy of Jacob's descendants and had joined Nebuchadnezzar in plundering Jerusalem. They even expanded their territory into southern Judah, inhabiting an area later called Idumea, the birthplace of Herod, the king. Because of their actions toward Israel, Edom's fate was foretold by the prophet: *I have made Esau bare. . . . and he is not* (49:10-12).

Judgment was then pronounced *against Babylon . . . the land of the Chaldeans. . . . there comes up a nation against her, which shall make her land desolate* (50:1-3).

Not only the release of Israel from captivity is foretold but the Israelites will eventually repent and accept their Messiah Jesus *in a perpetual covenant that shall not be forgotten* (50:4-5).

We can expect the forces of evil to discourage us in an effort to destroy our faith in God. However, God is not glorified by our fears, doubts, or frustrations. We must keep our eyes on the promises of God that have never failed. Consequently, there is never a valid reason to allow the pressures and problems of life to depress or frustrate us. In fact, despondency is a sin. *Count it all joy when you fall into divers temptations* (various trials); *Knowing this, that the trying of your faith works patience. But let patience have her perfect work, that you may be perfect and entire, wanting nothing. . . . Blessed is the man that endures temptation: for when he is tried, he shall receive the crown of life, which the Lord has promised to them that love Him* (James 1:2-4,12).

Thought for Today: God will hear the prayer of any repentant sinner.

Christ Revealed: As the Redeemer Who pleads our cause (Jeremiah 50:34). *Blessed* (praised and extolled and thanked) *be the Lord God of Israel; for He has visited and redeemed His people* (Luke 1:68). *It is Christ . . . Who is even at the right hand of God, Who also makes intercession for us* (Romans 8:34).

For definitions of unfamiliar words in today's Bible reading, see pages 468-480.

In Today's Reading
Judgment of Babylon; fall of Jerusalem; captivity of Judah

The spectacular empire of the Chaldeans surpassed anything the world had ever known. Its capital, Babylon, appeared invincible, with walls over 300 feet high and wide enough for chariots to ride two abreast. The empire was enjoying absolute rule over all the nations when Jeremiah declared that *Babylon is suddenly fallen. . . . your end is come. . . . Babylon shall become heaps* (ruins) *. . . without an inhabitant* (Jeremiah 51:8-62).

As foretold by the prophet, the Babylonian capital "suddenly fell." This was on the night that *Belshazzar the king. . . . saw the part of a hand that wrote . . . on . . . the wall of the king's palace. . . . your kingdom is finished* (Daniel 5:1,5,26). After the fall of Babylon, Cyrus, the conquering king of the Persian Empire, issued a decree urging the Jews to rebuild the Temple in Jerusalem. Most of the older generation that had been taken captive to Babylonia had died. The new generation was prospering under the new Persian rule and, consequently, only a small number felt a desire to leave.

The unwillingness of the majority of the Jews to forsake the luxuries of Babylon for the poverty and hardships they would experience in returning to Jerusalem has a modern-day parallel. How accurately this describes some who love the pleasures of the world and will not respond to the invitation of Christ, Who said: *If any man will come after Me, let him deny himself, and take up his cross daily, and follow Me* (Luke 9:23).

Many who seemingly consent to be "followers" of Christ drop out when things become difficult. Jesus illustrated this in His parable concerning the seed sown in stony places and among thorns. He likened such people to those who, *when tribulation or persecution arises because of the Word, by and by he is offended,* and of others *the care of this world, and the deceitfulness of riches, chokes the Word* (Matthew 13:21-22). Is it possible for a person to *take up his cross daily* (Luke 9:23), and yet devote his time, tithes, and talents to personal pleasures on the Lord's Day?

There is no man that has left house, or brethren . . . or lands, for My sake, and the Gospel's, But he shall receive a hundredfold now in this time . . . with persecutions; and in the world to come eternal life (Mark 10:29-30).

Thought for Today: We are to live in the world but not by its standards.

Christ Revealed: As the Creator of the universe (Jeremiah 51:15). *All things were created by Him, and for Him* (Colossians 1:16).

For definitions of unfamiliar words in today's Bible reading, see pages 468-480.

INTRODUCTION TO THE BOOK OF
Lamentations

The Book of Lamentations is an expression of Jeremiah's deep sorrow over the sins of his people that eventually resulted in the destruction of the Temple of God and the kingdom of Judah. Jeremiah knew the inevitable consequences of Judah's disobedience. *Jerusalem has grievously sinned; therefore she is removed. . . . The LORD has . . . poured out His fierce anger. . . . For the sins of her prophets, and the iniquities of her priests* (Lamentations 1:8; 4:11,13).

Jerusalem was the only place on earth where God accepted sacrifices made to Him. The Temple gave the people a false sense of security. Added to that, Jerusalem was *the city of the great King* (Psalm 48:2). But, ignoring the Word of God resulted in sin and, for those sins, the Israelites were subjected to horrors of deprivation, disease, suffering, starvation and, finally Jerusalem itself was defeated and destroyed. Even more pathetic than the massive loss of life and destruction of the city, however, was the destruction of the sacred Temple where God had dwelt (Lamentations 2:19-22; 4:8-10; also Exodus 25:22; II Chronicles 7:1-2).

> *No time, no time to study*
> *to meditate and pray,*
> *And yet much time for doing*
> *In a fleshly, worldly way;*
> *No time for things eternal,*
> *But much for things of earth;*
> *The things of little worth.*
> *Some things, tis true, are needful,*
> *But first things come first;*
> *And what displaces God's own Word*
> *Of God it shall be cursed.*
>
> *—M.E.H.*

WISDOM

Let the Word of Christ dwell in you richly in all wisdom; teaching and admonishing (urging) one another in psalms and hymns and spiritual songs, singing with grace in your hearts to the Lord (Colossians 3:16).

And that from a child you have known the Holy Scriptures, which are able to make you wise to salvation through faith which is in Christ Jesus (II Timothy 3:15).

IN TODAY'S READING
Jeremiah's lamentation over Jerusalem's destruction

Jeremiah was deeply grieved that the holy city of Jerusalem had *become as a widow! she that was great among the nations, and princess among the provinces, how is she become tributary! She weeps sore* (bitterly) *in the night, and her tears are on her cheeks . . . she has none to comfort her: all her friends have dealt treacherously with her, they have become her enemies. Judah is gone into captivity* (Lamentations 1:1-3). Jeremiah tells us why Jerusalem was reduced to such deplorable destruction: *The LORD has afflicted her for the multitude of her transgressions* (1:5).

The prophet Jeremiah compared the once wealthy, secure, and proud Israelite to a widow who had lost her husband. The loving Lord was the generous Provider and powerful Protector of Israel, but the people rejected Him. As a widow, Jerusalem was now alone, weeping in the night, with no one to comfort her: *Jerusalem has grievously sinned* (1:8). The Covenant of God with Israel required willing obedience to His Word, but they had not kept their part of the Covenant. Spiritual neglect eventually led the Israelites to lose not only their personal liberty, but also the precious privilege to let the world know the One True God Who expects them to reject their idols and worship their Creator.

We too have one supreme reason for living, and it is not to obtain financial security, popularity, or material success, or to look forward to the next vacation. The question that needs to be addressed is: Will we read how we must live to please our Creator, or suffer the consequences? Pity the person who is wasting the few short years of his life chasing social and financial goals, but failing to achieve the purpose for which God created him.

Jesus asked a sobering question: *Why call Me Lord, Lord, and do not the things which I say?* (Luke 6:46). Obviously, you can't do something you don't know, so, read His Guide to Life.

We must all appear before the judgment seat of Christ; that every one may receive the things done in his body, according to that he has done, whether it be good or bad. Knowing therefore the terror of the Lord, we persuade men (II Corinthians 5:9-11).

Thought for Today: *I will say to the Lord, my Refuge and my Fortress, my God, in Whom I trust* (Psalm 91:2).

Christ Revealed: By Jeremiah's sorrow over the destruction of Jerusalem (Lamentations 1:12-22). Jesus expressed His sorrow for Jerusalem's failure to come to Him before it fell again (Matthew 23:37; Luke 13:34).

For definitions of unfamiliar words in today's Bible reading, see pages 468-480.

IN TODAY'S READING
God's mercy; punishment of Zion;
the faithful grieve over their disaster and confess their sins

The prophet Jeremiah was one of the greatest prophets in biblical history, and few have suffered so much public humiliation, rejection, and hostility. For more than 40 years, he warned the Israelites to believe Moses and follow the Law or to face the judgment of God for their sins. Eventually, because they failed to repent, they faced the inevitable destruction of their glorious Temple and Jerusalem, the city of God.

God does not permit suffering just for the sake of punishment. It always has a twofold purpose: first, as **judgment upon sin**, but, second, to allow the offenders the **opportunity to repent and commit their lives to Him**. We can truly praise the Lord that He forgives us of all our sins when we repent and confess them to Him (I John 1:9). Jeremiah the prophet assures us: *Though He cause grief, yet will He have compassion according to the multitude of His mercies* (Lamentations 3:32).

After the destruction of the Temple, there was a realization of the awfulness of sin and the consequences of disregarding God's Word. The Israelites had assumed that God's Covenant promise would continue while their Covenant responsibility was being ignored. The prophet pleaded: *Let us search* (examine) *and try our ways, and turn again to the LORD* (3:40). Jeremiah called for a national confession of sin, repentance, and obedience to God's Word.

The once-powerful kingdom of Judah was now subjected to every form of humiliation. Its people had to beg for bread from foreigners, pay for drinking water, helplessly stand by and watch their children taken as slaves into heavy, forced labor, and know that these heathen soldiers had *ravished the women in Zion, and the maids in the cities of Judah* (5:11). Can we feel the heartbreak of the weeping prophet as he expresses his sorrow: *The crown is fallen from our head: woe to us, that we have sinned!* (5:16).

The righteous always suffer in the midst of a wicked nation; but, for the Christian, suffering should open our eyes to the true values of life. *We have had fathers of our flesh which corrected us. . . . they verily* (truly) *for a few days chastened us after their own pleasure* (judgment); *but He* (God) *for our profit, that we might be partakers of His holiness* (Hebrews 12:9-10).

Thought for Today: God's Word imparts insight into true values.

Christ Revealed: As the merciful Savior (Lamentations 3:22). *Keep yourselves in the love of God, looking for the mercy of our Lord Jesus Christ to eternal life* (Jude 1:21).

For definitions of unfamiliar words in today's Bible reading, see pages 468-480.

INTRODUCTION TO THE BOOK OF
*E*ZEKIEL

Ezekiel lived in Jerusalem during the great reformation period that followed the discovery of the Law in the Temple. This was during the reign of Josiah, the last godly king of Judah (II Kings 22:8-20; 23:1-29). After Josiah's death, the people chose his fourth son Jehoahaz as their king. He was also known as Shallum (23:30-34; I Chronicles 3:15, Jeremiah 22:10-12). Just three months later, Pharaoh-necho took him in chains to Egypt, and set up Josiah's second son Eliakim as king over Judah (II Kings 23:31-34; II Chronicles 36:1-4). Pharaoh changed Eliakim's name to Jehoiakim (II Kings 23:34-36). He was subject to Pharaoh-necho for about four years (Jeremiah 46:2); then Nebuchadnezzar defeated the Egyptians.

In the same year that he defeated Egypt, Nebuchadnezzar seized control of Jerusalem, stripped the capital and the Temple of its treasures and most of its golden vessels, and took many of the young royalty of Judah as captives to Babylon. Among them were Daniel and his three friends (Daniel 1:1-3,6; also Ezekiel 33:21).

Nebuchadnezzar left Jehoiakim to be his puppet ruler. Jehoiachin, Jehoiakim's 18-year-old son (also known as Jeconiah and Coniah), succeeded him and continued his father's evil policies (II Kings 24:8-9). After only three months, Jehoiachin was also taken captive to Babylon, along with Ezekiel and ten thousand influential leaders and craftsmen.

Ezekiel's captivity began about eight years after Daniel was taken to Babylon. Ezekiel was placed at Tel-Abib near the Chebar River, an irrigation canal which routed water from the Euphrates in a large semicircle through the countryside until it rejoined the Euphrates. Ezekiel prophesied for about 22 years (Ezekiel 1:2; 29:17).

Nebuchadnezzar then appointed Mattaniah, the third son of Josiah, to govern Judah and renamed him Zedekiah (II Kings 24:17; I Chronicles 3:15). During this time, Ezekiel's message was directed to his fellow captives as well as to the people remaining in the promised land. Both groups rejected Ezekiel's message. He eventually foretold the destruction of Jerusalem. After about 10 years, Zedekiah rebelled against Nebuchadnezzar and, as foretold by Ezekiel, Nebuchadnezzar once again attacked Jerusalem, broke down its walls and, this time, he destroyed the Temple built by Solomon. *None remained, save the poorest sort of the people of the land* (II Kings 24:8-16,18 – 25:21; II Chronicles 36:11-21).

The key thought in this book is the heart cry of our Creator, revealing the personal nature of a loving, caring Creator God! *They shall know that I am the LORD their God* (Ezekiel 28:26; 39:22; 39:28).

In Today's Reading
Ezekiel's vision of God's control of world affairs;
his call; warning of judgment

*A*s a captive of Nebuchadnezzar and far from the promised land, Ezekiel could not offer sacrifices to God according to the Law. But to Ezekiel's great joy, *the Word of the LORD came expressly to . . . the priest . . . in the land of the Chaldeans by the river Chebar; and the hand of the LORD was there upon him* (Ezekiel 1:3).

In Ezekiel's first vision, *a whirlwind came out of the north, a great cloud, and a fire infolding itself* (flashing forth), *and a brightness was about it. . . . Also out of the midst thereof came the likeness of four living creatures. And . . . they had the likeness of a man* (1:4-5). The cherubim (angelic beings) were fulfilling the perfect will of God.

Each of the four cherubim had wings and hands and four different faces. These heavenly beings typified Jesus Christ as seen in the four Gospels. The lion represented the ruler of the animal kingdom and symbolized the royalty and supreme majesty of Jesus Christ the King as presented in Matthew. The ox represented the most valuable domesticated animal and signified strength and patient service as the Servant of God, symbolic of Jesus Christ as presented in Mark. The face of man represented the humanity of Christ as perfect, fully human, yet fully divine as presented in Luke. The eagle was admired for its superior ability to swiftly rise into the heavens above all enemies on earth and represented the deity of Jesus as revealed in John. The swiftness of the eagle also represented Christ, Who is quick to bring protection, provision, or judgment, in a moment when needed.

The cherubim stood beside the wheel within a wheel (1:16), in which one wheel was revolving north-south and the other east-west. Since the cherubim faced all directions simultaneously, they were prepared to instantly obey the will of God in any direction of flight (1:9,12,17).

The Lord will protect and direct the lives of His people, just as He did Ezekiel. Their greatest need was spiritual food and daily guidance from His Word. *Man shall not live by bread alone, but by every Word that proceeds out of the mouth of God* (Matthew 4:4).

Thought for Today: Regardless of our circumstances, we should trust the Lord and expect a good outcome.

Christ Revealed: In a *likeness as the appearance of a Man,* Who sat upon the throne (Ezekiel 1:26-28). This foreshadowed God appearing as a Man, *the Man Christ Jesus* (I Timothy 2:5).

For definitions of unfamiliar words in today's Bible reading, see pages 468-480.

In Today's Reading
Famine, pestilence, and sword; remnant to be spared;
vision of the glory of God; vision of slaying in Jerusalem

ourteen years after Nebuchadnezzar's initial conquest of the kingdom of Judah, life in Jerusalem seemed to have returned to normal.
Consequently, the people would not believe Ezekiel, who was in
Babylon, when he prophesied concerning Jerusalem: *Your altars shall
be desolate. . . . the cities shall be laid waste* (Ezekiel 6:4-6). Even the
Israelites who were captive in Babylon were sure that God would protect Jerusalem and the only Temple on earth where His Presence dwelt.

But Ezekiel continued to warn them: *He that is in the field shall die
with the sword; and he that is in the city, famine and pestilence shall devour him* (7:15). What a horrifying prophecy!

Fourteen months after his first vision (1:1-2), Ezekiel reported: *The
Spirit . . . brought me in the visions of God to Jerusalem* (8:1-5). The
prophet then saw in his vision *the great abominations* (detestable things)
*that the house of Israel commits. . . . wicked abominations. . . . there sat
women weeping for Tammuz* (the Babylonian god of fertility). . . . *men,
with their backs toward the Temple of the LORD, and . . . they worshiped
the sun* (8:6,9-14,16). As a result of their disobedience to the Word of
God, the Israelites had *filled the land with violence* (8:17). The people
also would not believe his second vision that showed God's reason for
the horrifying judgment that was to come upon Judah and Jerusalem.

We face a similar situation with our overemphasis on material success and a refusal to read the Word of God to learn why He created us,
how He expects us to live, and what He expects us to do.

Wealth was never meant to be selfishly accumulated or to be lavished on ourselves. God entrusts people with wealth, *that you, always
having all sufficiency in all things, may abound to every good work* (II
Corinthians 9:8). Having a right attitude of the heart is all important
since both rich and poor can lust after more possessions.

The Holy Spirit warns: *They that will be rich fall into temptation and
a snare* (trap), *and into many foolish and hurtful lusts, which drown men
in destruction and perdition* (damnation) (I Timothy 6:9).

Thought for Today: *Godliness with contentment is great gain* (I Timothy 6:6).

**Christ Portrayed: By the man clothed in linen (Ezekiel 9:2-11) represents Christ as
High Priest, marking His people to be spared from the flaming sword of vengeance.
*Seeing then that we have a great High Priest, that is passed into the heavens,
Jesus the Son of God, let us hold fast* (firmly) *our profession* (confession) (Hebrews
4:14; also Revelation 7:2-3).

For definitions of unfamiliar words in today's Bible reading, see pages 468-480.

In Today's Reading
Glory of the Lord leaving the Temple; judgment upon lying leaders;
the promise of Israel's restoration and renewal; captivity near

*E*zekiel's vision revealed the dispatching of seven men, one to spare the faithful minority and six to slay the idolatrous majority of Israelites. *One man . . . clothed with linen* marked the foreheads of all who remained faithful to the Lord (Ezekiel 9:2-7). *Then the glory of the LORD departed from off the threshold of the House, and stood over the cherubims. And the cherubims lifted up their wings, and mounted up from the earth . . . and every one stood at the door of the east gate of the LORD's House* (10:18-19).

Ezekiel observed the leaders of Jerusalem who, it seemed, were being blessed and called upon to remain in charge as the favored people, while so many others had been taken captive. But in reality, many of the deprived captives in Babylon eventually learned, through suffering, to repent of their pagan idolatry and trust in the Lord God of Israel. God promised a great future to those who were loyal to Him. As Ezekiel prepared to leave the Temple, he saw the Presence of the Lord, Who rested just above the Mercy Seat of the Ark of the Covenant in the Holy of Holies, slowly leaving the place where He had once chosen to dwell (Exodus 25:22).

As *the glory of the LORD went up from the midst of the city* (Ezekiel 11:23), it reluctantly left *the city which the LORD did choose out of all the tribes of Israel, to put His Name there* (I Kings 14:21). It appears the Israelites were so involved in their religious activities they were not aware that God had forsaken them.

The Lord again gave Ezekiel a prophecy that reached far into the future: *I will put a new Spirit within you; and I will take the stony heart out of their flesh, and will give them a heart of flesh: That they may walk in My statutes* (decrees), *and keep My ordinances (commands), and do them: and they shall be My people, and I will be their God* (Ezekiel 11:19-20; also 36:26-27). **It is thrilling to know that Ezekiel was also speaking to Christians.** The Apostle Paul wrote: *You are no more strangers and foreigners, but fellowcitizens with the saints* (believers), *and of the household of God; And are built upon the foundation of . . . Jesus Christ Himself being the Chief Corner Stone* (Ephesians 2:19-20).

Thought for Today: True satisfaction and purpose are found only in Christ – never in material things.

Christ Revealed: As the One Who gives *a new Spirit* (Ezekiel 11:19). This is the promise fulfilled when we accept Jesus as Savior and Lord of our lives. *God has sent forth the Spirit of His Son into your hearts* (Galatians 4:4-7).

For definitions of unfamiliar words in today's Bible reading, see pages 468-480.

$\mathcal{J}_N$ $\mathcal{T}_{\text{ODAY'S}}$ $\mathcal{R}_{\text{EADING}}$

Judgment pronounced upon elders of Israel and Jerusalem;
parable of the vine; promises of future blessings under New Covenant

---

$\mathcal{A}$lthough the Israelites regularly offered sacrifices to God, they also worshiped the heathen idols of other nations. Consequently, the Israelites were brought under the control of Nebuchadnezzar, who took thousands of them captive. Once again, certain *elders of Israel* (Ezekiel 14:1) came to consult Ezekiel, as if they desired to know the will of God. But the Lord revealed their hypocrisy to Ezekiel, saying: *These men have set up their idols in their heart. . . . Thus says the Lord GOD; Repent, and turn yourselves from your idols; and turn away your faces from all your abominations* (detestable practices). *. . . That the house of Israel . . . may be My people, and I may be their God* (14:3,6,11).

To illustrate their one purpose as the people of God, the Lord presented a parable to Ezekiel: *How is the vine tree* (the grapevine which was often used by God to illustrate the Israelites) *more than any tree . . . of the forest? Shall wood be taken thereof to do any work? or will men take a pin* (stake) *of it to hang any vessel thereon? Behold, it is cast into the fire for fuel* (15:2-4; also Genesis 49:22; Deuteronomy 32:32; Psalm 80:8-11; Jeremiah 2:21; Hosea 10:1). Every Israelite knew that the grapevine was valued only for its fruit and was worthless for making anything useful or of lasting value.

The vineyard of the LORD of hosts is the house of Israel (Isaiah 5:7). Ezekiel also spoke of the vine as representing Israel, chosen of God to let the world know there was only One True God, Who would bless all who honored Him by keeping His Word. But *the vine* had failed to produce fruit; consequently, the only alternative was for it to be uprooted and *cast into the fire* (Ezekiel 15:4,7). This illustrated the Israelites being uprooted from the promised land and forced to live in Babylon.

The righteous judgment of God upon those in Jerusalem had to be consistent with the great privileges they had willfully forsaken. But the principles of God's Word are still true today. *No whoremonger, nor unclean person, nor covetous man, who is an idolater, has any inheritance in the Kingdom of Christ and of God. Let no man deceive you with vain words: for because of these things comes the wrath of God upon the children of disobedience* (Ephesians 5:5-6).

Thought for Today: Consider your priorities today. Are they wrapped up in the things of the world or committed to serving the Lord?

Christ Revealed: In the *everlasting Covenant* (Ezekiel 16:60). *He is the Mediator of a better Covenant* (Agreement) (Hebrews 8:6).

For definitions of unfamiliar words in today's Bible reading, see pages 468-480.

In Today's Reading

Parable of the eagles; judgment upon bad conduct;
blessings for good conduct; sorrow over the leaders of Israel

*E*zekiel was given another parable: *A great eagle* (Nebuchadnezzar) *with great wings . . . full of feathers, which had divers* (many) *colors, came to Lebanon, and took the highest branch of the cedar: He cropped off the top of its young twigs, and carried it into a land of traffic* (traders); *he set it in a city of merchants* (Ezekiel 17:1-4).

This parable illustrates the vast extent of Nebuchadnezzar's dominion. The eagle's feathers represent the great number of nations he had conquered. Removing *the highest branch* symbolized Jehoiachin king of Judah, and *a city of merchants* was Babylon where he would be taken captive.

There was also another great eagle with great wings and many feathers (Egypt): *and, behold, this vine did bend her roots toward him* (17:7). The Lord God told Ezekiel to tell the people: *Thus says the Lord GOD; Shall it prosper? shall he not pull up the roots thereof . . . that it wither?* (17:9). The purpose of this important prophecy was to warn King Zedekiah not to betray his oath of submission to Nebuchadnezzar by forming an alliance with Egypt. The vow made to Nebuchadnezzar and sworn to in God's Name was binding (Numbers 30:2, II Chronicles 36:13). Zedekiah was warned, but chose unwisely to disobey God's instruction.

In the ninth year of his reign, King Zedekiah made a military treaty with Egypt. As a consequence, Nebuchadnezzar besieged Jerusalem and the people suffered many months of famine and pestilence before the city and Temple were utterly destroyed.

Nebuchadnezzar's invasion of Judah could have been averted if Zedekiah had honorably kept his vow. We too are obligated to keep promises, even when they are made with the unsaved (Psalm 15:4.) There are always consequences when we break our promises, whether it be a marriage vow or a business transaction. *If a man vow a vow* (make a promise) *to the LORD, or swear an oath to bind his soul* (obligate himself) *with a bond; he shall not break his word* (Numbers 30:2).

When you vow a vow to God, defer not to pay it; for He has no pleasure in fools: pay that which you have vowed (Ecclesiastes 5:4-6).

Thought for Today: All who love the Lord will keep His Commandments.

Christ Revealed: As the One Whose forgiveness provides life everlasting (Ezekiel 18:20-22). *For God so loved* (the people of) *the world, that He gave His only begotten Son* (Jesus), *that whosoever believes in Him should not perish, but have everlasting life* (John 3:16).

For definitions of unfamiliar words in today's Bible reading, see pages 468-480.

ℐN 𝒯ODAY'S ℛEADING

God's refusal to be consulted by the elders; history of rebellious
Israel; its defeat by Babylon and scattering among the heathen

𝒯he king and the religious leaders of Judah had expressed growing
hatred for the prophet Jeremiah because of his messages of judgment
against them. There comes a time when God says: *They shall call upon
Me, but I will not answer* (Proverbs 1:28). It was now too late to pray for
God to spare Jerusalem from destruction. However, Ezekiel records:
Certain of the elders of Israel came to inquire (ask for guidance) *of the
LORD, and sat before me* (Ezekiel 20:1). Then God gave Ezekiel the following message: *I will not be inquired of by you . . . . I chose Israel. . . . But
they rebelled against Me. . . . they despised My judgments . . . for their
heart went after their idols* (20:3,5,8,16). Following this, Ezekiel received
a terrifying message from the Lord for Israel: *I am against you, and will
draw forth My sword. . . . to give it into the hand of the slayer* (21:3,11).

Ezekiel's prophecy of the sharpened sword was a message of impending destruction. King Zedekiah, the *profane wicked prince of Israel*
(21:25), and the people would soon be captured. Jerusalem and the
Temple would be destroyed by Nebuchadnezzar, who, no doubt, congratulated himself on his triumph in Judah. But, he was unknowingly
being used to fulfill God's judgment upon His rebellious people. This
is a reminder that *the lot is cast into the lap; but the whole disposing
thereof is of the LORD* (Proverbs 16:33).

No king has been anointed to sit on the throne of David in Israel
for the past 2500 years. As Ezekiel foretold: *Thus says the Lord GOD;
Remove the diadem* (turban), *and take off the crown. . . . I will overturn,
overturn, overturn, it: and it shall be no more, until He come Whose right
it is; and I will give it* (to) *Him* (Ezekiel 21:26-27). In the time of Jesus, an
Edomite named Herod was merely a puppet king appointed by Rome
to govern only the Jews of Judea. The promised land will continue to
exist without a king until the return of Jesus Christ as *King of kings, and
Lord of lords* (I Timothy 6:15).

Thought for Today: God is full of compassion toward all who hear His call, repent,
and turn to Him "today" – tomorrow could be too late.

Christ Revealed: As the One Who will gather His people from all nations and *will
purge out the false from the true* (Ezekiel 20:34-38). *When the Son of Man shall
come in His glory, and all the holy angels with Him, then shall He sit upon the
throne of His glory: And before Him shall be gathered all nations: and He shall
separate them one from another, as a shepherd divides his sheep from the goats.
. . . And these* (goats) *shall go away into everlasting punishment: but the righteous
into life eternal* (Matthew 25:31-46; also 3:12).

For definitions of unfamiliar words in today's Bible reading, see pages 468-480.

IN TODAY'S READING

Sins of Israel enumerated; parable of two sisters;
parable of the boiling pot; death of Ezekiel's wife

On the very day that God revealed to Ezekiel that his precious wife, *the desire* (delight) *of your eyes,* was to die, God also said: *Yet neither shall you mourn nor weep, neither shall your tears run down* (Ezekiel 24:16). Ezekiel was told by the Lord that, after his wife's death, he was to refrain from all the conventional signs of mourning for the dead. It was not that he was to be insensitive to the death of his wife. But, his own personal grief was to give way to the far greater heartbreak over the death of God's nation and the destruction of His Temple which took place the same day Ezekiel's wife died. *Thus says the Lord GOD; I will bring up a company upon them, and will give them to be removed and spoiled* (plundered). *And the company . . . shall slay their sons and their daughters. . . . and you shall bear the sins of your idols: and you shall know that I am the Lord GOD* (23:46-47,49).

News of Ezekiel's unusual reaction to his wife's death must have spread quickly, for the people asked: *Will you not tell us what these things are to us?* (24:19). Then came the tragic news from Ezekiel: *Thus says the Lord GOD; Behold, I will profane My Sanctuary, the excellency of your strength . . . and your sons and your daughters whom you have left shall fall by the sword. . . . when this comes, you shall know that I am the Lord GOD* (24:21-24).

Eventually, a messenger who had escaped the devastation of Jerusalem arrived in Babylon to report the city's destruction (33:21). The Israelites' acceptance of false gods and their indifference to the Word of God had brought about the destruction of Jerusalem and the death of their own sons and daughters, just as they had been forewarned by Jeremiah in Jerusalem and by Ezekiel in Babylonia (Galatians 6:7-8).

Often we see people grieving over material losses, but showing little concern for their own or their children's eternal welfare. Jesus said that His disciples should not be preoccupied with earthly things, not even our daily needs: *For all these things do the nations of the world seek after: and your Father knows that you have need of these things. But rather seek first the Kingdom of God and His righteousness; and all these* (material and otherwise) *things shall be added to you* (Luke 12:30-31).

Thought for Today: Allow Christ to truly be Lord of your life.

Christ Revealed: In the denunciation of Israel's false prophets (Ezekiel 22:25-28). Compare them with those Christ spoke against the scribes and Pharisees. *Woe to you, scribes and Pharisees* (Matt. 23:13-36).

For definitions of unfamiliar words in today's Bible reading, see pages 468-480.

IN TODAY'S READING
Gentile nations judged; judgment on Tyre's king and the fate of
Satan who inspired him; future regathering of Israel

*T*yre was situated on the Mediterranean Sea and was one of the rich-
est cities of the world. Its wealth was not gained from war, like that of
Babylon, but from commercial business. Its fleet of ships was the greatest
of all nations. Ezekiel prophesied: *The Word of the LORD came to me . . . I
am against you, O Tyrus* (Ezekiel 26:1,3). God foretold that Tyre would
be fully destroyed, not only because of its immoral idolatry, but also
because it was rejoicing over the downfall of Jerusalem and that its
competition no longer existed. It was saying: *Aha, she is broken . . . I
shall be replenished* (grow rich), *now* (that) *she is laid waste* (26:2).

Only God, Who rules over every detail on earth, would be able to
say: *They shall destroy the walls of Tyrus, and break down her towers: I will
also scrape her dust from her, and make her like the top of a rock. It shall be a
place for the spreading of nets in the midst of the sea: for I have spoken. . . .
you shall be built no more* (26:4-5,14). Nebuchadnezzar destroyed the
mainland city. During that long siege, the city's administration and wealth
was moved to the offshore island section of the city. But, more than two
centuries later, Alexander the Great besieged Tyre, which was then just
an island city nearly half a mile from the mainland. Since Alexander had
no fleet, his men used the stones from the walls of the ancient mainland
city to build a causeway to reach the island and destroy it exactly as
prophesied: *You shall be no more* (26:20-21).

The attitude of Tyre should be a warning to those who rejoice when
their competition goes bankrupt, or to the "Christian" who resents the
success of his "rivals" in the church or in the marketplace. Christians
have much to repent of here. Our gossip does more damage than we
can imagine when we rejoice over the so-called "failures" of others. Of
course, with God, there is **no failure**. *Now the works of the flesh . . . are
these; Adultery, fornication, uncleanness, lasciviousness* (sensuality), *Idolatry, witchcraft, hatred, variance* (discord), *emulations* (jealousy), *wrath,
strife, seditions* (dissensions), *heresies, Envyings, murders, drunkenness,
revellings, and such like: of the which I tell you before, as I have also told
you in time past, that they which do such things shall not inherit the Kingdom of God* (Galatians 5:19-21).

Thought for Today: When tempted, determine in your heart to remain faithful to God.

Christ Revealed: As the One Who will rule over the destruction of Satan at the end of
time: *I will bring forth a fire . . . it shall devour you* (Ezekiel 28:18-19). As Jesus
reigns following the Great White Throne Judgment, *the devil* (Satan) *. . . was cast
into the lake of fire* (Revelation: 20:1-10,14).

For definitions of unfamiliar words in today's Bible reading, see pages 468-480.

In Today's Reading

Egypt's defeat by Babylon foretold; Assyria's fall as a warning
to Egypt; lamentation (great sorrow) over Egypt's fall

*A*bout a year after the Babylonians had surrounded Jerusalem in
their plan to starve them into submission, Ezekiel foretold the end of
Egypt as a great nation. God said to him: *Son of man, set your face against
Pharaoh king of Egypt, and prophesy against him, and against all Egypt.
. . . because they have been a staff of reed* (worthless support) *to the house
of Israel. . . . Behold, I will bring a sword upon you, and cut off man and
beast out of you. And the land of Egypt shall be desolate and waste. . . .
neither shall it be inhabited forty years* (Ezekiel 29:2-11).

Although Egypt would no longer be a great power of the world, it
would not be utterly destroyed as Babylon would be. Ezekiel foretold:
*At the end of forty years I will gather the Egyptians. . . . into the land of
their habitation* (origin); *and they shall be there a base* (lowly) *kingdom.
. . . neither shall it exalt itself any more above the nations: for I will diminish them, that they shall no more rule over the nations* (29:13-15). Egypt
has remained an unimportant nation over the centuries. It stands as a
witness to the supreme authority of God.

At the time of the Exodus, the ten plagues forced the Egyptians to
acknowledge that their own gods were powerless against the One True
God. This should have caused Egypt and particularly, Israel, to reject
their idols and worship the One True God of creation.

God brought judgment upon Israel, Judah, Tyre, Sidon, Egypt, and
other nations to cause them to realize *that I am the* LORD (29:9). This
phrase is mentioned 66 times in this book alone to point out the importance of obeying the Word of God.

A future time of redemption and restoration was also foretold: *In
that day will I cause the horn* (strength) *of the house of Israel to bud forth*
(29:21). The horn is a symbol of power (I Samuel 2:10; Psalm 92:10). As
prophesied, the people of God, both Jew and Gentile, have a future
destiny of glory with Jesus as their Messiah.

*God . . . has. . . . given Him a Name which is above every name: That at
the Name of Jesus every knee should bow, of things in heaven, and things
in earth . . . And that every tongue should confess that Jesus Christ is Lord,
to the glory of God the Father* (Philippians 2:9-11).

Thought for Today: Boasting robs the Lord of His glory. Praise Him for blessings.

Christ Revealed: By the *Word of the* LORD **(Ezekiel 29:1).** *In the beginning was
the Word* **(Jesus),** *and the Word was with God, and the Word was God* **(John
1:1). God . . .** *has in these last days spoken to us by His Son* **(Hebrews 1:1-2).**

For definitions of unfamiliar words in today's Bible reading, see pages 468-480.

𝒥N 𝒯ODAY'S 𝒭EADING

Jerusalem's destruction; justice of God's dealing; reproof of the
false shepherds; destruction of Edom; restoration of Israel foretold

𝒢od addressed Ezekiel as *a watchman to the house of Israel*; and said
to Him: *Therefore you shall hear the Word at My mouth, and warn them
for Me* (Ezekiel 33:7). The Israelites who remained in Jerusalem, as well
as the captives in Babylon, disregarded Ezekiel's warnings that God
would destroy Jerusalem if they refused to repent of their sinful ways.
But, the Jews in Babylon complained that the death of their kindred in
Jerusalem and the destruction of their homeland were inconsistent with
the promise of God's Covenant. Then the Lord said: *Your people say,
The way of the Lord is not equal* (right): *but. . . . When the righteous turns
from his righteousness, and commits iniquity* (sin), *he shall . . . die. . . . But
if the wicked turn from his wickedness . . . he shall live* (33:17-19).

When the inevitable judgment had taken place as foretold by
Ezekiel, the Lord told him to say: *You . . . lift up your eyes toward your
idols, and shed blood: and shall you possess the land? . . . you work abomination* (do detestable sins) *. . . As I live, surely they . . . shall fall by the
sword, and . . . die of the pestilence. For I will lay the land most desolate.
. . . they shall know that I am the LORD* (33:25-29). This was all fulfilled as
prophesied by Ezekiel on the day of his wife's death (24:18,25-26). *And it
came to pass in the twelfth year of our captivity . . . one that had escaped
out of Jerusalem came to me, saying, The city is smitten* (33:21).

Ezekiel proclaimed that holy living was the Israelites' responsibility in their Covenant relationship with God. This was rejected by those
unwilling to forsake their sins. Times have not changed; living a godly
life is equally unpopular today with many "professing Christians" who
love what the world can offer for the gratification of the earthly nature
(I John 2:15-17). Like the Israelites, many people today talk about the
love of God while ignoring His command to act righteously. *As you
have yielded your members* (body parts) *servants to uncleanness and to
iniquity unto iniquity* (sins leading to more sins); *even so now yield your
members servants to righteousness to holiness* (sanctification). *. . . for the
end of those things* (sin) *is death* (Romans 6:19,21).

Thought for Today: Sinful conduct cannot bring lasting satisfaction.

Christ Revealed: As the Shepherd (Ezekiel 34:23). Jesus said: *I am the Good Shepherd, and know My sheep* (John 10:14).

For definitions of unfamiliar words in today's Bible reading, see pages 468-480.

In Today's Reading
Valley of the dry bones; prophecy against Gog;
vision of a restored Israel

After Nebuchadnezzar destroyed Jerusalem in 586 BC, most of the Israelites who survived were scattered throughout Babylonia among exiles from many heathen nations. Since the Temple and City of God were destroyed, they abandoned hope for the restoration of their homeland.

It was at this time of national hopelessness that Ezekiel was given a new vision and recorded: *The hand of the LORD was upon me, and carried me out in the Spirit of the LORD, and set me down in the midst of the valley which was full of bones* (Ezekiel 37:1). The bones were dry and bleached, having been there for some time. *And He said to me, Son of man, can these bones live? And I answered, O Lord GOD, You know. Again He said to me, Prophesy upon these bones, and say to them: O you dry bones, hear the Word of the LORD. Thus says the Lord GOD to these bones; Behold, I will cause breath to enter into you, and you shall live* (37:3-5).

As a nation, Israel was literally and spiritually dead and without hope of restoration. However, like the dry bones, it was not buried. Ezekiel continued to prophesy and *there was a noise, and behold a shaking, and the bones came together, bone to his bone* (37:7). Ezekiel proclaimed the Word of God, *and the breath came into them, and they lived, and stood up upon their feet, an exceeding great army* (37:10). Although the Israelites were saying: *Our hope is lost: we are cut off* from the land of promise (37:11), this army assured Israel of future restoration.

Ezekiel then was commanded to proclaim the good news: *I am the LORD . . . And shall put My Spirit in you, and you shall live, and I shall place you in your own land* (37:13-14). After more than 2500 years, the Israelites do exist as a nation within the promised land and God will soon fulfill His promise to King David. Israel's Messiah King, Jesus Christ, will rule the world from Jerusalem (Isaiah 2:1-4).

Dry bones also describe our sinful human nature, apart from the transforming, life-giving power of the Holy Spirit. Eternal life is made possible when we confess and repent of our sins and invite Jesus to be Lord of our lives. *For by grace are you saved through faith; and that not of yourselves: it is the gift of God: Not of works, lest any man should boast* (Ephesians 2:8-9).

Thought for Today: Jesus is coming soon! What a great and glorious day that will be!

Christ Revealed: As the One Who made possible the resurrection from the grave (Ezekiel 37:12). *For the Lord Himself shall descend from heaven with a shout . . . and the dead in Christ shall rise first* (I Thessalonians 4:13-18; also John 11:25; Revelation 1:18).

For definitions of unfamiliar words in today's Bible reading, see pages 468-480.

$\mathscr{I}$N $\mathscr{T}$ODAY'S $\mathscr{R}$EADING
Vision of the future Temple

$\mathscr{A}$few years after the vision of dry bones, Ezekiel received another vision. *In the five and twentieth year of our captivity . . . in the fourteenth year after that the city was smitten, in the self-same day the hand of the LORD was upon me. . . . In the visions of God He brought me into the land of Israel, and set me upon a very high mountain* (Ezekiel 40:1-2). This new vision looked far into the future, where Ezekiel beheld a glorious Temple, far more magnificent than the Temple built by Solomon.

The measurements of the grounds and the many details concerning the building and its unusual architectural design are recorded; but no instruction was given to Ezekiel regarding who would build it or when it would be built. In striking contrast, God gave Moses detailed instructions for building the Tabernacle and even the names of the craftsmen who were to build it in the wilderness (Exodus 25:9; 31:1-11). But Zechariah foretold: *Thus speaks the LORD of hosts: Behold the man Whose Name is The BRANCH* (Jesus Christ) *. . . He shall grow up out of His place, and He shall build the Temple of the LORD: Even He shall build the Temple of the LORD; and He shall bear the glory, and shall sit and rule upon His throne; and He shall be a priest upon His throne: and the counsel of peace shall be between them both* (Zechariah 6:12-13).

Almost 2000 years have passed since the Romans destroyed the Temple, with no recovery of the Brazen Altar, Laver of Brass, Pure Gold Candlestick, Table of Showbread, or Altar of Incense. The Ark of the Covenant, representing the Presence of God, disappeared in 586 BC, when Nebuchadnezzar destroyed Jerusalem.

The altar and the priests offering sacrifices for the sins of the people had all foreshadowed Jesus Christ, His atonement for our sins, and our relationship with Him through His sacrifice on the cross. Through the Romans, God removed the opportunity for the Jews to offer further sacrifices. These laws were *imposed on them until the time of reformation. But Christ being come a High Priest . . . by a greater and more perfect Tabernacle . . . by His own blood He entered in once into the Holy Place, having obtained eternal redemption for us* (Hebrews 9:10-12; compare John 4:21-24; Galatians 3:23-25; Colossians 2:17).

Thought for Today: We always seek first after what our hearts treasure most – whether it is the Lord or the things of the world – it can't be both.

Christ Revealed: Through the Temple (Ezekiel ch. 40). Christ indwells His people who have become temples of God (I Corinthians 6:19-20; II Corinthians 6:16-17).

For definitions of unfamiliar words in today's Bible reading, see pages 468-480.

IN TODAY'S READING

Vision of God's glory filling the Temple; ordinances for the priests; land for the sanctuary and the city described

In a vision, Ezekiel had witnessed the departure of *the glory of the God of Israel* sfrom the magnificent, but now destroyed, Temple built by Solomon (Ezekiel 9:3; 10:4,18-19; 11:22-23). Jerusalem and the once glorious kingdom of Israel were only memories. The Israelites had chosen to ignore God's Word and were actually worshiping idols, the sun, and all sorts of creatures in the Temple that had been dedicated to God alone (8:5-17).

Consequently the Israelites were enslaved in a heathen land. Again Ezekiel received a vision of a future Temple, far greater than Solomon's, where the glory of the Lord would return to dwell. Ezekiel was *brought . . . to the gate . . . that looks toward the east: And, behold, the glory of the God of Israel came from the way of the east: and His voice was like a noise of many waters: and the earth shined with His glory. . . . And the glory of the LORD came into the House by the way of the gate whose prospect* (face) *is toward the east. So the Spirit took me up, and brought me into the inner court; and, behold, the glory of the LORD filled the House* (43:1-2,4-5).

In this vision, the Lord of Glory entered His new Temple by the very way through which He had departed from the old Temple (compare 10:19 and 11:22-23). The Eastern Gate led straight to the Temple entrance of the eternal King, Who said: *I will dwell in the midst of the children of Israel for ever, and My Holy Name, shall the house of Israel no more defile* (43:7). The emphasis of this vision is the importance of holiness in the lives of the people of God.

The physical Temple had foreshadowed the life and ministry of Christ. In the millennium there will be no need for types or symbols because God the Father and Jesus Christ, Whom the symbols represented, will be present. Our concern should not be how and when the prophecies will be fulfilled; but above all else we should be concerned that our body, mind, and spirit be prepared for the Lord's return. *Know you not that you are the temple of God, and that the Spirit of God dwells in you? If any man defile the temple of God, him shall God destroy; for the temple of God is holy, which temple you are* (I Corinthians 3:16-17).

Thought for Today: Determine that today others will see Christ in you.

Christ Revealed: As the *glory of the Lord* (Ezekiel 43:4). Jesus is *the brightness of His* (God's) *glory, and the express image of His Person* (Hebrews 1:3).

For definitions of unfamiliar words in today's Bible reading, see pages 468-480.

$\mathcal{I}$N $\mathcal{T}$ODAY'S $\mathcal{R}$EADING

Worship of the prince; river flowing from the Temple;
boundaries and divisions of the land; gates of Jerusalem

$\mathcal{T}$he first part of Ezekiel's final vision from God described the *Temple* (Ezekiel 40 – 43); the second part described the worship and the character of the worshipers (44 – 46). The final part tells us of life-giving waters that *issued out from under the threshold* (doorway) *of the house eastward* (47 – 48) and of the boundaries and divisions of the land. The further this water flowed, the deeper it became. Among other things, it symbolizes our continued walk with the Lord for, as we experience more and more the all-sufficiency of His provision, we come to realize that His supply for all of our needs is abundant and unlimited.

The description of the land and the city are very different from either ancient or present-day, geographical Israel. This is a vision anticipating the glorious future that all believers in Jesus as the Messiah will experience. All who know and love Him as their Savior will enjoy the new promised land during the millennial reign of our Lord Jesus Christ.

Ezekiel was led by his guide to the front of the Temple. The water apparently emerged from under the Eastern Gate as a small stream that flowed *a thousand cubits,* a little less than one-third of a mile (47:2-3). Ezekiel then records: *The man . . . brought me through the waters.* Ezekiel states that it was ankle-deep. The same process was repeated at a second and at a third distance, each measuring *a thousand cubits.* At these locations, the water was found to be *to the knees* and then *to the loins* (47:4). At a fourth distance of *a thousand* cubits (47:5), the water had become *a river that could not be passed over* because of its depth.

Water provides life for the trees which bear wholesome fruit (47:9,12). This is what the Holy Spirit does in the lives of those who yield to Him. We begin to experience His gracious supply as a small stream which flows out from Christ the Fountainhead, and it continues to increase in preciousness as we daily walk in the light of His Word.

Our loving Father has provided His people with *a pure river of water of life, clear as crystal, proceeding* (flowing) *out of the throne of God and of the Lamb,* the Lord Jesus Christ. . . . *And whosoever will, let him take the water of life freely* (Revelation 22:1-17).

Thought for Today: The living water is available to all who *thirst for righteousness* (Matthew 5:6).

Christ Revealed: Through the river of living waters and in *the name of the city,* one of the names of God, *Jehovah (Yahweh)-Shammah* meaning: *The LORD is there* (Ezekiel 47:1-12; 48:35; also Revelation 21 -- 22).

For definitions of unfamiliar words in today's Bible reading, see pages 468-480.

Introduction To The Book Of
Daniel

The first chapter of Daniel is written in Hebrew, but chapters 2 – 7 are in Aramaic, the common language of the Israelites during their stay in Babylon as we as the common language spoken when Jesus was on earth. Chapters 1 – 7 describe Daniel and some of his fellow exiles who remained faithful to God despite life-threatening pressures. These *children of Israel, and of the king's seed* (royal family), *and of the princes* were among the first captives taken to Babylon (Daniel 1:1-17).

In chapters 8 – 12, Daniel **writes in Hebrew** concerning future events. Daniel's ministry covered the entire period of Judah's Babylonian captivity. He served as an official in the courts of both the Chaldean and Medo-Persian dynasties. He wrote during a time when the Jews were suffering great sorrow over the loss of life and of all their possessions in Jerusalem. The Book of Daniel gave comfort to the exiles and assurance of Israel's eventual triumph over its enemies. His writings were probably the basis for the wise men who hundreds of years later entered Jerusalem, saying: *Where is He that is born King of the Jews? for we have seen His star in the east, and are come to worship Him* (Matthew 2:2).

Only Daniel, through his God-given ability, could interpret the meaning of the giant image in Nebuchadnezzar's dream in chapter 2. This was the way that God used to move him into a position of administrative prominence. Nebuchadnezzar's dream image in chapter 2 and the first of Daniel's visions in chapter 7 both give similar outlines of the empires of Babylon, Medo-Persia, Greece, and Rome. These are the nations that would successively rule the world from the time of Nebuchadnezzar *until the times of the Gentiles be fulfilled* (Luke 21:24). Near the end of this present age, the Antichrist will make *war with the saints* (Daniel 7:21), the faithful followers of the One True God. Then Jesus Christ will return and establish His Kingdom, *which shall never be destroyed* (2:44). The Stone cut without hands, which ultimately *became a great mountain, and filled the whole earth* (2:34-35), refers to Jesus.

This book reveals the sovereign control of God over all individuals, as well as world governments. Soon His Kingdom will fill *the whole earth.* Although it is far easier to get excited over details of future events, obedience is clearly the central theme and of primary importance in this great book. Jesus quoted Daniel when He spoke of the *abomination of desolation* (Matthew 24:15; Mark 13:14; compare Daniel 9:27; 11:31; 12:11) and of the *great tribulation* (Matthew 24:21; compare Daniel 12:1).

TWO VIEWS OF GOVERNMENTS THAT RULE DURING "THE TIMES OF THE GENTILES"

A stone was cut out without hands, which smote (struck) the image upon its feet ... and broke them ... in pieces [2:34,44-45]

NEBUCHADNEZZAR'S DREAM [DANIEL 2:31-45]
DANIEL'S VISIONS [DANIEL 7:1-9]

THE WORLD'S POINT OF VIEW

A dazzling giant to be admired and achieved at any price: *The lust of the flesh, and the lust of the eyes, and the pride of life* (one's lifestyle) [I John 2:15-17].

FROM GOD'S POINT OF VIEW

The world system is full of pride, selfishness, greed, and cruelty, but is only temporary: *The world passes away, and the lust thereof: but he that does the will of God abides forever* [I John 2:15-17].

BABYLON is represented by *this image's head ... of fine gold* [7:4; see also 2:31-32,37-38; 7:17]. The head of gold in Nebuchadnezzar's dream was seen in Daniel's vision as a lion with eagle's wings. Both the head of gold and the lion represent Nebuchadnezzar, the king who conquered Israel, which represents the earthly Kingdom of God.

MEDO-PERSIA is represented in Nebuchadnezzar's dream by *its breast and its arms of silver* [7:5; also 2:32,39; 7:17; 8:3-8; 11:1-2]. But, in Daniel's vision, they were seen as a bear with three ribs in its mouth. The bear was Medo-Persia.

GREECE is represented in Nebuchadnezzar's dream by *its belly and thighs of brass* [7:6; also 2:32,39; 7:17; 8:5-8,21-22; 11:3-20]. In Daniel's vision, the stomach and thighs of brass were seen instead as a leopard with four wings of a bird on its back. Like a leopard, Greece was swift in conquering the known world under the youthful Alexander the Great. In Daniel's second vision, he saw a ram and a he-goat [8:5-8]. The one-horned goat [Greece] trampled the ram [Medo-Persia] to pieces. After his death, Alexander's kingdom was divided among his four generals, represented by the four heads of the leopard.

ROME is represented by *its legs of iron* [7:7:8; also 2:33,40-44; 7:23-24], which Daniel interpreted from Nebuchadnezzar's dream [2:33,40-43]. They were the two great divisions of Rome. They are seen in Daniel's vision as a dreadful beast with iron teeth, ten big horns and one little horn. After defeating Greece, Rome [the beast] was the fourth great empire to rule the world.

REVIVED FROM ROME [The New World Order] [10 toes – *part of iron and part of clay*] [7:7:8; also 2:33,40-44; 7:7-8,23-24] – This confederacy will consist of 10 kings. In his intent to destroy Christianity and rule the world, one day soon the antichrist [the little horn of 7:24] will defeat three of the ten kingdoms of this confederation. Ultimately, the New World Order, under the antichrist, will be destroyed by Jesus Christ [the Stone of 2:45] who will then set up His 1000 year earthly kingdom for Israel and all of His true followers.

313

𝒥ɴ 𝒯ODAY'S 𝓡EADING

Daniel rejects king's food; Nebuchadnezzar's dream interpreted by
Daniel; Shadrach, Meshach, and Abednego saved out of fiery furnace

𝒮oon after their capture, Daniel and other selected Israelite captives were assigned new names which would identify them as citizens
of Babylon. This was an attempt to remove their identities as children
of God. The king's intent was that these select men be taught to think
and live like Babylonians. Daniel means "God is Judge," but his
Babylonian name Belteshazzar means "Prince of Baal." As Daniel heard
his new name called day after day, it was intended to remind him that
the comfort, self-esteem, and high position he enjoyed in his new society were all the result of his being the "Prince of Baal."

*Nebuchadnezzar dreamed dreams, wherewith his spirit was troubled.
. . . The king commanded to call . . . the Chaldeans, for to show the king his
dreams. . . . The Chaldeans answered before the king, and said, There is not
a man upon the earth that can show the king's matter* (Daniel 2:1-2,10).
But, after Daniel and his friends prayed, the secret was revealed to
Daniel in a night vision and he proclaimed to the king that *there is a God
in heaven that reveals secrets, and makes known to the King Nebuchadnezzar
what shall be in the latter days* (2:18-19,28).

Daniel revealed to Nebuchadnezzar that the giant image in his
dream represented successive kingdoms that would rule the world. The
head was of fine gold and represented Nebuchadnezzar. *Its breast and
its arms of silver* symbolized the Medo-Persian Empire, which would
become the next dominating world power. The Grecian Empire, represented by *its belly and its thighs of brass* came next. The fourth empire, with *its legs of iron, its feet part of iron and part of clay* (2:32-33),
depicted the Roman Empire. The Roman Empire will be revived as a
one-world government in the end times. But it will be destroyed at the
return of Christ, Whose kingdom *shall never be destroyed* (2:44). The
exact details may not be clear, but it is vitally important to be prepared
for the soon coming of our King. *For now we see through a glass, darkly;
but then face to face: now I know in part; but then shall I know even as
also I am known* (I Corinthians 13:12; compare Acts 1:7).

Thought for today: Jesus holds today and all your tomorrows.

Christ Revealed: As *the Stone that smote the image* (Daniel 2:35). *The Stone* **is Jesus
Christ (Acts 4:11; Ephesians 2:20; I Peter 2:4-8).**

For definitions of unfamiliar words in today's Bible reading, see pages 468-480.

𝒥N 𝒯ODAY'S 𝓡EADING
Nebuchadnezzar's second dream and Daniel's interpretation;
Belshazzar's feast; Daniel in the lions' den

𝓑elshazzar ruled Babylon near the end of the 70-year-long Jewish exile. On the night that the Medo-Persian army invaded Babylon to defeat and execute Belshazzar, he was celebrating a great feast with *a thousand of his lords. . . . they brought the golden vessels that were taken out of the Temple . . . in Jerusalem: and . . . drank in them. . . . and praised the gods of gold, and of silver* (Daniel 5:1-4).

Suddenly the *fingers of a man's hand* (5:5) appeared and wrote on the wall. Belshazzar panicked *and his knees smote* (struck) *one against another* (5:6). His astrologers and soothsayers could not interpret the message. In desperation, Belshazzar summoned Daniel who boldly proclaimed: *This is the interpretation . . . God has numbered your kingdom, and finished it* (5:26). That night *Darius . . . took the kingdom* (5:31).

Darius decided *to set over the kingdom a hundred and twenty princes. . . over the whole kingdom; And over these, three presidents; of whom Daniel was first.* Because of envy, the other presidents and princes said to the king: *All . . . have consulted together to establish a royal statute . . . that whosoever shall ask a petition of any god or man for thirty days, save of you , O king, he shall be cast into the den of lions* (6:1-2,7-8). Without realizing its real purpose, the king signed the decree.

Now when Daniel knew that the writing was signed, he went into his house; and his windows being open in his chamber (room) *toward Jerusalem, he kneeled upon his knees three times a day, and prayed, and gave thanks before his God, as he did beforetime* (6:10). Daniel could have reasoned that, since he was not asked to worship an idol, why not cooperate *for thirty days* or just pray in secret? We need to ask ourselves: "If a similar decree were issued today, would it make a difference if we were told by government officials that we could not worship in church on the Lord's Day?" Yes, Daniel ended up in the den of lions but, afterwards he was able to testify to the king: *My God has sent His angel, and has shut the lions' mouths* (Daniel 6:22).

Thought for Today: Pride blinds the mind to the will of God.

Christ Portrayed: By Daniel – a stone was rolled across the mouth of the den of lions and set with the king's seal (Daniel 6:16-17). There was a stone rolled across the mouth of the cave where Jesus was buried and it too was set with an official seal (Matthew 27:63-66). As Daniel came forth unscathed, so Jesus came forth from the dead proclaiming the saving power of God (Revelation 1:18).

For definitions of unfamiliar words in today's Bible reading, see pages 468-480.

In Today's Reading

Daniel's vision of the beasts; vision of the ram and goat;
Daniel's prayer for his people; vision of 70 weeks

After the awesome grandeur of Nebuchadnezzar's dream of world governments is described (Daniel 2:19-45), the Lord reveals through Daniel, another dream that exposes man's selfish ambition and use of cruel, savage power. All these governments controlled the world at different times. Daniel said: *I saw in my vision . . . and, behold, the four winds of the heaven strove upon the great sea* (Daniel 7:2).*The great sea* is fallen humanity with its fierce competition and godless instability. The *four winds* illustrate the impact of selfish ambition and greed.

Four great beasts came up from the sea, diverse (different) *one from another* (7:3). The beasts correspond to the kingdoms of Babylon, Medo-Persia, Greece, and Rome. *The first beast* (Babylon) *was like a lion, and had eagle's wings* (7:4). As the head of the great image of Nebuchadnezzar's dream was gold, so the lion represented the king among animals. *And behold another beast* (Medo-Persia), *like a bear* (7:5), represented the empire which would later conquer Babylon.

The third beast, *like a leopard, which had upon the back of it four wings of a fowl,* represented the Grecian Empire. The *four wings* illustrate the speed with which Alexander the Great conquered the ancient world.

The *fourth beast was diverse from all the beasts that were before it; and it had ten horns* (the ten nations of the revived Roman Empire). This final beast was *dreadful and terrible* (terrifying), *and strong exceedingly; and it had great iron teeth: it devoured and broke in pieces, and stamped the residue* (ruthless expansion) *with the feet of it* (7:7).

The *ten horns* (7:24) correspond to the ten toes *on the feet* of Nebuchadnezzar's *great image* and represent a confederation of ten future world rulers, followed by *another little horn* (king) (7:8). This *little horn* represents the Antichrist who *shall speak against the Most High, and shall wear out* (oppress) *the saints* (believers) (7:25) who will be destroyed by "the Stone" (2:35, 44-45), Christ, Who *shall come to be glorified in His saints* (Christians), *and to be admired in all them that believe* (II Thessalonians 1:10).What a glorious time that will be!

Thought for Today: Living for Jesus provides satisfaction beyond compare.

Christ Revealed: As the *Son of Man* (Daniel 7:13-14). The truth of this vision was confirmed by our Lord as He spoke of His promised return. *They shall see the Son of Man coming in the clouds of heaven with power and great glory* (Matthew 24:30).

For definitions of unfamiliar words in today's Bible reading, see pages 468-480.

$\mathcal{I}$N $\mathcal{T}$ODAY'S $\mathcal{R}$EADING

Heavenly messenger detained; prophecy of kingdoms
from time of Daniel to the Antichrist; great tribulation

$\mathcal{T}$he kingdoms of this world eventually erupt into open hostility toward God and His people. Daniel foretold that during the period of the
revived Roman Empire terrible persecution would take place.

The Antichrist *shall exalt himself, and magnify himself above every
god, and shall speak marvellous things* (blasphemies) *against the God of
gods, and shall prosper till the indignation* (wrath) *be accomplished* (Daniel
11:36). Jesus speaks of an *abomination of desolation, spoken of by Daniel
the prophet* (Mark 13:14).

There have been *many antichrists* over the past 2000 years, as the
Apostle John foretold (I John 2:18); and the driving force of all antichrists
is to destroy the Kingdom of God. *There shall be a time of trouble, such
as never was since there was a nation . . . and at that time your people shall
be delivered, every one that shall be found written in the book* (Daniel 12:1).

But Daniel also said: *I heard, but I understood not: then said I, O my
Lord, what shall be the end of these things? And He said, Go your way,
Daniel: for the words are closed up and sealed* (kept secret) *till the time of
the end* (12:8-9). Daniel admitted that there was much in his prophecy
that he did not understand, yet it was intended that he share what was
revealed to him with all whose faith is in the eventual glorious outcome.

Daniel's prophecy reminds us to be prepared for the soon return of
Christ, when He shall reign and rule over all the world. *Let no man
deceive you by any means: for that day shall not come, except there come a
falling away first, and that man of sin be revealed* (II Thessalonians 2:3).
The time will come when it seems that the wicked one has triumphed,
*Even him, whose coming is after the working of Satan with all power and
signs and lying wonders* (2:9). *Then shall that wicked one* (Satan) *be revealed, whom the Lord shall consume* (slay) *with the spirit of His mouth,
and shall destroy with the brightness of His coming. . . . Now our Lord
Jesus Christ Himself . . . Comfort your hearts, and establish you in
every good word and work* (II Thessalonians 2:8,16-17).

Thought for Today: There is no need to fear since our Creator loves us.

Christ Revealed: As the One *Who lives for ever* (Daniel 12:7). As One of the Three
expressed Persons of the Trinity, Jesus Christ always has been and always will be.
Jesus said to them, Verily, verily (truly, truly), *I say to you, Before Abraham was, I
am* (John 8:58). *I am Alpha and Omega* (Christ), *the Beginning and the Ending, says
the Lord, Who is, and Who was, and Who is to come, the Almighty* (Revelation 1:8,
also 4:8).

For definitions of unfamiliar words in today's Bible reading, see pages 468-480.

Introduction To The Book Of
Hosea

Hosea lived in the northern kingdom of Israel and prophesied for about 50 years during the reigns of *Uzziah, Jotham, Ahaz, and Hezekiah, kings of Judah, and . . . Jeroboam the son of Joash, king of Israel* (Hosea 1:1).

It appears that, during Hosea's ministry, the northern kingdom was experiencing material prosperity and an expansion of its territory. This was primarily due to the decline of Syria and Moab, which resulted in the northern kingdom gaining control of the major east-west trade routes in the region. In the meantime, the golden calf worship centers, erected many years earlier in the cities of Bethel and Dan, had prepared the way for the immoral worship of Baal and Ashtoreth, resulting in Israel's further spiritual corruption and decline (I Kings 12:28-32; also Hosea 2:13; 10:5-6; 13:2).

Hosea endured deep humiliation because of his unfaithful wife Gomer. Her **harlotry illustrated how Israel had broken her covenant relationship with God,** just as an adulterous wife who chooses other lovers is unfaithful to her mate in the marriage covenant (Hosea 2:7-13). Hosea's forgiving love toward his unfaithful wife and the restoration of their marriage was an example to Israel of how God, in His mercy, would restore His blessings upon the nation, if only they would return to Him and be faithful (2:8,15-16; 10:12; 11:8-9; 12:6; 14:1,4).

Some who call themselves "Christians" are like Israel, guilty of spiritual hypocrisy (4:1-2), adultery (4:2,11; 7:4), false dealings (10:4; 12:7), idolatry (4:12-13; 8:5; 10:1,5; 13:2), and drunkenness (4:11; 7:5), as a result of ignoring the Word of God (4:4,10; 8:14). The history of Israel should serve as a warning that His righteous judgment will fall upon the unbelieving.

Does thy sacrifice seem useless
As you humbly serve the Lord?
Yes, to one who is most faithless
And ignores His Holy Word.

But to one who really knows Him
And His mighty Word of power
Nothing his sight of faith can dim
Even in the trying hour.

—M.E.H.

ℐN ℱODAY'S ℛEADING

Israel compared to an unfaithful wife;
judgment upon adulterous Israel;
Jehovah's (Yahweh's) withdrawal from His people; repentance urged

*J*eroboam II was king of the northern kingdom. The moral and spiritual level of the Israelites had become so low as to embrace *sodomites* (male cult prostitutes) . . . *and . . . all the abominations* (detestable practices) *of the nations which the LORD cast out* (of the promised land) (I Kings 14:24). Not one of the 19 kings of the northern kingdom of Israel attempted to lead the people to worship in Jerusalem as God had instructed. It was under these circumstances that *the Word of the LORD . . . came to Hosea. . . in the days of Jeroboam . . . king of Israel. . . . I will break the bow of Israel. . . . God said . . . I will no more have mercy upon the house of Israel* (Hosea 1:1-6).

The Lord spoke against His people through Hosea *because there is no truth, nor mercy, nor knowledge of God in the land. By swearing, and lying, and killing, and stealing, and committing adultery, they break out* (with no restraint) (4:1-2). **God revealed the consequences of Israel's sin, saying:** *Because you have rejected knowledge, I will also reject you, that you shall be no priest to Me: seeing you have forgotten the Law of your God, I will also forget your children* (4:6).

Israel's kings as well as its political and religious leadership ignored the importance of obedience to the Word of God. Jesus Christ set the example of how important the Old Testament should be to us. After 40 days of fasting, He was tempted of the devil, who said: *If You be* (Since You are) *the Son of God, command that these stones be made bread. But He answered and said, It is written, Man shall not live by bread alone* (physical necessities), *but by every Word that proceeds out of the mouth of God* (spiritual necessities) (Matthew 4:3-4; compare Deuteronomy 8:3). By quoting this Old Testament Scripture, our Lord revealed the "Key to Victory" over satanic deceptions. We can have that same victory over Satan when we allow *every Word that proceeds out of the mouth of God* to become a vital part of our daily lives (Matthew 4:4).

Thought for Today: Love for the Lord is expressed when we forgive others.

Christ Revealed: Through Hosea's love for his unworthy, sinful wife (Hosea 3:1-5). Our Lord Jesus not only loved us *while we were yet sinners,* but He also died the death of shame for us on Calvary so that all He possessed might become ours (Romans 5:8; 8:32; II Peter 1:3). *I will betroth you to Me for ever* (Hosea 2:19).

For definitions of unfamiliar words in today's Bible reading, see pages 468-480.

In Today's Reading
Israel's sin rebuked and captivity foretold;
Israel's immediate ruin but ultimate blessing

The northern kingdom of Israel did *not return to the LORD their God,
nor seek Him. . . . Ephraim also is like a silly dove without heart: they call
to Egypt; they go to Assyria* (Hosea 7:10-11) for national security rather
than trust the Lord according to His Word.

Israel's leaders had *gone up to Assyria. . . . Israel has forgotten his
Maker. . . . They have deeply corrupted themselves. . . . their glory shall fly
away like a bird. . . . they shall be wanderers among the nations* (8:9,14; 9:9,
11,17). The Lord gave a heartrending plea for Israel to return to Him
before they were destroyed: *It is time to seek the LORD* (10:12). Feel God's
heartbreak as He says: *I drew them with . . . bands of love* (11:4). He
lovingly pleaded: *O Israel, return to the LORD your God; for you have
fallen by your iniquity* (sin) (14:1).

Israel had foolishly put its trust in heathen nations and false gods
(5:13; 7:11; 8:9-10) and in its own ability to manipulate peace and security (12:8), rather than in the One Who is the only true source of security. Still, we see the willingness of the Lord to show mercy, as He always does to any repentant sinner, when He said: *I will heal their back-
sliding, I will love them freely* (14:4). The final words of the prophet Hosea
before the Israelites were conquered and carried away by the Assyrians
are a reminder to all of us: *The ways of the LORD are right, and the just
shall walk in them: but the transgressors shall fall therein* (14:9).

When we repent, turn from our sins, receive Jesus as our Savior, and
let the indwelling Holy Spirit control our lives, we are freed from the
power of Satan, sin, and spiritual death. *If we say that we have fellowship with Him, and walk in darkness, we lie, and do* (practice) *not the
truth. . . . these things write I to you, that you sin not. And if any man
sin, we have an Advocate* (Defender, Defense Attorney) *with the Father, Jesus Christ the righteous: And He is the propitiation* (appease-
ment, legal satisfaction) *for our sins: and not for ours only, but also for
the sins of the whole world* (I John 1:6; 2:1-2).

Thought for Today: Those who rejoice in the Lord can rejoice in tribulation.

Christ Revealed: In the son who was called *out of Egypt* (Hosea 11:1). This prophecy
is twofold: one is a historical reference pertaining to Israel (Ex. 4:22-23); and the other
is prophetic, looking to the sojourn of Christ as a child in Egypt (Matt. 2:14-15).

For definitions of unfamiliar words in today's Bible reading, see pages 468-480.

Introduction To The Book Of
JOEL

The future end-time *Day of the LORD* is mentioned five times (Joel 1:15; 2:1,11,31; 3:14) and Judah is mentioned six times (3:1,6,8,18-20). But, since the ten-tribed northern kingdom is not mentioned, we assume that it had already been destroyed by the Assyrians.

Joel prophesied a warning to Jerusalem of a coming national disaster, a result of the nation's departure from the Word of God. Joel likened this *Day of the LORD* to an invasion of locusts sweeping through the country, devouring the crops, stripping every leaf from the trees, and leading to a severe famine. Some believe this prophecy refers to real locusts. Others believe it illustrates invading armies. Probably it was both. But, the fact is, the kingdom of Judah faced destruction because it ignored the Word of God. Joel foretold of a *nation* (the Babylonians) . . . *strong, and without number. . . . He has laid My vine waste, and barked* (cut the bark from) *My fig tree: he has made it clean* (completely) *bare, and cast it away; the branches* (people) *thereof are made white* (like the dry bones of Ezekiel's vision) (1:6-7). The vine and the fig tree provided the most-valued edible produce of the land. They both illustrate Israel's relationship to God. The destruction of the trees, which demanded years of patient labor, was a national calamity, as productiveness was a token of peace and divine favor. The vine was the emblem of prosperity and peace (Psalm 80:8; Isaiah 5:1-5).

Joel prophesied invaders that were *a great people and a strong; there has not been ever the like, neither shall be any more after it, even to the years of many generations* (Joel 2:2). They would invade the land and leave *behind them a desolate wilderness; yea, and nothing shall escape them* (2:3). Because of the impending doom, the Lord appealed to the Israelites to repent and *turn . . . even to Me with all your heart* (2:12).

The prophet also foretold of a future *Day of the LORD* (2:11) when afterward God would pour out His *Spirit upon all flesh* (people) (2:28). We are now living in the *last days*, which began on the Day of Pentecost when *they were all filled with the Holy Spirit* (Acts 2:4,17). The Apostle Peter clearly declared: *This is that which was spoken by the prophet Joel* (2:16).

Joel's prophecy also foretells the time of the Lord's judgment, saying: *I will also gather all nations, and will bring them down into the valley of Jehoshaphat* (Joel 3:2). Many scholars believe that this *valley* is located on the eastern side of Jerusalem and is known as the Kidron (means gloomy) Valley, as well as the *valley of decision* (judgment) (3:14).

Soon, the nations that oppose the Kingdom of God will assemble for war; but it will be their day of judgment. *Then shall Jerusalem be holy* (set apart), *and there shall no strangers pass through her any more. . . . for the LORD dwells in Zion* (3:17,21).

ℐN ℐODAY'S ℛEADING
Plague of locusts; Joel's call to repentance; day of the Lord;
the Holy Spirit; restoration of Israel; judgment on nations

*J*oel warned of the impending destruction of Jerusalem. In mercy, *the Word of the LORD . . . came to Joel . . . . Blow . . . the trumpet in Zion, and sound an alarm in My holy mountain* (Joel 1:1; 2:1). The trumpet was often used to announce solemn days and feasts, and by watchmen to warn of approaching danger (Numbers 10:1-10). But, the sins of the Israelites were even more serious than the approaching enemies. Because of their sins, God could not bless them or protect them. *The Day of the LORD comes . . . a great people. . . . nothing shall escape them. . . . Therefore . . . turn . . . to Me with all your heart, and with fasting, and with weeping, and with mourning* (Joel 2:1-12).

The one condition for forgiveness and acceptance by the Lord is genuine repentance. True repentance is threefold. First, it is a sorrow for one's sin against God, as well as against others; second, it is a turning to the Lord, asking His forgiveness for all sins; and third, it is forsaking sin to live a life pleasing to Jesus Christ as Savior and Lord.

On the Day of Pentecost, the Apostle Peter preached the prophetic meaning of Joel's words, saying: *Whoever shall call on the Name of the Lord shall be saved* (Acts 2:21). He concluded his message by saying: *Repent, and be baptized every one of you in the Name of Jesus Christ for the remission of sins, and you shall receive the gift of the Holy Ghost* (Spirit). *For the promise is to you, and to your children, and to all that are afar off* (2:38-39). We are among those *that are afar off.*

The prophet Joel also foretold of the final *Day of the LORD* that is yet to take place: *Alas for the day! for the Day of the LORD is at hand, and as a destruction from the Almighty shall it come* (Joel 1:15). It will bring to a close the miserable rule of sinful mankind and finally usher in the glorious reign of Jesus Christ, the righteous King of Peace.

Jesus foretold there will come a time soon when *all the tribes of the earth . . . shall see the Son of Man coming in the clouds of heaven with power and great glory* (Matthew 24:30).

Thought for Today: The Holy Spirit works in our lives to the extent that we yield to His will as revealed in His Word.

Christ Revealed: As the One Who said: *I will pour out My Spirit upon all flesh* (people) (Joel 2:28) – fulfilled in part on the Day of Pentecost and still being fulfilled today (Acts 2:16-18).

For definitions of unfamiliar words in today's Bible reading, see pages 468-480.

Introduction To The Books Of
Amos & Obadiah

Amos was not a priest, nor was he trained in the prophetic schools; he was merely a shepherd and a caretaker of sycamore (fig) trees near the small mountain village of Tekoa. But, in obedience to the Word of God, he became a prophet (Amos 1:1; 7:14). Tekoa was located about 10 miles south of Jerusalem, in the area known as the wilderness of Judea, in the southern kingdom of Judah. However, God called Amos to preach in the northern kingdom of Israel (1:1; 3:9; 7:7-17). In obedience to this call, Amos traveled north about 22 miles to Bethel, the southern location of Israel's two golden calf worship centers. He then boldly denounced their religious idolatry and social evils (2:6-8; 3:9-10; 4:1-5).

If they continued to disregard God's Word, they were told the destruction of the kingdom would be inevitable: *Israel is fallen* (5:1-6). During this time, Uzziah was king of Judah, Jeroboam II was king of Israel, and the prophets Micah, Isaiah, Hosea, and Jonah were prominent. Both kingdoms were prospering materially and militarily (II Kings 14:23,25; II Chronicles 26:1-16), and nothing looked more unlikely to be fulfilled than the warnings of this simple country herdsman. (God works through the humble of the world.) The Israelites' prosperity and success only led to more immorality and injustice. But, according to the prophetic Word of God, about 30 years later, in 722 BC, the northern kingdom of Israel was invaded and destroyed by the Assyrians.

Obadiah is the shortest book in the Old Testament but it has a profound message. Its twofold subject is the punishment of God upon Edom and the ultimate establishment of the Kingdom of God on earth.

The territory of Edom extended south, below the Dead Sea, and along the Arabah (a desert plain). The land of Edom was also called Mount Seir because of the rugged range of mountains that dominated it, chief of which was Mount Seir. The mountains jutted upward about 3500 feet above the desert floor and more than 4500 feet above sea level. Edom's capital was the illustrious red-rock city of Sela, or Petra, which was situated securely in the midst of limestone mountain peaks. It was considered very secure because of the narrow passageway through the rocky mountain that led into Petra. Edom's fortified cities were located on an important caravan route between Egypt, in the south, and Syria, Assyria, and others, in the north.

The prophet foretold the destruction of the Edomites, who had followed their ancestor Esau's example of disregard for godly values and of intense hatred toward the Israelites. The Edomites had aided Nebuchadnezzar in destroying Jerusalem when they should have shown compassion and protected the Israelites, since both were descendants of Abraham and Isaac (Obadiah 1:10; Deuteronomy 23:7).

> ## In Today's Reading
> Judgments pronounced on Judah, Israel, and surrounding
> nations; Jehovah's (Yahweh's) sorrow over Israel's future captivity

Amos was only a farm laborer from the village of Tekoa in Judah, but he was willing to speak for God against sin even beyond the borders of the southern kingdom. He delivered his prophecy of impending judgment in Bethel, the site of one of Israel's two false worship centers and one of several residences of King Jeroboam II in the northern kingdom. This took place at a time when the northern kingdom was prospering financially and expanding its boundaries. Since the people of Israel were proud of their prosperity, it must have seemed ridiculous to hear this "outsider" shout: *Hear this word that the LORD has spoken against you, O children of Israel . . . I will punish you for all your iniquities* (sins). . . . *An adversary there shall be even round about the land; and he shall bring down your strength from you, and your palaces shall be spoiled* (plundered) (Amos 3:1-2,11). Because of their sins, destruction was inevitable; but, Amos' message concerning the coming judgment of God was completely ignored (2:6-8; 5:11-12).

Amaziah, the non-Levitical paid priest of King Jeroboam II, was quick to get word to the king about this disagreeable prophet from the southern kingdom. He interpreted the words of Amos to mean that Jeroboam would die by the sword; but the prophet had only stated what God had said: *I will rise against the house of Jeroboam with the sword. . . . Amaziah said to Amos . . . go, flee . . . into the land of Judah* (7:9-12). The prophecy *against the house of Jeroboam* was fulfilled when Zachariah, Jeroboam's son, was assassinated by Shallum after reigning only six months. Shallum took his place, but he only reigned for one month before he, in turn, was murdered by Menahem (II Kings 15:8-10,13-14).

God often uses ordinary people like Amos to proclaim His message. It is not what we possess in talents, nor how popular we may be, but how **obedient** we are that qualifies us to be used by the Lord.

For you see your calling, brethren, how that not many wise men after the flesh, not many mighty, not many noble, are called: But God has chosen the foolish things of the world . . . base things . . . which are despised . . . That no flesh should glory in His presence (I Corinthians 1:26-29).

Thought for Today: The Holy Spirit will provide His strength in anyone who willingly yields to Him.

Christ Revealed: As the Creator of the universe (Amos 5:8). *By His Son . . . He made the worlds* (Hebrews 1:2-3; also Revelation 4:11).

For definitions of unfamiliar words in today's Bible reading, see pages 468-480.

The Edomites had been hostile to the Israelites for centuries from the time Esau (Edom) forfeited his family birthright and was replaced by his brother Jacob (Israel). The prophet Obadiah foretold the eventual triumph of Israel, as well as the complete destruction of Edom: *For your violence against your brother Jacob shame shall cover you, and you shall be cut off for ever. . . . for the LORD has spoken it* (Obadiah 1:10,18).

Esau had moved to Mount Seir where the Edomites, his descendants, felt secure in their mountain fortress. Their self-sufficiency and disinterest in the will of God led them to ignore Obadiah's warning.

The Edomites conspired with Ammon and Moab against Judah and took Israelite captives. They also raided Judah in the days of King Ahaz to take even more captives to be their slaves (II Kings 8:20-22; II Chronicles 28:16-17). When Jerusalem was destroyed by the Babylonian army, some of the Jewish escapees tried to flee out of the land; but, the Edomites took advantage of the fleeing Israelites and blocked roads, robbed them, and delivered the refugees to the Babylonians (Obadiah 1:12-14). Because of their treachery, God foretold that Edom would be utterly destroyed (1:9-10,18).

About four years after the fall of Jerusalem, Nebuchadnezzar's army swept through Ammon, Moab, and Edom. Edomite refugees fled to the western area of their country south of Judea. They then made incursions northward into Judea, taking part of that land. This territory became known as Idumaea, from which later came Herod, the Roman-appointed puppet king who sought to kill the Child Jesus. Eventually, the Edomites disappeared from history, just as Obadiah had foretold. Unlike the prophecy against the Edomites, Obadiah foretold that Judah would recover and one day would again *possess their possessions* (1:15-17).

The absolute justice of God and our assurance of His faithfulness encourage us to know that the principles of right and wrong never change. Jesus expressed the inevitable spiritual law of God's Kingdom: *As you would that men should do to you, do also to them likewise* (Luke 6:31).

Thought for Today: Give God the credit for accomplishments, a safeguard against pride.

Christ Revealed: As the *Plumbline* (Amos 7:7-8). A plumb line is an instrument used in measuring an absolutely straight vertical line. Christ alone is qualified to walk in the midst of His people, measuring and exposing good and bad, true and false (Revelation 2 and 3).

For definitions of unfamiliar words in today's Bible reading, see pages 468-480.

Introduction To The Book Of
Jonah

Jonah was a prominent prophet in the northern kingdom of Israel during the prosperous but evil reign of King Jeroboam II. He foretold the great military success of Jeroboam over the Syrians (II Kings 14:25).

The Book of Jonah is the historical account of the prophet's mission to Nineveh, the capital of Assyria and Israel's great enemy. Because of this, Jonah at first failed to comply when God commanded him to prophesy of Nineveh's coming destruction as a result of their great wickedness. Undoubtedly Jonah was delighted that God would destroy them. But, after a series of horrifying events, he obeyed. Then he was unhappy when the king and the people of Nineveh repented and God, in His great mercy, withdrew His judgment from them. This book reveals *that God is no respecter of persons* (Acts 10:34). His compassion still extends toward all who will repent, turn from their sins, and worship Him.

The Book of Jonah reveals that God is concerned about Gentiles, just as He is about Jews – for both are eternally lost apart from having faith in Jesus Christ as their Savior, Who proclaimed: *I am the Way, the Truth, and the Life: no one comes to the Father, but by Me* (John 14:6).

Not what I do, Lord, nor what I say,
But what I am, Lord, matters today.
Busy with nothing we fill up the years,
Hurrying, worrying, gathering tears.

Why can't I learn, Lord, that power is within,
Why can't I see, Lord, the waste of my sin?
If I could be, Lord, growing in soul,
Seeing each day, Lord, more clearly the goal.

If I could live, Lord, discerning Thy face,
Ever more strongly held by Thy grace;
So take and mold, Lord, this heart of mine,
Till it shall be, Lord, like unto Thine!

—M.E.H.

$\mathcal{I}$N $\mathcal{T}$ODAY'S $\mathcal{R}$EADING

Jonah's effort to avoid God's will; His second commission;
Nineveh repents; Jonah's displeasure

$\mathcal{T}$he Lord commanded Jonah: *Arise, go to Nineveh, that great city, and cry* (preach) *against it; for their wickedness is come up before Me. But Jonah rose up to flee to Tarshish from the presence of the LORD* (Jonah 1:2-3). Jonah was probably delighted with the good news that the judgment of God would soon fall upon Nineveh. He could not believe that the mercy and love of God would extend even to Israel's enemies. So, he decided not to be a missionary to Nineveh. He must have felt fortunate when, on the very day he arrived in Joppa, he discovered a ship sailing to Tarshish, the most remote of the Phoenician trading places, and in the opposite direction from Nineveh.

For a while, events seemed to favor Jonah's "vacation plan" and gave him such peace of mind that he was soon *fast asleep* on the ship (1:5). However, favorable circumstances when avoiding the will of God are only temporary and they never lead to a pleasant end. The sailors became fearful when a great storm arose. Then, hearing that Jonah was fleeing from God, in an effort to appease Him, Jonah was thrown overboard, only to be swallowed by a big fish. After three days of soul searching, a repentant Jonah was vomited onto dry land by the great fish. He then became the greatest evangelist of his day, and saw the entire city of Nineveh repent of its wickedness. God could have chosen another prophet and let Jonah sink to the bottom of the sea, but God was merciful, demonstrating His love toward both the prophet and the repentant people in Nineveh. The willingness of God to forgive even the greatest of sinners who repent was made known when Nineveh's king and his people repented and were spared from the destruction prophesied by Jonah.

Jesus confirmed the historic truth concerning Jonah when He proclaimed: *As Jonah was three days and three nights in the whale's* (great fish's) *belly; so shall the Son of Man be three days and three nights in the heart of the earth. The men of Nineveh shall rise in judgment with this generation, and shall condemn it: because they repented at the preaching of Jonah; and, behold, a greater than Jonah is here* (Matthew 12:40-41).

Thought for Today: The one thing gained by ignoring God is trouble.

Christ Revealed: By Jonah's experience in the great fish (Jonah 1:7 – 2:10). Jesus used this historical event as an illustration to tell of His death, burial, and resurrection when the Pharisees demanded a sign from Him to prove Who He was (Matthew 12:39-41; also I Corinthians 15:4).

For definitions of unfamiliar words in today's Bible reading, see pages 468-480.

Micah was just a countryman who lived in a small village in Judea, about 20 miles southwest of Jerusalem near Gath (Micah 1:14). He prophesied during the reigns of kings Jotham, Ahaz, and Hezekiah of Judah, at the same time that Isaiah was a prominent prophet in Jerusalem. Micah exposed the sins of both the kingdoms of Judah and Israel, and boldly proclaimed the destruction of Israel (1:6-7), as well as of Jerusalem and the Temple (3:12). He also foretold Judah's restoration. Undoubtedly, Hezekiah found the prophecies of both Isaiah and Micah about the Israelites' promised restoration of great comfort (Isaiah 1:1; 62:1-12; Micah 1:1; 7:11-20). Micah also gave a remarkable prophecy, not only that the Messiah would be born in *Bethlehem*, but also concerning His eternal existence (5:2).

The Book of Micah closes with a message of hope, declaring the ultimate fulfillment of the covenant blessing God had promised to Abraham (7:20). Micah's prophecy confirms that without exception God requires obedience to His Word: *He has showed you, O man, what is good; and what does the LORD require of you, but to do justly, and to love mercy, and to walk humbly with your God?* (Micah 6:8).

> *"Tomorrow he promised his conscience,*
> *Tomorrow I mean to believe.*
> *Tomorrow I'll live as I ought to;*
> *Tomorrow my Savior receive.*
>
> *Tomorrow, tomorrow, tomorrow*
> *Thus day after day it went on.*
> *Tomorrow, tomorrow, tomorrow*
> *Till youth like a vision had gone.*
>
> *Till age in its passion had written*
> *The message of fate on his brow,*
> *And forth from the shadows of death*
> *Came that pitiful syllable, now."*
>
> —M.E.H.

GOD'S WORD IGNORED

My people are destroyed for lack of knowledge: because you have rejected knowledge, I will also reject you, that you shall be no priest to Me: seeing you have forgotten the Law of your God, I will also forget your children (Hosea 4:6).

Whoso despises the Word shall be destroyed: but he that fears (respects) *the Commandment shall be rewarded* (Proverbs 13:13).

ℐN ℐODAY'S ℛEADING

Impending judgment against Israel and Judah; future deliverance
of a remnant; birth of Christ foretold; Lord's judgment and mercy

ℰxcept for David, all the kings of Judah were born in Jerusalem –
the City of God. But, 700 years before Jesus was born, the prophet Micah
was led to prophesy: *You, Bethlehem Ephratah, though you be little among
the thousands of Judah, yet out of you shall He come forth to Me that is to
be ruler in Israel; Whose goings forth have been from of old, from everlasting* (eternity) (Micah 5:2).

At the God-appointed time, *there went out a decree from Caesar
Augustus, that all the world should be taxed. . . . Joseph also went up from
Galilee, out of the city of Nazareth, into Judaea, to the city of David, which
is called Bethlehem* (Luke 2:1,4). As a descendant of King David, Joseph
had to go to David's hometown of Bethlehem to register. In issuing his
command from Rome, Caesar could only have thought of his own kingdom. However, God used the heathen emperor's authority to fulfill
Micah's prophecy.

The most significant statement of Micah's prophecy is: *Whose goings forth have been from of old, from everlasting.* This proclaims the
deity and eternal existence of the Redeemer King Jesus. He could not
have been the Savior of mankind and suffer for the sins of the world if
He had a sinful nature like everyone else. Because of this, Jesus the Son
of God, was born of the virgin Mary without a human father.

Therefore, the angel Gabriel announced to Mary: *You shall conceive
in your womb, and bring forth a Son, and shall call His Name JESUS. He
shall be great, and shall be called the Son of the Highest. . . . and of His
Kingdom there shall be no end. Then said Mary to the angel* (Gabriel), *How
shall this be, seeing I know not a man? And the angel answered and said to
her, The Holy Spirit shall come upon you, and the power of the Highest
shall overshadow you: therefore also that holy thing* (Holy One) *Who shall
be born of you shall be called the Son of God* (Luke 1:31-35).

As descendants of Adam, we all have inherited his sinful nature
since *by one man's* (Adam's) *disobedience many were made sinners, so by
the obedience of One* (Jesus) *shall many be made righteous* (Romans 5:19).

Thought for Today: Wise men seek Jesus regardless of what others do.

Christ Revealed: As the *Ruler in Israel* (Micah 5:2) Who was to be born in Bethlehem.
Jesus Christ was born in Bethlehem as *the Son of the Highest: and the Lord God
shall give to Him the throne of His father David* (Luke 1:32-33; 2:4-6).

For definitions of unfamiliar words in today's Bible reading, see pages 468-480.

INTRODUCTION TO THE BOOKS OF
Nahum & Habakkuk

Nahum probably lived just before the defeat of Assyria, possibly during the same period as Zephaniah. Both prophesied after Isaiah, toward the end of the reign of Judah's sinful King Jehoiakim (II Kings 23:34 – 24:5; Jeremiah 22:17). Both prophets foretold the destruction of Nineveh as a result of its cruelties, oppressions, adulteries, and witchcraft (Nahum 1:1-14; Zephaniah 2:13-15). Its destruction had been delayed about 150 years because of its repentance following Jonah's message of judgment (Jonah 3:5-10). Eventually, the people reverted to their sinful ways.

The Assyrian Empire destroyed the northern kingdom of Israel in 722 BC, but in turn Assyria, was conquered by the Babylonians about 100 years after Nahum's prophecy. As Nahum had foretold, Assyria is extinct.

Habakkuk lived during the time when Nebuchadnezzar was conquering the world. He probably prophesied in Judah during the later years of Josiah's rule and into the reign of King Jehoiakim. Unlike his godly father Josiah, Jehoiakim *did that which was evil in the sight of the LORD* (II Kings 23:37). Habakkuk cried out against the moral corruption of idolatrous Judah which prevailed in his day. He foretold how God would permit the ruthless Babylonians to bring judgment on Judah. During those horrifying times, *the just shall live by his faith*, became the watchword of the faithful (Habakkuk 2:4; and the major theme of Romans 1:16-17; Galatians 3:11; Hebrews 10:38).

The Book of Habakkuk encourages all believers to accept, by faith, every situation, trusting that righteousness and justice will ultimately triumph according to the righteous judgment of the One True God.

Live out Thy life, Oh Christ, each day
In this poor body made of clay,
Reveal again, through me, dear Lord
The mighty power of Thine own Word.

—M.E.H.

GUIDE

Your Word is a lamp to my feet, and a light to my path (Psalm 119:105).

In Today's Reading
Prophecy and fulfillment of Nineveh's destruction;
vision of coming woes; Habakkuk's prayer

*A*bout 150 years had passed since the revival of Jonah's day when all of Nineveh repented and fasted (Jonah 3:5-10). However, as the years passed, several generations of Ninevites failed to teach their children about the One True God Who had spared their lives, so they returned to their sinful behavior. The time had now come for God to judge them. Judah was oppressed by Assyria, but the prophet Nahum foretold its freedom if the Israelites remained faithful to God. He appealed to them: *O Judah . . . perform your vows: for the wicked shall no more pass through you; he is utterly cut off* (Nahum 1:15).

Assyria was probably the most brutal of all the ancient heathen nations, and its capital Nineveh had greatly enriched itself by wars. Through Nahum, God forewarned: *Woe to the bloody city! it is all full of lies and robbery. . . . Nineveh is laid waste. . . . the sword shall cut you off* (3:1,7,15). Nineveh was destroyed exactly as foretold. That once-mighty city is still *laid waste* as a witness to the accuracy of the Word of God.

Habakkuk foretold the coming judgment that God would bring on His idol-worshiping people in Judah by using Babylon to punish them. He also foretold the judgment of God upon Babylon for its destruction of Judah: *O LORD, You have ordained them* (Judah) *for judgment; and, O mighty God, You have established* (ordained) *them for correction* (Habakkuk 1:12; compare II Corinthians 4:17).

Since we do not know all the facts, in the midst of our numerous, perplexing injustices, where too often evil seems to triumph, we should not express doubt in the *Holy One* (Habakkuk 1:12) by asking: "Why me," or "Why did He allow this to happen?" God is just as uncompromising toward sin today as He was then. Yet the Lord always forgives even the most sinful person who truly repents and turns to Him. All mankind will one day realize that the justice and mercy of *the LORD is good, a strong hold* (refuge) *in the day of trouble; and He knows* (loves) *them that trust in Him* (Nahum 1:7). We expectantly look forward to that day when *the earth shall be filled with the knowledge of the glory of the LORD* (Habakkuk 2:14; compare Romans 1:17; Galatians 3:11; Hebrews 10:38; 11:1-6).

Thought for Today: Religious activity is no substitute for godly living.

Christ Revealed: As the One Whom even the sea obeys (Nahum 1:4). Jesus *rebuked the winds and the sea* (Matthew 8:26-27).

For definitions of unfamiliar words in today's Bible reading, see pages 468-480.

Introduction To The Books Of
ZEPHANIAH, HAGGAI, & ZECHARIAH

Zephaniah probably influenced King Josiah in his godly reformation, which began in the 8th year of Josiah's reign in Judah (II Chronicles 34:3-7).

Zephaniah foretold the fall of Jerusalem perhaps 35 years before it took place (Zephaniah 1:4-13). He warned of *a day of wrath* (anger), *a day of trouble and distress, a day of wasteness and desolation. . . . because they have sinned against the LORD* (1:15,17). The prophet then appealed to the kingdom of Judah to repent: *Seek you the LORD, all you meek* (humble) *of the earth, which have wrought* (carried out) *His judgment* (2:3). God assured them that He would, in His time, graciously restore the nation.

Zephaniah also prophesied that Christ would come in power and glory. Known as *the great Day of the LORD* (1:7,14), that end-time event is referred to 13 times in these three chapters. The *Day of the LORD* will be *a day of wrath* (1:15,18) upon all evildoers; but it will be a blessed "homecoming" for the faithful (3:14,17).

Zephaniah, Nahum, Habakkuk, and Jeremiah prophesied at the same time. The period of Israel's history in which they lived is recorded in the Books of Ezra, Nehemiah, and Esther. They were among the last prophets who spoke for God before the 70-year Babylonian captivity.

Both Haggai and Zechariah were born in Babylon during the exile and went to Jerusalem some time after King Cyrus of Medo-Persia gave the decree to return and rebuild the Temple. Haggai and Zechariah began preaching in Jerusalem about 15 years after that decree.

Zechariah joined Haggai in encouraging the Jews to give first priority to their spiritual responsibility to rebuild the Temple: *The elders of the Jews built, and they prospered through the prophesying of Haggai the prophet and Zechariah. . . . They built, and finished it* in about four years (Haggai 1:1; Ezra 6:14-15). It was the preaching of the Word of God that turned the Israelites from their attitude of indifference toward spiritual needs to a willingness to carry out the will of the Lord. A major turning point in anyone's life comes when he realizes the power of God's Word and appropriates it into his daily decisions and actions.

The *Angel of the LORD* is prominent in this book (Zechariah 1:11-12; 3:1,5-6; 12:8). The second coming of Christ is foretold in 6:12 and 14:3-21. Zechariah foretold more about Christ than any other prophet except Isaiah. (Note 3:8; 9:9,16; 11:11-13; 12:10; 13:1,6.)

In Today's Reading

The Lord's judgment; future destruction of the Gentile nations;
the people urged to rebuild the Temple; unfaithfulness reproved

The Israelites who had returned from Persia with Zerubbabel started to rebuild the Temple in Jerusalem with great enthusiasm. But, when their Samaritan enemies greatly opposed them, they began building their own homes and working in their fields. Their personal interests contributed to their failure to put God first in their lives. No doubt, "legitimate" excuses were given for stopping the construction of the Temple.

As the people built their homes and developed their businesses, time to rebuild the Temple looked hopeless. Zerubbabel must have been discouraged as he thought of how much there was to do, how few willing workers there were, and how threatening the opposition was. While the Israelites continued to hope for better times, about 15 years passed and nothing more was accomplished for the Lord.

Then God moved upon the prophet Haggai to proclaim *the Word of the LORD* (Haggai 1:3-11, Ezra 5:1). Two months later, Zechariah also began proclaiming *the Word of the LORD* (Zechariah 1:1).

Haggai first announced: *Thus speaks the LORD of hosts, saying, This people say, The time is not come, the time that the LORD's House should be built. Then came the Word of the LORD by Haggai the prophet, saying, Is it time for you . . . to dwell in your ceiled* (paneled) *houses, and this House lie waste* (remain in ruins)? *. . . Consider your ways* (Haggai 1:2-5).

Upon hearing *the Word of the LORD*, the people renewed their interest in rebuilding the Temple, the one place designated by God for His people to worship Him. This time they ignored the threats of their enemies and *the elders of the Jews built, and they prospered through the prophesying of Haggai the prophet and Zechariah. . . . And they built, and finished it, according to the Commandment of the God of Israel* (Ezra 6:14). The Temple was completed in just four years.

Without *the Word of the LORD* as a standard, we subsequently fall prey to deception. Reading the Word of God renews our love for His Word and imparts spiritual strength needed to put Him first in our lives.

The Comforter, Who is the Holy Spirit, Whom the Father will send in My Name, He shall teach you all things, and bring all things to your remembrance, whatsoever I have said to you (John 14:18,26).

Thought for Today: Today, let us speak to someone about the Lord and how He has changed MY life.

Christ Revealed: As *King of Israel, even the LORD* (Zephaniah 3:15; compare John 1:49).
For definitions of unfamiliar words in today's Bible reading, see pages 468-480.

In Today's Reading

High priest resisted; Zechariah's visions of the candlestick
(lampstand), flying scroll, four chariots;
disobedience resulting in captivity

Zechariah foretold the glorious promise of the presence of God when the Israelites would be inspired to *sing and rejoice . . . for, lo, I come, and I will dwell in the midst of you, says the LORD* (Zechariah 2:10).

The Lord spoke through Zechariah who prophesied the restoration of the Jewish nation; he also declared: *Many nations* (people of every nationality) *shall be joined to the LORD in that day, and shall be My people: and I will dwell in the midst of you* (2:11).

Often we come to the end of our resources and lose confidence in our own abilities before we learn to trust in the Lord. It was at just such a time that an angel said to Zechariah: *This is the Word of the LORD to Zerubbabel, saying, Not by might, nor by power, but by My Spirit, says the LORD of hosts. Who are you, O great mountain* (authority)? *before Zerubbabel you shall become a plain* (4:6-7).

Zerubbabel, governor of Judah (Haggai 1:1), had been told to rebuild the Temple. Joshua (not Joshua of the conquest) was the high priest (Zechariah 3:1). These two are types foreshadowing our Lord as both king and priest (Matthew 2:2; Hebrews 5:1-10).

The work of God is not accomplished *by might,* nor *by power,* meaning not merely by human intelligence, zeal, or finances, *but by My Spirit, says the LORD of hosts.* The indwelling presence of the Holy Spirit is indispensable in living a true Christian life or accomplishing the will of God. *The Man Whose Name is The BRANCH* (Jesus Christ). . . *Even He . . . shall sit and rule upon His throne; and He shall be a priest upon His throne: and the counsel of peace shall be between them both. . . . And they that are far off shall come and build in the Temple of the LORD, and you shall know that the LORD of hosts has sent Me to you. And this shall come to pass, if you will diligently obey the voice of the LORD your God* (Zechariah 6:12-13,15).

And beginning at Moses and all the prophets, He (Jesus) *expounded* (explained) *to them in all the Scriptures the things concerning Himself* (Luke 24:13-27).

Thought for Today: Jesus will return *to be admired by all* (II Thessalonians 1:10).

Christ Revealed: As *My Servant the BRANCH* (Zechariah 3:8). Christ was brought into the world in the fullness of time, and *took upon Him the form of a servant* (Philippians 2:7). But He will soon return as the *righteous Branch* to reign as King (Jeremiah 23:5).

For definitions of unfamiliar words in today's Bible reading, see pages 468-480.

In Today's Reading

Restoration of Jerusalem promised; judgment on neighboring nations; Zion's future King and Jerusalem's future deliverance

Although his prophetic message was fulfilled centuries later, in great anticipation, Zechariah proclaimed: *Rejoice greatly . . . shout, O daughter of Jerusalem: behold, your King comes to you: He is just, and having salvation; lowly, and riding upon . . . a colt the foal of an ass* (Zechariah 9:9). This prophecy was fulfilled as Jesus entered Jerusalem during the last week before His crucifixion. *A very great multitude. . . . cried, saying, Hosanna to the Son of David: Blessed is He that comes in the Name of the Lord; Hosanna in the highest* (Matthew 21:8-9). The cry of *Hosanna* by the people (meaning "save us") was rejected by the jealous religious leaders who, instead, insisted that Jesus be crucified (Mark 14:1; 15:13).

Zechariah also foretold details concerning Judas, Jesus' betrayer, and his transactions with the religious leaders, saying: *I said to them, If you think good, give me my price* (wages, reward); *and if not, forbear. So they weighed for my price thirty pieces of silver* (Zechariah 11:12). Jesus, the true King of kings, was rejected and betrayed for a mere *30 pieces of silver* just as prophesied – the price of a mere slave (Exodus 21:32; compare Matthew 26:15). Israel will soon recognize its Messiah as Zechariah foretold: *I will pour upon the house of David, and upon the inhabitants of Jerusalem, the Spirit of grace and of supplications: and they shall look upon Me Whom they have pierced, and they shall mourn . . . as one that is in bitterness for his firstborn* (Zechariah 12:10; compare Romans 11:26-27).

Zechariah also foretold the end of our present sinful age: *Behold, the Day of LORD comes. . . . I will gather all the nations against Jerusalem to battle. . . . Then shall the LORD go forth, and fight against those nations. . . . And His feet shall stand in that day upon the Mount of Olives, which is before Jerusalem on the east. . . . And the LORD shall be King over all the earth* (Zechariah 14:1-4,9).

We are all prone to waste time speculating on future events and to forget what Jesus said to His disciples when they asked: *Lord, will You at this time restore again the kingdom to Israel? And He said to them, It is not for you to know the times or the seasons, which the Father has put in His own power. But you shall . . . be witnesses to Me . . . to the uttermost part of the earth* (Acts 1:6-8).

Thought for Today: Where God guides He provides.

Christ Revealed: As King as a Servant sold for *30 pieces of silver* (Zechariah 9:9; 11:12). *They covenanted with him for thirty pieces of silver* (Matthew 26:15).

For definitions of unfamiliar words in today's Bible reading, see pages 468-480.

Introduction To The Book Of
*M*alachi

It is unknown at what time Malachi prophesied; but, it is certain that Malachi's desire was for the Israelites to renew their covenant relationship with God. A spirit of worldliness prevailed among the Israelites just as it does in our communities today. Malachi pointed out the sins that separated the Israelites from experiencing the blessings of God and he appealed to them to repent (Malachi 3:7).

In chapter 1, Malachi first pleaded with Israel to return in full repentance to the Lord Who loved them. Then, in chapter 2, he appealed to the priests, pointing out their hypocrisy. And, in chapter 3, he prophesied of both the coming Messiah and John the Baptist probably 400 years before the Christian era: *Behold, I will send My messenger, and he shall prepare the way before Me: and the Lord, Whom you seek, shall suddenly come* (3:1; Luke 7:27). Finally, like other prophets before him, Malachi foretold *the coming of the great and dreadful Day of the LORD* (Malachi 4:5), when *all the proud . . . and all that do wickedly* will be destroyed. *But to you that fear* (reverence) *My Name shall the Sun of Righteousness arise with healing in His wings* (4:1-2).

Perhaps you've wondered why
Sore trials come your way,
Or murmured when dark clouds of grief
Obscured the light of the day.

God says the trial of your faith
More precious is than gold;
And He'll reward His servants true
With blessings manifold.

So trust in Him, His Word is sure
And infinite His love;
Oh, child of God, press on in faith –
Your Father reigns Above.

–M.E.H.

Helmet

And take the helmet of salvation, and the sword of the Spirit, which is the Word of God (Ephesians 6:17).

In Today's Reading
The Lord's love for Jacob; the sins of the priests;
Israel's unfaithfulness rebuked;
the Day of the Lord and final judgment

The first generation of Israelites that returned to Jerusalem with Zerubbabel to rebuild the Temple was dead, and the following generations had lost sight of the purpose God had for them as His people.

Malachi declared that God may not always be fully understood, but He is questioned only by those who reject or neglect His Word, saying: *If you will not hear, and if you will not lay it to heart . . . says the LORD of hosts, I will even send a curse upon you* (Malachi 2:2).

Malachi left no room for excuses when he declared that the Israelites were thieves. He boldly asked: *Will a man rob God? Yet you have robbed Me. . . . In tithes and offerings* (3:8). He then pronounced the inevitable judgment of God: *You are cursed with a curse: for you have robbed Me, even this whole nation* (3:9).

The people were *cursed with a curse* because the tithes belonged to God for the spiritual needs of the people and the support of the priesthood. They had ignored the command to *honor the LORD with your substance, and with the first-fruits of all your increase* (Proverbs 3:9; Exodus 22:29; II Chronicles 31:5).

Returning one-tenth of all our *increase* (income) to God expresses our faith that all we are and all we have belong to the Lord, and tithing demonstrates our love and gratitude to Him as our Savior and Lord.

More than 500 years before the Law was given, tithing was introduced by Abraham, *the father of all them that believe* (Romans 4:11), who brought a tenth of everything to *the priest of the Most High God* (Genesis 14:18-20). When we refuse to return *to God the things that are God's* (Matthew 22:21), we keep for ourselves what God has said is for proclaiming the Gospel of Christ. Is it greed, selfishness, indifference, or just a stubborn refusal to be obedient to what the Word of God clearly states? The seriousness of this sin can be seen in the severity of the famine that Israel was experiencing: *You are cursed with a curse: for you have robbed Me* (Malachi 3:9).

The Christian is to give *not grudgingly, or of necessity* (under compulsion): *for God loves a cheerful giver* (II Corinthians 9:7).

Thought for Today: Faith is demonstrated by obedience to the Word of God.

Christ Revealed: *The Lord, Whom you shall seek, shall suddenly come to His Temple* (Malachi 3:1; Mark 11:15-17), which meant that Jesus was the promised Messiah.

For definitions of unfamiliar words in today's Bible reading, see pages 468-480.

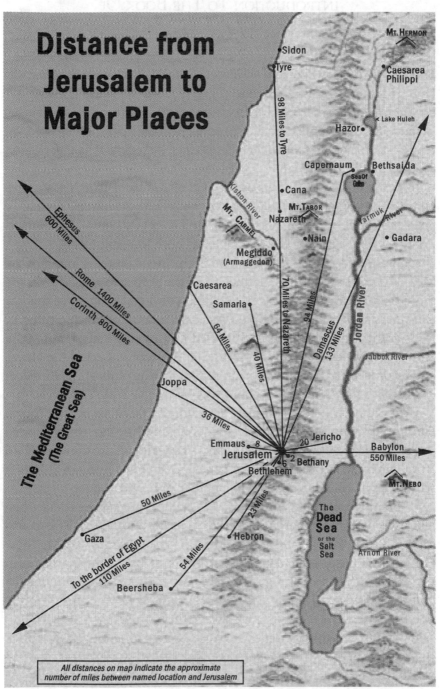

Distance from Jerusalem to Major Places

Sidon

Tyre

MT. HERMON

Caesarea Philippi

98 Miles to Tyre

Lake Huleh

Hazor

Capernaum

Bethsaida

Sea Of Galilee

Cana

MT. TABOR

Nazareth

Nain

Gadara

Yarmuk River

Kishon River

MT. CARMEL

Megiddo (Armaggedon)

70 Miles to Nazareth

94 Miles

Jordan River

Caesarea

Samaria

64 Miles

40 Miles

Damascus 133 Miles

Jabbok River

The Mediterranean Sea (The Great Sea)

Ephesus 600 Miles

Rome 1400 Miles

Corinth 800 Miles

Joppa

36 Miles

Emmaus 8

Jerusalem

20 Jericho

Babylon 550 Miles

2 Bethany

6 Bethlehem

MT. NEBO

50 Miles

23 Miles

The Dead Sea or the Salt Sea

Gaza

Hebron

Arnon River

To the border of Egypt 110 Miles

54 Miles

Beersheba

All distances on map indicate the approximate number of miles between named location and Jerusalem

You shall be witnesses to Me both in Jerusalem,
and in all Judea, and in Samaria,
and to the uttermost part of the earth (Acts 1:8)

Introduction To The Book Of
$\mathcal{M}$ATTHEW

The Gospel of Matthew was written by a Jew who was also known as Levi. He was a despised tax collector who worked for the Roman government (Matthew 10:3; Mark 2:14; Luke 5:27). Matthew presents Jesus as the fulfillment of all Messianic prophecy. In the opening sentence, we read: *The book of the generation of Jesus Christ, the Son of David, the Son of Abraham* (Matthew 1:1).

Matthew identifies Jesus as the *Son of Abraham* which associates Him with the Covenant that God had made with Abraham, saying: *In you shall all families of the earth be blessed* (Genesis 12:3; 17:7; II Samuel 7:8-17). *All families of the earth* includes both Jew and Gentile.

Since the focus of Old Testament Scripture is on the coming of the Messiah and His kingdom, Matthew used the phrase *Kingdom of Heaven* more than 30 times, *Son of David* 10 times, and *that it might be fulfilled which was spoken* at least 9 times. As confirmation of the anointing of Jesus as the Messiah, the Holy Spirit led Matthew to record more than 20 of His miracles. Matthew has more than 100 references to Christ Jesus and records ten of His parables that begin with the phrase: *The Kingdom of Heaven is like* (Matthew 13:24,31,33,44-45,47,52; 20:1; 22:2; 25:1,14).

The Sanhedrin kept complete genealogical archives of the descendants of Abraham and David. These enemies of Christ never questioned Jesus' ancestry. Both Joseph's and Mary's genealogies are the same from Abraham to David. Then Joseph's genealogy follows through Solomon while Mary's traces from Nathan, another of David's sons.

To remove all doubt as to Who Jesus is, Matthew records that, when Jesus was baptized, there was *a voice from heaven, saying, This is My beloved Son, in Whom I am well pleased* (3:17). Sometime later, Matthew also records the spectacular transfiguration of Christ during His conversation with Moses and Elijah, when *a voice out of the cloud . . . said, This is My beloved Son, in Whom I am well pleased; hear . . . Him* (17:2-5). The transfiguration completed Jesus' Galilean ministry. He then traveled south toward Jerusalem where He knew He would be crucified, *and the third day . . . rise again* (20:19).

It was on the Mount of Olives (Luke 24:50), 40 days after His resurrection, that Jesus told His disciples: *Go . . . teach* (disciple) *all nations, baptizing them in the Name of the Father, and of the Son, and of the Holy Spirit: Teaching them to observe all things whatsoever I have commanded you* (Matthew 28:19-20).

IN TODAY'S READING
Ancestry of Jesus; His birth; wise men; flight into Egypt;
ministry of John; baptism of Jesus; first apostles called

The birth of Jesus Christ was on this wise: When as His mother Mary was engaged to Joseph, before they came together, she was found with child of the Holy Spirit (Matthew 1:18).

The amazing *wise men from the east*, perhaps from Babylon, were led by a star *to Jerusalem,* where they inquired: *Where is He that is born King of the Jews? for we have seen His star in the east, and are come to worship Him* (2:1-2). It is probable that these men had studied the prophecies of Daniel who, during the captivity, gave a detailed explanation of the number of years before the Messiah would be born (Daniel 9:25-26).

It must have taken the *wise men* some length of time after the birth of Christ to arrive in Bethlehem, since we read: *When they were come into the house, they saw the young Child with Mary His mother, and fell down, and worshiped Him* (Matthew 2:11). Finding the prophesied King in the house as a *young Child* rather than a babe in the manger indicates several months or more had passed after the birth of Jesus.

The *wise men* had *come to worship Him* (2:2). Their worship included three gifts (2:11). First, they offered *gold,* the most fitting gift for *the King of kings, and the Lord of lords* (I Timothy 6:15). Then, they offered *frankincense,* a sweet perfume used on the Altar of Incense in the Temple, symbolic of prayer ascending to God. It was a fitting gift for a priest, for this King would be our *High Priest* (Hebrews 4:14), *Who also makes intercession for us* (Romans 8:34) before God. They also offered *myrrh,* which signified that He was destined to die; myrrh was often used as a burial spice (John 19:39).

In the providence of God, their gifts also provided adequate re-sources for Joseph and Mary's journey and stay in Egypt, whee they remained *until the death of Herod: that it might be fulfilled which was spoken of the Lord by the prophet, saying, Out of Egypt have I called My Son* (Matthew 2:15; Hosea 11:1). Then they *dwelled in . . . Nazareth* (where Jesus lived until He was about 30 years old) (Matthew 2:23).

Thought for Today: Genuine love is expressed when we willingly give our time and tithes to the Lord.

Cross References: For Matthew 1:23: See Isaiah 7:14. Matthew 2:6: See Micah 5:2. Matthew 2:15: See Hosea 11:1. Matthew 2:18: See Jeremiah 31:15. Matthew 3:3: See Isaiah 40:3.

For definitions of unfamiliar words in today's Bible reading, see pages 468-480.

ℐN 𝒯ODAY'S ℛEADING

Temptation by Satan; Sermon on the Mount; the Beatitudes;
believers likened to salt and light; Jesus' teaching on the Law,
divorce, oaths, giving, fasting

ℱollowing His baptism in the Jordan River, Jesus was *led up of the Spirit into the wilderness to be tempted of the devil* (Matthew 4:1). First, the devil suggested an easy, self-serving way in which Jesus might satisfy His hunger (appealing to the lust of the flesh). But Jesus, knowing that submission to the will of God must be the basis for all decisions, quoted Scripture saying: *It is written, Man shall not live by bread alone, but by every Word that proceeds out of the mouth of God* (4:4; Deuteronomy 8:3). The word *tempt* carries the thought of "try or prove." Such testing is a necessary part of our lives for it reveals our true character. *When He had fasted forty days and forty nights, He was afterward hungry. And when the tempter came to Him, he said, If* (Since) *You be the Son of God, command that these stones be made bread* (Matthew 4:2-3). The abilities God has bestowed upon us are meant to be used for His honor and glory.

Satan's second temptation came in *the holy city . . . on a pinnacle of the Temple* (Matthew 4:5). Satan suggested that Jesus should leap down into the midst of the people and present Himself as a super-human Messiah, appealing to the pride of life. Satan quoted Scripture to support this temptation, saying: *He shall give His angels charge concerning You. . . . lest at any time You dash Your foot against a stone* (4:6; Psalm 91:11-12). The devil frequently appears religious by quoting Scripture, but only the portions which fit his scheme. Jesus responded: *You shall not tempt the Lord your God* (Matthew 4:7).

In Satan's final attempt to seduce Jesus to sin, he *shows Him all the kingdoms of the world . . . And said . . . All these things will I give You, if You will fall down and worship me.* The devil suggested an easy way by which Jesus might avoid all the pain and suffering of the cross and yet rule *all the kingdoms of the world.* Even one exception would make Jesus a sinner. When we allow for one exception, it usually leads to another, etc. Jesus' reply was: *It is written, You shall worship the Lord your God, and Him only shall you serve* (Matthew 4:8-10).

Thought for Today: The poor in spirit are rich in spiritual blessings.

Cross References: For Matthew 4:4: See Deuteronomy 8:3. Matthew 4:6: See Psalm 91:11-12. Matthew 4:7: See Deuteronomy 6:16. Matthew 4:10: See Deuteronomy 6:13. Matthew 4:15-16: See Isaiah 9:1-2. Matthew 5:21: See Exodus 20:13. Matthew 5:27: See Exodus 20:14. Matthew 5:31: See Deuteronomy 24:1. Matthew 5:33: See Numbers 30:2. Matthew 5:38: See Exodus 21:24. Matthew 5:43: See Leviticus 19:18.

For definitions of unfamiliar words in today's Bible reading, see pages 468-480.

OLD TESTAMENT QUOTED BY CHRIST – PARTIAL LIST

MATTHEW	OLD TESTAMENT PASSAGE	OCCASION
4:4	Deut. 8:3	40-Day Temptation
4:7	Deut. 6:16	
4:10	Deut. 6:13	
5:21	Ex. 20:13; Deut. 5:17	Sermon on the Mount
5:27	Ex. 20:14; Deut. 5:18	
5:31	Deut. 24:1	
5:33	Lev. 19:12; Num. 30:2; Deut. 23:21	
5:38	Ex. 21:24; Lev. 24:20; Deut. 19:21	
5:43	Lev. 19:18; Deut. 23:6; 25:19	
9:13	Hos. 6:6	Response to His Critics
11:10	Mal. 3:1	Concerning John
12:7	Hos. 6:6	Response to His Critics
13:14-15	Isa. 6:9-10	Why Speaks in Parables
15:4	Ex. 20:12; 21:17; Lev. 20:9; Deut. 5:16	Response to His Critics
15:7-9	Isa. 29:13	Response to His Critics
19:4-5	Gen. 1:27; 2:24	Sacredness of Marriage; Response to His Critics
21:16	Psa. 8:2	Triumphal Entry
21:42,44	Psa. 118:22-23	"Builders" Rejected
27:46	Psa. 22:1	On the Cross

MARK	OLD TESTAMENT PASSAGE	OCCASION
7:6-7	Isa 29:13	Sermon on the Mount
7:10	Ex. 20:12; 21:17; Lev. 20:9; Deut. 5:16	
10:6	Gen. 1:27	Response to His Critics
10:7-8	Gen. 2:24	Response to His Critics
12:29-30	Deut. 6:4-5	Response to His Critics
12:36	Psa. 110:1	Teaching Concerning David's Son

LUKE	OLD TESTAMENT PASSAGE	OCCASION
4:4	Deut. 8:3	40-Day Temptation
4:8	Deut. 6:13	
4:12	Deut. 6:16	
4:18-19	Isa. 61:1-2	Nazareth Synagogue
7:27	Mal. 3:1	Concerning John
19:46	Isa. 56:7	The Temple Cleansing
23:46	Psa. 31:5	On the Cross

JOHN	OLD TESTAMENT PASSAGE	OCCASION
6:45	Isa. 54:13	Response to His Critics
8:17	Deut. 17:6	Response to His Critics
10:34	Psa. 82:6	Response to His Critics
15:25	Psa. 35:19; 69:4	Last Supper

> ### IN TODAY'S READING
> Conclusion of the Sermon on the Mount;
> preaching and miracles of Jesus; call of Matthew

Jesus warned: *Beware of false prophets . . . in sheep's clothing* (Matthew 7:15). Without a doubt, eternal life is a free gift from God – *not of works, lest any man should boast* (Ephesians 2:9). But, it is also true *that faith without works is dead* (James 2:20). Teaching is false when it offers eternal life without discipleship as a qualification for attaining heaven. To clarify one difference between true prophets and false prophets, our Lord said: *Not every one that says to Me, Lord, Lord, shall enter into the Kingdom of Heaven; but **he that does the will of My Father** Who is in heaven* (Matthew 7:21). However, the evidence of being a true Christian is more than doing great things; it is **being obedient** to the Lord Jesus Christ.

Our Lord spoke a parable: *Whosoever **hears these sayings of Mine, and does them**, I will liken* (compare) *him to a wise man, which built his house upon a rock . . . and the floods came, and the winds blew, and beat upon that house; and it fell not: for it was founded upon a rock. And every one that **hears these sayings of Mine, and does them not**, shall be likened* (compared) *to a foolish man, which built his house upon the sand . . . and the floods came, and the winds blew, and beat upon that house; and it fell: and great was the fall of it* (7:24-27).

Obedience is twofold: First, **one hears** *these sayings of Mine*, and **then one acts** on *these sayings of Mine*. The wise and the foolish are both giving much thought and labor to their activities – one to laying up treasures in heaven, but the other to achieving human goals. When our desire is to please Christ, His Word will be the supreme rule of life and will lead us to avoid the snares of self-will, pride, and greed. Through His Word alone, guided by the Holy Spirit, we are enabled to live each day being accountable to our Creator.

It is impossible to relive wasted years, but it is always possible to turn from sinking sand to build upon the eternal rock. *For other foundation can no man lay than that is laid, Which is Jesus Christ. Now if any man build upon this Foundation . . . Every man's work shall be made manifest* (known) *. . . because it shall be revealed by fire; and the fire shall try* (test) *every man's work of what sort it is* (I Corinthians 3:11-13).

Thought for Today: Having the mind of Christ purifies our thoughts (Philippians 2:5).

Cross References: For Matthew 7:23: See Psalm 6:8. Matthew 8:4: See Leviticus 13:49; 14:2. Matthew 8:17: See Isaiah 53:4. Matthew 9:13: See Hosea 6:6.

For definitions of unfamiliar words in today's Bible reading, see pages 468-480.

$\mathscr{I}$N $\mathscr{T}$ODAY'S $\mathscr{R}$EADING
Mission of the 12 apostles; John the Baptist's questions;
Jesus pronounces judgment on unrepentant cities; great invitation

When Jesus saw the multitudes, He was moved with compassion on them, because they fainted, and were scattered abroad, as sheep having no shepherd. Then says He to His disciples, The harvest truly is plenteous (plentiful), *but the laborers are few; Pray . . . the Lord of the harvest, that He will send forth laborers into His harvest* (Matthew 9:36-38). In answer to this need, Jesus chose just 12 ordinary men whom He taught, saying: *I send you forth as sheep in the midst of wolves: be . . . wise as serpents, and harmless as doves* (10:16-17). Christian persecution, often in the form of pressure to compromise, tests our sincerity. Times of peace often cause the *sheep* to be indifferent but, during persecution, the *sheep* discover they must depend on the Shepherd. Wolves are the natural enemy of sheep. Although *wolves* (false prophets) in human form sometimes appear to be *sheep* (7:15), their indifference to His Word becomes apparent. Like Satan (4:5-6), they only quote the few verses that support their agenda.

The Christian is given a "sheep-like" nature, symbolic of innocence and dependence, not of cowardice. Sheep, by their very nature, are in need of a shepherd or they will wander off and easily become prey to many enemies. Still worse, if one wanders, the entire flock may aimlessly follow. There is never safety in numbers for sheep; a shepherd is always necessary. *All we like sheep have gone astray* (Isaiah 53:6) and need the *Good Shepherd* (John 10:11,14) to guide us each day.

With Christ, the Christian can stand boldly in the face of the fiercest enemy. He assures us: *Fear not them which kill the body, but are not able to kill the soul: but rather fear Him Who is able to destroy both soul and body in hell* (Matthew 10:28). The Christian has no reason to expect kindness from a hostile world when his Master faced fierce enemies during His earthly life. Jesus said to His followers: *If you were of* (belonged to) *the world, the world would love his own: but because you are not of the world, but I have chosen you out of the world, therefore the world hates you. . . . they will also persecute you* (John 15:19-20).

Thought for Today: The meek are patient when faced with difficulties (Matthew 5:5).

Cross References: For Matthew 10:11, 35-36: See Micah 7:6. Matthew 11:5: See Isaiah 35:5; 61:1. Matthew 11:10: See Malachi 3:1. Matthew 11:23: See Ezekiel 26:20; 31:14; 32:18,24. Matthew 11:29: See Jeremiah 6:16.

For definitions of unfamiliar words in today's Bible reading, see pages 468-480.

In Today's Reading

Jesus, Lord of the Sabbath; controversy with Pharisees;
unpardonable sin; Christ's death and resurrection foretold;
His true kin

*J*esus was confronted by the Pharisees who criticized His disciples, saying: *Behold, Your disciples do what is not lawful to do on the Sabbath day* (Matthew 12:2). Jesus responded: *I say to you, That in this place is One greater than the Temple. . . . For the Son of Man is Lord even of the Sabbath day* (12:6-8). The Old Testament worship system foreshadowed the life and ministry of Jesus Christ as well as His Church. Israel had been commanded to keep the last day of the week, the Sabbath, as a day of rest to commemorate God's *work of creation* in six days (Exodus 20:9-11).

The Sabbath, as well as all Jewish worship days, which were also Sabbaths or holy convocations, were *a shadow of things to come*. The early Church recognized this and, in commemoration of Christ's resurrection, *upon the first day of the week . . . the disciples came together to break bread* (Acts 20:7). A few years later, the Apostle Paul was led to write: *Upon the first day of the week let every one of you lay by him in store, as God has prospered him, that there be no gatherings* (collections) *when I come* (I Corinthians 16:2).

Most Christians assemble to worship the Lord Jesus Christ on the first day of the week. Jesus rose from the grave on *the first day of the week* (Mark 16:9). In this way, we honor Him as Lord of our lives by putting Him first in every week. The Sabbath day of rest has its counterpart in the New Covenant *that in all things He might have the preeminence* (first place). *. . . Let no man therefore judge you in meat* (food), *or in drink, or in respect of a holyday* (festival), *or of the new moon, or of the Sabbath days: Which are a shadow of things to come* (Colossians 1:18; 2:16-17).

The Passover, commemorating Israel's freedom from Egyptian bondage, was replaced at Christ's final Passover, when He instituted the Lord's Supper. As Jesus and the apostles were eating the Passover meal, *Jesus took bread, and blessed* (gave thanks to God for) *it, and broke it, and gave it to the disciples, and said, Take, eat; this is My body. And He took the cup, and gave thanks, and gave it to them, saying, Drink . . . all of it* (from it, all of you); *For this is My blood of the New Testament* (Covenant), *which is shed for many for the remission of sins* (Matthew 26:26-28).

Thought for Today: *The fear of the LORD is the beginning of wisdom* (Proverbs 9:10).

Cross References: For Matthew 12:7: See Hosea 6:6. Matthew 12:18-21: See Isaiah 42:1-4. Matthew 12:40: See Jonah 1:17.

For definitions of unfamiliar words in today's Bible reading, see pages 468-480.

*I*N *T*ODAY'S *R*EADING

Jesus' parables; execution of John the Baptist; feeding of 5,000;
Jesus walks on the water

*I*n the first parable of Jesus that Matthew recorded, Jesus described four kinds of responses from those who hear His Word. The true disciple of Christ is represented by the *good ground* that received seed, which in turn brings forth fruit even to *a hundredfold* (Matthew 13:8-23). His second parable was of *tares* (weeds) that grew in the same field with wheat but produced no fruit (13:24-30). The *tares* look identical to wheat as they grow. In its young stages, only the expert can tell the difference. But, when these weeds reach maturity, there is no head exposing its lack of value. In this parable, the Master said: *Let both grow together until the harvest* (13:30). Jesus explained that *the field is the world; the good seed are the children of the kingdom* (13:38).

The *tares* represent those who outwardly appear to be converts to Christ, but who have never truly received Jesus as Savior and Lord of their lives. They may join the church, give their tithes, and deceive members of the church, but not Christ. It may seem startling to read that *the Son of Man shall send forth His angels, and they shall gather out of His kingdom all . . . which do iniquity; And shall cast them into a furnace of fire: there shall be wailing and gnashing of teeth* (13:41-42).

No one expects to be hurled into a lake of fire, where there is weeping and wailing and gnashing of teeth forever. Jesus said: *Narrow is the way, that leads to life, and few . . . find it* (7:14). These few have characteristics that are not true of the majority of people. They recognized that they were sinners and needed a Savior, and they asked the Lord to forgive them of their sins, and to make Him the Lord of their lives. They look forward to attending worship services on Sunday.

To *believe on the Lord Jesus Christ, and . . . be saved* (Acts 16:31), means much more than a mental assent to the fact – it's a way of living. *Continue in the faith grounded and settled, and be not moved away from the hope of the Gospel, which you have heard* (Colossians 1:22-23).

Thought for Today: Our faith is strengthened as we obey God's Word – the *Source* of faith.

Cross References: For Matthew 13:14-15: See Isaiah 6:9-10. Matthew 13:32: See Psalm 104:12; Ezekiel 17:23; 31:6; Daniel 4:12. Matthew 13:35: See Psalm 78:2. Matthew 13:41: See Zephaniah 1:3. Matthew 13:43: See Daniel 12:3.

For definitions of unfamiliar words in today's Bible reading, see pages 468-480.

𝒥N 𝒯ODAY'S 𝓡EADING

Scribes and Pharisees rebuked; 4,000 fed; the leaven;
Peter's confession; transfiguration of Jesus; the disciples' unbelief

𝒞aesarea Philippi was the location of the famous Pan, Greek god representative of all gods of paganism as well as the Baal god, considered to be a "lord of heaven and earth." It was located about 25 miles north of the Sea of Galilee. It is situated at the foot of the southern slope of Mount Hermon, with its snow-capped peak 9000 feet above sea level, the "highest mountain" in the promised land (Matthew 17:1). Many believed that the transfiguration of Christ took place here.

In the midst of large numbers of idol worshipers, Jesus asked His disciples: *Whom do men say that I the Son of Man am?* In response to His question, the disciples answered: *Some say that You are John the Baptist: some, Elijah; and others, Jeremiah, or one of the prophets.* But when He said: *But whom say you that I am?* – without hesitation, Peter said: *You are the Christ, the Son of the living God* (16:13-16).

Our Lord then introduced the word Church for the first time (Matthew 16:18). A "church," is a community of ones who are caring brothers and sisters in fellowship with one another and with Christ Who is the Head of the Church. The Church is composed of people redeemed by His blood and committed to Jesus as their Savior and Lord under the discipline of the Word of God. They recognize their responsibility to help one another in living their covenant relationship with Christ since the Church is the Body of Christ (I Corinthians 12:27).

Strange as it may seem, some of the followers of Christ disregard their responsibility to fellowship with other believers on the Lord's Day. Unknown to them, their spiritual influence with their own family becomes weak and ineffective. Still worse, too often they desecrate the Lord's Day for selfish pleasures.

In striking contrast, *Christ also loved the Church, and gave Himself for it; That He might sanctify and cleanse it with the washing of water by the Word, That He might present it to Himself a glorious Church, not having spot, or wrinkle, or any such thing; but that it should be holy and without blemish* (Ephesians 5:25-27; also I Corinthians 1:10)).

Thought for Today: Our worship is never in vain when we worship our Lord as God.

Cross References: For Matthew 15:4: See Exodus 20:12; 21:17; Leviticus 20:9; Deuteronomy 5:16. Matthew 15:8-9: See Isaiah 29:13. Matthew 16:27: See Psalm 62:12; Proverb 24:12.

For definitions of unfamiliar words in today's Bible reading, see pages 468-480

ℐN 𝒯ODAY'S 𝓡EADING

Humility; the lost sheep; forgiveness; marriage and divorce;
rich young ruler; workers in the vineyard; two blind men healed

𝒫eter asked a far more important question than he realized when he inquired of Jesus: *Lord, how often shall my brother sin against me, and I forgive him? till seven times? Jesus said to him, I say not to you, Until seven times: but, Until seventy times seven* (Matthew 18:21-22).

Peter thought he was being generous in suggesting *seven times.* This was twice as many times as required by the traditions of the scribes, plus one more, for a total of *seven times.* Unwillingness to forgive everyone of their sins against us while, at the same time, expecting Christ to forgive us of all our sins against Him everyday for a lifetime is, a fatal sin. He has warned *if you forgive not men their trespasses, neither will your Father forgive your trespasses* (6:15).

The Lord gives an illustration of a servant who owed *ten thousand talents* to his king (18:24). The amount was impossible to repay even in a lifetime. *The servant therefore fell down, and worshiped him, saying, Lord, have patience with me, and I will pay you all. Then the lord of that servant was moved with compassion, and loosed* (released) *him, and forgave him the debt. But the same servant went out, and found one of his fellow servants, which owed him a hundred pence* (mere pennies compared to 10,000 talents): *and he laid hands on him . . . saying, Pay me what you owe. And his fellow servant fell down at his feet, and besought him, saying, Have patience with me, and I will pay you all. And he would not: but went and cast him into prison* (18:26-30). When his lord was made aware of what took place, he *was angry, and delivered him to the tormentors, till he should pay all that was due to him. So likewise shall My Heavenly Father do also to you, if you from your hearts forgive not every one his brother their trespasses* (18:31-35).

When the fear of God is considered, we find it much easier to forgive others. *Let all bitterness, and wrath, and anger, and clamor, and evil speaking, be put away from you, with all malice: And be kind one to another, tenderhearted, forgiving one another, even as God for Christ's sake has forgiven you* (Ephesians 4:31-32; also Matthew 6:14-15).

Thought for Today: Live for the Lord now and you will enjoy eternity with Him.

Cross References: For Matthew 18:16: See Deuteronomy 19:15. Matthew 19:4: See Genesis 1:27; 5:2. Matthew 19:5: See Genesis 2:24. Matthew 19:7: See Deuteronomy 24:1-4. Matthew 19:18: See Exodus 20:13-16; Deuteronomy 5:17-20. Matthew 19:19: See Exodus 20:12; Leviticus 19:18; Deuteronomy 5:16.

For definitions of unfamiliar words in today's Bible reading, see pages 468-480.

In Today's Reading

Jesus' triumphal entry; Temple cleansed; fig tree cursed; authority of Jesus questioned; parables; taxes; the greatest commandment; weeping and gnashing of teeth in eternal darkness

*O*n Monday preceding His crucifixion, and just one day after His triumphant entry into Jerusalem, *Jesus went into the Temple of God, and cast out all them that sold and bought. . . . And said to them, It is written, My House shall be called the house of prayer; but you have made it a den of thieves* (Matthew 21:12-13; see Isaiah 56:7).

The chief priests were outraged and dispatched a delegation to interrupt Jesus *as He was teaching, and said, By what authority do You these things?* (Matthew 21:23). They were referring to His accepting all the praise that the multitude had given Him as the Messiah, as well as questioning who gave Him authority to dismiss their money changers. For these reasons they conspired to kill Him (26:4).

The Temple belonged to God, Who was in their midst. Jesus' cleansing of the Temple illustrates the cleansing that Christ alone brings into our lives through His atoning blood (26:28; I John 1:7; Revelation 1:5).

After pronouncing His judgment upon the Temple activities, *Jesus spoke to them again by parables, and said: The Kingdom of Heaven is like to a certain king, which made a marriage for his son . . . . The wedding is ready. . . . Go therefore into the highways, and as many as you shall find, bid to the marriage. . . . And when the king came in to see the guests, he saw there a man which had not on a wedding garment. . . . Then said the king to the servants . . . cast him into outer darkness; there shall be weeping and gnashing of teeth* (Matthew 22:1-13).

Because eternal separation from God is so final and so terrifying, Jesus said more about the horrifying torments of eternal hell as a *lake of fire* (Revelation 20:10) than all the writers of the New Testament combined. In this parable, Jesus exposes all who assume they are good enough for heaven. The Apostle Paul said: *There are many unruly and vain talkers and deceivers . . . . They profess that they know God; but in works they deny Him, being . . . disobedient, and to every good work reprobate* (Titus 1:10,16).

Thought for Today: True humility includes an attitude of gentleness with others.

Cross References: For Matthew 21:5: See Isaiah 62:11; Zechariah 9:9. Matthew 21:9: See Psalm 118:26. Matthew 21:13: See Isaiah 56:7; Jeremiah 7:11. Matthew 21:16: See Psalm 8:2. Matthew 21:33: See Psalm 80:8; Isaiah 5:1-2. Matthew 21:42: See Psalm 118:22-23. Matthew 22:24: See Deuteronomy 25:5. Matthew 22:32: See Exodus 3:6. Matthew 22:37: See Deuteronomy 6:5. Matthew 22:39: See Leviticus 19:18. Matthew 22:44: See Psalm 110:1.

For definitions of unfamiliar words in today's Bible reading, see pages 468-480.

In Today's Reading
Hypocrisy denounced; destruction of the Temple foretold;
signs of Christ's return

Following the cleansing of the Temple and the denouncing of the religious leaders as hypocrites, the Lord sat with His disciples on the Mount of Olives and foretold: *Many false prophets shall rise, and shall deceive many. And because iniquity* (lawlessness) *shall abound, the love of many shall wax* (become) *cold. But he that shall endure to the end, the same shall be saved. And this Gospel of the Kingdom shall be preached in all the world for a witness to all nations; and then shall the end come. . . . Heaven and earth shall pass away, but My words shall not pass away* (Matthew 24:11-14,35). Like the Pharisees of old, the *false prophets* today substitute contemporary opinions and situation ethics for the authority of God's Word.

On the Mount of Olives, just three days before His crucifixion, our Lord foretold the destruction of the Temple. It was destroyed about 40 years after His resurrection. He also spoke of His future return from heaven, saying: *Of that day and hour knows no man, no, not the angels of heaven, but My Father only* (24:36). He also warned: *Watch therefore: for you know not what hour your Lord does come. . . . Therefore be . . . ready: for in such an hour as you think not the Son of Man comes* (24:42,44).

Jesus made no attempt to give details concerning the soon destruction of Jerusalem, nor the more distant end of the age. But these words from the King emphasized the importance of always being prepared by speaking a parable of two servants. Jesus said: *Who then is a faithful and wise servant, whom his lord has made ruler over his household, to give them meat in due season? Blessed is that servant, whom his lord when he comes shall find so doing. . . . But . . . if that evil servant shall say in his heart, My lord delays his coming; And shall begin to smite* (beat) *his fellow servants, and to eat and drink with the drunken; The lord of that servant shall come in a day when . . . he is not aware of . . . and appoint him his portion with the hypocrites: there shall be weeping and gnashing of teeth* (Matthew 24:45-51).

Thought for Today: God is concerned about the inward condition of the heart as well as our daily conversation and attitudes.

Cross References: For Matthew 23:39: See Psalm 118:26. Matthew 24:15: See Daniel 9:27; 11:31; 12:11. Matthew 24:29: See Isaiah 13:10; 24:23; 34:4; Ezekiel 32:7; Joel 2:10,31; 3:15; Zephaniah 1:15. Matthew 24:30: See Daniel 7:13. Matthew 24:31: See Deuteronomy 30:4; Isaiah 27:13; Zechariah 2:6. Matthew 24:38: See Genesis 6:3-5; 7:7.

For definitions of unfamiliar words in today's Bible reading, see pages 468-480.

In Today's Reading

Parables; plot to kill Jesus; Jesus anointed; Lord's Supper;
Christ's agony and prayer; Judas' betrayal; Jesus' trial; Peter's denial

*J*esus represented Himself in a parable saying: *The Kingdom of Heaven is as a man travelling into a far country, who called his own servants, and delivered to them his goods. And to one he gave five talents, to another two, and to another one; to every man according to his several* (own) *ability; and immediately took his journey* (Matthew 25:14-15). These talents did not belong to the servants, but remained the property of their master. They were to be his managers (stewards) of the *goods* entrusted to them. The *goods* of this parable represent the opportunities and abilities that God has given to us and that He expects us to use for His Kingdom.

The servant who received *five talents* recognized that what he had received belonged to his master. On the day of judgment he said: *Lord, you delivered to me five talents: behold, I have gained beside them five talents more* (25:20).

And likewise he that had received two, he also gained other two (25:17). He was not expected to gain five since he had been given according to his own ability. Both faithfully doubled their talents and both were equally commended.

The third servant had received *one* talent. He put forth no effort for his master. Instead, he *went and dug in the earth, and hid his lord's* (master's) *money* (25:18). His effort for "earthly security" was inexcusable. He tried to excuse himself like the person today who shows great diligence working in the secular world, but says: "I'm too busy now. I'll serve the Lord at some more convenient time, or after I retire."

The consequences of neglecting the opportunities to serve his master were irreversible; there was no second chance to relive his life. The master declared: *Cast you the unprofitable servant into outer darkness: there shall be weeping and gnashing of teeth* (Matthew 25:30; compare 8:12; 22:13; 24:51).

We can choose to ignore our opportunities to serve Him, withhold our tithes, and desecrate the Lord's Day; but, without an exception, *every one of us shall give account of himself to God* (Romans 14:12). *You are not your own? For you are bought with a price: therefore glorify God in your body, and in your spirit, which are God's* (I Corinthians 6:19-20).

Thought for Today: Christians receive and enjoy a spiritual experience as they help others (Titus 3:8).

Cross References: For Matthew 26:31: See Zechariah 13:7. Matthew 26:64: See Psalm 110:1; Daniel 7:13.

For definitions of unfamiliar words in today's Bible reading, see pages 468-480.

In Today's Reading
Judas' suicide; Jesus before Pilate;
Jesus' crucifixion, burial, and resurrection; Great Commission

The resurrection of Jesus gave His disciples the key to understanding that their King and His Kingdom were both eternal. *Jesus came and spoke to them, saying, All power* (authority) *is given to Me in heaven and in earth. Go . . . therefore, and teach all nations, baptizing them in the Name of the Father, and of the Son, and of the Holy Spirit: Teaching them to observe all things whatsoever I have commanded you* (Matthew 28:18-20).

When we are baptized *in the Name of the Father, and of the Son, and of the Holy Spirit,* we proclaim the fullness of the Godhead. Thus, by public baptism, we confess to the world that God is our *Heavenly Father.* The phrase *and of the Son* is our witness to the world that Jesus is now Savior and Lord of our lives. Upon our confession, *the Holy Spirit* becomes our indwelling Sanctifier, Comforter, and Guide throughout life (John 14:26; 16:13). This confirms the Trinity of the Godhead and proclaims One God expressed in Three Persons.

Being *born again* (3:3,7) by His Spirit is a supernatural experience which changes the heart and transforms the life to one of daily worship and service to the Lord. This does not mean that we will reach perfection in this life; but as Peter urged: *Desire the sincere milk of the Word, that you may grow thereby* (I Peter 2:1-2). The Lord has provided just one Book and His Holy Spirit to tell us how to live and what He expects us to do. Titus proclaimed: *With all authority . . . that, denying ungodliness and worldly lusts, we should live soberly, righteously, and godly, in this present world; Looking for that blessed hope, and the glorious appearing of the great God and our Savior Jesus Christ; Who gave Himself for us, that He might redeem us from all iniquity* (lawlessness), *and purify to Himself a peculiar* (special) *people, zealous of good works* (Titus 2:12-15). Without exception we all at times fail the Lord but, let us say with Paul: *Forgetting those things which are behind, and reaching forth to those things which are before, I press toward the mark* (goal) *for the prize of the high calling of God in Christ Jesus* (Philippians 3:13-14).

Thought for Today: "If God is your partner, you had better have BIG Plans."

Cross References: For Matthew 27:5-10: See Zechariah 11:12-13. Matthew 27:34: See Psalm 69:21. Matthew 27:35: See Psalm 22:18. Matthew 27:39: See Job 16:4; Psalm 109:25; Lamentations 2:15. Matthew 27:43: See Psalm 22:8. Matthew 27:46: See Psalm 22:1.

For definitions of unfamiliar words in today's Bible reading, see pages 468-480.

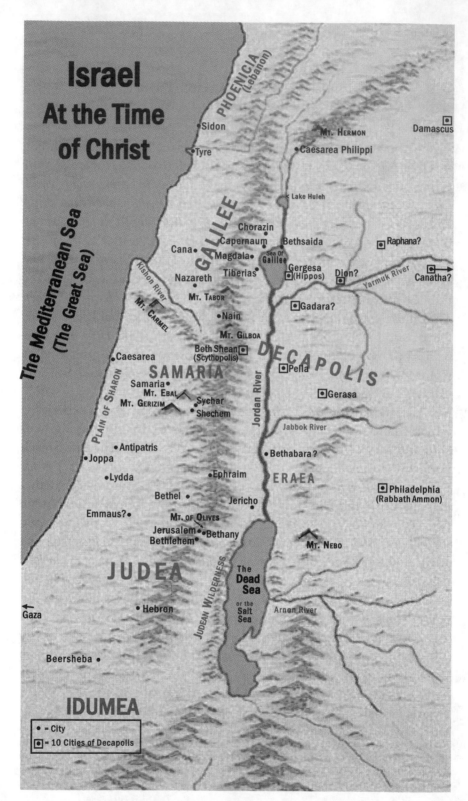

Israel
At the Time
of Christ

The Mediterranean Sea
(The Great Sea)

PHOENICIA
(Lebanon)

Sidon

Tyre

MT. HERMON

Damascus

Caesarea Philippi

Lake Huleh

GALILEE

Chorazin
Capernaum
Bethsaida

Cana
Magdala
Sea Of Galilee

Nazareth
Tiberias

Gergesa
(Hippos)

Dion?

Raphana?

Yarmuk River

Canatha?

MT. TABOR

Nain

Gadara?

MT. GILBOA

Caesarea

Beth Shean
(Scythopolis)

DECAPOLIS

SAMARIA

Samaria
MT. EBAL
MT. GERIZIM

Sychar
Shechem

Pella

Gerasa

Jordan River

Jabbok River

Antipatris

Joppa

Lydda

Ephraim

Bethabara ?

PERAEA

Philadelphia
(Rabbath Ammon)

Bethel

Jericho

Emmaus?

MT. OF OLIVES

Jerusalem
Bethlehem

Bethany

MT. NEBO

JUDEA

JUDEAN WILDERNESS

The
Dead
Sea
or the
Salt
Sea

Hebron

Arnon River

Gaza

Beersheba

IDUMEA

• = City
⊡ = 10 Cities of Decapolis

Introduction To The Book Of
$\mathcal{M}$ARK

The Holy Spirit directed Mark to emphasize the deity of Jesus as the perfect Servant of God. Five times He is called either *Son of God, Son of the Most High God,* or *Christ, the Son of the Blessed* (Mark 1:1; 3:11; 5:7; 14:61; 15:39). The first verse of the Book of Mark reads: *The beginning of the Gospel of Jesus Christ, the Son of God* (1:1). To confirm Jesus as *the Son of God,* Mark records about 20 of His miracles, demonstrating Jesus' authority over demons, nature, disease, and death (1:21-28; 1:29-31; 1:32-34; 1:40-45; 2:3-12; 3:1-6; 4:35-41; 5:1-20; 5:25-34; 5:22-24,35-43; 6:31-44; 6:45-50; 6:51-54; 7:24-30; 7:31-37; 8:1-9; 8:22-26; 9:2-10; 9:14-29; 10:46-52; 11:12-14,20-26; 16:1-11; 16:19-20).

Mark also describes Jesus as *the Son of Man came . . . to give His life a ransom for many* (10:45); the Faithful Servant of God – a Man of action, always busy doing and working, using such terms as *immediately* (at once), *straightway,* and *forthwith* (shortly), which Mark used over 40 times. His servanthood is portrayed in such passages as: *The Son of Man came not to be ministered to* (served), *but to minister* (serve) (10:45). The Holy Spirit also led Mark to record nine parables (2:21; 2:22; 4:1-20; 4:21-22; 4:26-29; 4:30-32; 9:50; 12:1-12; 13:28-31; 13:32-37).

Only in Mark are the hands of Jesus so prominent. Only Mark records that his town folk said: *Even such mighty works are wrought by His hands* (6:2). All these are symbolic of the work of a servant. None of the other Gospels refer to Jesus' hands as in the following Scriptures: Mark 1:31; 8:23,25; 9:27; 7:33.

There is no genealogy of Jesus, no mention of His birth, or the wise men, and nothing about His childhood or youth, since none of these are of interest in the account of a servant's life.

No other Gospel describes Jesus taking *a child . . . in His arms* (9:36).

Mark also refers to Jesus as *Master* (Teacher, Rabbi) 15 times (4:38; 5:35; 9:5,17,38; 10:17,20,35; 11:21; 12:14,19,32; 13:1; 14:14,45).

In contrast to Mark, Matthew provided no explanation of Jewish customs because he was appealing to Jews. But Mark was appealing to Gentiles so he was led to explain many Jewish customs and teachings which non-Jewish readers might be unfamiliar with (Mark 2:18; 7:3-4; 14:12; 15:42), also Judean geographic names and plants (1:13; 11:13; 13:3), and the value of Jewish coins in Roman money (12:42).

IN TODAY'S READING
Ministry of John the Baptist; baptism and temptation of Jesus;
His Galilean ministry; twelve apostles chosen; the unpardonable sin

God had directed Moses to *command the children of Israel, that they put out of the camp every leper. . . . that they defile not their camps, in the midst whereof I dwell* (Numbers 5:2-3). No disease occupies so much space in the Scriptures as leprosy. Strangely, it first appears as just a white, then pink spot. As leprosy slowly progresses, it becomes loathsome, and often fatal in its effects. It illustrates how insignificant sin may seem at first, but, if continued, its consequences are devasting.

A leper eventually loses sensitivity to pain. Still worse, as leprosy progresses, fingers and toes decay and fall off. For centuries, lepers were incurable – they were considered the untouchables of society.

One of these pitiful outcasts boldly made his way to Jesus – *beseeching* (begging) *Him, and kneeling down to Him, and saying to Him, If You will, You can make me clean* (Mark 1:40). When the leper said: *If You will,* he had no doubt that Jesus could heal him. But he doubted His willingness to do so since leprosy was much worse than just a hopeless disease, it made him ceremonially unclean. It was not "Could He?" but "Would He?" *Jesus, moved with compassion, put forth His hand, and touched him, and said to him, I will; be . . . clean* (1:41).

Matthew records that this leper *worshiped Him* (Matthew 8:2), and Luke said that he *fell on his face* before Him (Luke 5:12). Only Mark tells us that Jesus was *moved with compassion* and that His loving hand reached out to this defiled leper and *touched him*. Jesus was *moved with compassion,* one of the deepest of human emotions and a true expression of the loving heart of Jesus. Jesus' touch expressed compassion, expressed through His Word: *Be . . . clean* (Mark 1:41; Luke 5:13). Today Jesus says: *Now you are clean through the Word which I have spoken to you* (John 15:3). Faith in God comes through hearing His Word (Romans 10:17).

Once saved, like the cleansed leper who *began to publish it much* (Mark 1:45), you too will want to tell others what Jesus has done for you.

As we observe sinners all about us and see how sin is destroying the spiritual lives of people, it is important to also remember that *the Lord is . . . long-suffering . . . not willing that any should perish, but that all should come to repentance* (II Peter 3:9).

Thought for Today: The greater the pressures, the more time we must give to prayer.

Cross References: For Mark 1:2: See Malachi 3:1. Mark 1:3: See Isaiah 40:3.

For definitions of unfamiliar words in today's Bible reading, see pages 468-480.

In Today's Reading
Jesus' parables; the storm stilled; a legion of demons cast out;
Jairus' daughter raised

*J*esus described in a parable four kinds of responses from those who hear His Word, saying: *Behold, there went out a sower to sow. . . . Some* (seed) *fell by the way side, and the fowls of the air came and devoured it* (Mark 4:1-4). This means that some people respond to the Gospel with self-destroying indifference. They represent the hearer who expresses no concern for spiritual values but is open to pleasures and self-indulgence. *Satan comes immediately, and takes away the Word that was sown in their hearts* (4:15).

Others who hear His Word are like seed sown *on stony ground* (4:5). At first they are receptive, but soon lose interest. *These are they . . . who, when they have heard the Word, immediately receive it with gladness; And have no root in themselves, and so endure but for a time: afterward, when affliction or persecution arises for* (because of) *the Word's sake, immediately they are offended* (4:16-17). "Stony places" means solid rock beneath a shallow covering of soil. These "converts" appear promising and full of life; but confronted with a lifestyle that is inconsistent with the Christian life, or persecution because of the Word of God, they immediately quit.

Other "converts" are like seed *sown among thorns; such as hear the Word, And the cares of this world, and the deceitfulness of riches, and the lusts of others things entering in, choke the Word, and it becomes unfruitful* (4:18-19). Such people seem to recognize the true worth of Christ and eternal life, but have never made a break from their past. When the things of the world that keep a person from being devoted to the Lord are not weeded out, it they gradually take control of their hearts and spiritual interests are eventually crowded out.

But a more serious group of people who hear the Word of God are like seed *sown on good ground; such as hear the Word, and receive it, and bring forth fruit, some thirtyfold, some sixty, and some a hundred* (4:20). By faith, these people break up their *stony* places, removing the things that hinder spiritual growth. They root out the weeds and thorns of mixed motives, and they bear much fruit.

Jesus has said to all: *I am the Vine, you are the branches: He that abides in Me, and I in him, the same brings forth much fruit* (John 15:5).

Thought for Today: It is not *what* a person possesses that is important, but *who* possesses him.

Cross Reference: For Mark 4:12: See Isaiah 6:9-10; Jeremiah 5:21; Ezekiel 12:2.

For definitions of unfamiliar words in today's Bible reading, see pages 468-480.

IN TODAY'S READING
Apostles sent out; John the Baptist beheaded; 5,000 fed;
Jesus walks on water; rebuke of the Pharisees;
faith of a Syrophoenician woman

The Pharisees insisted the Law be observed as the scribes interpreted it; they believed in the Old Testament Scriptures, but they followed *the tradition of the elders* more than the Scriptures (Mark 7:3). They believed that Jesus' disciples were defiled because they did not ceremonially wash before eating as prescribed by former scribes in *the tradition of the elders*. It should have been a wake-up call to hear Jesus say: *Well has Isaiah prophesied of you hypocrites . . . This people honors Me with their lips, but their heart is far from Me. . . . teaching for doctrines the commandments of men. . . . Making the Word of God of none effect through your tradition* (7:6-8,13).

Later, Jesus explained to His disciples: *Whatsoever thing from outside enters into the man, it cannot defile him. . . . For from inside, out of the heart of men, proceed evil thoughts, adulteries, fornications, murders, Thefts, covetousness, wickedness, deceit, lasciviousness* (sensuality), *an evil eye, blasphemy* (slander), *pride, foolishness: All these evil things . . . defile the man* (Mark 7:18-23).

Satan often suggests evil thoughts, but they only become sin when we accept them and dwell upon them. We are deceived if we assume there is no harm in dwelling upon sinful thoughts as long as they are never verbalized or physically carried out. The Holy Spirit led the Apostle Paul to write: *The carnal* (worldly) *mind is enmity* (hostile) *against God: for it is not subject to the Law of God* (Romans 8:7).

Christians have the responsibility, and the ability, because of the indwelling Holy Spirit, to be overcomers of sinful thoughts: *Casting down imaginations, and every high* (proud) *thing that exalts itself against the knowledge of God, and bringing into captivity every thought to the obedience of Christ* (II Corinthians 10:4-5). A commitment to read through the Word of God with a desire to please the Lord will produce inward changes in conduct and attitudes that will affect all that we say and do. *This I say then, Walk in the Spirit, and you shall not fulfill the lust of the flesh* (Galatians 5:16).

Thought for Today: Our unspoken thoughts express the true desires of our hearts.

Cross References: For Mark 7:6-7: See Isaiah 29:13. Mark 7:10: See Exodus 20:12; 21:17; Leviticus 20:9; Deuteronomy 5:16.

For definitions of unfamiliar words in today's Bible reading, see pages 468-480.

ℐN ℐODAY'S ℛEADING
Feeding 4,000; leaven explained; healing blind man;
Peter's confession of faith; Jesus' death and resurrection foretold;
transfiguration; disciples unable to heal boy;
dispute over who is greatest, the terrifying torments of eternal hell

*J*esus and His disciples had been in the famous idol-worshiping town of *Caesarea Philippi* (Mark 8:27 – 9:1). It was here that Jesus *asked His disciples: Whom do men say that I am? And they answered, John the Baptist: but some say, Elijah; and others, One of the prophets. And He says to them, But whom say you that I am? And Peter answered . . . You are the Christ* (8:27-29).

A short time later, Jesus invited the people to follow Him, but with certain qualifications, saying: *Whosoever will come after Me, let him deny himself, and take up his cross, and follow Me. For whosoever will save his life shall lose it; but whosoever shall lose his life for My sake and the Gospel's, the same shall save it. For what shall it profit* (benefit) *a man, if he shall gain the whole world, and lose his own soul? Or what shall a man give in exchange for his soul? Whosoever therefore shall be ashamed of Me and of My words in this adulterous and sinful generation; of him also shall the Son of Man be ashamed* (8:34-38).

It was in this same region that, six days later, Jesus and three of His disciples went up on a *high mountain . . . and He was transfigured before them. . . . And there appeared to them Elijah with Moses: and they were talking with Jesus* (9:2-4). Moses and Elijah were now in the presence of their Messiah. At this momentous event, the two Old Testament prophets spoke with Jesus about *His decease* (dying) *which He should accomplish at Jerusalem* (Luke 9:31). Moses, representing the Law, and Elijah, representing the prophets, appeared to honor Jesus prior to His suffering, death on the cross, and physical resurrection.

Peter made the mistake of suggesting they *make three tabernacles; one for You, and one for Moses, and one for Elijah. For he knew not what to say* (Mark 9:5-6). However, since Jesus Christ is the Only Begotten Son of God, He alone is worthy of our worship and obedience (Revelation 4:9-11). Nothing, or no one, can replace or equal a personal communion with Him as our Lord.

After Peter's *three tabernacles* suggestion, *a Voice came out of the cloud, saying, This is my beloved Son: hear Him* (Mark 9:7).

Thought for Today: The worship, love, and loyalty that is due Christ is not to be shared with anyone else.

Cross References: For Mark 8:18: See Ezekiel 12:2. Mark 9:44,46,48: See Isaiah 66:24.

For definitions of unfamiliar words in today's Bible reading, see pages 468-480.

IN TODAY'S READING
Jesus on divorce; children blessed; rich young ruler;
blind Bartimaeus healed; triumphal entry; cleansing the Temple

King Herod arrested John the Baptist, *and bound him, and put him in prison for Herodias' sake, his brother Philip's wife. For John said to him, It is not lawful for you to have her. . . . And he sent, and beheaded John in the prison* (Matthew 14:3-4,10). In an effort to have Jesus arrested and, hopefully, executed by Herod, the Pharisees asked Jesus: *Is it lawful for a man to put away his wife?* (Mark 10:2). Jesus was not intimidated, but quoted the Word of God, saying: *From the beginning of the creation God made them male and female. For this cause shall a man leave his father and mother, and cleave to his wife; And they two shall be one flesh: so then they are no more two, but one flesh. What therefore God has joined together, let not man put asunder* (divorce) (Mark 10:6-9; Genesis 2:24).

The foremost responsibility in a marriage relationship rests with the husband, who is to love his wife, *even as Christ also loved the Church, and gave Himself for it* (Ephesians 5:25). Although numerous imperfections exist within the Church, Jesus does not give up on the Church and seek some other means of uniting people to follow Him. Furthermore, Jesus doesn't force anyone to be in submission to Him. The husband's conduct toward, and compassion for, his wife need to be like that of Christ for His Church. Christ leads the way and sets the perfect example in compassion, kindness, and forgiveness.

When a man is in submission to Christ, he prepares the way for his wife to desire to be in submission to him: *Therefore as the Church is subject to Christ, so let the wives be to their own husbands in every thing* (5:24). It is imperative that a wife feel secure in her husband's love. It is his responsibility to let her know by word and action how very important she is to him.

God created the world and put Adam in charge of it. He created Eve to be Adam's helpmate. Husband and wife are a team and should be *kind one to another, tenderhearted, forgiving one another, even as God for Christ's sake has forgiven you* (Ephesians 4:32).

Thought for Today: A helpmate is a working partner who provides support.

Cross References: For Mark 10:6: See Genesis 1:27; 5:2. Mark 10:7-8: See Genesis 2:24. Mark 10:19: See Exodus 20:12-16; Deuteronomy 5:16-20. Mark 11:9: See Psalm 118:26. Mark 11:17: See Isaiah 56:7; Jerermiah 7:11.

For definitions of unfamiliar words in today's Bible reading, see pages 468-480.

In Today's Reading

Wicked tenant farmers; paying taxes to Caesar; the resurrection;
greatest commandment; widow's offering; signs of the end

*J*esus was questioned by a scribe, who asked: *Which is the first*
(foremost) *Commandment of all?* (Mark 12:28). Jesus answered him by
quoting Deuteronomy 6:4-5. *The first of all the Commandments is, Hear,*
O Israel; The Lord our God is One Lord: And you shall love the Lord your
God with all your heart, and with all your soul, and with all your mind, and
with all your strength (12:29-30). Jesus then quoted Leviticus 19:18,
saying: *And the second is like* (it), *namely this, You shall love your neighbor*
as yourself. There is no greater Commandment than these (12:31).

The Hebrew word *Elohenu* is translated in English as *our God*. However, God chose to use the plural form, *Elohim*, meaning G*ods*, 2500
times in reference to Himself as the Self-Existent, One True God. This,
then, is what the sacred proclamation to Israel literally says: *Hear, O*
Israel; The Lord our Gods is One Lord. Furthermore, the Hebrew word
for *One* used here is also a solemn declaration that the Lord is a plurality
in unity. *One* (*'echad*) is a word which expresses *one* in the collective
sense. It signifies a compound unity – not an absolute unity. For
example, God said: *Man . . . and . . . wife . . . shall be one flesh* (Genesis 2:24).
Even with numerous children, they are still called *one* family. The *one*
Tabernacle (Exodus 36:13) included many individual parts. However,
there is a Hebrew word for *one* in the sense of an absolute one. It is the
word *yacheed* and this word is never used to express the Godhead,
although it is used many times in Scripture.

This truth exposes the ignorance of all who refuse to recognize Jesus
as the One True God, the Creator of all things. The Holy Spirit guided
the Apostle Paul to write of Jesus: *For by Him were all things created, that*
are in heaven, and that are in earth (Colossians 1:16). Those who reject
Jesus as God and the Holy Spirit as the One Who *will guide you into all*
truth (John 16:13) are, in fact, rejecting the revelation of God Himself as
God the Father, God the Son, and God the Holy Spirit. Jesus left no doubt
as to Who He was when He said: *I and My Father are One* (John 10:30;
also 5:18; 12:45; 14:9-11,20).

Thought for Today: Pray today for those in authority.

Cross References: For Mark 12:1: See Isaiah 5:2. Mark 12:10-11: See Psalm 118:22-23.
Mark 12:19: See Deuteronomy 25:5. Mark 12:26: See Exodus 3:3-6. Mark 12:29: See
Deuteronomy 6:4. Mark 12:30: See Deuteronomy 6:5. Mark 12:31: See Leviticus 19:18.
Mark 12:32: See Deuteronomy 4:35. Mark 12:33: See Deuteronomy 6:5; Hosea 6:6. Mark
12:36: See Psalm 110:1. Mark 13:14: See Daniel 9:27; 11:31; 12:11. Mark 13:24: See Isaiah
13:10. Mark 13:26: See Daniel 7:13. Mark 13:27: See Deuteronomy 30:4; Zechariah 2:6.

For definitions of unfamiliar words in today's Bible reading, see pages 468-480.

In Today's Reading
Jesus' last Passover; Gethsemane; Peter's denial; Jesus before Pilate;
Jesus' crucifixion, burial, resurrection, and ascension

*S*imon, a leper who had been healed by Jesus, lived in Bethany, a small town less than two miles south of Jerusalem on the slope of the Mount of Olives. Just a few days before Jesus was crucified, Simon invited Him and the apostles to his home for supper. As they sat eating, *there came a woman having an alabaster box of ointment of spikenard* (perfume) *very precious* (costly); *and she broke the box, and poured it on His head* (Mark 14:3; also Matthew 26:6-13; John 12:1-8).

This *ointment of spikenard* was valued at *more than 300 pence* – about a year's wages for a common laborer (Mark 14:5; Matthew 20:2). John records that it was Judas who spoke up, saying: *Why was not this ointment sold . . . and given to the poor? This he said, not that he cared for the poor; but because he was a thief, and had the bag* (money purse), *and bore what was put therein* (John 12:5-6). To Judas, anything that was poured out upon Jesus was wasted; he coveted the money that the ointment might have brought. Jesus replied: *Let her alone: against the day of My burying she has kept this. For the poor you always have with you; but Me you have not always* (12:7-8).

The lost opportunity to sell the ointment and pocket the money, coupled with the strong rebuke from Jesus and the great honor bestowed upon Mary, probably angered Judas, who *went to the chief priests* (Mark 14:10). Judas' reason for being one of the 12 apostles became clear when he said to the chief priests: *What will you give me, and I will deliver Him to you?* (Matthew 26:15-16). *When they heard it, they were glad, and promised to give him money* (Mark 14:11). The betrayal, and even the amount paid to Judas, had been foretold by one of the Lord's prophets 600 years earlier: *I said to them . . . give Me My price . . . So they weighed for My price thirty pieces of silver* (Zechariah 11:12).

Our generation is no different than in the time of Jesus. Human nature remains the same. Every person must make the personal choice whether to accept or to reject Jesus as Savior and Lord of their lives. The question asked by Pilate must still be answered: *What shall I do then with Jesus Who is called Christ?* (Matthew 27:22).

Thought for Today: What you decide to do with Jesus determines your eternal destiny.

Cross References: For Mark 14:27: See Zechariah 13:7. Mark 14:62: See Psalm 110:1; Daniel 7:13. Mark 15:24: See Psalm 22:18. Mark 15:28: See Isaiah 53:12. Mark 15:29: See Psalm 22:7-8. Mark 15:34: See Psalm 22:1. Mark 16:19: See Psalm 110:1.

For definitions of unfamiliar words in today's Bible reading, see pages 468-480.

INTRODUCTION TO THE BOOK OF
Luke

Luke was a Gentile who addressed this book, as well as the Book of Acts, to Theophilus, which means "friend of God." He proclaimed a universal Gospel to everyone who desires to be called a "friend of God" when he recorded the message the angel gave to the shepherds at the time of Christ's birth: *Fear not: for, behold, I bring you good tidings of great joy, which shall be to all people* (Luke 2:10). Luke revealed that the purpose for Jesus leaving heaven was *to seek and to save that which was lost* (19:10; also 1:68; 2:11,38; 24:21). Luke was known as *the beloved physician* (Colossians 4:14).

Luke emphasizes the divinity of Christ even in His perfect humanity. The perfect humanity of Jesus is revealed as Luke presents Jesus as the Son of Man. The phrase *Son of Man* is mentioned 25 times in this book. Luke also proclaimed the full deity of Jesus as the virgin-born Son of God as he traced the genealogy of Jesus through His mother Mary back to the creation of the first man, Adam. Through the actual, physical genealogy of Mary, Christ is linked with all mankind.

No other Gospel provides as many details of the humanity of Jesus as the Book of Luke does. He tells us about the parents and the birth of John the Baptist, Jesus' cousin who was just 6 months older than Jesus (Luke 1:36). He also gives the details of the journey of Mary and Joseph to Bethlehem where Jesus was born (2:1-7). Only Luke records that Jesus was *laid . . . in a manger* (2:7); was presented for circumcision in the Temple (2:21-24); conversed with the teachers (rabbinic scholars) at the age of twelve (2:42-46); and that *Jesus increased in wisdom and stature, and in favor with God and man* (2:52).

Luke also reveals the human dependence of Jesus upon His Heavenly Father in prayer (3:21; 5:16; 6:12; 9:16,18,28-29; 10:21; 11:1; 22:17,19; 23:46; 24:30). This points out the vital importance for all of His followers to realize how dependent upon God we are to accomplish His will through prayer. Only Luke records the disciples asking: *Lord, teach us to pray* (11:1), or Jesus teaching *that men ought always to pray, and not to faint* (lose heart) (18:1). The parable of the unjust judge and the widow (18:2-8), and the parable of the midnight appeal: *Friend, lend me three loaves* (11:5-13) are found only in Luke. All of these teach the importance of continuing to pray until the need is met.

Luke demonstrates that the Gospel is for everyone, even Samaritans (Luke 17:11-19).

In Today's Reading
Virgin birth of Jesus foretold; Mary's visit to Elisabeth;
Mary's praise to God; birth of John the Baptist

---

*J*esus would have been born with the sinful nature of Adam if Joseph had been His biological father. This would have made Jesus a sinner like all mankind and, thus, unable to be the sinless substitute for our sins. But Gabriel, the angelic messenger of good news, came to Mary and said: *Hail, you that are highly favored, the Lord is with you. . . . behold, you shall conceive in your womb, and bring forth a Son, and shall call His Name JESUS. He shall be great, and shall be called the Son of the Highest: and the Lord God shall give to Him the throne of His father David. . . . the power of the Highest shall overshadow you . . . that Holy Thing* (One) *Who shall be born of you shall be called the Son of God* (Luke 1:28,31-32,35).

Luke records that Mary was deeply *troubled at his saying* (1:29). Joseph also was troubled when he learned Mary was pregnant and contemplated a private divorce. *The angel of the Lord appeared to him in a dream, saying, Joseph, you son of David, fear not to take to you Mary your wife: for that which is conceived in her is of the Holy Spirit. And she shall bring forth a Son, and you shall call His Name JESUS* ("Jesus" in Hebrew is the same as "Joshua" meaning "Jehovah (Yahweh) delivered" – Savior): *for He shall save His people from their sins* (Matthew 1:20-21). How comforting this must have been to Mary. Instead of living under suspicion, there was a miraculous confirmation to Joseph of her virginity.

About 700 years before, Isaiah foretold: *Behold, a virgin shall conceive, and bear a Son, and shall call His Name Immanuel* (God With Us). *. . . to us a Child is born . . . the government shall be upon His shoulder: and His Name shall be called Wonderful, Counselor, The Mighty God, The Everlasting Father, The Prince of Peace* (Isaiah 7:14; 9:6). Jesus' birth revealed His unique nature as both God and Man.

The prophet Micah had foretold that the Messiah, *Whose goings forth have been from of old, from everlasting* (Micah 5:2), would be born in Bethlehem of Judah. This small town, about six miles south of Jerusalem, was called the city of David, for that is where David was born.

Zechariah . . . prophesied, saying, Blessed be the Lord God of Israel; for He has visited and redeemed His people (Luke 1:67-75).

Thought for Today: *We beheld His glory . . . full of grace and truth* (John 1:14).

Cross References: For Luke 1:17: See Malachi 4:5-6. **Luke 1:50:** See Psalm 103:17. **Luke 1:53:** See Psalm 107:9. **Luke 1:71:** See Psalm 106:10. **Luke 1:76:** See Malachi 3:1. **Luke 1:79:** See Isaiah 9:1-2; 59:8.

For definitions of unfamiliar words in today's Bible reading, see pages 468-480.

ℐN ᖶODAY'S ℛEADING

Jesus' birth; shepherds' adoration; Simeon's and Anna's prophecies;
Jesus in the Temple; John the Baptist; baptism of Jesus; Jesus' genealogy

---

The Passover brought Mary and Joseph to Jerusalem every year. The year Jesus was twelve years old, in the busy preparation for returning home after the feast, Mary and Joseph, *supposing Him to have been in the company* (group), *went a day's journey; and they sought Him among their kinsfolk* (relatives) *and acquaintance. And when they found Him not, they turned back again to Jerusalem, seeking Him. And it came to pass, that after three days they found Him in the Temple, sitting in the midst of the doctors* (teachers), *both hearing them, and asking them questions* (Luke 2:44-46).

After finding Him in the Temple, Mary said: *Son, why have You thus dealt with us? behold, Your father and I have sought You sorrowing* (2:48). Jesus calmly explained to Mary His reason for being in the Temple, saying: *How is it that you sought Me? knew you not that I must be about My Father's business?* (2:49). Jesus made it very clear Who His real Father was. Devotion to His Heavenly Father's interests drew Him to the Temple; but His submission to the will of His Father also caused Him to return to Nazareth where He *was subject* (obedient) *to them* (2:51).

In this age of rebellion, many young people are not disciplined to be in subjection to their parents or to anyone else. Honoring and obeying God-ordained parental authority *is the first commandment with promise* (Ephesians 6:2). Parents who are in submission to God have a responsibility to their children to spiritually train them – especially by personal example, through daily devotions, and by regular attendance in a Bible-teaching church on the Lord's Day. Pity the parents who rebel against restrictions which are placed on them on the job, at church, or in the community. Such people may even think they have a right to be independent of God-ordained authority, yet they still expect their children to be obedient to various authorities.

Let every soul (person) *be subject to the higher powers* (governmental authorities). *For there is no power but of God: the powers that be are ordained of* (established by) *God. Whosoever therefore resists the power, resists the ordinance of God: and they that resist shall receive to themselves damnation* (condemnation) (Romans 13:1-2).

Thought for Today: The certainty that all of God's Word will be fulfilled is the foundation of our Christian faith.

Cross References: For Luke 2:23: See Exodus 13:2,12. Luke 2:24: See Leviticus 12:8. Luke 2:32: See Isaiah 9:2; 42:6; 49:6. Luke 3:4-6: See Isaiah 40:3-5.

For definitions of unfamiliar words in today's Bible reading, see pages 468-480.

ℐN ℐODAY'S ℛEADING
Temptation of Jesus; His teachings; healings;
the miraculous catch of fish; other miracles; the call of Matthew

---

Some think they can worship God just as well while on the lake fishing or at home resting as they can in church. In contrast, Jesus recognized the need to honor God by regularly attending worship services. We read that *He taught in their synagogues* while in Galilee (Luke 4:15). *And He came to Nazareth, where He had been brought up: and, as His custom was, He went into the synagogue on the Sabbath day* (4:16). Jesus was invited to speak, *And there was delivered to Him the Book of the prophet Isaiah. And . . . He found the place where it was written, The Spirit of the Lord is upon Me, because He has anointed Me to preach the Gospel to the poor; He has sent Me to heal the brokenhearted, to preach deliverance to the captives, and recovering of sight to the blind, to set at liberty them that are bruised. . . . And He closed the Book, and He gave it again to the minister, and sat down* (4:17-20; Isaiah 61:1-2).

The Scripture Jesus read contained a clear mention of all three Persons of the Trinity – the Holy Spirit, the Father, and the Anointed One.

The people were amazed, *And the eyes of all them that were in the synagogue were fastened on Him. And He began to say to them, This day is this Scripture fulfilled in your ears* (Luke 4:20-21). They marveled at His *gracious words* (4:22), but knew He clearly referred to Himself as the Messiah Who had been foretold by Isaiah and other prophets beginning with Genesis 3:15. You can imagine how startled they were when Jesus said that He Whom they assumed to be *the son of Joseph* (Luke 3:23) was really their long awaited Messiah.

The congregation listening to Jesus was so infuriated at His equating Himself with God that they disrupted the worship service, seized Jesus, and attempted to put Him to death for blasphemy by pushing Him over a rocky precipice. *But He passing through the midst of them went His way* (4:28-30). Luke emphasized that Christ is God (the Messiah).

How easy it is to be mistaken when we follow emotions rather than the truth revealed in God's Word. In contrast to the Jews of Nazareth, later the Jews in Berea *received the Word with all readiness of mind*, for they *searched the Scriptures daily, whether those things were so* (Acts 17:11).

Thought for Today: Just think! You have the privilege to work for your Creator.

Cross References: For Luke 4:4: See Deuteronomy 8:3. Luke 4:8: See Deuteronomy 6:13. Luke 4:10-11: See Psalm 91:11-12. Luke 4:12: See Deuteronomy 6:16. Luke 4:18-19: See Isaiah 61:1-2. Luke 5:14: See Leviticus 13:1-3.

For definitions of unfamiliar words in today's Bible reading, see pages 468-480.

ℐN 𝒯ODAY'S ℛEADING
Jesus and the Sabbath; 12 apostles chosen; Sermon on the Mount;
healing and miracles; John the Baptist's question; Jesus anointed

𝒲e all have sinned beyond our ability to count, and we should be deeply thankful that our Heavenly Father forgives us when we repent of our sins. If we are truly grateful, we will approach everyone who sins against us with the same mercy and compassion that we receive from the Lord. Jesus, Who knows how the human heart tends to be hypocritical, warned: *Why behold . . . the mote* (speck) *that is in your brother's eye, but perceive not the beam that is in your own eye? . . . You hypocrite, cast out first the beam out of your own eye, and then you shall see clearly to pull out the mote that is in your brother's eye* (Luke 6:41-42).

It is our responsibility to recognize *the mote* (evil) for what it is, but we must first consider our own *beam* (negative attitudes and criticism of others). Only then are we qualified to help others with their needs.

A heart of compassion and concern to help others is in striking contrast to those who overlook their own faults and failures, but who rarely miss an opportunity to gossip about someone else's conduct or failures. We are prone to imply evil motives to others' actions, and may even exaggerate them. Thankfully, God is a merciful God, Who fully forgives us when we repent of our sins. But, we tend to judge ourselves by our good intentions and others by their mistakes. Since we expect God's mercy toward us, it makes a vital demand upon us to extend that same mercy to others. *If you forgive not men their trespasses, neither will your Father forgive your trespasses* (Matthew 6:15).

Criticism is often an act of self-righteousness in an attempt to build one's own self-esteem by putting others down. Also, it is easy to jump to conclusions without hearing or caring about all the facts. We have an amazing ability to misjudge the thoughts and actions of others. Judgmental people thrive on faultfinding and find something wrong with everything that is said or done by another whom they would love to belittle. It is this self-righteousness that Jesus spoke of when He said: *Cast out first the beam out of your own eye.* Then the love of Christ can be expressed through us.

If anyone is *overtaken in a fault* (sin), *you which are spiritual, restore such a one in the spirit of meekness; considering yourself, lest you also be tempted* (Galatians 6:1).

Thought for Today: It is unjust to criticize anyone – even those whose efforts fall short of what we expect. We answer to Christ for our own lives.

Cross References: For Luke 7:22: See Isaiah 61:1. Luke 7:27: See Malachi 3:1.

For definitions of unfamiliar words in today's Bible reading, see pages 468-480.

> ## *In Today's Reading*
> Jesus' teachings; more miracles; 12 apostles sent forth;
> 5,000 fed; Peter's confession; transfiguration of Christ

*J*esus put the sincerity of would-be disciples to the test when *a certain man said to Him, Lord, I will follow You wherever You go. And Jesus said to him, Foxes have holes, and birds of the air have nests; but the Son of Man has no where to lay His head* (no place to sleep) (Luke 9:57-58). The *foxes* illustrate the clever ones and the *birds of the air* illustrate the worldly. Jesus pointed out to this man that, if he chose to follow Him, he could expect hardships. Jesus was also saying that He was not attached to earthly possessions, nor could His followers expect any guarantee of earthly resources.

And another also said, Lord, I will follow You; but let me first go bid them farewell, which are at home at my house. And Jesus said to him, No man, having put his hands to the plow, and looking back, is fit for the Kingdom of God (9:61-62). Our Lord did not welcome volunteers who were only willing to join Him on their own terms; serving Christ requires a lifetime commitment. Love dictates that there be no compromise in following Him. Jesus was not then, nor is He now, in the midst of a membership drive, nor is He counting converts to prove His success.

Self-seekers and compromisers are often misled, believing there will be a more convenient time when they can choose to follow the Lord. Their excuses reveal that they have divided hearts. Some lack the "single eye" of devotion to Christ where, by comparison, all else in this world is of little importance. Others fail to put Christ first in their daily decisions and, yet, all who do will discover that the satisfaction of self-denial far exceeds fleeting earthly rewards. Each of us needs to consider whether there is someone in our life or something in our heart that is keeping us from giving Christ, His Word, and His will, first place in our lives.

Jesus warned: *The Kingdom of God is near at hand. Verily* (truly) *I say to you. . . . Heaven and earth shall pass away: but My words shall not pass away. And take heed to yourselves, lest at any time your hearts be overcharged with surfeiting* (self-indulgence), *and drunkenness, and cares of this life, and so that day come upon you unawares* (suddenly) (Luke 21:31-34).

Thought for Today: Worldly ambitions fade into insignifance when we devote ourselves to knowing the Lord by reading His Word.

Cross Reference: For Luke 8:10: See Isaiah 6:9.

For definitions of unfamiliar words in today's Bible reading, see pages 468-480.

𝒥N 𝒯ODAY'S 𝑅EADING
Seventy sent out; Good Samaritan; Martha and Mary; teaching on prayer; Pharisees denounced

A scribe who was an official interpreter of both the Mosaic Law and the traditions of the elders, *stood up, and tempted Him, saying, Master, what shall I do to inherit eternal life?* (Luke 10:25). Jesus replied: *What is written in the Law?* He answered: *You shall love the Lord your God with all your heart, and with all your soul, and with all your strength, and with all your mind; and your neighbor as yourself.* And Jesus said: *You have answered right: this do, and you shall live. But he, willing to justify himself, said to Jesus, And who is my neighbor?* (10:26-29).

Jesus illustrated the answer by saying: *A certain man went down from Jerusalem to Jericho, and fell among thieves, who stripped him of his raiment* (clothing), *and wounded him, and departed, leaving him half dead. And by chance there came down a certain priest that way: and when he saw him, he passed by on the other side. And likewise a Levite, when he was at the place, came and looked on him, and passed by on the other side. But a certain Samaritan, as he journeyed . . . when he saw him, he had compassion on him . . . and bound up his wounds . . . and brought him to an inn, and took care of him. . . . Which now of these three . . . was neighbor to him that fell among the thieves? And he said, He that showed mercy on him. Then Jesus said to him, Go, and do likewise* (Luke 10:30-37).

My *neighbor* is anyone who needs my compassion and whom I have the opportunity and ability to help. It does not matter what his position, race, or religion may be. We are simply to enter into the feelings of another's sufferings or misfortunes as God has done for us (Hebrews 4:15). Whatever is mine actually belongs to God and whatever belongs to God should be shared with my neighbor because my neighbor was also created by and in the image of God.

All of us need to be reminded of our Lord's answer to the lawyer's question. *What must I do to inherit eternal life?* Jesus caused him to recognize that the evidence of eternal life within us is a desire to **obey** God's Word. Jesus said: *A new commandment I give to you, That you love one another; as I have loved you, that you also love one another. By this shall all men know that you are My disciples, if you have love one to (for) another* (John 13:34-35).

Thought for Today: It is one thing to serve God, but quite another to show compassion to those who are less fortunate than we are.

Cross References: For Luke 10:27: See Leviticus 19:18. Luke 10:28: See Leviticus 18:5.

For definitions of unfamiliar words in today's Bible reading, see pages 468-480.

In Today's Reading
Warnings against greed, hypocrisy; parables, healings, and teachings

The Lord illustrated the deceptive danger of covetousness by telling this parable: *The ground of a certain rich man brought forth plentifully: And he thought within himself, saying, What shall I do, because I have no room where to bestow* (store) *my fruits? . . . I will pull down my barns, and build greater* (larger); *and there will I bestow all my fruits and my goods. And I will say to my soul, Soul, you have much goods laid up for many years; take your ease, eat, drink, and be merry. But God said to him, You fool, this night your soul shall be required of you: then whose shall those things be, which you have provided?* (Luke 12:16-20). By hard work in the highly-respected occupation of farming, this man had become wealthy. There is no hint that he had gained his wealth by dishonest methods. His soul-destroying sin was that he spent his lifetime in self-gratification. God called him a *fool*, and then added: *So is he that lays up treasure for himself, and is not rich toward God* (12:20-21).

We Christians should not allow material desires to distract us from doing the will of God. **We are not to worry about our future needs.** As important as food, clothing, and shelter are to maintaining life, our first concern should always be to *seek . . . first the Kingdom of God, and His righteousness* (Matthew 6:33). By keeping our priorities right, we prepare ourselves to be all that our Lord wants us to be to accomplish the purpose for which He created us.

How we use our time and talents is an expression of our Christian faith. Christ taught that life is truly fulfilling by loving, serving, and giving to extend the Good News to a lost world. Regardless of how much or how little talent, or possessions we may have or acquire, as good stewards we should prayerfully consider what Jesus would have us do with them.

You, O man of God . . . follow after righteousness, godliness, faith, love, patience, meekness (gentleness). *Fight the good fight of faith, lay* (take) *hold on eternal life, whereto you are also called, and have professed a good profession* (confession) *before many witnesses* (I Timothy 6:11-12).

Thought for Today: If we are truly concerned about God's interests, He will take care of ours.

Cross References: For Luke 13:27: See Psalm 6:8. Luke 13:35: See Psalm 118:26.

For definitions of unfamiliar words in today's Bible reading, see pages 468-480.

*I*N *T*ODAY'S *R*EADING

Humility; more parables; prodigal son; rich man and Lazarus;
the joy of eternal life with Abraham; the horror of eternal hell

*O*ur Lord illustrates the two alternatives in life. The first choice is a self-centered son who demanded freedom from his father's authority, and then *took his journey into a far country, and there wasted his substance* (inheritance) *with riotous living. . . . when he had spent all . . . he began to be in want* (faced starvation) (Luke 15:13-16).

A wise alternate choice is illustrated by this prodigal son when *he said . . . I perish* (die) *with hunger! I will arise and go to my father, and will say to him, Father, I have sinned against heaven, and in thy sight* (15:17-18).

The word "prodigal" means a waster; the young man *wasted* his father's substance. After he repented, his father made him aware of the seriousness of his former life as a sinner when he said: *This my son was dead, and is alive again; he was lost, and is found. And they began to be merry* and enjoy fellowship with each other (15:24).

Just as the prodigal son discovered that his father's love was far greater than he had previously realized, so too will every repentant sinner discover that the Heavenly Father is waiting with great compassion to forgive all who come to Him.

Jesus then told of a rich man who never recognized that he had "wasted" his life, even though he had become "very successful." But, *in hell . . . being in torments. . . . he cried . . . I am tormented in this flame* (Luke 16:23-24). It was only then he discovered that hell was eternal and that, between him and Abraham, there was a *great gulf fixed* (16:26). The rich man's preoccupation with success crowded out any desire to use his abilities or resources for the glory of God. The foremost purpose of our brief life on earth is to prepare for an endless eternity, and then do what we can to provide spiritual food for others.

Since the believer's true *conversation* (citizenship) *is in heaven* (Philippians 3:20), we dare not make secular goals, material gain, and physical satisfactions our priorities. All mankind, rich or poor, has one thing in common – physical death will open the door to either the joy of eternal life or the horrors of eternal hell. *Therefore we ought to give the more earnest heed to the things which we have heard. . . . How shall we escape, if we neglect so great salvation?* (Hebrews 2:1,3).

Thought for Today: Are you a prodigal? The Father is lovingly awaiting to welcome you.

Cross Reference: For Luke 16:15: See Proverbs 21:2.

For definitions of unfamiliar words in today's Bible reading, see pages 468-480.

*N*o one question could be of greater importance than that of *a certain ruler* (Luke 18:18) who *came . . . running, and kneeled to Him* (Jesus) (Mark 10:17). He was a *young man* (Matthew 19:20,22) and possessed great wealth. Kneeling before Jesus, he asked: *Good Master, what shall I do to inherit eternal life? And Jesus said to him. . . . Do not commit adultery, Do not kill, Do not steal, Do not bear false witness, Honor your father and your mother* (Luke 18:18-27; also Matthew 19:16-30; Mark 10:17-31). No one ever addressed a scribe or a rabbi as *Good Master* – only God was called good. Three Gospels report that he recognized Jesus as more than just another Teacher, but as the *Good Master* (Teacher). He knew that, beyond this physical life, there was an eternity that he wanted to inherit.

In response to his most vital question: *What must I do,* Jesus told him: *You lack one thing: sell all that you have, and distribute to the poor, and you shall have treasure in heaven: and come, follow Me. And when he heard this, he was very sorrowful: for he was very rich* (Luke 18:22-23). This should not be twisted to mean that eternal life can be earned by self-effort or sacrificial giving. Eternal life can only come from Him Who *loved us, and washed us from our sins in His own blood* (Revelation 1:5). He was unwilling to let Jesus be Lord of his life. He would not give up the influence, prestige, and financial security that his wealth provided. He was a good man, and very religious, but sadly he was eternally lost.

The Bible does not condemn people just because they are rich, but, *charge* (instruct) *them that are rich in this world, that they be not high-minded* (conceited), *nor trust in uncertain riches, but in the living God, Who gives us richly all things to enjoy; That they do good, that they be rich in good works, ready to distribute, willing to communicate* (share); *Laying up in store for themselves a good foundation against the time to come, that they may lay hold on eternal life* (I Timothy 6:17-19).

Your daily decisions and your lifestyle reveal what you really believe. The young ruler illustrates why Jesus said: *Narrow is the way, which leads to life, and few there be that find it* (Matthew 7:14).

Thought for Today: Read His Word. *He shall direct your paths* (Proverbs 3:6).

Cross Reference: For Luke 18:20: See Exodus 20:12-16; Deuteronomy 5:16-20.

For definitions of unfamiliar words in today's Bible reading, see pages 468-480.

In Today's Reading

Jesus and Zacchaeus; triumphal entry; cleansing the Temple;
parable of wicked tenants; paying taxes;
the resurrection; Jesus' authority

The Pharisees conspired against Jesus with the cooperation of the nonreligious political party called the Herodians, a group which urged Israel's submission to Rome (Matthew 22:16). These opposite-thinking groups of people hypocritically sent an investigative committee from the Sanhedrin, pretending to be interested in following Jesus. They said to Jesus: *Master, we know that You say and . . . teach the way of God truly: Is it lawful for us to give tribute* (taxes) *to Caesar, or not?* (Luke 20:21-22). Since the majority of Jews deeply resented paying taxes to the Roman government, this "committee" was sure the crowd would quickly turn against Jesus if He said "Yes." And the Pharisees could also say He was not the Messiah of Israel if He taught subjection to a Gentile government. But, if He said "No," the Herodian party could then accuse Him of conspiracy against the Roman government and Pilate could have Him arrested for treason.

But He perceived their craftiness, and said to them, Why tempt Me? Show me a penny (a Roman coin that was an accepted currency among Jews). *Whose image and superscription* (inscription) *has it? They answered . . . Caesar's. And He said to them, Render* (Give) *therefore to Caesar the things which are Caesar's.* The rest of His comment came as a stinging rebuke to their hypocrisy when He added: *And to God the things which are God's* (20:23-25). While the image upon a coin is representative of governmental authority, we must also submit to a higher authority because we are created *in the image of God* (Genesis 1:26-27). This means that the words of Jesus are still just as true for us today.

Some misguided citizens accept the benefits of government but avoid paying taxes. They ignore the two reasons for paying them. Christians are to pay required taxes and obey the law, but they also pay them as a requirement to please God. We simply cannot ignore His clear command to: *Submit yourselves to every ordinance of man for the Lord's sake: whether it be to the king, as supreme; Or to governors, as to them that are sent by him for the punishment of evildoers* (I Peter 2:13-14).

Thought for Today: Oh, to hear Jesus say, "Well done!"

Cross References: For Luke 19:38: See Psalm 118:26. Luke 19:46: See Isaiah 56:7; Jeremiah 7:11. Luke 20:17: See Psalm 118:22. Luke 20:28: See Deuteronomy 25:5. Luke 20:37: See Exodus 3:6. Luke 20:42-43: See Psalm 110:1.

For definitions of unfamiliar words in today's Bible reading, see pages 468-480.

In Today's Reading

The widow's offering; signs of the end; Jesus' last Passover;
the Lord's Supper; prayer in the garden; Jesus' arrest; Peter's denial

The Israelites' annual Passover meal was a reminder that the blood of an innocent lamb and obedience to the Word of God had made it possible for their ancestors to be redeemed from death, set free from Pharaoh and Egyptian slavery, and to enjoy freedom in the promised land.

On the evening of the Passover, Jesus *took bread, and gave thanks, and broke it, and gave to them* (His 12 disciples), *saying, This is My body which is given for you: this do in remembrance of Me. Likewise also the cup after supper, saying, This cup is the New Testament in My blood, which is shed for you* (Luke 22:19-20). At this Passover, our Lord identified Himself with the sacrificial Passover Lamb.

The Lord's Supper is a reminder that Jesus' death on the cross delivered us from Satan, and set us free from the condemnation for our sins to receive eternal life. This ordinance is so sacred that the Holy Spirit emphasized its importance through the Apostle Paul who wrote: *The Lord Jesus the same night in which He was betrayed took bread: And when He had given thanks, He broke it, and said, Take, eat: this is My body, which is broken for you: this do in remembrance of Me* (I Corinthians 11:23-25). It is of the utmost importance that we consider carefully that our Lord said: *This do in remembrance of Me.* He did not make a suggestion but a command. Jesus reminds all His followers: *Why call Me, Lord, Lord, and do not the things which I say?* (Luke 6:46). And again He said: *If a man love Me, he will keep My words* (John 14:23).

The Lord wanted us to know that His death on the cross made the difference for us between spending eternity in *the lake of fire* (Revelation 20:14-15) or in heaven with Him (John 3:16; 14:2-3). The Lord's Supper is a continuing reminder that there is forgiveness for all who, by faith, accept Jesus' atoning sacrifice as the only means of receiving eternal life. It is also a time to consider what attitudes of ill will toward others, revenge, and lust need to be confessed and forsaken. The Lord's table is a reminder that *whosoever shall eat this bread, and drink this cup of the Lord, unworthily, shall be guilty of the body and blood of the Lord. But let a man examine himself, and so let him eat of that* (the) *bread, and drink of that* (the) *cup* (I Corinthians 11:27-28).

Thought for Today: We need to express forgiving love in our hearts toward all offenders.

Cross References: For Luke 21:27: See Daniel 7:13. Luke 22:37: See Isaiah 53:12. Luke 22:69: See Psalm 110:1.

For definitions of unfamiliar words in today's Bible reading, see pages 468-480.

$\mathscr{I}$N $\mathscr{T}$ODAY'S $\mathscr{R}$EADING

Jesus before Pilate and Herod; His crucifixion and resurrection;
ministry of the risen Christ; His commission; His ascension

$\mathscr{S}$ome of the women who were followers of Jesus watched as He died on the cross, and then watched as the body of their beloved Lord was hastily laid in the rock-hewn tomb of Joseph of Arimathea. *That day was the preparation. . . . And the women. . . . returned, and prepared spices and ointments; and rested the Sabbath day according to the Commandment* (Luke 23:54-56). *Now upon the first day of the week, very early in the morning* (24:1), on their way to the tomb, these women were greatly concerned about *who shall roll away the stone from the door of the sepulcher* (tomb)? *. . . the stone . . . was very great* (large) (Mark 16:3-4). They soon discovered that their concern had already been taken care of by an angel.

Matthew recorded the terror experienced by the Roman guards who had been assigned to watch the sealed tomb, when *the angel of the Lord descended from heaven, and . . . rolled back the stone from the door, and sat upon it* (Matthew 28:2,4). When the women came to the tomb to complete the burial procedures, *they entered in, and . . . . behold, two men stood by them in shining garments: And. . . . said to them, Why seek the living among the dead? He is not here, but is risen: remember how He spoke to you when He was yet in Galilee, Saying, The Son of Man must be delivered into the hands of sinful men, and be crucified, and the third day rise again* (Luke 24:3-7). Excitedly, the women rushed to the disciples to relate their thrilling discovery.

These women had no thought of deserting their Lord in death, even though a hostile crowd had crucified Him. Our love for the Lord Jesus and His Word should enable us to overcome any temptation to be intimidated by unbelievers. Neither the women, nor the apostles, were expecting such a glorious experience on that resurrection morning. God always has better things in store for us than we think possible, *that He would grant you, according to the riches of His glory, to be strengthened with might by His Spirit in the inner man. . . . And to know the love of Christ, which passes knowledge, that you might be filled with all the fullness of God. Now to Him that is able to do exceedingly abundantly above all that we ask or think, according to the power that works in us, To Him be glory in the Church by Christ Jesus throughout all ages, world without end. Amen.* (Ephesians 3:16,19-21).

Thought for Today: God is merciful to all who ask.

Cross References: For Luke 23:30: See Hosea 10:8. Luke 23:34: See Psalm 22:18.

For definitions of unfamiliar words in today's Bible reading, see pages 468-480.

PRAYER ANSWERED

If you abide (live) *in Me, and My words abide in you, you shall ask what you will, and it shall be done to you* (John 15:7).

Then have we confidence toward God. And whatsoever we ask, we receive of Him, because we keep (obey) *His Commandments, and do those things that are pleasing in His sight* (I John 3:21-22).

If you keep (obey) *My Commandments, you shall abide* (remain, live) *in My love; even as I have kept My Father's Commandments, and abide in His love* (John 15:10).

Introduction To The Book Of
John

The Holy Spirit guided the Apostle John to reveal the true nature and purpose of Jesus Christ, both as perfect man and as deity, One with God the Father in the creation of all things. The Gospel of John begins by declaring: *In the beginning was the Word, and the Word was with God, and the Word was God. The Same was in the beginning with God. All things were made by Him; and without Him was not any thing made that was made* (John 1:1-3).

God further revealed Himself when *the Word was made flesh, and dwelt among us, and we beheld His glory, the glory as of the Only Begotten of the Father, full of grace and truth* (1:14).

John revealed Jesus as the prophesied, sinless *Lamb of God, Who takes away the sin of the world* (1:29; Isaiah 53:7). The religious leaders *sought the more to kill Him, because He . . . said . . .* (1) *that God was His Father, making Himself equal with God* (John 5:18); (2) in knowing *all things* (vs 20); (3) in judging, *the Father . . . has committed all judgment to the Son* (vs 22); (4) in receiving honor *even as they honor the Father* (vs 23); (5) in imparting *everlasting life* (vss 24-25); (6) in being self-existent, *as the Father has life in Himself; so has He given to the Son to have life* (the source of life) *in Himself* (vs 26); and (7) in resurrecting, *the Son makes alive whom He wills* (vss 21,28-29).

Jesus declared: *I and My Father are One. . . . he that has seen Me has seen the Father* (10:30; 14:9). He also spoke of *the glory* which He had with the Father *before the world was* (17:5). Jesus also revealed Himself as the eternal *I AM* of the Old Testament (Exodus 3:14) with eight *I am* statements: *I am the Bread of Life* (John 6:35); *Before Abraham was, I am* (8:58); *I am the Light of the world* (8:12); *I am the Door. . . . by Me if any man enter in, he shall be saved* (10:7-9); *I am the Good Shepherd* (10:11); *I am the Resurrection, and the Life* (11:25); *I am the Way, the Truth, and the Life: no man comes to the Father, but by Me* (14:6); and *I am the True Vine . . . . If a man abide not in Me, he is cast forth as a branch . . . and men gather them, and cast them into the fire* (15:1-2,6).

Jesus said to His followers: *Abide* (Remain) *in Me. . . . keep* (obey) *My Commandments* (15:4,10). *If you continue in My Word, then you are My disciples indeed; And you shall know the Truth, and the Truth shall make you free* (8:31-32). The purpose of John is clear. *These are written, that you might believe that Jesus is the Christ, the Son of God; and that believing you might have life through His Name* (20:31).

In Today's Reading
Deity of Christ; John the Baptist; the Lamb of God;
first miracle in Cana; cleansing of the Temple; Nicodemus

There was a man of the Pharisees, named Nicodemus, a ruler of the Jews: The same came to Jesus by night (John 3:1). This prominent rabbi probably wanted an uninterrupted conversation with Jesus, so he chose to see Him at night. He was a member of the Sanhedrin, the council which controlled the religious life of Israel, yet he confessed to Jesus: *Rabbi, we know that You are a teacher come from God* (3:2).

Jesus said to Nicodemus: *Except a man be born of water and of the Spirit, he cannot enter into the Kingdom of God. That which is born of the flesh* (human parents) *is flesh; and that which is born of the Spirit is spirit (sons of God* v. 1:12) (3:5-6). *You must be born again (of God v. 1:13) (3:7).* To illustrate how essential it is to be *born again* (eternal life), Jesus reminded him of when the Israelites, near the end of their 40 years of wilderness wandering, once again complained about their circumstances. So, the Lord sent fiery serpents among them. Thousands of people died. When the people cried out to God, He commanded Moses to make a serpent of brass and lift it up on a pole. The people could only be healed by turning their eyes and looking up at the brazen serpent (Numbers 21:5-9). Jesus then said: *As Moses lifted up the serpent in the wilderness, even so must the Son of Man be lifted up: That whosoever believes in Him should not perish, but have eternal life* (John 3:14-15). *He that believes in Him is not condemned* (judged): *but he that believes not is condemned already, because he has not believed in the Name of the Only Begotten Son of God* (3:18). The serpent was made of brass since brass is a biblical symbol of judgment.

The one who is *born again* of the Holy Spirit loves the things he once ignored, and he now hates the things he once desired. When we were born the first time, we received the sinful nature of our parents, which was inherited from Adam. When we are *born again* into the family of God, we receive His divine nature. Therefore: *Walk as children of light: (For the fruit of the Spirit is in all goodness and righteousness and truth;) proving what is acceptable to the Lord* (Ephesians 5:8-10).

Thought for Today: The most insignificant person by the world's standards is precious in the eyes of God.

Cross References: For John 1:23: See Isaiah 40:3; Malachi 3:1. John 2:17: See Psalm 69:9.

For definitions of unfamiliar words in today's Bible reading, see pages 468-480.

In Today's Reading
Jesus and the Samaritan woman; miracles of healing;
Jesus answers the Jews

The sheep gate where lambs were bought for sacrifice was located at the northeast area of the Temple court in Jerusalem. Nearby *the sheep market* (is) *a pool, which is called . . . Bethesda, having five porches* (John 5:2). At this pool *lay a great multitude of impotent* (sick, invalid, and physically disabled) *folk* (5:3). It was believed that the first to enter the pool of water after *an angel* stirred up the water would be cured (5:4). The Great Physician approached this crowd of helpless sufferers, but no one recognized Him.

In this crowd of helpless people was *a certain man . . . which had an infirmity thirty and eight years* (5:5). What possibility was there that anyone would care if he were ever healed? When this man expressed his hopelessness, Jesus looked beyond the man's problem and asked him to do something about it, saying: *Rise, take up your bed, and walk. And immediately the man was made whole, and took up his bed, and walked* (5:7-9).

Like this man, you and I once were spiritually helpless. We should be eternally grateful that Jesus did not pass us by but asked us if we wanted to be made whole. Jesus cares for even the most helpless, desiring that they will all recognize Him as Savior and Lord. They may be popular athletes, intellectual leaders such as Nicodemus, pitiful prostitutes like the woman at the well, or any other lost person.

This was on the day *there was a feast of the Jews* (5:1). Some believe this was the Passover, which would be very fitting. But others believe it was Pentecost (Deuteronomy 16:1-11), the day on which believers were first filled with the Holy Spirit and empowered to be witnesses *to the uttermost part of the earth* (Acts 1:8; 2:1-4).

The sheep gate illustrates Jesus, *the Lamb of God, Who takes away the sin of the world* (John 1:29). The pool called *Bethesda* means "house of mercy or grace." It is only through the compassion of Christ that any lost sinner, without exception, can find mercy and grace by accepting His sacrifice on the cross for our sins.

The Apostle Paul reminds us that we once were *children of wrath,* but we have been cleansed from our sins and given a new nature with the privilege to *put on the new man, which after God is created in righteousness and true holiness* (Ephesians 2:3; 4:24).

Thought for Today: Temporal "satisfactions" may "quench our thirst" momentarily, but they will never truly satisfy.

For definitions of unfamiliar words in today's Bible reading, see pages 468-480.

IN TODAY'S READING
Feeding 5,000; Jesus, the Bread of Life; Feast of Tabernacles;
Jesus forgives the adulteress; Jesus, the Light of the World

---

*J*esus entered *into the Temple* (Court), *and all the people came to Him; and He sat down, and taught them* (John 8:2). Jesus was rudely interrupted by *the scribes and Pharisees* who *brought to Him a woman. . . . They said to Him, Master, this woman was taken in adultery, in the very act. Now Moses in the Law commanded us, that such should be stoned: but what do You say?* (8:3-5). They brought this woman to Jesus, not because they were shocked at her conduct or grieved that the Law of God had been broken, but *that they might have* (a reason) *to accuse Him* (8:6). Had He said: "Let her go," they could accuse Him of compromising with sin and breaking the Mosaic Law. If He said: "Stone her," He would break Roman law and be accountable to Rome.

Jesus brought conviction to each one of the woman's accusers when He said: *He that is without sin among you, let him first cast a stone at her* (8:7). *And they which heard it . . . went out one by one, beginning at the eldest . . . Jesus was left alone, and the woman standing in the midst* (8:9). Then Jesus said to her: *Woman, where are . . . your accusers? has no man condemned you? She said, No man, Lord. And Jesus said to her, Neither do I condemn you: go, and sin no more* (8:10-11). Following this hypocritical interruption by these self-righteous religious leaders, Jesus resumed His teaching, saying: *I am the Light of the World: he that follows Me shall not walk in darkness, but shall have the Light of life* (8:12).

It is possible to follow *the Light of the World* for the wrong motives. During a time when someone faces a prison sentence or terminal cancer, they may "appear" to sincerely accept Jesus as Savior and Lord. However, let health return, or let there be a change of circumstances for the better, and their true motive becomes evident. All who were truly *born again* remain faithful. Others will be seen as once-zealous professors of faith as they revert to their self-centered ways. Such people are only temporarily "reformed" and have not been *transformed by the renewing of their minds* (Romans 12:2). In striking contrast with the hypocrites are those who, regardless of circumstance, remain faithful to Jesus. *Whoso keeps His Word, in him verily* (truly) *is the love of God perfected: hereby know we that we are in Him* (I John 2:5).

Thought for Today: To know what is right, and not live it, is sin.

Cross References: For John 6:31: See Exodus 16:4; Psalm 78:24. John 6:45: See Isaiah 54:13.

For definitions of unfamiliar words in today's Bible reading, see pages 468-480.

---

*T*he religious authorities in Israel were considered the shepherds of Israel; but they were false, self-serving leaders, as Ezekiel had foretold: *Woe be to the shepherds of Israel that do feed themselves! should not the shepherds feed the flocks?* (Ezekiel 34:2). Ezekiel then revealed the True Shepherd: *I will set up one Shepherd over them, and He shall feed them, even My servant David. . . . And I the LORD will be their God and My servant David a prince among them. . . . I will make with them a Covenant of Peace* (34:23-25).

Jesus identified Himself with the prophecy of Ezekiel when He said: *I am the Good Shepherd: the Good Shepherd gives His life for the sheep. . . . a hireling . . . sees the wolf coming, and leaves the sheep, and flees: and the wolf catches them, and scatters the sheep. . . . I am the Good Shepherd. . . . I lay down My life for the sheep* (John 10:11-15).

One of the distinguishing marks of a Christian is recognizing the need for guidance and a desire to follow the Good Shepherd. *The sheep follow Him: for they know His voice. And a stranger they will not follow, but will flee from him* (10:4-5).

The Holy Spirit led the Apostle Paul to write: *Now the God of peace, that brought again from the dead our Lord Jesus, that Great Shepherd of the sheep, through the blood of the everlasting Covenant, Make you perfect in **every good work to do His will**, working in you that which is well-pleasing in His sight, through Jesus Christ; to Whom be glory for ever and ever* (Hebrews 13:20-21).

Jesus also said: *I give to them eternal life; and they shall never perish, neither shall any man pluck them out of My hand. My Father, Who gave them (to) Me, is greater than all* (John 10:28-29). Here Jesus reveals Himself as both coequal and coeternal with God the Father. How comforting it is to be assured that we have Jesus the Good Shepherd caring for us.

The Apostle Peter foretold: *When the Chief Shepherd (Christ) shall appear, you shall receive a crown of glory that fades not away* (I Peter 5:4).

Thought for Today: Christians, like sheep, need to stay near the Shepherd in order to be protected from the deceptions of the world.

Cross Reference: For John 10:34: See Psalm 82:6.

For definitions of unfamiliar words in today's Bible reading, see pages 468-480.

$\mathscr{I}$N $\mathscr{T}$ODAY'S $\mathscr{R}$EADING

Raising of Lazarus; Pharisees' plot to kill Jesus;
Mary's anointing of Jesus' feet; triumphal entry;
Jesus' answer to the Greeks

$\mathscr{T}$hroughout the years of Jesus' ministry, we often see Him with-drawing Himself from public notice, and bidding *His disciples that they should tell no man that He was Jesus the Christ* (Messiah) (Matthew 16:20). When He raised the daughter of Jairus, He *charged them straitly* (strictly) *that no man should know it* (Mark 5:43). When they came down from the Mount of Transfiguration, He instructed His disciples *that they should tell no man what things they had seen, till the Son of Man were risen from the dead* (9:9). The reason for this can be seen because, when the 5,000 who were miraculously fed by two fish and five loaves of bread planned *to make Him a king, He departed again into a mountain Himself alone* (John 6:15). When His unbelieving brethren urged Him to *show* Himself *to the world. . . .* Then Jesus said to them: *My time is not yet come* (7:4,6).

Now Jerusalem was crowded with worshipers who had come from Judea, Samaria, Galilee, and as far away as Greece. They came early in order that they might be ceremonially qualified to partake of the feast: *The Jews' Passover was near at hand: and many went out of the country up to Jerusalem . . . to purify* (cleanse) *themselves* (11:55-56) as well as to see Jesus.

As Jesus made His public entry into Jerusalem, the religious leaders were overwhelmed by the immense crowd that followed Him, and they were heard to say: *Behold, the world* has *gone after Him* (12:19). At the God-appointed time, Jesus openly and rightly accepted the acclaim of the multitude that He was their Messiah.

The prophet had foretold almost 500 years earlier: *Rejoice greatly, O daughter of Zion; shout, O daughter of Jerusalem: behold, your King comes to you . . . lowly, and riding upon an ass, and upon a colt the foal of an ass* (Zechariah 9:9). Israel's True King now officially presented Himself to the nation as fulfilling that prophecy. *Many believed on Him; but because of the Pharisees they did not confess Him, lest they should be put out of the synagogue: For they loved the praise of men even more than the praise of God* (John 12:42-43).

Thought for Today: We should live so others can see Christ living in us.

Cross References: For John 12:13: See Psalm 118:26. John 12:15: See Zechariah 9:9. John 12:38: See Isaiah 53:1. John 12:40: See Isaiah 6:9-10; Exodus 4:21.

For definitions of unfamiliar words in today's Bible reading, see pages 468-480.

In Today's Reading
Jesus washes the disciples' feet; Jesus foretells His betrayal,
His death, and His second coming; Holy Spirit promised

The eleven apostles were convinced that Jesus was the Messiah. Along with the multitudes, they too had joined in shouting: *Hosanna: Blessed is the King of Israel* (John 12:13). But, Jesus had earlier said that He must *suffer many things of the elders and chief priests and scribes, and be killed* (Matthew 16:21). At that moment, the disciples were "fearful" because Jesus had said He was leaving them. The apostles were also troubled that He had said that one of their own number would betray Him (John 13:21-22).

Some of the most comforting words of Jesus were spoken at the very moment that the religious leaders were planning how to kill Him and He knew it. With the utmost calm He said: *Let not your heart be troubled: you believe in God, believe also in Me. . . . I go to prepare a place for you. . . . I will come again, and receive you to Myself; that where I am, there you may be also. . . . Peace I leave with you, My peace I give to you: not as the world gives, give I to you. Let not your heart be troubled, neither let it be afraid* (14:1-3,27).

The picture is much clearer to us 2,000 years later, as we read the full story. However, like the disciples, occasionally, each of us is faced with fears of what tomorrow may bring. When we are facing financial loss, divorce, disease, handicaps, or other "things" that happen to those who love the Lord, we need to remember that the Lord knows how to take care of our tomorrows. We too can have the utmost confidence in our Lord's comforting words: *Let not your heart be troubled: you believe in God, believe also in Me* (14:1).

We must choose whether we will or will not allow "our hearts to be troubled." Every disappointment offers an opportunity to overcome stress, fear, and depression, and to develop patience and faith in Him.

Beloved, think it not strange concerning the fiery trial (painful ordeal) *which is to try* (test) *you, as though some strange thing happened to you: But rejoice, inasmuch as you are partakers* (sharers) *of Christ's sufferings* (I Peter 4:12-13).

Thought for Today: We need to be thankful for the ministry of the Holy Spirit in and through us.

Cross References: For John 13:18: See Psalm 41:9. John 15:25: See Psalm 35:19; 69:4.

For definitions of unfamiliar words in today's Bible reading, see pages 468-480.

*I*n *T*oday's *R*eading

Jesus' prayer of intercession; His betrayal and arrest; Peter's denial;
Jesus before high priests; Jesus condemned; Barabbas released

*A*fter the Passover meal, Jesus began praying: *Father, the hour is come; glorify* (honor) *Your Son. . . . I have glorified* (honored) *You on the earth. . . . I have manifested* (made known) *Your Name to the men which You gave Me . . . and they have kept Your Word* (John 17:1,4-6). All true believers should unite in glorifying the *Father* and Christ our Lord, and in keeping His Word.

Jesus continued praying for all who would believe on Him, *that they may be one, even as We are One* (17:20-22). Jesus and the eleven disciples then went to the Mount of Olives. Jesus knew that Judas would soon arrive with the religious leaders who would lead the hostile mob and the Roman military to crucify Him. Just moments later, all of Jesus' followers forsook Him.

Satan is the *accuser of our brethren* (Revelation 12:10); but it is comforting to know that Jesus sees far more in His followers than we see in ourselves or in each other. He knew His disciples would leave Him; but He loved them and forgave them.

The difference between the weakest of Jesus' disciples and the worldly, unsaved person is revealed in Jesus' prayer to His Father in heaven: *I have given to them the words which You gave Me; and they have received them, and have known surely that I came out from You, and they have believed that You did send Me* (John 17:8). Notice the order: *The words which You gave Me, I have given to them,* and *they have received them.* This emphasizes that *faith comes by hearing, and hearing by the Word of God* (Romans 10:17). Faith and spiritual discernment are imparted as we daily meditate upon the Word of God. As the psalmist recorded: *A good understanding have all they that do His Commandments* (Psalm 111:10).

Jesus also prayed to the Heavenly Father to *keep through Your own Name those whom You have given Me* (John 17:11). How comforting to know that His prayer included everyone of us as He prayed: *I have given them Your Word. . . . They are not of the world, even as I am not of the world. Sanctify* (keep holy for God's service) *them through Your truth: Your Word is Truth. . . . Neither pray I for these alone, but for them also which shall believe on Me through their word* (John 17:14,16-20).

Thought for Today: We receive the joy of the Lord as we share His love.

Cross Reference: For John 17:12: See Psalm 41:9.

For definitions of unfamiliar words in today's Bible reading, see pages 468-480.

Post-Resurrection Appearances of Christ

Who Sees Him	Where	When	Reference
Mary Magdalene, Mary the mother of James, & Salome, Joanna & other women	At the tomb	Early Sunday morning	Matt. 28:1-10 Mark 16:1-8; Luke 24:1-11
Mary Magdalene	In the garden	Early Sunday morning	Mark 16:9-11; John 20:11-18
Two disciples	Road to Emmaus	Midday Sunday	Luke 24:13-32; Mark 16:12-13
Peter	Jerusalem	Sunday	Luke 24:34; I Cor. 15:5
Ten Apostles	Upper room	Sunday evening	Luke 24:36-43; John 20:19-23
Eleven Apostles	Upper room	One week later	Mark 16:14 John 20:24-29; I Cor. 15:5
Seven Apostles	Fishing in Galilee	Dawn	John 21:1-14
Eleven Apostles . . . disciples/ 500 followers	Galilee	Much later	Matt. 28:16-20; Mark 16:15-18; John 21:1-24; I Cor. 15:6
Disciples, principle women, Jesus' brothers, & others	Mount of Olives	40 days after the resurrection	Luke 24:46-53; Acts 1:3-14
Saul of Tarsus	Road to Damascus	Midday, years later	Acts 9:1-9; 22:1-8; 26:12-18; I Cor.15:8
James		Much later	I Cor. 15:7

> ## ℐN ℐODAY'S ℛEADING
> Christ's crucifixion, burial, resurrection, and post-resurrection
> appearances to His disciples; Peter's allegiance reaffirmed

*J*udas led the mob and the Roman soldiers to arrest Jesus. After His arrest, they *led Him away to Annas first . . . father-in-law to Caiaphas, which was the high priest that same year* (John 18:13).

According to the Word of God, the *high priest* was to be a direct descendant of Aaron and was to retain his office until death (Exodus 40:15; Numbers 35:25). However, Rome appointed a new *high priest* every year. Annas was *high priest* through Aaronic ion, but was deposed by Rome. He was succeeded by his son-in-law Caiaphas who was the "official" *high priest* according to Rome. However, many people still considered Annas to be the true *high priest*.

Jesus, the prophesied *Lamb of God, Who takes away the sin of the world* (John 1:29), was led first to the Jewish and then the Gentile-appointed high priests. With Caiaphas were the scribes, the elders, the chief priests *and all the council* (Matthew 26:57,59). In response to the question by the high priest regarding His deity, Jesus said: *Hereafter shall you see the Son of Man sitting on the right hand of power, and coming in the clouds of heaven* (26:64). Understanding that Jesus was claiming to be the Messiah, Caiaphas ripped his robe of authority as a sign of righteous indignation and shouted: *What further need have we of witnesses? behold, now you have heard His blasphemy* (26:65). Caiaphas based his decision on what God had said to Moses: *He that blasphemes the Name of the LORD, he shall surely be put to death* (Leviticus 24:16). *When they had bound Him, they . . . delivered Him to Pontius Pilate the governor* (Matthew 27:2).

Pilate knew Jesus was innocent of any criminal offense and said: *I find in Him no fault at all* (John 18:38). But, the religious leaders cried out violently: *Crucify Him, crucify Him. . . . He ought to die, because He made Himself the Son of God. . . . If you let this Man go, you are not Caesar's friend* (19:6-12). Pilate had to choose between Jesus *the Son of God* and the angry crowd; he chose the "religious" authorities. When a person compromises what is right for fear of losing his job or anything else, he has taken the first step on the road to eternal hell. Jesus said: *No servant can serve two masters* (Luke 16:13).

Thought for Today: Every Christian is responsible to tell of God's forgiving love.

Cross References: For John 19:24: See Psalm 22:18. John 19:36: See Exodus 12:46; Psalm 34:20. John 19:37: See Zechariah 12:10.

For definitions of unfamiliar words in today's Bible reading, see pages 468-480.

INTRODUCTION TO THE BOOK OF
Acts

The Book of Acts is a continuation of the Gospel of Luke. The Gospel of Luke ends with the Ascension (Luke 24:51), while the Book of Acts begins with the Ascension of Christ. It includes over 10 recorded appearances of Christ during the 40 days following His physical resurrection. His parting words to His disciples before *He was taken up. . . . into heaven* (Acts 1:9-11) are of utmost importance: *You shall receive power, after that the Holy Spirit is come upon you: and you shall be witnesses to Me . . . to the uttermost* (farthest) *part of the earth* (1:8).

As recorded in Acts, throughout the first 30 years of the Church, on every occasion, a believer was baptized following a confession of Jesus as Lord and Savior (Matthew 28:18-20; Mark 16:16; Acts 2:38,41; 8:12-13,36,38; 9:18; 10:47-48; 16:15,33; 18:8; 19:5).

The first 12 chapters of this book focus on the Apostle Peter and the first church in Jerusalem and conclude with his remarkable experiences among Gentiles in Samaria who became believers in Jesus as their Savior.

Beginning with the stoning death of Stephen, intense persecution began against the church (7:59 – 8:4). Saul of Tarsus was one of the chief leaders of this persecution of all who accepted Jesus as the prophesied Messiah (the Anointed One). These believers would later be called Christians (disciples of Christ) (11:26).

After his remarkable conversion, Saul, both a Jew and a Roman citizen by birth, dedicated his life to Christ for worldwide evangelism. He became known as the Apostle Paul, his Roman name, as he ministered to a Gentile world. He made his headquarters in Antioch of Syria, a Gentile city, which became the center of world evangelism. Acts 13:1 through 21:26 describe the events of Paul's three missionary journeys.

From Acts 21:27 to the end of the book, we have details of Paul's arrest and his transfer to Rome to appear before Emperor Nero. The book ends with Paul still under house arrest in Rome after two years (28:30). Prominent throughout this book is "the Word," which refers to the recorded Scriptures (2:41; 4:4,29,31; 8:4,14,25; 10:36-37,44; 11:1,16,19; 12:24; 13:5,7,26,44,46,48-49; 14:3,25; 15:7,35-36; 16:6,32; 17:11,13; 18:11; 19:10,20; 20:32). The Holy Spirit is referred to more than 40 times, as He fills, guides, and sustains Christians, and prayer is mentioned over 30 times. This book demonstrates how vital the Word of God, prayer, and the Holy Spirit are in the life of every believer and in the collective Body of Christ, His Church.

ℐN ᒍODAY'S ℛEADING

Ascension of Christ; promise of the Lord's return;
Matthias chosen to replace Judas;
coming of the Holy Spirit at Pentecost; Peter's sermon

𝒯he Feast (Festival) of Unleavened Bread portrayed the sinless Savior, Who is the *Bread of Life* (John 6:35,48) and was celebrated in conjunction with the Passover. The lamb without blemish offered as a sacrifice at Passover also typified Jesus, the perfect *Lamb of God* (1:29,36).

The third festival of Passover week was First-fruits. It was celebrated on the Sunday following the Passover observance. It was on the day of First-fruits that Jesus arose: *Now is Christ risen from the dead, and become the first-fruits of them that slept* (died) (I Corinthians 15:20).

The second major festival for which every male was to appear annually before God was 50 days later, *the morrow after the seventh Sabbath* (rest day) following First-fruits (Leviticus 23:15-16). It was the Feast of the Harvest and celebrated the first ingathering of the crops.

This festival became known to Christians as Pentecost (Greek: pent→kost→) from the Greek word for 50 (pent→konta). On that day, being filled with the Holy Spirit and quoting the prophetic Scriptures (Joel 2:28-29), Peter boldly proclaimed that *God has made that same Jesus, Whom you have crucified, both Lord and Christ* (Acts 2:36). Then the crowd said to Peter and the apostles: *Brethren, what shall we do? Then Peter said to them, Repent, and be baptized every one of you in the Name of Jesus Christ for the remission of sins, and you shall receive the gift of the Holy Spirit. For the promise is to you, and to your children, and to all that are afar off, even as many as the Lord our God shall call* (to be saved) (2:37-39). *And they continued steadfastly in the apostles' doctrine* (teaching) *and* (the) *fellowship, and in* (the) *breaking of* (the) *bread, and in* (the) *prayers* (2:42).

The required offering on Pentecost consisted of two loaves of leavened bread (Leviticus 23:17). These loaves, which represented both Jewish and Gentile believers, included leaven, symbolizing sin, since everyone except Jesus has sinned. The separate identities of the ground grains blended into a oneness, symbolizes all believers who lose their individual identities to become the Bride of Christ – His Church (Ephesians 5:21-32; I Corinthians 12:27). The Apostle Paul later declared: *There is neither Greek nor Jew . . . but Christ is all, and in all* (Colossians 3:11).

Thought for Today: We need to tell others about the joy of Christian fellowship.

Cross References: For Acts 1:20: See Psalm 69:25; 109:8. Acts 2:17-21: See Joel 2:28-32. Acts 2:25-28: See Psalm 16:8-11. Acts 2:34-35: See Psalm 110:1. Acts 3:22-23: See Deuteronomy 18:15,18-19. Acts 3:25: See Genesis 12:3; 22:18.

For definitions of unfamiliar words in today's Bible reading, see pages 468-480.

In Today's Reading
Peter and John imprisoned; believers share their possessions;
Ananias and Sapphira; seven helpers chosen; Stephen's arrest

 oyalty to the Lord and love for one another permeated the first
Church. *The multitude of them that believed were of one heart and of
one soul; neither said any of them that any of the things which he
possessed was his own; but they had all things common. . . . as many as
were possessors of lands or houses sold them, and brought the prices of
the things that were sold, And laid them down at the apostles' feet: and
distribution was made to every man according as he had need* (Acts
4:32,34-37). Undoubtedly, this was a great encouragement to the
congregation because most Jews who confessed Jesus as the Messiah
had probably lost their jobs. There is no mention of anyone being
required to sell his property or to share his wealth.

Ananias and his wife Sapphira also sold a piece of property; but,
they gave only a part of the proceeds to the Church while implying they
were giving everything just as others had done (5:1-2). The property
was theirs to dispose of as they chose. All giving was voluntary (5:4).
But, the "generous gift" of Ananias and Sapphira was a lie to the Body
of Christ – the Church (John 8:44; Revelation 21:8; Jeremiah 17:9).

The problem today is even more serious, not because Christians
keep part of the proceeds of a sale, but because many refuse to give even
a tithe (10%) of their income, the minimum that God requires for the
ministry of His Word. Tithing is not an option we have; it is a debt we
owe. **God rightfully owns all that He created**, but He only requires
us to return to Him one-tenth of what He has entrusted to us, thereby
acknowledging that we are only stewards (managers) of His property.
This principle was demonstrated by Abraham over 500 years before the
Law was given (Genesis 14:20; Hebrews 7:1-2). Later, the Law stated:
All the tithe (tenth portion) *of the land, whether of the seed of the land,
or of the fruit of the tree, is the LORD's: it is holy* (set apart) *to the LORD*
(Leviticus 27:30).

The Holy Spirit also directed Luke to write that you can't outgive
God, Who said: *Give, and it shall be given to you; good measure, pressed
down, and shaken together, and running over, shall men give into your
bosom. For with the same measure that you mete withal* (measure
anything) *it shall be measured to you again* (Luke 6:38).

Thought for Today: Nothing is impossible. Put your trust in God. (See Philippians 4:13.)

Cross References: For Acts 4:11: See Psalm 118:22. Acts 4:25-26: See Psalm 2:1-2.

For definitions of unfamiliar words in today's Bible reading, see pages 468-480.

In Today's Reading
Stephen's speech; his martyrdom; Saul's persecution of
Christians; Simon, the sorcerer; Philip and the Ethiopian

Stephen was a deacon in the Church at Jerusalem who knew the
Old Testament Scriptures. He boldly reminded the unbelieving authorities: *You always resist the Holy Spirit: as your fathers did, so do
you. Which of the prophets have not your fathers persecuted? and they
have slain them which showed before of the coming of the Just One; of
Whom you have been now the betrayers and murderers* (Acts 7:51-56).

With the same hatred which had caused the crucifixion of Christ,
the angry authorities dragged Stephen *out of the city, and stoned him.*
As he was dying, *he . . . cried with a loud voice, Lord, lay not this sin
to their charge* (7:57-60). Stephen could have avoided death by saying
nothing, but he made it clear that they were responsible for crucifying
Jesus, *the Just One.* Stephen's faith and forgiving attitude in the face of
death was the same as his Savior's on the cross and it surely must have
made a powerful impression on those who witnessed Stephen's love
toward his murderers. In the same spirit of love, we too need to pray
for those who despitefully treat us. Those who seem to be our enemies
today may someday be saved if we express the love of Christ to them
as Stephen did to his persecuters.

*At that time there was a great persecution against the church which
was at Jerusalem* (8:1). Instead of discouraging believers, persecution
resulted in a great missionary movement as Jesus' followers dispersed
throughout the region. Philip, who was also a deacon in the first
Church, was led by the Holy Spirit to meet an Ethiopian official on his
way home. As he read the Book of Isaiah, God led Philip to explain to
the Ethiopian how the prophecy of Isaiah 53:7-8 had been fulfilled in
Jesus of Nazareth. On learning that Jesus was the Messiah-Savior, the
Ethiopian asked to be *baptized. . . . Philip said, If you believe with all
your heart, you may. And he answered and said, I believe that Jesus
Christ is the Son of God. . . . and he baptized him. . . . the eunuch. . . .
went on his way rejoicing* (Acts 8:36-39).

Thought for Today: Christ desires to control all of your thoughts every day.

Cross References: For Acts 7:3: See Genesis 12:1. Acts 7:27-28: See Exodus 2:14. Acts 7:32:
See Exodus 3:6. Acts 7:33-34: See Exodus 3:5,7-8,10. Acts 7:37: See Deuteronomy 18:15. Acts
7:40: See Exodus 32:1. Acts 7:42-43: See Amos 5:25-27. Acts 7:49-50: See Isaiah 66:1-2. Acts
8:32-33: See Isaiah 53:7-8.

For definitions of unfamiliar words in today's Bible reading, see pages 468-480.

$\mathscr{I}$N $\mathscr{T}$ODAY'S $\mathscr{R}$EADING
Conversion of Saul; Dorcas raised from the dead;
visions of Peter and Cornelius; Gentiles receive the Holy Spirit

$\mathscr{S}$aul of Tarsus was a sincere Pharisee determined to stamp out the followers of Jesus whom he considered religious blasphemers worthy of the death penalty. So he obtained letters from the high priest to go about 135 miles to Damascus in Syria to arrest Christians who had fled from Jerusalem. He stated *that if he found any of this Way* (followers of Jesus), *whether they were men or women, he might bring them bound to Jerusalem* (Acts 9:2), where they could be tried for heresy and put to death.

As he neared Damascus, *suddenly there shined round about him a light from heaven: And he fell to the earth, and heard a voice saying to him, Saul, Saul, why persecute . . . Me? And he said, Who are You, Lord? And the Lord said, I am Jesus Whom you persecute* (9:3-5). Three days later, the Lord spoke to Ananias, a disciple of Christ who lived in Damascus, saying to him: *Arise, and go into the street which is called Straight, and inquire . . . for one called Saul, of Tarsus: for, behold, he prays, And has seen in a vision a man named Ananias* (9:11-12).

Ananias replied to the Lord: *I have heard . . . how much evil he has done to Your saints* (followers) *at Jerusalem. . . . But the Lord said to him, Go your way: for he is a chosen vessel to Me, to bear My Name before the Gentiles, and kings, and the Children of Israel: For I will show him how great* (many) *things he must suffer for My Name's sake. And Ananias . . . entered into the house; and putting his hands on him said, Brother Saul, the Lord, even Jesus . . . has sent me, that you might receive your sight, and be filled with the Holy Spirit. . . . and he* (Paul) *received sight forthwith, and arose, and was baptized* (9:13-18).

At about the same time, Peter also had a vision which caused him to realize *that God is no respecter of persons* (10:34). Speaking to Gentiles at the home of Cornelius, Peter declared: *To Him give all the prophets witness, that through His Name whosoever believes in Him shall receive remission of sins. While Peter yet spoke these words, the Holy Spirit fell on all them which heard the Word* (10:43-44). After they were filled with the Holy Spirit, Peter asked: *Can any man forbid water, that these should not be baptized, which have received the Holy Spirit as well as we? And he commanded them to be baptized in the Name of the Lord* (10:47-48). *By one Spirit we are all baptized into one Body* (I Corinthians 12:13,27).

Thought for Today: Live for God and He will give you His best.

For definitions of unfamiliar words in today's Bible reading, see pages 468-480.

In *Today's* *Reading*
Peter's report to the Jerusalem church; death of James;
Peter's imprisonment and deliverance; death of Herod;
Paul's first missionary journey

*S*aul of Tarsus was born a Jew, but he was also a Roman citizen by birth in the town of Cilicia, a Roman province (Acts 16:37-38). His family, it seems, had considerable wealth. Following the prescribed study of the Scriptures in Tarsus, Saul was selected for further rabbinic studies in Jerusalem as a student of the famous Rabbi Gamaliel (22:3). Paul later shared with the Galatian Christians that he was *exceedingly zealous of the traditions of my fathers* (beliefs of past rabbis passed down as authoritative) (Galatians 1:14).

After he accepted Jesus as the Messiah, he changed his Hebrew name Saul to his Roman (Gentile) name Paul to identify himself better with Gentiles. On his first missionary journey, *Paul and his company . . . departed from Perga . . . to Antioch in Pisidia*, a Roman province of Galatia in what is now Turkey. They *went into the synagogue on the Sabbath day, and sat down. And after the reading of the Law and the prophets* (Acts 13:13-15), they were invited to speak. Paul chose prophetic Scriptures to prove that Jesus was the Messiah. He began with a review of how *the God of . . . Israel chose our fathers. . . . raised up to them David to be their king. . . . Of this man's seed* (offspring) *God has according to His promise raised to Israel a Savior, Jesus. . . . Their rulers, because they knew Him not. . . . desired . . . Pilate that He should be slain. And when they had fulfilled all that was written of Him, they took Him down from the tree, and laid Him in a sepulcher* (tomb). *But God raised Him from the dead* (13:17,22-23,27-30).

Through Christ's death and resurrection, we receive eternal life. But, being saved and *justified from everything* is far more than just choosing a better way of life. First, it is realizing the awfulness of sin as an offense against God, having real sorrow for our sins and a sincere desire to be delivered from those sins. This is followed by a decision to live life by avoiding and resisting sin through the power of the Holy Spirit. Paul declared: *By Him all that believe are justified from all things, from which you could not be justified by the Law of Moses* (Acts 13:39).

Thought for Today: Share what Jesus means to you with someone today. (See Mark 8:38.)

Cross References: For Acts 13:22: See I Samuel 13:14; Psalm 89:20. Acts 13:33: See Psalm 2:7. Acts 13:34: See Isaiah 55:3. Acts 13:35: See Psalm 16:10. Acts 13:41: See Habakkuk 1:5. Acts 13:47: See Isaiah 49:6.

For definitions of unfamiliar words in today's Bible reading, see pages 468-480.

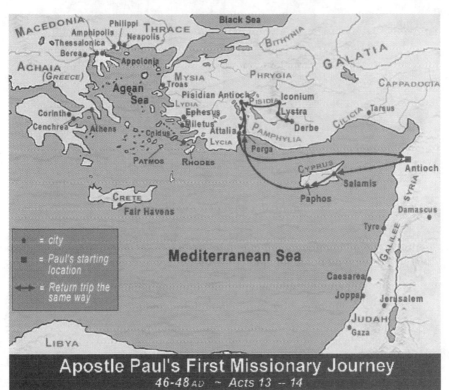

Apostle Paul's First Missionary Journey
46-48 AD ~ Acts 13 -- 14

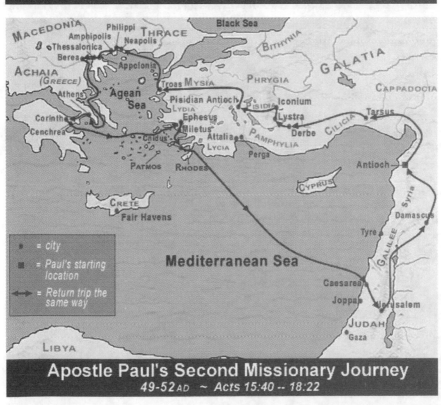

Apostle Paul's Second Missionary Journey
49-52 AD ~ Acts 15:40 -- 18:22

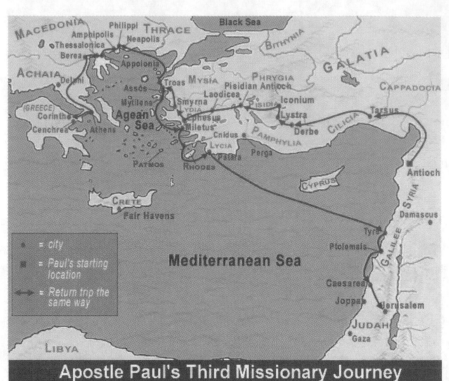

Apostle Paul's Third Missionary Journey
53-58 AD ~ Acts 18:22 -- 21:17

Apostle Paul's Trip to Rome
59-63 AD ~ Acts 27:1 -- 28:16

EVENTS IN THE LIFE
OF THE APOSTLE PAUL

TARSUS – The capital of Cilicia was the birthplace of Paul (the Roman name for Saul). He was a Jew, but also a Roman citizen by birthright (Acts 16:37-38; 22:3-29). He grew up in the Hellenistic (Greek) culture of Tarsus, which had both Hebrew tradition and Greek culture. Located in the province of Cilicia in Asia Minor, Tarsus was one of the three greatest universities in the world. It was the Athens of the eastern Mediterranean and Alexandria in Egypt. **JERUSALEM** – Paul received his Old Testament education in Jerusalem from Gamaliel, the greatest Hebrew intellectual educator of the time, according to *the perfect manner of the Law of the fathers* (22:3; compare 5:34-40). The first mention of Paul in the New Testament was at the stoning of Stephen, when *Saul was consenting to his death* (7:58-61). He persistently persecuted Christians and *made havoc of the Church* (8:3; 9:1).

CONVERSION TO CHRIST – Saul obtained a commission from the high priest to go to Damascus and persecute believers. On the way, blinded by a brilliant light, Saul *heard a voice saying to him, Saul, Saul, why persecute Me? . . . I am Jesus* (9:4-5). After Saul received Christ, he was *filled with the Holy Spirit. . . . and was baptized* (9:17-18). **ARABIA** – He *immediately . . . went into Arabia* (possibly near Mount Sinai) *and returned again to Damascus* (Galatians 1:16-17). *Then was Saul certain days with the disciples which were at Damascus. And immediately he preached Christ in the synagogues, that He is the Son of God. . . . proving that Jesus is the very Christ* (Acts 9:19-20,22). **JERUSALEM** – *After three years* (Galatians 1:18) certain Jews of Damascus determined to kill Saul, but he escaped (Acts 9:25) and went to Jerusalem (about 133 miles from Damascus) where he saw Peter and James (Galatians 1:18-19) and *spoke boldly in the Name of the Lord Jesus . . . but they* (the Jews) *went about to slay him. . . . When the brethren, they brought him down to Caesarea, and sent him forth to Tarsus* (Acts 9:26,29-30). **TARSUS** – Later, Barnabas, knowing how Paul had preached boldly in the Name of Jesus, both in Damascus and Jerusalem – went to Tarsus and brought Paul to Antioch (about 100 miles southeast of Tarsus) (11:25-26).

ANTIOCH – Paul joined *Barnabas, and Simeon that was called Niger, and Lucius of Cyrene, and Manaen* (13:1). A famine was prophesied *throughout all the world* (11:28) and the disciples sent Barnabas and Saul with money for their brethren *in Judea* (11:27-30). In Jerusalem, Paul met with *James, Cephas, and John, who seemed to be pillars* in the Church (Galatians 2:1-20) – possibly 14 years after Paul's first journey to the church in Jerusalem. On their return from Jerusalem to Antioch, they brought with them John Mark, a cousin of Barnabas (Acts 12:25). **ANTIOCH** – In Syria (13:1-3), Paul and Barnabas were set apart by the church at Antioch, as commanded by the Holy Spirit, for missionary work among the Gentiles. Antioch was the starting point for all three of Paul's great missionary journeys. Barnabas and Saul were *sent forth by the Holy Spirit* (13:4). They took John Mark with them, and departed for Seleucia and then for Cyprus. **CYPRUS** (13:1-4) – The native land of Barnabas (4:36), an island in the Mediterranean Sea about 60 miles from Syria. **SALAMIS** (13:5) – Paul preached in the synagogues in this eastern port. He and Barnabas traveled through the island (about 100 miles) to Paphos.

PAPHOS (13:6-7) – Sergius Paulus, the Roman "deputy" (governor) became a believer (13:12). *Paul and his company* then sailed to Perga. **PERGA** (13:13) – The capital of the province of Pamphylia was about 180 miles north of Paphos. John Mark deserted them and returned to Jerusalem. Paul and Barnabas proceeded on to Antioch. **ANTIOCH** (13:14-41) – This Antioch was located in Pisidia, about 120 miles north of Perga. Here *the Word of the Lord was published throughout all the region* (13:49). But the unbelieving Jews *raised persecution against Paul and Barnabas, and expelled them out of their coasts* (13:50). The Apostles then followed the Roman Road about 100 miles to Iconium. **ICONIUM** (13:51) – Iconium was the capital of Lyconia where *a great multitude both of the Jews and also of the Greeks believed* (14:1). Paul and Barnabas stayed a *long time* (14:3), until a mob attempted to stone them, then fled about 20 miles to Lystra.

LYSTRA (14:6) – Lystra was a small rural town of Lycaonia where Timothy lived and *there they preached the Gospel* (14:7). Soon, hostile Jews from Antioch in Pisidia and Iconium arrived and raised such opposition to Paul's preaching that the people stoned him, dragged him out of the city, and left him for dead (14:19); but Paul revived. Timothy probably witnessed Paul's preaching and the cruel stoning. The next day Paul and Barnabas went to the small town of Derbe. **DERBE** (14:20-21) – Derbe, *where they had preached the Gospel*, was about 30 miles to the southeast. They then returned through Lystra, Iconium, and Antioch in Pisidia where they appointed elders in every church (14:21-23). Paul and Barnabas then returned to Perga.

PERGA (14:25) – Paul and Barnabas preached the Word of God; then went to Attalia and sailed to Antioch in Syria, completing Paul's first missionary journey. **ANTIOCH in Syria** (14:26) – Paul and Barnabas remained here several years. **JERUSALEM** – The church at Antioch sent Paul and Barnabas with other believers to Jerusalem where they testified how God had saved the Gentiles.

ANTIOCH – Paul and Barnabas returned to Antioch, *teaching and preaching the Word of the Lord* (15:22,35). Barnabas left and sailed home to Cyprus (15:39). Paul then chose Silas to accompany him to the places where he had preached the Word on his first journey (15:40).

SECOND MISSIONARY JOURNEY

SYRIA AND CILICIA – Being *recommended by the brethren*, they left Antioch and journeyed by land *through Syria and Cilicia* (15:40-41). Here Paul strengthened the faith of the churches. **DERBE THEN LYSTRA** (16:1-3) – Here Timothy joined them *as they went through the cities. . . . so were the churches established in the faith* (16:4-5). **PHRYGIA AND GALATIA** (16:6) – As they continued through these territories, they *were forbidden by the Holy Spirit to preach the Word in Asia*. They moved on toward Mysia. **MYSIA** (16:7-8) – Once again, being forbidden by the Spirit to continue the intended journey to Bithynia, they passed by Mysia and came to Troas.

TROAS (16:8) – Here Luke joined them (16:10). Paul had a vision of a man asking him to come to Macedonia. Immediately they boarded a ship and sailed *to Samothracia and the next day to Neapolis*. **NEAPOLIS** (16:11 – Modern Kavalla)

– From there they went 10 miles inland to the Macedonian city of Philippi.
PHILIPPI (16:12) – Lydia of Thyatira – a businesswoman, a *seller of purple* – was baptized, along with her family (16:13-15). These were the first converts in Europe. Soon afterward, Paul and Silas were severely beaten, im-prisoned, and miraculously released at night (16:16-24). The jailer was converted and baptized, along with his household (16:22-34). Luke remained in Philippi while Paul, Silas, and Timothy went on to *Thessalonica, where there was a synagogue of the Jews*.
THESSALONICA (17:1 – Capital of Macedonia, about 100 miles away) – *Paul. . . went in to them, and three Sabbath days reasoned with them out of the Scriptures. . . . And some of them believed* (17:2,4). Then a mob *set all the city on an uproar. . . . and the brethren immediately sent away Paul and Silas by night to Berea* (17:5-10), about 50 miles away.

BEREA (17:10) – The people *received the Word with all readiness of mind, and . . . many of them believed* (17:11-12). But radical opposition incited by those from Thessalonica caused Paul to immediately depart (17:14). Paul and the others went to Athens while Silas and Timothy remained in Berea. **ATHENS** (17:15) – This was one of the great learning centers in the ancient world. Seeing widespread idolatry throughout the city, Paul *disputed . . . in the synagogue . . . and in the market daily. . . . Then certain philosophers* took him to Mars Hill (Areopagus) where he urged them *to seek the Lord . . . Who commands all men every where to repent* (17:17-32). A few believed. Paul then went to Corinth. **CORINTH** (18:1) – Corinth was a great seaport city where Paul met Aquila and his wife Priscilla. Silas and Timothy soon joined him, and *Paul was pressed in the Spirit, and testified to the Jews that Jesus was Christ* (18:5). *Crispus, the chief ruler of the synagogue, believed on the Lord . . . and many of the Corinthians hearing believed, and were baptized* (18:8). Paul remained in Corinth for more than a year and a half (18:11); then sailed with Aquila and Priscilla to Ephesus. **EPHESUS** (18:19) – This magnificent city had a population of over 225,000. After a short ministry in the synagogue, Aquila and Priscilla remained there, but Paul left by sea and *landed at Caesarea*, going on to Jerusalem to keep the *feast* (18:18-22). He then returned to Antioch. **ANTIOCH IN SYRIA** (18:22) – Paul had been gone for three or four years. He remained *some time* (18:23), perhaps a year. He then left on his third missionary journey with Timothy as his coworker.

THIRD MISSIONARY JOURNEY

GALATIA AND PHRYGIA (18:23) – Leaving Antioch they traveled through all the country of Galatia and Phrygia and came to Ephesus. **EPHESUS** (19:1) – Paul taught daily for about two years in the school of Tyrannus (19:9-10). *Mightily grew the Word of God and prevailed* (19:20). Paul sent Timothy and Erastus to Macedonia, but he remained in Ephesus until Demetrius, a silversmith, caused a riot (19:23-41). Paul then left for Macedonia. **MACEDONIA** (20:1) – Paul encouraged the believers in the places he visited on his former journey. He then went on to Greece. **GREECE** (20:2) – Paul stayed three months, probably visiting the churches on the way to Corinth. He intended to sail from there to Syria, but learned of a plot to kill him (20:3). So he went back through Macedonia to Philippi.

PHILIPPI (20:6) – There he was joined by Luke. They sailed together and, in five days, came to Troas. **TROAS** (20:6) – Paul and Luke remained here seven days, then departed – Paul on foot, but sending the others by ship to Assos where he joined them to sail on to Miletus (20:13-15). **MILETUS** (20:15) – Here the elders of the church at Ephesus met with him (20:17-38). Paul then sailed past Rhodes to Patara. **PATARA** (21:1) – Here they changed ships, embarking on one going directly to Phoenicia (21:2). Passing to the south of Cyprus, they landed at Tyre.

TYRE (21:3) – The disciples here warned Paul not to go on to Jerusalem (21:4). But, after praying with them, he boarded a ship and continued on to Ptolemais. **PTOLEMAIS** (21:7) – They stayed here for a day and had fellowship with other believers. The next day they went on to Caesarea. **CAESAREA** (21:8) – They stayed with Philip, the evangelist. Agabus foretold that Paul would be imprisoned if he went to Jerusalem (21:10-11). **JERUSALEM** – Paul was welcomed by the brethren (21:15-17). But he was seized by a mob because of mistaken identity (21:29,38), beaten, arrested, bound with chains (21:32-33), and imprisoned. The Lord appeared to him, saying: *Be of good cheer . . . you must bear witness of Me also at Rome* (23:11). After Paul's nephew over-heard a plot to kill him (23:12-30), Paul was taken to the Roman governor Felix at Caesarea (23:32-33).

CAESAREA (24:1 – 26:29) – Paul's accusers were Ananias the high priest with the elders and an orator named Tertullus (24:1-26). Paul remained a prisoner in Caesarea for two years (24:27). The high priest appealed to Festus, the successor of Felix, for a hearing in Jerusalem (25:1-9); but Paul appealed to *stand at Caesar's judgment seat* (25:10-11) so Festus had him present his defense before King Agrippa (25:22 – 26:29). Both Festus and Agrippa agreed that Paul *does nothing worthy of death*, but, because he had appealed to Caesar, Paul was transported by ship to Rome (26:30-32).

ENROUTE TO ROME (27:1 – 28:11) – The ship sailed south of Crete and passed Salmone *to a place which is called The Fair Havens* (27:7-8). After *they sailed close by Crete . . . there arose against it a tempestuous wind* (27:13-14). During the storm, Paul had a vision of *the angel of God* (27:23-24), and was told that the ship would *be cast upon a certain island*; and, as the ship broke up during the storm, *they escaped all safe to land* (27:26-44). On the island of Melita, Paul was bitten by a deadly viper, but *he shook off the beast into the fire, and felt no harm* (28:5). While there, Paul also healed the father of Publius (28:8-9). *After three months, they departed in a ship to Alexandria. . . . and went toward Rome* (28:11-14).

ROME (28:16-31) – Though Paul was still a prisoner, as a Roman citizen he was granted permission to dwell in his own rented house and continued to preach for two years. During that time, he probably wrote Ephesians, Philippians, Colossians, and Philemon. Since there is no clear statement in Scripture that he was freed, we assume his trial took place and Nero had him placed in the Mamertine Prison where he wrote the second letter to Timothy, saying: *The time of my departure is at hand. I have fought a good fight, I have finished my course, I have kept the faith: Hereafter there is laid up for me a crown of righteousness, which the Lord, the Righteous Judge, shall give me at that day: and not to me only, but to all them also that love His appearing* (II Timothy 4:6-8).

Continued from page 392

ℐN ℐODAY'S ℛEADING
Paul and Barnabas at Iconium; stoning of Paul at Lystra;
return to Antioch; journey with Silas; Paul's Macedonian
vision; conversion of Lydia; conversion of Philippian jailer

---

*A*lmost everywhere Paul and Barnabas traveled, *an assault was made . . . to use them spitefully* (wrongfully), *and to stone them* (Acts 14:5). In Iconium, about 90 miles east of Pisidian Antioch, violent opposition again erupted when Paul told them that Jesus was the Messiah foretold by the prophets. He fled from Iconium and went about 20 miles to Lystra where his attention was drawn to a crippled man. *Paul . . . steadfastly beholding him, and perceiving that he had faith to be healed, said with a loud voice, "Stand upright on your feet." And he leaped and walked* (14:9-10). Upon seeing this miraculous healing, the people were convinced that *the gods have come down to us in the likeness of men* (14:11). Paul and Barnabas strongly objected to being made objects of idolatrous worship (14:12-18).

Following this event, *certain Jews from Antioch and Iconium, who persuaded the people, and, having stoned Paul, drew him out of the city, supposing he had been dead. However, as the disciples stood round about him, he rose up, and came into the city: and the next day he departed with Barnabas to Derbe*, where they made many disciples (14:19-20).

Later, Paul made a brief reference to his sufferings for Christ, saying: *We must through much tribulation enter into the Kingdom of God* (14:22; also 9:16). Whenever there is a true spiritual awakening and people are being saved, without exception, Satan will seek to disrupt, discourage, and destroy the effect. So, we too should not be surprised that, following our best efforts to serve the Lord, Satan will seek to discourage us through hardships and even disappointments from those of whom we expected encouragement. Paul, the man God chose to write most of our New Testament, faced many dangers; but still he could write: *I know both how to be abased* (made low), *and I know how to abound* (have abundance): *every where and in all things I am instructed both to be full and to be hungry, both to abound and to suffer need. I can do all things through Christ Who strengthens me* (Philippians 4:12-13).

Thought for Today: To be guided into all truth, we must read and obey all the Truth.

Cross Reference: For Acts 15:16-17: See Amos 9:11-12.

For definitions of unfamiliar words in today's Bible reading, see pages 468-480.

ℐN ℐODAY'S ℛEADING

Jewish opposition; Paul and Silas in Berea; Paul on Mars Hill, at Corinth, at Ephesus; Priscilla and Aquila; the silversmiths

The Apostle Paul and his coworker Silas were brutally beaten by a mob in Philippi and thrown into prison. However, through God's intervention, they were released the next day. Paul was no quitter, *and when they had seen the brethren, they comforted them, and departed. . . . to Thessalonica* (Acts 16:40 – 17:1). Wherever he went, he always attended a Jewish synagogue. *Paul, as his manner was, went in to them, and three Sabbath* (Rest) *days reasoned with them out of the Scriptures, opening and alleging* (giving evidence), *that Christ must needs* (necessarily) *have suffered, and risen again from the dead; and that this Jesus, Whom I preach to you, is Christ. And some of them believed* (17:2-4).

When the unbelieving religious leaders became aware of these conversions, they were outraged and started a riot. Immediately afterwards, Paul left by night and traveled southwest to Berea. Upon arrival, they *went into the synagogue of the Jews. These were more noble than those in Thessalonica, in that they received the Word with all readiness of mind, and searched the Scriptures daily, whether those things were so. Therefore many of them believed* (17:10-12). Confessing Jesus as their Messiah was a monumental decision that would affect all aspects of their lives – family, friends, and business associates. Their dedication to the truth should encourage everyone, regardless of religious training, to study all the Scriptures with a sincere desire to know the Truth it reveals.

Our Creator has allotted each of us with only one lifetime to prepare for our eternal destiny. We have a dual responsibility – to become the person He wants us to be in order to accomplish the purposes for which He created us. Think how tragic it will be for those who fail to fulfill the will of God, wasting their few short years achieving material, social, and financial goals for self-gratification. God has provided one perfect Guidebook – His Word. Obey it and follow Jesus as our Savior and our God (I Timothy 2:5).

The times of this ignorance God winked at (overlooked); *but now commands all men every where to repent: Because He has appointed a day, in . . . which He will judge the world in righteousness* (Acts 17:30-31).

Thought for Today: Praise the Lord! His ways are always best.

Word Studies: 17:19 Areopagus = the Athenian council which met on Mars Hill; 17:29 Godhead = the Trinity -- God the Father, God the Son, God the Holy Spirit.

For definitions of unfamiliar words in today's Bible reading, see pages 468-480.

In Today's Reading

Paul's mission to Macedonia and Greece; raising of Eutychus
from death; message to the Ephesian elders; seized in the Temple

The Apostle Paul met with the Ephesian elders at Miletus, saying:
*I go bound in the spirit to Jerusalem, not knowing the things that shall
befall* (happen to) *me there: Save* (Except) *that the Holy Spirit witnessed in every city, saying that bonds and afflictions abide* (await) *me.
But none of these things move me, neither count I my life dear to
myself, so that I might finish my course with joy, and the ministry,
which I have received of the Lord Jesus, to testify* (solemnly affirm) *the
Gospel of the grace of God* (Acts 20:22-24).

The indwelling Holy Spirit will strengthen us to withstand our
trials and temptations as He did for Paul. Jesus promised believers: *I will
pray the Father, and He shall give you another Comforter, that He may
abide* (remain) *with you for ever* (John 14:16). We have not been left alone,
but are *strengthened with might by His Spirit in the inner man* (Ephesians
3:16). With the assurance of the indwelling Presence of the Holy Spirit,
we can face life with certainty concerning our future. This enables us to
enjoy a deep, inward peace that comes from God (John 14:27). We experience a contentment that *passes all understanding* (Philippians 4:7),
one that outward circumstances cannot affect. Because God, Who is
merciful and loving, is within us, we can respond with love and mercy
for others that sweeps away all prejudice, jealousy, hate, and envy. No
opposition can rob us of the peace God bestows when we permit Christ
the King to reign over our emotions. Though we have not always
permitted Christ to rule our emotions, we can say: "Though I'm not
what I ought to be, I'm not what I used to be; thanks to Christ, I'm
becoming what I was intended to be."

Spiritual growth takes place as we give, not just material things,
but what people need most, our love, our forgiveness, and our
understanding. In doing this, we are becoming more like Jesus. Paul
never denounced the evil Roman Emperor Nero, but he prayed for him.
Even as a prisoner in Rome, Paul wrote: *I exhort therefore, that, first
of all . . . prayers, intercessions, and giving of thanks, be made for all
men; For kings, and for all that are in authority; that we may lead a
quiet and peaceable life in all godliness and honesty. For this is good and
acceptable in the sight of God our Savior; Who will have all men to be
saved, and to come to the knowledge of the truth* (I Timothy 2:1-4).

Thought for Today: *This is the day the LORD has made; let us rejoice and be glad in
it* (Psalm 118:24).

For definitions of unfamiliar words in today's Bible reading, see pages 468-480.

In Today's Reading

Paul before the Sanhedrin (religious rulers); Jews vow to kill Paul;
Paul sent to Felix; Paul before Festus; his appeal to Caesar

When the Apostle Paul arrived in Jerusalem, the religious leaders *stirred up all the people* with false accusations: *This is the man, that teaches . . . against the people, and the Law, and this place* (Acts 21:27-28). In response, an angry mob seized Paul and tried to kill him, but he was rescued from their violence by Roman soldiers. He was then allowed to speak in his own defense to the Jews. When Paul mentioned his commission by Jesus to go to the Gentiles, they immediately considered him a traitor to their religion, and angrily shouted: *Away with such a fellow from the earth: for it is not fit that he should live* (22:22).

When the Sanhedrin authorities failed to convict Paul, religious zealots decided to take the law into their own hands and murder him (23:12-15). *Paul's sister's son* overheard their wicked plan to murder Paul and told the Roman captain, who then had Paul secretly transferred by night to Felix, the Roman governor of Judea residing at Caesarea (23:16-35).

During his several years' confinement in Caesarea, Paul was tried before three powerful rulers of the Roman Empire who listened to what he had to say about his faith in Jesus Christ. He faithfully *reasoned of righteousness, temperance* (self-control), *and judgment to come* (24:25). Each of his judges had a different reaction as Paul spoke of the *judgment to come*. His first judge Felix *trembled* (24:25) and so only heard him from time to time. Later, his second judge Festus exposed his indifference when he exclaimed in a *loud voice, Paul, you are beside yourself* (26:24). And, for whatever he may have meant, his third judge Agrippa said: *Almost you persuade me to be a Christian* (26:28). Whether Agrippa's words were sincere, or sarcastic, as some think, is not important – the outcome was the same. As far as we know, none of these men received Christ as Savior and Lord of their lives and, consequently, all were eternally lost.

There is only one convenient time to repent and receive Christ as Savior and Lord: *Behold, now is the day of salvation* (II Corinthians 6:2).

Thought for Today: Christ gave His all for us; let's give Him our all that He might live His life through us.

Cross Reference: For Acts 23:5: See Exodus 22:28.

For definitions of unfamiliar words in today's Bible reading, see pages 468-480.

---

*I*N *T*ODAY'S *R*EADING
Paul's defense before Agrippa; his voyage to Rome; storm at sea;
shipwreck at Melita (Malta); Paul at Rome

---

*W*hen Saul of Tarsus confessed his faith in Jesus Christ as the risen Savior and Messiah, Festus, the new Roman governor of Judea, exclaimed in *a loud voice, Paul, you are beside yourself. . . . But he* (Paul) *said I am not mad . . . but speak . . . the words of truth* (Acts 26:24-25).

Since Paul, as a Roman citizen, had appealed his case to Caesar, Festus placed him in the custody of *one named Julius, a centurion of Augustus' band* (27:1). Julius was to take Paul safely to Rome to stand trial before Nero, the Roman Emperor. They set sail and, after a brief docking at Sidon, continued along the northern coast of Cyprus. Stormy winds kept them from making much progress. On reaching *The Fair Havens* in Crete (27:8), Paul urged them to stay there during the winter months. He warned: *I perceive that this voyage will be with hurt* (danger) *and much damage, not only of the lading* (cargo) *and ship, but also of our lives;* but the majority of the people on board urged Julius to continue on to *Phenice, and there to winter; which is a haven* (harbor) *of Crete* (27:10-12).

Shortly afterwards, furious hurricane winds beat upon them. After two stormy weeks, their ship began to sink off the coast of Melita. *Paul stood forth in the midst of them, and said. . . . "Be of good cheer: for there shall be no loss of any man's life among you, but of the ship. For there stood by me this night the angel of God, Whose I am, and Whom I serve, saying, 'Fear not, Paul; you must be brought before Caesar: and, lo, God has given you all them that sail with you'"* (27:21-24). From this experience we learn that our judgment is only as good as our source of information.

Our life's voyage, like Paul's, may also be filled with violent storms. We may experience physical, financial, or emotional "shipwreck" and *all hope that we should be saved* may appear to be gone (27:20). But, there will come a day when the tempests we have weathered will seem insignificant compared to what God has accomplished through our faithfulness. Because of Christ, Paul could confidently say: *I take pleasure in infirmities, in reproaches, in necessities, in persecutions, in distresses for Christ's sake: for when I am weak, then am I strong* (II Corinthians 12:10; also Romans 5:1-5).

Thought for Today: There is no guarantee that you can accept Christ tomorrow because you may not have a tomorrow.

Cross Reference: For Acts 28:26-27: See Isaiah 6:9-10.

For definitions of unfamiliar words in today's Bible reading, see pages 468-480.

Introduction To The Book Of
*R*omans

The Christian life is progressively revealed in the Book of Romans. The main theme is *the Gospel of Christ: for it is the power of God to salvation to every one that believes. . . . For therein is the righteousness of God revealed from faith to faith: as it is written, The just shall live by faith* (Romans 1:16-17; compare Habakkuk 2:4).

Chapters 1 – 3 establish three facts: 1. *The wrath of God is revealed from heaven against all ungodliness and unrighteousness* (Romans 1:18); 2. *Both Jews and Gentiles . . . are all under sin* (3:9-11); 3. *By the deeds of the Law there shall no flesh* (person) *be justified* (3:20).

Chapters 4 – 5 explain that the righteous God has provided the only way for anyone to be forgiven of all their sins: *Jesus our Lord . . . was delivered* (put to death) *for our offenses, and raised again for our justification. Therefore being justified by faith, we have peace with God through our Lord Jesus Christ* (4:24-25; 5:1).

Chapter 6 explains the meaning and importance of believer's baptism: *So many of us as were baptized into Jesus Christ were baptized into His death? Therefore we are buried with Him by baptism into death: that like as Christ was raised up from the dead by the glory of the Father, even so we also should walk in newness of life* (6:3-4).

Chapters 7 – 8 reveal the conflict that exists between the believer's new spiritual nature and the old fleshly (sinful) nature. The victory is also revealed: *If Christ be in you, the body is dead because of sin; but the Spirit is life because of righteousness. . . . Therefore, brethren, we are debtors* (under obligation), *not to the flesh, to live after the flesh. If you live after the flesh, you shall die: but if you through the Spirit do mortify* (put to death) *the deeds of the body, you shall live* (8:10,12-13).

Chapters 9 – 11 declare a universal Gospel (Good News) to all mankind: *There is no difference between the Jew and the Greek: for the same Lord over all is rich to all that call upon Him. For whoever shall call upon the Name of the Lord shall be saved* (10:12-13).

Chapters 12 – 16 contain guidelines for spiritual growth and insight: (1) *Present your bodies a living sacrifice . . . to God*; (2) *Be not conformed to this world*; (3) *Be transformed by the renewing of your mind, that you may prove* (discern) *what is the good, and acceptable, and perfect, will of God* (12:1-2).

Paul emphasizes how important the Old Testament is to an understanding of the nature of God and of the Christian life: *For whatsoever things were written beforetime were written for our learning* (15:4).

ℐ𝓃 𝒯ODAY'S ℛEADING

Paul's desire to visit the Christians in Rome; both Jews and
Gentiles under condemnation; righteousness through faith

---

*S*atan and all unbelievers will be cast into the eternal *lake of fire*
(Revelation 20:10,13,15). However, *the wrath of God is . . . against all
ungodliness and unrighteousness of men, who hold the truth. . . . God has
showed it to them. . . . so that they are without excuse . . . when they knew
God, they glorified Him not as God, neither were thankful . . . their
foolish heart was darkened. Professing themselves to be wise, they
became fools, And changed the glory of the incorruptible God into an
image made like to corruptible man. . . . Wherefore God also gave them
up to uncleanness through the lusts of their own hearts, to dishonor their
own bodies between themselves* (Romans 1:18-27).

Three times we read that *God gave them up* to their degrading
passions (1:24,26,28). There are some who view sex as no more than a
physical appetite to be satisfied. But, Christ has said: *The fearful, and
unbelieving, and the abominable, and murderers, and whoremongers
. . . shall have their part in the lake which burns with fire* (Revelation
21:8). Sex is a gift from God which can only bring lasting satisfaction
and fulfillment within **the marriage relationship of one man with
one woman.**

In most of the world there is a disturbing and growing ignorance of
the Bible, the only Book which reveals sin for what it is – rebellion against
God. He alone has the right to set the standard for righteousness.

There is also a growing neglect of the Church and a tendency to use
the Lord's day and His tithe for self-centered pleasures. Doing so
usually leads to excuses for sin that remove any sense of guilt.

There is no victory over sexual perversion until it is seen for what
it really is, not as sickness or as an alternative lifestyle, but as sin. The
Good News is that, *now we are delivered from the Law, that being dead
wherein we were held; that we should serve in newness of* (the) *Spirit, and
not in the oldness of the letter* (Romans 7:6).

Thought for Today: God desires to take care of your life. Trust Him.

Cross References: For Romans 1:17: See Hab. 2:4. Romans 2:24: See Isaiah 52:5. Romans
3:4: See Psalm 51:4. Romans 3:10: See Psalm 14:1. Romans 3:11: See Psalm 14:2. Romans
3:12: See Psalm 14:3. Romans 3:13: See Psalm 5:9. Romans 3:14: See Psalm 10:7. Romans
3:15: See Isaiah 59:7. Romans 3:16-17: See Isaiah 59:7-8. Romans 3:18: See Psalm 36:1.

For definitions of unfamiliar words in today's Bible reading, see pages 468-480.

ℐN ᵀODAY'S ℛEADING
Salvation, righteousness through Jesus Christ; sin through
Adam; Christians under grace, not Law; baptism explained

The more we understand the horrible suffering and death of Jesus and the glory and power of His resurrection, the more we will desire to *walk in newness of life*, daily manifesting the life of Christ. *Therefore we are buried with Him by baptism into death: that like as Christ was raised up from the dead by the glory of the Father, even so we also should walk in newness of life. For if we have been planted together in the likeness of His death, we shall be also in the likeness of His resurrection: Knowing this, that our old man is crucified with Him, that the body of sin might be destroyed, that hereafter we should not serve sin* (Romans 6:4-6).

To commit ourselves only to the *likeness of His death,* of bearing the cross, and of self-denial, would produce a very dismal view of following Christ. It is the glorious indwelling power of His physical resurrection that not only frees us from sin's control but also daily encourages and strengthens us to *walk in newness of life.* Followers of Christ accept the fact that sin is no longer to be our master and that we are *dead indeed to sin. . . . Let not sin therefore reign in your mortal body, that you should obey it in the lusts thereof* (6:11-12). This does not mean we no longer sin, but that we are **enabled to overcome** sin!

Let not sin therefore reign (control) *in your mortal body, that you should obey it in the lusts* (evil desires) *thereof. . . . but yield yourselves to God, as those that are alive from the dead* (6:12-13). Our old "natural" man is still capable of yielding to the sinful desires of the flesh. But, Christ has made it possible for us to experience the reality of being *more than conquerors through Him* (8:37).

Jesus' life in us makes the difference: *Know you not, that to whom you yield yourselves servants to obey, his servants you are to whom you obey; whether of sin to death, or of obedience to righteousness?* (6:16). *But now being made free from sin, and become servants to God, you have your fruit to holiness, and the end everlasting life* (Romans 6:22).

Thought for Today: Sin only has power over us when we allow it.

Cross References: For Romans 4:3: See Genesis 15:6. Romans 4:7-8: See Psalm 32:1-2. Romans 4:17: See Genesis 17:5. Romans 4:18: See Genesis 15:5. Romans 7:7: See Exodus 20:17; Deuteronomy 5:21.

For definitions of unfamiliar words in today's Bible reading, see pages 468-480.

In *Today's* *Reading*
Law of life in the Spirit; suffering versus future glory;
Israel's failure because of unbelief; a means of mercy to Gentiles

*W*hen we accept Christ as Savior and Lord of our lives, we receive the spiritual nature of God and sincerely desire that *the righteousness of the Law might be fulfilled in us, who walk not after the flesh, but after the Spirit. For they that are after the flesh do mind the things of the flesh. . . . Because the carnal* (fleshly) *mind is enmity* (hostile) *against God: for it is not subject to the Law of God* (Romans 8:4-5,7). Praise God we don't have to be ruled by our carnal nature: *If you live after the flesh, you shall die: but if you through the Spirit do mortify* (put to death) *the deeds of the body, you shall live* (8:13).

True repentance results in a change of heart and lifestyle. This change should manifest itself in our becoming involved in sharing the Good News, supporting mission ministries, and becoming involved in a local church when physically able. Sadly, some people join a church, attend worship services, give generously, and assume that their good works are sufficient for entrance into heaven. But, they may only be expressing *a form of godliness, but denying the power thereof* (II Timothy 3:5). God is concerned first with what we are, then with what we do for Him.

Set your affection (mind) *on things above, not on things on the earth. . . . Mortify* (Put to death) *therefore your members which are upon the earth; fornication, uncleanness, inordinate* (unnatural) *affection, evil concupiscence* (desire), *and covetousness, which is idolatry: For which things' sake the wrath of God comes on the children of disobedience: In the which you also walked some time, when you lived in them. But now you also put off all these; anger, wrath, malice, blasphemy* (slander and abusive statements against God), *filthy communication out of your mouth. Lie not to one another, seeing that you have put off the old man with his deeds; And have put on the new man, which is renewed in knowledge after the image of Him that created him* (Colossians 3:2,5-10).

Thought for Today: Regardless of the circumstances, *I will praise the LORD at all times* (Psalm 34:1).

Cross References: For Romans 8:36: See Psalm 44:22. Romans 9:7: See Genesis 21:12. Romans 9:9: See Genesis 18:10. Romans 9:12: See Genesis 25:23. Romans 9:13: See Malachi 1:2-3. Romans 9:15: See Exodus 33:19. Romans 9:17: See Exodus 9:16. Romans 9:25: See Hosea 2:23. Romans 9:26: See Hosea 1:10. Romans 9:27-28: See Isaiah 10:22-23. Romans 9:29: See Isaiah 1:9. Romans 9:33: See Isaiah 28:16. Romans 10:5: See Leviticus 18:5. Romans 10:6-7: See Deuteronomy 30:12-13. Romans 10:8: See Deuteronomy 30:14. Romans 10:11: See Isaiah 49:23. Romans 10:13: See Joel 2:32. Romans 10:15: See Isaiah 52:7. Romans 10:16: See Isaiah 53:1. Romans 10:18: See Psalm 19:4. Romans 10:19: See Deuteronomy 32:21. Romans 10:20: See Isaiah 65:1. Romans 10:21: See Isaiah 65:2.

For definitions of unfamiliar words in today's Bible reading, see pages 468-480.

IN TODAY'S READING
Israel still to be saved; duties of a Christian in personal life,
in the church, in society, toward government

To be a Christian is to receive a new nature – the nature of God. *You must be born again* (John 3:7). Then the indwelling Holy Spirit enables us to let Christ control our lives instead of our controlling our own lives under our old master Satan.

It is only reasonable that we should live each day manifesting Christ's resurrection life, free from Satan's control. The Apostle Paul wrote: *Present your bodies a living sacrifice, holy, acceptable to God, which is your reasonable service. And be not conformed to this world: but be transformed by the renewing of your mind, that you may prove what is that good, and acceptable, and perfect, will of God* (Romans 12:1-2).

As we read through the Bible and obey it, God's Word becomes our spiritual food and our source of strength and spiritual insight to accomplish His will. Just as physical food is assimilated into our bodies to provide good health and physical strength, so the indwelling Holy Spirit strengthens our spiritual lives through His Word that we might be healthy in our spiritual lives. The Holy Spirit alone can *guide you into all truth* (John 16:13). However, He will not guide us into *all truth* if we refuse to read *all truth* from Genesis through Revelation. We are either a slave to sin and under the influence of Satan or a child of God and captive of His control over our lives. This is true freedom. The Word of God enlightens, then empowers us to overcome our former way of life. *Know the Truth, and the Truth shall make you free* (John 8:32).

We daily live in the midst of many voices calling for our attention. We will always be tempted to satisfy our self-serving, fleshly desires. We also need to daily be on guard against allowing "good things," or even "good people," to occupy our time and keep us from the best God has for us. Life is far too short to allow material possessions and the desire for worldly accomplishments to dominate our lives. Our opportunities to serve the Lord and to be prepared to meet Him will soon end. *See then that you walk circumspectly* (carefully), *not as fools, but as wise, Redeeming the time, because the days are evil* (Ephesians 5:15-16).

Thought for Today: When we are controlled by the indwelling Holy Spirit, we are pleasing to God.

Cross References: For Romans 11:3: See I Kings 19:10,14. Romans 11:4: See I Kings 19:18. Romans 11:8: See Isaiah 29:10. Romans 11:9-10: See Psalm 69:22-23. Romans 11:26-27: See Isaiah 59:20-21; Jeremiah 31:33. Romans 11:34: See Isaiah 40:13. Romans 11:35: See Job 41:11. Romans 12:19: See Deuteronomy 32:35. Romans 12:20: See Proverbs 25:21-22. Romans 13:9: See Exodus 20:13-17; Leviticus 19:18.

For definitions of unfamiliar words in today's Bible reading, see pages 468-480.

In Today's Reading
Law of love concerning doubtful things; Jewish and Gentile believers
share the same salvation; Paul's desire to visit Rome; personal greeting

*E*ven now, Christ is making intercession on our behalf because of
our weaknesses and temptations (Hebrews 7:25; Romans 16:25-27).

Not one person in history, except Jesus, has lived without sin. Since
we do not know the hearts of anyone, we are warned: *Who are you that
judges another man's servant? to his own master he stands or falls. Yea,
he shall be held up: for God is able to make him stand* (Romans 14:4).

We then that are strong ought to bear the infirmities (imperfections)
*of the weak, and not to please ourselves. Let every one of us please his
neighbor for his good to edification* (being built up). *For even Christ
pleased not Himself* (15:1-3). The greatest example of how we are to live
our lives is Jesus Christ, Who unselfishly took all our sins upon
Himself, suffering insult, persecution, and a cruel physical death on the
cross for our sake. His personal sacrifice demonstrated the Christian
way to deal with people for their good and God's glory.

The "stronger" brother will willingly put aside his personal desires
and lovingly consider how to strengthen his "weaker" brother without passing judgment, so as not to give Satan a foothold through
division or self-righteousness.

When we allow Christ to be Lord of our lives, it results in a sincere,
compassionate concern for others, not only for a weaker brother or
sister in Christ, but for the lost as well. Spiritual discernment leads us
to be understanding of others and their situations. The admonition *to
bear the infirmities* of others requires compassion and active involvement on the part of mature Christians.

While it is true that God judges sin and makes it clear that we must
reprove, rebuke, exhort (encourage) *with all long-suffering and doctrine*
(teaching) (II Timothy 4:2), our loving Lord is also saying to those
who represent Him: *Be . . . merciful, as your Father also is merciful*
(Luke 6:36). *By this shall all men know that you are My disciples, if you
have love one to* (for) *another* (John 13:35).

Thought for Today: Giving–not getting–is the key to our receiving blessings from God.

Cross References: For Romans 14:11: See Isaiah 45:23. Romans 15:3: See Psalm 69:9.
Romans 15:9: See Psalm 18:49. Romans 15:10: See Deuteronomy 32:43. Romans 15:11:
See Psalm 117:1. Romans 15:12: See Isaiah 11:1,10. Romans 15:21: See Isaiah 52:15.

For definitions of unfamiliar words in today's Bible reading, see pages 468-480.

Introduction To The Books Of
I & II *C*orinthians

There was little apparent acceptance of Jesus as the promised Messiah and Savior from sin by either the Jews or Gentiles in Athens (Acts 17:17,23,30-34). The Apostle Paul departed for Corinth, located about 50 miles to the west. He stayed in Corinth a year and a half (18:11). During that time, he supported himself through his profession of tent making, working with Aquila and Priscilla. They were a Jewish couple who had fled Rome because of Emperor Claudius' edict forcing all Jews to leave (18:1-3), and had a church in their home (I Corinthians 16:19).

Corinth was the capital of the Roman province of Achaia and was one of the most prominent cities in Greece, with a population estimated at more than 400,000. From there Paul concluded his second missionary journey by making a brief stop in Ephesus (Acts 18:18-19).

On his third missionary journey, Paul returned to Ephesus (I Corinthians 16:8), where he received disturbing reports concerning problems in the Corinthian church (1:11; 5:1; 7:1; 11:18). It was divided into four factions (1:12) and some members were openly living immoral lives (5:1-13). Responding out of great concern and love, Paul was directed by the Holy Spirit to explain how everything we do should be *to the glory of God* (10:31). A primary purpose of I Corinthians was to clarify the importance of *the Lord's Supper. . . . For as often as you eat this bread, and drink this cup, you do show* (proclaim) *the Lord's death till He come* (11:20,26). Paul gave the most detailed explanation of the Lord's Supper recorded in Scripture (11:23-34). The nine ministry gifts of the Holy Spirit are set forth in chapters 12 – 14; and, in chapter 13, the Holy Spirit led Paul to record the incomparable definition of love. The purpose and need for the resurrection of Christ follows in chapter 15.

A primary purpose of II Corinthians was to commend the disciplinary action taken by the church against the sins of its members.

In chapters 8-9, Paul expounded upon the principles and purposes of giving and urged participation in a financial collection for the saints in Judea. During the years that followed Paul's departure, there seems to have been a clique that developed within the church which was antagonistic toward his leadership and questioned his credentials (chapters 10 – 12). A major theme of II Corinthians is the ministry of reconciliation. Paul also appealed to them to be *reconciled to God* (5:14-21).

In Today's Reading
Grace and faithfulness of God; problems at Corinth;
Christians, as temples of God; authority of apostles

The church at Corinth was divided over who was the most accurate spiritual leader. Paul did not agree that he was right with those who preferred his views and that Apollos and Peter needed to give way to him, and he wrote: *Who then is Paul, and who is Apollos, but ministers by whom you believed, even as the Lord gave to every man?* (I Corinthians 3:5). We are not competitors, but *laborers together* (3:9). In writing to the Romans, Paul illustrated this divisive attitude by saying: *One man esteems one day above another: another esteems every day alike. Let every man be fully persuaded in his own mind* (Romans 14:5).

We are members of the Body of Christ. Our foremost concern should be that we *be perfectly joined together in the same mind and in the same judgment. . . . Is Christ divided?* (I Corinthians 1:10,13). All of us need each other, as together we can fulfill the Lord's will in the Body of Christ through our prayers, tithes, gifts, talents, and witnessing to others. No one should feel either indispensable or inadequate, for all *are one* (3:8) in Christ.

It takes every Christian to make up the Body of Christ, which is the Church, and, without exception, everyone is needed: *We being many are . . . one Body: for we are all partakers of* the *one Bread* (10:17), and *we are laborers together with God* (3:9).

This leaves no room for envying another person's ability or usefulness, nor for being puffed up with pride as if we had done anything of ourselves. Both jealousy and pride dishonor Christ and destroy the spirit of unity. The differences are often ignored because the real problem is not recognized.

It is important to recognize that Paul was not expecting uniformity of views, but for oneness of Spirit in the midst of differences. *The wisdom that is from above is first pure, then peaceable, gentle, and easy to be entreated, full of mercy and good fruits, without partiality, and without hypocrisy. And the fruit of righteousness is sown in peace of them that make peace* (James 3:17-18).

Thought for Today: Don't find fault with the gifts God has bestowed on others.

Cross References: For I Corinthians 1:19: See Isaiah 29:14. I Corinthians 1:31: See Jeremiah 9:24. I Corinthians 2:16: See Isaiah 40:13. I Corinthians 3:19: See Job 5:13. I Corinthians 3:20: See Psalm 94:11.

For definitions of unfamiliar words in today's Bible reading, see pages 468-480.

In Today's Reading
Immorality and other sins condemned;
guidelines for marriage and Christian conduct

*I*t was reported to Paul that one member of the church in Corinth was committing fornication or adultery with *his father's wife* (I Corinthians 5:1), which seems to mean that he had an ongoing sexual relationship with his stepmother. Whether his father was still alive is not indicated. Paul admonished them to immediately excommunicate the offending member: *In the Name of our Lord Jesus Christ . . . To deliver such a one to Satan for the destruction of the flesh, that the spirit may be saved in the day of the Lord Jesus* (5:4-5).

The uppermost consideration is not only how our lives affect our relationship with God, but also equally important are our church, families, and Christian friends.

When leaders of a church body allow obvious ongoing sin among its members, it encourages a sinner to excuse his own sin and continue to influence others to follow his immoral lifestyle.

If we believe what God has said in His Word about sin, there is accountability for it. Consequently, the decision to say or do nothing, merely in the interest of "harmony," is in opposition to what the Holy Spirit led Paul to write: *I have written to you not to keep company, if any man that is called a brother be a fornicator, or covetous, or an idolater, or a railer* (reviler), *or a drunkard, or an extortioner; with such a one no not to eat. . . . put away from among yourselves that wicked person* (5:11-13). *And such **were** some of you* (6:11). The key word here is WERE because all who have truly received Christ as Savior and Lord should have forsaken their sins.

Because of the inevitable results of sin, Paul continued to write: *Be not deceived: neither fornicators, nor idolaters, nor adulterers, nor effeminate, nor abusers of themselves with mankind, Nor thieves, nor covetous, nor drunkards, nor revilers, nor extortioners, shall inherit the Kingdom of God* (I Corinthians 6:9-10).

Thought for Today: To neglect the Word of God is to neglect God Himself.

Cross References: For I Corinthians 6:16: See Genesis 2:24. I Corinthians 9:9: See Deuteronomy 25:4.

For definitions of unfamiliar words in today's Bible reading, see pages 468-480.

In Today's Reading
Guidelines for worship; the Lord's Supper; spiritual gifts;
charity (love), the greatest gift

*S*urprising as it may seem to the world, from God's point of view it is more important to be known for your loving-kindness, thoughtfulness, and consideration of others than for being a famous evangelist, preacher, or teacher. *Though I speak with the tongues of men and of angels, and have not charity* (love), *I am become as sounding brass, or a tinkling cymbal* (1 Corinthians 13:1).

It is also more important to be known for one's love, as God loves, than for being the most prominent prophetic speaker in the world. Paul went on to reveal this God-given ability to love: *Though I have the gift of prophecy* (forth-telling or fore-telling), *and understand all mysteries, and all knowledge; and though I have all faith, so that I could remove mountains, and have not charity, I am nothing* – worthless to God (13:2).

Charity suffers long, and is kind (13:4). It *vaunts not itself,* does not brag with inflated ideas of its own importance, meaning it does not insist on its own way and is never rude to anyone. Neither is it self-seeking, quick to take offense, or resentful. Love does not think evil of anyone. This God-kind of love is very patient – never envious or boastful.

Another dimension of love is that it *does not behave itself unseemly, seeks not her own, is not easily provoked, thinks no evil* (13:5), meaning it is tactful, charitable, and willing to forgive. Love has a way of making us more concerned for the feelings and rights of others and less preoccupied with our own. The love of God keeps us from always trying to grab the best for ourselves or taking advantage of others.

Love also has a way of keeping us from listening to people who are anxious to pass on the latest gossip about the faults and failures of other brothers or sisters in Christ.

Love *bears all things . . . endures all things* (13:7) without getting frustrated or angry. *Charity never fails* (13:8), regardless of whether it is for friends, difficult people, or strangers. *Every one that loves is born of God, and knows God. He that loves not knows not God; for God is love* (I John 4:7-8).

Thought for Today: When you love the Lord, love for others will be its natural overflow.

Cross References: For I Corinthians 10:7: See Exodus 32:6. I Corinthians 10:26: See Psalm 24:1.

For definitions of unfamiliar words in today's Bible reading, see pages 468-480.

In Today's Reading
Spiritual gifts; resurrection of Christ;
collection for the Jerusalem saints

*I*t is a triumphant fact *that Christ died for our sins according to the Scriptures; And that He was buried, and that He rose again the third day according to the Scriptures* (I Corinthians 15:3-4). For the Christian, death is not the end of life, but only the beginning of a magnificent, eternal future with our wonderful Lord. *We shall all be changed, In a moment, in the twinkling of an eye, at the the last trump: for the trumpet shall sound, and the dead shall be raised incorruptible, and we shall be changed* (15:51-52).

Paul concluded his glorious thoughts on the return of the Lord Jesus by saying: *Therefore, my beloved brethren, be steadfast, unmovable, always abounding in the work of the Lord, forasmuch as you know that your labor is not in vain in the Lord* (it is always profitable) (15:58). While Paul wrote of a joyful eternity with Christ, the Apostle John wrote of the coming judgment for all unbelievers. *I saw a great white throne, and Him that sat on it. . . . And I saw the dead, small and great, stand before God; and the books were opened: and another book was opened, which is the Book of Life: and the dead were judged out of those things which were written in the books according to their works. . . . And whosoever was not found written in the Book of Life was cast into the lake of fire* (Revelation 20:11-15).

Christians have the utmost confidence that, *if the Spirit of Him that raised up Jesus from the dead dwell in you, He that raised up Christ from the dead shall also quicken* (make alive) *your mortal bodies by His Spirit that dwells in you* (Romans 8:11).

Our threefold purpose for living is to become the person that God planned for us to be so that we may accomplish His will for us on earth and be prepared for the triumphant splendor of heaven. Concerning heaven, the words of Jesus have brought precious comfort to millions when He said: *Let not your heart be troubled. . . . I go and prepare a place for you, I will come again, and receive you to Myself* (John 14:1.3).

Thought for Today: Christians will live with Christ forever. What a precious assurance!

Cross References: For I Corinthians 14:21: See Isaiah 28:11-12. I Corinthians 15:3-4: See Hosea 6:2. I Corinthians 15:25: See Psalm 110:1. I Corinthians 15:27: See Psalm 8:6. I Corinthians 15:32: See Isaiah 22:13. I Corinthians 15:45: See Genesis 2:7. I Corinthians 15:54: See Isaiah 25:8. I Corinthians 15:55: See Hosea 13:14.

For definitions of unfamiliar words in today's Bible reading, see pages 468-480.

*E*arthen vessels (clay pots) have very little value of their own. Their essential worth depends upon what they contain. If they are left empty, they have no purpose for existence. However, if they are filled with gold, their value increases dramatically. The body of a Christian is compared to an ordinary clay pot and the precious treasure it contains is *Christ in you, the hope of glory* (Colossians 1:27). *We have this treasure in earthen vessels* (II Corinthians 4:7) and are precious to God and responsible to Him as dispensers of His life-producing Word. Many would assume that no one had more spiritual authority than Paul, yet he wrote: *Not for that we have dominion over your faith, but are helpers of your joy: for by faith you stand* (1:24). The Corinthians were responsible to God, not to Paul, just as any Christian is only responsible to God in matters of faith.

Being accountable to God includes how we respond to experiences common to many of God's children: *We are troubled on every side, yet not distressed; we are perplexed* (puzzled), *but not in despair; Persecuted, but not forsaken; cast down, but not destroyed; Always bearing about in the body the dying of the Lord Jesus, that the life also of Jesus might be made manifest* (known) *in our body* (4:8-10). Since the Holy Spirit dwells in every Christian, we are expected to express His characteristics during every trial and suffering. We can also face trials and suffering with the confidence that our Lord is lovingly working out what is best for our eternal good.

Trials and troubles, in whatever form, are necessary for spiritual growth; without them, we would not exercise our faith or develop spiritual insight and strength (Acts 14:22; I Peter 1:6-7). Just as it was necessary for Jesus to die, we too must die to self-love and become willing partakers of His sufferings.

Our light affliction (trouble), *which is but for a moment, works for us a far more exceeding and eternal weight of glory; While we look not at the things which are seen, but at the things which are not seen: for the things which are seen are temporal; but the things which are not seen are eternal* (II Corinthians 4:17-18).

Thought for Today: We are called to *share in the sufferings of the Messiah* (I Peter 4:13).

Cross References: For II Corinthians 3:13: See Exodus 34:33. II Corinthians 4:13: See Psalm 116:10.

For definitions of unfamiliar words in today's Bible reading, see pages 468-480.

In Today's Reading
Living by faith; ministry of reconciliation;
believers not to be unequally joined with unbelievers;
Paul's ministry; the grace of giving

*N*o one would deny that we are living in a day of deception and compromise, and, unfortunately, Christians are tempted to search for satisfaction through what the world has to offer. To provide answers for this problem, Paul earnestly asked five questions that deserve our prayerful consideration because they have eternal consequences for us. *Be not unequally yoked together with unbelievers: for what fellowship has righteousness with unrighteousness? and what communion has light with darkness? And what concord* (harmony) *has Christ with Belial* (Satan)? *or what part has he that believes with an infidel* (unbeliever)? *And what agreement has the Temple of God with idols? for you are the Temple of the Living God* (II Corinthians 6:14-16).

Since there is a real danger of being caught up with world views that press upon us daily, James was led to warn us that *whosoever therefore will be a friend of the world is the enemy of God* (James 4:4). This is important to remember, since the believer and the unbeliever each have a different master. Paul was led to write: *If you then be risen with Christ, seek those things which are above, where Christ sits on the right hand of God. Set your affection* (mind and emotion) *on things above, not on things on the earth* (Colossians 3:1-2).

The Christian's call is to *come out from among them, and be separate, says the Lord, and touch not the unclean* (unfit) *thing; and I will receive you, And will be a Father to you, and you shall be My sons and daughters, says the Lord Almighty* (II Corinthians 6:17-18). To *come out from* means, among other things, that we should avoid becoming involved with unbelieving friends or joining in activities that keep us from being our best for Christ and His Church, even though we are called to love all people as God does.

Paul went on to say: *Having therefore these promises, dearly beloved, let us cleanse ourselves from all filthiness of the flesh and spirit, perfecting holiness in the fear of God* (II Corinthians 7:1).

Thought for Today: It is only by the grace of God that we *are* anything or can *do* anything of eternal value.

Cross References: For II Corinthians 6:2: See Isaiah 49:8. II Corinthians 6:16: See Leviticus 26:11; Ezekiel 37:27. II Corinthians 6:17: See Isaiah 52:11. II Corinthians 8:15: See Exodus 16:18.

For definitions of unfamiliar words in today's Bible reading, see pages 468-480.

In Today's Reading

Paul's spiritual authority; warning against false teachers;
Paul's suffering; his thorn in the flesh; his plans to visit Corinth

*P*aul often faced rejection from hostile enemies of Christ and occasionally from believers as well. He recalled: *Of the Jews five times received I forty stripes* (lashes) *save one. Thrice I was beaten with rods, once was I stoned, thrice I suffered shipwreck, a night and a day I have been in the deep; In journeyings often, in perils of waters, in perils of robbers, in perils by my own countrymen, in perils by the heathen, in perils in the city, in perils in the wilderness, in perils in the sea, in perils among false brethren; In weariness and painfulness, in watchings* (sleepless nights) *often, in hunger and thirst, in fastings often, in cold and nakedness. Beside those things that are outside that which comes upon me daily, the care* (concern) *of all the churches* (II Corinthians 11:24-28). After his conversion, Paul lived with only one purpose, to *preach the Gospel in the regions beyond* (10:16).

We too have the high calling to reach out in love to all people with the Good News of eternal life. Surely everyone should have the opportunity of hearing, at least once, that at death they are destined to either eternal death in the lake of fire or eternal life in heaven. Even though our lives and good works are very commendable, our Creator Jesus Christ said: *I am the Way, the Truth, and the Life: no one comes to the Father, but by Me* (John 14:6). Have you ever seriously thought what it means for your friends or loved ones to die without being saved?

The dividing line between the sheep and the goats, the weeds and the wheat, the saved and the lost rests upon one fact; Jesus assured us that, *if a man keep* (obey) *My saying, he shall never see* (experience) *death* (8:51).

It is of utmost importance that we consider our priorities. Do they bring us closer to the Lord and His purpose for our lives or take us further away from Him? *When the Son of Man shall come. . . . before Him shall be gathered all nations: and He shall separate them . . . as a shepherd divides his sheep from the goats. . . . Then the King shall say to them on His right hand, Come . . . inherit the kingdom prepared for you from the foundation of the world* (Matthew 25:31-34).

Thought for Today: *Rejoice. . . . be encouraged . . . be at peace, and the God of love and peace will be with you* (II Corinthians 13:11).

Cross References: For II Corinthians 9:9: See Psalm 112:9. II Corinthians 10:17: See Jeremiah 9:24. II Corinthians 13:1: See Deuteronomy 19:15.

For definitions of unfamiliar words in today's Bible reading, see pages 468-480.

November Daily Topical Reference Index

Introduction To The Book Of
Galatians

The Apostle Paul writes this letter *to the churches of Galatia* (Galatians 1:2) to refute false teachings regarding salvation. Paul calls it *another Gospel, which is not another* (1:6-7). They were being drawn away, not to a superior form of the same Gospel, but to something which was essentially a different gospel *which would pervert the Gospel of Christ.* The Greek verb here translated as *pervert* means, literally, to twist a thing around, or reverse it. They were twisting the *one and only Gospel of Christ*, and reversing its meaning into something which it never meant at all.

Paul does not leave us in any doubt as to the nature of the Galatian defection. His first words are: *I marvel that you are so soon removed from Him Who called you into the grace of Christ to another Gospel.* They were erring from that absolutely distinctive doctrine of the one true Gospel, that the eternal salvation of the soul is altogether of Divine *grace* in Christ.

This group of churches included Pisidian Antioch, Iconium, Lystra, and Derbe, in different districts within the Roman province of Galatia. False teachers were persuading some believers that circumcision and keeping the ceremonial laws given through Moses were essential for both Jew and Gentile to become Christians. *As many as desire to make a fair show in the flesh, they constrain* (compel) *you to be circumcised; only lest they should suffer persecution for the cross of Christ. For neither they themselves who are circumcised keep* (obey) *the Law; but desire to have you circumcised, that they may glory* (boast) *in your flesh* (6:12-13).

ENLIGHTENS

The entrance of Your words gives light; it gives understanding to the simple (Psalm 119:130).

INSTRUCTS

All Scripture is given by inspiration of God, and is profitable for doctrine, for reproof, for correction, for instruction in righteousness: That the man of God may be perfect, thoroughly furnished to all good works (II Timothy 3:16-17).

FOOD

*It is written, Man shall not live by bread alone, but by **every Word** that proceeds out of the mouth of God* (Matthew 4:4).

In Today's Reading
Only one Gospel; Paul's rebuke of Peter;
justification by faith, not the Law; the Law, our guide to Christ

*T*his letter forever settles the fact that there is but one way to avoid eternal hell and to be assured of eternal life in heaven for both Jew and Gentile. *Our Lord Jesus Christ . . . gave Himself for our sins, that He might deliver us from this present evil world, according to the will of God and our Father* (Galatians 1:3-4). We are reminded that no one deserves or earns the right to heaven by keeping *the Law*. We can only *be justified by the faith of Christ, and not by the works of the Law: for by the works of the Law shall no flesh* (man) *be justified. But if, while we seek to be justified by Christ, we ourselves also are found sinners, is therefore Christ the minister of sin? God forbid* (2:16-17). The full meaning of God's grace and undeserved loving-kindness was revealed when Jesus died on the cross that we might be delivered from the judgment of our sin and eventually be in heaven with Him.

Since no one has the ability to keep the Law of God, *Christ has redeemed us from the curse of the Law, being made a curse for us* (3:13). These facts lead us to recognize our great need of a Savior. *The Law was our schoolmaster to bring us to Christ, that we might be justified by faith. But after that faith is come, we are no longer under a schoolmaster* (3:24-25). Instead, we are led and empowered by the indwelling Holy Spirit to be *the children of God by faith in Christ Jesus. For as many of you as have been baptized into Christ have put on Christ. There is neither Jew nor Greek, there is neither bond nor free, there is neither male nor female: for you are all one in Christ Jesus. And if you be Christ's, then you are Abraham's seed, and heirs according to the promise* (3:26-29).

We are commissioned to reach our world with the Good News that Jesus Christ, the sinless Son of God, took our place and died for our sins. The Lord *has delivered us from the power of darkness, and has translated us into the kingdom of His dear Son* (Colossians 1:13). Our true citizenship is now in heaven, and we await Jesus' soon return. *The government shall be upon His shoulder: and His Name shall be called Wonderful, Counselor, The Mighty God, The Everlasting Father, The Prince of Peace* (Isaiah 9:6).

Thought for Today: We fear men so much because we fear God so little.

Cross References: For Galatians 3:6: See Genesis 15:6. Galatians 3:8: See Genesis 12:3,22:18. Galatians 3:10: See Deuteronomy 27:26. Galatians 3:11: See Habakkuk 2:4. Galatians 3:12: See Leviticus 18:5. Galatians 3:13: See Deuteronomy 21:23.

For definitions of unfamiliar words in today's Bible reading, see pages 468-480.

*J*N *T*ODAY'S *R*EADING
The two Covenants of Law and promise; liberty of the Gospel;
fruit of the Spirit

*T*he Apostle Paul recorded seventeen sins: *Now the works of the flesh are manifest* (evident), *which are these; Adultery, fornication, uncleanness, lasciviousness* (sensuality), *Idolatry, witchcraft, hatred, variance* (discord), *emulations* (jealousy), *wrath, strife, seditions* (dissensions), *heresies, Envyings, murders, drunkenness, revellings, and such like: of the which I tell you before, as I have told you in time past, that they which do such things shall not inherit the kingdom of God* (Galatians 5:19-21).

Sexual immorality, which includes adultery and fornication, heads the list. These sins include intercourse between any unmarried man and woman, as well as the vile perversions of sex, such as homosexuality, sodomy, and lesbianism. Sexual sin is one of the most deceptive sins of our day and destroys God-ordained marriage relationships.

However, *the works of the flesh* also include everything that defiles our mind, body, or spirit, such as sexually explicit magazines, television programs, and movies; immoral jokes; and evil thoughts, speech, or actions.

Idolatry includes greed and anything or anyone other than God Himself that determines our conduct. The object of idolatry could include money, an occupation, a person, or personal pleasure. Though these may not be evil in themselves, if they occupy the time and the loyalty which God deserves, they actually are idols.

Not to be overlooked is *witchcraft*, which includes horoscopes, palm reading, hypnotism, seances, and other acts of the occult.

Also on the list are *hatred, variance, emulations, wrath, strife, seditions, heresies* (5:20). *Strife and seditions* include rivalry and discord, while *envyings* include jealousy and the obsession to excel above others at any cost. All these spring from selfish attitudes of the heart.

We can give thanks to God that *they that are Christ's have crucified the flesh with the affections* (passions) *and lust* (5:24). We are no longer enslaved to these works of the flesh, but are endowed with the Holy Spirit and can bear His fruit, which are *love, joy, peace, long-suffering, gentleness, goodness, faith, meekness, temperance* (Galatians 5:22-23).

Thought for Today: Perhaps the failure we see in another person's life is a reflection of the hidden sin of self-righteousness in our own hearts.

Cross References: For Galatians 4:27: See Isaiah 54:1. Galatians 4:30: See Genesis 21:10. Galatians 5:14: See Leviticus 19:18.

For definitions of unfamiliar words in today's Bible reading, see pages 468-480.

Introduction To The Book Of
ＥPHESIANS

Beginning his third missionary journey, Paul returned to Ephesus and stayed there for about two years, preaching and teaching (Acts 19:1,8-10;20:31). During this time, a great number of people renounced the false worship of Diana and became Christians. Paul focuses attention on how God makes us alive in Christ Jesus. He reminds us: *You have He quickened* (made alive), *who were dead in trespasses and sins; Wherein time past you walked according to the course of this world, according to* (Satan) *the prince of the power of the air, the spirit that now works in the children of disobedience. . . . fulfilling the desires of the flesh and of the mind; and were by nature the children of wrath* (Ephesians 2:1-3). All of us are to be involved in the *perfecting* (equipping) *of the saints, for the work of the ministry, for the edifying* (building up) *of the body of Christ* (4:12). You are to be *renewed in the spirit of your mind . . . which after God is created in righteousness and true holiness* (4:23-24).

In contrast to those who walk in newness of life in Christ are those who *walk . . . as other Gentiles walk, in the vanity* (futility) *of their mind, Having the understanding darkened, being alienated from the life of God through the ignorance that is in them, because of the blindness of their heart* (4:17-18). We are warned that *no whoremonger, nor unclean person, nor covetous man, who is an idolater, has any inheritance in the Kingdom of Christ and of God* (5:5).

Ephesians teaches us to prepare for spiritual warfare, to *put on the whole armor of God, that you may be able to stand against the wiles* (schemes) *of the devil. For we wrestle not against flesh and blood, but against principalities, against powers, against the rulers of the darkness of this world, against spiritual wickedness in high places. Wherefore take to you the whole armor of God, that you may be able to withstand in the evil day, and having done all, to stand. Stand therefore, having your loins girt* (belted) *about with truth, and having on the breastplate of righteousness; And your feet shod with the preparation of the Gospel of Peace; Above all, taking the shield of faith, wherewith you shall be able to quench* (put out) *all the fiery darts* (arrows) *of the wicked. And take the helmet of salvation, and the sword of the Spirit, which is the Word of God* (6:11-17). The Book of Ephesians leads us to see how powerful the Word of God is in helping us to overcome *the wiles of the devil* (6:11). It is our protection from evil, but also includes our offensive weapon and the one Jesus used to defeat the temptations of the devil (Matthew 4:4). Ephesians 4:1-16 is a magnificent explanation of what our Christian ministry is to be.

𝓘N 𝓣ODAY'S 𝓡EADING
Spiritual blessings in Christ; prayers of Paul; unity of believers;
Paul's mission to the Gentiles

𝓣he God Who created all mankind has chosen us to be His children. In fact, *He has chosen us in Him before the foundation* (beginning) *of the world, that we should be holy and without blame before Him. . . . In Whom we have redemption through His blood, the forgiveness of sins, according to the riches of His grace* (Ephesians 1:4,7). No person or power can cheat us out of the very best that God has planned for our lives. As we daily read and study His Word with a desire to do His will, we can then pray and depend upon the Holy Spirit to guide our lives *according to the eternal purpose* (plan) *which he purposed* (planned) *in Christ Jesus our Lord* (3:11).

Before Christ came to earth, only the Jews had a Covenant relationship with God. *At that time you were without Christ, being aliens from the commonwealth of Israel, and strangers from the Covenants of promise, having no hope, and without God in the world* (2:12). Jews and Gentiles alike who receive Christ as Savior and Lord then have a Covenant relationship with God. *Through Him we both have access by one Spirit to the Father* (2:18).

In A.D. 70, God used the Roman general Titus to destroy the Temple, the Brazen Altar of Sacrifice, and the functions of the high priest. These merely foreshadowed the Messiah Jesus Who became the only Means through which a person could approach the One True Holy God to worship Him, *for we have boldness and access with confidence by the faith of Him* (3:12).

Is it any surprise that Satan will deceptively seek to keep us too busy doing "good" things in his effort to keep us from reading God's Word which will make our prayers effective? Because of our love for the Lord, the true believer looks forward to a daily dialog of prayer (talking to God) and reading His Word (God talking to us).

I pray *that Christ may dwell in your hearts by faith; that you, being rooted and ground in love, May be able to . . . know the love of Christ, which passes knowledge, that you might be filled with all the fullness of God* (Ephesians 3:17-19).

Thought for Today: Prayer is a powerful force that goes beyond our limited human wisdom and strength.

Cross References: For Ephesians 1:22: see Psalm 8:6. Ephesians 2:17: see Isaiah 57:19. For definitions of unfamiliar words in today's Bible reading, see pages 468-480.

In Today's Reading

Exhortations on unity; spiritual gifts; the importance of holiness;
walk in love; marriage, symbolic of the Church;
duties of children; armor of God

When we let the love of Christ flow through us and manifest His loving-kindness to everyone without discrimination, then we enjoy His bountiful blessings. We are to overcome all thoughts of resentment and ill will without exception. *Let all bitterness, and wrath, and anger, and clamor, and evil speaking, be put away from you, with all malice* (Ephesians 4:31). Instead, *be kind one to another, tenderhearted, forgiving one another, even as God for Christ's sake has forgiven you* (4:32).

Wrath and anger are often demonstrated in an outburst of abusive language as a reaction against someone who disagrees with our views. Sadly, when some people are offended they are unwilling to forgive. Equally serious is the sin of *slander* which is one of the seven sins that God hates the most (Proverbs 6:16-19).

The presence of any of these evils destroys our peace of mind, grieves the Holy Spirit, and affects our relationship with God. However, if we allow the Holy Spirit to rule our lives, feelings of anger are overcome.

Instead of thoughts of bitterness, revenge, and anger, we should see this as an opportunity to pray for those who wrong us. An example is Stephen, who prayed while he was being stoned to death. *He kneeled down and cried with a loud voice, Lord, lay not this sin to their charge* (Acts 7:60).

Every Christian is a representative of the Lord Jesus Christ and is responsible to respond with His love toward all who, by their words, attitudes, or actions, are unlovely. He is the Head of His Body the Church and we are that Body. It is under His direction that the whole Body is fitted togther perfectly to work in harmony *for the perfecting* (equipping) *of the saints* (believers), *for the work of the ministry, for the edifying* (building up) *of the Body of Christ. Till we all come in unity of the faith, and of the knowledge of the Son of God, to a perfect* (mature) *man, to the measure of the stature of the fullness of Christ* (Ephesians 4:12-13).

Thought for Today: Those who love the Lord keep His Commandments.

Cross References: For Ephesians 4:8: See Psalm 68:18. Ephesians 4:25: See Zechariah 8:16. Ephesians 4:26: See Psalm 4:4. Ephesians 5:31: See Genesis 2:24. Ephesians 6:2-3: See Exodus 20:12; Deuteronomy 5:16.

For definitions of unfamiliar words in today's Bible reading, see pages 468-480.

VICTORY OVER SATAN ASSURED

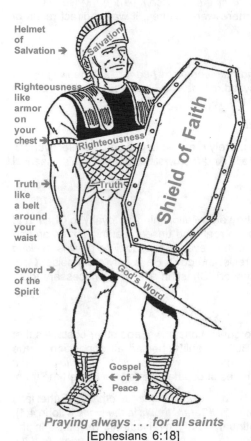

Helmet
of
Salvation →
Salvation

Righteousness
like
armor
on
your
chest →
Righteousness

Truth →
like
a belt
around
your
waist
Truth

Sword →
of the
Spirit
God's Word

Shield of Faith

Gospel
← of →
Peace

Praying always . . . for all saints
[Ephesians 6:18]

Be strong in the Lord, and in the power of His might. Put on the whole armor of God, that you may [successfully] be able to stand against [all] the wiles [strategies, strength, and deceits] of the devil. For we wrestle not against flesh and blood, but against principalities, against powers, against the rulers of the darkness of this world, against spiritual wickedness [forces of evil] in high places. Wherefore take to you the whole armor of God, that you may be able to withstand in the evil day [when you are tempted], and having done all, to stand [Ephesians 6:10-13].

Jesus' victory over Satan during His 40 days in the wilderness was accomplished as He quoted Scripture. And He reminds us that *man shall not live [victoriously] by bread alone [physical needs that supply physical strength], but by every Word that proceeds out of the mouth of God* [Matthew 4:4]. "Every Word" begins in Genesis.

Every piece of the *armor of God* illustrates the Word of God. Never is there a time when the Christian soldier can put aside his *armor* and say: "The battle is won." We are to *fight the good fight of faith* [I Timothy 6:12], and *faith comes by hearing, and hearing by the Word of God* [Romans 10:17]. *The Word of God is quick [living] and powerful . . . a discerner [judge] of the thoughts and intents of the heart* [Hebrews 4:12]. *It is God [through His Word] Who works in you both to will and to do of His good pleasure* [Philippians 2:13].

We overcome in the great conflict with worldliness as the soldier of Christ when we *put on the whole armor of God* [Ephesians 6:11]. Furthermore, there are no alternatives, no substitutes. College degrees, theology, and psychology are all powerless to prepare the soldier for spiritual warfare. It is futile to put on only half the *armor*, for Satan and his tactics are sure to aim his *fiery darts [arrows]* at the most vulnerable spot [6:16]. We're all inclined to fortify ourselves against certain selected sins and neglect the areas in which we think of ourselves as most secure. But the Lord warns: *Wherefore let him that thinks he stands take heed [care] lest he fall* [I Corinthians 10:12]. God knows all the enemy forces that we face, and He knows our weaknesses and has provided full protection and complete armor for us to be victorious – *more than conquerors through Him Who loved us* [Romans 8:37].

Verse 10: *Be strong in the Lord*

These are the same words that God spoke to Joshua: *Be strong*. Joshua was able to conquer the kings in the promised land in just seven years. His secret of strength is pointed out in Joshua 1:8: *This Book of the Law shall not depart out of your mouth but you shall meditate therein day and night, that you may observe to do according to all that is written therein: for then you shall make your way prosperous, and then you shall have good success.* The key to Joshua's conquest of the promised land is evident: *So did Joshua; he left nothing undone of all that the Lord commanded Moses* [11:15]. Israel's history illustrates that whenever there were failures, it was a direct result of ignoring the Word of God.

In the power of His might

To be overcome by sin is a faith failure, and *faith comes by hearing, and hearing by the Word of God* [Romans 10:17]. Pray as David did: *Open You my eyes, that I may behold wondrous things out of Your Law* [Psalm 119:18].

Verse 11: *Put on the whole armor of God*

We cannot provide our *armor*, but we are merely required to put it on. Its effectiveness depends entirely upon the One Who made it. And *the whole armor of God* is essential for a victorious Christian life.

Stand against the wiles of the Devil

The purpose of Satan [the devil] is to destroy our relationship and loyalty to Christ and make us ineffective as His soldiers. Satan is real, and unseen satanic forces around us are seeking to discourage and then to defeat every Christian. The devil is *seeking whom he may devour* [I Peter 5:8]. But, resist the devil. He is only a big noise. God, through His Word, has made available to every Christian everything necessary to be an overcomer.

Verse 12: *For we wrestle not against flesh and blood*

Our conflict may appear to be with men, organizations, laws, and other obstacles that seek to hinder our Christian activities. But, in reality, behind all opposition to the Gospel is Satan – *against principalities, against powers, against the rulers of the darkness of this world.* This darkness is the result of satanic efforts to pervert the truth.

Christ [is] . . . Far above all principality, and power, and might, and dominion [Ephesians 1:20-21] and *greater is He that is in you, than he [Satan] that is in the world* [I John 4:4]. The normal Christian life is one of continual victory over satanic assaults. In the natural man, there is a desire for *the lust of the flesh, and the lust of the eyes, and the pride of life [one's lifestyle]* [I John 2:15-17]. However, *if you live after [according to] the flesh, you shall die: but if you through the Spirit do mortify [put to death] the deeds of the body, you shall live* (Romans 8:13).

Verse 13: *Take to you the whole armor of God, that you may be able to withstand in the evil day [when you are tempted]*

The evil day of temptation will come but at a time when we least expect it.

and having done all, to stand

Our reason for failure is *friendship of the world. . . . whosoever therefore will be a friend of the world is the enemy of God* [James 4:4]. Jesus said: *No man can serve two masters* [Matthew 6:24]. We must decide who and what we are living for. James wrote: *A double minded man is unstable in all his ways* [James 1:8]. And Paul wrote: *Therefore, my beloved brethren, be you steadfast, unmovable, always abounding in the work of the Lord, forasmuch as you know that your labor is not in vain in the Lord* [I Corinthians 15:58].

Verse 14: *Having your loins girt [belted] about with truth*

The *belt* was often made of linen, wide enough for several folds that could carry valuables around the waist. Such is the Word of God, wrapped around us, encompassing our life, involving our whole being, preparing us to be effective.

The words *with truth* have a twofold meaning. One: it denotes the whole truth of God's Word in order to know His will and to accomplish His purposes.

The second meaning is personal integrity – honesty, sincerity, devotion, and determination – the opposite of hypocrisy, indifference, half-heartedness or selfish motives.

Truth is our belt holding our valuables. Nothing short of God's truth is sufficient as we move into action against the *wiles of the devil.*

Having on the breastplate of righteousness

The *breastplate* of the Roman soldier was worn to protect his heart – the source of physical life. The *armor* of the Christian is here called *righteousness. Righteousness* is an attribute of *the Lord our Righteousness* [Jeremiah 23:6; 33:16].

The *breastplate* covers the heart, the motives, the desires of our inmost being. Jesus prayed: *Sanctify them through Your Truth: Your Word is Truth* [John 17:17]. His ultimate desire for every Christian is that He might *sanctify [make us holy] and cleanse [us] with the washing of water by the Word. . . . holy and without blemish [blameless]* [Ephesians 5:26-27].

Verse 15: *Your feet shod with the preparation of the Gospel of peace*

The *feet* must be protected to *run with patience [endurance] the race* [Hebrews 12:1]. To be *shod [sandaled]* has reference to the military sandals – a symbol *of the Gospel of peace.* The *Gospel of peace* keeps us moving forward in the never ending goal to win lost souls for Christ.

Verse 16: *Taking the shield of faith*

The Roman soldier's *shield* was a large, oblong instrument covering most of his body. But it was his responsibility to hold it. The *shield* becomes our overall protection. *This is the victory that overcomes the world, even our faith* [I John 5:4-5]. *Without faith it is impossible to please Him [God]* [Hebrews 11:6]. This *shield of faith* affirms our faith in the Bible as the infallible Word of God. We believe in God the Father; Christ, our Redeemer; and the Holy Spirit to *guide [us] into [all] the Truth* [John 16:13].

You shall be able to quench [extinguish] the fiery darts [arrows] of the wicked

Fiery darts were tipped with flammable materials, like a fire brand, and shot through the air. They were intended to cripple or put out of service the enemy. The *fiery darts* are temptations of covetousness, lust, immorality, pride, love of money, revenge, hate, bitterness, and strife that will cripple the Christian and put him out of commission as an active, effective soldier of Jesus Christ.

Verse 17: *Take the helmet of salvation*

The helmet is the head covering. It is *the helmet* that protected the head and allowed the Roman soldier to hold his head high and face the enemy. And it is *salvation* – the new birth experience – *born of . . . [His] Spirit* [John 3:5] – that causes us to look up in faith, knowing that our *salvation* is *not by works of righteousness which we have done, but according to His mercy He saved us* [Titus 3:5].

Furthermore, having accepted Christ as our Savior, as did the believers who listened to Peter on the day of Pentecost, we *gladly receive His Word [and are] baptized* [Acts 2:41]. His Word not only has the solution for gaining eternal life, but gives direction to overcome all of life's problems.

And the sword of the Spirit

The sword of the Spirit is the Word of God. That Word makes us aware of the *wiles [schemes, trickery] of the devil.* It is the soldier's weapon of offense against unbelief, covetousness, pride, hatred, and worldliness. The secret to spiritual effectiveness is determined by how much of God's Word is a living reality in our lives. We need to ask ourselves: "How big is our *sword*?" Is it the size of a toothpick – a few verses here and there?

Just as the good soldier does not make up his mind whether or not to fight or in which direction to move, so the good soldier of Christ must be familiar with and trained to use his *sword* under the authority of the Holy Spirit.

This same indwelling Holy Spirit *will guide you into all truth* [John 16:13]. But He cannot guide us into the truth that we have refused to read. There is no substitute for the Word of God. That is why the Holy Spirit led David to write: *I will . . . praise [give thanks to] Your Name for . . . You have magnified Your Word above all Your Name* [Psalm 138:2]. Only the Word of God is said to be the source of our new birth, *being born again* [I Peter 1:23; James 1:18]. Only the Word of God is said to be the source of our spiritual growth. *Desire the sincere [unadulterated, pure] milk of the Word, that you may grow thereby* [I Peter 2:2].

The church world has a thousand imitation swords -- one for every problem. You name it and someone has written a book about it. One of the greatest victories of Satan is keeping Christians busy reading "good" books that keep them from reading THE BOOK. The Bible was created for your profit, for *all Scripture . . . is profitable* [II Timothy 3:16].

Verse 18: *Praying always with all prayer and supplication in the Spirit, and watching thereto with all perseverance and supplication*

It becomes evident that the Christian soldier is not left defenseless. *The weapons of our warfare are not carnal [fleshly], but mighty through God to the pulling down of strong holds* [II Corinthians 10:4]. As God's Word becomes our way of life, our prayers are answered. Satan will do everything in his power to distract us from reading God's Word, living God's Word, and praying according to God's Word. *He that turns away his ear from hearing the Law [God's Word], even his prayer shall be abomination* [Proverbs 28:9].

The Christian's *warfare* never ends. It's 365 days of every year. There is no leave of absence, no vacation, no time off. It is a continual fight against *the lust of the flesh, and the lust of the eyes, and the pride of life [one's lifestyle]* [I John 2:16].

for all the saints

The Christian soldier is a volunteer in the King of kings' army – not for self-interests – but *for all saints*. It is of utmost importance that we pray for the leadership, pastors, evangelists, missionaries, our church, and heads of ministries. But it is of equal importance to pray for the weakest saint – the one who may have offended us. Difficulty in forgiving others indicates an inadequate view of our need of forgiveness from God. Jesus warned: *If you forgive not men for their trespasses [from your heart], neither will your Father forgive your trespasses* [Matthew 6:15; compare 18:21-35].

This points out the importance of heartfelt earnestness in prayer. When Jesus prayed: *I pray for them . . . which You have given Me; for they are Yours. . . . that they might have My joy fulfilled in themselves. I have given them Your Word. . . . They are not of the world, even as I am not of the world. Sanctify them through Your Truth. Your Word is Truth. As You have sent Me into the world, even so have I also sent them into the world. . . . That they all may be one. . . . That the love wherewith You have loved Me may be in them, and I in them* [John 17:9,13-14,16-18,21,26]. Oh, how we need to recognize the importance of heartfelt praying *for ALL the saints*!

Continued from Page 424

Introduction To The Book Of
Philippians & Colossians

The Apostle Paul was in Troas, in Asia Minor, on his second mission-ary journey when he received the call, in a vision, to carry the Good News into Macedonia, *to Philippi, which is the chief* (leading) *city of that part of Macedonia, and a colony: and we were in that city abiding certain days* (Acts 16:12). The church that grew out of his stay was the first one Paul established within Europe.

As he wrote this letter, Paul was a prisoner in the custody of the Roman Emperor Nero, but he called himself the Roman *prisoner of Jesus Christ*. Like Paul, we need to remember Who is in control of our lives (Ephesians 3:1; 4:1; II Timothy 1:8; Philemon 1:1,9). He assured the Philippians that Christ is the never-failing source of strength during adverse circumstances, saying: *I can do all things through Christ Who strengthens me* (Philippians 4:13). The key thought of this letter is: *Rejoice in the Lord always: and again I say, Rejoice* (4:4). *Joy, rejoice,* and *rejoiced* occur a total of 21 times in this short book (1:4,18,25-26; 2:2,16-18,28; 3:1,3; 4:1,4,10).

The city of Colossae was located in the Roman province of Asia Minor on the east/west trade route that ran from Ephesus to Tarsus, and then to Syria. In this brief letter, Paul focused on the fundamental doctrines of our faith in God, *Who has delivered us from the power of darkness, and has translated us into the kingdom of His dear Son: In Whom we have redemption through His blood, even the forgiveness of sins* (Colossians 1:13-14).

Paul also combated false teachings by confirming the deity of Christ and His supremacy over all things. *For by Him all things were created, that are in heaven, and that are in earth, visible and invisible, whether they be thrones, or dominions, or principalities, or powers: all things were created by Him, and for Him: And He is before all things, and by Him all things consist* (hold together). *And He is the Head of the Body, the Church: Who is the beginning, the Firstborn from the dead; that in all things He might have the preeminence* (first place) (Colossians 1:16-18).

Some of the Jewish converts felt they should continue to keep the Sabbath, but the Holy Spirit led Paul to write: *Let no man . . . judge you in meat* (food), *or in drink, or in respect of a holyday* (festival), *or of the new moon, or of the Sabbath* (Rest) *days: Which are a shadow of things to come; but the Body is of Christ* (2:16-17).

In Today's Reading

Paul's prayer for the Philippians; the privilege of suffering for Christ; unity gained by humility; exhortation to rejoice in the Lord

The Apostle Paul first preached in Europe in the city of Philippi. On the Sabbath, he went to a place of prayer by a river where he met Lydia, a businesswoman from Thyatira who was saved along with a few others, and a church was planted there (Acts 16:13-15). At a later date, as a missionary prisoner at Rome, Paul wrote to these converts: *According to my earnest expectation and my hope, that . . . Christ shall be magnified in my body, whether it be by life, or by death. For to me to live is Christ, and to die is gain* (Philippians 1:20-21).

His imprisonment in Rome gave him the opportunity to share the Good News about Jesus with the elite guard of the Roman Empire. This was a great opportunity to tell many of them about Jesus Who is the Messiah foretold of in the Scriptures, as there was a change of guard three or four times a day. He wrote to the Philippians: *The things that happened to me have fallen out* (turned) *rather to the furtherance of the Gospel; So that my bonds in Christ are manifest* (known) *in all the palace* (military headquarters), *and in all other places* (1:12-13).

Paul encouraged the church to hold *forth the Word of Life; that I may rejoice in the day of Christ, that I have not run in vain, neither labored in vain* (2:16). Our occupation in life may be in politics, the military, business, education, manual labor, or homemaking, but our primary concern should always be *that I have not run in vain, neither labored in vain*.

We all have a natural desire for physical comforts, security, and material things. However, in making our decisions, our first loyalty should be to Christ. There is a storehouse of spiritual wealth and peace in Him that makes all earthly possessions unimportant.

Paul had renounced a prominent career for a life of unceasing hardship and persecution which was destined to end in violent death. Knowing what the future held for him, he said: *I count all things but loss for the excellency of the knowledge of Christ Jesus my Lord: for Whom I have suffered the loss of all things, and do count them but dung* (rubbish), *that I may win Christ. . . . That I may know Him and the power of His resurrection, and the fellowship of His sufferings, being made conformable to His death* (Philippians 3:8,10).

Thought for Today: Happiness cannot result from an act of sin.

For definitions of unfamiliar words in today's Bible reading, see pages 468-480.

IN TODAY'S READING

The supremacy of Christ; reconciliation in Christ; warning
against false teaching; the new life in Christ; Christian virtues

---

*A*s we continue reading God's Word with a desire to please Him
in all of our decisions, the Holy Spirit guides us into a deeper revelation
of His will and His ways. There is no limit to the understanding,
strength, and endurance that are made available to every Christian.
Christ alone, through His Word, can reveal and meet all of our
spiritual needs. To help us grasp the importance of this, Paul wrote: *We
. . . do not cease to pray for you, and to desire that you might be filled
with the knowledge of His will in **all** wisdom and spiritual understanding; That you might walk worthy of the Lord to **all** pleasing, being
fruitful in every good work, and increasing in the knowledge of God;
Strengthened with **all** might, according to His glorious power, to **all**
patience and longsuffering with joyfulness; Giving thanks to the Father,
Who has made us meet* (qualified) *to be partakers of the inheritance of
the saints* (believers) (Colossians 1:9-12). Notice how often the word **all**
is used – **all** wisdom . . . **all** pleasing . . . **all** might. . . **all** patience.

What follows is the practical expression of the new life in Christ for
all believers. *Buried with Him in baptism, wherein also you are risen
with Him through the faith of the operation of God, Who has raised Him
from the dead. And you, being dead in your sins and the uncircumcision
of your flesh, has He quickened* (made alive) *together with Him, having
forgiven you all trespasses* (2:12-13). As evidence of this new life as
Christians, Paul encouraged the new believers to *mortify* (treat as
dead) *therefore your members which are upon the earth* (physical
nature); *fornication, uncleanness* (sexual immorality), *inordinate affection* (lust), *evil concupiscence* (desire), *and covetousness, which is idolatry: For which things' sake the wrath of God comes on the children of
disobedience* (3:5-6).

The Christian's strength in fulfilling God's will is the result of
letting *the Word of Christ dwell in you richly in all wisdom; teaching
and admonishing* (urging) *one another in psalms and hymns and
spiritual songs, singing with grace in your hearts to the Lord. And
whatsoever you do in word or deed, do all in the Name of the Lord Jesus,
giving thanks to God and the Father by Him* (3:16-17).

Thought for Today: The prayers of the upright are the Lord's delight.

For definitions of unfamiliar words in today's Bible reading, see pages 468-480.

Introduction To The Books Of
I & II Thessalonians

After being beaten and jailed in Philippi along with Silas and then miraculously delivered, the Apostle Paul arrived in Thessalonica on his second missionary journey (Acts 17:1). This was the capital of Macedonia (northern Greece) and its chief seaport and commercial center. Some Jews, and many Greeks, accepted Jesus during this time and a church was established. *For this cause* (reason) *also we thank God without ceasing, because, when you received the Word of God which you heard of us, you received it not as the word of men, but as it is in truth, the Word of God, which effectually works also in you that believe* (I Thessalonians 2:13).

Forced to leave Thessalonica because of violent opposition to his message, Paul journeyed to Berea, where he was well received. But, within a short time, fanatical Jews came from Thessalonica and again fiercely opposed him. He then went on to Athens, where he faced the indifference of the intellectuals and had little success (Acts 17:15-33; I Thessalonians 3:1). From there he went to Corinth (Acts 18:1).

In this first letter to the Thessalonians, Paul alludes five times to the return of Christ: 1:10; 2:19; 3:13; 4:15-16; 5:2-3. He earnestly urged them to be prepared for Christ's return and prayed for them, saying: *The very God of peace sanctify you wholly; and I pray God your whole spirit and soul and body be preserved* (kept) *blameless to the coming of our Lord Jesus Christ* (I Thessalonians 5:23).

In Paul's second letter to the Thessalonians, he foretold that *the Lord Jesus shall be revealed from heaven with His mighty angels, In flaming fire taking vengeance on them that know not God, and that obey not the Gospel of our Lord Jesus Christ* (II Thessalonians 1:7-8). Before Christ returns, evil and wickedness will become more intense under the control of *that man of sin,* the Antichrist (2:3; also Daniel 7:25). At that time there will be intense opposition to the Truth of God. Paul also warned that false teaching will cause a great falling away from the faith. *Let no man deceive you by any means: for that day shall not come, except there come a falling away first, and that man of sin be revealed, the son of perdition. . . . Whose coming is after the working of Satan with all power and signs and lying wonders, And with all deceivableness* (deception) *of unrighteousness in them that perish; because they received not the love of the Truth, that they might be saved* (II Thessalonians 2:3,9-10). The return of Christ is referred to more than 20 times in the 8 short chapters of these two letters.

The certainty of the believer's eternal life with Christ is based on the physical resurrection of Jesus Christ (I Corinthians 15:20-23). The Apostle Paul wrote: *If we believe that Jesus died and rose again, even so them also which sleep* (die) *in Jesus will God bring with Him. For this we say to you by the Word of the Lord, that we which are alive and remain to the coming of the Lord shall not prevent* (precede) *them which are asleep* (have died). *For the Lord Himself shall descend from heaven with a shout, with the voice of the archangel, and with the trump of God: and the dead in Christ shall rise first. Then we which are alive and remain shall be caught up together with them in the clouds, to meet the Lord in the air: and so shall we ever be with the Lord. Wherefore comfort* (encourage) *one another with these words* (I Thessalonians 4:14-18).

The return of Christ will be the greatest event since His ascension when, *while they beheld, He was taken up; and a cloud received Him out of their sight* (Acts 1:9). His return was confirmed at the time of His ascension by two witnesses from heaven: *This same Jesus, Who is taken up from you into heaven, shall so come in like manner as you have seen Him go into heaven* (1:11).

We can comfort fellow Christians, whose loved ones have been called home to be with the Lord with the assurance that soon, we will have a joyous reunion – not only with Christ, but also with all our redeemed loved ones. Our utmost confidence is in Jesus, our Lord, Who assured us: *Let not your heart be troubled: you believe in God, believe also in Me. . . . I go and prepare a place for you* (John 14:1,3).

There are no words to describe the glorious return of our Lord Jesus Christ. All of history is reduced to just two ages: the present age that began with Adam, and the age to come. You *know perfectly* (full well) *that the day of the Lord so comes as a thief in the night* (I Thessalonians 5:2). We are moving toward the appointed *day of the Lord.* This is the joyous anticipation of every Christian who is faithfully preparing and waiting for the triumphant return of our Redeemer.

Because of this assurance of Christ's return, *comfort* (encourage) *yourselves together, and edify* (build up) *one another, even as also you do* (I Thessalonians 5:11).

Thought for Today: Security is found in Christ not in the abundance of material things.

Cross References: For I Thessalonians 5:4: See Isaiah 35:4.

For definitions of unfamiliar words in today's Bible reading, see pages 468-480.

In Today's Reading
Encouragement in persecution; instruction concerning the day of the Lord; commandment to work

It grieves our hearts to realize that the vast majority of mankind is blindly rushing toward an eternal lake of fire, ignorant of the horrors of their impending doom and judgment. *To you who are troubled rest with us, when the Lord Jesus shall be revealed from heaven with His mighty angels, In flaming fire taking vengeance on them that know not God, and that obey not the Gospel of our Lord Jesus Christ: Who shall be punished with everlasting destruction from the presence of the Lord, and from the glory of His power* (II Thessalonians 1:7-9).

To be sure, much of the world has its heart set on gaining more and more of this life's luxuries and on increasing its income level compared to the year before. So they work harder or get a part-time job to pay for things they cannot afford. Their fears and frustrations continue to grow as the result of their inability to cope adequately with situations they can't change. This drive has, at times, led to physical and emotional exhaustion, depression, and what some call "burnout."

At times, we are all tempted to be influenced by this spirit of the world that deceives many *that perish; because they received not the love of the Truth, that they may be be saved. And for this cause God shall send them strong delusion* (unbelief), *that they* (unbelievers) *should believe a lie: That they all might be damned* (judged) *who believed not the Truth, but had pleasure in unrighteousness* (2:10-12). We need to remind ourselves daily that we are in a spiritual battle against satanic forces.

Without exception, those who choose to invest their lives in serving Christ receive true satisfaction beyond words to explain. This means they regularly read the whole counsel of God to be fully prepared, not merely for a heavenly future, but for present-day living and the ministry of God's Word in the use of our time, talents, and possessions.

The Apostle John tells us: *These are written, that you might believe that Jesus is the Christ, the Son of God; and that believing you might have life through His Name* (authority) (John 20:31).

Thought for Today: Jesus Christ is coming soon! It could be today.

Cross References: For Thessalonians 1:8 See Isaiah 1:28. II Thessalonians 2:3: See Daniel 7:25. II Thessalonians 2:4: See Ezekiel 28:2.

For definitions of unfamiliar words in today's Bible reading, see pages 468-480.

Introduction To The Books Of
I & II Timothy

In these two letters to Timothy, Paul emphasized that knowing the Scriptures was vital, both for worshiping the Lord, defeating the devil, and for living to please Him. Then Paul stressed that an important qualification of elders and deacons (leaders) was to be *a good minister* (servant) *of Jesus Christ, nourished up* (educated) *in the words of faith and of good doctrine* (teaching), *whereto you have attained. . . . If any man teach otherwise, and consent not to wholesome words* (biblical teaching), *even the words of our Lord Jesus Christ, and to **the doctrine which is according to godliness**; he is proud, knowing nothing* (I Timothy 4:6; 6:3-4). Because of ignorance of the Word of God, *the doctrine which is according to godliness* is unknown by many. Consequently, far too few are aware that, without holiness *no man shall see the Lord* (Hebrews 12:14); and *as obedient children, not fashioning yourselves according to the former lusts in your ignorance: But as He which has called you is holy, so be holy in all manner of conversation* (conduct) (I Peter 1:14-15).

In this first letter, Paul clearly states: *There is One God, and One Mediator* (Arbitrator) *between God and men, the Man Christ Jesus* (I Timothy 2:5). Paul admonished Timothy to remain faithful to Christ and His Word.

Shortly before his martyrdom in Rome, Paul wrote his second letter to Timothy, which was also the last letter that he wrote (II Timothy 4:6-7). Paul again urged his beloved Timothy, *son in the faith* (I Timothy 1:2), to *be strong in the grace that is in Christ Jesus* (II Timothy 2:1). He warned that failure to thoroughly study all the Scriptures would ultimately result in facing God *ashamed*. He encouraged Timothy to *study* (be diligent) *to show yourself approved to God, a workman that needs not to be ashamed, rightly dividing the Word of Truth* (2:15). God's Word alone provides godly wisdom to instruct us to know and do His will (3:15). Reading and obeying all the Scriptures is the only safeguard against deceptions which result from a mixture of truth and error. Paul declared the all-sufficiency of the Scriptures to reveal answers to all of life's problems. We must *preach the Word; be instant* (ready) *in season, out of season; reprove, rebuke, exhort* (encourage) *with all long-suffering and doctrine* (teaching). *For the time will come when they will not endure sound doctrine; but after their own lusts they shall heap to themselves teachers, having itching ears; And they shall turn away their ears from the truth, and shall be turned to fables* (myths, stories) (4:1-4).

In Today's Reading

Warning against false doctrine; thankfulness for mercy;
qualifications of church leaders; instructions about the widows
and the elderly; the good fight of faith

The Roman emperor Nero was ruthlessly persecuting Christians
and committing many of them to death at the time Paul wrote this letter
to Timothy. Yet, Paul emphasized the importance of Christians praying for those who were in authority over them, regardless of their
conduct. He wrote: *I exhort therefore, that, first of all, supplications,
prayers, intercessions, and giving of thanks, be made for all men; For
kings, and for all that are in authority; that we may lead a quiet and
peaceable life in all godliness and honesty* (I Timothy 2:1-2).

As we pray for world leaders, as well as for our local officials, we can
be sure our prayers will have an affect upon their actions, whether the
men themselves are godly or evil. *The king's heart is in the hand of the
LORD, as the rivers of water: He turns it wherever He will* (Proverbs 21:1).

When Peter and others were commanded by the religious authorities to stop telling that Jesus was the Savior of the world, as faithful
Christians, *Peter and the other apostles answered and said, We ought
to obey God rather than men* (Acts 5:29).

Christians should faithfully witness to the truth as revealed by
Christ in His Word, even when it could mean imprisonment or death.
While many *shall turn away their ears from the truth*, we must remain
faithful *in all things, endure afflictions* (II Timothy 4:4-5). The number
of those *suffering affliction* (James 5:10) and being martyred for their
faith in Christ continues to grow.

Later, Peter also emphasized the responsibility of Christians to be
law-abiding citizens, writing: *Submit yourselves to every ordinance of
man for the Lord's sake: whether it be to the king, as supreme; Or to
governors, as to them that are sent by him for the punishment of
evildoers, and for the praise of them that do well* (I Peter 2:13-14). The
New Testament provides no example to justify responding to corrupt
government with force or by not paying taxes. We are taught that it
is Satan who instigates rebellion, violence, and riots.

*For we ourselves also were sometimes foolish, disobedient, deceived,
serving divers lusts* (enslaved to various self-centered desires) . . . *living
in malice and envy, hateful, and hating one another. But . . . according
to His mercy He saved us* (Titus 3:3-5).

Thought for Today: Christians enjoy the peace of God regardless of circumstances.

Cross Reference: For Timothy 5:18: See Deuteronomy 25:4.

For definitions of unfamiliar words in today's Bible reading, see pages 468-480.

In Today's Reading
Exhortations to Timothy; the coming apostasy;
steadfastness in the Scriptures; the charge to preach

There was no hesitancy in Paul's conviction that he was *an apostle of Jesus Christ. . . . Who has saved us, and called us with a holy calling, not according to our works, but according to His own purpose and grace, which was given us in Christ Jesus before the world began* (II Timothy 1:1,9).

The name *Jesus* and the title *Christ* were used six times in the first two verses. The Good News of the Gospel of Jesus Christ is that He imparts eternal life to all who will receive Him by faith. Everything else that we do is incidental to the supreme purpose for which Jesus Christ came: *The Son of Man is come to seek and to save that which was lost* (Luke 19:10).

The Christian life may require us to endure *the afflictions of the Gospel* (II Timothy 1:8). However, we should not fear afflictions because *our Savior Jesus Christ . . . has abolished death, and has brought life and immortality to light through the Gospel* (1:10).

To deny Christ takes on many forms. Our lifestyle could be a form of denying Him. If, in the midst of a lost world, we remain silent in the presence of gross sin, we deny Him. To not do what we should in reaching the lost world with His Word is perhaps the most serious denial of all. We have been forewarned: *The time will come when they will not endure sound doctrine* (teaching); *but after their own lusts shall they heap to themselves teachers . . . And they shall turn away their ears from the truth, and shall be turned to fables* (myths, stories) (4:3-4).

Today, among some, a compromised Christianity supports human greed and lust for comfort, wealth, leisure, and material possessions. What a striking contrast this is to the *good soldier* who endures *hardness* (suffers hardships) and of whom Paul wrote: *No man that wars entangles himself with the affairs of this life; that he may please him who has chosen him to be a soldier* (II Timothy 2:3-4). *Wherefore take to you the whole armor of God, that you may be able to withstand in the evil day, and having done all, to stand. Stand therefore, having your loins girt about with truth, and having on the breastplate of righteousness . . . Above all, taking the shield of faith, wherewith you shall be able to quench all the fiery darts of the wicked* (Ephesians 6:13-14,16).

Thought for Today: The will of God does not lead where the grace of God does not provide.

Cross Reference: For II Timothy 2:19: See Numbers 16:5.

For definitions of unfamiliar words in today's Bible reading, see pages 468-480.

Paul had left Titus on the island of Crete and this letter was sent to instruct him to *set in order the things that are wanting, and ordain elders in every city, as I had appointed you* (Titus 1:5). Through Paul, the Holy Spirit clearly set forth qualifications for a bishop – an excellent guideline for all church leaders (1:6-9).

From prison in Rome, Paul wrote a personal letter to a man named Philemon, who may have been an influential Christian in Colossae and was possibly one of Paul's converts. It appears that Onesimus, a slave who belonged to Philemon, had run away and perhaps later became a convert to Jesus Christ through Paul's ministry in Rome. It is assumed that, after becoming a Christian, Onesimus agreed to return to his master in Colossae. This beautiful letter urged Philemon to receive Onesimus, not as a runaway slave, but as a beloved brother in the Lord, just as he would have received Paul himself (Philemon 1:16-17).

> We all have sinned against the Lord
> And stand condemned by His own Word,
> No prayer or plea of ours could win
> God's free forgiveness for all our sin.
>
> But Jesus came and took our place
> That He might save us by His grace;
> He bore our sins – so great and wide –
> That we, through Him, be justified.
>
> And as we plead Christ's work complete
> Upon the Cross – where He did meet
> Each claim of God's most righteous Law –
> God wipes away each sin and flaw.
>
> He speaks His peace within the heart
> And bids all guilt and fear depart,
> Counts, us accepted in His Son
> And sees the life of faith begun.
>
> May we, in gratitude and love,
> Seek e'er those things that are Above
> And let Christ live His life anew
> Through all who love His will to do.
>
> —M.E.H.

In Today's Reading

The qualifications of church officers; a warning against false
teachers; Christian conduct; Paul's appeal for Onesimus

The churches on the island of Crete needed spiritual leadership, so
Paul instructed Titus to ordain qualified men to fill these positions.
Such men were to *be blameless* (above reproach), *the husband of one
wife, having faithful* (believing) *children not accused of riot or unruly.
For a bishop must be blameless, as the steward of God; not self-willed,
not soon angry, not given to wine, no striker* (not violent), *not given to
filthy lucre* (not greedy for financial gain); *But a lover of hospitality, a
lover of good men, sober, just, holy, temperate* (disciplined); **Holding
fast the faithful Word** *as he has been taught, that he may be able by
sound doctrine both to exhort and to convince the gainsayers* (opposition) (Titus 1:6-9).

The Church belongs to Christ. His qualifications for spiritual
leaders must not be disregarded; man's alternative options are unacceptable to God. Paul's letter to Titus warns that leaders must be blameless
in their personal lives.

Paul gave instruction that older men and women should teach the
younger men and women, instructing them to forsake evil passions
and worldly ambitions, and to live honorably before the Lord. *The
Grace of God that brings salvation has appeared to all men, Teaching
us that, denying ungodliness and worldy lusts, we should live soberly*
(sensibly), *righteously, and godly, in this present world; Looking for
that blessed hope, and the glorious appearing of the great God and our
Savior Jesus Christ; Who gave Himself for us, that He might redeem us
from all iniquity* (lawlessness), *and purify to Himself a peculiar*
(special) *people, zealous of good works* (2:11-14). Our teaching must be
based upon the threefold work of Christ for His people as a result of His
death upon the cross. 1) He set us free – *redeemed us from all iniquity*
(vs 14); 2) He set us apart – *purified to Himself a peculiar people* (vs 14);
and 3) He made us to be *zealous of good works* (vs 14).

A Christian should always be *holding fast the faithful Word as he
has been taught, that he may be able by sound doctrine both to exhort
and to convince the gainsayers* (Titus 1:9).

Thought for Today: Attitudes of superiority or that another is inferior are evil.

For definitions of unfamiliar words in today's Bible reading, see pages 468-480.

Introduction To The Book Of
Hebrews

The authorship of this book is uncertain, but many Bible scholars assume that Paul wrote it while *in his own hired house* in Rome (Acts 28:30). However, the true Author of every book in the Bible is the Holy Spirit.

The Jews had the only true revelation of the One True God and the only divinely-appointed city and Temple for over a thousand years.

Following the persecution mentioned in Acts 8, persecution against Jesus' followers intensified. Some Christians were attempting to add Christianity to Judaism and some were in doubt as to what to do. Consequently, there are about 30 direct quotations and 50 allusions to the Old Testament in the Book of Hebrews to instruct Jewish believers how the Old Covenant had been fulfilled by Jesus, the Messiah, as foretold by the prophets.

The superiority of Christ and His New Covenant are the themes of the book. *God, Who at sundry times and in divers* (various) *manners spoke in time past to the fathers by the prophets, Has in these last days spoken to us by His Son, Whom He has appointed Heir of all things, by Whom also He made the worlds. . . . Therefore we ought to give more earnest heed to the things which we have heard, lest at any time we should let them slip* (drift away) (Hebrews 1:1-2; 2:1; also 3:3; 7:21-27).

The infallible *Word of God is quick* (living), *and powerful, and sharper than any two-edged sword, piercing even to the dividing asunder* (in two) *of soul and spirit, and of the joints and marrow, and is a discerner of the thoughts and intents of the heart* (4:12).

The word **better** (superior) is one of the key words in Hebrews. *For the Law made nothing perfect, but the bringing in of a **better** hope did; by the which we draw near to God. . . . But now has He obtained a more excellent* (superior) *ministry . . . He is the Mediator of a **better** Covenant which was established upon **better** promises* (7:19; 8:6).

The Ten Commandments were written on tablets of stone, but Christ's Covenant is written in *the hearts* of His disciples (8:10).

The Old Covenant, with its endless animal sacrifices, is in striking contrast to the New Covenant which required only One Sacrifice, the perfect Lamb of God (Revelation 5:6,12; 13:8). Christ's own sinless blood cleanses us from all our sins (Hebrews 9:12; 10:1-14).

Let us hold fast the profession of our faith without wavering; (for He is faithful that promised;) And let us consider one another to provoke (encourage) *to love and to good works* (10:23-24).

ℐɴ 𝒯ODAY'S ℛEADING
Why Christ assumed a human body; Christ's superiority to
angels and Moses; salvation; Christ, our High Priest

ℐt was angels who delivered Lot out of Sodom (Genesis 19:1-26);
angels ministered to Jesus following His 40-day fast (Matthew 4:11);
and an angel delivered Peter from prison (Acts 12:11). But, even more
comforting to us is to know that angels are *ministering spirits, sent
forth to minister for them who shall be heirs of salvation* (Hebrews 1:14).
Just think; that includes all who are *heirs of salvation.* Even when it
seems that Satan has devastated our lives, God, Who created and rules
the universe, is making the works of Satan and the wrath of men to
further His ultimate will for each one of us.

The importance of angels does not compare to the superiority of
Christ. *For to which of the angels said He at any time, You are My Son?*
(1:5). Yet, despite His eternal superiority as Creator of angels, because
of His great love for us, Jesus willingly *was made a little lower than the
angels for the suffering of death . . . that He by the grace of God should
taste death for every man. For it became* (was proper for) *Him, for
Whom are all things, and by Whom are all things, in bringing many
sons to glory, to make the Captain of their salvation perfect through
sufferings. . . . For verily* (truly) *He took not on Him the nature of angels;
but He took on Him the seed* (offspring) *of Abraham. Wherefore in all
things it behooved* (was best for) *Him to be made like to His brethren,
that He might be a merciful and faithful High Priest . . . to make
reconciliation for the sins of the people* (2:9-10,16-17).

Consider the honors conferred upon Moses who delivered Israel
from Egypt. Through him the whole Levitical order, the Tabernacle,
and the formal worship system were instituted; but Christ delivered all
who receive Him from eternal hell (John 3:16).

*Let us therefore fear, lest, a promise being left us of entering into His
rest, any of you should seem to come short of it* (Hebrews 4:1).

Thought for Today: When Christ, the Prince of Peace rules our hearts, we will not insist
on having things our way.

Cross References: For Hebrews 1:3: See Psalm 110:1; Hebrews 1:5: See Psalm 2:7; II Samuel
7:14. Hebrews 1:6: See Psalm 97:7. Hebrews 1:7: See Psalm 104:4. Hebrews 1:8-9: See Psalm
45:6-7. Hebrews 1:10-12: See Psalm 102:25-27. Hebrews 1:13: See Psalm 110:1. Hebrews
2:6-8: See Psalm 8:4-6. Hebrews 2:12: See Psalm 22:22. Hebrews 2:13: See Isaiah 8:18.
Hebrews 3:7-11: See Psalm 95:7-11. Hebrews 4:3: See Psalm 95:11. Hebrews 4:4: See
Genesis 2:2.

For definitions of unfamiliar words in today's Bible reading, see pages 468-480.

IN TODAY'S READING

Christ, the High Priest; appeal to believe; priestly order of
Melchizedek; Aaronic priesthood inferior to Christ's priesthood

How thankful we are that mercy is an attribute of God. It is one
of our greatest daily needs. Mercy is an expression of His willingness
to forgive sinners and deliver them from eternal hell. Mercy involves
love as well as a practical demonstration of compassion.

Because God is also holy, He must enforce the penalty for sin, and
the wages of sin is death (Romans 6:23). In the Old Testament, an
innocent, sinless lamb took the place of an Israelite and was slain in his
place for his sin. The devout Jew was continually reminded that *it is the
blood that makes an atonement for the soul* (Leviticus 17:11). But, the
need for numerous sacrifices ceased when Jesus, the innocent, sinless
Son of God, died on the cross for our sins and became the *Lamb of God,
Who takes away the sin of the world* (John 1:29).

He became the Author of eternal salvation to **all who obey Him**
(Hebrews 5:9). *By His own blood He entered in once into the Holy Place,
having obtained eternal redemption for us. . . . How much more shall the
blood of Christ, Who through the eternal Spirit offered Himself without
spot* (defect) *to God, purge* (cleanse) *your conscience from dead works to
serve the living God?* (9:12-14).

Since we so often fail to be all that we should be and deserve the
judgment of God, it is His mercy that gives a Christian assurance of a
continued relationship with Him. In turn, the true believer will
express mercy in his relationships with others because the Spirit of God
dwells in his heart. We have His promise: *Blessed are the merciful: for
they shall obtain mercy* (Matthew 5:7).

Truth, justice, and true mercy are inseparable. Jesus illustrated
mercy by telling of a Good Samaritan taking care of a helpless stranger
who had been beaten and left half dead (Luke 10:33-37).

Put on therefore, as the elect (chosen) *of God, holy and beloved,
bowels of mercies* (compassion), *kindness, humbleness of mind, meekness, long-suffering; Forbearing one another, and forgiving one another*
(Colossians 3:12-13).

Thought for Today: We can no more attain a worthwhile purpose in life apart from God than
the clay can become a useful vessel apart from the potter.

Cross References: For Hebrews 5:5: See Psalm 2:7. Hebrews 5:6: See Psalm 110:4. Hebrews
6:14: See Genesis 22:17.

For definitions of unfamiliar words in today's Bible reading, see pages 468-480.

In Today's Reading

The New Covenant; the perfect sacrifice of Christ compared to
temporary sacrifices under the Law; an appeal to remain faithful

The Tabernacle and worship system for Israel was revealed by God
to Moses on Mount Sinai. It consisted of numerous sacrifices which
could not cleanse from sin but only "cover" them temporarily. However, every detail of this vast worship system was symbolic of the future
single sacrifice of Christ on the cross. He replaced Israel's high priest,
priests, and all of the sacrificial worship system. God foretold through
His prophet of a future Covenant: *I will make a New Covenant with the
house of Israel, and with the house of Judah* (Jeremiah 31:31; compare
Hebrews 8:6-13).

Under the Old Covenant worship system, the *blood of goats and
calves* (9:12,19), which were innocent animals, was sacrificed daily for
worshipers' sins. But Christ, Who is God become Man, shed His own
blood and entered once and for all, not an earthly Holy of Holies, *for
Christ is not entered into the Holy Places made with hands, which are
the figures of the true; but into heaven itself, now to appear in the
presence of God for us* (9:24).

The Holy Spirit led the writer of Hebrews to point out here that the
Old Covenant had looked forward to a *greater and more perfect
Tabernacle* (9:10-11). The words *more perfect Tabernacle* refer to the
incarnate form of Jesus, since the Tabernacle's contents, as well as the
Tabernacle itself, symbolized Christ, His life, ministry, and death, as
did all of the sacrifices. Animal sacrifices are no longer acceptable
because *Christ being come a High Priest of good things to come, by a
greater and more perfect Tabernacle, not made with hands, that is to
say, not of this building; Neither by the blood of goats and calves but by
His own blood He entered in once into the Holy Place, having obtained
eternal redemption for us* (9:11-12).

The confession of our faith is a public acknowledgment that we
have renounced the world and its lusts to remain loyal to our Lord and
Savior Jesus Christ, Who has done so much for us. *God commends His
love toward us, in that, while we were yet sinners, Christ died for us*
(Romans 5:8).

Thought for Today: Yes, God is all-wise, all-powerful, and ever-present. How could we fear
the future?

Cross References: For Hebrews 8:5: See Exodus 25:40. Hebrews 8:8-12: See Jeremiah 31:31-
34. Hebrews 9:20-21: See Exodus 24:8. Hebrews 10:5-7: See Psalm 40:6-8. Hebrews 10:12-
13: See Psalm 110:1. Hebrews 10:16-17: See Jeremiah 31:33-34. Hebrews 10:30: See
Deuteronomy 32:35-36. Hebrews 10:37-38: See Habakkuk 2:3-4.

For definitions of unfamiliar words in today's Bible reading, see pages 468-480.

In Today's Reading
Worthy fruits of faith, patience, godliness;
warning against disobedience; service well-pleasing to God

The history of the people of God confirms that some endured hostile circumstances and suffering, yet remained faithful and fulfilled His will. In the "Heroes of Faith Hall of Fame" (Hebrews 11:1-38), we are given a review of some of them. *By faith Abraham, when he was tried* (tested), *offered up Isaac . . . Accounting that God was able to raise him up, even from the dead; from where also he received him in a figure. . . . By faith Moses . . . refused to be called the son of Pharaoh's daughter; Choosing rather to suffer affliction with the people of God, than to enjoy the pleasures of sin for a season* (short time); *Esteeming the reproach of Christ greater riches than the treasures in Egypt* (11:17-26). The Old Testament men and women listed in this chapter chose to obey God and to live godly lives, regardless of the outcome.

This reminds us of how much more our Savior has made available to us through the indwelling of the Holy Spirit and the full knowledge of the will of God through His written Word. Surely, we too can *lay aside every weight, and the sin which does so easily beset us, and . . . run with patience* (endurance) *the race that is set before us* (12:1). The runners who win the race of life are *looking to Jesus, the Author and Finisher of our faith; Who for the joy that was set before Him endured the cross, despising* (thinking little of) *the shame, and is set down at the right hand of the throne of God* (12:2). The Christian life demands self-denial, discipline, and wholehearted love for God and His Word. These characteristics distinguish the Christian from the self-indulgence practiced by the world. We must decide for ourselves, by a prayerful reading of the Scriptures and self-examination, if there are worldly hindrances to our spiritual lives that need to be eliminated.

The race of which Paul writes is a life of faithfulness and obedience. *He said to them all, If any man will come after Me, let him deny himself, and take up his cross daily, and follow Me* (Luke 9:23).

Thought for Today: *Let your heart keep My Commandments: For length of days, and long life, and peace, shall they add to you* (Proverbs 3:1-2).

Cross References: For Hebrews 11:18: See Genesis 21:12. Hebrews 12:5-6: See Proverbs 3:11-12. Hebrews 12:12: See Isaiah 35:3. Hebrews 12:26: See Haggai 2:6. Hebrews 13:5: See Joshua 1:5; also Deuteronomy 31:8. Hebrews 13:6: See Psalm 118:6.

For definitions of unfamiliar words in today's Bible reading, see pages 468-480.

Introduction To The Book Of
James

The author of this book identifies himself as *James, a servant of God and of the Lord Jesus Christ* (James 1:1). He was not one of the twelve apostles (Matthew 10:2-4), but appears to be the first presiding elder over the Jerusalem church (Acts 12:17; 15:13-21). Paul spoke of him as *James the Lord's brother* (Galatians 1:19).

James often quotes the Old Testament Scriptures, then proceeds to apply them to Christian living (James 2:8,23; 4:5-6); and he warns: *Whosoever therefore will be a friend of the world is the enemy of God* (4:4).

James presents a series of practical tests whereby we may recognize the genuineness of saving faith (2:14,17-18,20,22,24,26; 5:15). He admonished each believer *to keep himself unspotted from the world* (1:27).

James reminds us that we have become spiritual children of God by His Word of Truth, *which is able to save your souls. . . . Of His own will begat* (fathered) *He us with the Word of Truth, that we should be a kind of first-fruits of His creatures. . . . Wherefore lay apart* (rid yourselves of) *all filthiness and superfluity of naughtiness* (whatever wickedness still remains), *and receive with meekness the engrafted* (implanted) *Word, which is able to save your souls. But be doers of the Word, and not hearers only, deceiving your own selves* (1:21,18,21-22).

James also explains the great power of prayer by reminding us of Elijah. *The effectual fervent prayer of a righteous man avails* (accomplishes) *much. Elijah was a man subject to like* (the same) *passions as we are, and he prayed earnestly that it might not rain: and it rained not on the earth by the space of three years and six months. And he prayed again, and the heaven gave rain, and the earth brought forth her fruit* (5:16-18; also I Kings 17:1; 18:1,45).

PEACE

These things I have spoken to you, that in Me you might have peace. In the world you shall have tribulation (oppression): *but be of good cheer; I have overcome the world* (John 16:33).

Being justified by faith, we have peace with God through our Lord Jesus Christ (Romans 5:1).

BE FAITHFUL

But whoso keeps His Word, in him verily (truly) *is the love of God perfected: hereby know that we are in Him* (I John 2:5).

445

Christians to rejoice in trials; heeding the Word of God;
faith that works; dangers of the tongue; worldliness and pride;
warning to the rich; power of prayer

Some of us are inclined to tell others about all our sufferings and sorrows with a "Woe is me" attitude of despair, seeking sympathy from our listeners. Some are also prone to blame anyone, even God, for their problems. But James may surprise you because he wrote: *My brethren, count it all joy when you fall into divers temptations* (manifold trials); *Knowing this, that the trying* (testing) *of your faith works* (develops) *patience. But let patience have her perfect work, that you may be perfect and entire* (complete), *wanting* (lacking) *nothing* (James 1:2-4).

However, James also reminds us: *Blessed is that man that endures temptation* (remains faithful): *for when he is tried* (approved), *he shall receive the crown of life, which the Lord has promised to them that love Him. Let no man say when he is tempted, I am tempted of God: for God cannot be tempted with* (by) *evil, neither tempts He any man* (1:12-13). Trials in life may seem to be wasted time, but they are a great benefit to those who remain teachable and faithful. The fact is *the trial of your faith is much more precious than gold* (I Peter 1:7).

All of us need to be reminded to *draw near to God, and He will draw near to you* (James 4:8). Pity the poor soul who believes that it is only the devil who is giving him a hard time and, consequently, feels frustrated and distressed. All trials and assaults by Satan can only happen with the permission of God and should prompt us to praise the Lord, *knowing . . . that . . . our faith works* (develops) *patience.* We don't need to fear what may happen.

We possess the *whole armor* so that *you may be able to stand against the wiles* (schemes, trickery) *of the devil* (Ephesians 6:11). To withstand the devil during our trials, we must remember Paul's words of encouragement to the Ephesians: *Above all, taking the shield of faith, wherewith you shall be able to quench all the fiery darts of the wicked. . . . and the sword of the Spirit, which is the Word of God* (6:16-17). However, we must *put on the whole armor of God. . . . Praying always* (Ephesians 6:11,18).

Thought for Today: Sinful things blight our lives, but good things result from prayer, Bible reading, and obeying God's Word.

Cross References: For James 2:8: See Leviticus 19:18. James 2:11: See Exodus 20:13-14. James 2:23: See Genesis 15:6. James 4:6: See Proverbs 3:34.

For definitions of unfamiliar words in today's Bible reading, see pages 468-480.

INTRODUCTION TO THE BOOKS OF
I & II PETER

In writing these two letters, Peter obeyed two specific commands given to him by the Lord Jesus Himself. *I have prayed for you, that your faith fail not: and when you are converted, strengthen your brethren* (Luke 22:32). Then Jesus said *to him the third time, Simon, son of Jonah, love you Me? Peter was grieved because He said to him the third time, Love you Me? And he said to Him, Lord, You know all things; You know that I love You. Jesus said to him, Feed My sheep* (John 21:17).

Peter called himself *an apostle of Jesus Christ. . . . an elder, and a witness of the sufferings of Christ, and also a partaker* (sharer) *of the glory that shall be revealed* (I Peter 1:1; 5:1). He also mentioned that he was sending this letter from Babylon (5:13). In this first letter, he was writing to encourage the Christians who had fled their homeland because of persecution and had become *the strangers* (foreigners) *scattered throughout Pontus, Galatia, Cappadocia, Asia, and Bithynia* (1:1). He is urging them to *gird up the loins of your mind* (1:13). When they had hard work to do, they would gather up their robes and fasten them with their belts to keep them out of the way.

Throughout the past 2,000 years, Christians have been subjected to much suffering just as Jesus foretold (John 15:18). Peter affirmed this by writing: *You were called: because Christ also suffered for us, leaving us an example, that you should follow His steps* (I Peter 2:21).

The highlight of the first book is the importance of the Word of God as the only guide for living our life in Christ: *Being born again, not of corruptible seed, but of incorruptible, by the Word of God, which lives and abides for ever* (1:23). He further encouraged: *As newborn babes, desire the sincere* (unadulterated) *milk of the Word, that you may grow thereby* (2:2).

In the interval between the two letters, an even more critical situation of false teaching confronted the Church. Peter warned in his second book: *Brethren, give diligence to make your calling and election sure: for if you do these things, you shall never fall. . . . There were false prophets also among the people, even as there shall be false teachers among you, who secretly* (craftily) *shall bring in damnable* (destructive) *heresies, even denying the Lord that bought them, and bring upon themselves swift destruction. And many of them shall follow their pernicious* (destructive) *ways; by reason of whom the way of truth shall be evil spoken of* (II Peter 1:10; 2:1-2).

ᴵN ᴛODAY'S ᴿEADING
Call to Christian dedication; proper use of Christian liberty;
the example of Christ's suffering

$\mathcal{P}$eter referred to Christians as *elect . . . through sanctification of the Spirit, to obedience and sprinkling of the blood of Jesus Christ* (I Peter 1:2). "Sprinkling" alludes to the blood which was sprinkled on the Brazen Altar as a symbol of the people's obedience to God, as well as on the people as a symbol of God's acceptance of them (Exodus 24:1-11).

As Christians, we look forward to *an inheritance incorruptible* (imperishable), *and undefiled, and that fades not away, reserved in heaven for you, Who are kept* (protected) *by the power of God through faith to salvation ready to be revealed in the last time* (I Peter 1:4-5). However, during our brief lifetime in this world, Peter urged that we, *as strangers and pilgrims* (temporary residents), *abstain from fleshly lusts* (desires), *which war against the soul* (2:11).

Peter reminded us of the deception of sin, saying: *As obedient children, not fashioning* (conforming) *yourselves according to the former lusts in your ignorance: But as He Who has called you is holy, so you be holy in all manner of conversation* (behavior). . . . *Seeing you have purified* (cleansed) *your souls in obeying the truth through the Spirit to unfeigned* (genuine) *love of the brethren, see that you love one another with a pure heart fervently: Being born again, not of corruptible seed, but of incorruptible, by the Word of God, which lives and abides for ever. . . . the Word of the Lord endures for ever* (1:14-15,22-23,25).

Since the Bible is our source of guidance and strength, Peter urged all believers: *As newborn babes, desire the sincere milk of the Word, that you may grow thereby* (2:2). Peter points out that the nourishment of the Word is essential if we are to live *as obedient children*. This could only mean our surrender to the Lord's authority since it is always in our very best interest. Peter also describes Christians as *a spiritual house, a holy priesthood to offer up spiritual sacrifices, acceptable to God by Jesus Christ* (2:5). Each of us is a sacred temple for the indwelling Holy Spirit. In addition, we have been chosen to be *a peculiar people* (God's own); *that you should show forth the praises of Him Who has called you out of darkness into His marvelous light* (I Peter 2:9).

Thought for Today: Can others see a difference between your life as a Christian and your former life as an unbeliever?

Cross References: For I Peter 1:16: See Leviticus 11:44-45. I Peter 1:24-25: See Isaiah 40:6-8. I Peter 2:6-7: See Isaiah 28:16.; Psalm 118:22. I Peter 2:22: See Isaiah 53:9. I Peter 2:24: See Isaiah 53:4-5,12.

For definitions of unfamiliar words in today's Bible reading, see pages 468-480.

$\mathscr{I}$N $\mathscr{T}$ODAY'S $\mathscr{R}$EADING
Duties of husbands and wives; suffering and reward;
duties of the elders

$\mathscr{T}$here is just One Source of spiritual knowledge and strength. The Holy Spirit led the apostle to write: *If any man speak, let him speak as the oracles* (utterances) *of God; if any man minister* (serve), *let him do it as of the ability which God gives: that God in all things may be glorified through Jesus Christ, to Whom be praise and dominion for ever and ever. Amen* (I Peter 4:11). In contrast to the Word of God are the opinions, reasonings, cultures, and traditions of men. We must not minimize, modify, or ignore the only Guide to Life that our Creator has given as the standard by which we must live.

The last recorded words that Jesus spoke personally to Peter were on the shores of the Sea of Galilee, when Jesus asked three times: *Simon, son of Jonah, do you love Me? . . . Peter was grieved because He said to him the third time, do you love Me? And he said to Him, Lord, You know that I love You. Jesus says to him, Feed My sheep* (John 21:15-17). Peter fulfilled that commission by passing the Word along to all of us. Caring for, defending, guiding, and numerous other duties are needed by believers; but *feed My sheep* means to teach them all of God's Word, from Genesis through Revelation. All of us can be involved. Some write, edit, and print, while others support the distribution of the teaching ministries for Jesus, Who commanded us as well: *Feed My sheep*.

The underlying principle of most worldly endeavors is: "How much is in it for me?" This spirit of greed, pride, and power has so permeated everything in our age that even churches are not free from the danger of self-serving ambition. Because the Word of God is alive and never changes, and human nature remains unchanged, the message the Holy Spirit led the Apostle Paul to write to Timothy is still applicable to us today: *Before God, and the Lord Jesus Christ, Who shall judge the quick* (living) *and the dead at His appearing and His Kingdom; Preach the Word; be instant* (ready) *in season, out of season; reprove, rebuke, exhort* (encourage) *with all long-suffering and doctrine* (teaching) (II Timothy 4:1-2).

Thought for Today: Christian growth is evident when one finds satisfaction in helping others discover spiritual values.

Cross References: For I Peter 3:10-12: See Psalm 34:12-16. I Peter 5:5: See Proverbs 3:34.

For definitions of unfamiliar words in today's Bible reading, see pages 468-480.

IN TODAY'S READING
God's manifold graces; false teachers; certainty of Christ's return

This second letter begins with one significant thought: *God . . . has given to us all things that pertain to life and godliness, through the knowledge of Him Who has called us to glory and virtue* (II Peter 1:2-3). Peter's key thought is that a life of godliness is made possible by appropriating the *exceeding great and precious promises: that by these you may be* **partakers of the divine nature**, *having escaped the corruption that is in the world through lust* (1:4). It is of utmost importance that we recognize we are the body of Christ. *Now you are the body of Christ, and members in particular* (I Corinthians 12:27). *And beside this, giving all diligence* (earnestness), *add to your faith virtue; and to virtue knowledge; And to knowledge temperance* (self-control); *and to temperance patience; and to patience godliness; And to godliness brotherly kindness; and to brotherly kindness charity. For if these things be in you, and abound, they make you that you shall neither be barren nor unfruitful in the knowledge of our Lord Jesus Christ. But he that lacks these things is blind, and cannot see afar off, and has forgotten that he was purged* (cleansed) *from his old sins* (II Peter 1:5-9).

Since the first concern of God is for His children's moral and spiritual health, whatever in their lives is contrary to this necessarily brings about His loving discipline and correction. His holiness and His wrath against sin are inseparable. *For our light affliction* (trouble), *which is but for a moment, works for us a far more exceeding and eternal weight of glory* (II Corinthians 4:17). God has given us the freedom to choose to let "affliction" work for us or against us. *Beloved, seeing you know these things before, beware lest you also, being led away with the error of the wicked, fall from your own steadfastness* (II Peter 3:17-18).

The ultimate goal for the Christian is to become more Christlike. *Seeing you have purified* (cleansed) *your souls in obeying the truth through the Spirit to unfeigned* (sincere) *love of the brethren, see that you love one another with a pure heart fervently: Being born again, not of corruptible seed, but of incorruptible, by the Word of God, which lives and abides for ever* (I Peter 1:22-23).

Thought for Today: The Lord forgives all who desire to live for Him.

Cross Reference: For II Peter 2:22: See Proverbs 26:11.

For definitions of unfamiliar words in today's Bible reading, see pages 468-480.

Introduction To The Book Of
I John

The writer of this book did not identify himself. However, many believe him to be John, the apostle *whom Jesus loved* (John 13:23). The Holy Spirit's first and main theme is *the Word.*

John said that he and others had seen with their own eyes *the One Who was from the beginning, Whom we have heard . . . Whom we have looked upon, and our hands have handled, of the Word of Life* (I John 1:1). *He who says, I know Him, and keeps not His Commandments, is a liar, and the truth is not in him. But whoso keeps His Word, in him verily* (truly) *is the love of God perfected: hereby know we that we are in Him* (2:4-5).

John exposed "professing Christians" who continue to pursue *the lust of the flesh* (desire of the carnal nature), *and the lust of the eyes, and the pride of life* (2:16).

We are also reminded that love is the distinguishing characteristic of a Christian. The word *love* appears about 46 times in these five short chapters. The indwelling love of God causes a remarkable transformation in the lives of Christians. It imparts a desire to live in full obedience to the will of God, as revealed in His Word. *We know that, when He shall appear, we shall be like Him; for we shall see Him as He is* (3:2). Satan will do all he can through false teachers to divert an awareness in us that *every man that has this hope in Him **purifies himself**, even as He is pure* (3:3). Consequently, we are again warned against false teaching: *Believe not every spirit, but try* (test) *the spirits whether they are of God: because many false prophets are gone out into the world. . . . They are of the world: therefore speak they of the world, and the world hears* (believes) *them* (4:1,5).

*These things I have written to you that believe on the Name of the Son of God; **that you may know*** (and not be deceived by false prophets) *that you have eternal life* (5:13). Assurance of salvation and eternal life are prominent as seen by the number of references to the born again (2:3,5,29; 3:14,19,24; 4:13,16; 5:15,18-20).

Life

Of His own will begat (fathered) *He us with the Word of Truth, that we should be a kind of first-fruits of His creatures* (James 1:18).

Being born again, not of corruptible seed, but of incorruptible, by the Word of God, which lives and abides for ever (I Peter 1:23).

In Today's Reading
Fellowship with God; reality of and remedy for sin;
danger of anti-christs; children of God and righteousness;
loving one another

*M*ost of us know someone whom we admire and respect. Often we pattern our lives after that person. Our Heavenly Father has provided us with the incomparable Role Model of all history – Jesus Christ. Let us commit ourselves to following His example, even as John wrote: *If we say that we have fellowship with Him, and walk in darkness, we lie, and do not* (practice) *the truth: But if we walk in the Light, as He is in the Light, we have fellowship one with another* (I John 1:6-7).

There are some who say they have a relationship with Christ, but still *walk in darkness*. God directed John to write that they *lie*. The darkness of the natural mind is always more concerned about one's self, one's well-being and one's successes. But, the spiritually minded who *walk in the light as He is in the Light*, are first and foremost concerned that Christ be *exalted* in their thoughts, conduct, and conversation with others (II Corinthians 10:5; Romans 12:1-2).

A characteristic of *darkness* is a desire to be noticed. Such people receive a feeling of supremacy by drawing attention to themselves and seeking to dominate conversations. With others, *darkness* appears in the form of impatience, a sensitive spirit that is easily offended, a disposition to resent and retaliate when contradicted, or in impulses to criticize.

A jealous disposition, a secret spirit of envy, or a disposition to speak of the faults and failings of others rather than of their virtues are also characteristics of *darkness*. Some walk in *darkness* with a spirit of discouragement and self-pity and a determination to convey that spirit to everyone who will listen.

Pity the people who are so preoccupied with their own self-image and their ambitions that they are indifferent to reaching a lost world with the Good News that Jesus died to save them.

Let us be like King David who prayed: *Search me, O God, and know my heart: try me, and know my thoughts: And see if there be any wicked way in me, and lead me in the way everlasting* (Psalm 139:23-24).

Thought for Today: Those who harbor hatred do far more damage to themselves than they do to those whom they hate.

Cross References: For I John 1:8: see Ecclesiastes 7:20. I John 3:12: see Genesis 4:8.

For definitions of unfamiliar words in today's Bible reading, see pages 468-480.

In Today's Reading
How to test the spirits; an appeal for brotherly love;
the witness of the Spirit

*T*he Holy Spirit directed the Apostle John to write: *Beloved, believe not every spirit, but try* (test) *the spirits whether they are of God: because many false prophets are gone out into the world* (I John 4:1). Doctrinal deception is widespread and often difficult to discern. Jesus warned: *Not every one who says to Me, Lord, Lord, shall enter into the Kingdom of Heaven; but he that does the will of My Father Who is in heaven* (Matthew 7:21).

Many who believe they are *the children of the Kingdom shall be cast into outer darkness: there shall be weeping and gnashing of teeth* (8:12). The consequence of deception is horrifying. The majority of "religious" people will be *cast . . . into a furnace of fire: there shall be wailing and gnashing of teeth* (13:42). Nothing could be more consequential than to remove all doubt that we are included with the *few there be that find it* (eternal life) (7:14). Since it determines our destiny for eternity, we are told: *Examine yourselves, whether you be in the faith* (II Corinthians 13:5). Jesus warned: *Take heed that you be not deceived* (Luke 21:8). We are also warned: *Seducers* (imposters) *shall wax worse and worse* (progress from bad to worse), *deceiving, and being deceived* (II Timothy 3:13). John said: *This is the love of God, that we keep His Commandments. . . . For whoever is born of God overcomes the world: and this is the victory that overcomes the world, even our faith. Who is he that overcomes the world, but he that believes that Jesus is the Son of God?* (I John 5:3-5).

Born of God is far more than an intellectual acceptance of a theological doctrine. It affects the whole life – the heart as well as the head. It molds character and guides conduct. If our confession of faith that *Jesus is the Son of God* (4:15) is genuine, we have a desire to be obedient to His Commandments (5:2). We daily become involved with Jesus Who came into the world to *seek and to save that which was is lost* (Luke 19:10).

As we truly believe in Christ as the Son of God, the Savior of the world, we are partakers of His life and share in His victory. To His followers, Jesus promised: *In the world you shall have tribulation* (oppression): *but be of good cheer; I have overcome the world* (John 16:33). Consequently, *in all these things we* (too) *are more than conquerors through Him Who loved us* (Romans 8:37).

Thought for Today: The sincerity of our love for Christ can be measured by the kindness that we show to others.

For definitions of unfamiliar words in today's Bible reading, see pages 468-480.

INTRODUCTION TO THE BOOKS OF
II & III John & Jude

The writer of **II John** referred to himself as *the elder,* and the letter is addressed *to the elect lady and her children, whom I love in the truth; and not I only, but also all they that have known the truth* (II John 1:1). While some believe the letter was addressed to an individual, others believe that, since persecution was so intense at the time it was written, the author was actually writing to the Church, the Bride of Christ, and its members, whom he addressed as *children, whom I love in the truth.* He goes on to say: *I rejoiced greatly that I found of your children walking in truth, as we have received a commandment from the Father* (1:4). The importance of teaching the Word of God is emphasized. The word *truth* is used five times in the first four verses of II John.

In **III John**, the word *truth* is used 6 times in its 14 verses. Here we are introduced to three people: Demetrius, whom John praises; Gaius, a generous helper and colaborer in the work of the Lord; and Diotrephes, a man with exceptional abilities but who was a hindrance to the ministry. These men are examples of many today who are either helping or hindering the ministry of Christ.

Jude identifies himself as *Jude, the servant of Jesus Christ, and a brother of James* and he writes *to them that are sanctified by God the Father, and preserved in Jesus Christ* (Jude 1:1). Jude possibly was the Judas of Matthew 13:55 and Mark 6:3, and, therefore, the half brother of Jesus.

Jude's letter is devoted to exposing the fearful, deadly consequences of believing false doctrines and false teachers. *Certain men crept in unawares* (unnoticed), *who were before of old ordained to this condemnation, ungodly men, turning the grace of our God into lasciviousness* (unbridled lust), which is *denying the only Lord God, and our Lord Jesus Christ* (1:4). Since salvation is by grace and not of works, these ungodly men taught that Christians were not obligated to keep any Commandments even though Jesus said: *Why call Me, Lord, Lord, and do not the things which I say?* (Luke 6:46); and: *If you love Me, keep My Commandments* (John 14:15). Peter quoted from Leviticus 11:44-45: *It is written, Be holy: for I am holy* (I Peter 1:16). These men were active members of a church, but there was no evidence of the faith that overcomes sin. Also, the Apostle Paul wrote to warn against such apostasy: *How shall we, that are dead to sin, live any longer therein?* (Romans 6:2).

In Today's Reading
The commandment to love; warning against deceivers;
Diotrephes rebuked; judgment on false teachers

*I*n his brief but very important letter to all believers, Jude wrote: *It was needful for me to write to you, and exhort* (urge) *you that you should earnestly contend for the faith which was once delivered to the saints. For there are certain men crept in unawares . . . ungodly men, turning the grace of our God into lasciviousness, and denying the only Lord God, and our Lord Jesus Christ. . . . Woe to them!* (Jude 1:3-4,11). To *earnestly contend for the faith* implies not only the necessity of believing that *all Scripture is given by inspiration of God*, but that it alone is the final Word on all doctrine (II Timothy 3:16).

There is a superficial and deceptive unity being promoted today by some who have joined hands with religions that reject Jesus of Nazareth as the *Only Lord God, and our Savior Jesus Christ*. Such religions also deny either the total deity or the total humanity of Jesus. Some people assume there is but One God but that He is called by various names, such as Allah or Buddha. They ignorantly conclude that all religions are equally acceptable. Others say that, as long as you are sincere, it doesn't matter what you believe. You may be sincere, but Jesus said: *I am the Way, the Truth, and the Life: no man comes to the Father, but by Me* (John 14:6). And Peter proclaimed: *Neither is there salvation in any other: for there is no other name under heaven given among men, whereby we must be saved* (Acts 4:12). We are *looking for that blessed hope, and the glorious appearing of the great God and our Savior Jesus Christ* (Titus 2:13).

Jude warns that deceivers will be judged, *even as Sodom and Gomorrha, and the cities about them in like manner, giving themselves over to fornication . . . are set forth as an example, suffering the vengeance* (punishment) *of eternal fire* (Jude 1:7). *Woe to them! for they have gone in the way of Cain, and ran greedily after the error of Balaam for reward, and perished in the gainsaying* (rebellion) *of Core* (Korah) (1:11; Numbers 16:1-3,31-35).

Having been enlightened by this brief book, we can add a resounding "Amen" to Jude's closing statement: *Now to Him that is able to keep you from falling, and to present you faultless before the presence of His glory with exceeding joy, To the only wise God our Savior, be glory and majesty, dominion and power, both now and for ever* (Jude 1:24-25).

Thought for Today: Knowing and obeying God's Word is the only safeguard against being deceived by false teachings.

For definitions of unfamiliar words in today's Bible reading, see pages 468-480.

Introduction To The Book Of
Revelation

The aged Apostle John was imprisoned on Patmos (Revelation 1:9), a small, rocky island about ten miles long and six miles wide, which lies about 35 miles off the southwest coast of Asia Minor (modern-day Turkey). During this imprisonment, John received *the Revelation of Jesus Christ, which God gave to Him, to show His servants things which must shortly* (soon) *come to pass* (1:1). John was told: *What you see, write in a book, and send it to the seven churches which are in Asia; to Ephesus . . . Smyrna . . . Pergamos . . . Thyatira . . . Sardis . . . Philadelphia . . . Laodicea* (1:11). . . . *from Jesus Christ, Who is the Faithful Witness, and the First Begotten of the dead, and the Prince of the kings of the earth* (1:5; also 1:18; 2:8). This final message of Christ to His Church is exceedingly important. These seven churches represent the dangers that still confront Christians today. In addition, we learn the importance of being an "overcomer" and the glorious future that the Lord has prepared for us. As we read through this book, we will recognize the progression of the plan of God for His followers as the events of prophecy unfold.

Though we may not understand everything in this book, it is of utmost importance that we read it: *Blessed is he that reads, and they that hear the words of this prophecy, and keep those things which are written therein: for the time is at hand* (1:3). It should not be overlooked for it contains some of the most important warnings and some of the most precious promises of all Scripture. Since we can't keep something we have never read, we need to study it carefully. More than 300 symbolic terms throughout the Book of Revelation describe numerous events concerning Christ and His Church. His ultimate, glorious, and eternal reign is its primary theme. The symbols can be understood by referring to their use in over 500 references in the Old Testament.

There is danger of becoming so fascinated by the details of future events that we fail to see that the Book of Revelation is the unveiling of the Person and purpose of Jesus Christ. The key phrase is the book's first five words: *The Revelation of Jesus Christ.* We find the sacrificial title of Christ as *the Lamb* about 30 times in Revelation. Four aspects of Christ as *the Lamb* are seen in Revelation. In chapters 4 – 5, the worship of *the Lamb* is celebrated; in chapters 6 – 18, the wrath of *the Lamb* is detailed; the wedding of *the Lamb* as well as the great white throne judgment are revealed in chapters 19 – 20; and, in chapters 21 – and 22, the wife of *the Lamb* is described.

The last glorious event involving Christ on earth was His ascension – the next great event will be His soon return!

I *N* *T*ODAY'S *R*EADING
Greetings to the seven churches; a vision of the Son of Man;
His messages to the churches

---

*T*he seven churches of Asia Minor each received a letter dictated by Christ and recorded by John while he was on the island of Patmos. Since the character and conduct of churches and Christians is the same in every generation, the messages are just as vital and valid for us today.

Words of praise were given to the church at Ephesus for its sound doctrine. However, Christ said: *You have left your first love* (Revelation 2:4). Losing devotion to Christ usually happens gradually. Some become so involved in business, leisure activities, or even church responsibilities that the worship of Christ becomes mechanical and a mere formality. This charge is most serious: *Remember therefore from where you are fallen, and repent . . . or else I will come . . . and will remove your candlestick* (lampstand) *. . . except you repent* (2:5). Twice in one verse Jesus warned them to *repent.*

The letter sent to the church at Smyrna acknowledged that they were suffering: *I know your works, and tribulation, and poverty, (but you are rich)* (2:9). This church appeared destitute of the comforts of life. Some would be cast into prison, others would suffer persecution. But because of their loyal devotion, the Lord promised: *Remain faithful to death and I will give you a crown of life. . . . He that overcomes shall not be hurt by the second death* (2:10-11).

The letter Jesus Christ sent to the church at Pergamos said that they lived *where Satan's seat is: And you hold fast* (remain true to) *My Name . . . My faith* (2:13). However, some *hold the doctrine* (teaching) *of Balaam, who taught Balak to cast a stumbling block before the children of Israel . . . to commit fornication* (2:14). Jesus warned: *Repent: or else I will come quickly, and will fight against them with the sword of My mouth* (2:16).

False prophets like Balaam seem to have one thing in common; they are motivated by greed. Others today say they have a "special revelation of the truth" that must be the guide to biblical interpretation in the church. In Paul's letter to the Galatians, we are warned of such dangers: *If any man preach any other Gospel to you than that you have received, let him be accursed* (condemned) (Galatians 1:8-9).

Thought for Today: Our present burdens may often seem heavy, but the Lord always enables us to bear them.

Cross References: For Revelation 1:5: See Psalm 89:27. Revelation 1:6: See Exodus 19:6. Revelation 1:7: See Daniel 7:13; Zechariah 12:10. Revelation 2:7: See Genesis 2:9. Revelation 2:23: See Jeremiah 17:10. Revelation 2:27: See Psalm 2:9.

For definitions of unfamiliar words in today's Bible reading, see pages 468-480.

ℐN ℐODAY'S ℛEADING
Our Lord's messages to the churches at Sardis and Philadelphia;
disapproval of the church at Laodicea; the sealed book

𝒯he church in Sardis could boast that there were no false teachers, nor was false doctrine being taught; but there was an equally serious evil. The King Who knows all things announced: *To . . . the church in Sardis write . . . I know your works, that you have a name that you live, and are dead. Be watchful, and strengthen the things which remain, that are ready to die. . . . repent* (Revelation 3:1-3).

A few names . . . in Sardis . . . have not defiled their garments; and they shall walk with Me in white: for they are worthy. He that overcomes . . . I will not blot out his name out of the Book of Life (3:4-5). During His earthly ministry, Jesus had also said: *If you keep* (obey) *My Commandments, you shall abide* (remain) *in My love* (John 15:10).

Jesus commended the church in Philadelphia for their faithfulness, saying: *Behold, I have set before you an open door, and no man can shut it: for you have . . . kept My Word, and have not denied My Name. . . . I will also keep you from the hour of temptation* (testing), *which shall come upon all the world* (Revelation 3:8,10).

The majority of church members in Laodicea probably congratulated themselves on being moderate and broad-minded. They could pity the narrow-minded Christians in other churches. The Laodicean believers have prided themselves on their ability to compromise and make friends with those who hated Christ. But Jesus severely condemned this church: *So then because you are lukewarm, and neither cold nor hot, I will spew* (vomit) *you out of My mouth* (3:16). Our Lord explained that He chastened those whom He loved and appealed to them: *Be zealous* (earnest) *therefore, and repent* (3:19). Compromise is both self-deceiving and self-destructive.

Jesus, the Lord of His Church, is still knocking on doors of men's hearts with the same words of encouragement: *I stand at the door, and knock: if any man hear My voice, and open the door, I will come in to him, and will sup with him, and he with Me. To him that overcomes will I grant to sit with Me in My throne, even as I also overcame, and am set down with My Father in His throne* (Revelation 3:20-21).

Thought for Today: No one on earth can steal your treasures in heaven.

Cross Reference: For Revelation 3:5: See Exodus 32:32. Revelation 3:12: See Isaiah 62:2. Revelation: 4:2-3: See Ezekiel 1:28. Revelation 4:5: See Zechariah 4:2. Revelation 4:6: See Ezekiel 1:22. Revelation 4:7: See Ezekiel 1:10. Revelation 4:8: See Isaiah 6:2-3.

For definitions of unfamiliar words in today's Bible reading, see pages 468-480.

In Today's Reading
The seven seals; 144,000 sealed; the numberless multitude;
four trumpets sounded

The exile of John on Patmos and the suffering taking place in Smyrna (Revelation 2:8-10) are examples of the persecution that was intensifying against Christians throughout the Roman Empire.

However, we are thrilled to read one of the greatest promises of the Bible: *After this I beheld, and, lo, a great multitude, which no man could number, of all nations, and kindreds, and people, and tongues, stood before the throne, and before the Lamb* (Lord Jesus Christ), *clothed with white robes, and palms in their hands; And cried with a loud voice, saying, Salvation to our God Who sits upon the throne, and to the Lamb* (7:9-10). This multitude is the overcomers who are, at last, in the presence of their Lord and Savior. This revelation has strengthened the faith of many Christians who have faced fierce opposition from a hostile world.

Each generation of believers discovers that the defiance against Christ and biblical moral principles is becoming stronger, and the deceptions so subtle that, in our human strength and wisdom, we would easily lose heart. Down through the ages, those who have had their hearts set upon living for Jesus have always been a small minority. As Jesus foretold: *Narrow is the way, which leads to life, and few there be that find it* (Matthew 7:14). However, the total population of heaven will be *a great multitude, which no man could number*. These faithful Christians may not have had much of earth's pleasures, but life is exceedingly short compared to eternity. The trials we face now will seem insignificant compared to the glorious privilege of being in the presence of the King of kings for all eternity.

God deserves our highest praise for Who He is in Himself, and for His great love in giving us eternal life. *For the Lamb Who is in the midst of the throne shall feed them, and shall lead them to living fountains* (springs) *of waters: and God shall wipe away all tears from their eyes* (Revelation 7:17).

Thought for Today: Every day "Praise the Lord" for Who He is and what He has done for you!

Cross References: For Revelation 6:12: See Joel 2:31. Revelation 6:13: See Isaiah 34:4. Revelation 6:17: See Joel 2:11. Revelation 7:3: See Ezekiel 9:4. Revelation 7:17: See Ezekiel 34:23.

For definitions of unfamiliar words in today's Bible reading, see pages 468-480.

In Today's Reading

Fifth and sixth trumpets; the angel and the little scroll;
the two witnesses; the seventh trumpet

A voice from heaven directed the Apostle John: *Go and take the little book which is open in the hand of the angel which stands upon the sea and upon the earth. And I went to the angel, and said to him, Give me the little book. And he said to me, Take it, and eat it up; and it shall make your belly bitter, but it shall be in your mouth sweet as honey. And I took the little book out of the angel's hand, and ate it up; and it was in my mouth sweet as honey: and as soon as I had eaten it, my belly was bitter. And he said to me, You must prophesy again before many peoples, and nations* (Revelation 10:8-11).

John is first given a *little book,* symbolic of God's Word. Once it was digested, he was qualified to tell the world that the *little book* has a message that is exceedingly sweet to those who receive Christ as Savior. Eating all of it speaks of understanding and appropriating all the Scriptures into our lives (compare Ezekiel 2:8-9; 3:1-3).

Jesus then said: *I will give power to my two witnesses* (thought by some to be Moses and Elijah or Enoch and Elijah), *and they shall prophesy a thousand two hundred and threescore* (1260) *days, clothed in sackcloth* (Revelation 11:3). They will face overwhelming opposition. *And when they shall have finished their testimony* (witnessing), *the beast that ascends out of the bottomless pit shall make war against them, and shall overcome them, and kill them* (11:5-8). These *two witnesses* of Christ cannot be martyred until they *have finished their testimony.* Then, and only then, the enemies of God *shall . . . kill them. . . . And they that dwell upon the earth shall rejoice over them, and make merry, and shall send gifts to one another; because these two prophets tormented them that dwelt on the earth* (11:7,10).

Regardless of how fearful our future may appear, we can enjoy the peace of God, knowing that everything is under His control. *The seventh angel sounded; and there were great voices in heaven, saying, The kingdoms of this world are become the kingdoms of our Lord, and of His Christ; and He shall reign for ever and ever* (Revelation 11:15).

Thought for Today: Praise the Lord! Our work for the Lord cannot end until He allows it.

Cross References: For Revelation 9:2: See Joel 2:10. Revelation 9:4: See Exodus 12:2.; Revelation 9:6: See Joel 2:4. Revelation 9:7: See Joel 1:6. Revelation 10:6: See Nehemiah 9:6. Revelation 11:4: See Zechariah 4:12,14. Revelation 11:11: See Ezekiel 37:5.

For definitions of unfamiliar words in today's Bible reading, see pages 468-480.

In Today's Reading
The sun-clad woman; the dragon; a man-child;
the blood of the Lamb; the beasts

There appeared a great wonder (sign) *in heaven; a woman clothed with the sun, and the moon under her feet, and upon her head a crown of twelve stars. And she being with child cried, travailing in birth, and pained to be delivered. And there appeared another wonder in heaven; and behold a great red dragon, having seven heads and ten horns, and seven crowns upon his heads. . . . and the dragon stood before the woman which was ready to be delivered, for to devour her Child as soon as He was born. And she brought forth a Man Child, Who was to rule all nations with a rod of iron: and her Child was caught up to God and to His throne* (Revelation 12:1-5). This is reference to the birth and ascension of Jesus Christ.

The great dragon . . . that old serpent, called the devil, and Satan, which deceives the whole world (12:9) is always in opposition to the people of God. Satan is given four designations here: *Dragon* portrays his monstrous character as the enemy of God; *serpent* points out his deception as in the Garden of Eden; *devil* reminds us that he is a slanderer, and *Satan* means adversary. *Your adversary the devil . . . walks about, seeking whom he may devour* (I Peter 5:8). His most effective means of defeating a Christian are the "good" things that appeal to human nature. The world seeks success and happiness on earth through material things. But, only as we surrender to the Lord's will do satisfying blessings become our way of life. This is illustrated by *the woman* who *fled into the wilderness, where she has a place prepared of God, that they should feed her there* (Revelation 12:6). The trial of the remnant of God occurs in *a wilderness,* which also appears to be a desert-like moral condition of this world ruled by the *great red dragon* (Satan) (12:3). But, there is a precious peace in the desert that comes by leaving the results in the hands of our Creator. God is never defeated.

They overcame him (Satan) *by the blood of the Lamb, and by the word of their testimony* (witness); *and they loved not their lives to the death* (Revelation 12:11).

Thought for Today: Satan thrives on the biblical ignorance of saints.

Cross References: For Revelation 12:5: See Isaiah 66:7. Revelation 12:14: See Exodus 19:4. Revelation 13:1: See Daniel 7:8,24. Revelation 13:5: See Daniel 7:8.

For definitions of unfamiliar words in today's Bible reading, see pages 468-480.

The 7 Churches of Asia
(Revelation Chapters 2 & 3)

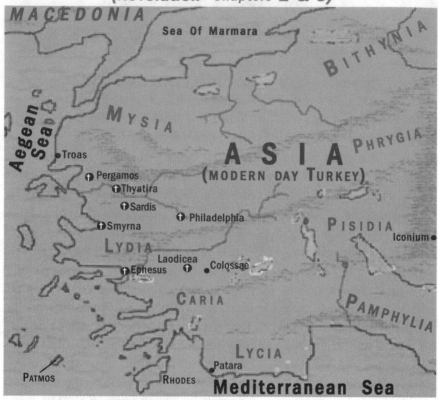

Abide - Abound

Art thou abiding in the Vine
In fellowship serene,
His Precious Word, thy daily Bread
With naught thy Lord between?

Doth thy heart yearn new heights to gain,
Yea! new depths to explore,
To mount on eagles' wings superb
In Faith and love to soar?

My Child, if thou wouldst e'er abound
In Jesus Christ, thy Lord,
Then truly thou must e'er abide
In God's own Holy Word.

—M.E.H.

In Today's Reading
The Lamb; messages of the three angels; harvest of the earth;
preparation for the seven vials (bowls) of wrath

In the midst of world chaos, John is led to report good news: *I looked, and, lo, a Lamb stood on the Mount Zion, and with Him a hundred forty and four thousand, having His Father's Name written in their foreheads. And I heard a voice from heaven, as the voice of many waters, and as the voice of great thunder: and I heard the voice of harpers harping with their harps. And they sung as it were a new song before the throne, and before the four beasts* (living creatures), *and the elders: and no man could learn that song but the hundred and forty and four thousand, which were redeemed from the earth. These are they which were not defiled with women; for they are virgins. These are they which follow the Lamb wherever He goes. These were redeemed from among men, being the first-fruits to God and to the Lamb* (Revelation 14:1-4). The Lamb is the triumphant Christ on Mount Zion, the location of His Temple. His sheep, whom Satan cannot deceive, are the undefiled.

Here is the patience of the saints (holy ones): *here are they that keep* (obey) *the Commandments of God, and the faith of Jesus. And I heard a voice from heaven saying to me, Write, Blessed* (divinely favored) *are the dead which die in the Lord from hereafter: Yea, says the Spirit, that they may rest from their labors; and their works do follow them* (14:12-13).

If a person has lived a respectable life, even though he or she was not devoted to Christ, at funerals we all want to assume that Jesus will welcome them into heaven. But to *die in the Lord* can only mean those for whom Jesus prayed: *They have kept Your Word. . . . They are not of the world, even as I am not of the world. Sanctify* (make holy) *them through Your Truth: Your Word is Truth* (John 17:6,16-17). Such are believers who have taken up Jesus' cross of daily self-denial (Luke 9:23) and are truly serving the Lord. Those of the world who have never been saved would have nothing in common with those praising the Lord with *many people in heaven, saying Alleluia; Salvation, and glory, and honor, and power, to the Lord our God* (Revelation 19:1).

Thought for Today: God's loving care for us is unlimited (Romans 8:38-39).

Cross References: For Revelation 14:7: See Psalm 146:6. Revelation 14:8: See Isaiah 21:9. Revelation 14:10: See Jeremiah 25:15; 51:7. Revelation 14:20: See Joel 3:13. Revelation 15:1: See Leviticus 26:21. Revelation 15:4: See Psalm 86:9; Isaiah 66:23; Jeremiah 10:7. Revelation 15:8: See I Kings 8:10-11.

For definitions of unfamiliar words in today's Bible reading, see pages 468-480.

IN TODAY'S READING
Babylon, the mother of abominations; the doom of
Babylon predicted; fall of Babylon

The Apostle John reported that *he carried me away in the Spirit, into the wilderness: and I saw a woman sit upon a scarlet colored beast, full of names of blasphemy, having seven heads and ten horns. . . . having a golden cup in her hand full of abominations* (detestable sins) *and filthiness of her fornication* (unfaithfulness). *And upon her forehead was a name written: MYSTERY, BABYLON THE GREAT, THE MOTHER OF HARLOTS AND ABOMINATIONS OF THE EARTH* (Revelation 17:3-5). Old Testament Babylon became the most magnificent capital city of the ancient world, and its king, Nebuchadnezzar, controlled the then-known world. During his conquests, he destroyed the kingdom of Judah, as well as the Temple of God and the holy city of Jerusalem.

BABYLON THE GREAT, THE MOTHER OF HARLOTS illustrates God-defying forces in politics and religion that will soon control the world. This apostate, federation of churches and world religions will give full support to the one-world political and economic system called the *scarlet colored beast,* which will be ruled by the Antichrist.

The *woman* and the *beast* represent the close alliance that exists between the world government, called the beast, and the harlot, Babylon, which pretends to be the true church.

This false church will promote the "equality of all religions." Eventually, together they will fiercely oppose Jesus Christ as the only way to obtain eternal life. The message of this superchurch will be based on social issues, humanitarian objectives, and lifeless formalism, and it will appeal to the majority of people.

The forces of the world *shall make war with the Lamb, and the Lamb shall overcome them: for He is Lord of lords, and King of kings: and they that are with Him are called, and chosen, and faithful* (17:14).

Daily our thoughts are upon being prepared for His return. Our Lord said: *Behold, I come quickly; and My reward is with Me, to give every man according as his work shall be* (Revelation 22:12).

Thought for Today: Praise the Lord, Jesus of Nazareth, the King of Peace will soon return.

Cross References: For Revelation 17:4: See Jeremiah 51:7. Revelation 17:12: See Daniel 7:20-24. Revelation 17:14: See Daniel 2:47. Revelation 18:2: See Jeremiah 50:39; Isaiah 21:9. Revelation 18:5: See Jeremiah 51:9. Revelation 18:7-8: See Isaiah 47:7-8; Zepheniah 2:15. Revelation 18:22: See Ezekiel 26:13. Revelation 18:24: See Jeremiah 51:49.

For definitions of unfamiliar words in today's Bible reading, see pages 468-480.

In Today's Reading
Marriage supper of the Lamb; Rider on the white horse;
Satan bound and doomed; great white throne judgment

I *saw heaven opened, and behold a white horse; and He that sat upon him was called Faithful and True* (the Lord Jesus Christ), *and in righteousness He does judge and make war* (Revelation 19:11). *And I saw the beast* (the Antichrist), *and the kings of the earth, and their armies, gathered together to make war against Him that sat on the horse, and against His army* (19:19).

Another scene takes place before *a great white throne, and Him that sat on it, from Whose face the earth and heaven fled away; and there was found no place for them. And I saw the dead, small and great, stand before God; and the books were opened: and another book was opened which is the Book of Life: and the dead were judged out of those things which were written in the books, according to their works. And the sea gave up the dead which were in it; and death and hell delivered up the dead which were in them: and they were judged every man according to their works. And death and hell were cast into the lake of fire. This is the second death. And whosoever was not found written in the Book of Life was cast into the lake of fire* (20:7,11-15). This is the final destination of Satan and all who reject Christ as Savior and Lord. God will not push His way into anyone's life. Repentance is a redemptive experience which leads to forgiveness. It buries the past under the blessed hope of tomorrow *and the glorious appearing of the great God and our Savior Jesus Christ* (Titus 2:13).

Think how joyous it will be for those who do repent and accept Jesus Christ as Savior and Lord of their lives, to see again their loved ones and all the saints of the ages: Abraham, Jacob, Joseph, David, and Paul. However, first, and best of all, we will meet Jesus, our wonderful Redeemer. *A voice came out of the throne, saying, Praise our God, all you His servants, and you that fear* (reverance) *Him, both small and great. And I heard as it were the voice of a great multitude, and as the voice of many waters, and as the voice of mighty thunderings, saying, Alleluia: for the Lord God Omnipotent* (All-Powerful) *reigns. Let us be glad and rejoice, and give honor to Him: for the marriage of the Lamb is come, and His wife has made herself ready* (Revelation 19:5-7).

Thought for Today: Satan distorts the facts, but the Word of God reveals the truth.

Cross References: For Revelation 19:2: See Psalm 19:9; Deuteronomy 32:43; II Kings 9:7. Revelation 19:5: See Psalm 115:13. Revelation 19:11: See Psalm 96:13. Revelation 19:16: See Deuteronomy 10:17. Revelation 19:18: See Ezekiel 39:4. Revelation 20:2: See Isaiah 24:22. Revelation 20:8: See Ezekiel 38:2,15. Revelation 20:12: See Daniel 7:10.

For definitions of unfamiliar words in today's Bible reading, see pages 468-480.

In Today's Reading
The new heaven and the new earth;
the heavenly Jerusalem; Christ's coming

The Lord did not leave us with uncertainty as to what lies beyond the grave. All true followers of Christ will dwell in *a new heaven and a new earth: for the first heaven and the first earth were passed away; and there was no more sea. And I John saw the holy city, new Jerusalem, coming down from God out of heaven, prepared as a bride adorned for her husband. And I heard a great voice out of heaven saying, Behold, the Tabernacle of God is with men, and He will dwell with them, and they shall be His people, and God Himself shall be with them, and be their God* (Revelation 21:1-3).

Our war against sin will soon end *and there shall be no more death, neither sorrow, nor crying, neither shall there be any more pain: for the former things are passed away* (21:4).

Just think! There will be no more crying, no physical distress, and no suffering; and no condemnation will press on our consciences. There will be no fear of evil for *there shall in no wise enter into it* (the holy city, new Jerusalem) *any thing that defiles, neither whatsoever works abomination* (foul, detestable thing), *or makes a lie: but they which are written in the Lamb's Book of Life* (21:27) will be there.

Oh! the joy that awaits us in its full realization. Praise His wonderful Name! We soon will be welcomed home by our wonderful Lord! *Having therefore these promises, dearly beloved, let us cleanse ourselves from all filthiness of the flesh and spirit, perfecting holiness in the fear of God.* And let us cast *down imaginations, and every high* (proud) *thing that exalts itself against the knowledge of God . . . bringing into captivity every thought to the obedience of Christ* (II Corinthians 7:1; 10:5).

We close this glorious revelation of Jesus Christ, having completed the reading of the entire God-given Guide to Life: *And the Spirit and the bride say, Come. And let him that hears say, Come. And let him that is thirsty come. And whosoever will, let him take the water of life freely* (Revelation 22:17).

Thought for Today: Death promotes Christians into everlasting life.

Cross References: For Revelation 21:5: See Isaiah 25:8. Revelation 21:23: See Isaiah 29:33. Revelation 21:25: See Isaiah 60:11. Revelation 21:27: See Isaiah 52:1. Revelation 22:2: See Ezekiel 47:12; Genesis 2:9. Revelation 22:3: See Zechariah 14:11. Revelation 22:12: See Isaiah 40:10. Revelation 22:13: See Isaiah 44:6; 48:12. Revelation 22:16: See Isaiah 11:1. Revelation 22:18: See Deuteronomy 12:32.

For definitions of unfamiliar words in today's Bible reading, see pages 468-480.

December Daily Topical Reference Index

THE POWER OF GOD'S WORD

Jesus Christ set the example of how important the Old Testament was to Him and should be to us. His emphasis started with the first recorded words of our Lord following His baptism. After 40 days of fasting, He was tempted of the devil, who said: *If You be* (Since you are) *the Son of God, command that these stones be made bread. But He answered and said, It is written, Man shall not live by bread alone* [physical necessities], *but by every Word that proceeds out of the mouth of God* [spiritual necessities] [Matthew 4:3-4; compare Deuteronomy 8:3]. By quoting this Old Testament Scripture, our Lord revealed the "Key to Victory" over satanic deceptions. We can have that same victory over Satan as we become familiar with *every Word that proceeds out of the mouth of God.*

---

*God's Holy Word has surely been
Inspired of God and not of men;
No power or eloquence of men
Could ere conceive God's wondrous plan.
Withstanding all the tests of time,
It stands unchanged, unique, sublime;*

– M. E. H.

APPROVED:
Study (Be diligent) *to show yourself approved to God, a workman that needs not to be ashamed, rightly dividing the Word of Truth* (II Timothy 2:15).

DISCIPLESHIP:
If you continue in My Word, then you are My disciples indeed: And you shall know the Truth, and the Truth shall make you free (John 8:31-32).

FAITH:
So then faith comes by hearing, and hearing by the Word of God (Romans 10:17).

FOOD:
Desire the sincere milk of the Word, that you may grow thereby (I Peter 2:2). (The strength of our spiritual life and our ability to please the Lord will be in exact proportion to the time we set aside to read through the Bible.)

Your words were found, and I did eat them; and Your Word was to me the joy and rejoicing of my heart (Jeremiah 15:16).

Neither have I gone back from the Commandment of His lips; I have esteemed the words of His mouth more than my necessary food (Job 23:12).

GOD'S ESTIMATE OF HIS WORD:
I will . . . praise Your Name for Your lovingkindness and for Your truth: for You have magnified Your Word above all Your Name (Psalm 138:2).

PRAYERS ANSWERED:
If you abide in Me, and My words abide in you, you shall ask what you will, and it shall be done to you (John 15:7).

Beloved, if our heart condemn us not, then have we confidence toward God. And whatsoever we ask, we receive of Him, because we keep His Commandments, and do those things that are pleasing in His sight (I John 3:21-22).

PRAYERS THAT ARE DETESTABLE:
He that turns away his ear from hearing the Law, even his prayer shall be abomination (detestable) (Proverbs 28:9).

SANCTIFICATION:
Sanctify them (kept holy for God's service) *through Your Truth: Your Word is Truth* (John 17:17).

Seeing you have purified (cleansed) *your souls in obeying the Truth through the Spirit to unfeigned* (sincere, genuine) *love of the brethren, see that you love one another with a pure heart fervently* (I Peter 1:22).

TRUTH:
The Word of God is quick (alive), *and powerful . . . and is a discerner of the thoughts and intents of the heart* (Hebrews 4:12).

ENDURES FOREVER:
Your Word is true from the beginning: and every one of Your righteous judgments endures for ever (Psalm 119:160).

But the Word of the Lord endures for ever. And this is the Word which by the Gospel is preached to you (I Peter 1:25).

Heaven and earth shall pass away, but My words shall not pass away (Matthew 24:35).

SUSTAINS:
Holding forth the Word of Life; that I may rejoice in the day of Christ, that I have not run in vain, neither labored in vain (Philippians 2:16).

Unless Your Law had been my delights, I should then have perished in my affliction (Psalm 119:92)

Word Studies

abated - disappeared; reduced

Abba - Father, an Aramaic Term

abhor - disregard, reject (Lev. 26:15); loathe, hate (Job 42:6; Is. 7:16)

abjects - slanderers (Ps. 35:15)

abominable/abominaton - defiled, unclean, detestable to God

abusers of themselves - sodomites

according to his months - every month

according to the manner - as pre- scribed by Law (Lev. 5:10)

accounted of - considered of value

accursed - devoted, set apart, as holy unto the Lord (Josh. 6:17-18)

activity - competence, skill (Gen. 47:6)

Adar - compares with Feb/Mar

addicted - devoted (1 Cor. 16:15)

adjure - solemnly put under oath

advertise - to inform (Ruth 4:4)

afflict your souls - humble yourselves, practice self-denial (Lev. 16:29)

affinity - an alliance (1 Kin. 3:1)

after - according to (Gen. 10:20); committed to (2 Sam. 15:13)

against - waiting to meet (Gen. 43:25; Ex. 7:15; Num. 10:21); opposite (Num. 8:2-3); before (2 Kin. 16:11)

Aha, aha - an expression of scorn

Alpha and Omega - the first and last letters of the Greek alphabet. Christ is saying he is everything A to Z

ambassage - delegation; representatives

Amen - So be it; It is true

amerce - to punish with a fine (Deut. 22:19)

Anathema - accursed (1 Cor. 16:22)

ancients - elders (Is. 24:23; Ezek. 7:26)

angle - hooks (Is. 19:8)

Anointed - Messiah (Hebrew) and Christ (Greek) (Ps. 2:2)

anon - immediately (Matt. 13:20; Mar. 1:30)

answerable - corresponding (Ex. 38:18)

answereth - corresponds (Gal. 4:25)

Apollyn - Destroyer (Rev. 9:11)

apothecary - perfumer (Ex. 30:25)

apparently - clearly (Num. 12:8)

appertaineth - belongs (Lev. 6:5)

appoint - name (Gen. 30:28); comfort (Is. 61:3)

Areopagus - name of the Athenian court or council which met on Mars Hill

Ariel - the lion city of Jerusalem (Is. 29:1)

arm - family (1 Sam. 2:31)

artificer - craftsman (Gen. 4:22)

artillery - small armor; weapons

asp - cobra (Is. 11:8)

assay - endeavor, attempt, venture (Deut. 4:34; Job 4:2; Acts 16:7; Heb. 11:29); be reluctant (1 Sam. 17:39)

assuaged - subsided (Gen. 8:1)

asunder - in two halves; apart

atonement - blood sacrifice that becomes covering for sin, resulting in reconciliation with God (Lev. 4:20); reconciliation (Rom. 5:11)

augment - increase (Num. 32:14)

austere - stern, harsh, exacting

avenger of blood - the nearest relative of the person slain who should avenge his death by destroying the slayer

averse - returning (Mic. 2:8)

avouched - openly declared (Deut. 26:17)

Baale of Judah - refers to the town of Kirjath-jearim (2 Sam. 6:2)

Baali - my lord and master (Hos. 2:16)

Baalim - idols of Baal (Judg. 3:7)

babbling - complaints (Prov. 23:29)

bade/badest - ordered/told

baldness - shaving their head as a sign of sorrow (Deut. 14:1)

band - a woven binding to keep it from tearing (Ex. 39:23); one of the ten divisions of the Ancient Roman Legion (Acts 10:1)

bands - painful diseases (Ps. 73:4); ensnared by deceit (Eccl. 7:26); punish- ment (Is. 28:22); unity (Zech. 11:7); ligaments (Col. 2:19; 1 Thes. 2:19)

bar - carrying frame (Num. 4:10)

barbarian/barbarous - foreigner/foreign

bare record - related what had happened

barked - broken, splintered (Joel 1:7)

bases - original foundation (Ezra 3:3)

battlement/s - guard railing/branches

be at charges with - pay the expenses of

beat off - handpick His "harvest" (Is. 27:12)

beauty - grace, good will (Zech. 11:7)

Beelzebub - the fly god idol of the Philistines meaning dung god or filth god, since the fly finds its food in refuse

Beer-sheba - well of oath (Gen. 26:33)

beeves - bullocks (Lev. 22:19)

begat - fathered

beguile - deceive, seduce

Belial, children/sons/daughter of - apostate evildoers (Deut. 13:13); sodomites (Judg. 19:22); sinful woman (1 Sam. 1:16)

belly - mind (Job 32:19)

beside ourselves - insane (2 Cor. 5:13)

besom - broom (Is. 14:23)

besought - asked (John 19:31)

bestowed - stationed (1 Kin. 10:26)

Bethel - House of God

bethink - think it over/learn a lesson

betimes - early in the morning (Gen. 26:31); diligently (Prov. 13:24)

betwixt - between (Gen. 30:36)

Beulah - married (Is. 62:4)

bewail - mourn (Deut. 21:13)

bewray - betray (Is. 16:3)

bier - coffin or stand for carrying a corpse

bishop - spiritual overseer (1 Tim. 3:31)

blast - spirit of bad fortune (2 Kin. 19:7)

blasting - blight; mildew (Hag. 2:17)

blaze - to make known (Mark 1:45)

blemish - defect; permanent injury

blindness of their hearts - closed minds

blood of Jerusalem - sins of Jerusalem of killing innocent prophets including Jesus Christ (Is. 4:4)

Bochim - weeping (Judg. 2:5)

bolled - in the bud (Ex. 9:31)

bolster - pillow; headplace (1 Sam. 26:7)

bondman/bondservant - slave

bonnets - headpieces; turbans

booths - temporary shelters (Neh. 8:14)

borders - ornaments (Song. 1:11)

borrow - ask (Ex. 11:2)

bosses - thick layers (Job 15:26)

botch - boils or sores (Deut. 28:27)

bottles - made of animal skins (Josh. 9:4)

bound in the bundle of life - protected in the cave of the living (1 Sam. 25:29)

bowed - swayed (2 Sam. 19:14)

bowels - your own body (Gen. 15:4); body (Gen. 25:23); heart (Gen. 43:30; Song. 5:4); whole being (Is. 16:11); emotions (Jer. 4:19); affections (2 Cor. 6:12); affection (Phil. 1:8)

bowels boiled - heart is troubled (Job 30:27)

bravery - beauty (Is. 3:18)

brawling - contentious (Prov. 21:9)

bray - beat (Prov. 27:22)

breaches - damaged places; gaps; breaks in the city wall (Amos 4:3)

bread - food (1 Kin. 21:5)

Breaker - Messiah (Mic. 2:13)

breaking in - flood (Job 30:14)

breaking up - breaking in (Ex. 22:2)

breath - spirit (Job 17:1)

brigandine(s) - armor (Jer. 46:4; 51:3)

bright - sharp (Jer. 51:11)

brother - one of their own people (Deut.

22:1); uncle (2 Chr. 36:10)

bruise - greatly injure or wound, literally break in pieces (Gen. 3:15)

bruit - report; rumor (Jer. 10:22; Nah. 3:19)

brutish - stupid (Prov. 12:1); cruel (Ezek. 21:31)

buckler - defender (2 Sam. 22:31); shield (Prov. 2:7; Song. 4:4)

buffet - discipline; hit with the fist

builded against - besieged (Lam. 3:5)

Bul - compares with Oct/Nov

bunches - humps (Is. 30:6)

burden - mournful oracle or prophecy

burning - brand as a slave (Is. 3.24); public fire to honor (2 Chr. 21:19; Jer. 34:5)

busybody - meddler, prying into

by and by - before long or soon

by their polls - each one individually

Cabul - unproductive wasteland

calves - calf idols (Hos. 10:5)

camphire - flowers (Song. 1:14)

candlestick - oil lamp; lampstand

cankered - corroded (James 5:3)

captivity - fortune (Job 42:10); captives (Hos. 6:11)

careful - concerned; anxious

carefulness - fearfulness and anxiety (Ezek. 12:18); diligence, seriousness (2 Cor. 7:11)

carelessly - securely (Is. 47:8; Ezek. 39:6)

carriage(s) - baggage

cast - placed (Gen. 21:15)

cast a cord make boundaries (Mic. 2:5)

cast about - deserted (Jer. 41:14)

cast clouts - worn-out clothes (Jer. 38:12)

cast up - highway to life (Jer. 18:15)

casteth not - does not miscarry (Job 21:10)

castles - settlements or camps (Gen. 25:16); fortresses, strongholds (2 Chr. 17:12)

caul - appendage on the liver (Ex. 29:22); lobe of fat (Lev. 3:4)

cauls, and their round tires - hairdos

celestial - heavenly (1 Cor. 15:40)

certify - inform (2 Sam. 15:28; Ezra 5:10)

chafed - angered (2 Sam. 17:8)

Chaldean - Babylonian

chambering - immorality (Rom. 13:13)

chamberlain/s - treasurer/officials

chambers - storerooms (Ezra 8:29); constellations (Job 9:9); dwelling place (Ps. 104:13)

champaign - flat open country

changed - scorched (Dan. 3:27)

chapiter - upper part, a cap which goes on top of a column (Jer. 52:22)

chapmen - merchant traders (2 Chr. 9:14)

chapt - dried up, parched (Jer. 14:4)

charge - admonish (Ex. 19:21); to fix responsibility, to commission (Deut. 3:28); responsibility (1 Kin. 4:28)

chargeable - burdensome (2 Sam. 13:25)

charged - commanded (Gen. 28:1)

charger - large dish, platter, or tray

charity - love (1 Cor. 13:1; Rev. 2:19)

chasten - humble (Dan. 10:12)

Chemarims - the priests in charge

cherish - attend, be of service as his nurse

chide/chode- find fault; quarrel/argued

chief - foremost men (2 Sam. 23:13); masters (Lam. 1:5)

children - young men (Dan. 1:4)

Chinneroth - also called Sea of Galilee

choler - furious anger/rage

churl/ish - cruel crafty men/rough, uncouth

circumspect - careful, cautious

clave - split (Gen. 22:3; Num. 16:31; 1 Sam. 6:14; Ps. 78:15); was passionately attracted to (Gen. 34:3)

clean - ceremonially undefiled (Lev. 15; Num. 19:11); entirely (Isa. 24:19; Zech. 11:17)

cleave - be joined (Gen. 2:24); cut (Lev. 1:17); remain faithful (Josh. 23:8)

clift - hollow opening (Ex. 33:22)

cloke - covering (John 15:22)

close - aloof, concealed (1 Chr. 12:1)

close places - fortresses or strongholds

clouted - patched (Josh. 9:5)

cloven - divided (Acts 2:3)

coast - territory border; surrounding region

cockatrice - viper (Is. 11:8)

cockle - weeds (Job 31:40)

cogitations - thoughts (Dan. 7:28)

collops of fat - figuratively speaking, bulging in prosperity (Job 15:27)

color - pretense (Acts 27:30)

come at - go near (Num. 6:6; Ezek. 44:25)

come without - go outside (Num. 35:26)

comely - lovely (Song. 2:14); proper (1 Cor. 11:13)

comfortably - encouragingly (2 Chr. 30:22); kindly and tenderly (Is. 40:2)

common - unholy (Acts 10:14)

commune - speak; discuss

communicate - meet the financial needs

communicate with - express your concern

compacted - true unity (Eph. 4:16)

companies - collection of idols (Is. 57:13)

compass - ledge (Ex. 27:5); go around (Num. 21:4); surround (2 Sam. 22:6; 2

Kin. 11:8; Ps. 116:3; Rev. 20:9)

compassion - lovingkindness (Rom. 9:15)

concision - false circumcision (Phil. 3:2)

concubine - a servant/secondary wife

concupiscence - evil desires of lust

condemned - taxed; fined (2 Chr. 36:3)

confounded - put to shame; disgraced

confusion - perversion (Lev. 18:23); dishonor, humiliation, shame (1 Sam. 20:30; Is. 30:3; Dan. 9:7; Ezra 9:7)

consecration - ordination (Lev. 8:33)

constrain - try to compel (Gal. 6:12)

consulted shame - brought dishonor

consumption - destruction (Is. 10:22)

contemn - defy; despise (Ps. 10:13)

conversant - associated (1 Sam. 25:15)

conversation - conduct (Ps. 50:23; Gal. 1:13; Eph. 4:22); citizenship (Phil. 3:20)

convey me - allow me to pass (Neh. 2:7)

convocation - holy/sacred assembly

coping - the top, the highest, coarse of stone on which the timber is laid

corn - grain

cornfloor - threshing floor (Hos. 9:1)

couchingplace - resting place (Ezek. 25:5)

council - Sanhedrin, the prosecuting body for both civil and religious crimes (John 11:47)

counsel - purpose, plan (Heb. 6:17)

countenance - be partial to (Ex. 23:3); face (Neh. 2:2)

countervail - justify, compensate

course - the assigned divisions of priests (Ezra 3:11); in turn (1 Cor. 14:27)

cover his border - establish his territory

cover his feet - take a nap (1 Sam. 24:3)

cover the ark - install the veil as a partition

cover with a covering - make an alliance

covering of the eyes - compensation

covert - protecting power (Ps. 61:4); shelter (Is. 32:2); hiding place (Jer. 25:38)

cracknels - cakes (1 Kin. 14:3)

crisping pins - money bags (Is. 3:22)

crowned - officials, princes (Nah. 3:17)

cubit - about 18 inches

cumbrance - burden of complaints (Deut. 1:12)

cunning - skillful; skilled; skill

cunning women - women skilled at weeping and mourning (Jer. 9:17)

curious - artistic; skillfully made

current money - legal note (Gen. 23:16)

curtains - tent; Tabernacle (1 Chr. 17:1)

cut down - silenced (Jer. 48:2)

cut off - excommunicated (Lev. 17:4);

destroyed; put to death

dam - mother

daughter - people (Jer. 46:11)

daughters - cities and villages (Ps. 48:11; Jer. 49:2)

day - fate (Job 18:20)

day of the Lord - the time of judgment upon the ungodly as well as the time of rejoicing for the faithful (Is. 2:12)

days are determined - allotted time to live is set (Job 14:5)

dayspring - dawn (Job 38:12)

dead dog - worthless person (2 Sam. 9:8)

dealt - distributed (2 Sam. 6:19)

dealt hardly - treated harshly (Gen. 16:6)

dearth - famine; drought

debate - contention; quarreling (Is. 58:4)

decayed - giving way (Neh. 4:10)

deceitfully - negligently; halfheartedly (Jer. 48:10)

decline after many - yield to the evil majority (Ex. 23:2)

decree - boundary (Prov. 8:29)

defiled - raped and dishonored (Gen. 34:2)

defraud - deprive (1 Cor. 7:5)

degree - reputation (1 Tim. 3:13)

delectable - cherished (Is. 44:9)

delicately - trembling with fear (1 Sam. 15:32)

deputed - appointed judge (2 Sam. 15:3)

derision - ridicule; laughingstock

describe - map out, survey (Josh. 18:6)

descry - spy out, keep a watch (Judg. 1:23)

desire of all nations - Christ, the Messiah

desolate - suffering for their guilt

device - scheme, plan, purpose, plot

devils - idols, demons (2 Chr. 11:15)

diadem - turban or headdress (Job 29:14)

diet - regular allowance (Jer. 52:34)

dirt - dung (Judg. 3:22)

disallowed - rejected (1 Pet. 2:4)

discomfited - defeated, caused to panic

discover - uncover

discover his father's skirt - commit adultery with his father's wife

discover itself - express itself (Prov. 18:2)

discover not a secret to another - do not betray another man's confidence

discover the face of his garment - strip off his outer garment (Job 41:13)

discreet - shrewd and discerning

disorderly - irresponsibly; undisciplined

dispensation - Divine Order (Eph. 1:10); special ministry (Eph. 3:2)

disposing - decision (Prov. 16:33)

dispossessed - drove out (Num. 32:39)

dissemble - act deceitfully (Josh. 7:11)

dissimulation - hypocrisy; insincerity

distress not - do not create a problem

ditch - reservoir (Is. 22:11)

divers - a double standard (Prov. 20:10); various (Heb. 13:9)

divide their tongues - bring confusion

divided by lot - assignment by drawing lots to determine the will of God (Prov. 16:33)

divination - wonder-working words of their own minds (Jer. 14:14)

divine - could discover by divination who stole it (Gen. 44:15); practice (Ezek. 13:23)

diviners - fortune-tellers (1 Sam. 6:2)

doctors - scholars, the Rabbis (Luke 2:46)

doubtful disputations - passing judgment on his opinions (Rom. 14:1)

dragon - serpent or crocodile (Ps. 91:13); large sea animal (Ps. 148:7); jackal or wolf (Job 30:29; Is. 43:20)

draught - sewer (Matt. 15:17); catch (Luke 5:9)

dreadful - awesome; holy (Rom. 14:1)

dress - tend or cultivate (Gen. 2:15); prepare (Gen. 18:7)

dried away - dissatisfied and discouraged

drop thy word toward - preach against

dropping - irritation (Prov. 19:13)

drought - heat (Gen. 31:40)

drove - herd (Gen. 32:16)

dukes - chiefs (Gen. 36:15)

dung it - fertilized it (Luke 13:8)

dureth - continues (Matt. 13:21)

durst - dares to; dared

dust - descendants (Num. 23:10)

dwell deep - hide in deeply concealed places (Jer. 49:8)

ear - plow (1 Sam. 8:12; Is. 30:24)

early - diligently; earnestly (Prov. 1:28)

earnest - pledge guarantee (Eph. 1:14)

ears ... opened - open to obedience

ears shall tingle - will be astonished with horror (2 Kin. 21:12)

earth divided - people became separated (Gen. 10:25)

earth upon his head - a sign of grief or mourning (1 Sam. 4:12)

Easter - a mistranslation of Passover

effect - fulfillment (Ezek. 12:23)

effectual - in its inworking, bringing the praying person to recognize the will of God (James 5:16)

effeminate - homosexual perversion

El-beth-el - the God of Bethel (Gen. 35:7)

emerods - tumors (Deut. 28:27; 1 Sam. 5:6)

eminent place - mound or high place for pagan shrine (Ezek. 16:31)

employed about - opposed to (Ezra 10:15)

emulation - jealousy (Rom. 11:14)

enchantment - fortune-telling or practice of witchcraft (Lev. 19:26)

engines of war - battering rams

enjoin - give orders; appoint (Job 36:23)

enlarged - filled with love (2 Cor. 6:11)

enquire at her mouth - ask her personally

enquired early - sought diligently

ensign - tribal banner; signal to rally, flag

ensue - pursue, go after (1 Pet. 3:11)

entreat - treat (Acts 7:6; 1 Thes. 2:2)

ephod - priestly garment (Ex. 39:2); shield or breastplate (Judg. 8:27)

Ephraim - Northern Kingdom (Jer. 7:15)

Ephratah - district in which Bethlehem was located

epistle - letter, message (Col. 4:16)

equal - compare (Lam. 2:13); fair (Ezek. 18:25)

equity - skill (Eccl. 2:21)

eschew - to shun, turn from (1 Pet. 3:11)

Esh-baal - another name for Ish-bosheth

espied - saw (Gen. 42:27); searched out, selected (Ezek. 20:6)

espoused - betrothed or engaged

espy - watch (Jer. 48:19)

estate - council (Acts 22:5)

Ethiopian - Cushite (2 Chr. 14:9)

even - twilight (Ex. 29:39)

evenings - desert wasteland (Jer. 5:6)

evidence - deed (Jer. 32:10)

evil - bad (Jer. 29:17); sinful (Matt. 6:23); wrong (John 18:23); the evil - Satan (John 17:15)

evil communications corrupt good manners - evil companions or associations ruin or defile good character (1 Cor. 15:33)

evil entreateth - cruelly took advantage of

evil travail - misfortunes (Eccl. 5:14)

evilfavouredness - serious defect

exacted - assessed, taxed (2 Kin. 15:20)

exacteth - demands (Job 11:6)

excellency - advantage (Eccl. 7:12); pride (Amos 6:8)

exchangers - bankers, moneylenders

exercise - concern (Ps. 131:1)

exorcists - claimed they could cast out evil spirits (Acts 19:13)

expected end - hopeful future (Jer. 29:11)

experiment - experience, proof, evidence

fain - desire to

faint - give up; lose courage; be distressed

fairs - wares (Ezek. 27:12)

fall (out) - turn out (Ruth 3:18; Phil. 1:12)

fall not out by the way - don't argue

fall (away) - desert (1 Chr. 12:19; Jer. 37:13)

falleth - surrenders (Jer. 21:9)

fame - news (Gen. 45:16)

familiar - close (Job 19:14)

familiar spirit - medium, spiritualist, witch, or fortune-teller (1 Sam. 28:7)

familiars - friends (Jer. 20:10)

famish - reduce to nothing (Zeph. 2:11)

fanners - destroyers (Jer. 51:2)

fast - securely (Judg. 16:11); firm (Prov. 4:13; 1 Cor. 16:13; 1 Thes. 3:8)

fast by - close by (Ruth 2:8)

fat - rich, good, the best (Gen. 49:20; 1 Chr. 4:40; Neh. 9:25; Ezek. 34:14); prosperous (Deu. 32:15); strong (Is. 58:11); well watered (Ezek. 45:15)

fat or lean - fertile or barren (Num. 13:20)

father - grandfather (Dan. 5:2)

fathers - ancestors (Deut. 11:21)

fear - includes deep respect, honor, devotion, reverential awe, an attitude of unconditional trust and submission (Prov. 9:10; Phil. 2:12; Rev. 14:7)

feign - pretend (2 Sam. 14:2; 1 Kin. 14:5)

fell - died (2 Sam. 21:9)

fell a lusting - was greedy for better things

fell unto me - came over and joined me

fell upon - murdered (1 Sam. 22:18)

feller - tree cutter (Is. 14:8)

fellows - female virgin companions

fellowship - pledge of partnership (Lev. 6:2)

fenced - knit (Job 10:11); dug up (Is. 5:2); fortified (Dan. 11:15)

fens - marshes (Job 40:21)

fetch a compass - make a turn or circuit; circle around

fetch his pledge - carry off his collateral

filled with - controlled by (Eph. 5:18)

fillets - ornamental thin bands around the pillars (Ex. 27:10)

filthy - corrupt (Ps. 53:3); rebellious, defiant (Zeph. 3:1); immoral (2 Pet. 2:7)

filthy lucre - financial gain (1 Tim. 3:8)

fire - oppression (Is. 43:2)

fires - dawning light (Is. 24:15)

firebrands - torches of flax on fire

flagons - cakes of raisins or grapes (Song. 2:5); bottles or jars (Is. 22:24)

flay - skin (Lev. 1:6)

flow together - be enlightened (Is. 60:5)

follow - pursue (2 Sam. 2:26; 1 Chr. 10:2)

folly - wicked conduct (Judg. 20:10)

for - instead of (Num. 8:18); have been like (Job 34:36)

forbear - refuse; neglect (Num. 9:13; Ezek. 2:5); do what you prefer (Jer. 40:4)

force of the Gentiles - wealth of the nations

forecast his devices - devise plans

forehead - attitude (Ezek. 3:8-9)

former - eastern (Dead Sea) (Zech. 14:8)

forswear - to swear falsely (Matt. 5:33)

forwardness - earnestness (2 Cor. 8:8); willingness (2 Cor. 9:2)

foundation - creation (Eph. 14:4)

foundations - principles of society based on the Word of God (Ps. 11:3); out of course - ignored (Ps. 82:5)

fourscore - 80

flowers - monthly period (Lev. 15:33)

frame - pronounce (Judg. 12:6); devise (Ps. 94:20); prepare (Jer. 18:11)

fray - frighten; terrorize; drive away

free born - born a Roman citizen (Acts 22:28)

fretted - provoked to anger (Ezek. 16:43)

fretteth - is resentful (Prov. 19:3)

fretting - contagious, spreading

frontlets - memorial symbol (Ex. 13:16)

froward - perverse (2 Sam. 22:27); cunning (Job 5:13); unfavorable; opposed (Ps. 18:26, second use); wrongful and false (Prov. 2:12; 8:8); obstinate and evil (Ps. 101:4); deceitful (Prov. 4:24)

frowardly - rebelliously (Is. 57:17)

fruit depart - miscarry (Ex. 21:22)

fuller - to bleach, make white, to clean

furbish - polish (Jer. 46:4; Ezek. 21:9)

furniture - saddle (Gen. 31:34); utensils, vessels (Ex. 35:14)

gainsay - speak against; contradict; faultfind

gall - bitter afflictions (Jer. 8:14)

gat him - returned (Num. 11:30)

gate - meeting place to transact legal or official business (Ruth 4:1)

gates - towns; of hell - the powers of Satan

gathering - obedience, respect (Gen. 49:10)

gazingstock - object of ridicule (Heb. 10:33)

ghost - spirit (Gen. 35:29)

gift - bribe (Ex. 23:8; Deut. 16:19)

gin - trap, snare (Job 18:9; Ps. 140:5)

gird up your loins - fasten the loose, flowing garments with a belt (2 Kin. 4:29)

girdle - interlaced belt (Ex. 28:8); apron (2 Kin. 1:8)

girt - clothed (2 Kin. 1:8); put on (John 21:7); wrapped around (Rev. 1:13)

glass - mirror (Is. 3:23; I Cor. 13:12)

gleaned - killed (Judg. 20:45)

glory - wealth (Gen. 31:1)

glory over me - the honor is yours to tell me

go to - come; listen (Gen. 11:3; Is. 5:5)

goads - pointed rods used to prod an animal

goats - civic/political leaders (Zech. 10:3)

Godhead - the Trinity — God the Father, God the Son, God the Holy Spirit

gods - earthly rulers and judges (Ps. 82:1); My representatives (Ps. 82:6)

good speed - success (Gen. 24:12)

goodman - a male head of a household

government - authority (Is. 22:21)

grave - engrave, inscribe (Ex. 28:9)

graven images - carved idols (Deut. 7:25)

great sea - Mediterranean Sea (Num. 34:6)

grieved - annoyed, incensed (Acts 4:2)

grievous - severe (Ex. 9:3); cruel (1 Kin. 12:4); harsh (Prov. 15:1); a hardship (Phil. 3:1)

grievousness - oppression (Is. 10:1)

grove - idol (Deut. 12:3); place of worship to the goddess Ashtaroth

guile - deceit; lie or deception

habergeon - sleeveless coat (Ex. 39:23)

haft - handle (Judg. 3:22)

hale - to take by force (Luke 12:58)

hallow - set apart, consecrate, sanctify (Ex. 40:9; 1 Kin. 8:64); cleanse (Lev. 16:19)

halt - limp (Gen. 32:31); waver (1 Kin. 18:21); lame or crippled (Mark 9:45)

halting - downfall (Jer. 20:10)

hand(s) - word (Ezra 10:19; Ezek. 17:18); care (Ps. 95:7)

hap was to light - happened to come

hard by - near, close (Lev. 3:9)

hardened their neck - were stubborn

hardly bestead - sorely distressed

harness/ed - armor/in military order

harts - deer (Lam. 1:6)

hasty fruit - first ripe fig (Is. 28:4)

hated - unloved (Gen. 29:31; Deut. 21:15)

haunt - location; haunt it - dwell there

health - salvation (Ps. 42:11)

heap/s - failure/ruins (Is. 17:11/Ps. 79:1)

heart - human mind (Dan. 7:4)

heart smote - conscience accused

heat - anger (Ezek. 3:14)

heath - dry bush (Jer. 17:6)

heave offerings - implies willing offerings

heave shoulder - thigh (Lev. 10:14)

heaved - offered (Num. 18:30)

hell: Sheol - the grave (Job 26:6); Gehenna - eternal destiny of the lost; indescribable torment (Luke 16:24; Mark 9:48; Matt. 10:28)

Hephzibah - My delight is in her (Is. 62:4)

heresy - a belief that is not the true religion

hew - to cut stones (2 Chr. 2:2)

hewn down - destroyed (Is. 33:9)

Hiddekel - Tigris (Gen. 2:14)

high - proud (Is. 10:12)

high arm - great power (Acts 13:17)

high day - early in the day (Gen. 29:7)

high hand - boldly (Ex. 14:8)

high heaps - road signs (pointing back to Israel) (Jer. 31:21)

high places - places/shrines for idol worship

hinder - western (Mediterranean Sea) (Zech. 14:8)

hindermost - last (Gen. 33:2; Jer. 50:12)

Hinnom - later called Gehenna, which Jesus used to illustrate the place of eternal punishment (2 Chr. 28:3)

hires - earnings (Mic. 1:7)

hiss - scoff, ridicule,shame (1 Kin. 9:8; Jer. 49:17; Jer. 25:9); signal (Zech. 10:8)

hoar - gray (1 Kin. 2:6; Is. 46:4)

hold - stronghold, safe place (1 Sam. 22:4)

holden - held fast (Job 36:8)

holes - sockets (Zech. 14:12)

hollow - socket (Gen. 32:25)

holpen - helped (Is. 31:3; Dan. 11:34)

holy - sanctified, set apart (Lev. 2:3)

Horeb - Sinai (1 Kin. 19:8)

horn/s - esteem; strength/military power

hosen - tunic or undergarments (Dan. 3:21)

Hoshea - Joshua (Deut. 32:44)

host - camp (Gen. 32:2); army (2 Sam. 17:25)

houghed - hamstrung, crippled (Josh. 11:9)

husbandmen - farmers (2 Kin. 25:12)

husbandry - the soil (2 Chr. 26:10)

hyssop - plant used for purging/cleansing

ignominy - dishonor (Prov. 18:3)

imagery - perverse idol imagination

images - household gods (Gen. 31:19); likenesses (1 Sam. 6:5); incense altars (Ezek. 6:4)

Immanuel - God with us (Is. 7:14)

immutability - unchangeableness

imperious - shameless (Ezek. 16:30)

importunity - unwanted persistence

impotent - helpless, crippled (Acts 14:8)

impudent - stubborn (Ezek. 2:4)

impute sin - hold sin against him (Rom. 4:8)

in my hand - in danger (Ps. 119:109)

in the ear - ripening (Ex. 9:31)

inclosings - settings (Ex. 28:20)

incontinent - without self-control

instant - insistent or persistent (Luke 23:23)

instantly - earnestly (Acts 26:7)

instruments - furniture (Ex. 25:9); yokes (1 Kin. 19:21); schemes (Is. 32:7)

inventions - deeds (Ps. 106:29); insight (Prov. 8:12)

inward/s - dearest, intimate/inner organs

Ishi - my husband (Hos. 2:16)

issue - offspring (Gen. 48:6); discharge (Lev. 15:2)

issues - escapes (Ps. 68:20)

JAH - an abbreviation of Jehovah — the Eternal, Self-Existent One — and corresponds to I AM THAT I AM

jangling - arguing (1 Tim. 1:6)

jealous - zealous (1 Kin. 19:14)

jealousy - fury (Is. 42:13); protective love (Zech. 8:2)

Jebus - Jerusalem (Judg. 19:11)

Jehovah-jireh - the Lord will provide

Jehovah-nissi - YHWH is my refuge

Jerubbaal - Gideon (1 Sam. 12:11)

Jeshurun - Israel as complacent people

Jewry - the Judean region (John 7:1)

jubilee - every fiftieth year, when all debts were canceled (Lev. 25:10ff)

judgment - justice (Ps. 111:7)

keep the charge - obey the regulations (Lev. 8:35); assist in the duties and assignments (Num. 8:26)

keeper of mine head - captain of my bodyguard (1 Sam. 28:2)

Kerioth - cities (Jer. 48:41)

kine - cattle; heifers

kine of Bashan - fat cows, raised in the best pasturelands — but here, it is used figuratively in referring to self-gratifying, sensual, influential women

know - rape and abuse (Gen. 19:5); have homosexual relations with (Judg. 19:22); have anything to do with (Ps. 101:4)

lade - load (Gen. 45:17; Luke 11:46)

laid waste - destroyed (Is. 64:11)

lament - commemorate (Judg. 11:40)

languisheth - wastes away, dies

lasciviousness - lustfulness (2 Cor. 12:21)

laver - basin, bowl used for washing

lay - take (Eccl. 7:2)

league - peace treaty; covenant

leap on the threshhold - rush into houses

to confiscate the property (Zeph. 1:9)
leasing - lies (Ps. 5:6)
leave - permission (Num. 22:13; John 19:38); forego (Neh. 10:31)
leaved gates - double doors (Is. 45:1)
lesser cattle - sheep (Is. 7:25)
let - rented (Mark 12:1); prevented (Rom. 1:13)
levy - forced labor (1 Kin. 5:13; 9:15)
liberal - noble (Is. 32:5)
licence - opportunity (Acts 25:16)
liers - secret ambush (Judg. 20:29)
lieth out - extends (Neh. 3:25)
lift up the head - exalt themselves (Ps. 83:2); pardon (Jer. 52:31; 2 Kin. 25:27)
lifted up mine hand - promised, vowed
lighted upon - came to (Gen. 28:11); spoken against (Is. 9:8)
lightly - ignorantly (Gen. 26:10)
lightness - shameless behavior (Jer. 3:9); vain boasting (Jer. 23:32)
like - equal (Ex. 30:34; Deut. 18:8)
liking - in appearance (Dan. 1:10)
lintel - the crosspiece at the top of the door
list - choose, desire (Mark 9:13; James 3:4)
loins - waist (2 Chr. 10:10; Ezek. 47:4)
loins girded - dressed for a journey
looked on - gloated over (Obad. 1:12)
loose the loins - weaken (Is. 45:1)
lucre - money (1 Sam. 8:3)
lunatic - one affected by the moon, such as epilepsy (Matt. 17:15)
lusty - strong fighters (Judg. 3:29)
lying vanities - vain idols (Ps. 31:6); false worship (Jon. 2:8)
Magor-missabib - terror on every side
Mahanaim - two camps (Gen. 32:2)
make inquiry - reconsider (Prov. 20:25)
mammon - material things (Matt. 6:24)
mantle - robe (1 Sam. 28:14; Ezra 9:3)
mar - ruin (Jer. 13:9)
Mara/h - bitter/bitterness
Maranatha - the Lord is coming!
mark - notice (Ruth 3:4; 1 Kin. 20:22); record (Ps. 130:3)
Massah (and sometimes) **Meribah** - tempted the Lord to slay them because of their faultfinding (Ex. 17:7)
matrix - womb (Ex. 13:12; Num. 3:12)
maw - stomach (Deut. 18:3)
mean - commoner (Is. 2:9); unimportant (Acts 21:39)
meat - food (Gen. 1:29; 9:3; Lev. 25:6; Joel 1:16; John 4:8); grain/cereal (Ezek. 45:24); a meal (Matt. 9:10)

meddle - associate (Prov. 20:19)
meet - qualified (Deut. 3:18); justly due (Prov. 11:24); right (Jer. 26:14; Phil. 1:7; 2 Thes. 1:3); worthy (1 Cor. 15:9)
melt - test by affliction (Jer. 9:7); scatter (1 Sam. 14:16); be weary from grief (Ps. 119:28)
menstealers - people who enslave (control) others (1 Tim. 1:10)
mete - measure; parcel out
Midian - the descendants of Abraham through his second wife Keturah
Millo - mound of earth raised as a fortress
minish - make fewer in number (Ex. 5:19)
minister - servant (Matt. 20:26)
mischief - harm; evil intent; malice
mite - a very small unit of money
mitre - headdress, turban (Ex. 29:6)
mock - abuse (Jer. 38:19); deceive (Matt. 2:16)
moderation - humility and reputation for graciousness (Phil. 4:5)
mortify - put to death (Col. 3:5)
mote - small speck, dirt, dust or splinter
mother - grandmother (2 Chr. 15:16)
motions of sins - sinful passions or cravings
mount - mound for fortification (Jer. 6:6)
mountain - power (Jer. 51:25)
mourneth - dries up (Is. 24:7)
murrain - pestilence or disease (Ex. 9:3)
mystery - hidden purpose of God (Eph. 3:3)
nail - secure hold (Ezra 9:8)
nail of the tent - large tent peg (Judg. 4:21)
naked - out of control (Ex. 32:25)
nakedness of the land - weak points of our defense (Gen. 42:9)
narrowly look upon - gaze at (Is. 14:16)
naturally - sincerely (Phil. 2:20)
navel - body (Prov. 3:8)
nephews - grandsons or other descendants
nether - lesser or bottom; lower
Nethinims - Temple attendants or servants
new moon - Passover Feast (Ps. 81:3)
ninth hour - 3 p.m.
nitre - a wound (Prov. 25:20); strong lye soap (Jer. 2:22)
No - the city of Thebes in Egypt
noise - report (Jer. 10:22; Mark 2:1)
Noph - Memphis, ancient capital of lower Egypt
notable - notorious (Matt. 27:16)
obeisance - bowing in respect
oblation - offering, gift (Lev. 7:14); Holy Place (Ezek. 45:7); contribution (Ezek. 45:13); sacred district (Ezek. 48:20)

occupy - use (Judg. 16:11); do business (Luke 19:13)

offend - be held guilty (Jer. 2:3); cause to sin (Matt. 18:6)

ofttimes - often (Matt. 17:15; John 18:2)

omnipotent - all-powerful

opened thy feet - played the harlot

oppress - cheat, defraud (Lev. 25:14)

oracle - inner room, Holy of Holies (1 Kin. 6:5); Temple (Ps. 28:2)

oracles - the Scriptures (Rom. 3:2)

order the child - teach; train (Judg. 13:12)

order the lamps - tend to; keep burning

ouches - mountings or settings for precious stones (Ex. 28:11; 39:13)

ought - anything (Ex. 22:14; John 4:33); whatever (Lev. 19:6); sin (Num. 15:30)

out of hand - at once (Num. 11:15)

outlandish - foreign (Neh. 13:26)

outwent - went farther than or ahead of

over against - in front of; opposite

overcharge - be too severe (2 Cor. 2:5)

overran - outran (2 Sam. 18:23)

owls - ostriches (Is. 43:20)

Palestina - Philistia; Philistines

paps - breast (Luke 23:29); chest (Rev. 1:13)

passion - suffering and death (Acts 1:3)

patrimony - family property (Deut. 18:8)

peculiar - special (Ex. 19:5)

peeled - rubbed bare (Ezek. 29:18)

peep - whisper (Is. 8:19)

penury - poverty (Prov. 14:23; Luke 21:4)

peradventure - suppose; perhaps

perdition - destruction

perfect - blameless; mature; complete

Pharaoh - title of the monarchs of Egypt

phylacteries - small boxes containing Scripture texts worn by Jews as a reminder to keep the Law (Matt. 23:5)

pictures - carved figures that were objects of worship (Num. 33:52)

pilled - peeled (Gen. 30:37)

pillows - magic protective charms (Ezek 13:18,20)

pipes - flutes (1 Kin. 1:40)

pit - cistern (Jer. 41:9)

pitched - encamped (Ex. 17:1)

pitiful - compassionate (Lam. 4:10)

place - settle, establish (Ezek. 37:26); trace (Dan. 2:35)

plagues wonderful - extraordinary afflictions (Deut. 28:59)

platted - shaped (John 19:2)

play - hold a contest (2 Sam. 2:14);

show joy (2 Sam. 6:21)

play the men - show courage

played with his hand - played the harp

pleasant bread - desirable food (Dan. 10:3)

pleasant pictures - religious imagery

pleasant vessel - valuable vesesel

pledge - news (1 Sam. 17:18)

polled - cut (2 Sam. 14:26)

porter - gatekeeper; doorkeeper

portion - part or property; inheritance

possess the gate - overcome, be victorious

posts - couriers (Esth. 3:15; 8:10)

pots - sheepfolds (Ps. 68:13)

potsherd - piece of broken pottery (Job 2:8); earthen vessel (Prov. 26:23; Is. 45:9)

prating against - ridiculing (3 John 1:10)

prating fool - self-sufficient know-it-all

prayed - urged (John 4:31)

precious - rare, scarce (Is. 13:12)

presbytery - the elders (1 Tim. 4:14)

prevent - trap (2 Sam. 22:6); overtake (Job 30:27); go/come before (Ps. 59:10); speak before (Matt. 17:25)

prey - prize of war; prize (Jer. 21:9; 45:5)

prince of this world - Satan (John 12:31)

privily - unobserved; secretly

privy to - aware of in your own heart

profane - common (Ezek. 42:20); guilty of violating or breaking the law (Matt. 12:5)

prolong the perfection - reap the harvest

proper good - personal treasure

propitiation - atoning sacrifice, Mercy Seat

protest - warn (Gen. 43:3; 1 Kin. 2:42)

prove - test (Ex. 16:4; Judg. 3:4; 2 Chr. 9:1)

provender - straw and fodder (Judg. 19:19)

prudence - spiritual insight (Eph. 1:8)

publican - tax collector (Luke 5:27)

publisheth afflictions - announces disaster

puffeth - makes light (Ps. 10:5)

pulse - vegetables (Dan. 1:12)

purge - cut back (John 15:2); declare ceremonially clean (Mark 7:19)

purifying - religious cleansing ritual

purloining - stealing, pilfering, embezzling

purtenance - inner organs of an animal

push - drive (Deut. 33:17); gore (1 Kin. 22:11)

put away - divorce (Ezek. 44:22)

putteth his mouth in the dust - speaks humbly (Lam. 3:29)

quarter - own way (Is. 47:15); a region (Mark 1:45)

quaternion - unit of four soldiers (Acts 12:4)

quicken - give life (Ps. 80:18; John 6:63)

quiet - strong (Nah. 1:12)

quit - guiltless (Ex. 21:28); no longer
bound (Josh. 2:20); be courageous (1
Sam. 4:9; 1 Cor. 16:13)
quite - completely (Ex. 23:24)
Rabsaris - the chief financial official
Rabshakeh - chief officer
Raca - worthless one, said in contempt
Rahab - poetic name for Egypt (Ps. 89:10)
rail (on) - belittle; denounce; insult; slander
raiment - clothing
raised - awakened (Song. 8:5)
ranges - hearth (Lev. 11:35)
ravening - viciousness, covetousness
ravished - delighted (Prov. 5:19)
receipt of custom - tax collector's office
recompence in the same - fair return
record - witness (Phil. 1:8)
redound - abound (2 Cor. 4:15)
reins - inner self (Ps. 26:2); waist (Is. 11:5)
remission/remit - forgiveness/forgive
rend - to tear or pull apart
renowned - chosen representatives
rent - tore/torn (Gen. 37:34; 2 Sam. 1:2);
split apart (1 Kln. 13:3); rope (Is. 3:24)
repent - renunciation and sorrow for sin,
turning to the Lord for forgiveness and a
desire to obey the Lord (II Cor. 7:10);
change to the opposite direction
reproach - disgrace; rebuke
reprobate - impure, rejected (Jer. 6:30)
reputation - high esteem (Phil. 2:29)
requite - repay (Deut. 32:6; 2 Sam. 2:6)
rereward (rearward) - rear guard
reserve - keep safe (Jer. 50:20)
residue - balance; remainder
resort - gather (Mark 10:1)
respect - approval (Gen. 4:4); concern
(Ex. 2:25); obedience (Ps. 119:6)
rest - burial (Job 17:16)
reward - bribes (Is. 5:23)
ribband - cord (Num. 15:38)
ride - put in harness (Hos. 10:11)
riotous - gluttonous (Prov. 23:20)
rising - swelling (Lev. 13:2)
river - middle of the valley (2 Sam.
24:5); Euphrates (Ezra 7:21; 8:36; Is.
8:7; Jer. 2:18)
road - raid -- i.e., fighting (1 Sam. 27:10)
roar - cry, groan
rod - chastisement (Job 9:34); tribe (Ps.
74:2); authority (Mic. 6:9)
roll - scroll; record (Zech. 5:1)
room - stead, place, position
rude in speech - unskilled as an orator
ruleth with God - is faithful to God

rushing - shouting (Ezek. 3:12)
sabbath day's journey - a little over one-
half mile which was the extent a Jew
was to travel from home on the Sabbath
subbaths - cessation of activity (Lam. 1:7)
sacrilege - petty theft of sacred things
salt sea - also called Dead Sea (Josh. 12:3)
saluted - greeted; embraced (Luke 1:40)
sanctify - set apart, consecrate, make holy
sanctify Me - hold Me in reverential honor
sardius - ruby (Ex. 39:10)
saving health - salvation (Ps. 67:2)
savour - fragrance (Song. 1:3); satisfaction (2 Cor. 2:14)
scourged - whipped, flogged (Mark 15:15)
scrip - pouch; small bag or purse
sea - large bronze laver at which the
priests ceremoniously cleansed their
hands and feet before entering the
Tabernacle (Jer. 27:19)
sea of the Philistines - Mediterranean Sea
sea of the plain - area of the Dead Sea
seed - descendants, offspring, children
seer - prophet (2 Sam. 15:27)
seethe - boil (Deut. 14:21; Zech. 14:21)
Selah - the rock fortress city of Petra (just
south of the Dead Sea) (2 Kin. 14:7)
sepulchre - grave, tomb
served themselves of them - enslaved them
servile work - work at your occupations
set - take to (Ex. 7:23); expose (Hos. 2:3)
set at nought - reject; discredit; look
down upon
set forward - oversee (Ezra 3:8)
set light - dishonor (Deut. 27:16)
setteth thee on - incited or influenced you
settle - ledge (Ezek. 43:14, 20)
settled his countenance - stared intensely
sever - set apart; select
several house - separated house
severally - individually (1 Cor. 12:11)
shadow - protection (Gen. 19:8)
shadowing shroud - forest shade
shambles - meat market (1 Cor. 10:25)
shamefacedness - modest behavior
Shebah - oath (Gen. 26:33)
sheepcote - pasturelands; protecting sheep
sheets - linen garments, like shirts
Sheshach - Babylon
shipping - boats (John 6:24)
shoot out the lip - ridicule, hurl insults
sick of love - lovesick (Song. 2:5)
sickness - menstrual period (Lev. 20:18)
signet - ring bearing a seal with which
documents were stamped to officially

give personal authority (Gen. 38:18)

signification - meaning (1 Cor. 14:10)

Sihor - the Nile River (Jer. 2:18)

similitude - likeness; figure, shape, or form

simplicity - sincere faithfulness (2 Cor. 11:3)

sincere - pure, without a mixture (1 Pet. 2:2)

single - free from deceit; sincere

singular - special (Lev. 27:2)

Sitnah - enmity, anger (Gen. 26:21)

sixth hour - noon by Jewish time and 6 pm by Roman time

slack - negligent, lazy (Prov. 10:4); weak, powerless (Hab. 1:4; Zeph. 3:16)

sleep - be dead (Job 7:21)

sleep with his pledge - keep it overnight

slide - waver, fall (Ps. 26:1)

slideth back - stubborn (Hos. 4:16)

small cattle - sheep (2 Chr. 35:8; Is. 43:23)

smell - be pleased, take delight (Amos 5:21)

smite - defeat; crush (Deut. 7:2; Ps. 143:3)

smote - attacked; defeated; struck down; stabbed

snuffed - sneered (Mal. 1:13)

sober - of sound mind (2 Cor. 5:13)

sod(den) - boiled (Ex. 12:9; 2 Chr. 35:13)

softly - slowly (Gen. 33:14)

sojourn - live temporarily (Gen. 12:10)

solace - delight (Prov. 7:18)

solemn(ity) - appointed (time) (Deut. 31:10)

solemn days - appointed Feasts, festivals

sometimes - formerly (Eph. 2:13)

son of perdition - Judas Iscariot (John 17:12)

sons - descendants (1 Chr. 1:6)

soothsayer - fortune-teller (Josh. 13:22)

sorcery - witchcraft (Acts 8:9)

sore - afflictions (Ps. 38:11); severe(ly); fierce(ly); grievous(ly)

sore broken - severely crushed (Ps. 44:19)

sorrow(s) - pain, suffering (Gen. 3:16); toil, struggle to make a living (Gen. 3:17)

sottish - devoid of spiritual understanding

soul - person (Lev. 5:4); well-being (Prov. 29:10)

sounding - yearning affection (Is. 63:15)

span - about nine inches (Is. 40:12)

spikenard - perfume (Song. 1:12)

spirit of infirmity - disability (Luke 13:11)

spirits - motives (Prov. 16:2)

spoil - take the wealth of; plunder and rob

spoon - bowl (Num. 7:44)

sport - ridicule (Is. 57:4)

sporting with - caressing, expressing love to (Gen. 26:8)

sprinkle - purify by His blood (Is. 52:15)

squares - sides (Ezek. 43:17)

stablish - strengthen (2 Thes. 2:17)

staff - supply (Ezek. 5:16)

staff of reed - false support (Ezek. 29:6)

stairs - cliffs, steep places (Song. 2:14)

stalled - fattened (Prov. 15:17)

stand against the blood - fail to help when a neighbor's life is in danger (Lev. 19:16)

standing - pools of (Ps. 114:8)

staves - carrying poles; sticks; clubs; staffs

stay - support (2 Sam. 22:19); cease, do not move (2 Sam. 24:16); help (Prov. 28:17); rely (Is. 10:20; 48:2); leading men (Is. 19:13)

stayed - persuaded, restrained (1 Sam. 24:7); propped (1 Kin. 22:35); ceased flowing (2 Kin. 4:6); stopped (Ps. 106:30)

stays - armrests (1 Kin. 10:19; 2 Chr. 9:18)

stealeth - kidnaps (Ex. 21:16)

stiffnecked - stubborn; hardened

stirs - shoutings (Is. 22:2)

stock/stone - idols (Jer. 2:27)

stomacher - rich robe (Is. 3:24)

store - number (Gen. 26:14); food supply (Lev. 26:10); kneading trough or bread bin (Deut. 28:5)

stout - arrogant; harsh (Mal. 3:13)

stouthearted - stubborn-minded

straightway - immediately, without delay

strait - distress (2 Sam. 24:14); small (Is. 49:20); narrow, strict (Luke 13:24)

straitened - hindered (Prov. 4:12); limited (Mic. 2:7); restricted (Luke 12:50)

straitly - specifically (Gen. 43:7); strictly, definitely (1 Sam. 14:28)

straitly charged - sternly warned

straits - where there was no way out

strakes - strips (Gen. 30:37); marks (Lev. 14:37)

strange - improper, unholy (Num. 26:61); foreign, false (1 Sam. 7:3; 1 Kin. 11:1; Ezra 10:2; Ps. 137:4); alien (Job 19:3); repulsive (Job 19:17); adulterous (Prov. 5:3); awesome, unusual (Is. 28:21)

strange woman - harlot (Prov. 2:16)

strangers - foreigners (Neh. 13:30); exiles (1 Pet. 1:1)

strawed - scattered; spread (Mark 11:8)

streets - fields (Ps. 144:13)

strength - normal depth (Ex. 14:27); ability to resist (Is. 23:10); refuge (Nah. 3:11)

strengthened the hand(s) - encouraged; assisted (1 Sam. 23:16; Ezra 1:6)

strengtheneth - acts proudly (Job 15:25)

stretched out arm - mighty power

stricken - advanced (Gen. 24:1)

striketh hands - responsible for his neighbor (Prov. 17:18)

stripes - beatings; wounds

stripling - youth (1 Sam. 17:56)

stroke - case of dispute (Deut. 21:5)

strove - quarreled; contended; disputed

suborned - bribed; persuaded; influenced to do wrong (Acts 6:11)

subscribe evidences - sign deeds

substance - property (Ezra 10:8)

subtil - cunning, clever, shrewd, crafty (Gen. 3:1; 2 Sam. 13:3); deceitful (Prov. 7:10); treacherous (Acts 7:19)

subtilty - insight (Prov. 1:4)

suburbs - pasturelands (Num. 35:5)

succor/succour - help; assist

suffer - allow, permit, tolerate

suffer them - let them remain (Esth. 3:8)

sufficeth - will satisfy (John 14:8)

sum - census (Num. 1:2; 26:2)

sundered - separated (Job 41:17)

sunrising - eastern border (Num. 21:11)

sup - take something to eat and/or to drink (Luke 17:8); share spiritual food and fellowship (Rev. 3:20)

superfluity of - what remains (James 1:21)

superfluous - deformed (Lev. 21:18; 22:23); unnecessary (2 Cor. 9:1)

supplanted - taken the place of

suppliants - worshipers

sure - safe (Prov. 11:15)

sure house - lasting dynasty (1 Sam. 25:28)

sureties for - responsible for (Prov. 22:26)

surfeiting - overindulgence (Luke 21:34)

swaddled - reared and cared for

swaddling - to wrap with cloth, implying special care is given to Him

swaddlingband - wrapping

swallowed up - without restraint (Job 6:3)

swear/sware - promise/d solemnly

swearing - the curse of God (Jer. 23:10)

swellings - pride; self-assertion

tabering - beating (Nah. 2:7)

tabernacles - tents (Job 11:14)

tabernacles of bribery - houses of the bribetaker (Job 15:34)

tablets - perfume boxes (Is. 3:20)

tabret - object of contempt, ridicule (Job 17:6); tamborine (Is. 5:12)

taches - devices for fastening two parts together (Ex. 26:6)

taken - caught (John 8:3)

tale - quota, number (Ex. 5:8)

tare - mauled or mangled (2 Kin. 2:24)

tares - darnel; a weed (Matt. 13:25)

target - javelin (1 Sam. 17:22)

tarry - continue; stay (Lev. 14:8; Ps. 101:7)

Tartan - title of Assyria's commander in chief (2 Kin. 18:17)

tear themselves - prepare food, break bread

teareth him - violent convulsions

Tebeth - compares with Dec/Jan

tell - count (Gen. 15:5; Ps. 22:17; Ps. 147:4)

tempered - combined (1 Cor. 12:24)

tempest - storm (Is. 32:2)

tempt - test, try (Gen. 22:1)

tender - weak; inexperienced

tenons - clasps (Ex. 26:19)

tenor - general idea (Gen. 43:7)

tenth hour - 4 p.m.

teraphim - household idols (Hos. 3:4)

terrestrial - earthly (1 Cor. 15:40)

terrible - awesome; wonderful; fearful

terribleness - fierceness (Jer. 49:16)

testimony - Ark of the Covenant (Num. 17:10)

tetrarch - ruler of a fourth part or one of four rulers of a country or province

thankworthy - approved or acceptable

thigh - hip (Gen. 32:25)

thing - message (Dan. 10:1)

third hour - 9 a.m; **of the night** - 9 p.m

thitherward - toward (Jer. 50:5)

threescore - 60

throne of iniquity - workers of evil

thyine - scented wood (Rev. 18:12)

time no longer - no more waiting, delay

times - years (Dan. 4:16; 12:7); astrology (Lev. 19:26)

tire - turban (Ezek. 24:17)

Tirshatha - governor (Ezra 2:63; Neh. 10:1)

title - monument, grave marker (2 Kin. 23:17)

token/s - sign/testimony and experience

told out - assigned (2 Chr. 2:2)

torn him - thrown him into convulsions

touch a woman - have sexual relations

touching - concerning (Num. 8:26)

tow - straw or kindling to be burned

toward - near (Gen. 13:12); friendly/favorable to (Gen. 31:2; Jer. 15:1)

traffick - do business (Gen. 42:34)

train - royal attendants (1 Kin. 10:2); trailing robe (Is. 6:1)

translate - transfer (2 Sam. 3:10)

travail - give birth (Gen. 38:28; 1 Sam. 4:19); hardship (Ex. 18:8)

tributary - slave (Lam. 1:1)

tribute - an assessment; taxes (Num. 31:39; Rom. 13:6); forced labor (Josh. 17:13; 1 Kin. 4:6)

tried - proven true (2 Sam. 22:31)

trimmest - scheme (Jer. 2:33)

troubled - made trouble for (Gen. 34:30); confused, panicked (Ex. 14:24)

trow - trust, think, give acceptance to

try - examine, test (Lam. 3:40)

tumult - uproar, riot, disorderly disturbance

turn - restore (Job 42:10; Ps. 80:3)

thitherward - in that direction

turning - corner (Neh. 3:19)

turning leaves - hinged panels

twain - two (Mark 15:38)

unawares - unintentionally (Num. 35:15)

uncircumcised - ceremoniously defiled and forbidden (Lev. 19:23); those without a covenant with God (1 Chr. 10:4); heathen (Is. 52:1); unrepentant (Acts 7:51)

uncircumcised lips - poor speech

unclean - ceremonially defiled (Lev. 5:2)

undefiled - blameless (Ps. 119:1)

unfeigned - sincere; genuine; without hypocrisy (2 Cor. 6:6; 1 Tim. 1:5)

ungirded - unloaded (Gen. 24:32)

unicorn - wild ox (Num. 23:22; Job 39:9)

unleavened - without yeast (Lev. 2:4)

unsearchable - beyond our understanding

unseemly - rudely (1 Cor. 13:5)

untempered morter - whitewash

untimely - green, unripe (Rev. 6:13)

untimely birth - stillborn (Job 3:16)

untoward - sinful (Acts 2:40)

upbraid - rebuke, denounce, condemn

upholden - helped (Job 4:4)

Urim and Thummim - two objects kept in the high priest's breastplate and used for determining the will of God

usury - interest on money lent (Matt. 25:27)

utter - outer (Ezek. 47:2)

uttermost sea - Mediterranean Sea

vain - void of understanding (Prov. 12:11); morally misguided (Rom. 1:21); worthless

vainglory - boasting (Phil. 2:3)

vanities - worthless idolatry (1 Kin. 16:13)

vanity - dishonesty (Prov. 13:11; 30:8)

variance - a state of disagreement

vaunteth not itself - is not boastful

vehemently - angrily (Luke 11:53)

vein - mine (Job 28:1)

verity - truth (Ps. 111:7)

vesture - clothing; robe; garment

vexed - afflicted; distressed; grieved; tormented

vial - container; bowl or cup

victuals - provisions; food

vigilant - self-controlled (1 Tim. 3:2)

vile - undignified (2 Sam. 6:22); rotten (Jer. 29:17)

villany - disgraceful things (Jer. 29:23)

vine - Israel (Ps. 80:8)

viol/s - strings/harps (Is. 5:12/Amos 5:23)

virtue - healing power (Mark 5:30; Luke 6:19); power from a supernatural being (Luke 8:46)

visage - appearance (Is. 52:14)

visit - punish (Jer. 50:31); look after the needs (James 1:27)

wait (on) - serve, minister (in) (1 Chr. 6:32)

wall - moat (Dan. 9:25)

want - lack; be without (Ps. 23:1; Jer. 35:19)

wanton - seductive (Is. 3:16)

ward - duty (Neh. 13:30); custody; guarded house; guard post

wave them - present with a waving motion

wax - become; grow (Ps. 102:26)

weaken the hands - discourage, frighten

wealth - well-being (Ezra 9:12)

weigh - make smooth and straight (Is. 26:7)

wench - maidservant (2 Sam. 17:17)

whisperers - gossipers (Rom. 1:29)

whited wall - hypocrite (Acts 23:3)

wiles - treacherous/cunning deceit

will worship - self-inspired efforts at worship (Col. 2:23)

wimples - shawls (Is. 3:22)

winebibber - one who drinks wine

winked at - overlooked (Acts 17:30)

wise hearted - skillful, expert craftsman

wist - knew (Lev. 5:17; Mar. 14:40)

wit - see, know (Gen. 24:21; Ex. 2:4)

with - against (Gen. 14:9)

withs - small ropes (Judg. 16:7)

without - outside (Lev. 6:11; Ezra 10:13; John 18:16); independent of (1 Cor. 11:11); beyond (2 Cor. 10:13)

wonderful - horrible (Lam. 1:9; Dan. 8:24); mighty (1 Sam. 6:6)

wont - accustomed (Matt. 27:15)

work - concern (Prov. 16:11)

wormwood - bitterness (Lam. 3:15)

wot - know (Gen. 21:26; 44:15; Num. 22:6)

wreathed - joined together (Lam. 1:14)

wreathen - woven, braided, twisted

wrest - pervert; distort (Deut. 16:19)

wroth - exceedingly angry; furious

wrought - committed (Neh. 9:18); acted (Ezek. 20:9); prepared (2 Cor. 5:5)

yoke - burden (Acts 15:10)